COMPANY SECRETARY'S HANDBOOK

Twelfth edition

Douglas Armour FCG

icsa
The Chartered
Governance
Institute

First published 1995

Published by
ICSA Publishing Limited
Saffron House
6–10 Kirby Street
London EC1N 8TS

Typeset by Paul Barrett Book Production, Cambridge
Edited by Sheida Heidari
Cover designed by Anthony Kearney

British Library Cataloguing in Publication Data
A catalogue record for this book is available from the British Library

ISBN 978-1-86072-777-1

Contents

Foreword

The myriad of governance requirements coming from legislation, regulation, codes of practice and various other forms of guidance can be daunting to even the most seasoned of governance professionals. The role undertaken by company secretaries, and their team, can be wide-ranging and varied. On any given day, the company secretary might be working on board logistics and support, writing board papers, advising other members of the management team, writing policies, project managing the production of annual reports and organising general meetings. There may also be other professional disciplines reporting into them.

In practice, the company secretary is generally juggling any number of crucial tasks, for a number of stakeholders, usually with critical time pressures that also need to be met.

To fulfil the role to the full potential, there are a vast amount of governance requirements, for the organisation, most notably coming out of the Companies Acts, that need to be considered and complied with.

As anyone who has worked in a secretariat team will know, navigating the range of requirements can take time. The requirements are also nuanced according to the type of organisation you are dealing with, which Douglas Armour has usefully summarised in his Introduction, and how they are regulated, if at all.

For those who are not a company secretary, by profession, the range of requirements can be even more daunting. So whether you are a company secretary, director, solicitor or an accountant, the information within the *Company Secretary's Handbook* will soon prove itself to be invaluable in ensuring compliance.

Lyn Colloff, MBA, FCG, ACII
Chartered Secretary/Governance Professional

Preface

The object of writing this book is to provide a practical guide to company secretarial procedures undertaken by company secretaries, solicitors and accountants.

The book covers all of the core tasks generally associated with the work of the company secretary. The commentary is illustrated by Precedents for all key transactions and additional reference material is presented in the Appendices section. The book has a detailed contents list and index, and the text is fully cross-referenced. Key terms are highlighted in bold on first use, and defined in an end-of-book Glossary.

The twelfth edition reflects the law as at 1 July 2019. Chapters referring to the *Listing Rules*, *Prospectus Rules* and *Disclosure and Transparency Rules* refer to those rules as at 1 July 2019. Articles of association references throughout the book are to the Model Articles for companies incorporated under the Companies Act 2006 set out in SI 2008/3007. Whenever you are contemplating any course of action, it is always extremely important to check the provisions of the articles of association, as these vary from company to company.

All fees and charges are shown as at 1 July 2019.

In common with previous editions, this book is intended to be a *practical* guide to the legislation governing companies and company secretarial procedure. As with all legislation, the provisions of the Companies Acts and related legislation are open to interpretation and must be assessed in the context of the circumstances at hand, the articles of association of the company in question and any relevant shareholders' agreement or other ancillary agreements.

While every effort has been made to ensure the accuracy of the content of this book, neither the author nor the publisher can accept responsibility for any loss arising to anyone relying solely on the information contained herein.

Douglas Armour
October 2019

Introduction

Although this Handbook is aimed primarily at readers who already have a working knowledge of companies and company law, there will be some who are less familiar with the concept of the company as established in the United Kingdom.

For UK businesses, there are a number of different forms of entity available through which that business can trade. These include:

- sole traders;
- partnerships;
- limited liability partnerships;
- limited partnerships;
- friendly and provident companies;
- European Economic Interest Groupings; and
- companies incorporated under the Companies Acts.

This book is written for directors, company secretaries, managers and administrators, and their advisers, of the last category – companies incorporated under the Companies 2006 or previous Companies Acts. The vast majority of trading entities established in the UK are companies of one type or another, incorporated under the Companies Acts, as amended. Unless stated otherwise, a reference to a 'company' will mean to a company incorporated under the Companies Act 2006 and not to any other trading entity, whether known as a 'company' or not. References to 'the Companies Act', 'the Act' and section numbers with no act reference should be read as references to the Companies Act 2006, as amended.

Although there are three different types of company – companies limited by shares, limited by guarantee and unlimited companies – they all have certain basic characteristics. The overwhelming majority of companies are limited by shares.

Guarantee companies are best suited for use with charitable enterprises, although charities may also be registered as charitable incorporated organisations under Charities Acts (there is different legislation in England and Wales, Scotland and Northern Ireland), and sporting or social associations particularly where the membership is to be subject to an annual subscription. Unlimited companies will normally be utilised in the case of a professional company where limited liability is not permitted or where, for reasons of secrecy, the owners do not wish to publish their accounting information.

There are a number of different variations of companies limited by shares, the most common being private limited companies, followed by public limited companies. Less common forms include Community Interest Companies (CICs) and Right to Manage companies (RTMs).

Structure of the CA2006

The CA2006 is an extremely lengthy piece of legislation comprising 1,300 sections arranged in 47 Parts together with 16 Schedules. The primary legislation is supported and updated by an increasing number of statutory instruments as well as changes deriving from EU directives and Regulations.

The 47 Parts are grouped into ten areas as follows:

Part	Summary
1–7	Fundamentals of what a company is, formations and company names
8–12	Shareholders and directors
13–14	How companies may take decisions
15–16	Directors' accountability to shareholders
17–25	Share capital, capital maintenance, annual returns and company charges
26–28	Company reconstructions, mergers and takeovers
29–39	Regulatory framework, application to companies not formed under the Companies Acts and other company law provisions
40–42	Disqualification of overseas directors, business names and statutory auditors
43	Transparency obligations
44–47	Miscellaneous and general

Territorial extent

Unlike previous companies legislation, the CA2006 applies to all UK companies.

Northern Ireland

Company law remains a transferred matter from Northern Ireland and accordingly the CA2006 could be separately amended or repealed. References in the CA2006 to any provisions restating or replacing provisions originally contained in CA1985, CA1989 or C(AICE)2004 should be read as references to the corresponding provisions in the Companies (Northern Ireland) Order 1986, the Companies (Northern Ireland) Order 1990 or the Companies (Audit, Investigations and Community Enterprise) Order 2005.

Scotland

Company law is a reserved matter and consequently applies equally to Scottish companies. However, the CA2006 also contains non-company law provisions, some of which are devolved matters. These devolved matters were given legislative consent by the Scottish Parliament on 16 March 2006.

The devolved matters are:

- changes to the regulation of business names in Part 41 reflecting the changes contained in Part 5 which are a reserved matter;
- statutory guidance issued by the Lord Advocate in Scotland to prosecutors and enforcement agencies in relation to the new offence of knowingly or recklessly causing an audit report to be misleading, false or deceptive (s. 509);
- audit exemption requirements for Scottish charities (s. 1175); and
- giving the Auditor General for Scotland power to specify public bodies for his audit (s. 483).

Wales

Company law is not a matter transferred to the Welsh assembly and so there are no devolved matters.

Crown dependencies

To reflect the existing jurisdiction of the Takeover Panel, Part 28 of the CA2006 contains provisions enabling it to be extended by Order in Council to the Isle of Man or any of the Channel Islands.

Table of abbreviations

ABI	Association of British Insurers
AGM	annual general meeting
AIM	Alternative Investment Market
AR	AIM Rules
BACS	Bankers' Automated Clearing System
BEIS	Department for Business, Energy & Industrial Strategy
CA1985	Companies Act 1985
CA1989	Companies Act 1989
CA2006	Companies Act 2006
CCSS	CREST courier and sorting service
CDDA1986	Company Directors Disqualification Act 1986
CIC	Community Interest Company
CIS	Community Interest Statement
CJA1993	Criminal Justice Act 1993
CMA	Competition and Markets Authority
CSPO	Company Secretarial Practice Online, the official ICSA information service
DCLG	Department of Communities and Local Government
DPA2018	Data Protection Act 2018
DTR	Disclosure and Transparency Rules
EA2002	Enterprise Act 2002
ECD	Excluded Company Declaration
EDC	electronic data capture
EEA	European Economic Area
EPA1985	Enduring Powers of Attorney Act 1985
ERMs	Exchange Regulated Markets
FA1986	Finance Act 1986
FCA	Financial Conduct Authority
FRC	Financial Reporting Council
FSMA2000	Financial Services and Markets Act 2000
GAAP	Generally Accepted Accounting Principles
GDPR	General Data Protections Regulations
IA1986	Insolvency Act 1986
IAS	International Accounting Standards
IASB	International Accounting Standards Board
ICSA/The Institute	The Institute of Chartered Secretaries and Administrators
ICTA1988	Income and Corporation Taxes Act 1988
IFRS	International Financial Reporting Standards
IR1986	Insolvency Rules 1986

ISD	Investment Services Directive
LLP	limited liability partnership
LR	Listing Rules
MCA2005	Mental Capacity Act 2005
MiFID	Markets in Financial Instrument Directive
NCA	National Crime Agency
NE RFI	NEX Exchange Rules for Issuers
NED	non-executive director
PCA	person closely associated
PDMR	person discharging managerial responsibilities
POCA2002	Proceeds of Crime Act 2002
RIE	Recognised Investment Exchange
RIS	regulatory information service
RTM	Right To Manage (company)
SAIL	Single Alternative Inspection Location
SBEE2015	Small Business, Enterprise and Employment Act 2015
SDRT	Stamp Duty Reserve Tax
SEAQ	Stock Exchange Automated Quotation system
SEATS PLUS	Stock Exchange Alternative Trading Service
SETS	Stock Exchange Electronic Trading Service
SRO	self-regulatory organisation
UCITS	Undertaking for Collective Investment in Transferable Securities
UKLA	UK Listing Authority

About the author

Douglas Armour is a senior manager and governance team leader at Intertrust London, which provides company secretarial and governance services to a portfolio of capital market SPVs. Douglas provides advice both internally and externally to colleagues and clients. He was company secretary of Equiniti Group plc from January 2015 until July 2016, assisting with the progression from private equity ownership through its IPO and admission to the London Stock Exchange in October 2015. Prior to this, Douglas was a director of Equiniti David Venus Limited, which became part of the Equiniti Group in 2009. In that role, he was responsible for ensuring that changes in legislation, corporate governance, listing rules and best practice were disseminated not only internally to the company secretarial teams, but also across the wider Equiniti Group and externally to clients.

With more than 30 years at Equiniti David Venus, he has experience in all aspects of company secretarial and corporate governance compliance for companies of all sizes, from owner-managed private organisations to FTSE 100 companies.

A Fellow of the ICSA since 1996, he writes and contributes to a number of respected company secretarial practice reference works, including the Company Secretary's Handbook, Company Secretary's Checklists and the Company Compliance and Administration Study Text for The Chartered Governance Qualifying Programme.

1 – The company secretary

Introduction

The role of the **company secretary** can encompass all areas of a **company**'s activities, depending on the size and nature of the company, and the qualifications and experience of the individual. These activities can be divided into three principal categories.

The board

The company secretary should ensure that proper board procedures are in place and are adhered to, and that all relevant papers are circulated to board members in advance of meetings. They should also provide practical support and guidance, particularly to non-executive directors, and monitor and guide the company's corporate governance policies.

The company

The company secretary should ensure the company's compliance with relevant legislation and codes of conduct specific to the company's business activities. The company secretary will often provide a central source of information to the board and senior executives.

The members

The company secretary is often the primary point of contact for members and institutions, particularly in matters related to corporate and environmental governance.

Background

The origins of the company secretary begin with the Joint Stock Act 1856. This Act established the procedures for the **formation** of a **limited company** by registering the memorandum and **articles of association**, and established the dual system of ownership and management. The Act also contained provisions for the secretary to the company. In these early years, the position held no responsibilities or duties.

Indeed, in a court case in 1887,[1] the Master of the Rolls, Lord Esher, stated that 'A secretary is a mere servant; his position is that he is to do what he is told, and no person can assume that he has any authority to represent anything at all'.

It was not until the Companies Act 1948 that the company secretary was recognised as an **officer** of the company alongside the **directors** and all companies were required to appoint a company secretary. There were no specific duties; however, the company secretary was authorised to sign prescribed forms on behalf of the company and make statutory declarations as to matters of fact concerning the company.

The position of the company secretary gradually gained formal recognition as a responsible officer under a succession of Acts including the Trade Descriptions Act 1968, the Taxes Management Act 1970 and the Unsolicited Goods Act 1971.

1971 was a good year for company secretaries, as at a Court of Appeal[2] judgement, Salmon LJ stated that the position of the company secretary was formally noted as being the 'chief administrative officer'.

This was expanded upon in the same hearing by the then Master of the Rolls, Lord Denning, who stated:

> A company secretary is a much more important person nowadays than he was in 1887. He is an officer of the company with extensive duties and responsibilities. This appears not only in the modern Companies Acts, but also by the role which he plays in the day-to-day business of companies. He is no longer a mere clerk. He regularly makes representations on behalf of the company and enters into contracts on its behalf which come within the day-to-day running of the company's business. So much so that he may be regarded as held out as having authority to do such things on behalf of the company. He is certainly entitled to sign contracts connected with the administrative side of a company's affairs, such as employing staff, and ordering cars, and so forth. All such matters now come within the ostensible authority of a company's secretary.

Further recognition of the importance of the role of the company secretary came in the Companies Act 1980, which required company secretaries of public companies to be qualified either by professional qualification or by prior experience.

In 1992, the key role of company secretaries in good corporate governance was recognised in a report issued by a committee chaired by Adrian Cadbury, titled 'Financial Aspects of Corporate Governance', but universally referred to as the Cadbury Report. This report was launched followed a number of corporate governance failures including Maxwell Corporation, BCCI and Polly Peck.

In 2008, the role of the company secretary took a backward step. As part of the programme to deregulate companies in the general review of Company Law, the 2006 Companies Act saw the position of the company secretary become optional for private companies.

The 2018 Edition of the UK Corporate Governance Code reinforced and further recognised the role of the company secretary as being responsible for advising their boards on all governance matters in addition to having a key role in assisting the board chair with regular evaluation of the board as a whole and of individual directors.

The position does not in itself involve the exercise of management responsibility and if, as many do, the company secretary is to have powers of management, these will come from some other executive office.

A corporate body may, subject to certain restrictions, be appointed company secretary. A **partnership** may be appointed company secretary in the name of the firm. In England and Wales, where partnerships do not have corporate status, this has effect as an appointment of all the partners as joint secretaries. In Scotland, where partnerships do have corporate status, the partnership may be appointed company secretary in its own right.

It is also possible to appoint deputy or assistant company secretaries, who may act in the office of company secretary if that office is vacant or there is no company secretary capable of acting (s. 274).

The office of company secretary

With effect from 6 April 2008, only **public companies** are required to appoint a company secretary (s. 271). **Private companies** will be able to appoint a company secretary, if they wish to do so, and the following provisions apply equally to both private and public companies (s. 270).

As discussed more fully below, the duties of the company secretary are not specified in detail in the Companies Acts. However, in various sections of the Companies Acts, the company secretary is named as one of the people who may sign prescribed forms on behalf of the company, make statutory declarations and sign the **confirmation statement**. Additionally, the company secretary is recognised as a responsible officer by the Taxes Management Act 1970, the Trade Descriptions Act 1968, the Unsolicited Goods and Services Act 1971 and the Data Protection Act 2018.

The company secretary is an officer of the company as defined by ss. 1121 and 1173, and consequently may incur personal responsibility for not complying with requirements of the Act affecting the company.

As well as the statutory requirements, a company's articles of association may contain provisions with regard to the appointment, resignation or removal of the company secretary.

Qualifications

The company secretary of a private company need have no professional or other qualification, or have any previous experience.

In the case of a public company, s. 273 provides that the directors must take all reasonable steps to ensure that the company secretary is a person who appears to have the knowledge and experience necessary to discharge the functions of company secretary, and who also meets other requirements laid down in that section.

Persons qualified to be the company secretary of a public company under these provisions include:

- a barrister, advocate or solicitor, called or admitted in any part of the UK;
- a member of various professional bodies, including the Institute of Chartered Secretaries and Administrators (ICSA), and members of various accountancy bodies in England and Wales, Scotland and Ireland;
- a person who is a member of any other professional body who appears to the directors to be capable of discharging the functions of the company secretary; and
- a person who, for at least three of the five years immediately preceding their appointment as company secretary, held the office of company secretary of another public company.

Prohibited appointments

The auditor of a company and any employee of the auditor may not be appointed as company secretary (s. 1214).

The sole director of a company is no longer prohibited from being appointed as its company secretary. However, there is little to be gained in practice from doing so, as any documents requiring signature by a sole director and the company secretary cannot be signed by the same person acting in both capacities (s. 280). Accordingly, while it is now possible for a private company to have one person as sole director and shareholder, it is still necessary for another person to be appointed either as company secretary or as an authorised signatory to execute certain documents or to witness the execution of those documents.

Appointment

A corporate body may, subject to certain restrictions, be appointed company secretary. A partnership may be appointed company secretary in the name of the firm. In England and Wales, this has effect as an appointment of all the partners as joint secretaries. In Scotland, where partnerships have corporate status, the firm may be appointed company secretary in its own right. It is also possible to appoint deputy or assistant company secretaries, who may act in the office of company secretary if that office is vacant or there is no company secretary capable of acting (s. 274).

Following the coming into force of the Limited Liability Partnerships Act 2000, a **limited liability partnership** (LLP), as a corporate body, whether registered in England and Wales or in Scotland, can be appointed as company secretary.

The appointment process is the same for private and public companies. On **incorporation** of a new company, the person named as company secretary on Form IN01 (not obligatory for a private company) is deemed to have been appointed as the first company secretary of the company (ss. 12 and 16). Form IN01 is delivered to the **Registrar of Companies** for **registration**, together with the memorandum and articles of association of the company. Subsequent appointments – or in the case of a private company, this may be the first appointment – are made by the directors in accordance with the provisions of the articles of association (see precedent 33). The following action should be taken:

1 At a meeting of the directors or by **written resolution**, the directors must resolve to appoint a new company secretary. Where the new appointment is to replace an incumbent company secretary rather than to fill a vacancy, the **resolution** will also include the replacement of the previous company secretary, be it by way of resignation, retirement, removal or another cause.
2 The particulars relating to the new company secretary must be entered in the company's register of secretaries (s. 275) and notified to the Registrar of Companies on Form AP03 (Appointment of Secretary) or Form AP04 (Appointment of Corporate Secretary) within 14 days of the appointment (s. 276). The form can be filed either in paper form or electronically.
3 If the company secretary is to be an authorised signatory of the company's bank account, notification of the change of company secretary and a specimen signature should be sent to the bank, together with any additional verification of identity documents required by the bank.
4 If thought appropriate, announcement of the new appointment should be made to the company's staff, suppliers and customers.
5 A formal **service contract** should be drawn up for signature by the company and by the company secretary.
6 If the company has an insurance policy covering officers of the company against the liabilities that they may incur in carrying out their duties, the insurance company should be notified, usually at renewal, of the appointment of the new company secretary.
7 In the case of a company with publicly traded **shares**, the company secretary should be supplied with the company's rules governing transactions in its securities, if any, which should comply with the terms of the Market Abuse Regulations, Disclosure and Transparency Rules, and the Listing, AIM or NEX Rules, as appropriate.

Duties

None of the Companies Acts or most articles of association specifically define the powers of a company secretary. As a consequence, the position has been considered by the courts at various times. As discussed on page 2, the concept of the ostensible authority attaching to the office of the company secretary was established by the courts in 1971. Although matters falling within this administrative function are not explicitly set out or defined, this ostensible authority will often extend to the employment of staff, the company's premises, data processing and other office machinery, printing and stationery requirements, and the acquisition, maintenance and sale of company vehicles. If the company secretary is responsible for data processing, their responsibilities will be governed by the Data Protection Act 2018 and the General Data Protection Regulations, especially if they are the person appointed Data Protection Coordinator for the company. However, without express authority, the company secretary's responsibilities will not extend to negotiating trading **contracts**, e.g. sale or purchase of goods and materials or production machinery, which are matters affecting the company's business operations and will, in most cases, be the responsibility of other managers. In many companies, the company secretary may be the appropriate person and be authorised to sign contracts relating to such matters on behalf of the company.

If a company secretary acts beyond their authority, whether express or ostensible, the company will be bound by such acts, but the company secretary may be held liable by the company for any loss incurred as a result.

The Company Secretaries Group of the ICSA considered the duties of the company secretary and published a guide distinguishing between the core duties that all company secretaries should perform and those additional duties that they may be called upon to undertake, as set out below.

Board meetings

Coordinating the operation of the company's formal decision-making and reporting machinery; formulating meeting agendas with the chairman and/or chief executive; attending and minuting meetings; maintaining minute books; certifying copies of minutes; and ensuring that correct procedures are followed (see Chapter 9).

General meetings

Originating and obtaining internal and external agreement to all documentation for circulation to shareholders; coordinating the administration and minuting of meetings; and ensuring that correct procedures are followed (see Chapter 8).

Articles of association

Ensuring that the company complies with its articles of association; drafting and incorporating amendments in accordance with correct procedures. The articles are now deemed to incorporate all clauses previously found in the **memorandum of association**, with the exception of the **subscriber** clause (see Chapter 3).

General compliance

Monitoring and ensuring compliance with relevant legal requirements, particularly under the Companies Acts (see Chapter 7).

UKLA, AIM and NEX requirements

Monitoring and ensuring compliance with the *Listing Rules* and *Disclosure and Transparency Rules*, *AIM Rules* and *NEX Exchange Primary Rules*; managing relations with the UK Listing Authority, Stock Exchange or NEX Exchange through the company's advisers; releasing information to the market; ensuring the security of unreleased, price-sensitive information; and making applications for listing and admission of additional issues of securities (see Chapters 15, 16 and 18).

Statutory registers

Maintaining the following statutory registers:

1. **members** (see also 'Share registration' below) – ss. 113, 114;
2. company **charges** – ss. 877, 891 and 892;
3. directors – s. 162;
4. directors' usual residential addresses – s. 165;
5. secretaries – s. 265;
6. **debenture** holders (if applicable) – s. 743; and
7. people with significant control register (PSC Register) – s. 790M.

Private companies can elect to keep their statutory registers on the central register maintained by Companies House (see Chapter 7).

Statutory returns

Filing information with the Registrar of Companies to report certain changes regarding the company or to comply with requirements for periodic filing. Of particular importance in this regard are:

1. confirmation statement;
2. report and accounts (see also next item);
3. amended articles of association;[3]
4. returns of **allotments and statements of capital**;
5. notices of appointment, removal and resignation of directors or the company secretary;
6. notices of removal or resignation of the auditors;
7. change of registered office; and
8. notification of the creation or satisfaction of charges.

(See Chapters 7, 13, 14 and 22.)

Report and accounts

Coordinating the publication and **distribution** of the company's annual report and accounts and interim statements in consultation with the company's internal and external advisers; and, in particular, preparing the **directors' report** and strategic report (see Chapters 9 and 10).

Share registration

Maintaining the company's register of members; dealing with **transfers** and other matters affecting shareholdings; and dealing with queries and requests from shareholders (see Chapter 13).

Shareholder communications

Communicating with the shareholders (e.g. through circulars); payment of **dividends** and interest; issuing documentation regarding rights issues and capitalisation issues; general shareholder relations; and relations with institutional shareholders and their investment protection committees (see Chapter 13).

Shareholder monitoring

Monitoring movements on the register of members to identify any apparent 'stake building' in the company's shares by potential **takeover** bidders; and making inquiries of members as to beneficial ownership of holdings.

Share and capital issues and restructuring

Implementing changes in the structure of the company's share and loan **capital**; and devising, implementing and administering directors' and employees' share participation schemes (see Chapter 13).

Acquisitions and disposals

Participating as a key member of the company team established to implement corporate acquisitions and disposals; and protecting the company's interests by ensuring the effectiveness of all documentation and that due diligence disclosures enable proper commercial evaluation prior to completion of a transaction (see Chapter 16).

Corporate governance

Reviewing developments in corporate governance, and advising and assisting the directors with respect to their duties and responsibilities in order to ensure compliance with their personal obligations under company law and, if applicable, stock exchange requirements as well as any disclosure obligations under either the UK Corporate Governance Code or the Wates Principles (see Chapter 17).

Non-executive directors

Acting as a channel of communication and information for non-executive directors (see Chapter 6).

Company seal

If the company has a company seal, ensuring its safe custody and proper use.

Registered office

Establishment and administration of the registered office; receipt, coordination and distribution of official correspondence received by the company at its registered office; and ensuring the provision of facilities for the public inspection of documents.

Subsidiary companies

The administration of **subsidiary** companies; and implementing changes to, and maintaining a record of, the group's structure.

Resignation or removal

Subject to any service contract in force, the company secretary may resign by notice in writing to the board (see precedent 34). The board may remove the company secretary and replace that person by simple majority (see precedent 35). Any termination will be subject to the terms of any service contract and removal of an individual from the office of company secretary need not necessarily also require termination of employment.

Whether the company secretary has resigned or been removed from office, the following procedures should be followed:

1. In the case of a removal, the directors must approve a resolution to remove the company secretary, either at a meeting or by written resolution.
2. The fact of the resignation or removal of the company secretary must be entered in the company's register of directors and secretaries, and notified to the Registrar of Companies on Form TM02 within 14 days of the resignation or removal. The form can be filed either in paper form or electronically (see Chapter 7).
3. If the company secretary is an authorised signatory on the company's bank account, notification of the change in company secretary should be given to the bank.
4. A new company secretary must be appointed to a public company as soon as practical and the procedure on appointment outlined above should be followed. As the position is optional for a private company, there is no such urgency if a replacement company secretary is to be appointed.

Change of particulars

Although many pre-2009 companies will have a combined register of directors and company secretaries under the Companies Act 2006 (CA2006), the register of secretaries kept by a company is treated as a separate register in accordance with s. 162 and s. 275, respectively. The company secretary has a duty to notify the Registrar of Companies of any changes in their particulars under s. 276.

Entries in the register of secretaries must comply with the obligation in s. 277(1)(b) to state a service address which may be their residential address, but need not be.

Deputy, assistant or joint company secretaries

The directors may appoint an assistant or deputy company secretary (s. 274). This person may be appointed and removed by resolution of the directors, subject to any provisions contained in the company's articles of association. There is no requirement for the appointment to be notified to the Registrar of Companies.

Rather than an assistant or deputy company secretary, some companies may wish to appoint one or more joint company secretaries. Details of any joint company secretaries must be notified to the Registrar of Companies (s. 276). Appointment or removal of a joint company secretary is carried out in the same way as for a sole company secretary, and will be by resolution of the directors (see precedent 33).

Notes

1. *Barnett, Hoares & Co v South London Tramways Co* [1887].
2. *Panorama Developments (Guildford) Ltd v Fidelis Furnishing Fabrics Ltd* [1971].
3. CA2006 introduces a new civil penalty of £200 for failure to comply within 28 days following the receipt of the notice requiring the company to deliver a copy of its amended articles.

2 – Company incorporation

Introduction

In most cases, company incorporation (registration or formation) is a relatively straightforward process and can be undertaken without any legal training, although the majority of companies are formed either by specialist registration **agents** (also referred to as formation or incorporation agents) or increasingly directly with Companies House, using their web incorporation service (http://ewf.companieshouse.gov.uk).

This chapter looks at the most common forms of incorporation and the differences between them, the process of incorporation (including the issue of company and business names) and the documentation that must be filed with the Registrar of Companies in order for the company to begin trading. It also covers the procedures necessary for re-registering existing companies under different corporate structures.

Although falling outside the scope of this book, there are alternatives to incorporating a company under the Companies Act. Anyone setting up in business may wish to consider trading as a sole trader, as an unregistered unlimited partnership or as a registered limited liability partnership. The choice between incorporating or trading without limited liability will depend on the desire to keep the financial status of the business secret and/or the different taxation regimes applying to companies and unincorporated entities.

What is a company?

Corporate persona

A company is a legal entity in its own right, separate from that of its owners (members/shareholders) or managers (directors). Accordingly, a company can enter into contracts and own assets in its own name, unlike a sole trader or a partnership, which does not have a legal identity separate from the owner in whose name(s) all contracts and assets are made/held.

Like a natural person, a company has a 'home' address, where legal documents and notices may be served. This address is known as its registered office and, among other things, determines the company's VAT and corporation tax office and the tax office dealing with any PAYE. This is the official address for serving of official notices, including notice of court action against the company to recover monies owed.

When a company is formed, there is an obligation to register information with the Registrar of Companies, and subsequently to register changes to this information. This will include the names and addresses of the persons forming the company and the company's registered office.

Ownership

All companies are owned by their members. In companies limited by shares, these will be the shareholders; companies limited by **guarantee** will be owned by their guarantors; and **unlimited companies** can have shareholders or some other method of determining the proportion in which the company is owned. The majority of companies are limited by shares, either as private limited companies (usually referred to as 'limited companies'), or public limited companies (more usually referred to as 'public' or 'plc' companies).

Liability

The phrase 'limited' refers to the liability of the owners (the members/shareholders) for the **debts** of the company. Members of limited companies, whether limited by shares or guarantee, have limited liability for the debts of the company. The amount of their liability is limited to the amount agreed to be paid for the shares on their issue by the company. Accordingly, once shares are fully paid, members have no further liability. The majority of shares are issued as fully paid shares and accordingly there is no liability on the part of the owners for any trading or other debt of the company.

The liability of a guarantor of a company limited by guarantee is limited to the amount of their guarantee and is usually some nominal amount such as £10.

Members of unlimited companies, as the name implies, have no limit on their liability to meet the debts of the company, should it fail.

Management

The management of all companies, regardless of type, is undertaken on behalf of the members by the directors. Directors need not be members, although in the majority of private companies the members and the directors will be the same group of individuals.

Even where they are members, the directors have a duty to manage the affairs of the company for the benefit of the membership as a whole and not just some part of the membership.

Although certain individuals cannot be appointed as directors of companies, including bankrupt and disqualified directors, there are no qualifications required to act as a director of a company and no need to show any previous management experience.

Failure to act properly as a director may lead to serious consequences, including disqualification from acting as a director. The Companies Act 2006 has for the first time set out core duties of the directors (see Chapter 6).

Company secretary

All public companies are required to have a company secretary, while private companies may choose to have a company secretary but are not required to. The company secretary of a private company need have no qualifications or previous experience. Company secretaries of public companies are required to be a member of one of a group of professional bodies or to have appropriate experience.

Articles of association

The articles of association detail the provisions relating to the regulation of the company in terms of the rights of its members and the authority of the directors.

The Companies Act provides three sets of model articles of association appropriate for private companies limited by shares, private companies limited by guarantee and public companies, and these are referred to as model articles.

Although there are very many regulations in the model articles setting out the rights of members and their relationship to the company, there are very few details concerning the rights of directors and their relationship with the company. Accordingly, while there are strict timescales for giving notice to shareholders to convene shareholders' meetings, directors' meetings are convened on reasonable notice, which can vary not only from company to company but also on the matter to be considered.

Previous Companies Acts provided a model set of articles suitable for private, public and guarantee companies in the form of tables appended to the Acts. The model articles for companies limited by shares was the first of these tables (Table A) and as a consequence they are often referred to as Table A. Even where the model articles are changed, the articles of any particular company will remain the articles and references to the model articles are to the version of the model articles applicable at the time of incorporation, until such time as they are changed by the company shareholders.

Share dealing, mergers and acquisitions

A company raises capital by issuing shares in the company to investors in return for money. These shares may subsequently be sold by the shareholders. Shares in public limited companies may be quoted on the Stock Exchange or NEX Exchange Main Board, where they are freely traded.

A company may wish to expand its business or avoid competition by merging with or acquiring another company.

Accounts and auditors

Incorporation as a limited company brings with it responsibilities to prepare and publish **annual accounts**, and for larger companies to have the accounts reviewed by an auditor. The prime reason for publishing accounts is so that potential trading partners can assess the risks of doing business, since if the business fails, the owners have no liability to meet the debts.

Dissolving the company

A company may have a limited lifespan and may eventually be wound up. This is the process of closing the company's affairs, selling any property and equipment, settling any liabilities and distributing any surplus funds to the owners. If the company is unable to pay its debts while it is trading, it may go into **liquidation**, administration or receivership. In these cases, an outside party is appointed to oversee the winding-up so as to secure as much funds as possible to meet the debts of the company. In most cases, there will be no surplus funds remaining for distribution to the owners.

Table 2.1: Types of trading entity

Factors to consider	*Plc*	*Ltd*	*Unltd*	*Guarantee*	*LLP*	*Unincorporated*
Profit	✓	✓	✓		✓	✓
Not for profit				✓		
Liability of members limited	✓	✓		✓	✓	
Liability of members unlimited			✓			✓
Financial information confidential			✓			✓
Financial information public	✓	✓		✓	✓	
Profits to be assessed for tax on owners					✓	✓
Profits to be assessed for tax on trading vehicle	✓	✓	✓	✓		
Shares to be offered to the public >100 persons	✓					
Shares to be offered to a defined restricted membership		✓	✓	✓	✓	✓

Matters to consider when incorporating a company

Table 2.1 summarises the various types of trading entities available and the range of factors to consider when incorporating a company.

Types of companies

There are five types of companies that may be incorporated, but the majority of companies are formed limited by shares. Companies limited by shares may be private companies or public companies. Companies limited by guarantee and unlimited companies can only be registered as private companies (ss. 4 and 5). The differences between private and public companies are discussed on pages 17–19. The company secretary should also be aware of other forms of incorporation, as follows.

Community Interest Company

Community Interest Companies (CICs) are private companies limited by shares or by guarantee that have lodged a Community Interest Statement, either at the time of incorporation or subsequently. CICs are also required to have an asset lock provision under which the assets and profits must be permanently retained within the CIC and used solely for the benefit of the community. The assets and profits may be transferred, but only to another organisation that has an asset lock. A CIC cannot obtain charitable status.

Right to Manage company

Right to Manage companies (RTMs) were introduced under the Commonhold and Leasehold Reform Act 2002. These are private companies limited by guarantee which must adopt articles of association prescribed by the RTM Companies (Model Articles) (England) Regulations 2009 (SI 2009/2767). RTMs enable long leaseholders in blocks of flats to take over the management of their building.

The name of such a company must end with 'RTM Company Limited' or the Welsh equivalent.

The Department of Communities and Local Government (DCLG) is responsible for RTM companies in England. A Welsh RTM company must adopt articles of association prescribed by the RTM Companies (Model Articles) (Wales) Regulations 2011 (SI 2011/2680). RTM companies do not exist in Scotland or Northern Ireland.

Companies limited by guarantee

This is a form of incorporation mainly used by charitable or non-profit-making organisations. For a company to be registered as a charity, it must be formed as a company limited by guarantee. Registered charities can convert their company to a CIC, but will lose their charitable status.

Unlimited companies

These are mainly used by professional practices and some special types of trading organisations where corporate status with perpetual succession is required. The advantage of perpetual succession is that the company carries on notwithstanding the changes in the membership of the company that will inevitably occur from time to time. This form of company can also be used to keep financial information secret at the 'price' of losing limited liability for the owners, since unlimited companies are not required to file accounts with the Registrar of Companies.

Limited liability partnerships

Created in April 2001 (and outside the scope of this book), this form of corporate body combines the organisational flexibility and taxation regime of a partnership with the financial disclosure and **creditor** protection regime of a limited company. A limited liability partnership combines the roles of owner and manager into one category of member. Unlike a limited company, a limited liability partnership must have at least two members.

Differences between companies limited by shares and those limited by guarantee

The main differences between companies limited by shares and companies limited by guarantee are that in the case of a company limited by guarantee, the following conditions apply:

1. Although members do not buy shares in the company, if the company is wound up, they guarantee to pay an amount to the company in order that it may meet some or all of its liabilities. The amount of the guarantee is usually a nominal amount and is frequently as little as £10.
2. Companies limited by guarantee may only be formed without **share capital** and all guarantee companies incorporated since 1 July 1985 are private companies. Before 22 December 1980, a guarantee company could be formed with or without share capital (CA1985 s. 1(4)), and before July 1985, guarantee companies with a share capital could also be public companies if they met the appropriate conditions (CA1985 s. 1(3)).
3. The memorandum of the company must be in the relevant form set out in Schedules 1 and 2 of the Companies (Registration) Regulations 2008 (SI 3014). Schedule 1 is for companies with a share capital and Schedule 2 is for companies without.
4. Different sets of model articles are prescribed under the Companies Act for private companies limited by shares and limited by guarantee.
5. The members of the company are the original subscribers to the memorandum of association, and any other persons whom the directors may approve for membership and who agree to be members.

6 If the company is non-profit-making, it may be permitted to omit the word 'limited' from its name (s. 60). An application for exemption can be made as part of the incorporation process using the relevant part of Form IN01.
7 Notwithstanding the exemption from including the word 'limited' from its name, the company is required to disclose on business letters and order forms that it is a limited company (s. 82).
8 The Secretary of State may withdraw the exemptions and require the company to include the word 'limited' in its name (s. 64) if they consider that the company no longer complies with the criteria to qualify for exemption.

Differences between companies limited by shares and unlimited companies

The main differences between companies limited by shares and unlimited companies are that in the case of an unlimited company, the following conditions apply:

1 Members of unlimited companies are liable for the company's liabilities without limit.
2 Unlimited companies must always be private companies (s. 4(2)).
3 Any transfers of shares must be on the 'common' form of transfer, which is signed by both **transferor** and **transferee**, and not the form prescribed under the Stock Transfer Act 1963, which requires only the signature of the transferor. (The transferor is the person who wishes to sell/pass on their shares to another person; the transferee is the person who is acquiring those shares, thereby becoming a member of the company.)
4 Unlimited companies are exempt from filing accounts with the Registrar of Companies unless they are a **holding company** of a limited company or a subsidiary of a limited company (s. 448).

Public companies and private companies

The definitions of public and private companies set out in s. 4 are as follows:

1 A public company is limited by shares (or limited by guarantee with a share capital, provided it was incorporated prior to 22 December 1980), complying with the following conditions:
   (a) the **certificate of incorporation** states that the company is a public company;
   (b) the company must have been registered or re-registered as a public company on or after 22 December 1980.
2 A private company is a company that is not a public company.

Additional requirements for public companies

The following is a summary of the main requirements on public companies that do not apply to private companies. Although this list is not exhaustive, it is clear that the legislative burden on public companies is greater than that for private companies.

1 The name of a public company must end with the words 'public limited company', 'plc' (or 'Public Limited Company' or 'PLC'), or the Welsh equivalent.
2 A public company must have an issued share capital with a nominal value of not less than the authorised minimum, which is currently £50,000 or the prescribed euro equivalent (ss. 761 and 763), before it can commence business or borrow (see point 3).
3 The issued shares must be paid up to not less than 25% of their nominal value, together with the whole of any premium (s. 761(3)). The **share premium** is the excess amount, if any, paid for a share over its nominal value.
4 Only public companies may offer their shares or debentures to the public (s. 755).
5 Strict rules are imposed on public companies to ensure that full value is given for any shares allotted (ss. 584–609).
6 A public company must file its accounts with the Registrar of Companies within six months of the end of its **financial year** (ss. 441 and 442(2)(b)).
7 A public company must have at least two directors, one of whom may also be the company secretary (s. 154).
8 A public company must appoint a company secretary (s. 271). The company secretary of a public company must be suitably qualified (s. 273).
9 A public company must hold **annual general meetings**.
10 A public company must lay its financial accounts before its shareholders and reappoint its auditors.
11 A public company may not approve resolutions by written resolutions of its members (s. 288), unless this is authorised by its articles of association.
12 There are strict regulations on a public company's ability to purchase its own shares or provide financial assistance for the purchase of its own shares. In particular, a public company may not fund the purchase of its own shares out of capital.
13 Although private companies need not have restrictions on the transfer of their shares, many do in order to retain ownership with the existing shareholders. Such provisions also provide protection from a disgruntled shareholder who might wish to sell shares to an 'outsider' or competitor. A public company whose shares are traded on a market (i.e. LSE, AIM or NEX) cannot, with one exception, place restrictions on the transferability of its fully paid shares. Public companies whose shares are not traded can adopt similar provisions to

private companies. The exception relates to companies whose articles contain a provision requiring a specified percentage of their shares to be held by UK residents.

14 The election of directors in a **general meeting** must be dealt with by separate rather than composite resolutions (s. 160(1)).

15 Public companies do not qualify as small or medium-sized companies.

16 Listed public companies must propose a resolution at their annual general meeting to approve the directors' remuneration report (s. 439).

17 The directors of public companies and private companies with more than one class of share may only be given authority to issue additional shares pursuant to s. 551 for a maximum of five years.

18 The articles of association of a public company may not contain a blanket exclusion of the **pre-emption rights** on the issue of new shares (s. 567).

19 While quoted companies are no longer required to produce an operating and financial review, many choose to do so voluntarily. The legal requirement for companies to produce a business review in their directors' report applies to all companies except 'small' companies.

20 Public Listed **companies** are required to draw up their financial results using International Accounting Standards.

21 For a company whose shares are admitted to a regulated market, a member who holds shares on behalf of another person may nominate them to enjoy information rights in respect of those shares (ss. 146–153).

22 The articles of a public company must contain specific authority before the directors can authorise a transaction or arrangement where a director has a conflict of interest (s. 175(5)).

How to form a company

Registration

Registration is the process by which a company is incorporated and becomes a legal entity separate from its owner(s) (i.e. the shareholders). This process is commonly referred to as registration, incorporation or formation. This is the case even with a private company, which may have only one shareholder. This principle is stated in s. 7(1):

> A company is formed under this Act by one or more persons – subscribing their names to a memorandum of association . . . and complying with the requirements of this Act as to registration.

Registration is effected by delivering the relevant documentation to the Registrar of Companies. Guidance (GP1) on incorporating a company is available from the Registrar by post or from the Companies House website (see Directory).

Registration can be undertaken in three ways:

1 Electronic software filing using an approved software product. The filing fee is £10 for the standard service or £30 for the guaranteed same-day service. Standard incorporations are usually processed within 24 hours.
2 Paper filing. The filing fee is £40 for the standard service or £100 for the guaranteed same-day service. Standard incorporations are usually processed within five working days.
3 Web Incorporation Service. The filing fee is £12 and there is no guaranteed same-day service. This service is only applicable for companies adopting the model articles without amendment and those not adopting a company name that requires approval.

Registration of private limited companies

These are the most commonly formed companies.

The first step is to find a suitable name. An index of company names is kept by the Registrar of Companies and must be checked to make sure that the proposed name will not be the same as or too similar to the name of any existing company.

The name should not be one to which the Registrar or other persons are likely to take exception (see Appendix 4). When a name has been selected, the documents listed below, having been completed and executed, must be sent to Companies House (New Companies Section, Cardiff for English/Welsh companies and Edinburgh for Scottish companies – see Directory).

If registration is required for a specific date, this can be accomplished by submitting the registration documents together with a covering letter to that effect. As a standard incorporation is usually processed in five days or fewer, it is suggested that the paper be submitted at least ten days before the required date. Alternatively, registration can be effected on a same-day basis (see page 22).

1 *Memorandum of association*. There must be at least one subscriber to the memorandum, who must agree to take at least one share in the company. The number of shares that each subscriber has agreed to take is shown against their name in the memorandum. One witness must sign against the name of each subscriber. A subscriber to the memorandum need not necessarily be an individual; it may be a corporate body, in which case the memorandum is signed by someone duly authorised on its behalf. The memorandum for a private company limited by shares must be in the form contained in Schedule 1 of the Companies (Registration) Regulations 2008 (SI 2008/3014).
2 *Articles of association*. All companies must register articles of association and a section concerning articles of association is provided on Form IN01, which is used when making an application to incorporate a company. This provides three options: (i) to adopt the relevant set of model articles in their entirety; (ii) to adopt the relevant set of model articles with modification; or (iii) to adopt an entirely bespoke set of articles.

3 *Form IN01*. Details of the proposed company must be submitted on Form IN01, 'Application to register a company'. Details to be provided include the proposed name, situation of the registered office, details of the proposed secretary (if any) and directors, together with their service address.
4 *Name approval*. Formal approval of the name of the company (if required) (see Chapter 4).
5 *Registration fee*. A cheque payable to Companies House for the registration fee of £10 (£50 for a same-day service). Where the documents are submitted electronically using the software filing or WebFiling facility, the filing fee is £8 (£30 for the same-day service).

The company's memorandum and articles of association delivered to the Registrar of Companies prior to incorporation may be in the Welsh language, provided the registered office is to be located in Wales, but must be accompanied by an English translation. This must be certified as being a correct translation by a notary public or solicitor.

If all is in order, the Registrar of Companies will issue a certificate of incorporation bearing the date of incorporation, the company's registered number and stating that the company is a private company. The certificate should be kept safely, but duplicate certificates of incorporation can be obtained from the Registrar of Companies for a fee (£15, or £50 for a same-day certified copy).

A private company may commence business as soon as it is incorporated.

Registration of public companies

The documents to be sent to the Registrar of Companies for the formation of a public company are the same as those for a private company.

A public company must have at least two directors (s. 154) and a company secretary. The Registrar's certificate of incorporation states that the company is a public company. Unlike a private company, a public company cannot immediately commence business on the issue of the certificate of incorporation or exercise any of its borrowing powers. Before this can happen, the company must deliver the 'Application for a trading certificate for a public company' (Form SH50), following which the Registrar will issue the trading certificate, confirming that the company complies with s. 761 of the Act concerning the capital requirements of public companies. This application includes confirmation that the authorised minimum share capital has been subscribed, giving details regarding the payment for the shares and certain other matters. The authorised minimum requires that each share issued by a public company must be paid up as to a minimum of 25% of its nominal value and 100% of any premium (s. 761). The Registrar is entitled to rely on the statement of compliance as sufficient evidence of the matters stated in it.

The issue of the trading certificate by the Registrar of Companies means that the company can commence its business and exercise any of its borrowing powers. If it does so before the issue of the certificate, the company and any officer in default may be liable to criminal penalties, although the transactions are not affected. In such an event, the Secretary of State may call upon the company to comply with the provisions of s. 761 within 21 days. If the company fails to do so, any party to the transaction who has sustained loss or damage may claim against the directors, who are jointly and severally liable to indemnify that party.

Registration of a Community Interest Company

The legislation under which CICs may be registered is contained in the Companies (Audit, Investigations and Community Enterprises) Act 2004 and the Community Interest Company Regulations 2005, SI 2005/1788. Along with the usual forms and documents required to incorporate a company, there are additional requirements for the incorporation of a CIC, as follows.

The memorandum and articles must comply with the provisions of Part 3 of the Community Interest Company Regulations 2005. These requirements set out details of the asset lock and other features of a CIC.

The name of the CIC must, if it is not a public company, end with the words 'Community Interest Company' or 'CIC'. If the registered office is situated in Wales, the Welsh equivalent may be used instead: 'Cwmni Buddiant Cymunedol' or 'CBC'. If the CIC is a public company, the name must end with 'Community Interest Public Limited Company' or 'Community Interest plc', or their Welsh equivalent: 'Cwmni Buddiant Cymunedol Cyhoeddus Cyfyngedig' or 'Cwmni Buddiant Cymunedol ccc'.

A CIC must clearly demonstrate how it will meet the community interest test. One way it can do this is to define closely its objects, rather than using the general commercial objects clause.

Form CIC36 is the Community Interest Statement (CIS) (C(AICE) 2004 s. 27). The CIS is to confirm that the company will benefit the community; it sets out the intended activities of the CIC and demonstrates how these will benefit the community. The Regulator will rely on the CIS in determining whether the proposed company is eligible for CIC status.

The final document is the Excluded Company Declaration (ECD) in the form approved by the Regulator. The purpose of the ECD is to confirm that the company is not excluded from being eligible from being a CIC. Excluded activities include involvement in political activities, lobbying for changes in legislation and activities for the benefit of a restricted segment of the community.

Additional supporting information may also be provided in an accompanying letter. The incorporation documents are all filed at Companies House. The filing fee for incorporating a CIC is £35. As the Regulator must confirm that the proposed company meets the eligibility criteria for a CIC, same-day incorporations are not possible.

Same-day registration

The registration of private or public companies is usually effected within five days of receipt of the registration documents by post, or within 24 hours where one of the online services is used. Registration can also be effected on the date of documents receipt if they are sent to Companies House (Cardiff) or the London office, addressed to the 'New Incorporation Section – same day incorporations', or if the online service is used by selecting the same-day option. The fee for a same-day registration is £100 for paper filings and £30 for electronic filings. In practice, the documents need to be received by midday for the company to be registered on the same day (3.00pm for electronic submissions).

Companies' registered numbers

On incorporation, every company is allocated a registered number; this consists of one or more sequences of figures or letters. The Registrar has the power to change a company's registered number but, for a period of three years following notification of a new registered number, the company may use either the old number or the new one on business letters and order forms (s. 1066).

Changing the status of a company

Re-registration

Provided certain conditions are met, companies incorporated as private limited companies can re-register as public companies and vice versa.

The following changes of status are permitted:

1. Private to public (unless previously re-registered as unlimited) (s. 90).
2. Public to private limited (s. 97).
3. Private limited to unlimited (unless previously re-registered as limited) (s. 102).
4. Unlimited to limited (unless previously re-registered as unlimited) (s. 105).
5. Public to unlimited (unless previously re-registered as limited or unlimited) (s. 109).

Re-registration of a private company as a public company

A private company meeting the necessary conditions can re-register as a public company (s. 90). The re-registration must be approved by **special resolution** and application made to the Registrar.

To qualify for re-registration as a public company, the company must have:

1. at least two directors (s. 154), one of whom must be a natural person (s. 155); and
2. issued at least £50,000 of share capital, in nominal value, of which all of any premium and at least 25% of the nominal value on each share must be paid (the authorised minimum) (s. 91).

A balance sheet must be prepared for a date not more than seven months prior to the date of the application together with an unqualified **audit** report, made up to a date not more than seven months prior to the date of application (s. 92). If the company has previously taken advantage of the audit exemption (see page 152) and has not prepared audited accounts, it must prepare audited accounts prior to its application for re-registration. If the auditor's report is qualified, the auditor must confirm that the qualification is not material for the purposes of establishing that the net assets are not less than the aggregate of the called-up share capital and undistributable reserves (s. 92(5)).

The auditor must report that the balance sheet shows that the net assets are not less than the aggregate of the share capital and any undistributable reserves (s. 92(1)(c)).

If, between the date of the balance sheet and the date of application for re-registration, the company has issued shares for non-cash consideration, a report confirming the value of the consideration in terms of s. 1150 must be prepared (s. 93).

Where the company has insufficient share capital in issue, it is common practice to undertake a capitalisation issue at the same time as the special resolution to re-register the company is proposed. The procedure for re-registering a private company as a public company is as follows:

1 The directors, at a board meeting, resolve to convene a general meeting or circulate a written resolution to approve a special resolution that the company be re-registered as a public company, to alter the articles of the company to state that the company is to be a public company and to make other amendments necessary for the articles to conform with the requirements for a public company (see precedent 12). This includes changing the name of the company to end with the appropriate suffix, e.g. 'public limited company', a permitted abbreviation or the Welsh alternative.
2 When the special resolution has been passed, an application is submitted to the Registrar of Companies on Form RR01 ('Application by a private company for re-registration as a public company'), signed by a director or the company secretary. The resolution must be filed within 15 days of its passing. The following documents must accompany the application:
   (a) a copy of the special resolution approving the re-registration;
   (b) a printed copy of the articles as altered by the special resolution;
   (c) a copy of the auditors' written statement in relation to s. 92(1)(c);
   (d) a copy of the relevant balance sheet, together with a copy of an unqualified auditors' report on it;
   (e) if shares have been allotted by the company between the relevant balance sheet date and the passing of the special resolution, other than for cash, a report with regard to the valuation of any asset in consideration for which the shares were allotted (s. 93(2)(a));
   (f) if there is no company secretary appointed, a statement of the company's proposed secretary in accordance with s. 95 needs to be completed on section 2 of the application; and

(g) a cheque in respect of the re-registration fee payable of £20. If it is proposed to change the name as well as re-register the company, the fee increases to £30. The fee for same-day re-registrations or re-registrations and change of name are £50 and £100, respectively.

3 If the application is approved, the Registrar of Companies will issue a certificate of incorporation stating that the company is a public company. When the certificate is issued, any alterations to the memorandum and articles take effect.

4 See 'Change of company name' (Chapter 4) for guidance on other matters to be dealt with.

Re-registration of other types of company as public companies

Unlimited companies may be re-registered as public companies (s. 90(1)). They cannot, however, re-register as a public company if they have previously re-registered as an unlimited company (s. 90(2)(e)).

Re-registration of a public company as a private company

As the provisions regulating public companies are more stringent than those for private companies, it is not necessary for the directors to ensure that the company meets any requirements prior to putting an appropriate resolution to the shareholders. The procedure to re-register a public company as a private company is as follows:

1 The directors, at a board meeting, resolve that a general meeting be convened to pass a special resolution that the company be re-registered as a private company and making such other alterations to the articles as required. This includes a change of the name of the company, deleting the suffix 'public limited company' or any abbreviation and substituting the word 'Limited' (see precedent 13).

2 When the special resolution has been passed, a copy must be sent to the Registrar of Companies within 15 days.

3 If holders of not less than 5% of the issued share capital or a group of not fewer than 50 of the company members object to the change, they may apply to the court for cancellation of the special resolution within 28 days of its being passed (s. 98(1)–(3)). Shareholders who voted in favour of the resolution are barred from calling for the cancellation of the resolution. If such an application is made, the Registrar of Companies must be informed immediately on Form RR03 (s. 99(1)). The court will either cancel or confirm the resolution, and a copy of the court order must be lodged with the Registrar within 15 days of the order being made, or such longer time as the court may allow (ss. 98(3) and 99(3)).

4 Assuming that no application for cancellation is made or if the special resolution is confirmed by court order, application for re-registrations should be submitted to the Registrar of Companies on Form RR02 ('Application by a

public company for re-registration as a private limited company') and signed by a director or the company secretary. The form must be accompanied by the following documents:

(a) a printed copy of the special resolution;
(b) a printed copy of the articles, as altered by the special resolution. If all the company's shareholders voted in favour of the resolution, the application may be made immediately following the meeting; and
(c) a cheque in respect of the re-registration fee payable of £20. If it is proposed to change the name as well as re-register the company, the fee increases to £30. The fee for same-day re-registrations or re-registrations and change of name are £50 and £100, respectively.

5 If the Registrar of Companies is satisfied that the application is valid, they will issue a certificate of incorporation appropriate to a company that is not a public company. The alterations to the articles take effect upon the issue of the certificate.
6 See 'Change of company name' (Chapter 4) for guidance on other matters to be dealt with. The above procedure is for voluntary re-registration.
7 All public companies, whether Listed or not, are subject to the City Code on Takeovers and Mergers (see Chapter 21). The Code provides protection to shareholders in the event of a takeover or merger.

Provided the company was not a Listed company or offered any of its shares to the public in the previous ten years by re-registering as a private company, the company may no longer fall within the scope of the City Code. Although not a statutory or City Code requirement, unlisted public companies with external shareholders are recommended to contact the Takeover Panel if they are proposing to re-register as a private company. The Takeover Panel will be concerned to ensure that shareholders are made aware that in the event of re-registration, they will lose the protection afforded by the City Code. For contact details, see the Directory.

Re-registration of private limited company as unlimited

A private limited company may re-register as an unlimited company (s. 102), unless it has previously re-registered as a limited company (s. 102(2).

The procedure to re-register a private limited company as a private unlimited company is as follows (s. 103):

1 The directors, at a board meeting, resolve that a general meeting be convened or written resolutions circulated to pass a resolution that the company be re-registered as a private unlimited company and making such other alterations to the articles as required. This includes a change of the name of the company, deleting the suffix 'limited' or any abbreviation and substituting the word 'Unlimited' (see precedent 87). The resolution to re-register as an unlimited company must be approved by all members (s. 102(1)(a)). If the company

was incorporated prior to 1 October 2009, the opportunity can be taken to remove the now redundant clauses contained in its memorandum of association.

2 When the resolution has been passed, a copy must be sent to the Registrar of Companies within 15 days.

3 Application for re-registration should be submitted to the Registrar of Companies on Form RR05 ('Application by a private limited company for re-registration as an unlimited company') and signed by a director or the company secretary. The form must be accompanied by the following documents:
   (a) a printed copy of the resolution;
   (b) a printed copy of the articles, as altered by the special resolution
   (c) the prescribed form of assent for re-registration signed by all the members (this form has no number but is available on application to Companies House or by downloading a copy (https://assets.publishing.service.gov.uk/government/uploads/system/uploads/attachment_data/file/341151/proFormaFormOfAssentForReRegistrationOfPrivateLimitedCompanyAsUnlimited.pdf); and
   (d) a cheque in respect of the re-registration fee payable of £20. If it is proposed to change the name as well as re-register the company, the fee increases to £30. The fee for same-day re-registrations or re-registrations and change of name are £50 and £100, respectively.

4 If the Registrar of Companies is satisfied that the application is valid, they will issue a certificate of incorporation appropriate to a company that is an unlimited company. The alterations to the articles take effect upon the issue of the certificate.

5 See 'Change of company name' (Chapter 4) for guidance on other matters to be dealt with.

Re-registration of unlimited company as private limited company

An unlimited company may re-register as a limited company (ss. 105 and 106); however, a limited company which has previously re-registered as an unlimited company cannot later re-register as a limited company (s. 105(1) and (2)).

The procedure to re-register a private unlimited company as a private limited company is as follows (s. 106):

1 The directors, at a board meeting, resolve that a general meeting be convened or written resolutions circulated to pass a special resolution that the company be re-registered as a private limited company, either by shares or guarantee, and making such other alterations to the articles as required. This includes a change of the name of the company, deleting the suffix 'unlimited' or any abbreviation and substituting the word 'Limited' (see precedent 88). If the company was incorporated prior to 1 October 2009, the opportunity can be

taken to remove the now redundant clauses contained in its memorandum of association.

2 When the resolution has been passed, a copy must be sent to the Registrar of Companies within 15 days.

3 Application for re-registration should be submitted to the Registrar of Companies on Form RR06 ('Application by an unlimited company for re-registration as a private limited company') and signed by a director or the company secretary. The form must be accompanied by the following documents:
   (a) a printed copy of the special resolution;
   (b) a printed copy of the articles, as altered by the special resolution
   (c) a statement of guarantee, if appropriate; and
   (d) a cheque in respect of the re-registration fee payable of £20. If it is proposed to change the name as well as re-register the company, the fee increases to £30. The fee for same-day re-registrations or re-registrations and change of name are £50 and £100, respectively.

4 If the Registrar of Companies is satisfied that the application is valid, they will issue a certificate of incorporation appropriate to a company that is a private limited company. The alterations to the articles take effect upon the issue of the certificate.

5 Within 15 days of the re-registration a statement of capital must be submitted unless that information has already been submitted statement of capital and initial shareholdings under s. 10 or a statement of capital (s. 108).

6 See 'Change of company name' (Chapter 4) for guidance on other matters to be dealt with.

3 – Articles of association

Introduction

As the basic constitutional documents of a company, the articles of association provide the framework within which a company must operate. The articles of association are the rules and regulations by which the internal affairs of the company and the relationships between the company, its directors and its members are governed.

Many topics of interest and importance relating to the running of a company are referred to in passing as, in practical terms, there are very few matters which can be determined by reference to the articles alone. Forfeiture of shares is one exception, as it has no statutory basis.

The articles are put in place when a company is incorporated remain that company's articles, unless they are amended by resolution of the shareholders.

Memorandum of association

Every company must have a memorandum and the form of this is prescribed by legislation. It contains a statement from the subscribers (being the founder members) that they wish to be formed into a company pursuant to the memorandum.

Under previous Companies Acts, the memorandum set out any restrictions on the activities the company could undertake, as companies were only permitted to exercise certain powers provided these were permitted by the memorandum or articles of association. An important change introduced by the Companies Act 2006 was to reverse this, and companies can now undertake any (lawful) activity and exercise any authority of the company, provided there are no restrictions in the articles of association.

With the exception of the subscriber clause, all other clauses previously contained in a company's memorandum of association are now deemed to form part of the articles of association, and any references to giving specific powers to the company or directors now serve as a limit on those powers.

A common example is the share capital clause. The Companies Act removed the requirement for companies to have an authorised share capital, which previously stipulated the maximum number of shares that the company could issue.

Unless removed, these legacy clauses now serve as a restriction on the otherwise unlimited number of shares that a company can issue (see page 196).

Articles of association

Every company must also have articles of association. The articles are the regulations governing a company's internal management. As such, there is more freedom about what the articles contain and they can – and for companies with non-director members, should – be tailored to suit a company's particular circumstances.

Importantly, under the Companies Act, the articles constitute a contract between each of the members and can be enforced as if signed by each individual member (s. 33(1)). They set out the relationship between the company and its members, and the requirements of the articles must be observed.

They must be printed and numbered in consecutive paragraphs, registered at the time of the incorporation of the company and signed by the subscribers.

Model articles

The Companies (Model Articles) Regulations 2008 prescribe model articles for private companies limited by shares, public companies and guarantee companies. The relevant model articles will automatically be the articles for companies formed under the Companies Act 2006, which do not register their own articles of association, or which register their own articles but do not exclude the model articles in whole or in part. As a result, the articles of a company usually contain a combination of the articles registered upon incorporation and those model articles not specifically excluded or amended by the company's own articles.

Previous Companies Acts incorporated Tables A to F, which were the model forms for both the memorandum and articles of association. Table A contained the default articles of association for a company limited by shares. Accordingly, the previous model articles were simply referred to as Table A, even though in reality there were 19 different versions of Table A from 1856 until the final version created in 2008.

Companies incorporated under those earlier Companies Acts will have adopted some version of Table A and these regulations will continue to apply to those companies. When reading a company's articles that incorporate Table A, it is essential to establish which version of Table A applies, by reference to the date of adoption of the articles currently in force. It will usually be indicated quite clearly at the start of the articles which version of Table A applies and whether any specific clauses in Table A are excluded or varied.

The articles can only very rarely be said to constitute the last word on any particular issue. They must generally be viewed against a broader framework of company law. Given that law is always evolving, it is quite usual for the articles to refer to the legislation in force at the time of their adoption, but also to encompass any later changes.

There is no magic formula for determining whether the constitutional documents or the statutory provisions take precedence. In very broad terms, the articles cannot stipulate requirements or procedures that are less stringent than the statutory position where this would or could result in some loss of rights for the shareholders. Sometimes the Companies Acts permit the articles to contain more detailed or challenging requirements than are prescribed by law, such as allowing the delivery of proxies up to the time scheduled for a general meeting, or requiring longer notice to be given of a general meeting than is required by company law. Sometimes statute does not conceive of this possibility at all. While this may seem a little confusing, the exact position should become clear by detailed review of the relevant clauses of the Companies Acts.

Further, many of the statutory provisions that have come into force recently cannot automatically be read into a company's articles. In such cases, the articles need to be amended before use can be made of the new provisions. For example, the Companies Act does not require private companies to hold an annual general meeting. The company's articles might contain a provision requiring the holding of an annual meeting, since under previous Companies Acts, all companies were required to hold an annual general meeting. In such a case, the company will continue to have to hold an annual meeting until such time as the articles are amended.

From 28 April 2013, a change to the model articles has been brought about by provisions in the Mental Health (Discrimination) Act 2013, insofar as it removes model article 18(e) from the model articles for private companies to tackle discrimination in this area of law. Additionally, model articles for public companies have also been amended to remove any such discrimination (article 22(e) of the model articles).

As such, all model articles adopted for private and public companies incorporated after 28 April 2013 should omit any reference to termination of a director's appointment on grounds of mental health.

Bespoke articles

Certain types of company adopt specialised forms of articles which depart further from the model articles. These include subsidiaries, residents' management companies, and charitable and non-profit-making organisations. CIC companies are required to modify their articles to comply with provisions of Part 3 of the Community Interest Company Regulations 2005.

Listed, AIM and NEX companies will usually disapply the model articles in their entirety, and will adopt a comprehensive set of articles drawn up to meet their specific needs and requirements.

Companies may also wish to adopt articles relating to the rights of shareholders so as to create different classes of shares with different rights attaching to each class. Broadly speaking, these rights can be split into voting rights, dividend rights, rights on the return of capital and rights relating to the issue of new shares or the transfer of existing shares.

Companies limited by guarantee usually adopt bye-laws in addition to the articles. These are essential where the company operates a membership separate from its shareholders or guarantors. Often there will be different types of membership and differing levels of annual subscriptions. The articles would not be an appropriate document in which to set out rules and regulations relating to the membership and internal regulations of the organisation and, accordingly, these are set out in a separate document.

Shareholder agreements

Increasingly, companies are putting some rules of internal management into shareholder agreements rather than into articles. Shareholder agreements are contracts between the parties entering into it. As such, they are completely distinct from the articles. Articles are automatically a contract between a company and each of its members. However, a shareholder agreement is merely a contract between those persons who are parties to it. It is therefore essential that any person joining the company as a member agrees to become a party to the shareholder agreement, because failure to do so means that they are not bound by the agreement, nor can they enforce it against a party to it. Shareholders' agreements commonly include a clause that stipulates that **allottees**, transferees and transmittees must agree to be bound by the terms of the agreement before the allotment, transfer or transmittal of shares is completed.

While articles of association constitute a public document, shareholder agreements are generally viewed as being confidential. It is arguable that certain provisions of a shareholder agreement (such as anything that purports to vary a provision stated in the company's articles) should be filed at Companies House. Sections 29 and 30 provide that copies of all agreements agreed to by all the members, that would not otherwise have been effective unless passed by a special resolution, should be filed at Companies House within 15 days of being made. In the absence of any judicial authority on this point, it is likely that shareholder agreements will continue to be treated as purely private documents.

While a shareholders' agreement may contain a number of provisions that also appear in the articles, there are a number of other matters that shareholders might prefer to include only in the shareholders' agreement so that they are not available on the public record. Examples of such matters include: transferability of shares in a range of different circumstances, including circumstances that are to be regarded as 'permitted transfers' (e.g. transfers from or to founder members of the company or their family members); restrictive covenants on the company and the parties; or the company's distribution policy.

Under section 21(1), unless the provisions in the articles are more stringent, a company can change its articles by passing a special resolution. A shareholders' agreement, however, can only be changed in accordance with the manner set out in the contract itself, or, if the contract is silent, by obtaining the agreement of all parties to it. As hinted at above, a company can choose a higher threshold of approval that needs to be obtained before its articles can be changed – for example, by requiring unanimity – but this could be restrictive from a practical perspective on a day-to-day basis, especially if the company's shareholder base is large. It is also quite common to find provisions in the shareholders' agreement that impose some additional requirements with regard to amendment of the articles – for example, that approval must be given by a particular shareholder (often the majority investor) as well as the 75% majority being met.

Controlling shareholders agreements

In order to provide greater protection for minority shareholders in companies with a majority shareholder, premium listed companies with a shareholder or a concert party of shareholders holding 30% or more of the company's voting rights ('a controlling shareholder') must enter into a legally binding controlling shareholders agreement, or relationship agreement which, as a minimum, must contain three undertakings:

- that transactions and the arrangement between the company and the controlling shareholder will be conducted on an arm's length basis on normal commercial terms;
- that the controlling shareholder will not take any action that would prevent the company from complying with its obligations under the Listing Rules; and
- that the controlling shareholder will not seek any shareholder resolutions the purpose of which is intended or appears to be intended to circumvent the proper application of the Listing Rules.

The FCA has confirmed that the intention is to ensure as far as possible that inappropriate relationships do not develop.

Issuers with a controlling shareholder must confirm in their annual report that they have entered into a controlling shareholders agreement, the extent to which the parties to the agreement have complied with the terms and explanation for any non-compliance.

(For more information, see Chapter 16.)

Alteration of articles

The articles may be altered by amending the wording of one or more of the articles, deleting or adding articles, or adopting a completely new set of articles to take the place of the original ones. Articles may be amended in any way subject to the following:

1 When the court deals with an unfair prejudice application under section 994, it is open to the court to alter the company's articles and to prohibit any alteration of that amended article without its consent.
2 An amendment to the articles cannot increase the liability of any member unless the member agrees in writing, before or after the amendment has taken place (s. 25).

3 If the amendment seeks to vary **class rights**, it will not be valid unless the resolution has also been passed at a class meeting of the members of that class. In addition, members who voted against the resolution and who hold between them at least 15% of the shares of the class in question have 21 days to object to the court (s. 633).
4 Any amendment must be bona fide for the benefit of the company and not a potential fraud on minority shareholders.

In order to amend the articles, a special resolution must be passed as follows:

1 The directors in a board meeting resolve to convene a general meeting to consider the special resolution, to approve a circular to members explaining the reasons for the alterations and, in the case of a Listed company, to approve a **three-way proxy** form (*LR 9.3.6*) (see precedents 5 and 7).
2 All amendments in wording may be included in the resolution (see precedent 11). However, if it is intended to adopt new articles, the circular will usually summarise the main provisions and state that a copy of the proposed articles is available for inspection, either at the company's registered office or at the office of the company's solicitors, from the time the notice is sent to members to the date of the meeting.
3 If a significant proportion of the shares are held by financial institutions, e.g. insurance companies and pension funds, it may be appropriate to obtain confirmation that the proposed new articles are acceptable. This may be particularly relevant where changes are proposed to require greater involvement of shareholders, in line with the company's corporate governance strategy.
4 A certified copy of the resolution must be sent to the Registrar within 15 days of the meeting. This must be accompanied by a printed copy of the articles as amended or a certified copy of the new articles, as appropriate (s. 26(1)).
5 (*Listed, AIM and NEX companies only*) Two prints of the resolution and of the new or amended articles must be sent to the Financial Conduct Authority (FCA) for publication through the document-viewing facility (*LR 9.6.2*).
6 A reprint of the memorandum and revised articles incorporating a copy of the special resolution should be prepared or, alternatively, copies in stock should be suitably amended. Copies of the reprinted memorandum and articles or amended copies should be sent to directors of the company, its auditors, solicitors and others known to use copies of the memorandum and articles.
7 Copies of the amended articles must be sent to any members on request (s. 32(1)(a)).
8 Where a number of amendments dealing with separate matters are proposed, it may be appropriate to deal with those by different resolutions rather than bundled together. In this way, shareholders can consider each matter separately and vote on each amendment as appropriate.

Entrenchment of articles

As previously noted, the Companies Act has changed the structure of companies' constitutional documents, and provisions previously found in the memorandum of association are now incorporated in the articles of association. This change has made it possible for the provisions previously found in the memorandum, and which could not therefore be changed, to be altered by special resolution. To provide continuing protection for those clauses, the concept of entrenchment has been introduced by s. 22.

As a consequence, companies will no longer be able to provide that a certain provision can never be repealed or amended. For example, a company with charitable aims might use entrenchment to ensure that profits cannot be distributed to its members, rather than relying on charity law or using the community interest company vehicle.

However, following consultation, the government has decided that there is some uncertainty that s. 22(2) might have unintended consequences as regards changes to class rights that are subject to a separate regime set out in s. 630. As a result, s. 22(1) was not brought into force and remains delayed.

A company must give notice to the Registrar when an entrenching provision is included in its articles (whether on formation or subsequently), or where the company's articles are altered by order of a court or other authority so as to restrict or exclude the power of the company to amend its articles to amend or remove those powers (s. 23).

Where a company amends any entrenched provisions in its articles, it must send to the Registrar the resolution or court order making or evidencing the amendment (s. 24), together with a 'statement of compliance' on Form CC01 or CC02, depending on whether the amendment is to include or exclude entrenchment provisions, respectively. This must certify that the amendment has been made in accordance with the company's articles (including any provision for entrenchment) or, where relevant, in accordance with any order of the court or other authority.

Format and content of the articles

The articles must form one document, comprise numbered consecutive paragraphs and, in the case of the articles registered at the time of the incorporation of the company, be signed by the subscribers.

A company is free to adopt or amend the contents of its articles in any way it wishes, subject to the provisions being lawful and not conflicting with any provisions of the Companies Acts or any other rule of law.

Typically, where the model articles are not adopted, the articles will include some or all of the following provisions.

Preliminary

There will usually be a few initial clauses stating that the model articles do not apply, setting out details of any defined words or expressions and that the Companies Act in force at the time of adoption and any modifications to the Companies Act thereafter will apply to the company.

Office

Details of where the registered office must be located.

Share capital

Details of the class name(s) and nominal value of the company's shares. The Companies Act 2006 removed the concept of authorised share capital and, as a consequence, the articles are not required to state an authorised capital amount. Companies may, however, choose to impose a restriction on the maximum number of shares that can be issued, although shareholders can be protected by limiting the directors' authority to issue shares and by requiring pre-emption provisions to be observed.

It is normal to state that any new shares will rank equally with existing shares of the same class.

The members will be given authority, subject to passing an **ordinary resolution**, to undertake a consolidation, cancellation or subdivision of shares, stating the default position to be followed where a consolidation results in the creation of fractions of shares.

The articles will also normally allow members to undertake reduction of capital and purchase of own shares, and any conditions concerning reduction of capital and purchase of own shares. These usually replicate or adopt the conditions set out in the Companies Act, but additional conditions can be imposed.

Class rights and meetings

Where there are more than one class of shares or the shares are not to have unfettered rights (such as no right to dividends), then details of the restrictions, enhancements and variation in rights must be set out in the articles. If the articles are silent on any particular right, then the shares must be treated equally in respect of that right.

The articles will also contain clauses setting out: the protection for shareholders of different classes with either enhanced or restricted rights; that their rights may not be changed without their consent as a class; and the process required to hold class meetings. These would tend to be the same procedures as for general meetings, with appropriate changes to take account of the meeting being a class meeting.

Shares

Provided the company is permitted to do so by its articles, it may pay commission on the issue of new shares up to a maximum of 10% of the issue price (ss. 552 and

553). In practice, this provision is rarely used other than by public companies issuing shares under a **prospectus**, where commissions may be offered to financial intermediaries or as an incentive to apply early.

Directors may only exercise the company's power to allot additional shares if permitted to do so by the directors or by resolution of the members, unless the allotment relates to shares being allotted in relation to an employee share scheme or the granting of a right to convert securities into shares (ss. 549 and 551(1)). The director(s) of a private company with only one class of shares is/are deemed to have authority to allot those shares, subject to any restriction in their articles (s. 550). The model articles contain no restriction.

Directors of private companies with more than one class of shares or of public companies may only exercise the company's power to allot shares as permitted by the articles of association or by resolution of the members. Authorisation must state the maximum number of shares that may be allotted and the date on which it will expire, which must not be longer than five years after the date of incorporation, if contained in the articles, or the date of approval of the resolution giving the authority (s. 551(3)). The authority may be given, varied, renewed or withdrawn by ordinary resolution.

In addition to provisions permitting the directors to exercise the company's power to allot shares, the articles may also contain provisions excluding the pre-emption rights on the allotment of shares contained in s. 561. These statutory pre-emption rights may be excluded entirely by the articles of a private company (s. 567), or may be excluded by special resolution of the members for specific allotments or where there is general authority to allot shares (ss. 570 and 571) (see Chapter 13 for further details on share allotments).

Share certificates and uncertificated holdings

Articles 24 and 25 of the model articles for private companies limited by shares set out the requirements relating to share certificates. Under these articles, each shareholder is entitled to one or more certificates in respect of the shares they hold and the certificate(s) must be provided free of charge. The minimum basic information to be shown on the share certificate is:

- how many shares the certificate is for and what class they are;
- the nominal value of the shares;
- that the shares are fully paid up; and
- any distinguishing numbers assigned to the shares.

A share certificate may not cover holdings in more than one class. Joint holders are only entitled to one share certificate between them. Certificates must be sealed or executed in any other way provided for by law (e.g. signed by one director and witnessed or signed by two officers).

A shareholder is entitled to a replacement certificate where the original is damaged, defaced, lost, stolen or destroyed. Where a certificate is damaged or defaced, the certificate should be returned to the company. Where the certificate cannot be found, the shareholder will usually be asked to sign an indemnity (see precedent 70). Often such indemnity has to be joined in by a bank or insurance company, but sometimes the requirement is waived. While it is generally good practice for replacement certificates to be clearly marked as such, there is no such requirement in the model articles that this be done.

Where the company's shares are permitted to be held in uncertificated form, the articles must contain the necessary provisions dealing with the holding of shares in dematerialised form.

If shares have been allotted partly paid, the articles should contain provisions stating the procedure to follow, in order that the directors can call upon those members to pay up the balance outstanding. This process is called making a call on the shares. The articles will also make provisions on the actions available to the company in the event of the call not being paid, including liability of joint holders, interest on unpaid calls and the right of the company to create a lien on the shares.

Lien on shares

In the event of a call on partly paid shares not being paid, the articles will usually allow the directors to take a lien over the shares. If the call remains unpaid, the directors will have the power to sell those shares and give good title to the person purchasing them.

Forfeiture of shares

If shares have been issued as nil paid, the articles should contain additional provisions in case a call remains unpaid, allowing the company to forfeit the shares for non-payment. Unless there is this authority in the articles, there is no right for shares to be forfeited.

Where shares have become liable to forfeiture, the articles would typically contain a provision allowing the non-paying member to surrender the shares.

Transfer of shares

Unless members are to have an unrestricted right to transfer shares to anyone they wish, the articles of a private company will routinely contain restrictions on the right to transfer. In many cases these restrictions will require any shares to be sold to be offered to existing members in proportion to the number of shares already held and in priority to the shares being offered to any non-shareholders.

A company whose shares are admitted to trading on the main market, AIM or NEX will not be permitted to have any pre-emption rights on the transfer of shares.

With the rise of computerised registers of members and the use of record dates, it is becoming increasingly less common for the register of members to be closed to allow any pending transactions to be processed prior to the declaration of a dividend or similar corporate event.

When presented with an instrument of transfer, the directors must either register the transfer or notify the intending transferor of the refusal to do so (s. 771). This notification must be made within two months of the transfer form being lodged with the company (s. 771(1)).

Tag-along rights do not feature in the model articles, and therefore need to be specifically included in a company's articles or shareholder agreements if they are considered necessary and appropriate. The inclusion of tag-along rights in a company's articles or in a shareholder agreement gives minority shareholders a measure of comfort about what will happen when the majority shareholder wishes to sell shares in circumstances that would lead to a change of control of the company.

In such circumstances, tag-along rights ensure that the shares can only be sold if the proposed buyer offers to buy all the other shares in the company on the same (or better) terms as the original offer. The articles also need to include a clause that prevents completion of the sale in the event that the seller fails to comply with the provisions of the tag-along clause. The company will also be empowered to refuse to register the transfer in the buyer's name unless a compliant offer has been made to the minority shareholders.

Drag-along rights may also be included in a company's articles or in a shareholders' agreement. As with tag-along rights, since they are not dealt with in the model articles, inclusion of such rights in a shareholders' agreement or the company's articles is the only way of ensuring they apply.

Drag-along rights compel a majority shareholder to bring all the other shareholders with them when they accept an offer to buy their shares that would result in a change of control of the company. This ensures that the prospective buyer can acquire the entire company. Inclusion of these rights is generally at the behest of the majority shareholder, keen to ensure they do not miss out on an opportunity to sell their investment because the buyer refuses to proceed with a transaction that would see minority shareholders remaining in situ. When drafting such clauses, consideration should be given as to whether there should be any exclusions to the general rule, as there may be circumstances in which minority shareholders need not be compelled to sell their holdings.

General meetings

The articles will contain detailed provisions dealing with the holding of general meetings.

Notice of general meetings

Although the Companies Act lays down minimum notice periods for meetings and the definition of clear days' notice that will apply, these can be amended by the articles, which may provide for either a longer notice period or a different, longer definition of clear days' notice. In particular, it should be noted that the Companies Act reduced the notice period for general meetings. The articles of an older company, however, may well reproduce the notice periods contained in the former Acts, in which case those longer notice periods will apply until such time as the articles are amended.

Proceedings at general meetings

In addition to detailed provisions for convening general meetings, the articles will contain detailed provisions for the conduct of meetings including the quorum requirement, procedures to be followed in the event a quorum is not present or maintained, power of the chairman to adjourn the meeting, who can act as chairman, details on who can vote and the method of voting (including right to call for a poll vote, conduct of the poll and time allowed for conducting the poll).

Voting rights

Particularly in cases where the company has more than one class of shares, the articles will contain detailed provisions setting out the different voting rights of members and how they may exercise those rights if they are not able to attend the meeting in person.

A significant change introduced by the Companies Act was the right of members to appoint one or more proxies and that a **proxy** need not also be a member in their own right. Previously many companies restricted the right to the appointment of one proxy, but any provisions to this effect are no longer valid.

Corporations acting by representatives

Rather than appointing proxies, many corporate shareholders will appoint a corporate representative. Unlike the appointment of a proxy, the appointment of a corporate representative does not require registering with the company in advance of the meeting. The appointee should take with them a letter on headed stationery confirming their appointment.

Directors

The articles will contain details of the appointment process for directors, and the maximum or minimum number of directors (if any).

Increasingly, if the directors are required to hold a share qualification, details will need to be stated in the articles. Some companies, in particular those undertaking services that require a specific qualification, such as architecture or dentistry, may include requirements that the directors must hold a specified professional qualification.

The articles may contain provision for the payment of fees to directors in addition to any remuneration they might receive for their executive duties.

There are extensive provisions in the Companies Act relating to directors' interests in contracts, and there will often be additional provisions in the articles and in particular provisions allowing directors to participate in discussions and decisions, provided they had declared any interests.

Appointment and retirement of directors

In addition to the statutory provisions, the articles of most companies will provide that the directors may fill any vacancies up to any maximum number permitted by the articles. Public companies will also have provisions setting out the arrangements for directors to retire by rotation at each annual general meeting (AGM). A public company without any shares admitted to a public market may well exclude rotation provisions, while those companies with shares traded on the main market, AIM or NEX might require their directors to retire by rotation, one third each year. Listed companies are recommended by the **UK Corporate Governance Code** to have their directors retire by rotation every year, and increasingly Listed companies are amending their articles to include this provision.

Alternate directors

There are no provisions within the Companies Act to allow directors to appoint alternates. Accordingly, directors can only do so if specifically authorised by the articles of association. The articles will need to include provisions setting out details of how a director can appoint an alternate, who may be appointed if any further consent is required. A typical position would be that a director can appoint an alternate by notice in writing to the board. The appointment of another director as alternate needs no further consent, but the appointment of a non-director requires the consent of the other directors. Where directors receive fees for attendance at meeting or other directors' fees, there may also be provisions stipulating how (if at all) the entitlement to any fee is split. The articles should also refer to the rights, duties and responsibilities of any person appointed as an alternate.

The model articles for a public company contain provisions for the appointment of **alternate directors**. The model articles for a private company do not.

Proceedings of directors

Unlike members' meetings, the Companies Act is for the most part silent on directors' meetings and accordingly the articles must contain all necessary provisions, which will usually include:

- power to convene directors' meetings;
- quorum for a board meeting;
- resolutions in writing;
- powers of directors to act notwithstanding reduction below minimum number;
- appointment of chairman;
- appointment of and delegation of powers to committees;
- proceedings of committees; and
- validity of acts of directors.

Borrowing powers

For companies incorporated under the Companies Act, the directors will have full authority to exercise the powers of the company to borrow and secure loans against the company's assets, unless restricted by the articles of association. This is a departure from the previous position, which authorised the directors to exercise those powers to the extent permitted by the articles. For the majority of companies, this is perfectly acceptable and no additional provisions are required.

Larger companies and those with external shareholders (in particular, Listed, AIM and NEX companies) will restrict the directors' power to borrow or secure the assets of the company. This limitation is often stipulated as a multiple of the net asset value of the company rather than a specific amount, and accordingly the actual limit will vary over time.

If the directors breach these powers, third parties will usually be protected and the company will be unable to void the contract, but it will be able to seek to recover any losses from the directors concerned.

Secretary

Articles for public companies and some private companies will contain provisions relating to the appointment of a company secretary. Where a private company does have these provisions, care must be taken to ensure that the wording does not require the company to appoint a company secretary, as if the articles do contain such a clause, this will stop the company taking advantage of the exemption for private companies contained in the Companies Act.

If the company is likely to appoint assistant or deputy company secretaries, and for those individuals to have specific duties, these will need to be allowed for in the articles, as there are no statutory provisions in the Companies Act.

The seal

Although the requirement for all companies to have a company seal was dropped by the Companies Act 1989, some companies do still maintain a company seal and the articles should include provisions governing its use. In particular, most Listed, AIM and NEX companies will have a company seal, as the bulk issue of share certificates is much easier with the use of a security seal, which does not require the signature of a director or company secretary. A security seal, however, can only be adopted if the company has a company seal (s. 50).

Dividends

Although the Companies Act contains provisions setting out the basis on which a company may distribute profits and the calculation of **distributable profit**, the articles will need to contain provisions specifying the mechanics of making payments, including:

- power to declare dividends;
- dividends payable in any currency;

- power to pay interim and fixed dividends;
- share premium account;
- dividends not to bear interest;
- deduction of debts due to company;
- unclaimed and retained dividends;
- payment of dividends *in specie*;
- receipts by joint holders;
- method of payment of cash dividends;
- cheques etc. to be at sole risk;
- right to stop sending dividend warrants by post; and
- power to specify record dates.

Shares in lieu of dividend

There is no statutory right for companies to offer shares in lieu of cash dividends and these powers will need to be specified in the articles.

Notices and documents

The statutory provisions for the issue of notices and documents are regularly amended by the articles of association, particularly in respect of the definition of clear days' notice and deemed receipt of notices after posting, detailed provisions on issue of notices and other documents by electronic communication and members with addresses outside the UK.

The articles may also detail provisions covering situations where there is disruption to the postal service, allowing for the use of a record date to determine the right to receive notices and permitting the issue of notice without a manuscript signature.

Untraced shareholders

A company will usually seek the power to stop sending notices and documents where the members has moved without providing their new address, and ultimately the right to sell shares held by these 'lost' shareholders, but only after reasonable efforts have been made to locate them.

Destruction of documents

There are circumstances in which a company may destroy certain documents, such as cancelled share certificates and transfer documents. (For more information on retention of documents, see page 111.)

Indemnity and insurance

Any provision by which a company provides an indemnity for a director against any liability, whether as a result of negligence, default, breach of duty or breach of trust, is invalid, subject to some limited exceptions, one of which is the purchase of directors' and officers' insurance (s. 232(2)).

Practice and procedure

Memorandum and articles of association

Typical practice is to have a combined memorandum and articles of association in one document. Usually, the combined document will comprise a front page stating the company's name and number, the heading 'Memorandum and Articles of Association' and who compiled the same – although this last part is an option. Following the front page is typically the memorandum in the form described previously, followed by the articles (whether model articles or bespoke articles).

4 – Company names

Introduction

Every company must be registered with a unique name. The company will not be registered by the Registrar of Companies if the name is 'the same as' an existing name on the index of names or where it does not bear the appropriate status, i.e. limited. A name will not be registered if it is offensive or if its use constitutes an offence (s. 53). When searching the index online, the Companies House website offers the facility for a Company Name Availability Search, which can identify 'same as' company names.

The name of the company does not need to appear as a separate clause in the memorandum or articles of association, but it does need to appear in the title of the document for identification purposes.

The members of the company may change the name of the company by special resolution (s. 78), and provided there is authority in the articles of association by any other means (s. 79). Typically this will be by authorising the directors to approve the change by directors' resolution.

A name will not be approved if it gives the impression that the company is connected with central or local government, or contains an expression which may only be used with the approval of the Secretary of State (ss. 54 and 55) unless written approval has been obtained from the appropriate authority. From 31 January 2015, two statutory instruments came into effect which revised and reduced the number of 'sensitive' words, and set out in detail the characters and punctuation that may form part of a company's name. They are the Company, Limited Liability Partnership and Business Names (Sensitive Words and Expressions) Regulations 2014 (SI 2014/3140) ('the Sensitive Words Regulations') and the Company, Limited Liability Partnership and Business (Names and Trading Disclosures) Regulations 2015 (SI 2015/17) ('the Names and Trading Disclosures Regulations'). The regulations apply equally to companies, limited liability partnerships and unincorporated businesses.

The lists of words or expressions requiring justification set out in schedule 2 of the Sensitive Words Regulations are reproduced in Appendix 5 (page 539). Many common examples of previously restricted words are now permitted without the need for justification, including European, International, Group and Holding.

Except in limited circumstances, it is not possible to register a name which is the 'same as' an existing registered name. The exceptions are set out in reg. 8 of the Names and Trading Disclosures Regulations; they are that the existing company consents to the proposed name and that the two entities are in the same group. 'Same as' refers to the name taking into account words or expressions which are excluded for the purposes of establishing if a proposed name is the same as an existing name.

Company names

If it is a private company, the company's name must end with the word 'Limited', 'Unlimited' or the relevant abbreviation, unless advantage has been taken of s. 60 to omit the word 'Limited' or 'Ltd'. The name of a public company must end with the words 'public limited company' or 'plc' or, if preferred, 'Public Limited Company' or 'PLC' (s. 58). A company limited by guarantee may apply to omit the word 'Limited' or its abbreviation from its name (s. 60).

If the registered office of the company is to be situated in Wales, the company may, if it wishes, have the Welsh equivalents of 'Limited', 'Unlimited' or 'public limited company' in its name ('cyfyngedig', 'anghyfyngedig' and 'cwmni cyfyngedig cyhoeddus', respectively).

Additional requirements apply in the case of companies incorporated outside Great Britain that have a place of business (including a share registration office) in Great Britain (s. 1047). The Secretary of State may require an overseas company to use a different name in Great Britain (s. 1048) if its name is the same as or similar to an existing company registered in Great Britain.

Control of company names

It is the responsibility of the persons forming the company or the directors, in the case of a proposed change, to check the Company Registration Office's index of names maintained at Companies House. This facility also enables the searcher to check whether any specific name will be considered too similar to an existing name. In particular, the following should be noted:

1 A company will not be registered by the Registrar of Companies if the name is 'the same as' an existing name on the index of names or where it does not bear the appropriate status, i.e. 'Limited' in the case of a private company or 'public limited company' (or an abbreviation) in the case of a public company. A name will not be registered if it is offensive or if its use constitutes a criminal offence (s. 53).
2 A name will not be approved if it gives the impression that the company is connected with central or local government, or contains an expression which may only be used with the approval of the Secretary of State (ss. 54 and 55)

unless written approval has been obtained from the appropriate authority (see Appendix 5).

3 Where a company has been registered with a name which is 'the same as' or 'too like' a name shown on the Company Registration Office's index, within 12 months of the registration the company may be directed by the Secretary of State to change its name within such period as they may specify (ss. 67 and 68). This period is extended to five years of registration where the company has provided, for the purpose of registration, information that is misleading or that has not fulfilled assurances given at the time of registration (s. 75). At any time after registration, the Secretary of State may direct a company to change its name within six weeks, or such longer period as they may allow, where the company's name is so misleading in regard to the nature of its activities as to be likely to cause harm to the public (s. 76).

4 There are detailed guidance notes on the provisions regarding company names, which may be obtained from the Registrar of Companies on request or downloaded from the Companies House website (see the Directory).

Company names adjudicator

Any person may object to the Company Names Tribunal, part of the Intellectual Property Office, that a name is the same as or similar to a name they are associated with or have goodwill in (ss. 68–74). These provisions of the Act provide a remedy for parties who are aggrieved by the registration of a company name in circumstances where they suspect the name has been registered in order to extract money or to prevent the aggrieved party from registering the name.

Cases are heard by the company names adjudicators, who must announce their decision within 90 days and can order a company to change its name.

The existing owner of the registered company name can rely upon the following defences:

- that the name was registered before the applicant started to use the name or the event upon which the applicant relies to show it has goodwill or reputation in the name; or
- that the company is operating under the name or is planning to do so and has incurred substantial start-up costs, or has previously operated using the name but is now dormant; or
- that the name was registered in the ordinary course of a company formation business and the company name is available for sale to the applicant on the standard terms of that business (an 'off the shelf company'); or
- that the name was chosen in good faith; or
- that the interests of the applicant are not adversely affected to any significant extent.

Application is made using Form CNA1 and must be accompanied by a fee of £400. Further information and the application form can be found on the Company Names Tribunal website (www.ipo.gov.uk/cna.htm).

Change of company name

A company may change its name by special resolution of its members or, if permitted by its articles of association, by resolution of the directors or by any other means as provided in the company's articles of association (s. 77). The change of name takes effect on the issue of a certificate of incorporation or certificate of change of name by the Registrar of Companies.

The detailed procedure for the change of name of a public company by special resolution is as follows (some of these steps are not relevant for private companies):

1 The proposed new name is checked against the Company Registration Office's index of names and approval of the name obtained if required.
2 The directors resolve to circulate a written resolution or convene a general meeting to consider the special resolution to change the name (see precedents 6 and 8). Alternatively, for a public company, the resolution to change the name can be done as special business at an annual general meeting. If provided by the articles of association, the directors can resolve to change the company themselves.
3 The directors approve a circular explaining to all members, and persons nominated by members under ss. 145 or 146 to receive notices, the reason for the proposed change of name and, if a general meeting is to be convened, a notice is sent to the members. If the change of name is to be approved at an annual general meeting, the explanation can be included in the directors' report.
4 (*Listed companies only*) A form of three-way proxy must be sent out with the notice of meeting (*LR 9.3.6*) (see precedent 7).
5 (*Listed, AIM and NEX companies only*) It is no longer necessary, in most instances, for proof copies of notices, resolutions, proxy forms or circulars to be vetted and approved by the UK Listing Authority prior to issue, provided the documents comply with the requirements laid down by the *Listing, AIM or NE RFI* and are certified by the company's sponsor as so doing. However, two copies of the circular, notice and proxy form must be submitted to the document-viewing facility, together with any required letter(s) of compliance, no later than the date of issue to shareholders (*LR 9.6.1*). In the case of an AIM or NEX company publication, this is done by way of an announcement via a **regulatory information service** (*AR 10* and *20, NE RFI 35, 38*).
6 A certified copy of the special resolution should be prepared for filing with the Registrar of Companies immediately following the meeting, certified by the signature of the chairman, together with the fee payable for a change of name (£10 if filed on paper, £8 if filed electronically). If the change of name is urgent,

it can be processed by Companies House on a same-day basis, on payment of an increased filing fee of £50 (£30 if filed electronically). In practical terms, the resolution needs to be with Companies House by midday in order for the change to be effective on the same day. It is desirable that the resolution for change of name be sent to the Registrar separately from any other resolutions that may need to be registered in order to avoid delay.

7 (*Listed companies only*) Copies of the special resolution must also be sent to the document-viewing facility at the same time as it is sent to the Registrar of Companies (*LR 9.6.2*).

8 A certificate of incorporation on change of name is issued by the Registrar. The change of name has legal effect from the date of the certificate and not the date of the resolution (s. 81(1)).

9 (*Listed, AIM and NEX companies only*) Once the change of name is effective, the company must make an announcement via a regulatory information service and forward a copy of the change of name certificate to the FCA (*LR 9.6.19*). AIM companies must make an announcement via a regulatory information service (*AR 17*).

10 The new name must be displayed outside the registered office and other places of business and elsewhere, such as on the company vehicles or on the packaging of its products.

11 The company's stationery must also be reprinted, or at least overprinted, with the new name where this is feasible. If the new stationery is to be prepared in advance, it is wise to avoid substantial expenditure in case the Registrar raises any objections to the new name. The company's website (if it has one) and e-mail must be updated with the new name (regulation 6(2) of The Companies (Trading Disclosures) Regulations 2008 (SI 2008 No. 495)).

12 If the company has a company seal, or a security seal, new seal(s) incorporating the new company name must be adopted by the board of directors.

13 Banks and other organisations with which the company has dealings may require the production of the certificate of incorporation on change of name certified by the company secretary. If an official copy of the certificate is required, this can be obtained from the Registrar.

14 The special resolution must be attached to all copies of the memorandum and articles held in stock.

15 It is necessary in this case to file a new copy of the memorandum and articles with the Registrar of Companies. However, all persons known to be in possession of a copy of the company's memorandum and articles – e.g. the directors and the company's auditors and solicitors – should be sent a print of the special resolution to be attached to their copies.

16 If the change of name was directed by the Secretary of State, the same procedure applies, but no change-of-name fee is payable.

Trading disclosures

The company's name must be displayed outside every office or place of business and engraved on the company's common seal (if it has one). Place of business includes a share transfer or share registration office.

In addition, the company's full name must be shown on all business letters, website and e-mail and other documents, as specified in the Companies (Trading Disclosures) Regulations 2008 (SI 2008/495), including publications, cheques, orders for goods and services on behalf of the company, invoices and receipts. The place of registration and the registered number of the company as shown on the certificate of incorporation must also be shown on business letters, website and e-mail and order forms, together with the address of the registered office. In addition, if a company has a website, it must disclose the VAT number if the company is registered for VAT, regardless of whether the website is used to sell goods or services or not.

It is not necessary to show the amount of the share capital on business letters, but if this is done, the reference must be to the paid-up share capital.

The names of directors need not be shown on business letters, but if it is desired to do so, the names of all the directors must be stated, not just one. However, it would still be in order for a letter to be signed by a director with that title under their signature without showing the names of all the directors on the paper (regulation 8 of the Companies (Trading Disclosures) Regulations 2008 (SI 2008/495)).

If it is intended that directors of the company should have headed paper stating their office, it is essential that care is taken not to breach the provisions. Although it is acceptable to show that the letter is from the 'Office of the Chairman', it would not be acceptable to state from the 'Office of Mr J. Smith, Director', unless the names of the other directors were also shown. It is not necessary for the names to appear with equal prominence, merely that they are all legible.

If the company has its registered office in Wales and uses the Welsh equivalent of 'Limited', or 'public limited company' in its name ('cyfyngedig' and 'cwmni cyfyngedig cyhoeddus', respectively), the fact that the company is limited must be stated in English on its stationery, bill heads and other official documents. It must also be included in a notice displayed at every place of business of the company.

Business names

If a company carries on business under a name which is not its corporate name, it must comply with the provisions of ss. 1192–1207. These are as follows:

1 Although the controls on 'same' or 'too like' names do not apply in relation to business names (but see below), names implying connection with central or local government or containing certain words and expressions may be used only with the written approval of the Secretary of State (ss. 1193 and 1194). If

the business name is used on business letters, written orders for goods, invoices, etc., the full name of the company must also be stated and an address within the United Kingdom at which service of any document relating to the business will be effective must be given (ss. 1201 and 1202).

2 The full name of the company must be displayed in all premises where the business is carried on under the business name so that customers or suppliers may refer to it. The name must also be given immediately in writing to any person doing business with the company who may request it (ss. 1204 and 1202(2)).

Failure to comply with any of the above provisions renders any officer of the company responsible liable to criminal penalties. In addition, if the provisions have not been complied with, the company may not be able to enforce contracts made under the business name (ss. 1205 and 1206).

Although the restrictions on 'same' or 'too like' company names do not apply to business names, care must be taken not to infringe any trademarks or to use an existing name of a company operating in the same or a similar industry. Use of an existing name might lead to an action for 'passing off'. This is where one company is seen to be benefiting from the reputation of another established business by using the same or a very similar name and 'passing itself off' as that other business.

Care must also be taken not to infringe any existing trademark registrations which might take precedence over a registered or business name.

There is no official register of business names, although a number of commercial enterprises purport to offer such a service, usually for a fee.

5 – Members

Introduction

A company is owned by its members. For companies with a share capital, there is a transparent structure with ownership being divided between the members according to the proportion of shares they hold. Companies limited by shares are overwhelmingly the most common form of company and as a consequence, the terms members and shareholders have become synonymous with each other.

For companies limited by guarantee, the members guarantee the company's debts, usually limited to a nominal amount. In general, although guarantors are the members, they are not true owners of the business, but should be viewed as trustees holding ownership temporarily until this is passed on to the next trustee. Guarantors are usually not entitled to participate in profits or distribution of surplus assets, and in the event of a guarantee company ceasing to trade or being wound up, any assets remaining must be passed to another guarantee or charitable company with similar objects. However, this need not be the case and it is necessary to examine the memorandum and articles of association if a distribution of income (dividend) or capital is proposed, to ensure that this is permitted under the company's constitution.

Unlimited companies without a share capital will have some other method of determining ownership which will typically be a members' agreement similar in content to a partnership agreement setting out the members' rights to vote, share in profit, shares in assets and contribution to assets, in the event that the company is unable to settle its debts.

Who can be a member

The subscribers to the memorandum of association are deemed to have agreed to become members of the company and, on registration of the company, their names should be entered in the register of members and in the People with Significant Control (PSC) Register, if appropriate. A person may subsequently become a member by applying for new shares or by the transfer or transmission to them of shares already in issue and the entry of their name in the register of members. Two criteria must be met to become a member: first, the person must agree to be a member; and second, they must be entered as a member in the register of members (s. 112). Both requirements must be met before a person is regarded as a member of the company.

As long as there is no provision to the contrary in the articles, any legal person such as a company may hold shares in a company. The articles of some companies, however, exclude certain categories of person from membership, e.g. persons who are not able to give a declaration of British nationality. At the same time, it is necessary to ensure that in the case of a registered company, for example, the company's articles of association do not preclude the holding of shares in other companies.

However, an unincorporated body like a partnership, club or association not registered under the Act should not be accepted as a member of the company, because it does not possess legal personality. If such a body wishes to hold shares, these should be registered in the name of an individual or individuals, or a person having a legal personality such as a bank nominee or a trustee company.

Similarly, the holder of an office should not be accepted as a member in that capacity unless it is an office created by statute, such as the Treasury Solicitor or the Accountant General. Some public officers are legally deemed to be a corporation, e.g. the Public Trustee, and as such may be registered as members of companies.

Shares should not be registered in the name of an English partnership. They should be held in the names of two or more partners and no reference should be made in the register of members to the partnership. Scottish partnerships, however, have legal personality and may, therefore, be registered in the firm's name as members of the company. Shares held by a limited liability partnership can be registered in the name of the limited liability partnership, as it is a corporate body with a legal persona.

Shares in a company may be held by a number of persons in a joint account. However, some articles of association limit the number of persons who may be so registered. In the case of a Listed company, the maximum number of joint holders is not permitted to be fewer than four.

Unless a subsidiary company is acting only as personal representative or trustee without having any beneficial interest in the shares or acting as an authorised dealer in securities, a subsidiary company is not permitted to be a member of its holding company (s. 136). Section 139 makes provisions to enable a company's subsidiary company to act as trustee for a group employee share scheme or pension scheme. There is, however, no prohibition on the holding of shares by a subsidiary in its holding company if it held shares in that company before it became its holding company. However, in this case, the subsidiary is not permitted to vote at meetings of the holding company (s. 137(4)). It would not be lawful for any further shares in the holding company to be allotted to such a subsidiary company, a situation that could arise if the holding company undertook a capitalisation issue.

Single-member companies

All companies limited by shares, subject to any contrary provision in its articles, need have only one shareholder (s. 7(1)). The Companies (Single Member Private Limited Companies) Regulations 1992, SI 1992/1699 reduced the minimum number of shareholders required for a private limited company from two to one. The Companies Act dropped the requirement for a public company to have at least two members with effect from 1 October 2007. Any company incorporated prior to the coming into effect of these provisions may need to amend their articles of association if these specifically state that the company must have two or more shareholders. Any rule of law requiring a private company to have two members has been modified by the statutory instrument.

Any sole shareholder may also be a sole director of a private company. Any company reducing its membership to one must, when updating the register of members, add a note stating that the company has only one member and the date on which the change occurred (s. 123). If a company with only one member increases its membership, a note should be added to the register of members stating this fact, together with the date on which the change occurred (s. 123, see precedent 81).

Section 318 provides that for a single-member company, notwithstanding any provision in a company's articles, one member present by person or by proxy shall constitute a valid quorum. Additionally, as the discipline of duly convening meetings for a single-member company is cumbersome, it is in order for a single member to take decisions normally requiring a meeting, provided that any decisions are formally recorded in writing (s. 357). Any agreements made between a single member and a sole director who is also the member must be set out in a written memorandum or recorded in the minutes of the next meeting of the board of directors (s. 231). Although this provision applies only to contracts other than in the normal course of business, to prevent any innocent omission it is recommended that a written record be kept of all contracts between the company and a sole member/director. It may also be appropriate for the director to declare their interest in the matter pursuant to the articles of association.

Minors as members of a company

Since becoming a member of a company may involve the assumption of liabilities in respect of the shares held, it is not considered good practice to accept minors as members of a company in their own name, as their responsibilities would be voidable during their minority (i.e. under the age of 18 in England, Wales and Northern Ireland; see below for details of the position in Scotland). This is especially important where the shares are partly paid, as this imposes an obligation to pay any calls that may be made by the directors.

The articles of association may give express power to reject allotments and transfers in the name of a minor, but if not, a right of rejection is conferred by general law. Accordingly, the company may repudiate the contract for the allotment of new shares, and in the case of a transfer, the transferor may be reinstated as the holder of the shares. It may come to light at some later stage that a minor is a member of the company and until any repudiation or rejection of their membership, any minors can enjoy the full rights of membership. Rejection of a minor can take place only during that person's period of minority. The *Listing Rules* (*LR 2.2.4*, *AIM Rule 32* and *NEX Rule 2c*) require that the articles of association of companies contain no restrictions on the transfer of fully paid shares, although the right of rejection is maintained under the general rule of law. From a practical point, especially for publicly traded companies, minors may well become members of the company without the company's knowledge.

Any member transferring shares to a minor, even in ignorance, is liable for any future calls on those shares while the minor is still the registered holder and a minor. Any person who procures the acquisition of shares and their registration in the name of a minor makes themselves liable to indemnify any transferor in respect of any future calls.

In Scotland, persons are pupils until the age of 12 (girls) or 14 (boys), after which they become minors until the age of 18. Pupils have no capacity to contract, although their guardian (tutor) may contract on their behalf. Minors who live independently and hold themselves out as having reached the age of 18 have the capacity to contract. If a minor has a guardian (curator), contracts will normally be made only with that person's approval.

A pupil or minor who validly acquires shares is able to reduce (cancel) the contract not only while still a pupil or minor, but until the age of 22 (this additional age limit does not apply to business contracts). In order to reduce the contract, the pupil or minor only has to show that the contract was unreasonable.

Where shares have been incorrectly registered in the name of a minor and a sale or transfer of the shares is required, a parent or guardian will need to obtain a Court Order, typically a Vesting Order or General Form of Judgement, to enable a sale or transfer to proceed. The Court Order is required to ensure the sale is being done in the best interests of the shareholder, the 'minor', as they cannot deal with the transaction for themselves, and is carried out under the authority of the court.

How many shares must be issued?

A private company need only issue one share, and there is no minimum nominal or **paid-up capital** requirement.

Public companies are required to issue at least £50,000 or the prescribed euro equivalent, in nominal value of shares, with each share at least 25% paid up as to its nominal value and 100% of any premium (ss. 761 and 763) before commencing to trade, and to maintain this minimum capital at all times. A public company could issue only one share and in order to meet the minimum capital requirement, it would need to have a nominal value of not less than £50,000 or the prescribed euro equivalent.

Members' rights

Where all members are to have equal rights, the company need only have one class of shares. It is only where members or groups of members are to have different rights that the company's share capital will need to be divided into different classes.

Classes of shares

The articles of association will set out the division of shares into different classes, with the respective rights of each of the classes being stated. There is a statutory requirement for determining what the classes are called and while many share classes provide a clue to their rights or restricted rights, e.g. non-voting shares or fixed dividend shares, other classes may simply be distinguished as 'A' **ordinary shares** and 'B' ordinary shares. The most common classes into which shares of a company may be divided are as follows.

1 Ordinary shares which rank after the preference shares as regards dividends and return of capital but carry voting rights not normally given to holders of **preference shares**, unless their preferential dividend is in arrears. These shares constitute the company's 'risk capital' – i.e. each year, the directors declare a dividend to be paid on the ordinary shares out of the profits of the company. If the company does well, the dividends will be good and increase year by year; but if the company does badly, the dividends may be reduced or even (in a very bad year) omitted entirely. The word 'ordinary' is commonly omitted from the description of the shares in the articles of association where a company only has one class of shares in issue. In some companies the risk capital is called 'deferred shares' or 'deferred stock'.
2 Ordinary shares, which are non-voting shares, usually distinguished from the voting shares by calling them 'non-voting' or 'A' shares. Some companies have classes of ordinary shares which have restricted voting rights. In both cases, however, the shares otherwise have similar rights to those of the other ordinary shares as in point 1 above.
3 Preference shares, which carry a preferential right to a fixed rate of dividend and, on a winding-up, to return of capital with or without a premium, together with arrears of dividend. They constitute part of the company's share capital, and repayment of capital on preference shares would rank ahead of repayment of capital on the ordinary shares (or the deferred shares or deferred stock) in a liquidation. The fixed rate of dividend is expressed as a percentage of the nominal value of the shares and not the issue price. Holders of preference shares get the same rate of dividend year in and year out, unless in any year the

profits of the company are insufficient to pay the preference dividends, which, of course, take priority over payment of dividends on the ordinary shares.

4 Cumulative preference shares, which provide that if in any year the profits of the company are insufficient to pay the dividend on the preference shares, the dividends not paid will be paid in subsequent years, together with the previous year's (or years') dividend(s), when the company's fortunes improve. The payment of such arrears would rank ahead of payment of dividends on the ordinary shares.
5 Redeemable preference shares or cumulative redeemable preference shares, which will be redeemed by the company at their nominal or par value (i.e. the face value) at some stated date in the future. The amount of the repayment, however, is the actual nominal value of the shares, e.g. £1 preference shares would be redeemed at £1 per share, notwithstanding that the market value of the shares might be higher or lower than this amount.
6 Debentures and loan stocks, which are in effect loans to the company by investors who receive a fixed rate of interest on the debenture or loan stock. They are mentioned here, although they are not a class of share, since they are frequently met with when considering a company's financial structure. Generally, debentures are secured loans on the assets of the company, whereas loan stocks are normally unsecured.

Payment of the interest on debentures and loan stocks ranks ahead of the payment of preference dividends and ordinary dividends. They would also rank ahead of preference and ordinary shares in repayment of capital in a liquidation. It should be noted, however, that debentures and loan stocks do not form part of the company's capital, although quite often they are colloquially referred to as 'loan capital'. The company's capital is confined to the company's share capital, which includes preference shares as well as ordinary shares.

Rights attaching to a class of shares

The rights attaching to all shares will be stated in the articles of association. The most common rights differentiating one class from another are as follows:

- *Right to vote*: the right to attend and vote at meetings may be restricted or enhanced.
- *Right to receive dividend*: the right can be to a preferential dividend, whether fixed or not, or can be that dividends may be declared on any individual class or all, at the directors' discretion, or that a particular class has no right to dividend.
- *Right to capital on a winding-up or a return of capital*: the right to capital is often linked to the right to dividend. A class of shares with enhanced dividend rights may have restricted rights to any further benefit in an increase in asset value of the company. The right will vary from the right to the return of the amount paid up on each share to full participation in the retained profit.

- *Right of pre-emption on transfer and allotment*: these rights will affect the shareholders' ability to realise their investment and their protection from dilution in the event of an issue of shares of the same class.
- *Right of redemption*: normally given to shares carrying enhanced dividend rights but no right to capital, redemption rights allow investor to realise their investment at a predetermined date or following a stipulated formula.
- *Right to conversion*: normally to ordinary shares: like redemption rights, rights to conversion are usually given to shares carrying enhanced dividend rights but no other rights, enabling realisation at some future time.

A company can create classes of shares with as many or few rights as it wishes. The rights will often depend on the investor where new capital is being invested to enable an existing business to expand. Although the majority of rights attaching to shares can be altered whether the shares have been issued or not, it is not possible to convert issued shares that were not redeemable into **redeemable shares**.

Variation of rights

The Companies Act provides that the rights attached to a class of shares or members shall be varied in accordance with the provisions of the company's articles of association, or, if the company's articles do not make provision for the variation of class rights, in accordance with the provisions of Chapter 9 of Part 17 of the Act. This allows a company to specify less demanding procedures for varying class rights in its articles of association.

Section 630 provides that class rights may only be varied by the written consent of the holders of at least three-quarters in nominal value of the issued shares of the relevant class, or if a special resolution passed by the holders of that class sanctions the variation. Where the company's articles impose a higher threshold for consent to the variation of class rights, the company must comply with the more onerous regime. Section 631 provides that for companies without share capital consent in writing from at least three-quarters of the members of that class, a special resolution passed at a separate general meeting of the members of that class sanctioning the variation will be required to vary class rights.

Holders of not less than the aggregate of 15% of the issued shares of a class (or 15% of the members of a class in the case of a company without a share capital) who did not consent to, or vote in favour of, the variation may apply to the court for it to be cancelled within 21 days of the resolution consenting to the variation being passed. In this case, the variation will not take effect until it is confirmed by the court. The application may be made by one or more of these shareholders (or members) on behalf of those entitled to make the application. The court will disallow the variation if it is satisfied that the variation would unfairly prejudice the holders (or members) concerned; otherwise, the court will confirm the alteration (ss. 633 and 634). A copy of the court order must be filed with the Registrar within 15 days of it being made.

Companies creating new classes of shares or members, or varying the rights of existing classes of shares or members, are required to notify the Registrar of the particulars of the rights created or affected within one month of the date of variation (ss. 636–640).

Protection from unfair prejudice

Directors have a **fiduciary** duty under **common law** and under s. 172(1) to act in the interests of the members as a whole, and can be held liable in the event that they act for the benefit of a subgroup of members or for their own benefit rather than the members as a whole or even at all.

Any member of a company may apply to the Court on the basis that either the company's affairs are being or have been conducted in a manner that is unfairly prejudicial to the interests of members generally or of some part of its members (including at least themself), or that an actual or proposed act or omission of the company is or would be prejudicial (s. 994).

It is important to note that the claimant must be able to demonstrate that the conduct complained of is both unfair and prejudicial to the interest or rights of the members or some part of the members of the company.

Conduct may be unfair even in circumstances where there has been no bad faith or no intention to be unfair or prejudicial. The test is objective and there is no need to show that anybody acted in bad faith or with the intention of causing prejudice. The courts will regard the conduct as unfair if a hypothetical reasonable bystander (the so-called man on the Clapham omnibus) would believe it to be unfair.

The conduct must be prejudicial to the complainant's interests in their capacity as a member of the company. The court does, however, take a broad view of what constitutes members' rights.

If the court find in favour of a complainant and agree that unfair prejudice has occurred, the Act sets out several remedies available to the court (s. 996(2)) in addition to a general provision to make any order it deems appropriate (s. 996(1)):

- regulate the conduct of the company's affairs in the future;
- require the company to refrain from doing or continuing an act complained of, or to do an act which it has omitted to do;
- authorise civil proceedings to be brought in the name and on behalf of the company by such person/s and on such terms as the court may direct;
- require the company not to make any, or any specified, alterations in its articles without the leave of the court; and
- provide for the purchase of the shares of any members of the company by other members or by the company itself and, in the case of the purchase by the company itself, the reduction of the company's capital accordingly.

The power to authorise civil proceedings subject to terms directed by the court can be a particularly useful remedy for the complainant as it not only enables an action to be pursued by the company, but also means the costs of the action will be borne by the company.

The most common remedy is to order that the shares held by the members whose interests have been prejudiced be purchased by those who caused the unfair prejudice.

Ordering that shares of a private company be purchased can cause considerable problems since the shares, not being traded, have no established market value and there are many conflicting methods of valuation. Although the court will not necessarily stipulate the valuation method to be used, they will often oblige the valuer to value the company at the date the prejudice initially took place and on the basis that the prejudicial conduct had not taken place.

Derivative action claims

The Companies Act introduced a derivative action procedure, making it easier for members to sue directors or others for a broader range of acts or omissions than was previously possible under common law (ss. 260–269). Due to the different legal systems in England, Wales, Northern Ireland and Scotland, the legislation is split, with ss. 260–264 applicable to proceedings brought in England, Wales or Northern Ireland, and ss. 265–269 applicable to proceedings brought in Scotland. The provisions themselves are intended to have the same effect in all territories.

Grounds for bringing a derivative action

A derivative action claim may only be brought under the provisions of the Companies Act or under a court order, and may be brought in respect of an actual or proposed act or omission involving negligence, default, breach of duty (including the codified duties described on pages 74–76) or breach of trust. The claim may be brought by a member whether the cause of action arose before or after they first became a member (ss. 260 and 265).

Application for permission to continue derivative claim

A member who has brought proceedings must apply to court for permission to continue the claim.

If a company has brought a claim and that claim could be continued as a derivative action claim, a member may apply to the court to continue the claim as a derivative action claim on the grounds that:

- the manner in which the company brought or is continuing the claim is an abuse of a process of the court; or
- the company has failed to prosecute the claim diligently; or
- it is appropriate for the member to continue the claim.

The court must dismiss the claim if the evidence filed by the member does not disclose a ***prima facie*** case for giving permission. In dismissing a claim, the court may make any consequential order it considers appropriate, including a costs order.

If the evidence does disclose a *prima facie* case, then the court may give directions as to the evidence to be provided by the company and may adjourn the proceedings to allow that evidence to be obtained (ss. 261, 262, 266 and 267).

Grounds for permission to continue

On hearing the permission application, the court must refuse permission to continue the claim if a person seeking to promote the success of the company for the benefit of its members would not continue the claim or if the conduct complained of has been authorised or ratified by the company (i.e. the members). On any resolution to ratify a director's negligence, default, breach of duty or breach of trust, the votes of those members personally interested in the ratification must be disregarded.

In exercising its discretion to allow an action to be continued, the court must consider:

- whether the member is acting in good faith;
- the importance a director promoting the success of the company would attach to continuing the claim;
- whether the conduct would be likely to be authorised or ratified by the company;
- whether the company has decided not to pursue the claim; and
- whether the applicant should pursue a remedy in their own right instead of on the company's behalf.

The court must have particular regard to the evidence of independent members in deciding whether to grant permission (ss. 263 and 268).

Application to continue action brought by another member

Where a member has commenced a derivative action against the director's claim, another member may apply to the court to continue the claim on the grounds that:

- the manner in which the first member brought or is continuing the claim is an abuse of a process of the court; or
- the first member has failed to prosecute the claim diligently; or
- it is appropriate for the second member to continue the claim.

The court must dismiss the claim if the evidence filed by the member does not disclose a *prima facie* case for giving permission. In dismissing a claim, the court may make any consequential order it considers appropriate, including a costs order.

If the evidence does disclose a *prima facie* case, then the court may give directions as to the evidence to be provided by the company and may adjourn the proceedings to allow that evidence to be obtained (ss. 264 and 269).

6 – Directors

Introduction

The definition of a director contained in s. 250 is very general. It states that a director is any person who occupies the position of director, by whatever name called. This is clearly illustrated in companies where the senior executive director will often have the job title Chief Executive Officer (CEO) whereas a 'client services director' in most instances will not be a board director at all.

A **shadow director** is a person who is effectively directing the affairs of the company but who is not called 'director' (s. 251).

The definition refers to any person rather than any individual and thus will include corporate bodies having a legal persona. In this way, it is possible for one company to be appointed a director of another company. SBEE2015 was intended to introduce a general prohibition on the appointment of corporate directors however at the time of writing those provisions had not been brought into effect.

This chapter looks in detail at types of directors, how they are appointed, resign or are removed, and at their powers, duties, liabilities and disclosure requirements.

Appointment

Eligibility

There are only two eligibility criteria in the Companies Act to satisfy when appointing directors:

1 There must be at least one natural person appointed as a director at all times (s. 155).
2 On appointment, the person being appointed must be at least 16 years old (s. 157).

A company's articles of association may, however, contain additional eligibility criteria. For example, directors might be required to hold a minimum number of shares or a particular professional qualification relevant to the business. A company carrying on business as a registered auditor may require that all directors are capable of being appointed as auditors in their own right. It is very common for the directors of a residents' management company to be required to be property owners or tenants of the particular development.

Provided the two Companies Act eligibility criteria, together with any criteria in the company's articles, are met, anyone may be appointed to the office of director, provided they are not specifically prohibited. These prohibited persons are as follows:

- A bankrupt person may not be appointed as a director. If a director becomes bankrupt after appointment, they must immediately resign, unless leave to continue is given by the courts (CDDA1986, s. 11).
- A person who has had a disqualification order made against them may not act as a company director, unless leave has been given by the courts (CDDA1986, ss. 2 and 5).
- The auditor of a company cannot also be a director or company secretary of that company (s. 1214).
- The director of an insolvent company cannot, without the leave of the court, be appointed as a director of a company with a 'prohibited' name (IA1986, s. 216).

In addition, the Act and articles of association may provide further instances where appointment may not be made or may cease – for example:

1. If the person is suffering from a mental disorder and is admitted to hospital under the Mental Health Act 1983, a court order is made on the grounds of mental disorder or a register medical practitioner gives a written opinion that the person has become physically or mentally incapable of acting as a director for a period of at least three months (Private Model Articles reg. 18(d)(e)). From 28 April 2013, a change to the model articles has been brought about by provisions in the Mental Health (Discrimination) Act 2013 insofar as it removes model article 18(e) from the model articles for private companies to tackle discrimination in this area of law. Additionally, model articles for public companies have also been amended to remove any such discrimination (article 22(e) of the model articles).
2. If a receiving order has been made against the director or proposed director, or if they compound with their creditors generally (Private Model Articles reg. 18(c)).
3. If the maximum number of directors permitted by the articles has been reached.
4. The articles of a company incorporated before January 2007 may require directors to retire annually upon reaching the age of 70. This reproduced the effect of CA1985 s. 293, which has now been repealed, and companies should consider removing such a clause which may be unenforceable under age discrimination legislation.

Procedure for appointment

The first directors of a company are those whose names are entered on Form IN01 on the incorporation of a company. Subsequent appointments as directors are governed by the provisions of the company's articles of association. These usually provide that the board itself may or the members in general meeting may fill any casual vacancies or appoint additional directors up to the maximum number permitted by the articles.

For public companies and any private company that chooses to hold annual general meetings, elections or re-elections of directors following **retirement by rotation** must be approved in general meeting (Public Company Model Articles reg. 21). Also, at the company's first annual general meeting, all the directors retire from office and have to be re-elected by the members at the meeting (model articles of a public company reg. 21(1)).

A casual vacancy is one arising from the death or resignation of a director. Once it has been established that the proposed replacement is willing to be appointed (consent is formally required by signature of the consent-to-act section of Form AP01 or AP02), the procedure for appointing a director to fill a casual vacancy is as follows:

1 The board resolves to appoint the new director (see precedent 14).
2 The company secretary confirms to the newly appointed director their appointment by the board and deals with the following:
   (a) requesting personal particulars, including date of birth, which are required to complete Form AP01 or AP02 (there are different forms to be completed by natural persons and corporate entities) and to make the necessary entry in the register of directors (s. 162). The date of birth is required for all directors (s. 163(f)). Although the full date of birth must be provided to Companies House, only the month and year of birth are placed on the public record;
   (b) Form AP01 or AP02 is no longer required to be signed by the appointee signifying their consent to act, but instead is signed on behalf of the company confirming that the appointee has consented to act. Alternatively, details of the new appointment may be made online either using an appropriate software package or via the Companies House website. Pre-registration is required for both these services;
   (c) as Forms AP01 and AP02 no longer contain a consent to act declaration, formal consent to be appointed as a director should be obtained from new directors. Without this consent, it may be difficult to prove that the person has consented to be appointed and if there is a dispute, application can be made to the Registrar of Companies for the appointment to be struck out (see page 71);
   (d) if the director will be signing cheques on the company's behalf, requesting a specimen signature to be sent to the company's bank;

(e) informing the director of any share or other qualifications that must be acquired under the articles and the time allowed in which to do this;
(f) inviting the director to give a general or specific notice of their interests in contracts with the company (ss. 182 and 185);
(g) providing dates of forthcoming board meetings;
(h) enquiring how the director wishes their remuneration to be paid, e.g. sent to their home address or paid direct into their bank account, including information regarding their PAYE coding and National Insurance contributions (if they are already paying the maximum contributions in connection with another employment, they should obtain and submit to the company a certificate of exemption from contributions);
(i) providing general information about the business of the company if the newly appointed director is not already involved in the company. Copies of the articles of association, reports and accounts for recent years and interim reports and circulars should be made available, if required; and
(j) (*Listed, AIM and NEX companies only*) providing a copy of the company's rules for securities transactions, if any, and asking the director to acknowledge receipt.

3 (*Listed, AIM and NEX companies only*) A regulatory information service should be notified of the appointment by the end of the business day following the decision to appoint the director (*LR 9.6.11, AIM Rule 17, NEX Rule 70*). Details of the director's other business activities must be disclosed to a regulatory information service within 14 days. Details of any interests in shares of the company must also be disclosed within five days of their appointment. A NEX company should announce this information as soon as possible.

4 If appropriate, a press announcement should be sent to newspapers or through the company's press agents.

5 On receipt of the relevant information from the director, the necessary entries in the register of directors and the register of directors' residential addresses. The completed Form AP01 or AP02, whether on paper or electronic, must be sent to the Registrar of Companies within 14 days of the date of appointment. There may also be other matters to attend to, depending on the circumstances.

6 Where a director is not required to have a share qualification, it is usual for the articles to provide that the director may receive notice of, and attend and speak at, general meetings of the company. As a non-shareholder, they would not otherwise have such power except if acting as chairman of the meeting.

7 If the company has an insurance policy covering directors and officers of the company against liabilities incurred in carrying out their duties, the insurance company should be notified of the appointment of the new director, either at the time of appointment or at renewal, depending upon the wording of the policy.

Directors' addresses

Directors are required to give details of a service address for the receipt of official notices. The service address can be their usual residential address, but if it is not, details of their usual residential address must be provided on Form AP01, on appointment, or any subsequent change in their usual residential address on Form CH01. Companies House verifies the address details supplied against the Post Office database and will reject any that appear to be an office address. Accommodation addresses and PO Box numbers cannot be used, as clearly these are not residential addresses. Companies House does not place the residential address information on the public file unless it has reason to believe that mail addressed to the service address is being returned, not being actioned or not being forwarded to the individual concerned.

Although the residential address is not placed on the public file at Companies House, if the Company takes advantage of the option to use the central registry as their statutory books (see Chapter 7), this will result in the residential address information and full date of birth information being available to anyone who searches the public records.

Alternate directors

There is no provision in the Act authorising a director to appoint an alternate to act on their behalf in their absence, so alternates may be appointed only if the articles specifically provide for this.

Article 25 of the model articles for a public company make provision for a director to appoint another director to be their alternate, or they may appoint any other person as their alternate subject to that person being approved by the board of directors (see precedent 16). The model articles for private companies and companies limited by guarantee do not provide for the appointment of alternate directors.

Alternate directors are included in the definition of 'director' in s. 250 and their particulars should be entered in the register of directors and secretaries, and filed with the Registrar of Companies on Form AP01. This form does not differentiate between the appointment of a person as a director or as an alternate director; however, it is possible to enter 'alternate director' in the occupation field if preferred.

Accordingly, a search of the records at Companies House will reveal alternate directors' appointments as well as those of directors, without any distinction. They are subject to the same rules as directors with regard to disclosure of interests in shares of traded companies and related party transactions with the company. Their names must also be shown on letterheads if it is company practice to show the names of directors on such stationery. An alternate director may act only in the *absence* of the appointing director: it is not a complete assignment of office by the director.

Shadow directors

A person not being formally appointed as a company director but who nevertheless either controls the management of the company or on whose instructions the directors act is a 'shadow director' of the company and is deemed to be a director of the company for all purposes (s. 251). The appointment of a shadow director should be notified on Form AP01; however, the requirement for the company to confirm that the appointee has consented to act might prove difficult, as by their very nature, shadow directors are unlikely to consent formally. In such circumstances it is recommended that the form be submitted to Companies House with a covering note explaining the circumstances of the 'appointment'.

Although directors will often act on the recommendations of their professional advisers, this would not normally imply that those advisers were shadow directors, provided that their advice is limited to a particular part of the business such as accounts or commercial property transactions. A professional adviser giving wide-ranging assistance on areas outside the scope of their engagement runs the risk of being a shadow director.

Minimum number of directors

A public company must have at least two directors and a private company must have at least one director (s. 154). All companies must have at least one director who is a natural person (s. 155).

The articles may stipulate that there must be a higher minimum number of directors. If, for any reason, the number of directors falls below this number, the remaining directors have the power to fill a casual vacancy or to convene a general meeting only for the purpose of allowing the shareholders to appoint an additional director(s). If, for any reason, it is not discovered that the number of directors has fallen below the minimum number, once the number has been restored it is recommended that the board ratify the decisions made while there were insufficient directors. Provided the acts being ratified were within the board's authority, they can be ratified by the board. In such circumstances, many companies will also seek ratification by the shareholders to ensure that the decisions are not queried in the future.

Defective appointment of directors

If the appointment of a director is found to be defective in any way, s. 161 provides that, for the protection of third parties, any earlier acts made by the person acting as a director remain valid. Section 239 provides that the members of the company may ratify prior acts of directors either individually or collectively for acts of negligence, default or breaches of duty or trust.

Disputed appointments

SBEE2015 introduced a new process which came into force in April 2016 under which a director can dispute their appointment or amend details filed in respect of their appointment and make application to Companies House for the appointment to be struck out (s. 1095(4A)).

Application is made using Form RP06. The Registrar will enquire of the company to ascertain whether consent was given or not; where consent cannot be proved, the appointee's details will be removed from the record. The process can only be used in respect of appointment from Form AP01 or AP02 received by Companies House on or after 6 April 2016.

Managing directors and other executive directors

The appointment of directors as managing or executive directors is governed by provisions contained in the company's articles, giving the directors power to appoint such directors, to determine the terms of their appointment and remuneration, and to delegate to them such powers of the board as may be desired (Private Model Articles reg. 19, Public Model Articles reg. 23). Since the office of managing director is normally a full-time executive appointment, it is good practice for this appointment to be governed by a formal service agreement, rather than just a note of the principal terms, so that the remuneration and other benefits associated with the appointment may be made clear. The agreement should also contain any provisions relating to confidentiality and some control over the director's activity, in the event of their leaving the service of the company. The contracts of directors who also hold salaried executive positions with the company should specify whether the remuneration stated in the contract is exclusive or inclusive of directors' fees. For a smaller company, the terms of appointment could be set out in the minutes of the board appointing the director and a letter sent to the director containing a copy of the minutes and asking them to confirm acceptance of the proposed appointment in writing.

The articles normally give the board of directors power to revoke any appointment of a managing director, subject to the terms of any service agreement with the company. The appointment would also cease if the director ceased to be an employee of the company for any reason.

Non-executive directors

A non-executive director (NED) is a member of the board of directors without executive responsibilities in the company. The role of non-executives is to contribute skills and experience to board decision making that might not otherwise be available, and to provide a suitable balance of power in the boardroom. Most smaller companies will have no need to appoint non-executive directors, but the role of NEDs is seen as increasingly important for larger, Listed companies, and the issue of the balance between executive and non-executive directors on boards has become a key tenet of good corporate governance practice (see Chapter 17). Where appointed, NEDs have the same powers, duties and liabilities as executive directors.

Special types of director

Some companies' articles provide for the board to appoint persons to offices with the word 'director' as part of their title, e.g. divisional director, associate director. Such a person is not a director within the meaning of s. 250 and is not entitled to attend board meetings. Such a person is not subject to the statutory responsibilities and liabilities of a director, provided that they do not represent themselves as being a director, in terms of the Companies Act, in dealings with third parties. It can be misleading to appoint officials with the word 'director' in their job titles when they are not subject to the legal duties of a director. However, the practice is sometimes followed in order to give an added measure of status to senior executives to facilitate their dealings with customers and suppliers, especially if the company has substantial dealings in overseas territories.

Local boards are also sometimes formed by companies under provisions contained in their articles. These persons are not full directors for the purposes of the Companies Act 2006.

Contracts of employment

A director's employment contract (often referred to as a service contract) that cannot be terminated other than for breach of contract within a period of two years must be approved by the shareholders in general meeting (s. 188) (see precedent 17).

Shareholders' approval may be given by an ordinary resolution passed at a general meeting, provided that a written memorandum setting out the terms of the proposed agreement or a copy of the service contract is available for inspection by members of the company at the registered office for a period of not less than 15 days prior to the date of the meeting. Companies are required at all times to keep copies of directors' service contracts available for inspection by members, at an address specified for that purpose by the company (s. 228).

In accordance with the UK Corporate Governance Code, Listed, AIM and NEX companies are encouraged to have service agreements with their directors with a notice period of not more than one year (code provision D1.5) (see Chapter 16).

Powers of directors

The directors of a company are authorised by the articles of association to manage the business of the company and to exercise the company's powers (Private and

Public Model Articles article 3). This seemingly unlimited authority is usually balanced by the fact that this authority is subject to the provisions of the Companies Acts, the company's articles of association, by resolution of the members, internal policies and the directors' service contracts.

The power of the directors is given to the board collectively and not individually. Directors are usually also given power to delegate any or all of their power to one or more persons or one or more committees consisting of one or more directors (Private and Public Model Articles, regulation 5, see precedent 24).

Matters reserved for the board

For many companies there is no practical difference between the composition of the senior executive management team and the board of directors. However, in larger companies and especially listed companies executive directors will very much be a minority on the board of directors and there will be an executive committee below the board of directors which undertakes the day-to-day management of the business and implementation of the strategy agreed by the board of directors.

In exactly the same way that delegation of board authority to its committees must be fully documented the same is true of separation of the roles and responsibilities of the board and executive management. With this division of responsibilities, it is essential that there is a clear demarcation of matters that are the responsibility of the board and those matters delegated to the executive management team.

The directors should identify categories of matters as well as specific items which require the prior approval of the board of directors. The schedule is most often referred to as the 'matters reserved for the board'. The directors should also lay down procedures to be followed in the rare circumstances where a decision is required before the next directors' meeting.

As a basic principle, all material contracts, and especially those not in the ordinary course of business, should be referred to the board of directors for decision prior to the commitment of the company.

The directors should approve definitions of the terms 'material' and 'not in the ordinary course of business'.

Where there is any uncertainty regarding the materiality or nature of a contract, it is best practice for that contract to be brought before the board of directors for consideration.

Duties

A director's prime duty, which they hold together with their fellow directors, is to manage the company for the benefit of its members. The directors may delegate some or all of their powers to particular directors (perhaps constituting a committee of the board) and/or other senior officers in the company, but they cannot delegate their duties.

Although the Companies Act is clear that directors' prime duty is to the company members the Act notes that they must also have regard to the interests of employees, customers, suppliers, the community and the environment. The evolution of corporate governance places greater emphasis on the interests of these non-member stakeholders and while not overruling the Companies Act provisions places greater obligations on directors of larger companies to explain how they have exercised their powers and fulfilled their duties. Introduced for financial years beginning on or after 1 January 2019, s. 414(CZA) requires directors of large companies to describe how they have exercised their duty under s. 172.

The Companies Act 2006 introduced seven duties of directors. These duties codified, with some amendments, existing case law.

1. To act within their powers (s. 171)

Directors must act in accordance with the company's constitution and only exercise powers for the purposes for which they are conferred. The company's articles of association should be consulted to ascertain the extent of a director's powers and any limitations placed upon them.

2. To promote the success of the company (s. 172)

A director must act in the way they consider, in good faith, would be most likely to promote the success of the company for the benefit of its members as a whole, and in doing so have regard (among other matters) to:

- the likely consequences of any decision in the long term;
- the interests of the company's employees;
- the need to foster the company's business relationships with suppliers, customers and others;
- the impact of the company's operations on the community and the environment;
- the desirability of the company maintaining a reputation for high standards of business conduct; and
- the need to act fairly as between members of the company.

3. To exercise independent judgement (s. 173)

4. To exercise reasonable care, skill and diligence (s. 174)

The duties imposed by ss. 173 and 174 require that a director owes a duty to exercise the same standard of care, skill and diligence that would be exercised by a reasonably diligent person with the general knowledge, skill and experience that may reasonably be expected of the person carrying out the same functions as a director in relation to that company (an objective test); and the general knowledge, skill and experience that the director actually has (a subjective test).

For example, a finance director would be expected to have a greater knowledge of finance issues than, say, the HR director (the objective test); but if the HR director is also a qualified accountant, then they would be expected to have a greater knowledge than would normally be expected of a HR director, although not necessarily the same knowledge as the finance director (the subjective test).

5. To avoid conflicts of interest (s. 175)

Directors must avoid situations in which they have or might have a direct or indirect interest that conflicts or might conflict with the interests of the company. Of particular importance are conflicts relating to property, information or opportunity, regardless of whether the company could take advantage of such opportunities (s. 175(2)).

The duty does not apply to conflicts arising out of transactions or arrangement between the company and the director.

Where the company is a private company, authorisation may be given by resolution of the directors, provided there is nothing in the company's articles of association that invalidated the authorisation (see precedent 18).

Where the company is a public company, authorisation may be given by resolution of the directors, provided there is specific authority in the company's articles of association that permits directors to authorise such transactions (see precedent 18).

Such authorisation, whether for a private or public company, is only valid if the necessary quorum for a meeting of the directors is present excluding the director with the conflict of interest and without that director voting (s. 175(6)).

6. Not to accept benefits from third parties (s. 176)

Directors must not accept a benefit from a third party being given by virtue of their being a director or due to any action or inaction by the director.

Benefits received by a director from a person by whom their services are provided are not to be regarded as paid by a third party.

The duty is not infringed if the acceptance of the benefit cannot reasonably be regarded as likely to give rise to a conflict of interest.

7. To declare interests in any proposed transaction or arrangement (s. 177)

A director must declare the full nature and extent of any direct or indirect interest in any proposed transaction or arrangement before that transaction or arrangement is entered into. The declaration may be given at a meeting of the directors or by notice in accordance with ss. 184 or 185.

Where a previous notification or interest becomes inaccurate or incomplete, additional notification(s) must be made.

Notification is not required where the director is not aware of the interest or is not aware of the transaction or arrangement.

Notification is not required where the nature of the interest is such that it cannot reasonably be regarded as likely to give rise to a conflict of interest, to the extent that the other directors are already aware of the interest without requiring specific notification or where the transaction relates to the director's service contract.

Directors of companies whose shares are publicly traded also have additional non-Companies Act duties and responsibilities, and these are considered in Chapter 16.

Liabilities

Directors properly exercising the powers of the company and acting as agents for the company will not incur personal liability in the event of a breach of contract. However, directors may incur personal liability if they have given personal guarantees or if they have not made it clear that they are acting as agent of the company and not in a personal capacity.

There are also a number of circumstances under which a director may be personally liable to the company or third parties from a breach of duty or statutory offence, including:

- acting as a director while disqualified (CDDA1986 s. 15);
- a director of an insolvent company carrying on a business with a company with a prohibited name (IA1986 ss. 216, 217);
- employing illegal immigrants (AIA1996 s. 8);
- evasion of VAT (FA1986 ss. 13 and 14);
- failure to show company name on correspondence, cheques, etc. (ss. 83 and 84);
- fraudulent preference (IA1986 ss. 238–240);
- fraudulent trading (s. 993);
- irregular share allotment (ss. 563 and 579);
- making false statement in a prospectus (FSMA2000 s. 90);
- non-observance of pre-emption rights on allotment (ss. 563 and 572);
- public company trading prior to issue of trading certificate (s. 767);
- trading with intent to defraud (IA1986 s. 213);
- wrongful trading (IA1986 s. 214); and
- health and safety offences (HSWA1974 s. 37).

Member action

As considered in Chapter 5, members may take legal action against the directors under an action for unfair prejudice or as a derivative action claim.

Unfair prejudice

Any member of a company may apply to the court on the basis that either the company's affairs are being or have been conducted in a manner that is unfairly prejudicial to the interests of members generally or of some part of its members (including at least themself), or that an actual or proposed act or omission of the company is or would be prejudicial (s. 994).

It is important to note that the claimant must be able to demonstrate that the conduct complained of is both unfair and prejudicial to the interest or rights of the members or some part of the members of the company.

Derivative action claims

Sections 260–269 introduce a derivative action procedure, making it easier for shareholders to sue directors or others for a broader range of acts or omissions than was possible under common law.

Due to the different legal systems in England, Wales, Northern Ireland and Scotland, the legislation is split, with ss. 260–264 applicable to proceedings brought in England, Wales or Northern Ireland, and ss. 265–269 applicable to proceedings brought in Scotland. The provisions themselves are intended to have the same effect in all territories.

A derivative action claim may only be brought under the provisions of the Companies Act or under a court order, and may be brought in respect of an actual or proposed act or omission involving negligence, default, breach of duty (including the codified duties described above) or breach of trust. It may be brought by a member whether the cause of action arose before or after they first became a member (ss. 260 and 265).

Vacation of office

The office of director is vacated on the death of the office holder or under a provision in the articles of association of the company. Such a provision might be that the directors are appointed for a fixed term and, on expiry of that term, their appointment automatically ceases.

Vacation of office may also arise under statute, as follows:

1. If the director becomes bankrupt, unless the court permits the appointment to continue (CDDA1986 s. 11).
2. If the director is disqualified from being a director by court order (CDDA1986, ss. 1–6, as amended). A register of such disqualification orders is maintained by the Secretary of State for inspection by the public (CDDA1986 s. 18).
3. The appointment of a person as a director who has not attained the age of 16 is void (s. 159).

Under the articles, further methods of vacating office may be specified as follows:

- Where the articles stipulate any qualifying criteria and that criteria has not been met, the office of director would be vacated at the conclusion of the qualifying period.
- In the case of a company where the director reaches the relevant age limit set out in its articles, the office of director would be vacated at the conclusion of the next following annual general meeting.
- *Resignation*. This will usually take effect from the date on which the letter of resignation is received by the company, unless this states some subsequent date on which the resignation is to become effective. To be effective, the resignation does not need to be accepted by the board, unless the articles provide otherwise.
- *Absence*. If the director is absent from board meetings for some specified period (often six months) without leave of absence. In order to monitor the operation of any such article, therefore, the secretary should arrange for the board to grant leave of absence where it is known that a director is likely to be absent for a period exceeding six months, e.g. because of overseas travel on the company's business or because of long illness.
- If a receiving order is made against a director or the director compounds with their creditors generally.
- If an order is made by the court on grounds of mental disorder.
- If the director is removed from office, e.g. by a notice signed by all co-directors or by any holding company.

Retirement by rotation (public companies only)

The model articles for public companies provide for the retirement of one-third of the total number of directors by rotation every year (Public Model Articles, reg. 21). There is no general requirement in the Act for directors to retire by rotation at annual general meetings. It is usual for the articles to provide that a person appointed as a director by the board to fill a casual vacancy, or as an additional director, must be re-elected at the next following annual general meeting of the company. Such retirements and elections are not taken into account in determining the directors who are to retire by rotation at that meeting (Public Model Articles, reg. 21(b)).

For a Listed company, the UK Corporate Governance Code recommends that all directors should offer themselves for re-election every year (see Chapter 16). The procedure to be followed for the retirement of directors by rotation depends on the wording of the articles, but typically will be as follows:

1. At the first annual general meeting of the company, all the directors must retire and be elected by the members (see precedent 19).

2 At subsequent annual general meetings, one-third of the directors or, where the number is not an exact multiple of three, the number nearest to one-third retire from office. Directors who are retiring because they have been appointed since the last annual general meeting and directors who are excluded from the retirement by rotation provision (e.g. managing directors) are not taken into account for this purpose. Some companies' articles provide that the number of directors to retire by rotation shall be one-third of the directors or, if their number is not three or a multiple of three, then the number nearest to but not exceeding one-third shall retire. For example, in the case of a board of directors consisting of eight directors, under such provisions, three directors would retire; under these alternative articles, only two directors would retire.
3 The directors to retire at any annual general meeting are those who have been in office longest since their last election. If two or more persons became directors on the same day, those to retire (unless they otherwise agree among themselves) shall be determined by lot.
4 Directors retiring by rotation are eligible for re-election, but the company in general meeting may elect some other person to take that director's place.
5 In public companies, the resolutions at a general meeting for the appointment or reappointment of directors must be voted on individually unless those at the meeting first agree unanimously that the appointments or reappointments may be made by a single resolution (s. 160).

Removal of directors

The members may remove a director at any time by ordinary resolution (see precedent 20), regardless of anything to the contrary in the articles or any agreement with the director (s. 168). Removal, however, does not deprive the director of any rights they may have to compensation or damages payable in respect of the termination of their appointment as a director.

Special notice must be given to the company of the intention to propose such a resolution (see precedent 21). A copy of the notice must be sent to the director concerned, to give them the opportunity to make representations in writing to the company and to request that these be circulated to the members.

Where such special notice is received by the company, care must be taken to ensure that the requirements of s. 169 are strictly complied with. It may be advisable to obtain legal advice as to the precise procedure. In the case of a public company, a resolution could be proposed at the next annual general meeting. In all other cases, the removal will be dealt with at a general meeting and special notice must be given to the company of the intention to propose a resolution to remove a director not less than 28 days prior to the meeting, as specified in s. 168(2).

Articles of association may not exclude the provisions of ss. 168 or 169, but may make additional provisions for removal of directors, such as by unanimous resolution of the other directors or by written notice of the holding company.

A private company may not use the written resolution procedure to remove a director, which must be by way of a resolution approved at a general meeting (s. 288).

No directors

Many private companies have only one director and, if this sole director were to resign or die, any shareholder may request the company secretary to convene a shareholders' meeting to appoint a new director.

This would also be the case if a company with more than one director found itself with no directors as a result of mass resignations or some accident resulting in their deaths. In this scenario, it would be quite likely that all the shareholders would also have died, as in many private companies, all shareholders are also directors. In such circumstances, it would be prudent to include a provision in the articles of association allowing the executors of a deceased shareholder to nominate new director(s) in the event of there being no directors (see precedent 22).

The Secretary of State has power under s. 156 to give a direction as to the procedure to follow to appoint a new director or directors.

The UK Corporate Governance Code recommends that all directors offer themselves for re-election each year (see Chapter 16). Accordingly, it is possible, although unlikely, that all the directors could be voted out of office. As a consequence, some Listed companies have introduced amendments to their articles to ensure the company is not left with no directors. One possible scenario is that the executive directors are deemed reappointed, but with restricted powers in order to convene a general meeting to appoint new directors and to exercise such other powers as are necessary to ensure the company remains as a going concern.

Procedural issues

A number of administrative matters must be dealt with when a director ceases to hold office.

1. The board should formally minute the vacation of office (see precedent 23).
2. The date of ceasing to be a director must be recorded in the register of directors.
3. A notice on Form TM01, TM02 or the electronic equivalent should be sent to the Registrar of Companies within 14 days of the date of vacation of office.
4. Any fees for the period to the date of cessation of office should be paid to the director or, if deceased, to their personal representatives. HM Revenue & Customs should be informed of the cessation of fees.
5. If the name of the director is shown on company stationery, it should be removed.
6. (*Listed, AIM and NEX companies only*) A regulatory information service must be notified as appropriate.

7 It may be appropriate to issue a press release.
8 If the director was authorised to sign cheques, the bank should be informed.

The director should be requested to return all documents and other company property to the company. If they had the use of a company car, arrangements should be made for its return to the company.

Disqualification

Directors may be disqualified under the CDDA1986 either automatically, resulting from a defined event, or where application has been made to the court that a person is unfit to be a director.

A person who has been disqualified may not, during the period of disqualification, be a director, liquidator, **administrator**, receiver or manager of a company, whether directly or indirectly, without the consent of the court.

Contravention of a disqualification order is a criminal offence punishable by up to two years' imprisonment or an unlimited fine. Application for disqualification is made under the appropriate provision of the CDDA1986, and disqualification may be automatic or discretionary.

Disqualification for unfitness

The court is obliged to disqualify a person who was or is a director of an insolvent company where their conduct makes them unfit to be involved in the management of a company.

A director can be found unfit to be a director as a result of either their actions or inaction.

Disqualification on conviction

The courts may make a disqualification order if a person has been convicted of an indictable offence in connection with the management, promotion, formation or liquidation of a company.

Disqualification for breach of statutory obligations

A disqualification order may be made for persistent failure to file accounts or annual returns or other documents required to be filed with Companies House, or failing to keep statutory records.

Disqualification for fraudulent or wrongful trading

A disqualification order may be made against a person if, during the course of a winding-up, it appears that they are guilty of an offence under s. 993 for fraudulent trading or have committed some other offence or breach of duty, or where the director is required to make a contribution to the company's assets for insolvent trading.

Disqualification in the public interest

The Secretary of State has power to apply to the courts for a disqualification order on the grounds of public interest. This would usually follow from an enquiry by the **Department for Business, Energy & Industrial Strategy** inspectors.

Disqualification undertaking

The Secretary of State may, where an individual would otherwise be subject to disqualification proceedings under CDDA1986 ss. 7 and 8, accept a disqualification undertaking from that person. The maximum periods of such a disqualification undertaking is two years if in respect of a matter subject to CDDA1986 s. 7, and 15 years if relating to offences under CDDA1986 s. 8 (CDDA1986 s. 1A).

Competition disqualification order

The court must make a disqualification order (maximum 15 years) against a person if a company of which that person is a director commits a breach of competition law and the court considers the conduct of that person makes them unfit to be concerned in the management of a company (CDDA1986 s. 9A).

Competition undertaking

The Office of Fair Trading or the specified regulator may accept a disqualification undertaking from a person in circumstances where the OFT or the regulator believes a company of which that person is a director has committed a breach of competition law and that person's conduct makes them unfit to manage a company (CDDA1986 s. 9B).

Interests in contracts

Where a director is directly or indirectly interested in a contract or a proposed contract with the company, they must declare the nature of their interest at a meeting of the directors. Private Model Article 14 and Public Model Article 16 impose restrictions on a director in voting on a matter in which they are personally interested. The type of interest relevant for this purpose is widely defined and includes contracts by the company with any other company of which the director is also a director. However, if the director's interest in a contract arises merely because they are a minor shareholder in another company that is a party to the contract, this would not constitute a declarable interest, provided the shareholding was not material – e.g. less than 5% of the voting capital.

A useful procedure for a director to give general notice of interests is given by ss. 182–185 (see precedent 15).

Where notice of an interest is given in writing, it must be given by the director to each other director in hard copy by post or by hand, or by such other means as may be agreed between them. Written notice of an interest is deemed to form part of the proceedings of the next meeting of the directors (s. 184).

A director may give general notice, either at a directors' meeting or in writing, of an interest in or with another company, firm or person and that will constitute a declaration of an interest in any future transaction or arrangement with that company, firm or person.

Where the director required to give a notification is a sole director, such notification must be in writing (s. 186).

Material transactions between the company and its directors must be disclosed in the company's accounts. The Companies Act 2006 imposes restrictions on substantial property transactions between companies and their directors, as discussed below.

In the case of Listed companies, it is usual to find that the articles include a provision prohibiting the directors to vote on all but a few matters in which they have an interest. Such allowable interests include arrangements for approved pension schemes, and directors' and officers' insurance schemes. Non-disclosable transactions with companies, where the interest is in that company's share capital, are limited to holdings not exceeding 1%.

Substantial property transactions

A director of a company or of its holding company may not enter into any arrangement to acquire from or transfer to the company a 'non-cash asset' without prior approval of the members by ordinary resolution passed in general meeting (s. 190) (see precedent 31).

The restriction on substantial property transactions extends to persons connected with a director and to shadow directors, and requires that, where a director or connected person is also a director of the holding company, additional approval in general meeting of the holding company be sought.

A 'substantial non-cash asset' is defined in s. 191 as any asset of the company if its value is greater than £5,000 and which is also in excess of 10% of the company's net asset value or £100,000 (whichever is the lower). Transactions exceeding this limit require approval by the members.

The net asset value is determined by reference to the most recent statutory accounts or, if there are none, to the company's aggregate called-up share capital.

Transactions not requiring approval

Exemptions for transactions not requiring approval in general meeting include:

- a non-cash asset valued at less than £5,000;
- an arrangement between a wholly owned subsidiary and either the holding company or a fellow wholly owned subsidiary;
- an arrangement where the company is being wound up (except a **members' voluntary winding-up**); or

- in circumstances where the director is acquiring the asset in their capacity as a member of the company and not as a director, i.e. issue of shares pursuant to a rights issue.

While such transactions do not require approval of the members by ordinary resolution in general meeting, they must still be approved and formally recorded in the minutes of a meeting of the board of directors.

Disclosure requirements

A transaction approved pursuant to s. 190 is likely to be 'material' and will require disclosure in the company's accounts.

The UK Listing Authority normally requires that, other than small transactions, transactions between directors and a Listed company are the subject of a circular to members and require prior approval of the members in general meeting (*LR 11.1 and 11 Annex 1*).

Contravention of s. 190

Where requirements of s. 190 are contravened and a transaction does not receive the necessary approval, the director or connected person and any other directors who authorised such arrangements or transaction are liable to account to the company for any direct or indirect gain made from the transaction, and jointly indemnify the company from any loss or damage resulting from the transaction.

The transaction or arrangement may also be voidable at the instance of the company (s. 195(2)).

However, where advance approval was not obtained, the transaction can be affirmed by members in general meeting within a reasonable period thereafter (s. 196).

Loans to directors

A company may not make loans to its directors or connected persons or to directors of its holding company, nor may it give guarantees or other securities for such loans or enter into credit transactions for the benefit of the director, unless it has been approved by members (ss. 197–214). Although a loan that is outstanding when a person is appointed a director is permitted to continue, any additional amounts of principal or rolled-up interest would come within the prohibitions.

Additional restrictions apply to public companies and companies that are members of a group containing a public company. **Quasi-loans** to directors and loans or quasi-loans to connected persons of directors of such companies are prohibited. A quasi-loan is a transaction under which one party pays a sum for someone else, or agrees to reimburse expenditure incurred by someone else, on the terms that that person will reimburse the person making the payment or where the circumstances give rise to a liability on that person to reimburse the payer.

A director's 'connected persons' are family members as defined in s. 253, including spouse, civil partner, parents, children or stepchildren, but excluding grandparents, grandchildren, siblings, aunts, uncles, nieces and nephews, even if they live at the same address. A connected body corporate is defined in s. 254 as any company of which they have at least 20% control or the trustees or any settlement for the benefit of such persons.

The exceptions that apply to a company making loans or quasi-loans to directors or persons connected with them without members' approval are strictly limited and are as follows:

1 An advance of up to £50,000 may be made to a director to enable them to meet expenditure incurred for the purpose of the company or to enable them to perform their duties properly (s. 204).
2 Approval is not required where the company meets the expenses in defending an action in connection with an alleged negligence, default or breach of duty or trust, provided the amounts are repayable on conviction, judgement being given against the director or being refused relief (s. 205).
3 Approval is not required where the company meets the expenses in defending an action or investigation brought by a regulatory authority in connection with an alleged negligence, default or breach of duty or trust. The company may not fund the payment of any fines imposed on the director personally (s. 206).
4 A loan or quasi-loan is permissible, provided that the amount concerned does not exceed £10,000 (s. 207(1)).
5 A credit transaction for an amount not exceeding 15,000 is permitted (s. 207(2)).
6 A transaction entered into in the ordinary course of the company's business, provided that the value of the transaction and the terms on which it is made are not more favourable than those that would be offered to a person of similar financial status unconnected with the company (s. 207(3)).
7 Special exemptions apply for loans made by money-lending companies (including banks) in the ordinary course of their business, provided the value of the loan and any terms are not different to those imposed to a person not connected with the company but otherwise under similar circumstances (s. 209).

The provisions prohibiting unauthorised loans to directors contained in the Companies Act are detailed, and reference should always be made to the legislation in the Act and (if thought desirable) legal advice taken. In particular, care should be taken if reliance is placed on the exemption relating to advances to enable a director to carry out their duties properly, as there is potential for this exemption to be abused.

Political donations

Companies may not make a political donation to a political party or other political organisation or incur any political expenditure unless that donation or expenditure has been approved in advance by its members or, in the case of a wholly owned subsidiary, by its holding company (s. 366, see precedent 32). Approval is not required where the aggregate amount of political donations and political expenditure does not exceed £5,000 for the 12-month period ending on the date the donation is made or expenditure incurred (s. 378).

The resolution must specify the maximum amount that may be donated or the maximum amount of expenditure that may be incurred (s. 367). Unless the resolution specifies an earlier date, the authority has effect for a maximum of four years, commencing on the date the resolution is passed (s. 368).

The directors of the company at the time of any unauthorised donation or expenditure are liable to repay the amount of the unauthorised donation or expenditure, and are also liable to compensate the company for any loss or damage incurred (s. 369).

Where a company has made unauthorised donations or incurred any expenditure, members holding at least 5% of the nominal value of the company's issued shares or 50 members may bring an action to enforce repayment of those amounts and any compensation. The costs of the action can be reclaimed by the members from the company only by way of a court order (ss. 370–372).

Donations and subscriptions to trade unions (other than donations to a trade union's political fund), trade associations, all-party parliamentary groups and groups specified by regulation are exempted, as these groups are not political parties or political organisations (ss. 374–377).

7 – Corporate compliance

Introduction

Directors' duties are defined in a number of statutes, and are supplemented by additional common law duties which have evolved over the years and which come under the headings of their fiduciary duty to the company and a duty of skill and care. Directors' prime duties are discussed in Chapter 6. This chapter considers compliance duties as well as duties under other legislation. It should be noted, however, that there are many legislative provisions applicable to particular business types and markets, and this book can only deal with a general overview of the more common provisions.

In general, as noted in Chapter 6, directors are required to exercise the powers of the company for the benefit of the company and its members as a whole. There are, however, circumstances when this general rule is superseded. For example, under certain circumstances, the directors must take account of the interests of the employees (s. 172(1)(b)). Where a company cannot avoid insolvency, directors are required to take account of the interests of the company's creditors. There will also be occasions when, as agents for individual members, directors have a duty to act in the best interests of those members individually.

The principal compliance issues relating to accounts and audit, *Listing Rules*, London Stock Exchange and NEX Markets and corporate governance are dealt with in Chapters 11, 12, 15, 16, 17 and 19. This chapter discusses compliance issues concerning statutory registers and filing obligations, authentication and retention of documents. It also looks at other compliance issues affecting the majority of companies including employees, health and safety, disability discrimination, data and consumer protection, the environment and financial matters.

It is the general duty of the company secretary to ensure compliance by the company with the provisions of the Companies Acts and the company's articles of association. However, company secretaries of large companies and groups, companies engaged in regulated markets and companies with shares admitted to trading on a public market will often also have a wider compliance role to fulfil.

Statutory registers

Every company is legally obliged to keep certain specified registers, books and records to reflect the operation of its business. It is the company secretary's primary responsibility to see that they are properly maintained and kept up to date.

Traditionally, companies incorporated by agents were supplied with a bound or loose-leaf book containing pro-forma registers for use by the company. As a consequence, the statutory registers of a company are frequently referred to as the statutory records or the statutory book(s).

Legal requirements

The Companies Act required that every company keep the following registers, books and records:

1. register of members – ss. 114 and 128D;
2. register of directors – s. 162;
3. register of directors' residential addresses – s. 165;
4. directors service contracts – s. 228;
5. directors' indemnities – s. 237;
6. books containing minutes of directors meetings, resolutions in writing of directors and decisions of a sole director – s. 248;
7. register of secretaries – s. 275;
8. books containing minutes of company meetings, resolutions in writing of members and resolutions of a sole member – s. 355;
9. accounting records – s. 386;
10. contracts for purchase of own shares – s. 702;
11. documents for purchase of own shares out of capital – s. 720;
12. register of debenture holders, if any – s. 743;
13. register of people with significant control – ss. 790M and 790Z;
14. report to members of investigation by public company into interests in its shares – s. 805;
15. register of interests in voting shares disclosed to a public company – s. 808; and
16. register of charges – s. 859Q.

There is no obligation to keep registers of individual share allotments or transfers. However, these are often included in bound and loose-leaf statutory books, and where these registers are kept, they must be made available for inspection as set out on page 97.

Register of members

Full details of the requirements to create and maintain the register of members as well as common transactions are dealt with in Chapter 18.

Register of directors

The register of directors must contain for each current and former director:

1. Name and former name. Former names need not be disclosed if not used in business or not used in the previous 20 years. Maiden names of married women need not be disclosed.
2. Service address. This can be an office or residential address. An office address is recommended to mitigate against identity theft. The address in the register of directors, which must be available for public inspection, should be the same as on the central register maintained at Companies House. In the case of a corporate appointment the address should be the registered or principal office.
3. Country of residency. For a corporate appointment this is the country of registration and registration reference (in the case of an EAA-registered company) or the legal form, law by which governed and the register on which the registration is entered, if any.
4. Nationality.
5. Business occupation, if any.
6. Date of birth.
7. Date of appointment.
8. Date of termination of appointment, if relevant.

Register of directors' residential addresses

This must contain details of each director's usual residential address and any changes to it. If the address stated in the register of directors is the director's usual residential address, then this fact can be entered in the register of directors' residential addresses, provided the entry does not use the phrase 'the company's registered office'.

Register of secretaries

The register of secretaries must contain for each current and former secretary:

1. Name and former name. Former names need not be disclosed if not used in business or not used in the previous 20 years. Maiden names of married women need not be disclosed.
2. Service address. This can be an office or residential address. An office address is recommended to mitigate against identity theft. The address in the register of secretaries, which must be available for public inspection, should be the same as on the central register maintained at Companies House. In the case of a corporate appointment the address should be the registered or principal office.
3. In the case of a corporate company secretary, there must also be entered detail so the register and registration reference (in the case of an EAA registered company) or the legal form, law by which governed and the register on which the registration is entered, if any.

4 Date of appointment.
5 Date of termination of appointment, if relevant.

Register of debenture holders

It is not a requirement of the Companies Act to keep a register of debenture holders; however, if a register is kept, it must comply with the requirements set out in ss. 743–748. These requirements broadly mirror the rights to request a copy of the register of members and the obligation of the company to ensure that the request is made for a proper purpose. These rights, as they apply to the register of members, are considered in Chapter 18.

If there is just one single debenture, an entry could be made in the company's register of charges, which would negate the need to keep a separate register of debenture holders. It is, however, convenient to keep a separate register where a series of debentures is issued.

Register of people with significant control

The register of people with significant control (the PSC Register) was introduced to provide greater transparency of ownership of UK companies (ss. 790A–790ZG). Up until its introduction on 6 April 2016, the majority of UK companies only needed to disclose details of the registered holder of their shares and not beneficial ownership.

All companies other than those qualifying for exemption under s. 790B are required to keep a PSC Register.

A PSC is anyone in the company who meets at least one of the conditions set out in the Register of People with Significant Control Regulations 2016 (SI 2016/339). Some companies will have no PSCs, while others may have several. The majority of companies will have one PSC, reflecting the fact that the majority of companies have a sole shareholder.

A PSC is a person who:

1 holds, directly or indirectly, more than 25% of the shares;
2 holds, directly or indirectly, more than 25% of the voting rights;
3 holds the right, directly or indirectly, to appoint or remove a majority of directors;
4 otherwise has the right to exercise, or actually exercises, significant influence or control over the company; and
5 has the right to exercise, or actually exercises, significant influence or control over the activities of a trust or firm which is not a legal person, the trustees or members of which would satisfy any of the four conditions above.

As noted above, the purpose of the PSC Register is to increase transparency in ownership and accordingly the register is of natural persons. As a result, where the immediate ownership is through another corporate entity or a trust, companies are required to move down to the next layer of ownership until the ultimate owner(s) are identified.

If the company does not have a PSC or has been unable to obtain confirmed details of their PSCs, one of a number of permitted statements must be entered into the PSC register and updated as required.

These permitted statements are as follows:

1 The company knows or has reasonable cause to believe that there is no registrable person or registrable relevant legal entity in relation to the company.
2 The company knows or has reasonable cause to believe that there is a registrable person in relation to the company but it has not identified the registrable person.
3 The company has identified a registrable person in relation to the company but all of the required particulars of that person have not been confirmed.
4 The company has not yet completed taking reasonable steps to find out if there is anyone who is a registrable person or a registrable relevant legal entity in relation to the company.
5 The company has given a notice under s. 790D of the Act which has not been complied with.
6 The addressee has failed to comply with a notice given by the company under section 790E of the Act.
7 The company has issued a restrictions notice under paragraph 1 of Schedule 1B to the Act.

Although in general, it is details of individual ownership that must be recorded in the PSC Register, there are two other types of entity that are permitted. Accordingly there are three types of ownership structure whose details must be entered into a company's PSC register. The categories are individual, registrable relevant legal entity (RLE) and other registrable person.

The information to be registered about each category of ownership is as follows:

- For an individual person:
  - the date the individual became a registrable person;
  - name;
  - country/state of residence;
  - nationality;
  - service address;
  - usual residential address (this is not shown on the public record);
  - date of birth (only the month and year is shown on the public record); and
  - the nature of their control over the company.
- For a registrable relevant legal entity (RLE) (such as a company):
  - the date that they became a registrable RLE;
  - corporate name;

  - address;
  - legal form of the corporate body;
  - governing law under which the RLE was registered;
  - place of registration (if applicable);
  - registration number (if applicable); and
  - the nature of their control over the company.
- For another registrable person (such as a corporation sole or local authority):
  - date on which they became a registrable person in relation to the company in question
  - name;
  - principal office;
  - the legal form of the person;
  - law by which they are governed; and
  - the nature of their control over the company.

Register of interests in voting shares disclosed to a public company

Companies are no longer required to keep registers of directors' interests in shares and public companies are no longer required to keep registers of interests of those holding 3% or more of its voting capital.

A public company does, however, have power under s. 793 to require any person whom it knows or has reason to believe is or was at any time in the previous three years interested in the relevant share capital of the company (i.e. voting shares) to supply information to the company as specified in the section. The information includes the identity of the persons interested in the voting shares in question and information as to whether such persons were parties to an agreement to which s. 824 relates (i.e. 'concert parties') (see precedent 82).

The company must maintain a register of interests disclosed to it pursuant to a disclosure request made under s. 793 (s. 808). The register must contain details of the date the request for information was made and the information disclosed to the company in pursuance of the notice.

The register kept pursuant to s. 808, often referred to as 'the s. 808 register', must be kept at the registered office or the SAIL address (see page 93).

Where a public company re-registers as a private company, it must retain and make any register kept under s. 808 available for inspection until the end of the period of six years after it ceased to be a public company (s. 819).

Unless the register has always been kept at the company's registered office, notice of where the register is located and any change in that place must be given to Companies House (s. 809). Unless the register is kept in a form that is itself an index, a separate index must also be maintained (s. 810).

Register of charges

Companies are no longer required to keep a register of charges for charges created on or after 6 April 2013. In place of this requirement, copies of charges (and any amendments to them) and instruments creating a charge must be made available for inspection at either the company's registered office or its SAIL address (ss. 859P and Q).

Minute books

There are no statutory requirements regarding the location of minute books of directors' meetings. Minutes of general meetings held after 1 November 1929 must be kept at the registered office.

The type of minute book kept by the company will depend on the size and procedures of the company concerned. For private companies, they may be kept in bound books, either handwritten or with typed sheets of paper pasted into the bound book with the pages serially numbered. It is convenient for the minutes to be numbered consecutively from number 1 upwards throughout the book. Thus in the first minute book, the minutes would be numbered 1.1, 1.2, 1.3, etc., in the second minute book, they would be numbered 2.1, 2.2, 2.3, and so on.

Larger public companies generally use loose-leaf minute books. Again, it is recommended that the pages are numbered serially and the minutes numbered consecutively. Some companies also maintain an index at the back of the minute book giving reference to the items covered by the minutes. The secretary must decide whether the time spent in indexing the minutes will serve any useful purpose.

Minutes of general meetings should be kept separate from board minutes, since members have a right to inspect the minutes of general meetings but not of board meetings (s. 358).

Location of records

There are particular requirements with regard to the place where various statutory records or records are kept and where they may be inspected.

As an alternative to the registered office address, companies can choose to keep and make available for inspection some or all of the records and registers at a **S**ingle **A**lternative **I**nspection **L**ocation, also referred to as the SAIL address.

As an alternative to the registered office or SAIL address, with effect from 30 June 2016, Schedule 5 of SBEE2015 amended the Companies Act to permit private companies the option of keeping the information that must be recorded in certain statutory registers on the public, central register, maintained by the Registrar of Companies.

The options available to a company for where to keep these registers and records are as follows.

Table 7.1: Records and locations

Record	*Registered office*	*SAIL address*	*Central Registry (private companies only)*
Register of members	✓	✓	✓
Historic register of members	✓	✓	
Register of directors	✓	✓	✓
Register of secretaries	✓	✓	✓
Register of directors' residential address	✓	✓	✓
Register of charges	✓	✓	
Register of interests in voting shares	✓	✓	
Register of debenture holders	✓	✓	
PSC Register	✓	✓	✓
Historic PSC register	✓	✓	
Company minutes and resolutions	✓		
Directors' minutes and resolutions	✓		
Accounting records			
Directors' service contracts	✓	✓	
Directors indemnities	✓	✓	
Contracts for purchase of own shares	✓	✓	
Documents re. purchases of shares out of capital	✓	✓	
Report into ownership of own shares	✓	✓	

SAIL address

Where a company takes advantage of the option to hold records and make them available for inspection at a SAIL address, notification must be given to the Registrar of Companies using Form AD03 within 14 days, indicating which of the registers are being kept at the SAIL address.

Use of central register

As noted above, a private company may elect to hold some or all of five of its statutory registers on the central register maintained by the Registrar of Companies, and once the registers are held on the central register it can subsequently elect to hold them itself. This option was introduced as a de-regulating measure primarily for the benefit of sole director/member companies. It is, however, available to all private companies.

Companies must opt in to make use of the central registry to keep any of their statutory registers and do so by opting in immediately on incorporation of the company by completing the appropriate section on the incorporation Form IN01 or at any time after incorporation by submitting the requisite form as follows:

- EH01 Register of directors
- EH02 Register of directors' usual residential addresses
- EH03 Register of secretaries
- EH04 PSC Register
- EH05 Register of members

Companies may opt out of using the central registry to keep all or some of their statutory registers at any time and do so by opting out by submitting the requisite form to Companies House as follows:

- EW01 Register of directors
- EW02 Register of directors' usual residential addresses
- EW03 Register of secretaries
- EW04 PSC Register
- EW05 Register of members

With the exception of the register of members, the Registrar maintains the company register(s) from the usual forms submitted notifying changes to the information, and no additional filings or notifications are required.

To maintain the register of members, it is necessary to notify the Registrar of changes to the members' details such as transfers of shares and changes of address using Form EH06.

Format of statutory registers

The statutory registers may be kept in manuscript or printed bound or loose-leaf hard copy or on computer or other non-legible electronic form, provided that adequate precautions are taken against falsification and that, in the case of non-legible records, they can be reproduced in hard copy for inspection (ss. 1134, 1135 and 1138). Although records may be inspected in electronic form, hard copy copies can be requested.

Data protection and company registers

The General Data Protection Regulation is pan-European legislation and is supported in the UK by the Data Protection Act 2018 (DPA2018). The Privacy and Electronic Communications Regulations (PECR) set out the principles, rights and obligations for the processing of personal data.

By virtue of holding and maintaining statutory registers, all companies process personal data and will meet the definition of a data controller (see below); therefore, they will need to register under the DPA2018 and pay an annual data protection fee. Unlike the previous data protection legislation there are very limited exemptions but also no need to provide details of the data processing being undertaken.

The following definitions are relevant to understanding compliance with GDPR and DPA2018:

- A 'data controller' means the natural or legal person, public authority, agency or other body which, alone or jointly with others, determines the purposes and means of the processing of personal data.
- 'Data processor' means a natural or legal person, public authority, agency or other body which processes personal data on behalf of the controller.
- 'Personal data' means any information relating to an identified or identifiable natural person.

Any company that only processes personal data within one or more of the categories below and for no other purpose is exempt from the requirement to pay a data protection fee:

- staff administration;
- advertising, marketing and public relations;
- accounts and records;
- not-for-profit organisation purposes;
- personal, family or household affairs;
- maintaining a public register;
- judicial functions; or
- processing personal information without an automated system such as a computer.

These exemptions are only in relation to payment of ICO fees and the provisions of protection will still apply.

Data controllers other than those only undertaking exempt processing must provide the following information to the ICO:

- the name and address of the controller;
- the number of members of staff;
- the turnover for the latest financial year; and
- any other trading names.

The names and contact details of the following people will be required:

- the person completing the registration process; and if different
- a relevant person in the organisation to contact on ICO matters.

The data protection fee depends on the size of the company measured in terms of turnover or numbers of staff. There are three different tiers of fees as set out in

Table 7.2. An organisation meets the Tier test if it meets either of the criteria for that Tier.

Table 7.2: ICO data protection fees

Tier	*ICO fee**	*Turnover not exceeding*	*Average number of employees not exceeding*
Tier 1	£40	£632,000	10
Tier 2	£60	£36m	250
Tier 3	£2,900	No limit	No limit

*Where paid by direct debit, the fee is reduced by £5.

Inspection of registers/documents

The Act not only stipulates where the statutory registers must be held, but also contains provisions regarding their inspection, other than the register of directors' residential addresses. Inspection of all the registers is free to members and, in the case of the historic register of charges, free to creditors. Anyone else may be required to pay a fee.

Requests to inspect the register of members or the PSC register must be accompanied by a statement identifying the person requesting the information and the purpose for which they require the information. If the company does not believe that the request is being made for a proper purpose, application may be made to the court for a direction either to supply the information or to order the company not to comply with the request. Any application to the court must be made within five days of the request being made.

The general position is that all the registers must be kept at and be available for inspection either at the registered office or a place of inspection.

The following registers and documents must be available for inspection:

- s. 114 (register of members);
- s. 162 (register of directors);
- s. 228 (directors' service contracts);
- s. 237 (directors' indemnities);
- s. 275 (register of secretaries);
- s. 358 (records of resolutions, etc.);
- s. 702 (contracts relating to purchase of own shares);
- s. 720 (documents relating to redemption or purchase of own shares out of capital by private company);
- s. 743 (register of debenture holders);
- s. 790N (register of people with significant control, excluding usual residential address information);

- s. 805 (report to members of outcome of investigation by public company into interests in its shares);
- s. 809 (register of interests in shares disclosed to public company);
- s. 877 (instruments creating charges and register of charges: England and Wales); and
- s. 892 (instruments creating charges and register of charges: Scotland).

The registers and other documents of a public company must be available for inspection for at least two hours between 9.00am and 5.00pm on business days.

The registers and other documents of a private company must be available for inspection for at least two hours between 9.00am and 3.00pm on business days and the company must be given two days' notice of inspection where such request is made during the notice period of a meeting or during the circulation period of a written resolution and ten days' notice at all other times.

Fees payable

The company is obliged to provide copies of certain registers and documents upon payment of a fee.

Fees in respect of inspection of registers by non-members

The fee relates to the inspection of the registers of members, register of interests in shares and register of debenture holders, and is £3.50 per hour or part thereof during which the register(s) is/are inspected.

Fees for provision of copies of entries in registers and copies of reports

The fees for copies of the registers of debentures, register of interests in voting shares and registers of debenture holders or members are:

- £1.00 for the first five entries;
- £30.00 for the next 95 entries or part thereof;
- £30.00 for the next 900 entries or part thereof;
- £30.00 for the next 99,000 entries or part thereof; and
- £30.00 for the remainder of the entries in the register.

The fee for provision of copies of trust deeds, service contracts and minutes is 10 pence per 500 words or part thereof.

Interests in shares (public companies only)

As noted above, a public company has power under s. 793 to require any person whom it knows or has reason to believe is or was at any time in the previous three years interested in the relevant share capital of the company (i.e. voting shares) to supply information to the company as specified in the section. The information includes the identity of the persons interested in the voting shares in question and information as to whether such persons were parties to an agreement to which s. 824 relates (i.e. 'concert parties') (see precedent 82).

The company must maintain a register of interests disclosed to it pursuant to a disclosure request made under s. 793 (s. 808).

The register must be open for inspection by any person free of charge. On payment of the prescribed fee, any person may request a copy of any entry in the register. Any person requesting to view or be sent a copy of the register or any entry must provide their name and address and the purpose for which the information is requested. Where the information is requested on behalf of a third party, their details and the purpose for which they require that information must also be disclosed (s. 811).

Where a company receives a request under s. 811 and it is satisfied that the request is for a proper purpose, it must supply the information requested or refuse the request if not satisfied. A person whose request has been refused may apply to the court. The court may order the company not to comply, and in the absence of such an order the company must provide the requested information. Where an application is made to the court, the applicant must notify the company that the application has been made and the company must make its best endeavours to notify any person whose details would be disclosed if the company was required to comply with the request under s. 811 (s. 812).

Entries in the register may only be removed six years after the date the entry was made (s. 816) or to remove incorrect information (s. 817).

Members holding not less than one-tenth of the paid-up capital of the company giving the right to vote at general meetings of the company may require the company to exercise its powers under the provisions of s. 793 (ss. 803 and 804). A report of the information received must be prepared and the members of the company requisitioning the company to make the investigation must be notified that the information is available for inspection at the company's registered office. Copies of the report must also be supplied on request. The report must be made available for inspection within 15 days of the conclusion of the investigation (s. 805(1)).

Failure to give information to the company under s. 793 by any persons may result in heavy penalties (ss. 794 and 797). It is of interest to companies to be aware of the identity of persons who hold significant holdings of voting shares in the company under the cloak of nominee names, not only to improve investor relations but also as this may be the prelude to a takeover bid for the company. If a person on whom a company serves a request for information does not provide the requested information within the time specified, the company can apply to the court for a direction that the shares be subject to restrictions (s. 794).

The effect of an order under s. 794 is that:

- any transfer of shares is void unless approved by the court pursuant to s. 800(3);

- the voting rights are no longer exercisable;
- no further shares may be issued in right of the holder of the shares or in pursuance of an offer made to the holder; and
- other than in liquidation, no payment may be made to the holder in respect of the holding whether capital or otherwise.

The court may make such provisions it deems appropriate to protect the position of third parties (s. 794(2)). The restrictions imposed by an order made under s. 794 may be relaxed by an application under ss. 799 and 800 made by the company or any aggrieved person.

In addition to an order placing restrictions on the shares, the court may make an order requiring the shares to be sold and may impose conditions on the sale (s. 801). The proceeds of any such sale must be paid into court to be held for the benefit of the beneficial owner(s) who may apply for payment (s. 802).

Companies Act statutory forms

Companies are required to ensure that changes to the company's corporate structure are notified to the Registrar of Companies for placing on public record. Additionally, companies must make a confirmation statement each year (s. 853A) (see below).

Conveniently, the companies forms incorporate, in the top left corner of the first page of every form, details of the relevant section number of the Companies Act 2006 under which the obligation to lodge the form arises. A list of the forms currently in use, and the periods in which they must be filed following the event to which they relate, is given in Appendix 3.

Copies of all statutory forms are available free of charge from Companies House and may be requested by post, telephone or via the Companies House website (see Directory, page 597). Many company incorporation agents and business stationers have their own, approved versions of most statutory forms. Approved versions are also available as part of most company secretarial software packages. Companies House has now made almost all forms available for completion and submission online from their website. For certain forms, such as the Confirmation Statement (Form CS01), there is a fee payable and the fee is reduced where the forms are submitted electronically.

In the past, Companies House has usually insisted that all hard copy forms filed bear an original signature. However, following a review and after seeking counsel's opinion, this policy was changed. Companies House has determined that it is acceptable for a person to authorise others to apply their signature to documents. There is a presumption that the use of an automated signature will be subject to internal controls. Accordingly, forms and documents will not be rejected simply because they do not have, or appear not to have, original signatures. This relaxation does not extend to allowing submission of documents by fax, due to issues relating to document quality.

There are a great number of circumstances under which the Registrar can reject documents if they are incorrectly completed and signed. For example, Companies House now frequently rejects documents that are illegible. In this case, illegible means not only documents that cannot easily be read, but also documents that are not capable of being captured electronically or where capture is possible but would result in an unacceptably large file (ss. 1068 and 1072).

Documents may be rejected if they contain shading, colour text or images or are printed on glossy paper. Ideally, documents should be printed or typed on white A4 paper.

CA2016 s. 1068 permits delivery of any document to the Registrar under any provision of the Companies Acts in such manner and in such form as the Registrar may direct.

Online filing

Many companies will find it more convenient to file their statutory forms electronically.

Electronic filing is available either by using the Companies House WebFiling service or by Software Filing using an approved third party software package or by developing their own bespoke in-house software solution.

There are no registration or electronic filing fees; however, the normal document submission or registration fees apply, although the fees generally are reduced for online filings.

WebFiling

Registering to use the WebFiling service is very simple, requiring the online registered of a username and password and then requesting an authentication code for the company or companies for which WebFiling is to be used. The authentication code is posted to the company's registered office address and so will need to be set up in advance. The authentication code acts as the confirmation signature on the forms.

Electronic filing has a number of advantages over paper-based filing, including:

- quicker;
- cheaper (online filing fees are usually lower than the paper-based equivalent filing);
- rejection rates are lower due to in-built checks, pre-population of data; and
- automatic confirmation of filing.

In addition, users of the WebFiling service can opt in to receive email reminders for submission of annual accounts and confirmation statement and can opt in to the **PRO**tected **O**nline **F**iling service (PROOF). PROOF combats corporate identity theft by making changes of registered office or director changes only notifiable using either WebFiling or Software Filing.

Software Filing

The Software Filing services allows companies to develop software solutions for them or their customers to file Companies House forms electronically.

The service works by the use of electronic transmission of documents to Companies House via an HTTPS link using Extensible Markup Language (XML). These documents must comply with the structure approved by the Registrar for electronic submission. Software Filing allows the filing of the same range of forms as the WebFiling service, and in addition some forms of accounts as well as incorporation documents.

Types of forms

With the exception of the annual confirmation statement and annual accounts, other statutory forms are only required because of a corporate event. Where forms or documents are required to be filed as a result of the more common types of event-driven filings, these are dealt with in the appropriate section of this book.

Filing of accounts and points to be aware of to ensure the accounts are not rejected are dealt with in Chapter 10.

Annual confirmation statement

For the vast majority of company secretaries, the confirmation statement will be the only company form with which they have to deal with during the course of the year. The obligation on companies to make an annual return is imposed by s. 853A(1).

Introduced as a deregulating measure, the confirmation statement is intended to offer an easier and more efficient way for companies to check and confirm information held by the Registrar of Companies rather than having to provide information in the form of the annual return, which for many companies remains unchanged from year to year.

All companies must make a confirmation statement up to a date not more than 12 months after the previous confirmation (or 12 months after incorporation), although a company may choose to make it up to an earlier date. The confirmation statement must be filed with the Registrar of Companies within 14 days of the confirmation date, together with a fee (currently £13 if filed online or £40 if filed in hard copy). If a company files more than one confirmation statement in any 12-month period, there is no fee payable for filing the second or subsequent statements.

The statement confirms that all information that the company is required to have delivered to the Registrar of Companies under s. 853A(2) (Relevant Events) (s. 853B) for the confirmation period to which it relates has been delivered or is being delivered at the same time as the confirmation statement. In addition to the statement concerning Relevant Events, companies must provide updated information primarily relating to their share capital, share ownership and beneficial ownership (ss. 853C–I).

Relevant Events

The confirmation statement confirms that any changes to the following either have already been delivered to the Registrar of Companies or are being delivered with the confirmation statement:

- registered office address;
- appointment, termination or change of details of directors (excluding residential address);
- appointment, termination or change of details of secretary (excluding residential address); and
- location of company registers.

Additional information updates

In addition to the Relevant Events statement, companies must provide details of any changes, since the previous confirmation statement, to the:

- SIC code;
- statement of capital;
- trading status of shares;
- shareholder information;
- company's PSC status if s. 790B(1)(b) applies to it; and
- PSC Register.

Where a private company has elected to hold some of all of the permitted registers on the central register held at Companies House, it must also notify any changes to the information needed to be recorded in those registers, including:

- its members;
- directors and their details, including their residential address;
- the secretary's details; and
- PSCs and their details.

Changes to statement of capital

If there have been no changes to the details of the statement of capital, the confirmation statement can just show that there have been no changes for the period covered by the statement.

If a revised statement of capital is required, full details must be provided even in respect of classes where there is no change. The statement of capital comprises:

- total number of issued shares;
- aggregate nominal value of issued shares;
- aggregate amount (if any) unpaid on any shares differentiating between nominal and any premium;

- for each class of shares:
  - narrative summary of the rights attaching to the shares;
  - total number of issued shares; and
  - aggregate nominal value of issued shares.

Trading status of shares

A confirmation if any of the company's shares were admitted to trading on a relevant market or any market outside the UK and if so whether they were so admitted and whether the company was subject to *DTR 5* throughout the confirmation period or part only (s. 853E).

Shareholder information

The information to be provided on shareholders varies depending on whether the company is a traded company or not. A traded company is one whose shares are traded on a public market such as the Main Market of the London Stock Exchange or AIM. Traded companies are required to publish details of their larger shareholders.

Non-traded company

With the exception of private companies keeping their register of members on the central register, non-traded companies must provide details of changes to the shareholders as follows:

- name of every person who was a member of the company at any time during the period since the previous confirmation statement;
- number of shares of each class held by each member at the date of the confirmation statement;
- number of shares of each class transferred during the period covered by the statement to or by another member; and
- date of registration of those transfers.

This shareholder information may be omitted if it is the same as the information filed with the previous confirmation statement (s. 853F(4)).

PSC register information

Unless the company opts to hold its PSC register on the central registry maintained by Companies House, it must provide the information on its PSC register with its confirmation statement.

When companies deliver their first confirmation statement, it must include all the information in the PSC register. For subsequent confirmation statements, companies need only notify details of any changes together with the date of change.

Restricted disclosure of PSC information

Where an individual has obtained protection from the disclosure of protected confirmation, that protection extends to the PSC Register information. Depending on the level of protection obtained, this will mean that either their usual residential address (URA) is protected, so it is not disclosed to credit reference agencies (s. 790ZF protection), or that all of their PSC information is protected from disclosure on the public record (s. 790ZG protection), or both.

If the company has an individual as a PSC whose URA is protected from being disclosed, this fact needs to be indicated on the confirmation statement.

If the PSC has applied for or been granted protection, so that none of their PSC details are disclosed on the public register (s. 790ZG protection), the confirmation statement can only be filed in hard copy form. A different version of the confirmation statement is used for this purpose and it is only available from the secure registers team.

Application under either s. 790ZF or s. 790ZG can only be made on a paper application which is only available by contacting the secure registers team.

The precise applications detail vary depending on the protection required; however, all applications require:

- a statement of the grounds on which the application is made;
- details about the applicant;
- details about the individual or individuals requiring protection; and
- details about the companies or proposed companies in question.

Additionally, evidence supporting the basis of the application must be provided such as evidence of actual or threatened attacks disruption, violence, intimidation or other targeting activists.

Applications for protection are subject to a fee, as follows:

- application under s. 790ZF to prevent disclosure of URA information £100
- abbreviated application under s. 243 or 790ZF to prevent disclosure of URA information £15
- application under s. 790ZG to prevent disclosure of all of a PSC's information £100
- combined application under ss. 790ZF and 790ZG £100

Accounting reference date – Form AA01

Companies may choose to shorten or extend their accounting year. A change in the accounting year must be authorised by the directors at a board meeting and Form AA01 must be filed at Companies House. The change is not effected until the form has been accepted for filing at Companies House.

A company's first accounting period must be longer than six months and must not exceed 18 months.

For further details, see Chapter 10.

Appointment of directors – Form AP01/AP02

Following incorporation, additional directors may be appointed in accordance with the regulations laid down by the company's articles of association.

The appointment of a director must be authorised by the directors at a board meeting and Form AP01 (individuals) or AP02 (Corporate) must be filed at Companies House within 14 days of the appointment.

For further details, see Chapter 6.

Directors ceasing to hold office – Form TM01/TM02

A director may cease to hold office in a number of ways, including resignation, removal, death, by statute and under the provisions of the articles of association.

Depending on the reason for the termination of the appointment of a director authority or noting at a board meeting may be appropriate. In all circumstances, Form TM01 (individuals) or TM02 (Corporate) must be filed at Companies House within 14 days of the termination.

For further details, see Chapter 6.

Registered office – Form AD01

A company's first registered office will be stated on Form IN01 when the company is incorporated. The registered office must be in the same part of the United Kingdom that the Company is registered in with the exception that companies registered in 'England and Wales' can chose to have their registered office in either England or Wales.

The directors must authorise any change in the registered office address (see precedent 9) and, to be effective, notice must be given to Companies House on Form AD01.

Any change does not become effective until the form is received and accepted as valid by the Registrar of Companies. The company's headed stationery must show the new registered office address not later than 14 days after the date that the notice was submitted to the Registrar of Companies.

Documents delivered to the old address within 14 days of the date of change are validly served on the company.

Registration of charges – Form MR01

Particulars of every charge to which the Companies Act 2006 applies must, within 21 days of its creation, be delivered for registration to Companies House on Form

MR01, together with a certified copy of any instrument creating or evidencing the charge.

For further details, see Chapter 20.

Allotment of shares – Form SH01

Within one month of the date of allotment, a return of allotments (Form SH01) should be filed with the Registrar of Companies. The form contains details of the shares being issued together with a statement of capital following the share issue.

For further details, see Chapter 12.

Additional Companies House filing requirements for resolutions

1 A copy of the following resolutions must be filed with the Registrar of Companies within 15 days of approval (ss. 29 and 30):
   - special resolutions;
   - resolutions or agreements which have been agreed to by all the members of a company but which, if not so agreed to, would not have been effective for their purpose unless passed as special resolutions;
   - resolutions or agreements which have been agreed to by all the members of some class of shareholders but which, if not so agreed to, would not have been effective for their purpose unless they had been passed by some particular majority or otherwise in some particular manner; and
   - all resolutions or agreements which effectively bind all the members of any class of shareholders though not agreed to by all those members.

2 A resolution passed by the directors under the direction of the court, to change the name of the company under s. 64.

3 A resolution passed by the directors to change the name of the company under s. 79.

4 A resolution of a company to give, vary, revoke or renew an authority to the directors for the purposes of ss. 550, 551 (allotment of relevant securities) (see precedent 45).

5 A resolution conferring, varying, revoking or renewing authority under s. 701 (market purchase of the company's own shares).

6 A resolution for voluntary winding-up, passed under IA1986 ss. 84(1) (a) or (b).

7 A directors' resolution to amend the articles of association of the company to allow title to securities to be transferred through CREST (reg. 16(6) of the Uncertificated Securities Regulations 1995, SI 1995/3272) (see precedent 66).

8 Forms IC01 or IC02 notification of intention to carry on business or cease to carry on business as an investment company.

Name change

Once the resolution has been passed, a copy of the resolution must be submitted to the Registrar within 15 days of the date of the meeting or effective date of the resolution in writing, as the case may be, together with the change of name fee (currently £10 for paper, £8 for electronic; same-day fee £50 for paper and £30 for electronic). The change of name is effective upon the date of the certificate of incorporation upon change of name issued by the Registrar of Companies.

Company accounts

Companies must deliver a signed copy of their accounts to the Registrar as follows (s. 442):

(a) private companies within nine months of the year-end; and
(b) public companies within six months of the year-end.

Listed companies may issue a preliminary announcement of their results and must publish their audited accounts as soon as possible after the year-end, but in any event not more than six months after the year-end (*LR 9.8.1*). A Listed company must announce and publish its interim results within 90 days of the end of the period to which it relates (*LR 9.9.3*). An AIM company must announce and publish its annual accounts within six months of the end of the financial year and its interim accounts within three months of the end of the period to which it relates (*AIM Rules 18* and *19*). A NEX company must announce and publish its annual accounts and interim accounts within five months and three months, respectively (*NE RFI 44*).

Auditors

Resignation

A copy of the notice of the resignation incorporating the s. 519 statement must be sent to the Registrar of Companies within 14 days by the company (s. 517).

Removal or non-reappointment

When an ordinary resolution has been passed to remove or not reappoint an auditor, notice must be given to the Registrar of Companies within 14 days (s. 512).

Execution of documents

For companies incorporated in England and Wales or Northern Ireland, a document is executed by (s. 44):

- by the affixing of its common seal; or:
- by signature by:
  - two authorised signatories; or
  - a director in the presence of a witness who attests the signature.

An authorised signatory is every director of the company and where appointed, the company secretary and any joint company secretary.

The above provisions do not apply to Scotland and Scottish companies.

Detailed provisions with regard to the execution of documents by Scottish companies, which also need not have a common seal, are contained in s. 48. These require that Scottish companies may sign or subscribe to documents in accordance with the provisions of the Requirements of Writing (Scotland) Act 1995 and, if so signed or subscribed, shall have effect as if given under seal or executed.

If a contract is entered into on behalf of a company by a person as agent for a company before the company has been formed, then, subject to any agreement to the contrary, the contract has effect as one entered into by the person purporting to act as agent for the company and they are personally liable on the contract (CA1985 s. 36C).

The company seal

A company need not have a common seal (s. 45). Whether or not a company has a seal, however, the following provisions apply with regard to the execution of documents (s. 44).

It is usual for a common seal (if one exists) to be kept by the company secretary, who will maintain a record of all documents to which the seal has been affixed. In the case of infrequent use of the seal, specific reference to the document sealed may be made in the minutes of the board meeting authorising the sealing (see precedents 9 and 83). If the seal is used frequently, it will be more convenient for the particulars of the documents sealed to be entered in a seal register and for this to be produced at each board meeting at which an appropriate confirmatory resolution will be passed.

It is common for modern forms of articles of association (e.g. reg. 49 of the Private Company Model Articles) for companies to pass a board resolution delegating authority for the use of the seal to various officers of the company. Other persons may be designated 'authorised signatories' to sign documents to which the seal has been affixed. If this procedure is followed, there is no need for the sealings to be confirmed by the directors at a board meeting, although a record of all documents sealed should be kept in a seal book/register.

Securities seal

A company which has a common seal may have a securities seal, which is a copy of the common seal with the addition on its face of the word 'Securities' and which can be used to seal certificates relating to the securities of the company (s. 50). This is particularly useful where the company has appointed an outside share registrar; the two principal benefits are firstly that the company may keep the use of its common seal (if it has one) under its own control, and secondly that share certificates sealed with a security seal do not also require a signature.

The provision allowing companies to have a securities seal came into force on 12 February 1979. Companies incorporated before that date may adopt and use a securities seal notwithstanding the contents of their articles of association or of any trust deed securing debenture stock specifying sealing in any other way.

Companies that intend to use a securities seal upon their share certificates must ensure that they also have a common seal even if they do not intend to use it, as the use of a securities seal is only permitted where the company has a common seal (s. 50). Provided the articles contain the relevant authority, the seal need not be a physical seal but can be printed or embossed. For share registrars, use of pre-printed security seals is becoming a popular means of sealing share certificates.

Official seal for use abroad

Subject to appropriate authority in the articles of association, a company with a common seal which transacts business abroad may have one or more official seals for use in overseas countries (s. 49). In order for such seals to be used validly, the company must appoint in writing under its common seal the person or persons in the territory concerned who will affix the official seal to documents in that country (see precedent 9). An official seal for use abroad is a copy of the common seal with the addition on its face of the name of the country in which it is to be used.

Instead of having a seal for use abroad, however, a company may grant a power of attorney to an individual in any place outside the United Kingdom to execute deeds on its behalf in that country. If the company has a common seal, the appointment of the attorney would be made by a document under seal (s. 47).

Authentication of documents

Another duty of the company secretary (or a director or other authorised officer of the company) is to authenticate by signature any document or proceeding which is required to be authenticated by the company.

The company secretary is frequently asked to provide certified copies of documents, resolutions, minutes, etc., and will usually do so by signing the document together with the words 'Certified to be a true copy' and the date of signature.

Retention of documents

The company secretary is often responsible for exercising control over the company's policy regarding the filing and retention of documents. The period of time for which documents should be retained depends on the nature of the document. Appendix 5 contains a schedule giving both statutory and suggested retention periods for a large number of documents, including company records and share registration documents.

Recent legal cases have demonstrated the necessity to have an effective document retention policy that is relevant to their business, that is adhered to by all parts of the business and that where litigation is anticipated, steps are taken to ensure documents are not destroyed either deliberately or in accordance with the normal operation of the policy.

When implementing or reviewing document retention policies, the following issues are relevant:

- **Legal and regulatory requirements**. Companies need to be aware of differing legal obligations and guidance on document retention including accounting, tax, company law, compliance, employment, insurance and health and safety. Some services such as financial services regulation have specific (longer) document retention requirements.
- **Data protection legislation**. In the EU, the Data Protection Directive broadly harmonised data protection within the EU, and retaining personal data for longer than is necessary may contravene this data protection legislation.
- **Electronic or original documents**. While electronic storage of document images is now increasingly the norm, there must be appropriate measures in place to be able to demonstrate that the image or file copy of an electronic original has not been altered. Documents under seal, stamped documents and documents of title in England and Wales should be kept in their original form. Although electronic files can be kept for many years, advances in technology might mean that the underlying software to read those files is no longer available after a few years and care needs to be taken that any archived files are capable of being reproduced in a readable format.
- **Statutory limitation periods**. Limitation rules rarely specify document retention periods. The limitation period can, however, be used to determine the type of documents needed to be retained to take or defend any legal action. Limitation periods vary considerably between countries and so retention policies may need to be country-specific.
- **Destruction of documents**. Certain documents should be kept in original form and never be destroyed, such as board minutes, documents under seal, tax documents and original documents that are the subject of court proceedings. However, there are other rules that mandate the destruction of documents after a certain period.

Modern slavery act statement

Companies, other than those qualifying as small or medium sized, that meet four criteria are required to publish an annual statement setting out the steps taken by the company to prevent modern slavery in their business and in their supply chain.(Modern Slavery Act 2015 (MSA2015) s. 54)

The four criteria are as follows (MSA2015 s. 54(2) and (12):

- It is a body corporate or partnership, wherever incorporated or formed.
- It carries on a business or part of a business in the UK.
- It supplies goods and services.
- Its annual turnover is at least £36m.

Although there is no timescale for the publication of the statement, the Home Office guidance notes that the statement should be made within six months of the financial year to which it relates. To meet the requirement, companies should undertake an annual assessment to determine whether the company meets the criteria, and review the company's policies and procedures for ensuring there is no modern slavery within the company or its supply chain

The statement, which should be formally approved by the directors, must be published on the company's UK website, if it has one. Groups may publish a statement in respect of the whole group or, where the group comprises distinct business divisions, separate statements may be more appropriate.

A company that does not have a website must provide a copy of the statement within 30 days of a written request for a copy being received.

Gender pay gap reporting

As established in 2017 by the Equality Act 2010 (Gender Pay Gap Information) Regulations 2017 (SI 172/2017), all companies with 250 or more employees must publish details of the relative pay rates for men and women in their business (the gender pay gap).

The gender pay gap is the difference between the average earnings of men and women, expressed relative to men's earnings. For example, 'women earn 15% less than men per hour'.

The legislation sets out comprehensive details of how the rates of pay are to be calculated so that all companies report in the same way. Ensuring a common methodology in calculating the data ensures accurate comparisons between companies and industry sectors. The gender pay gap data must relate to the pay paid to employees, including directors, in the pay period which includes the 'snapshot date' which is 31 March for public sector employers and 5 April for businesses and charities.

Qualifying companies must publish their gender pay gap data and a written statement on their external website, if they have one, and submit those figures to an online government portal. If the employer does not have an external website, the information can be made available on a group website or failing that on an internal intranet or otherwise circulated to employees.

The requirement to report falls on the employing entity, and for groups it may be that several subsidiaries have their own obligation to report their gender pay gap data. Groups may also publish aggregated group gender pay gap data but are not obliged to do so.

Companies with fewer than 250 employees may voluntarily report their gender pay gap data, but are not obliged to do so. Where voluntary disclosure is made, the same methodology in calculating the data should be used.

The online portal includes a template publication page, but companies can create their own provided it meets the template criteria.

The portal can be accessed at www.gov.uk/report-gender-pay-gap-data.

The gender pay gap data that must be published is:

- mean gender pay gap in hourly pay;
- median gender pay gap in hourly pay;
- mean bonus gender pay gap;
- median bonus gender pay gap;
- proportion of males and females receiving a bonus payment; and
- proportion of males and females in each pay quartile.

Payment practices disclosures

Payment practice and performance reporting was introduced by the UK government as part of its strategy to encourage prompt payment, especially to small suppliers. Large companies are required to submit details of their payment terms and actual performance to an online government portal every six months. The data collected is available to the public.

The obligation is individual to all companies, and accordingly groups may comprise one or more companies that are required to report their own payment practices (SBEE2015 s. 3 and The Reporting on Payment Practices and Performance Regulations 2017 (SI 395/2017).

A company falls within scope of the regulations if it meets any two of the following criteria at each of its previous two balance sheet dates:

- turnover of at least £36m (£43.2m gross);
- balance sheet total of at least £18m (£21.6m gross) (meaning the aggregate of amounts shown as assets; and
- at least 250 employees.

Turnover means the amounts received for the sale of goods and services, excluding financial services.

Qualifying companies are required to report in respect of each six month period commencing on the first day of its financial year and within 30 days of the end of each reporting period.

The following information must be provided:

- narrative description of standard payment terms including normal length of time for payment, maximum payment period and any changes to standard payment period and how suppliers have been notified or consulted in respect of any changes;
- description of the process to resolve disputes; and
- statistics showing average number of days to pay invoices from date of receipt of invoice, percentage of payments made in less than 30 days, between 31 and 60 days and in 61 days or more and the percentage of payments made within the agreed payment terms.

Confirmation by way of 'tick box statements' about:

1 whether suppliers are offered e-invoicing;
2 availability of supply chain financing;
3 whether a charge is made for the supplier to remain on a supplier's list and if so if a charge has been made in the reporting period; and
4 whether the business is a member of a payment code, and the name of the code whether the business is a member of a payment code, and the name of the code.

Other compliance and regulatory matters

Although other compliance and regulatory responsibilities lie outside the scope of this book, directors and company secretaries must familiarise themselves with a range of these. Although some regulations are specific to certain industries, there are a number of regulations common to most businesses, including those listed in Table 7.3.

Table 7.3: Legislation that applies to most businesses

Area	*Legislation*
Employment	■ National Minimum Wage Act 1998 ■ Working Time Regulations 1998 ■ Employment Rights Act 1996 ■ Pensions Act 2008 ■ Equality Act 2010
Mandatory employer's liability insurance	■ Employers' Liability (Compulsory Insurance) Act 1969
Disability discrimination	■ Equality Act 2010

Area	*Legislation*
Health and safety	■ Health and Safety at Work, etc., Act 1974. ■ Health and Safety (Display Screen Equipment) Regulations 1992 ■ Management of Health and Safety at Work Regulations 1999 ■ Manual Handling Operations Regulations 1992 ■ Personal Protective Equipment at Work Regulations 1992 ■ Provision and Use of Work Equipment Regulations 1998 ■ Reporting of Injuries, Diseases and Dangerous Occurances Regulations 1995 ■ Workplace (Health Safety and Welfare) Regulations 1992
The environment	■ Environmental Protection Act 1990 ■ Environment Act 1995 ■ Pollution Prevention and Control (England and Wales) Regulations 2000 ■ Climate Change Act 2008 ■ Natural Environment and Rural Communities Act 2006 ■ Clean Neighbouthoods and Environment Act 2005
Beneficial ownership/ nominee arrangements	■ Trustee Act 2000
Data protection	■ Data Protection Act 2018
Intellectual property, trade descriptions	■ Registered Designs Act 1949 ■ Patents Act 1977 ■ Patents Act 2004 ■ Copyright, Designs and Patents Act 1988 ■ Trade Marks Act 1994
Consumer credit and protection	■ Consumer Credit (EU Directive) Regulations 2010 ■ Consumer Protection from Unfair Trading Regulations 2008 ■ Consumer Credit Acts of 1974 and 2006 ■ Consumer Rights Act 2015
Competition	■ Competition Act 1998 ■ Enterprise Act 2002 ■ Enterprise and Regulatory Reform Act 2013

Area	*Legislation*
Taxation (corporation tax, VAT, NIC and PAYE)	■ Income Tax Act 2007 ■ Corporation Tax Act 2009 ■ Value Added Tax Act 1994 ■ Income Tax (Earnings and Pensions) Act 2003 ■ Social Security (Contributions and Benefits) Act 1992
Money laundering	■ Money Laundering, Terrorist Financing and Transfer of Funds Regulations 2017 ■ Criminal Finances Act 2017 ■ Proceeds of Crime Act 2002 ■ Money Laundering Regulations 2007 ■ Terrorism Act 2000

8 – Members' resolutions and general meetings

Introduction

The requirement for companies to hold general meetings of shareholders is laid down in the Companies Act 2006, and reinforced by the company's articles. The provisions of the Act cannot be overruled by a company's articles where the effect would be to deprive the members of any rights provided by statute. However, in instances where the procedure stipulated by the articles is merely different from the statutory position, the articles may still prevail. Care needs to be taken therefore to establish that the correct requirements have been observed. Many companies' articles are still based on Table A.

Approval of resolutions of the members of private companies may be sought by the written resolution process or by holding a general meeting. For the majority of private companies, which only have a few members, the written resolution process is likely to be used in the majority of cases, as holding a members' meeting is a much more time-consuming process.

Resolutions in writing

With a few exceptions, the members of a private company may pass any resolution that could be put to a general meeting by written resolution. The exceptions are:

1 removal of a director under s. 168; and
2 removal of an auditor under s. 510.

Written resolutions may be proposed by the directors using the procedure set out in s. 291 or by the members using the procedure set out in ss. 292–295 (s. 288).

A copy of the proposed written resolution must be sent by post or electronic means to all members entitled to attend and vote at a general meeting (s. 289).

A member signifies their agreement to a written resolution by returning to the company a document in hard copy or electronically, identifying the resolution and signifying their consent (s. 296).

A written resolution is approved when the requisite majority of members have signified their agreement, votes being calculated according to the number of shares held by each member (ss. 284 and 296).

If agreement has not been given within 28 days from the date the resolution was circulated, it is deemed to have lapsed and any consent given after that date has no effect (s. 297).

Copies of written resolutions circulated to members must also be sent to the company's auditor if it has one (s. 502(1)).

Resolutions proposed by directors

The company must send copies of the proposed resolution to all eligible members at the same time either in hard copy, by electronic means or by using a website (ss. 291(2) and (3)). Alternatively, if it can be accomplished quickly, the same copy can be circulated for signature, but to be valid, all sufficient signatures must be obtained within the 28-day window imposed by s. 297. The resolution must be accompanied by a statement informing the members of how to signify consent and the deadline for receipt of consenting copies (see precedent 4).

Resolutions proposed by members

Any member or members of a private company together holding not less than 5% of the total voting rights of the company may also request that a statement of not more than 1,000 words be circulated with the proposed resolution (see page 124). The company's articles may provide for a share ownership threshold of less than 5% (s. 292).

A company need not comply with such a request if the resolution, on being passed, would be ineffective by reason of inconsistency with legislation or the company's constitution or if it is frivolous, vexatious or defamatory (s. 292).

Where a valid request is received, copies of the proposed resolution and any accompanying statement must be circulated to all eligible members at the same time in hard copy, in electronic form or by means of a website within 21 days of receiving the request (s. 293).

The costs of circulating the proposed resolution and any statement must be met by the requisitionist(s) and unless the company has previously agreed to do so, the company need not comply with the requisition unless sufficient funds are deposited by the requisitionist(s) to meet the expenses (s. 294).

The company or other aggrieved person may apply to the court for an order not to comply with the request to circulate the proposed resolution and any statement on the grounds that the rights conferred by s. 292 are being abused (s. 295).

General meetings

The Act's requirements cover the convening of general meetings, notice of general meetings, proceedings to be followed at general meetings and the votes of members, including provisions for proxies for members unable or unwilling to attend in person.

There are three main types of general meetings:

1 annual general meetings (AGMs);
2 general meetings; and
3 class meetings of the holders of a particular class of the company's capital.

Convening a general meeting

The directors may convene a general meeting at any time of their choosing (s. 302).

Directors of a public company are required to convene an annual general meeting within six months of the end of the company accounting period, in order for members to receive the accounts (s. 336).

Members can require the directors to convene a general meeting and to propose resolutions and circulate statements (ss. 303 to 305) (see pages 124 and 138).

Notice of general meetings

The minimum periods of notice required for general meetings is specified in s. 307. These periods cannot be reduced by the company's articles, although the minimum periods can be extended.

Listed companies are required, where possible, to comply with the UK Corporate Governance Code, which contains a best practice requirement for notice of AGMs to be 20 working days in all cases.

The minimum notice periods specified in s. 307 are:

- general meeting of a private company: 14 days;
- annual general meeting of a public company: 21 days;
- general meeting of a public company that is not a traded company: 14 days.

For traded companies the notice periods are set out in s. 307A, as follows:

- general meetings where specified conditions are met: 14 days;
- all other general meetings: 21 days.

In order for a general meeting of a traded company to be held on 14 days' notice, the circumstances specified in s. 307A must be met. This section was inserted into the Act by the Companies (Shareholders' Rights) Regulations 2009 (SI 2009/1632). These circumstances are as follows:

- the meeting is not an annual general meeting;
- members are offered an electronic voting facility; and
- a special resolution has been passed to reduce the notice period to 14 days. This must have happened at either the immediately preceding annual general meeting or at a general meeting held since the last annual general meeting.

If all three conditions are met, the notice period will be 14 days. In all other cases, 21 days' notice will be required.

Special notice

Resolutions requiring special notice (s. 312):

- notice to company of intention to put resolution: 28 days;
- notice to members at same time as notice given to members of meeting.

However, great care needs to be taken as, while the model articles do not contain any provisions regarding notice periods, different notice periods which may have been adopted, varied or excluded by any particular company:

- general meeting of a private or public company to consider special resolutions or the appointment of a director: 21 days;
- annual general meeting of a public company: 21 days;
- all other general meetings of private or public company: 14 days.

If the company's articles impose longer notice provisions than are required by the legislation, they override the statutory notice periods.

Clear days

In all cases, the period of notice is expressed as clear days' notice. This means that the day on which the notice is served and the day on which the meeting is to be held are excluded (s. 360). The date on which the notice is deemed to be served varies with different companies' articles.

For example, if a private company wishes to hold a general meeting on 17 May, the latest date for posting the notice of meeting would be 1 May. The notice would be deemed to be served on 3 May and the 14 days counted from 4 May would expire on 17 May.

Agreement to short notice of meeting

There is a useful concession under s. 307(4) in circumstances where it is not possible (or desirable) to give the minimum period of notice required by subsections (1) and (2) of that section or by the articles under which a general meeting may be held on short notice.

Advantage of the concession, however, can usually be taken only by companies with a small number of members. It is good practice for the agreement to short notice to be in writing, so that there is no doubt that the meeting was validly called (see precedent 72). It should be noted that the provision does not allow the complete dispensation of giving notice and notice must still be given to all members, even if it is known that they cannot attend.

The number of members required to give valid consent to short notice is defined in ss. 307(5) and (6), which provides that for a private company, the requisite majority to agree to short notice is a majority in number of the members having a right to attend and vote at the meeting, and together holding not less than 90% of the share capital of the company. This 90% limit may be increased by the company's articles to not more than 95%. Thus, if in the case of a company with 100 shares, one member held 97 shares and three other members held one share each, the one member with more than 95% of the share capital could not hold the meeting at short notice, because they would not constitute a majority of the members. This provision protects minority members holding less than 10% of the shares.

For a public company, the percentage required for a general meeting is 95%.

In the case of an AGM, consent must be given by all the members entitled to attend and vote (s. 337(2)). Thus the concession is useful only to small public companies. The form of consent to short notice for an AGM should include agreement to accept the company's report and accounts (if necessary), even though they were not sent to members not less than 21 days before the date of the meeting, as required by s. 424.

Although not legally required, it may be advisable to obtain a letter of non-objection to the short notice from the company's auditors. Notice of all general meetings must be sent to the auditors under s. 502(2), which gives them the right to receive notice of and attend general meetings.

Entitlement to notice of general meetings

Subject to any provisions in the company's articles, notice is to be given to every member and director (s. 310

In addition, s. 310(2), reg. 27 (private company model articles) provide that executors or administrators of a deceased member or the trustee of a bankrupt member must be given notice, even though they may not have the right to vote at the meeting.

Surprisingly, the company secretary has no formal right to receive a copy of the notice or to attend general meetings. Holders of preference shares or non-voting shares will often not be entitled to receive notice of general meetings, as the articles will usually exclude both voting rights and the right to notice of meetings, and accordingly override the provisions of s. 310, unless, because of a particular event, they are entitled to vote at them. In practice, however, and especially in the case of Listed companies, notices will usually be sent to every holder of shares or debentures, whether or not the registered address of the holder is in the UK and irrespective of whether the securities held entitle that member to vote at the meeting. This is because, under ss. 431 and 432, every member and holder of debentures must be sent a copy of the report and accounts, and the notice of meeting is usually incorporated in this document. It is, however, usual practice to include an explanatory note stating that the notice is sent for information only to debenture holders, who are not entitled to attend and vote at the meeting.

For a class meeting, only the holders of the shares of that class are entitled to notice. Section 313 affords protection to the company in the case of accidental omission to give notice to any person entitled to receive it.

The model articles do not contain any provisions concerning entitlement to notice.

Content of notices

The notice must state the time, place and date of the meeting, and the general nature of the business to be transacted (s. 311) (see precedent 5). Where a special resolution is to be proposed, the notice must contain the text of the resolution and must state that the resolution is to be proposed as a special resolution (s. 283(6)). Since the directors normally instruct the company secretary to convene the general meeting, the notice is usually signed by the company secretary on behalf of the board (sometimes referred to as 'by order of the board').

Listed companies must follow the provisions of the *Listing Rules* (*LR 9.3.6, 7*) in regard to proxies, i.e. every member must be given the opportunity to vote for, against or abstain every resolution included in the notice (the so-called 'three-way proxy': see below). In order to facilitate this, resolutions in the notice of meeting should be numbered so that the numbers can be included on the proxy form, with boxes for the member to tick either for or against the resolution, or to abstain from voting.

Every notice must include a prominent statement which makes clear that the member entitled to attend and vote may appoint one or more proxies to attend, speak and vote on their behalf (s. 325). A proxy need not be a member of the company. Any provision in the company's articles requiring proxies to be lodged more than 48 hours (excluding any day that is not a working day) before the meeting is invalid (s. 327).

The notice of an AGM of a public company must state that the meeting is to be the AGM (s. 337).

Types of resolutions that may be passed at general meetings

At a general meeting, an ordinary resolution that may, in certain circumstances, require special notice to have been given (see below) may be passed as a special resolution.

Ordinary resolutions

A simple majority of those present and voting is all that is required to pass an ordinary resolution. The practical effect of this should be considered. If there are 12 members entitled to vote present at a meeting, the resolution would be passed if seven voted in favour and five against. The resolution would also be passed if nine of the 12 members abstained from voting, and of the three who did vote, two voted in favour of the resolution and one against.

Examples of this type of resolution include:

- alterations to the share capital under ss. 617 and 618;
- a capitalisation of profits;
- the grant of authority for the allotment of securities (ss. 550 and 551); and

- subject to provision in the articles, a resolution authorising the directors to offer shareholders the right to elect to receive new ordinary shares for the whole or part of a cash dividend.

Special resolutions

The majority required to pass a special resolution is one of not less than 75% of those voting. It is essential that the notice of the meeting states that it is intended to propose a resolution as a special resolution. Under CA1985, at least 21 clear days' notice had to be given. However, by s. 307, only 14 days' notice needs to be given of a general meeting at which a special resolution is to be passed. This does not apply to general meetings of traded companies, where 21 days' notice will still be required, unless a resolution reducing the notice period to 14 days has been passed (see page 119).

The type of business that must be dealt with by a special resolution is specified in the Act and/or the company's articles. It includes: alteration of the articles (s. 21); change of name (s. 77); disapplication of pre-emption rights (s. 571); and reduction of capital (s. 641).

The notice convening the meeting at which a special resolution is to be considered must include the full text of the resolution. With the exception of obvious typographical errors, the meeting cannot amend the wording of a special resolution (s. 283(6)).

Special notice

This must not be confused with special resolutions. Special notice of certain ordinary resolutions must be given to the company (s. 312), as follows:

- A resolution to remove an auditor before the expiration of their term of office (s. 510) (see precedent 73).
- Under s. 168, resolutions:
  - to remove a director before the expiration of their period of office (see precedent 20);
  - to appoint somebody in place of the director removed at the meeting at which they are removed (see precedent 74).

Special notice must be given to the company at least 28 days prior to the meeting.

The company is required to give notice of the resolutions of which special notice has been given to all members in the notice of meeting or, if not practicable, by advertisement in a newspaper or such other manner allowed by the articles, not less than 14 days before the meeting (s. 312(3)).

Where the special notice relates to a resolution proposed by the directors, such as the removal of an auditor, it is common practice for the special notice to be given by a director.

Circulation of members' statements or resolutions

Companies have a duty to circulate resolutions or statements of not more than 1,000 words with respect to that or any other business of the meeting if requested to do so by members (s. 314).

Companies have a duty to circulate resolutions if requested to do so by members (s. 338).

The request for circulation may be given by:

1 members holding not less than 5% of the total voting rights at the meeting concerned; or
2 no fewer than 100 members holding shares with an average paid-up value of not less than £100.

The request to circulate a statement must identify the statement to be circulated or the text of the resolution; it must be authenticated by the persons making it and must be received by the company at least one week prior to the meeting.

The company need not comply with the request if the effect of the resolution is ineffective, defamatory, frivolous or vexatious.

The cost of circulating the statement need not be met by those requesting it if it relates to an AGM and sufficient requests to require circulation are received prior to the end of the financial year. In all other cases, those seeking the circulation of the statement must meet the costs unless the company resolves otherwise. Unless the company has previously resolved to meet any costs, an amount reasonably sufficient to cover the costs must be deposited with the company not less than one week prior to the meeting, failing which the company need not circulate the statement (s. 316).

The company may apply to the courts for leave not to comply with the request if the company or an aggrieved person believes the request is of a defamatory nature or the rights under s. 314 are being abused (s. 317).

Annual general meetings

Annual general meetings of private companies

Under the Companies Act, private companies are no longer required to hold an annual general meeting.

Any private company required by its articles to hold an AGM will need to comply with the general provisions on meetings in Part 13 of the Companies Act, together with any more onerous requirements in its articles.

Members of private companies no longer have the statutory right to demand that the company holds an AGM, except by amending the articles to require this.

However, members of private companies holding 5% of the voting rights can requisition a general meeting (ss. 303–305) and members holding 5% of voting rights have a new right to requisition a written resolution (ss. 292–295).

Public companies: convening an annual general meeting

Every public company and every private company that is a traded company must hold an annual general meeting within the period of six months (nine months for a private traded company) commencing on its accounting reference date (s. 336).

In most cases, the directors convene the AGM (s. 302). Under s. 306, the court has power to order an AGM and may direct the manner in which it should be held and conducted. It is likely that a meeting convened under the direction of the court will be a general meeting rather than the AGM.

Business at annual general meetings

The following is the routine business of an annual general meeting:

- Receiving the report and accounts laid before the meeting, as required by ss. 437–438.
- The declaration of a dividend.
- The election of directors. (This will include both the election of directors who have been appointed since the last AGM and the re-election of directors who have retired by rotation, as required by the company's articles or the Act.)
- The reappointment and remuneration of the auditors.

Apart from routine business, any other business may also be undertaken at the AGM, for example:

- ordinary resolutions to increase the company's capital;
- special resolutions for any required alterations to the company's articles;
- authority to the directors to issue capital as required by s. 551;
- authority for the directors to disapply pre-emption rights (s. 571); and
- where it is company practice, and there is provision in the company's articles, to authorise the directors to offer shareholders the right to receive new ordinary shares instead of cash for all or part of any dividend.

'Other' business used to be described as 'special' business, but the model articles make no distinction between the two, hence the suggested use of the terms 'routine business' and 'other business'.

Additional requirement for quoted companies

Quoted companies must put a resolution at the meeting that receives the audited accounts for the approval of the directors' remuneration report (s. 439).

Receiving report and accounts

It is not appropriate for the minutes of an AGM (including a general meeting of a private company) to state: 'The report and accounts for the year ended 20XX were received and approved/adopted.' The Companies Act makes no provision for the report and accounts to be *approved/adopted* by the meeting (ss. 437–438). All that is legally required is that the accounts be laid before the meeting. Although there is no legal obligation to have any resolution at all, best practice is for shareholders to resolve to receive the accounts and to have the opportunity to question directors about them. The appropriate minute would be more correct if it stated: 'The report of the directors and audited accounts for the year ended 20XX were laid before the meeting' (or 'were received by the meeting').

There is a common misconception that shareholders approve the accounts and, by implication, can refuse to approve them. The accounts are the accounts of the directors; shareholders merely receive them. Shareholders have no right to reject accounts or request their amendment.

For a Listed company, any vote against receipt of the accounts would be taken as a vote of no confidence in the board.

Declaration of dividend

Where appropriate, a declaration of a final dividend is usually included in the resolution to receive the directors' report and accounts. The articles of the company will normally follow Public Model Article 70, which provides that the company may, by ordinary resolution, declare dividends in accordance with the rights of the members, but that no dividend shall exceed the amount recommended by the directors. Thus, although the accounts may show an amount of the proposed dividend, this could be reduced or even rejected by the members, whether the accounts are accepted or not.

The Private and Public Model Articles 30 and 70, respectively, authorise directors to pay interim dividends on their own authority.

Shareholders' right to propose directors at an AGM

Neither the Act nor the model articles contain explicit authority for members to propose the appointment of additional directors at a public company annual general meeting. The previous form of model articles did contain this authority. As noted above members do, subject to certain safeguards, have a general right to propose resolutions to be considered at a general meeting (s. 303). Additionally members of a public company have the right to propose resolutions for consideration at an AGM (s. 338) and members of a traded company have the right to propose business, other than a resolution for consideration at an AGM (s. 338A). In each case the request must state the general nature of the resolution or business, may include specific text of a proposed resolution and must be proposed by a member or members holding not less than 5% of the total voting rights or between them hold not less than 100 shares on which an aggregate of not less than £100 has been paid.

The request is not valid if:

1 it would, if passed, be ineffective,
2 it is defamatory of any person, or
3 it is frivolous or vexatious.

'Other' general meetings

Convening general meetings

Subject to the articles, general meetings may be convened at any time in order to transact business that needs to be dealt with. The directors may convene a general meeting under authority contained in s. 302. Alternatively, under s. 303, the directors may be required to call the meeting by a requisition of the members. The court also has authority under s. 306 to convene a general meeting.

Quorum at general meetings

The quorum for meetings is stipulated in s. 318 and provides that for a company with a sole shareholder, the quorum is one and that in all other cases, subject to any provisions in the company's articles of association, two members present in person or by proxy may constitute a quorum. A company's articles usually make provision for a procedure to be adopted in the event of a quorum not being present.

Some articles might require that if a quorum is not present within half an hour, or if a quorum ceases to be present after the commencement of the meeting, the meeting is adjourned to the same day, time and place in the following week or to such time and place (but not day) as the directors may decide. This regulation is frequently amended so that at the adjourned meeting, those shareholders present shall constitute a quorum even if below the 'normal' quorum.

Similar provisions for adjournment feature in the model articles (article 41 for private companies and article 33 for public companies), with the difference that there is no default adjournment to the same day, time and place in the following week. Rather, the chairman must either specify the time and place for the adjourned meeting, or state that the meeting will continue at such time and place as the directors may decide. In addition, for the adjourned meeting there is no reduced quorum provision.

Chairman at general meetings

Private Model Article 31 and Public Model Article 39 state that the chairman of the board will also be chairman for general meetings. If the chairman is not present, then another director (e.g. a deputy chairman or vice-chairman) takes the chair. In the absence of any director, one of the members present takes the chair.

Section 319 states that subject to any provisions in the company's articles, any member may be elected by the meeting to be chairman of that meeting. Section 328 permits a proxy holder to be elected chairman of the meeting subject to any provisions in the articles.

The role of the chairman at a shareholders' meeting is to ensure that the meeting is properly and fairly conducted, allowing all opinions to be expressed.

The company's articles will also usually give the chairman specific powers relating to the conduct of meetings which might include some or all of:

- authority to adjourn or close the meeting before the conclusion of all business – usually to be exercised in the event of disruption;
- a second, casting vote, in the event of the number of votes being cast for or against a resolution being equal;
- authority to call for a vote by way of a show of hands or on a poll;
- authority to exclude disruptive members and/or permit guests and other non-members to attend (but not vote); and
- discretion in the holding of a poll vote either at or following the meeting and process to be followed for conducting any poll vote.

The role of the company secretary at meetings

Preparation for an annual general meeting of a public company

As well as the routine business of annual general meetings outlined above, it is also routine business for companies with the appropriate provision in their articles to pass an ordinary resolution giving authority to the directors to offer shareholders the option to receive the whole or any part of their dividends in new ordinary shares rather than in cash.

Other items of non-routine business (e.g. alteration of articles) should be described in a separate circular to members dispatched with the notice of the meeting.

The venue for the meeting will probably have been fixed several months in advance, and the date of the AGM included in the programme of board meetings for the year and previously approved by the directors. Following receipt of the audited accounts, the following matters should be undertaken by the company secretary.

1. It is quite common for the report and accounts to incorporate the notice of the meeting as well as the chairman's statement. Three proof copies of the booklet containing the notice of meeting and the accounts will be required, and all three copies will require signature for each of the reports.
2. Send another copy of the report and accounts with the names of the signatories and dates printed in to the company's printers for a final proof prior to running off the bulk supply for dispatch to shareholders.
3. Advise the company's registrar (either the company's own in-house registrar or a firm of service registrars) of the amount of the recommended dividend, if any, in order that they may prepare the dividend warrants for dispatch to shareholders following approval at the AGM.
4. If a dividend is to be paid, the company should also arrange with its bankers for a dividend account to be opened, in which the money required to pay the dividend will be placed.

5 Prepare proxy forms for dispatch with the report and accounts to shareholders. These can be either separate cards inserted in the booklet or a tear-out page in the booklet.

6 The report and accounts will normally be sent directly to shareholders by the company's printers. They should be instructed as to the date on which posting should take place and whether the document is to be sent by first or second class post. The names of the signatories on the bulk printed supply should be printed in exactly the same way as the original signatures on the three signed copies, e.g. 'Albert Smith' and not 'A. Smith'.

7 One of the three signed copies of the report and accounts booklet will be placed in the company's directors' board minute book, one copy will be retained by the company's auditors and the third copy will be sent to the Registrar of Companies. The signed copy of the report and accounts for the Registrar of Companies could be sent either at the same time that these are dispatched to members or at a later date, within the time allowed by s. 442.

8 It is usual to invite the company's solicitor to attend the meeting. The company's auditors are entitled to attend under s. 502(2).

9 The forms of proxy returned by shareholders should be checked against the register of members. A report on the result of the proxy count should be made available for the board after the expiry of the deadline for receipt of proxies (usually 48 hours before the time of the meeting).

10 Consider the preparation of ballot papers in case a poll is demanded (for more detail, see below). It might be prudent to do this if many proxy cards have been returned with votes against any particular resolution(s).

11 If the chairman is going to make remarks at the meeting, additional to those contained in their statement in the report and accounts, prepare copies to give to the company's press agents at the meeting and, for Listed, AIM or NEX companies, to send simultaneously to a regulatory information service (see *LR 9.3.1*, *DR 2.2.1*).

12 A copy of the register of members should be available at the AGM. This is required in case it is necessary for persons attending the meeting to be identified, to ensure only those entitled to attend are present.

13 Provide attendance sheets for shareholders, the press, proxies and representatives of corporate shareholders who are attending the meeting under authority of s. 323.

14 Make available for inspection copies of the directors' service contracts.

15 Prepare an order of proceedings, setting out the various resolutions to be passed at the meeting. There is no requirement for resolutions to be seconded and it is perfectly in order for the chairman of the meeting to propose all resolutions with no seconder.

16 From the outset, always bear in mind practical considerations, such as making room bookings in good time, checking catering arrangements and finding out whether a photographer or video-conferencing facility is needed.

At the general meeting

The company secretary should first check that a quorum is present and then be ready to read the notice of meeting. If the meeting consents (and it usually does), this may be taken as read, since it will have been included in the report and accounts sent to all members. The auditor's report must cover the accounts laid before the meeting and state the name of the auditor and, where the auditor is a firm, the name of the person who signed it as senior statutory auditor. This will, of course, have been included in the booklet containing the report and accounts.

The company secretary will assist the chairman in counting the votes (if necessary) on a show of hands. This is not normally necessary, except in the case of a special resolution, where there might be some doubt about whether the necessary three-quarters majority of those attending and voting was achieved.

All proxies are entitled to speak at the meeting including demanding or joining in the demand for a poll vote on any resolution (ss. 324 and 329). The company secretary will often oversee the process if a poll is demanded on any resolution, to be taken either at or after the meeting (see page 134).

After the meeting

The minutes of the meeting should be prepared. It is not always necessary for these to be sent out in draft to the directors for comments, since the minutes will usually cover only routine business or such other business as may have been specified in the notice convening the meeting.

If payment of a final dividend is approved at the meeting, the necessary arrangements must be put in hand for its payment. Depending on the payment date, this may simply be to release electronic transfers and mailing of cheques already prepared, or to take a cut of the register of members at the record date and calculate the amounts due to individual members (see Chapter 19).

Traded companies must make a market announcement via a regulatory information service (RIS) of all resolutions, other than ordinary resolutions at an AGM, approved by the shareholders at a general meeting (*LR 9.6.18*).

Registration of resolutions with the Registrar of Companies

The resolutions that must be filed with the Registrar of Companies are specified in s. 29. These include all special resolutions, as well as the ordinary resolutions to authorise the allotment of securities (s. 551(9)) and to authorise a market purchase of the company's own shares (s. 701(8)).

Copies of resolutions must be filed with the Registrar of Companies within 15 days of approval.

Voting at general meetings

Initially, resolutions are put to the meeting for members to vote on a show of hands. If a resolution is defeated on a show of hands and the chairman is aware that there are a substantial number of proxy votes in favour of the resolution, they will demand a poll. On a show of hands, every member present in person or by proxy and entitled to vote has one vote only, irrespective of the number of shares held. On a poll, however, the number of shares held determines the number of votes the member may cast either in person or by proxy. In the event of an equality of votes, most articles of older companies give the chairman a casting vote. This regulation ceased to have effect for companies incorporated on or after 1 October 2007 for companies incorporated under the Companies Act 1985, and there is no corresponding article in the model articles for companies incorporated under the Companies Act 2006.

On the declaration by the chairman of whether the resolution has been carried or lost and an entry being made in the minute book to that effect, the validity of the resolution cannot be questioned (s. 320), and it is unnecessary to insert in the minute book the number of members voting for or against the resolution. However, before declaring that a special resolution has been passed, it is necessary to ensure that the requisite majority was present to pass such a resolution.

Abstaining

The increasing role of corporate governance and the need for shareholders, particularly institutional shareholders, to express their opposition to various aspects of a company corporate governance performance has seen an increasing use of abstentions on proxy forms. In law, an abstention is not a vote. However, abstentions can affect the outcome of a vote. If the majority is to be calculated by reference to the votes cast, then abstentions would not be counted. But if the majority is by reference to the total votes returned, then abstentions are counted and might very well prevent resolutions from being approved, as fewer than half the votes returned were in favour. If this were the case, abstentions would in effect be votes against a resolution. Sections 282(3), 282(4), 283(4) and 283(5), however, state that the majority on a poll is to be calculated by reference to the voting rights of the members who vote; accordingly abstentions have no effect. The ICSA has issued a guidance note which recommends that companies allow members to instruct their proxy to vote for or against a resolution, as at present, but also to allow them to indicate that the proxy has discretion on how to vote or that they should abstain from voting. In order to avoid confusion, it is suggested that abstentions should be rephrased as 'vote withheld'.

Corporate shareholders

A shareholder that is a corporate body may be represented at a company meeting by a person appointed as its representative by a resolution of the corporate body's directors under s. 323. Following the changes to proxy rights introduced by the Companies Act 2006, the only practical difference between a corporate representative and a proxy is that details of a proxy must be lodged in advance, whereas a corporate representative can bring their letter of appointment to the meeting.

Where shares are held by a nominee in one account for multiple beneficiaries, this can cause problems at a meeting if multiple corporate representatives are appointed without any clear instructions as to the votes that each represents.

Proxies

Under s. 324, an individual or corporate members of a company may appoint one or more proxies to attend, speak and vote both on a show of hands or a poll (s. 284). A proxy need not be a member of the company. Proxies are appointed for individual meetings or adjournments of it and have no other rights. The notice of a general meeting must state clearly the right of the members to appoint one or more proxies (s. 325).

For unlisted public companies and private companies, it is not obligatory to send proxy forms with notices of meetings. In general, this is done only if controversy is anticipated.

Where proxy forms are used, they must be issued to all members of the company and not just to those who favour the board (s. 326). The company may accept proxy forms lodged at the last minute, provided they are in an appropriate form. It is unlawful for a company to require proxies to be lodged with the company *more* than 48 hours prior to the time of the meeting (s. 327), excluding any days that are not working days. Proxies may be submitted in electronic form, but only to an address supplied by the company for that purpose (s. 333). Accordingly, sending a form of proxy by e-mail to the company secretary's normal e-mail address would not constitute a valid proxy.

A traded company must provide an electronic address for the receipt of proxies (s. 333A(1)).

At the meeting

Members who appoint a proxy may still attend the meeting and vote in person; attendance and voting at the meeting effectively revokes the proxy appointment. The right of a person appointing a proxy to attend and vote at a meeting is conditional upon this not being prohibited by the articles, but such a provision would be exceptional.

Three-way proxies

Listed companies must issue three-way proxy forms (*LR 9.3.6*). A three-way proxy includes provision for members to indicate which way they wish the proxy to cast their votes or to abstain from voting in the event of a poll being demanded. It must cover all the resolutions on the notice of meeting. The form must also state that, if it is returned without any indication as to how the proxy shall vote on any resolution, the proxy may exercise their discretion.

The proxy form cannot restrict the member to appointing the chairman or another director as their proxy; it must include provision for the member to appoint a proxy of their own choice. Corporate members will usually be satisfied with the appointment of a proxy, and will send a representative only if they wish the representative to comment at the meeting and vote on a show of hands.

Form and dispatch of proxy forms

The pattern of voting indicated on returned forms of proxy will show whether or not there is likely to be any disagreement on the business. The chairman will thus know in advance whether they should demand a poll in the event of a motion being defeated on a show of hands, since they will know whether the majority of proxies lodged with the company are in favour of the resolution.

It is usual for proxy forms to be in the form of pre-paid postcards. If there is to be a number of meetings following the AGM, e.g. a general meeting or a meeting of any particular class of the members, the proxy cards for those meetings are usually different colours, to facilitate sorting. Many companies' articles require that proxies must be lodged at the company's office not less than 48 hours before a meeting. The model articles are silent, relying on s. 327, which provides that the period of notice may not be longer than 48 hours (excluding any day that is a weekend or bank holiday), but may be shorter. It is also usual for articles to permit proxies to be lodged between an original meeting and an adjourned meeting. However, this can be done only if specifically provided for in the articles.

The address to which proxies are to be returned may be the company's office, which in most companies' articles is defined as the registered office of the company, or to some other place specified in the notice convening the meeting.

For example, if the share registration work of the company is carried out by a service registrar at a place other than the registered office, the proxies may be sent to the address of the registrar. It is worth noting that the model articles for public companies do not assume the company's office will be the registered office address, referring instead to a 'proxy notification address', which is the return address specified in the notice.

Notwithstanding anything contained in a company's articles or the model articles as adopted by the company, proxies may be submitted by an electronic communication to an address notified by the company for that purpose (ss. 333 and 333A).

In addition to providing numbered boxes for each resolution, so that the members can indicate with a tick whether they vote for or against a resolution, it is useful for the proxy form to include a phrase to the effect that, on any other business arising at the meeting (including any motion to amend a resolution or to adjourn the meeting), the proxy will act at their own discretion. The absence of such a sentence may be taken to preclude the proxy from voting on an amended resolution or on a resolution whether or not to adjourn the meeting. It also gives a proxy the power to vote on any matter which may arise in connection with the procedure of the meeting (see precedent 7).

Evaluation of proxies

The proxy cards should be sorted and scrutinised when they are received by the company or its registrar, to check that they have been properly completed. A running total should be kept of the votes for and against each resolution, as well as open votes. If the chairman of the company is appointed as the proxy, they will usually vote in favour of the resolutions. It should be noted that shareholders may limit their proxies to only part of their holdings and that they can appoint more than one proxy, each proxy appointed covering separate parts of their shareholding. Sorting proxy cards will be determined in the light of experience.

The proxy form should be signed personally by individual members. Corporate members must complete the proxy card in accordance with their own articles of association. This may be, for example, under seal if the company has a seal, or by a named individual appointed by board resolution to sign the proxy card on the company's behalf. In this case, the authority under which it is signed should be lodged with the proxy card if not already registered with the company. Although joint members have equal rights, some companies' articles provide for the joint members to be ranked in the order on which their names appear on the entry in the register of members with the first-named holder in the account (the 'senior'). Where two or more joint members exercise those rights, the company would act on the instructions of the 'senior' member. The Companies Act 2006 and the Private and Public Model Articles are silent on the exercise of voting rights by joint holders.

Unless stipulated by the articles, it is not necessary for signatures on proxy forms to be witnessed.

Incorrectly completed proxy forms must be rejected, but if there is time and if the shareholding is substantial, they should be returned for amendment. A proxy may be revoked by the lodgement of a subsequent appointment, provided that the appointment is received by the company in time prior to the meeting. A proxy lapses if the person who gave it dies prior to the meeting, provided that notice of the death is received by the deadline for receipt of proxies (i.e. usually 48 hours prior to the meeting).

Demand for a poll

The rules governing the demanding of a poll are laid down in the company's articles. The provisions of ss. 321 and 329 must also be taken into account, as they may render certain provisions void.

Section 321 provides that any provision in a company's articles is void if it were to exclude the right to demand a poll by:

1 not fewer than five members;
2 a member or members representing not less than one-tenth of the total voting rights of all the members with the right to vote at the meeting; or
3 a member or members holding shares conferring a right to vote at the meeting, being shares on which an aggregate sum has been paid up equal to not less than one-tenth of the total sum paid up on all the shares conferring that right.

Proxies are entitled to demand or join in the demand for a poll to be conducted.

For a demand for a poll to be valid, it must be called before or immediately on the declaration by the chairman of the result of the vote on a show of hands.

When a poll is demanded

When a poll is demanded, the chairman may, if appropriate, suggest that, since they hold proxies overwhelmingly in favour of the resolution, the person or persons requesting the poll should consider withdrawing their demand.

If the demand is not withdrawn, the validity of the demand should be checked by confirming that those who have demanded it are, in fact, shareholders or, for example, if the member demanding it is a single member, that they hold not less than one-tenth of the total voting rights. This is a task for the company secretary or (for larger meetings) scrutineers.

If the company secretary or the scrutineers advise that the poll has not been properly demanded, the chairman makes a statement to this effect and the meeting proceeds to its next business, or to a show of hands if the poll was requested before a vote by a show of hands has taken place. If the demand for the poll is valid and is not withdrawn, the chairman advises the meeting to this effect. If they have not already advised the meeting as to the proxy position when the poll was first demanded, they should now do so. Assuming the poll is still not withdrawn, the chairman announces the time for holding of the poll, e.g. either immediately, at the conclusion of the meeting or at a later date. It is usual practice for the poll to be held at the end of the meeting and for it to be kept open for one hour. The meeting then proceeds to its next business until the conclusion of business. At the end of the meeting, the chairman declares the meeting adjourned if the poll is to be taken then, or closes the meeting if the poll is to be taken at a later date. Where the poll is to take place, the chairman should inform the members of the procedure for the conduct of the poll. The chairman should explain that those who have appointed a proxy need not complete a ballot paper unless they wish to alter their vote.

Ballot papers must be distributed to those members present. Completed papers are handed to the company secretary/scrutineers. The scrutineers, especially if they are the company's auditors or registrars, will no doubt have their own instructions for checking ballot papers, verifying holdings and preparing a report and final certificate of the result of the poll for the chairman.

Publication of results of a poll

Quoted companies that are not traded companies must ensure that when a poll vote is taken, the following information is made available on a website (s. 341(1)):

1 date of the meeting;
2 text or description of the subject matter of the resolution; and
3 number of votes cast in favour and against.

Traded companies must ensure that when a poll vote is taken, the following information is made available on a website (s. 341(1A)):

1 date of the meeting;
2 text or description of the subject matter of the resolution;
3 number of votes cast;
4 proportion of the **issued capital** represented by those votes;
5 number of votes cast in favour and against; and
6 number of abstentions (if counted).

The information must be made available on the website in the case of a quoted company that is not a traded company as soon as reasonably practical and must be retained for a period of at least two years (s. 353). A traded company must make the information available within 16 days of the meeting, or the day following the declaration of the result, if later (s. 341(1B)).

Independent proxy report

Members of a quoted company may require the directors to obtain an independent report on any poll taken or to be taken at a general meeting (ss. 342–351). To be valid, the request for an independent report must be made by:

- a member or members together holding not less than 5% of the total voting rights; or
- not fewer than 100 members each holding shares on which, on average, there has been paid up the sum of at least £100.

The request may be in writing or electronic form, must identify the poll to which it relates, must be authenticated by those making the request and must be received no later than one week after the date on which the poll is taken (s. 342).

Procedural motions

Procedural motions are motions that are used to regulate the conduct of the business of the meeting. For the vast majority of routine meetings, they are never used. However, where contentious resolutions are proposed or where there is a vociferous element present, the use of procedural motions can be used to curtail discussion of a particular resolution.

As with many aspects of the legal system, the terminology of procedural motions has not changed over the years, and now sounds arcane and intimidating to those not used to it. There are six common procedural motions:

1 the closure (that the questions be now put);
2 next business (that the meeting proceed to the next business);
3 previous question (that the question be not now put);
4 postponement (version 1) (that the question lie on the table);
5 postponement (version 2) (that the matter be referred back to…); and
6 adjournment.

Speaking

Members and proxies entitled to attend and vote at a meeting are entitled to speak at the meeting.

Although those attending have the right to speak, they may be prevented from doing so in order to keep the meeting to a reasonable length or to maintain order. The chairman should ensure that all differing opinions on the matter under consideration are expressed and, in doing so, it should not be necessary for every person who wishes to speak to do so.

Traded companies must ensure that all questions put by members attending the meeting, and relating to the business of the meeting, are answered. The exceptions to this are in circumstances where: to do so would interfere with preparations for the meeting; the disclosure of confidential information is required; the answer has already been provided on a website in the form of an answer to a question; or it is undesirable in the interests of the company or the good order of the meeting for the question to be answered (s. 319A).

Adjournment of general meetings

Although the chairman may adjourn the meeting without the consent of the members if there is disorder, the power to adjourn a meeting usually rests with the members attending, who must give their consent. The model articles for public companies, article 33(6) provide that no business at an adjourned meeting shall be transacted other than that which could have been transacted at the original meeting. If the meeting is adjourned for more than 14 days, however, fresh notice of at least seven days, specifying the business to be transacted, must be given. When a resolution is passed at an adjourned meeting, it is deemed to have been passed on the date of the adjourned meeting rather than the date on which the original meeting was adjourned (s. 332).

If it is necessary to postpone or cancel a meeting after the notice of meeting has been issued, the correct procedure is to hold the meeting at the scheduled time and place, and for a resolution to be passed adjourning the meeting to a later date. A circular could be sent to shareholders explaining the reasons for the postponement, so that they do not waste their time in attending a purely formal meeting.

Requisitioned meetings

Directors are required to convene a general meeting if requested to do so by any member or members holding between them at least 5%, in nominal value, of the paid-up issued share capital of the company or, if the company does not have share capital, 5% of the voting rights.

The requisition must state the objects of the meeting, and must be authenticated by all the requisitionists. The requisition may consist of one or more copies signed by one or more requisitionists (see precedent 75). If the directors do not issue a notice to convene the meeting within 21 days, the requisitionists may convene the meeting themselves, provided they call it for a date not more than three months later. The directors are deemed not to have convened the meeting if they issue a notice convening a meeting for a date more than 28 days after the date of that notice. Any reasonable expenses incurred by the requisitionists in issuing a notice must be repaid by the company, which can retain the money out of the fees payable to the directors (ss. 304 and 305).

Class meetings

As the name implies, class meetings are meetings of holders of a certain class of the company's capital and are held in accordance with the articles of the company or conditions that attach to the securities concerned. Class meetings are required whenever the rights of the holders of the class are to be varied because of some action proposed by the company. Such variations may relate to a change in the voting rights attaching to the class or to changes proposed in a reorganisation of the company's share structure.

Subject to any provisions in the company's articles, the same rules for the holding of general meetings apply to class meetings, with the exception that there is no general power for members of a class to requisition a class meeting (ss. 334 and 335, see precedent 43).

9 – Directors' meetings and resolutions

Introduction

Unlike members' meetings, which are strictly governed in terms of notice periods, who may attend and speak, rules concerning voting and the differing majorities required for certain resolutions, the Companies Act is silent on how directors should conduct their meetings.

Private Model Article 16 and Public Model Article 19 permit directors to conduct their meetings as they see fit. Accordingly, there is no specific notice period and all decisions are based on a simple (50%) majority of those present or represented by an alternate and eligible to vote.

There are detailed provisions obliging directors to disclose their interest in matters being discussed and preventing abuse of their positions by running the company for their own benefit (see below), as well as ensuring that a proper record of directors' meetings is kept but little else.

Listed company directors are also required to comply with the Market Abuse Regulations and to comply with the provisions of the UK Corporate Governance Code or explain any departures from the Code (*LR 9.8.5 (5 & 6)*) (see Chapter 10 and Chapter 17).

In practice, public companies with external shareholders and large private companies will hold regular board meetings at which executive management strategy is determined. For the vast majority of private companies, formal board meetings are seldom held, and any formal resolutions are approved as written resolutions (see below). In this case, the management of the company is dealt with on a day-to-day basis by a series of informal discussions between the relevant directors with no formal written record.

Directors must ensure that they are fully aware of all decisions being reached in this informal manner, as they are collectively responsible for the company's activities. Ignorance is no excuse and, as seen earlier, in extreme circumstances can lead to disqualification and personal liability.

Board meetings are general discussion meetings and, unlike the formal structured nature of members' meetings, usually proceed on an informal basis. The chairman assesses whether the general view of the meeting should be incorporated into the minutes of the meeting as the decision of the board, either in narrative form or, where appropriate, as a formal resolution. If, however, the views of directors are fairly evenly balanced on the pros and cons of a particular course of action, it would be appropriate to put the matter to a formal vote.

The Act is only concerned with formal directors' meetings. Directors and in particular executive directors will also hold regular meetings in the form of executive committees and formal committees of the board.

Board meetings

Frequency and notice

Board meetings do not have to be held at fixed intervals and may be convened from time to time, as the directors see fit. Large companies will also usually have an executive committee, composed of executive directors, which meets between board meetings. Companies with non-executive directors will frequently have a schedule of regular board meetings planned many months in advance. For the vast majority of private companies, formal board meetings are seldom held with any formal resolutions approved as written resolutions. In these circumstances, the management of the company is dealt with on a day-to-day basis by a series of informal discussions between the relevant directors with no formal written record.

If meetings are not held on fixed dates, the chairman will usually instruct the company secretary to convene a meeting. It is, however, open to any director, either acting independently or by instructing the company secretary, to convene a board meeting. No specific length of notice is required. For some companies, reasonable or normal notice might be one week and for others, it might be much shorter. Even where meetings are held regularly in accordance with a fixed timetable, it is still appropriate to issue reminders, sending a copy of the agenda at the same time.

The notice of a directors' meeting will usually include the place, date and time for the meeting and an agenda of the general topics to be discussed (see precedent 25). The notice can be circulated in any manner appropriate to the company, e.g. verbally, by letter, fax, e-mail or by hand.

The matters to be discussed at a board meeting will naturally depend on the nature of the company's business and the number of directors. According to the size of the company, board papers and reports will either be circulated with the agenda or tabled at the meeting. Where any complex matters are to be considered, it is helpful to the directors, and in particular any non-executive directors, for board papers to be circulated in advance of the meeting.

Companies are required to keep minutes of meetings of their directors (s. 248) and it is essential that a proper record is kept of all decisions of the directors of the company.

The Act does not contain an explicit obligation to record and keep minutes of meetings of committees of the directors. Some company articles may have an explicit requirement to keep committee meeting minutes and it certainly is good practice to do so.

The Act and the articles are silent on the detail of what constitutes minutes and it is for each company to decide for itself the style, content and format of the minutes. At first sight, taking minutes shoulud be a straightforward task, but that is rarely the case in practice.

The company secretary sometimes needs telepathic abilities to interpret the mood of the meeting and the individuals present and the near invisible body language intended to indicate the detail of the minutes required or even whether minutes of the discussion are required at all. It is all too common after five minutes of feverish writing on the part of the company secretary on a sensitive subject for the main speaker to add the words '... and none of this is for the minutes...'. It is very rare indeed for the other directors present, or any of them, to disagree with that assertion.

It can be very useful for the company secretary to have a pre-meeting with the key directors, as this will often enable the company secretary to include in the minutes those key items that the director did not mention at the meeting but are known to all present and are important to be recorded as part of the decision-making process. The art of deciphering what was understood to be said rather than the words that in reality were said is one of the key differences between a good minute taker and someone who merely transcribes what was said.

There will be routine departures from the pre-agreed running order of the agenda with disproportionate time spent discussion minor matters while the main topic of the meeting is relegated to a brief discussion as those present prepare to leave the meeting. There will be many occasions where a new topic is introduced and discussed at length, but which no one present wants to be recorded.

Minutes of meetings of the directors that are authenticated by the chair of the next directors' meeting are evidence (in Scotland sufficient evidence) of the proceedings of the meeting (s. 249(1)). Provided the minutes have been properly recorded then until the contrary is proved, the meeting is deemed duly held and convened, the proceedings to have taken place and any appointments made at the meeting are deemed valid (s. 249(2)).

It is advisable to number minutes and resolutions serially to facilitate reference to any particular minute, if necessary. This may arise when the board is approving authorised cheque signatories, where it may be desired in the future to refer to the minute by its number and refer to the deletion or addition of certain names.

Chair

Private and Public Model Article 12 permits the directors to appoint one of their number to chair their meetings; in addition, some articles provide for the appointment of deputy chair and vice-chair (see precedent 26). A person appointed chair of the board will also usually take the chair at general meetings of the company and will often be referred to as chair of the company, although there is no provision for such an appointment (Private Model Article 39, Public Model Article 31).

Where the articles do not specify, s. 319 provides that any member or a proxy (s. 328) may be elected to take the chair at a general meeting.

Private Model Article 13 and Public Model Article 14 grant the chair of the directors' meetings a casting vote if there are equal votes for and against any resolution. This casting vote is in addition to any other votes that the chair may have. It is normal practice for the chair to use this casting vote to maintain the status quo on the grounds that there is no majority in favour of change. However, it is at the chair's discretion how to use the casting vote, if at all.

The style of minutes varies from company to company and from industry to industry. For those sectors that have an industry regulator, minutes of directors' meetings increasingly tend to be fuller, providing more detail of the discussion and reasons for decisions being reached together with challenges being raised by specific directors and actions taken to review those challenges.

Quorum

The quorum for board meetings is fixed as two directors (Private Model Article 11 and Public Model Article 10), unless the directors decide otherwise. If the company had only two directors and one resigns or dies, Private Model Article 11 and Public Model Article 10 provide that the sole continuing director may appoint another director (see precedent 27). This should be done formally by signing a suitable document, which is inserted in the directors' minute book (see precedent 1). Where the number of directors falls below the minimum required by the articles of association, the remaining director(s) have no power other than to appoint another director or directors, or to call a general meeting of the company at which another director or directors could be appointed.

Meeting participants need not all be present at the same physical location with virtual attendance possible using conference video, telephone or web streaming technology. Provided those participating are able to hear each other and contribute to the discussions and decisions, this is perfectly acceptable.

It is increasingly common, however, for private companies to incorporate in their articles a provision vesting all the company's authority in the hands of a sole or surviving director(s), even where their number has fallen below the minimum number stipulated elsewhere (see precedent 28).

Resolutions in writing

The Act makes no provision for directors to take decisions by written resolution and any such authority will derive from the articles or under common law. It is sometimes necessary for the directors to make a decision urgently, and Private Model Article 8 and Public Model Articles 17 and 18 provide that a resolution signed by all the directors entitled to attend a board meeting is as valid and effectual as if passed at a duly constituted board meeting (see precedent 29). If convenient, such a resolution could be a single document, which is signed by each director in turn. Alternatively, a separate copy of the resolution could be sent to each director for signature. The document or documents signed by the directors should be inserted in the directors' minute book.

It is now common practice for companies to adopt articles allowing directors to conduct meetings by video or telephone, either by a conference facility or by the chairman ascertaining the views of the directors individually. In addition, resolutions agreed by facsimile or e-mail are being used, although it is desirable for any written resolution to be signed to provide a permanent record.

By their nature, written resolutions only contain details of the decisions to be approved and may also contain a briefing of the relevant subject matter. Written resolutions do not, however, contain any discussion of the subject matter as there is no forum for any such discussion.

The Act does not contain an explicit obligation to record and keep written resolutions of the directors, where permitted by the articles. Some company articles may have an explicit requirement to keep written resolutions, and it certainly is good practice to do so.

Maintenance of minute books

Companies are required by s. 248 to maintain minutes of all meetings of the directors and for these to be available for inspection by any director. There is no provision or right for the members to have access to minutes of the meetings of the directors. (Members can, however, request to see minutes of members' meetings.) The taking of minutes, and their maintenance and safekeeping, is one of the core duties of the company secretary (see below).

Certification of minutes

Where a third party, such as the company's bank or landlord, requests to see a copy of a particular board resolution, it is clearly not advisable to submit the entire minutes of that meeting or even a particular page of the minutes, as these may contain confidential information. In such circumstances, it is normal for the resolution in question to be reproduced on a separate sheet and for the company secretary or a director to certify the extract as a true copy of the original minute (see precedent 30).

The role of the company secretary

The company secretary usually plays a central role in the preparations for, and management of, board meetings, and is responsible for any administration arising from the meeting.

Preparation for a board meeting

Prior to the board meeting, the company secretary should ensure the following tasks are done.

1 Issue a call for board papers to relevant directors and managers responsible for preparing the reports to the meeting.
2 Send a notice to each director stating the time, date and place of meeting with a copy of the agenda and supporting papers.
3 If any of the company's managers are to attend the whole or part of the meeting, e.g. the company's accountant, they should also be advised of the meeting and sent a copy of the agenda and supporting papers. If they are to attend only part of the meeting, they should be sent the papers for the relevant items only.
4 It is sensible for the company secretary to ensure that spare copies of the agenda and supporting papers are available at the meeting itself.
5 In preparing the agenda for the meeting, the company secretary should consider those items that come up on a recurring basis, e.g. half-yearly staff report, and if necessary, remind the appropriate department to have the report ready in time for circulation with the agenda. Matters on which no decision was reached at a previous meeting or which were deferred from a previous meeting should also be included in the agenda.
6 Sometimes the supporting papers will incorporate a formal resolution, which the board is to be asked to pass. This will save time when the minutes of the meeting are prepared.
7 Just before the meeting, arrangements should be made to ensure that everything necessary for the meeting is ready in the boardroom. It is also usual to have a copy of the company's articles of association, the Companies Act and other relevant material in the boardroom, in case it is necessary to refer to them during the meeting.
8 In the case of Listed companies, the opportunity is often taken to have schedules of transfers available for inspection by board members. For those companies with an active share register, these summaries will usually be restricted to the largest transfers, as otherwise the reports would be too lengthy to be of any use.

At the board meeting

1 For incorporation in the minutes, take a note of those directors present and report any apologies for absence.
2 Ensure that a quorum is present. If any item in which a director has an interest is to be considered, ensure that there will still be an independent, disinterested quorum to deal with it.
3 Take notes during the course of the meeting on any action decided on by the board and of its decisions reached, together with appropriate justification, if

necessary. The minutes should not be a verbatim record of what is said; if they were, this could cause complications.

4 It is usual to note in the minutes the arrival of any director after the proceedings have started or the departure of a director before the meeting has ended.
5 The chair may ask the company secretary to advise on any point of procedure regarding the conduct of the business of the meeting, but it would be appropriate for the company secretary to intervene in the meeting (unless they are themselves a director) only if the board were proposing to do something that was unlawful or contrary to the company's articles of association.
6 If a manager is to be called in for discussion of a specific item, ensure that they are ready to be called when that item is reached on the agenda.
7 If any confidential papers are left behind on the board table by the directors, these should be collected by the company secretary before staff come in to clear the room.

After the board meeting

1 (*Listed, AIM and NEX companies only*) If the company has made a decision with regard to the payment of a dividend on the company's ordinary shares, yearly or half-yearly accounts have been approved or a decision for the appointment or resignation of a director, a regulatory information service should be advised immediately by telephone or fax (*LR* 9.7.2). If necessary, a regulatory information service should also be advised of any decision to make an issue of shares or debentures or to postpone the payment of a preference dividend or of interest (*LR* 9.6.4, 9.7.2.2).
2 The company's managers should be notified of any action which the board require them to take, e.g. by sending a memorandum or letter to the managers concerned.
3 Make a note of any item that has been deferred for future consideration to ensure that it is not overlooked.
4 If the directors have asked for a report on a specific subject to be prepared for their next meeting, ensure that the manager responsible for preparing it is notified.
5 Prepare the minutes of the meeting, showing the names of the directors present, those whose apologies were noted, and the arrival and departure of any director who was not present at the beginning or end of the meeting.
6 The procedure to be followed after preparation of the minutes will vary from company to company. However, it is usual to send a copy of the draft minutes to every director present with a request that they return any comments by a given date, following which the minutes can be prepared in their final form for distribution to all directors.
7 If a director makes a comment about the wording of a particular minute, the alteration should be agreed with the chair, who will then mention the amendment at the subsequent board meeting before signing the minutes. Since the chair has agreed the amendment, it is unlikely that any director present at the

subsequent board meeting will object to the alteration. Other than obvious mistakes, alterations should be confined to what was said rather than what any particular director meant to say or, on reflection, would have preferred not to say.

Committees – types, purpose and composition

As noted above, boards comprising both executive and non-executive directors will often constitute committees of the board to provide more detailed, independent oversight of certain areas. Listed companies are recommended by the UK Corporate Governance Code to establish several standing board committees including audit, remuneration and nominations committees.

Model Articles Plc & Ltd regs. 5 and 6 provide that directors may delegate their powers to committees with such powers as the board may decide (see precedent 24). The proceedings of committees will follow those that apply to the board as a whole. In certain circumstances, it may also be desirable that the action taken by a committee should be validated by the directors or by the company in general meeting.

Board committees generally bring four main benefits to the company:

- member knowledge specialisation;
- committee specialism;
- better accountability; and
- more time to look into specific matters in more detail.

Certain non-executive directors will have been appointed due to their specialist knowledge which can be exploited by or is essential to the good operation of a committee. A good example of this is the appointment of an experienced accountant, ideally a current or former CFO to head the audit committee. Their specialist knowledge is critical to the proper functioning of the audit committee. Over time, other non-specialist members of committees will build a body of knowledge and be better able to interact with and make a positive contribution to the task of holding the executive team to account.

Coordinating the board's in-depth review of specialist areas such as remuneration policy, risk management or health and safety allows a better allocation of issues needing to be addressed by the board generally, enabling more efficient and effective working of the board as a whole.

Board committee structure enables improved individual accountability and responsibility of committee members. Many boards comprise 10 or more directors, and time pressures can make it difficult for all directors to contribute on all topics, especially where their views are similar to others. Some non-executives may also feel intimidated by detailed industry knowledge and experience of the executive directors or even the chair. However, within the committee structure they are more able to perform their oversight function with more time available, fewer participants and a degree of separation from the executive directors.

Board committees can devote more time to the detail of their area of responsibility than is possible for the full board. While the board makes use of committees to assist in its oversight of their area of interest, the full board retains responsibility for and makes the final decisions in all those areas.

For a Listed company, a majority of the members of these committees should be independent of the executive team and, especially in the case of the chair of each committee, have an appropriate level of qualification and experience. In two significant areas, the remuneration and audit committees, the membership should be entirely independent non-executives to provide, as far as possible, a neutral view to setting the executive remuneration policy and agreeing the scope and terms of the external audit, including the appointment of the external auditor.

The minutes of all meetings of committees of the board (or a written summary thereof) should be circulated to the board prior to its next meeting, and the opportunity should be given at that meeting for any member of the board to ask questions that are usually directed to the relevant committee chair.

It is a UK Corporate Governance Code recommendation that the work of the audit, remuneration and nomination committees be contained in the annual financial statements, and these normally take the form of a report to the members by each committee chair.

10 – Accounts

Introduction

All companies are required to keep accounting records that are sufficient to show and explain the company's transactions and to disclose, with reasonable accuracy, the company's financial position at any time (s. 386).

The directors are required to prepare accounts that give a true and fair view of the assets, liabilities, financial position and profit or loss of the company in respect of each financial period, usually a period of 12 months, and to circulate copies to their members (ss. 393, 423, see precedent 77).

The accounts for larger companies must be audited and the accounts of quoted companies must contain additional disclosures and information.

The Companies Act 2006 (Strategic Report and Directors' Report) Regulations 2013, which apply to all companies and to the accounts prepared for periods ending on or after 30 September 2013, introduce a requirement to prepare a strategic report as part of their annual report. The strategic report is separate to the directors' report, and its purpose and content do not differ significantly for the business review which it replaces.

In addition, the regulations have amended the disclosure requirements for the directors' report to remove certain disclosures, which, on the whole, were duplicated elsewhere in the accounts.

More recently, changes have been brought in under the Companies, Partnerships and Groups (Accounts and Reports) Regulations 2015 and the Accounting Directive: Companies, Partnerships and Groups (Accounts and Reports) Regulations 2015 relating to financial years beginning on or after 1 January 2016.

Accounting records

All companies are required to keep records of their financial transactions. The records must contain sufficient detail to enable the financial position of the company to be determined at any time, so that the directors can ensure that any profit and loss account or balance sheet complies with the requirements of the Companies Act or Article 4 of the IAS Regulations if they apply to the company (s. 386).

The records should contain all details of any income and expenditure, and a record of the company's assets and liabilities. If a parent company has a subsidiary undertaking not registered under the Companies Acts, it must ensure that sufficient records are maintained by or for the subsidiary in order to ensure that the profit and loss account and balance sheet of the parent company comply with the provisions of the Act.

The accounting records must be kept for a period of three years if the company is a private company and for six years if it is a public company (s. 388(4)).

If the accounting records are held at a location outside the UK, the company must send accounts and returns at least every six months and keep those in the UK (s. 388).

Accounting reference date

A company's first financial year begins on the day of its incorporation and ends on its accounting reference date, the end of the financial year. Each successive financial year begins the day following the date the previous balance sheet is made up to and ends on the next accounting reference date. The accounts may be made up to a date not more than seven days before or after the accounting reference date (s. 390(3)(b)). This flexibility is allowed to enable a company to arrange a year-end; stock count at a convenient time.

For a new company, the first accounting period starts on the day of incorporation and ends on the last day of the month in which the anniversary of its incorporation falls. The date on which an accounting period ends is known as the company's 'accounting reference date'. The directors may change the accounting reference date of the company, including its first, automatically allocated, date, provided that the first accounting period is not less than six months and that any period is not longer than 18 months (ss. 391(5), 392(5), see precedent 76). After the first period, a company can change its accounting reference date to as short a period as it wishes (s. 392).

If the company becomes a subsidiary undertaking or a parent company, the accounting periods for the two companies must – unless in the directors' opinions, there are good reasons against it – coincide (s. 390(5)). In these circumstances, if necessary, a company may extend its accounting reference period even if it has, in the previous five years, extended its accounting reference date (s. 392(3)).

The directors will determine any change in the company's accounting reference date and must notify the Registrar on the specified form (Form AA01). The change is not effective until the form is accepted for filing by the Registrar.

Changing the accounting reference date

A change in accounting reference date is made by notice to the Registrar, also using the specified form (currently Form AA01). A company can change its accounting reference date at any time, whether or not that period has already expired, provided the time allowed for filing the accounts for that period has not expired.

Extending the period

A period cannot be extended beyond 18 months and, except in certain specified circumstances, a company cannot extend its accounting reference date more than once in any five-year period (s. 392).

Care must be taken when extending a company's first accounting period to the maximum 18 months, as in most cases, simply adding six months to the existing accounting reference date will result in a period in excess of 18 months.

Shortening the period

A period may be shortened by any amount. There is no restriction on the number of times a company may shorten an accounting period provided the filing period of the accounting period being shortened has not expired and that it is the current or immediately preceding accounting period that is being shortened.

Preparation of individual accounts

Pursuant to s. 395, a company's individual accounts must comply with the provisions of CA2006 or International Accounting Standards (IAS) with respect to the form and content of the profit and loss account, balance sheet and any additional information that is required to be given. There is an overriding provision that the accounts must give a true and fair view of the state of the company's financial affairs. In circumstances where it is necessary to depart from the provisions of the Act or other provisions, such departure and the reasons for it must be noted in the accounts (s. 396(5)). In addition to Companies Act requirements, accounts must be prepared in accordance with accounting standards issued by the Accounting Standards Board (s. 464). These are stated in Financial Reporting Standards 100–105, applicable to accounting periods beginning on or after 1 January 2016.

Content

For accounting periods ending on or after 30 September 2013, Companies Act individual accounts must comprise (s. 396):

1 strategic report (s. 414A(1)), not applicable to small companies (s. 414A(2));
2 directors' report (s. 415);
3 a separate corporate governance statement (s. 419A) (only applicable to large-sized private companies, public and quoted companies);
4 balance sheet made up to the last day of the financial year;
5 profit and loss account covering the period of the accounts; and

6 additional information (other than companies qualifying as small) to be provided in the way of notes including: off-balance sheet arrangements (s. 410A); employee numbers and costs (s. 411); and directors' benefits (ss. 412, 413).

Preparation of group accounts

In addition to the requirement to prepare individual accounts, the directors of a company, if, at the financial year-end, it was a parent company, must prepare group accounts (s. 399), in accordance with the Companies Act provisions set out in s. 404, or IAS accounts (s. 406). These Companies Act group accounts consist of a consolidated balance sheet and a consolidated profit and loss account. The directors of the holding company can, if they so determine, decide not to consolidate the accounts of a subsidiary if it carries out a substantially different activity to the parent and consolidating the results would result in the true and fair view being obscured (s. 405).

Content

Companies Act group accounts must comprise (s. 404):

1 group strategic report (s. 414A(3));
2 group directors' report (s. 415);
3 a separate corporate governance statement (s. 419A) (only applicable to large-sized private companies, public and quoted companies);
4 consolidated balance sheet made up to the last day of the financial year (s. 404(1)(a));
5 consolidated profit and loss account covering the period of the accounts (s. 4040(1)(b));
6 individual profit and loss account unless the exemption set out in s. 408 is available and taken; and
7 additional information to be provided in the way of notes, including about: related undertakings (s. 409); (other than companies qualifying as small), off-balance sheet arrangements (s. 410A); employee numbers and costs (s. 411); and directors' benefits (ss. 412, 413).

Consistency of accounts

The directors of a parent company that prepares group accounts must ensure that the individual accounts of the parent and each subsidiary are prepared using the same financial reporting framework (s. 407).

Exemptions

There are a number of exemptions from the requirement of a parent company to prepare group accounts:

1 The parent company of a group qualifying as small need not prepare group accounts (s. 398).
2 If the parent is itself a subsidiary and its immediate parent undertaking is incorporated in a European Economic Area (EEA) state and prepares consolidated accounts including those of the subsidiary in question (s. 400).
3 If the parent is itself a subsidiary and its immediate parent undertaking is not incorporated in an EEA state and prepares consolidated accounts including those of the subsidiary in question (s. 401).
4 If all of its subsidiaries meet the conditions for exemption to be included in group accounts (s. 402).

In each case, although not required to prepare group accounts, the directors may do so if they wish. Exemption is not available to a company with shares Listed on the stock exchange of any EU member state.

Additional exemptions, set out in s. 405, apply where:

- the inclusion of the subsidiary accounts are not material, taken together if there is more than one subsidiary to be excluded from the consolidation, for the purposes of establishing a true and fair view;
- the exercise of control by the parent company is substantially restricted on a long-term basis;
- the necessary information to enable the consolidation to take place cannot be obtained without an unreasonable expense; or
- the parent company holds the shares with a view for resale and the company has not previously been included in any consolidated accounts of the parent.

Parent company

A parent company is defined in s. 1162 as one that:

- holds the majority of the voting rights in another company;
- is a member of another company and has the right to remove or appoint a majority of the directors;
- has the right to exercise dominant control either by a right contained in the articles of association or by a contractual arrangement;
- is a member of the company and controls a majority of the voting rights by agreement with other shareholders; or
- has a participating interest and either exercises dominant control or the affairs of both companies are managed together.

Content of strategic report

The directors of a company that is not small must prepare a strategic report to inform its members and help them assess how the directors have performed their duty under s. 172 to promote the success of the company.

The strategic report must contain:

1 a fair review of the company's business (s. 414C(2)(a));
2 a description of the main risks and uncertainties facing the company (s. 414C(2)(b).

The review must be a balanced and comprehensive analysis of the development and performance of the business during the year, and the position of the business at the year-end, consistent with the size and complexity of the business (s. 414C(3)).

The review must include appropriate financial and non-financial key performance indicators to aid an understanding of the business development, performance or position (s. 414C(4)). There are exemptions available to qualifying medium-sized private companies.

For companies that do not qualify as medium sized, the strategic report must contain a statement which describes how the directors have had regard to the matters set out in s. 172(1)(a)–(f) when performing their duty under s. 172.

For a quoted company, the strategic report must also include (s. 414C(7–10)):

1 main trends and factors likely to affect future development, performance or position of the company;
2 information on environmental matters;
3 company employees;
4 social and community interests;
5 a description of the company's strategy;
6 a description of the company's business model;
7 a breakdown of the gender of its directors, senior managers and employees; and
8 information on those third parties with which the company has contracts or arrangements essential to its business.

For a company that is traded, a banking company, an authorised insurance company or a company that carries out insurance market activities and has more than 500 employees, an additional non-financial statement is required. The statement must contain such information that is necessary for an understanding of the company's development, performance and position and the impact of its activity, relating to, at least:

1 environmental matters (including the impact of the company's business on the environment);
2 the company's employees;
3 social matters;
4 respect for human rights; and
5 anti-corruption and anti-bribery matters.

The information must include:

1. a description of the company's business model;
2. a description of the company's policies in relation to the matters mentioned in S. 414CB(1)(a)–(e) and any due diligence processes implemented by the company in pursuance of those policies;
3. a description of the outcome of those policies;
4. a description of the principal risks relating to the matters mentioned in subsection (1)(a)–(e) arising in connection with the company's operations and, where relevant and proportionate:
   a. a description of its business relationships, products and services which are likely to cause adverse impacts in those areas of risk, and
   b. a description of how it manages the principal risks; and
5. a description of the non-financial key performance indicators relevant to the company's business.

(ss. 414CA and 414CB)

The strategic report may contain items that would otherwise be required to be disclosed in the directors' report if they are of strategic importance (s. 414C(11)), and must contain references to or additional explanation of amounts included in the annual accounts (s. 414C(12)).

A group strategic report may, where appropriate, give greater emphasis to matters that are significant to its undertakings (ss. 414A(4) and 414C(13)).

The directors may exclude and not disclose information if, in their opinion, disclosure would be seriously prejudicial to the interests of the company.

Content of directors' report

The directors of the company must prepare a report containing, as a minimum:

- the names of those persons who were directors of the company during the financial year and details of any directors' indemnity insurance and the principal activities of the company in the course of the year (ss. 236 and 416(1));
- the amount of any proposed dividend (s. 416(3)) (except for small companies or companies that would be small if not part of an ineligible group (s. 415A);
- where audited, a statement that as far as each of the directors is aware, there is no relevant audit information not disclosed to the auditors and that they have taken the necessary steps to make themselves aware of any relevant audit information and whether it has been disclosed or not (s. 418(2));
- identification of any matters disclosed in the strategic report rather than in the directors' report (Sch. 7.1A); and
- information on political donations (Sch. 7.3(2) and 4(1) and Sch. 5.2(2) and 3(1)) (not applicable to subsidiaries of a UK incorporated company).

With the exception of small companies, an indication must also be disclosed, where material, of financial risk management objectives and policy, including any hedging of future transactions, exposure to price risk, credit risk, liquidity risk and cash flow risk, important events affecting the company or its subsidiaries, future developments, research and development activities and any branches established outside the UK (Sch. 7.6 and 7.7).

Quoted and public companies must also disclose details on the acquisition of own shares (Sch. 7.9).

Remuneration report

The directors of a quoted company must prepare a remuneration report in respect of each financial year (s. 420). (See Chapter 17.)

Corporate governance statement

Under the Companies Act 2006 (Accounts, Reports and Audit) Regulations 2009 (SI 2009/1581), large-sized private companies, public companies and quoted companies are required to prepare a separate corporate governance statement (i.e. not part of the directors' report) as part of their annual reports and accounts.

The separate corporate governance statement is defined by s. 472A (as inserted by the Regulations) as a statement required to be given by under rules 7.2.1 to 7.2.11 of the Disclosure and Transparency Rules (DTR).

(See Chapter 17.)

IAS accounts

The detailed provisions for IAS individual accounts or group accounts are beyond the scope of this handbook. The following general points should be noted where a company is preparing or is proposing to prepare IAS accounts.

Once a company has prepared IAS accounts for the first time, it can only revert to preparing Companies Act accounts if:

- the company becomes a subsidiary of an undertaking that does not prepare IAS accounts;
- the company ceases to have securities traded on a regulated market; or
- a parent undertaking of the company ceases to have securities traded on a regulated market.

Although the bulk of the Companies Act provisions relating to the form and content of accounts do not apply to companies preparing IAS accounts, those aspects of the Companies Act that deal with accounting provisions outside the scope of IAS will still apply. Accordingly, the provisions relating to disclosure requirements relating to staff numbers, directors' emoluments, directors' report and publication of accounts, audit and certain other disclosures remain applicable.

Liability for false or misleading statements

Directors are liable to compensate the company for any loss suffered by it as a consequence of any untrue or misleading statements or omission of any information they knew or should have known were untrue or misleading or where the concealment of information was dishonest (s. 463).

The directors are liable in respect of the information contained in:

- the strategic report (ss. 463(1) and 414D(2));
- the directors' report (ss. 463(1) and 419(3));
- the directors' remuneration report (see page 274); and
- Any separate corporate governance report.

Approval of strategic report

The strategic report must be approved by the board of directors and signed on their behalf by a director or the company secretary (s. 414D(1)).

Approval of directors' report

The directors' report must be approved by the board of directors and signed on their behalf by a director or the company secretary (s. 419).

If advantage has been taken of the small companies regime, a statement to this effect must be included immediately above the signature.

Approval of corporate governance statement

The separate corporate governance statement must be approved by the board of directors and signed on their behalf by a director or the company secretary (s. 419A).

Audit

All companies must have their annual accounts audited, unless the company is exempt from audit under:

- s. 477 – small companies;
- s. 479A – subsidiary exemption;
- s. 480 – **dormant companies**; or
- s. 482 – non-profit companies subject to public sector audit.

Small companies audit exemption

A company qualifies as small if it is not excluded and meets at least two of the following criteria:

- Its turnover for the year is not more than £10.2 million.
- Its balance sheet total for the year does not exceed £5.1 million.
- The average number of employees does not exceed 50.

A company qualifies as small in its first financial year or any subsequent year if it meets the conditions in that year and the year before.

Companies that meet any of the following conditions at any time during the financial year are excluded from the small companies regime:

- public companies;
- the company is an authorised insurance company, banking company, e-money issuer, ISD (Investment Services Directive) investment firm or UCITS (Undertaking for Collective Investment in Transferable Securities) management company;
- the company carries on insurance market activities; or
- the company is a member of an ineligible group.

Companies that have adopted Table A of the Companies Act 1948 (or earlier versions) and companies that adopted bespoke Articles of Association prior to 1 October 2009 may be required by their articles of association to appoint auditors. In these circumstances, the articles will need to be amended if the company wishes to take advantage of the audit exemption.

Subsidiary exemption

A company that is a subsidiary of a parent undertaking established under the law of an EEA state is exempt from the requirement to audit its accounts if the following conditions are met:

1 All members of the company must agree to the exemption in respect of the financial year in question (see precedent 85),
2 The parent undertaking must give a guarantee under s. 479C in respect of that year on Form AA06,
3 The company must be included in the consolidated accounts drawn up for that year or to an earlier date in that year by the parent undertaking in accordance with:
   a. the provisions of the Seventh Directive (83/349/EEC); or
   b. international accounting standards,
4 The parent undertaking must disclose in the notes to the consolidated accounts that the company is exempt from the requirements of this Act relating to the audit of individual accounts by virtue of this section (see precedent 86).
5 The directors of the company must deliver to the registrar on or before the date that they file the accounts for that year:
   a. a written notice of the agreement referred to in subsection (2)(a);
   b. the statement referred to in s. 479C(1);

c. a copy of the consolidated accounts referred to in subsection (2)(c);
d. a copy of the auditor's report on those accounts, and
e. a copy of the consolidated annual report drawn up by the parent undertaking.

Dormant companies

A dormant company is one that has had no significant accounting transactions as defined in s. 1169 since the end of its previous financial year or, in the case of a newly incorporated company, since its incorporation. The following transactions can be disregarded for the purposes of assessing the company's dormant status:

- payment for shares taken by the subscriber(s) to the memorandum and articles of association;
- fees paid to the Registrar of Companies; and
- civil penalties imposed by the Registrar of Companies (i.e. late filing penalties).

Any other transactions required to be entered in the company's accounting records will disqualify the company from claiming dormant status (e.g. bank interest/charges).

A company that would otherwise not be exempt from audit under s. 480 because it was a subsidiary undertaking, and was a public company or member of an ineligible group for any period in that year, may claim the exemption, provided it was dormant throughout that period (s. 394A) and all the members agree. A parent guarantee has been provided and it must be included in the consolidated accounts of its parent.

The dormant company exemption is not available to any company that:

- is required to prepare group accounts or if at any time during the financial year in question; or
- was an authorised insurance company, banking company, e-money issuer, a MiFID (Markets in Financial Instrument Directive) investment company or a UCITS management company, or it carried on insurance market activities.

Request for audit by members

As the exemption is automatic rather than optional, as in the case of **abridged accounts**, members holding between them 10% of the issued share capital or 10% of any issued class have the right to require that an audit is undertaken. If the company does not have a share capital, 10% of the members may exercise the right to require an audit. To require an audit, notice in writing must be deposited at the company's registered office during the financial period to which it relates and not later than one month before the end of the financial period for which the audit is requested (s. 476).

Charities

The rules regulating the preparation of accounts and auditing requirement for a company that is a registered charity are no longer contained in the Companies Act, but by regulations issued by the Charity Commission under powers contained in the Charity Act 2006.

Charities that meet the criteria for a small company are not eligible to take advantage of the provisions relating to the preparation of abridged accounts.

Auditor's report

Where a company is required to have its accounts independently audited, the company's auditor is required to report to the members on the accounts (s. 495(1)). The auditor's reports must contain:

1 an introduction identifying the accounts that were audited and the financial reporting framework used in their preparation;
2 the scope of the audit work undertaken and auditing standards used;
3 a statement of whether the accounts give a true and fair view:
   a. in the case of the balance sheet, of the state of the affairs of the company at the financial year-end;
   b. in the case of a profit and loss account, of the profit or loss of the company during the period; and
   c. in the case of group accounts, similar statements in respect of those undertakings whose results have been consolidated;
4 a statement of whether the accounts have been properly prepared in accordance with the stated financial framework;
5 a statement of whether the accounts have been properly prepared in accordance with the provisions of the Companies Act or the IAS Regulations, as appropriate;
6 a statement of whether in their opinion the information in the directors' report is consistent with the accounts;
7 if the company is a quoted company, a statement on the auditable part of the directors' remuneration report and whether that report has been properly prepared in accordance with the Companies Act (ss. 495–497); and
8 if the company must prepare a separate corporate governance statement, a statement that the company's disclosures made in accordance with DTR 7.2.5 and 7.2.6 (information about internal control and risk management systems in relation to financial reporting processes and about share capital structures) are consistent with the accounts.

The auditor's report must be either qualified or unqualified, and must include reference to any matter the auditor wishes to draw attention to without qualifying the report (s. 495(4)).

Every copy of the audit report that is published by the company must state the name of the auditor and, where the auditor is a firm, the name of the person who is the senior statutory auditor that signed the report (s. 505). There is limited exemption allowing the name of the auditor to be omitted if there are reasonable grounds to believe that the auditor or anyone associated with the auditor is at risk of violence or intimidation and that a resolution to that effect has been approved by members. Notification of the information withheld must be given to the Secretary of State (s. 506).

Publication, laying and delivery of accounts to members

Other than for small companies, copies of the full accounts must be sent to all members of the company, all debenture holders and all persons entitled to receive notice of general meetings. Companies qualifying as small may prepare abridged accounts for their members and file these at Companies House.

Private companies

Under CA2006, private companies are no longer required to hold annual general meetings, providing there is nothing to the contrary contained in their articles of association. However, they are still obliged to circulate the accounts to the members, debenture holders and any other party entitled to receive notice of general meetings. The accounts must be sent to members not later than the end of the period allowed for filing the accounts with the Registrar (usually nine months), or, if earlier, not later than the date the accounts were actually delivered to the Registrar (ss. 424, 442).

Public companies

The accounts must be issued to these persons not less than 21 days prior to the general meeting at which they are laid before the members unless all the members agree otherwise (CA1985 ss. 238, 424(3)).

The accounts must be laid before the members in general meeting no later than the end of the period allowed for filing the accounts with the Registrar (usually six months) (ss. 437, 442).

There is no requirement for the accounts of a public company to be approved by members; they must simply be laid before them in general meeting. Accordingly, the resolution put to members should simply be to receive the accounts for the year.

Quoted companies

A quoted company must also make its annual reports and accounts available on a website as soon as reasonably practical. The accounts must remain available on the website until the accounts for the following year are made available (s. 430).

Quoted companies – approval of remuneration report

Quoted companies are required to include within their accounts a remuneration report and a resolution to approve the remuneration report must be put to the meeting that receives the accounts (s. 439).

Quoted companies must have members' approval to their remuneration policy, which is subject to a binding shareholder vote at least every three years and an annual remuneration report, which is subject to an annual, non-binding vote of shareholders reporting on how the company has applied the policy.

Format of accounts

Companies taking advantage of the small companies regime have two accounts formats available to them set out in section B, Schedule 1 of the Small Companies and Groups (Accounts and Directors' Report) Regulations 2008 as amended by the Companies, Partnerships and Groups (Accounts and Reports) Regulations 2015.

Companies that qualify as medium-sized must prepare their accounts in accordance with Regulation 4 of the Large and Medium-sized Companies and Groups (Accounts and Reports) Regulations 2008.

Delivery of accounts to Companies House

Except as noted below, all limited companies must deliver a signed copy of their accounts, which need not be full accounts, whether audited or not, to the Registrar as follows:

- private companies within nine months of the year-end (s. 442);
- public companies within six months of the year-end (s. 442).

In the case of a financial year that is not 12 months, there are different provisions.

If the company's first accounting period is longer than 12 months, the period allowed for filing the accounts ends on the date nine or six months (as appropriate) after the first anniversary of the company's incorporation or, if later, three months after the end of the accounting reference period. For financial years beginning before 6 April 2008, the relevant period is ten or seven months after the anniversary of incorporation.

If the accounting period is shortened, the period allowed for filing the accounts is nine or six months, as applicable, or, if later, three months after the date of notice under s. 392 shortening the accounting period (s. 442).

Companies that are both dormant and a subsidiary can take advantage of an exemption not to file accounts with Companies House. Instead they are required to file a copy of their parent company accounts (s. 448A). In order to take advantage of this exemption, the following conditions must be met:

1 The company must qualify as dormant.
2 The company must be a subsidiary of a company incorporated within an EEA state.
3 All the members of the company must consent.
4 The parent company must give a guarantee in respect of the subsidiary's liabilities for that year under s. 448C.
5 The parent company must include a statement that the subsidiary has taken advantage of the exemption for that year.
6 The directors must deliver to Companies House within the period for filing the accounts:
   a. written notice of consent given by the members (s. 448A(2)(a));
   b. the statement referred to in s. 448C(1) on Form AA06;
   c. a copy of the parent company's consolidated accounts (s. 448A(2)(c));
   d. a copy of the auditor's report on those accounts; and
   e. a copy of the consolidated annual report of the parent company.

Late delivery of accounts

If accounts are delivered to the Registrar outside the period allowed for delivery in accordance with the provisions of s. 441, the company is subject to a late filing penalty calculated as shown in Table 10.1, under s. 453.

Table 10.1: Late delivery of accounts

	Private	*Public*
Less than one month late	£150	£750
Between one and three months late	£375	£1,500
Between three and six months late	£750	£3,000
More than six months late	£1,500	£7,500

Additionally, if the previous year's accounts were also late, the penalties in the following year double.

Accounts to be delivered – abridged accounts

Small-sized companies

Companies falling within the definitions of small-sized (see page 157) may deliver abridged accounts to the Registrar under s. 444. Unlike the previous abridged accounts regime, full accounts do not need to be prepared and issued to shareholders, who may be sent the abridged accounts instead. As noted above, certain companies that qualify as small may be exempt from the requirement to prepare audited accounts.

A company that qualifies as a small company may file abridged accounts consisting of:

1 an abridged version of the balance sheet;
2 an abridged profit and loss account;
3 notes to the above prepared in accordance with paragraphs 1A–1C of Schedule 1 to the Small Companies and Groups (Accounts and Directors' Report) Regulations 2008;
4 a statement immediately above the signature(s) of the director(s) that they have been prepared in accordance with the provisions applicable to companies subject to the small companies regime.

Adoption of the abridged accounts regime requires the unanimous consent of members.

Medium-sized companies

A medium-sized company is one that satisfies any two of the following conditions (ss. 465–467):

- Turnover must not exceed £36m.
- The balance sheet total must not exceed £18m.
- The average number of employees must not exceed 250.

Companies that meet any of the following conditions at any time during the financial year are excluded from the medium-sized companies regime:

- public companies;
- a company that has permission under Part 4 FSMA2000 to carry out a regulated activity;
- carries on insurance market activities;
- is a member of an ineligible group.

A group is ineligible under s. 467(2)) if any of the group companies:

- is a public company or a body corporate whose shares are admitted to a regulated market;
- is a company (other than a small company) that has permission under Part 4 FSMA2000 to carry out a regulated activity;
- is a company that is an authorised insurance company, banking company, e-money issuer, MiFID investment firm or UCITS management company; or
- carries on insurance market activities.

For the above purpose, a group company means any company that is either a parent or subsidiary undertaking.

A company qualifies as medium-sized in its first financial year or any subsequent year if it meets the conditions in that year and the year before.

If a company qualifies as medium-sized in one financial year but not in the next, it may still file abridged accounts in that second year, unless disqualified under s. 467. It will not be able to file abridged accounts in the third year unless it qualifies in that year as either small or medium-sized.

With effect from accounting periods beginning on or after 1 January 2016, a company that qualifies as a medium-sized company may no longer file abridged accounts, and accordingly full accounts must be filed.

The directors' report, balance sheet and auditor's report must have a live signature and state the name of the person who signed them.

Small and medium-sized groups

A parent company need not prepare, or deliver, group accounts if it qualifies as small. The aggregate figures for turnover not exceeding £10.2m net (£12.2m gross), balance sheet total not more than £5.1m (£6.1m gross) and average number of employees not exceeding 50 would, if applied to an individual company, qualify it as small-sized (s. 399(1)).

For a medium-sized group, the turnover must not exceed £36m net (£43.2m gross); the balance sheet total must not exceed £18m net (£21.6m gross); and the average number of employees must not exceed 250.

The reference to 'net' means those aggregate figures for turnover and balance sheet total with the set-offs and other adjustments made in accordance with s. 404. The reference to 'gross' turnover or balance sheet total means those aggregate figures prior to any set-off or other adjustment. The group accounts must satisfy the appropriate conditions on either a net or a gross basis, but not using one net and the other gross (ss. 383, 466).

If auditors certify that the parent company is eligible for qualification as either small or medium-sized, and group accounts are not prepared, the auditor's report must be attached to the individual accounts of the parent company (s. 445(4)). If advantage is taken of this exemption by the directors, there is no statutory provision by which the shareholders of the company can require that group accounts be prepared and laid before them.

Unquoted companies

By s. 446, an unquoted company must file accounts consisting of:

1. strategic report;
2. directors' report;
3. separate corporate governance statement;
4. profit and loss account;
5. balance sheet;
6. notes to the accounts; and
7. audit report, if the accounts are audited.

The directors' report, separate corporate governance statement, balance sheet and auditor's report must have a live signature and state the name of the person who signed them.

The provisions of s. 446 do not apply to an unquoted company that qualifies as small or medium-sized (s. 446(5)).

Quoted companies

A quoted company must file accounts consisting of (s. 447):

1 strategic report;
2 directors' report;
3 separate corporate governance statement;
4 directors' remuneration report;
5 profit and loss account;
6 balance sheet;
7 notes to the accounts; and
8 audit report, if the accounts are audited.

The strategic report, directors' report, separate corporate governance statement, directors' remuneration report, balance sheet and auditor's report must have a live signature and state the name of the person who signed them.

Unlimited companies

Unlimited companies do not need to file a copy of their accounts with the Registrar (s. 448) unless at any time during the period covered by the accounts, the company was:

- a subsidiary or a parent of a limited undertaking;
- a banking or insurance company (or the parent of such a company); or
- a member of a partnership governed by the laws of any part of Great Britain and all the other members of the partnership are either limited companies, limited liability partnerships or unlimited companies or a Scottish firm, each of whose members is a limited company.

Unaudited accounts

In addition to filing unaudited accounts at Companies House, whether abridged or not, a qualifying company must include a statement immediately above the signature(s) of the director(s) on the balance sheet that:

1 the company is eligible to prepare unaudited accounts and qualifies for audit exemption;
2 no notice from shareholders has been received by the company requesting that an audit be undertaken; and

3 the directors acknowledge their responsibilities to maintain proper accounting records and to prepare accounts that give a true and fair view of the company's position and have been prepared in accordance with the provisions of the Companies Acts.

Revised accounts

Directors of a company are permitted to prepare and issue revised accounts to replace accounts they believe are defective. If the original accounts have been circulated to shareholders or filed with the Registrar of Companies, then the only modifications required are in respect of those matters within the accounts that do not comply with the requirements of the Companies Act 1985 or IAS Regulations and any consequential amendments (s. 454).

Where accounts have been circulated to shareholders, or filed at Companies House, and it appears to the Secretary of State that they do not comply with the provisions of the Act, they may issue a notice giving the directors not less than one month in which to give an explanation or to prepare revised accounts (s. 455). If the directors do not give a satisfactory explanation or do not prepare revised accounts, the Secretary of State may make an application to the courts for an order directing the preparation of revised accounts (s. 456).

Additional reporting requirements for certain companies

The auditors of companies subject to statutory regulation are required to report directly to that company's regulators in certain circumstances. The companies concerned are:

- banks;
- building societies;
- insurance companies;
- friendly societies; and
- investment businesses regulated under FSMA2000.

The duty to report to a company's regulator arises in circumstances where the auditor concludes that a matter is relevant to the regulator's function, having regard to matters specified in statute or any related regulations, including rules of the regulator and where, in the auditor's opinion, there is reasonable cause to believe that a matter may be material to the regulator. Although this additional duty on auditors relates to their role as auditors, if the firm also undertakes non-audit services, those responsible for the audit work should request assurances from their colleagues that they are not aware of any matters that would require disclosure to the regulator.

Summary financial statements

The ability to issue summary financial statements was withdrawn for accounting periods ending on or after 30 September 2013; however, any company whose accounts have been audited may, subject to any provisions contained in its articles of association, issue the strategic report and supplemental material to its shareholders in place of the full statutory accounts (s. 426). Any shareholder receiving the strategic report and supplemental material may require that the full accounts be sent to them.

The strategic report and supplemental material may be made available on a website or sent by electronic communication to members who have supplied an address for that purpose.

The period allowed for the laying and delivery of the accounts must not have expired.

The strategic report and supplemental material must be approved by the board of directors and the original copy signed on their behalf by a director whose name must be stated on the copies issued to shareholders.

The strategic report and supplemental material must (s. 426A):

1 be derived from the full statutory accounts and contain a statement to that effect;
2 contain details of how a member can receive a copy of the full statutory accounts and reports;
3 state whether the full statutory accounts had a qualified audit report or not, and if so, set out the qualified statement in full together with any further material needed to understand the qualification;
4 state whether a statement under s. 496 was qualified or not and, if qualified, this statement must be reproduced in full together with any additional material needed to understand the qualification; and
5 (for a quoted company) include a copy of that part of the remuneration report which sets out the single total figure table.

Additional disclosure for Listed companies

All Listed companies must adopt International Financial Reporting Standards (IFRS).

The International Accounting Standards Board (IASB) has issued guidance in the form of IFRS1 to assist companies reporting under IFRS. The main requirements of IFRS1 are as follows:

1 Companies must comply with all IASB standards.
2 There are certain exemptions from the standards where the costs of implementation outweigh the benefit.

3 Retrospective application is prohibited particularly where the standard requires judgements to be made on circumstances where the outcome is now known.
4 Items held as hedged under GAAP (Generally Accepted Accounting Principles) may be held as hedged under IFRS provided the various hedge requirements were met from 1 January 2004.

The existing requirements for Listed, AIM and NEX companies require additional disclosure so as to ensure full disclosure of relevant information and to prevent a false market for the shares developing. The full requirements are contained in the *Listing, AIM* and NEX *Rules*, and include the following:

- Two copies of the accounts of a Listed company must be submitted to the UK Listing Authority (*LR 9.6.1*).
- Accounts to be published as soon as possible, and not more than six months after the year-end for Listed and AIM companies (*LR 9.8.1, AIM rule 19*). NEX companies must issue their accounts to shareholders within the normal Companies Act periods (six months if a plc or nine months if limited).

A Listed company must make disclosure of the following unless exemption is agreed to by the Financial Conduct Authority:

1 a statement of the amount of interest capitalised by the group during the period under review with an indication of the amount and treatment of any related tax relief;
2 any information required by *LR 9.2.18R* (publication of unaudited financial information);
3 details of any small related party transaction as required by *LR 11.1.10R(2)(c)*;
4 details of any long-term incentive schemes as required by *LR 9.4.3R*;
5 details of any arrangements under which a director of the company has waived or agreed to waive any emoluments from the company or any subsidiary undertaking;
6 where a director has agreed to waive future emoluments, details of such waiver together with those relating to emoluments which were waived during the period under review;
7 in the case of any allotment for cash of equity securities made during the period under review otherwise than to the holders of the company's equity shares in proportion to their holdings of such equity shares and which has not been specifically authorised by the company's shareholders:
   a. the details relating to the form and content of the accounts;
   b. the names of the allottees, if fewer than six in number, and, in the case of six or more allottees, a brief generic description of each new class of equity holder (e.g. holder of loan stock);

   c. the market price of the allotted securities on the date on which the terms of the issue were fixed; and
   d. the date on which the terms of the issue were fixed;
8. the information required by paragraph (7) must be given for any unlisted major subsidiary undertaking of the company;
9. where a Listed company has Listed shares in issue and is a subsidiary undertaking of another company, details of the participation by the parent undertaking in any placing made during the period under review;
10. details of any contract of significance subsisting during the period under review:
    a. to which the Listed company, or one of its subsidiary undertakings, is a party and in which a director of the Listed company is or was materially interested; and
    b. between the Listed company, or one of its subsidiary undertakings, and a controlling shareholder;
11. details of any contract for the provision of services to the Listed company or any of its subsidiary undertakings by a controlling shareholder, subsisting during the period under review, unless:
    a. it is a contract for the provision of services which it is the principal business of the shareholder to provide; and
    b. it is not a contract of significance; and
12. details of any arrangement under which a shareholder has waived or agreed to waive any dividends; and where a shareholder has agreed to waive future dividends, details of such waiver together with those relating to dividends which are payable during the period under review.

In the case of a Listed company incorporated in the UK, the following additional items must be included in its annual report and accounts (*LR 9.8.6*):

1. a statement setting out all the beneficial and non-beneficial interests of each director of the Listed company that have been disclosed to the company under Article 19 of the Market Abuse Regulations as at the end of the period under review, including:
   - all changes in the beneficial and non-beneficial interests of each director that have occurred between the end of the period under review and one month prior to the date of the notice of the annual general meeting; or
   - if there have been no changes in the period described above a statement that there have been no changes in the beneficial or non-beneficial interests of each director;
2. a statement showing, as at a date not more than one month prior to the date of the notice of the annual general meeting:
   - all information disclosed to the Listed company in accordance with s. 793; or
   - that there have been no disclosures, if no disclosures have been made;

3 a statement made by the directors that the business is a going concern, together with supporting assumptions or qualifications as necessary;
4 a statement setting out:
- details of any shareholders' authority for the purchase, by the Listed company, of its own shares that is still valid at the end of the period under review;
- in the case of purchases made otherwise than through the market or by tender to all shareholders, the names of sellers of such shares purchased, or proposed to be purchased, by the Listed company during the period under review;
- in the case of any purchases made otherwise than through the market or by tender to all shareholders, or options or contracts to make such purchases, entered into since the end of the period covered by the report; and
- in the case of sales of treasury shares for cash made otherwise than through the market, or in connection with an employees' share scheme, or otherwise than pursuant to an opportunity which (so far as was practicable) was made available to all holders of the Listed company's securities (or to all holders of a relevant class of its securities) on the same terms, particulars of the names of purchasers of such shares sold, or proposed to be sold, by the company during the period under review;

5 a statement of how the Listed company has applied the main principles of the UK Corporate Governance Code, in a manner that would enable shareholders to evaluate how the principles have been applied;
6 a statement as to whether the Listed company has:
- complied throughout the accounting period with all relevant provisions set out in of the UK Corporate Governance Code; or
- not complied throughout the accounting period with all relevant provisions set out in of the UK Corporate Governance Code and, if so, setting out:
  - those provisions, if any, it has not complied with;
  - in the case of provisions whose requirements are of a continuing nature, the period within which, if any, it did not comply with some or all of those provisions; and
  - the company's reasons for non-compliance; and

7 a report to the shareholders by the board which contains all the matters regarding the unexpired length of directors' service contracts where the directors is proposed for (re)election at the AGM, set out in *LR 9.8.8R*.

The report to the shareholders by the Board required by *LR 9.8.6R(7)* must contain details of the unexpired term of any directors' service contract of a director proposed for election or re-election at the forthcoming annual general meeting, and, if any director proposed for election or re-election does not have a directors' service contract, a statement to that effect.

11 – Auditors

Introduction

Every company that is not exempt, dormant or a non-profit making company subject to public sector audit must appoint an auditor, whose primary function is to report to the company's members on the statutory accounts prepared in accordance with ss. 394 or 399, for individual company accounts and group accounts, respectively (s. 475).

Where a company is exempt by virtue of being a small company, any member or members holding between them at least 10% in nominal value of the company's share capital may require an audit to be carried out (s. 476).

Scope of the statutory audit

Article 25a of the Statutory Audit Directive seeks to clarify the scope of the statutory audit. In particular, it notes that the statutory audit does not contain any assessment of the future viability of the company, nor any judgement on current or future efficiency or effectiveness of the management.

UK's competent authority

The FRC has been designated as the UK's competent authority and is given ultimate responsibility for regulatory tasks under the Statutory Audit Directive. The FRC continues to be the standard-setting body for auditors and is to conduct inspections, investigations and disciplinary cases in relation to the audits of PIEs. The FRC can delegate tasks to recognised supervisory bodies. Amendments to Schedule 10 of the Companies Act 2006 set out the conditions that bodies must fulfil to qualify as recognised supervisory bodies.

Choice of auditor

SATCAR 2016 reg. 12 provides that any contractual clauses that restricts the choice of auditor have no legal effect. The audit committees of audited entities are required to state that no such clause has been imposed on them from 17 June

2016 (ss. 485A(5)(c)(ii) and 489A(5)(C)(ii)). From 17 June 2017, PIEs must report to the FRC any third-party attempt to impose such a clause or otherwise influence auditor choice.

Exemption from audit

Small company exemption

A company that qualifies as small qualifies for exemption from audit unless:

- the members have requested an audit under s. 476; or
- the company is excluded from qualifying for exemption under s. 478.

A company that meets any two of the criteria set out in Table 11.1 is a small company (CA2006 s. 382(3)).

Table 11.1: Small company criteria

Threshold	*Turnover*	*Balance sheet total**	*No. of employees*
Individual accounts – not to exceed	£10.2m	£5.1m	50
Group accounts – not to exceed	£10.2m net or £12.2m gross**	£5.1m net or £6.1m gross**	50

* Balance sheet total means total of fixed and current assets

** Net means after any set-offs or other adjustments for group transactions and gross means without those set-offs and adjustments.

To be eligible to prepare and file small-sized company accounts for any given financial year, the company must be or have been small-sized during one or more of the following financial years:

- if the accounts are for the 1st year, in that year;
- for accounts for any other year, in that year and the previous year; or
- if the company fails to qualify in the year for which the accounts are being prepared, in the previous year.

(CA2006 s. 382)

The following companies are excluded from being treated as small-sized if at any time during the financial year, the company is:

- a public company;
- an authorised insurance company, banking company, e-money issuer, MiFID investment firm or UCITS management company;

- a company that carries out insurance market activities; or
- a member of an ineligible group.

(CA2006 s. 384(1))

A group is ineligible if any of its members are:

- a traded company;
- a corporate body whose shares are admitted to trading on a regulated market in an EEA state;
- a person (other than a small company) authorised under FSMA2000 to carry on a regulated activity;
- a small company that is an authorised insurance company, banking company, e-money issuer, MiFID investment firm or UCITS management company; or
- a person who carries on insurance market activity.

(CA2006 s. 384(2))

Subsidiary exemption

A company that is a qualifying subsidiary of a company incorporated in the European Economic Area (EEA) can claim exemption from audit. A subsidiary cannot claim the exemption if, at any time during the financial year, it was:

- a quoted company;
- an authorised insurance company, a banking company, e-money issuer, a MiFID investment firm or UCITS management company; or
- a special register body or employers association.

All the shareholders of the subsidiary must confirm that they agree to the subsidiary accounts not being audited. The parent company must guarantee all the liabilities of the subsidiary at the year-end.

The following must be filed at Companies House, together with the subsidiaries' unaudited accounts:

- written notice that all the members have agreed to the exemption;
- Form AA06; and
- a copy of the consolidated audited accounts of the holding company, including the audit report, and the notes to the accounts must include a statement identifying the subsidiaries exempt from audit (s. 479A).

Eligibility to be an auditor

Under the Statutory Auditors and Third Country Auditors Regulations 2016, the FRC was appointed as the Competent Authority with ultimate responsibility for regulatory matters under the Statutory Audit Directive with power to delegate authority to supervisory bodies.

A person or firm may be appointed as an auditor only if they are or it is a member of a recognised supervisory body and is eligible for appointment under the rules of that body (s. 1212). A firm may be a partnership or a corporate body.

A recognised supervisory body must have rules that prohibit a person from being eligible for appointment as an auditor, unless:

- any individual member holds an appropriate qualification;
- any firm is controlled by qualified persons and those individuals responsible for corporate audit work hold appropriate qualifications. An appropriate qualification and a qualified person is any person who, in accordance with Sch. 10, s. 7, holds:
  - a recognised professional qualification obtained in the UK; or
  - an approved overseas qualification and meets any additional criteria that may be required.

All recognised supervisory bodies must maintain a register of individuals and firms eligible for appointment as company auditors and of all individuals holding appropriate qualifications (s. 1239).

The register must be available for inspection at the principal UK office of the recognised body for at least two hours during normal working hours on every working day. The register must be arranged in alphabetical order and by reference to the appropriate supervisory body. The supervisory bodies are required to supply each other with all necessary information to ensure that each recognised body can properly maintain its register.

The recognised supervisory bodies are also required to maintain a register of the names and addresses of the directors or partners and members of each firm. Any amendments to the registers maintained by the supervisory bodies must be made within ten days of the change being notified to them. The five recognised supervisory bodies are:

- the Institute of Chartered Accountants of Scotland;
- the Institute of Chartered Accountants in England and Wales;
- the Institute of Chartered Accountants in Ireland;
- the Association of Chartered Certified Accountants; and
- the Association of Authorised Public Accountants.

A person is prohibited by s. 1214 from acting as auditor to any company of which they are an officer or employee, or a partner or employee of such a person or a member of a partnership of which that person is a partner.

An officer includes director, manager or company secretary (s. 1173(1)). Where an auditor is deemed to be an officer of the company by virtue of any provision of the Companies Acts, they are not prohibited from acting as auditor by virtue of s. 1214(5).

Appointment

Private company that is not a Public Interest Entitiy (PIE)

Unless the directors have reasonable grounds for believing that the company will qualify from exemption to appoint auditors, auditors must be appointed, for their first audited financial year, before the end of the period allowed for sending accounts to members or, if earlier, the date the accounts were sent to members. For subsequent years, the auditors must be appointed or reappointed within the period of 28 days commencing on the deadline for sending accounts to members or, if earlier, the date the accounts were actually sent to members. This period is known as the 'period for appointing auditors' (s. 485).

The directors may appoint the first auditor to the company. The directors may also appoint an auditor following a period during which the company was exempt from audit or to fill a casual vacancy caused by the resignation or death of the previous auditor (s. 485(3)).

In the normal course of events, the directors will make the initial appointment of auditor and the appointment is confirmed annually either by the members in general meeting or by there being no objection to the appointment automatically continuing in cases where no general meeting is held.

If a private company which is required to have an audit fails to appoint an auditor, the Secretary of State may appoint an auditor to fill the vacancy (s. 486). In circumstances where auditors have not been appointed, the company must give notice to the Secretary of State within seven days of the expiry of the period allowed for appointing auditors.

An auditor can only be appointed to a non-PIE private company pursuant to ss. 485 or 486, and may be deemed to be reappointed under s. 487.

Where no auditor has been appointed by the end of the next period allowed for appointing auditors, the auditor in office immediately before that time is deemed to have been reappointed unless:

- their appointment was made by the directors;
- the company's articles require actual reappointment;
- deemed reappointment is prevented by members under s. 488;
- a resolution to reappoint the auditors is lost; or
- the directors have resolved that no auditor should be appointed for the financial year in question.

Pursuant to s. 488, members holding between them at least 5% of the total voting rights may prevent the deemed reappointment of an auditor by giving notice in writing to that effect to the company before the end of the accounting reference period immediately prior to the time when the auditor would otherwise be deemed to be reappointed.

Public company that is not a PIE

Other than in the case of a dormant company, all public companies must appoint auditors. For their first financial year, auditors must be appointed before the meeting at which accounts are laid before the members. The first auditors would usually be appointed by the directors, but can be appointed by the members if the directors fail to do so (s. 489).

For subsequent years, the auditors must be appointed or reappointed at the conclusion of the meeting at which the accounts for the previous financial year are laid before the members (s. 489(2)).

The directors may also appoint an auditor following a period during which the company was exempt from audit or to fill a casual vacancy caused by the resignation or death of the previous auditor (s. 489(3)).

If a public company fails to appoint an auditor in accordance with the provisions of s. 489, the Secretary of State may appoint an auditor to fill the vacancy. The company must give notice to the Secretary of State within seven days of the conclusion of the meeting at which the previous accounts were laid before the members (s. 490).

An auditor can only be appointed as auditor of a non-PIE public company pursuant to ss. 489 and 490.

The appointment of an auditor to a public company does not automatically renew, and their appointment ceases at the conclusion of the meeting at which the accounts are laid before the members, unless they are reappointed (s. 491).

Audit of Public Interest Entities

The Statutory Audit Directive applies to PIEs, statutory auditors and audit firms. The Statutory Audit Directive was implemented in the UK through Parts 16 (Audit) and 42 (Statutory Auditors) of the Act and through a number of statutory instruments.

The Statutory Audit Directive was implemented in the UK through amendment to Parts 16 and 42 of the Act and the introduction of *DTR 7.1* and subsequently amended by an Amending Directive and also by the Audit Regulation, both of which were implemented by the Statutory Auditors and Third Country Auditors Regulations 2016 (SI 2016/649) (SATCAR2016).

A PIE is defined in s. 519A as a company that meets at least one of the following criteria:

- an issuer with any transferable securities admitted to trading on a regulated market;
- a credit institution; or
- an insurance undertaking.

AIM and NEX Exchange Growth Market are not regulated markets and accordingly companies whose shares are traded on those markets will not be PIEs unless they are also a credit institution or insurance undertaking.

It should be noted that the definition of a PIE refers to transferable securities rather than equity shares and accordingly the issuers of listed debt instruments are covered by the legislation even if their equity shares are not listed and traded.

Appointment of auditors by a PIE

The Statutory Audit Directive introduced mandatory audit firm rotation under which the same audit firm cannot be reappointed without a tender of the audit provision of audit services at least once every ten years and cannot be appointed if they have continuously held the office of auditor for a period of 20 years.

If an audit tender process has not been carried out in the previous ten years before the appointment by a PIE of an auditor, the audit committee must undertake a public tender process in accordance with ss. 485A, 485B, 489A and 489B. Article 16(3) sets out a detailed tender process to be followed by the audit committee. If the company does not have an audit committee, the directors must carry out the tender process, and it is for the directors to decide how to carry out that process.

Whether carried out by the audit committee or the directors, the opportunity to tender must be extended to at least two audit firms, either of which has a reasonable chance of being appointed.

For PIEs that have an audit committee, at the conclusion of the tender process the audit committee must make its recommendation to the full board of the preferred top two choices for auditor appointment and formally confirm that the recommendation is free from third party influence or contractual restriction. It is for the board as a whole to decide which of the two auditors to appoint. If the directors disagree regarding the preferred candidate of the audit committee, the directors must provide reasons.

Small or medium-sized enterprises within the meaning of Article 2(1)(f) the Prospectus Directive or, in the case of a public company, a company with a reduced market capitalisation within the meaning in Article 2(1)(t) of the Prospectus Directive are exempt from these provisions.

Audit tender and maximum engagement period for auditors

The maximum term of office for the auditor of a PIE is the longer of:

- ten years from the first day of the first financial year in respect of which the auditor was appointed (ss. 487(1C)(a) and 491(1C)(a));
- 20 years from the first day of the first financial year in respect of which the auditor was appointed, provided that a tender process has been held for at least one financial year which begins every ten years in that period (ss. 487(1C)(b) and 491(1C)(b)); or
- such other period not exceeding 20 years beginning with the first day of the first financial year in respect of which the auditor was appointed and ending on the last day of the relevant ten-year period (ss. 487(1C)(c) and 491(1C)(c)).

This means that PIEs must undertake a tender for their audit services at least every ten years, with no auditor being able to hold office for more than 20 years, unless extended by up to a further two years by the FRC in exceptional circumstances (ss. 487(1C) and 491(1C)). An extension cannot be granted if it would result in a period of office that exceeds 22 years.

The auditor of a PIE is not eligible for reappointment if within the previous four years they, or a member of the same network of auditors, have ceased to be auditor having held the appointment for the maximum engagement period (ss. 487(1E) and 491(1E)).

There are transitional provisions relating to the mandatory audit firm rotation requirements, as follows:

From 17 June 2020

- Where a PIE has been receiving audit services from the same auditor for 20 or more consecutive years at 17 June 2016, it will no longer be able to reappoint that auditor.

From 17 June 2023

- Where a PIE has been receiving audit services from the same auditor for more than 11 but less than 20 consecutive years at 17 June 2016, it will no longer be able to reappoint that auditor.

Appointment of partnership

Unless there is a clear statement to the contrary, the appointment of a partnership as auditor is an appointment of the partnership and not the individual partners (s. 1216). Where the partnership ceases, the appointment is treated as having been extended to:

- any person who succeeds to that partnership having previously carried it on in that partnership and is an eligible person; or
- any partnership eligible and that succeeds the partnership that has ceased. A partnership is treated as succeeding another partnership only if the partners are substantially the same or if the new partnership takes over substantially the whole of the business of the previous partnership.

A partnership established under the laws of England and Wales or Northern Ireland, or any other country where partnerships do not constitute a legal person, ceases whenever there is not only a change on a dissolution, but also a change in partners. Partnerships established under the law in Scotland do constitute legal persons and do not cease on a change of partners.

Many firms of auditors have incorporated as either limited companies or limited liability partnerships. As corporate bodies, these firms have legal persona and it is the corporate body that is appointed. Where a partnership ceases, wherever established, and no person or firm succeeds the appointment, the appointment may be extended by ordinary resolution of the members to any person or firm succeeding to the business of the previous firm or such part of the business as comprised the appointment (s. 1216(5)).

Where a person or firm is to be removed as auditor for whatever reason, special notice of that fact must be given to the members (s. 511).

Exempt companies

A company that is exempt from having its accounts audited is also exempt from the obligation to appoint auditors. It should be noted, however, that a private company becoming exempt from the audit requirement does not automatically terminate the appointment of existing auditors, and in such circumstances the directors should resolve that no auditors be appointed for the financial year (s. 487(2)(e)) (see precedent 79).

Remuneration of auditor

Remuneration of auditors appointed by the directors must be fixed by the directors. Remuneration of auditors appointed or reappointed by the members must be fixed by the members or in such other manner as the members may decide (s. 492). In practice, it is normal for the members to authorise the directors to fix the remuneration of the auditors. For a public company, this resolution is often combined with the resolution reappointing the auditors for the coming year when the current accounts are laid before the members (see precedent 73).

The amount of the auditors' remuneration in their capacity as auditors, including any expenses, must be disclosed in the accounts (ss. 493 and 494). Remuneration includes any cash value of any benefits in kind given to the auditors. In addition to remuneration for audit services, companies are required to disclose amounts paid to auditors and their associates for non-audit services such as financial or taxation services. Companies qualifying as small companies are exempt from the obligation to disclose auditors' remuneration and non-audit remuneration, and parent companies qualifying as medium sized are exempt from the obligation to disclose non-audit remuneration.

Rights and duties of auditors

Auditor's report

The auditor is required to report to the members on all accounts of the company that are in the case of a private company sent out to members and, in the case of a public company, laid before the members in general meeting (s. 495).

The report of the auditor must include an introduction identifying the accounts that have been audited and the financial framework applied, together with a description of the scope of the audit work carried out and the accounting standards adopted.

Audit report

The auditor's report must include:

1. the identity of the company the subject of the audit;
2. a description of the annual accounts being audited (including the period covered by those accounts);
3. a description of the financial reporting framework used in the preparation of the accounts; and
4. a description of the scope of the audit and confirmation of the auditing standards followed.

The auditor's report must:

1. be either unqualified or qualified;
2. include a reference to any matters to which the auditor wishes to draw attention by way of emphasis without qualifying the report;
3. include a statement on any material uncertainty relating to events that may cast significant doubt about the company's ability to continue to adopt the going concern basis of accounting; and
4. state the auditor's place of establishment.

In cases where joint auditors have been appointed, the auditor's report must be made jointly and state whether both auditors agree on matters in the auditor's report. If they do not agree, the report must include the opinions of each auditor and give their reasons for disagreement (s. 495(4)). A similar statement is required in relation to the auditor's report on the strategic report and directors' report, any separate corporate governance statement and in relation to the duties of the auditor (ss. 496(2), 497A(2) and 498(6)).

The audit report must be signed by both joint auditors (s. 503(4)).

Additional requirement for quoted company audit report

If the company is a quoted company, the auditor must also report on the auditable parts of the remuneration report and state whether, in their opinion, the directors' remuneration report has been properly prepared in accordance with the Act (s. 497).

The auditor must also report on the corporate governance statement and state in the audit report whether, in their opinion, the statement is consistent with the accounts (s. 497A).

Signing of audit report

The auditor's report must state the name of the auditor, and be signed and dated (s. 503).

In the case of an auditor who is an individual, the report must be signed by that individual. In the case of an auditor that is a firm, the report must be signed by the senior statutory auditor in their own name on behalf of the firm.

The senior statutory auditor is the person identified by the audit firm as such in relation to that particular audit, and must in their individual capacity be capable of being appointed as auditor of the company (s. 504).

Except as noted below, every copy of the audit report that is published must state the name of the auditor and, where appropriate, the name of the senior statutory auditor (s. 505).

There is limited exemption allowing the name of the auditor to be omitted if there are reasonable grounds to believe that the auditor or anyone associated with the auditor is at risk of violence or intimidation.

Duties of auditor

In carrying out an audit of a company's accounts, an auditor must carry out sufficient investigations so that they can form an opinion as to whether:

- adequate accounting records have been maintained;
- the accounts are consistent with the accounting records; and
- (in the case of a quoted company) the auditable part of the directors' remuneration report is consistent with the accounting records.

If, in the opinion of the auditor, one or more of these statements cannot be made, that fact must be stated in their report to members.

If the auditor does not obtain all the information or explanations they require, this fact must be stated in their report.

If the accounts do not contain the details of directors' remuneration, pensions and/or compensation for loss of office required by s. 412 or (for a quoted company) the details required by s. 421 relating to the auditable part of the directors' remuneration report, the missing information must be contained within the auditor's report (s. 498(4)).

If the directors have prepared accounts taking advantage of the regime available to small companies and, in the opinion of the auditor, the company does not qualify as a small company, this fact must be stated in the auditor's report (s. 498).

Rights to information and access

An auditor of a company enjoys certain statutory rights to information in connection with the exercise of their duties, and they include the following:

- A right of access at all times to the company's books, accounts and records and a right to require from the company's directors and officers such information and explanations as the auditor thinks necessary for the performance of their duties (s. 499(1)).

- The auditor is entitled to attend any general meetings of the company and to receive all notices and other communications relating to any general meeting. They may also speak on any business of the meeting that concerns them as auditor (s. 502).
- It is the duty of subsidiary undertakings incorporated in the UK and their auditors to give the auditors of the parent company such information and explanations as those auditors may reasonably require for the purposes of their duties as auditors of the parent company (s. 499(2)).
- A parent company, having a subsidiary undertaking that is not a body incorporated in the UK shall, if its auditors require, take all such steps as are reasonably open to it to obtain from the subsidiary such information and explanations as its auditors may reasonably require (s. 500).

It is an offence (punishable by fine and/or imprisonment) for an officer of the company, in conveying information and explanations required by the company's auditors, to make a statement that they know is misleading, false or deceptive in a material particular (s. 501).

Report to the audit committee

Article 11 of the Audit Regulation introduces a new requirement for the auditors to provide a detailed audit committee report, which must include:

1. identification of the audit partner(s) responsible for the audit;
2. if some of the audit work has been undertaken by another statutory auditor who is not a member of the same network, or has used the work of external experts, a statement of that fact and that the auditor has received confirmation from the other auditor or external expert regarding their independence;
3. a description of the scope and timing of the audit;
4. a description of the methodology used, including which balance sheet items have been directly verified and which have been verified based on system and compliance testing – any substantial variation in the weighting of system and compliance testing should be explained, even if the previous year's statutory audit was carried out by another auditor;
5. the quantitative level of materiality applied, including qualitative factors considered, to perform the statutory audit for the financial statements as a whole and, where applicable, the levels for particular transactions, balances or disclosures;
6. any significant deficiencies in the audited entity's internal financial control and/or accounting systems or, in the case of consolidated financial statements, that of the parent undertaking;

7 any significant matters identified during the audit involving actual or suspected non-compliance with applicable laws, regulations or the articles of association, considered to be relevant in order to enable the audit committee to fulfil its tasks;
8 any significant difficulties or matters encountered in the course of the statutory audit and that were discussed, verbally or in writing, with management; and
9 any other matters arising from the statutory audit that in the auditor's professional judgement, are significant to the oversight of the financial reporting process.

Non-audit fees

Article 4 of the Audit Regulation has introduced a cap on fees for non-audit services. The cap is expressed as a ratio to the audit fee and means that the auditor may not undertake non-audit services where the fee exceeds 70% of the average audit fees in the previous three consecutive financial years.

SATCAR 2016 requires subsidiaries that are audited by an auditor other than the auditor of the consolidated group accounts to make a disclosure in the notes to their own accounts, as their audit and non-audit fees will not have been disclosed in the consolidated disclosure in the group accounts.

Prohibition on non-audit services

Article 5 of the Audit Regulation contains a list of non-audit services that must not be provided by the statutory auditor.

These prohibited services include:

1 certain tax services;
2 bookkeeping and preparing accounting records and financial statements;
3 payroll services;
4 certain legal services;
5 services related to the entities internal audit function; and
6 certain human resources services.

Where an auditor provides non-audit services that are not prohibited, they must assess whether the provision of those services will have any effect on their audit independence.

Audit committees

The *Disclosure and Transparency Rules* include additional provisions relating to audit committees of Listed companies as follows:

- Listed companies must have a body or bodies (the 'audit committee'), responsible for performing the functions set out in *DTR 7.1.3(4)* (*DTR 7.1.1*).
- A majority of the members of the audit committee must be independent, at least one member of the audit committee must have competence in accounting or auditing, or both, and the members of the audit committee as a whole must have competence relevant to the sector in which the company is operating (*DTR 7.1.1A*).
- The chairman of the audit committee must be independent, and appointed by the members of the audit committee or by the board (*DTR 7.1.2*).

The role of the audit committee must include:

1. monitoring the financial reporting process and making recommendations or proposals to ensure its integrity;
2. monitoring the effectiveness of the company's internal quality control and risk management systems and, where applicable, its internal audit, regarding the financial reporting of the company, without breaching its independence;
3. monitoring the statutory audit of the annual and consolidated financial statements, in particular, its performance;
4. reviewing and monitoring the independence of the statutory auditor in accordance with paragraphs 2(3), 2(4), 3–8 and 10–12 of SATCAR 2016 Sch. 1 and article 6 of the Audit Regulation, and in particular the appropriateness of the provision of non-audit services to the company in accordance with article 5 of the Audit Regulation;
5. advising the board of the results of the statutory audit and explaining how the statutory audit contributed to the integrity of financial reporting and its role in that process; and
6. except when article 16(8) of the Audit Regulation is applied, being responsible for the procedure for the selection of statutory auditor(s) and recommending the statutory auditor(s) to be appointed in accordance with article 16 of the Audit Regulation (*DTR 7.1.3*).

The company must make a statement available to the public disclosing the composition of the audit committee or, if there is no audit committee, the body that undertakes those functions (*DTR 7.1.5*).

The company may include the statement required by *DTR 7.1.5* in any statement it is required to make under *DTR 7.2* (*DTR 7.1.6*).

In the FCA's view, compliance with provisions A.1.2, C.3.1, C.3.2, C.3.3 and C.3.83 of the UK Corporate Governance Code will result in compliance with *DTR 7.1.1–6* (*DTR 7.1.7*).

Additional auditor reporting requirements

The auditors of companies subject to statutory regulation are required to report direct to that company's regulators in certain circumstances. The companies concerned are:

- banks;
- building societies;
- insurance companies;
- friendly societies; and
- investment businesses regulated under FSMA2000.

The duty to report to a company's regulator arises in circumstances where the auditor concludes that a matter is relevant to the regulator's function, having regard to matters specified in statute or any related regulations, including rules of the regulator and where, in the auditor's opinion, there is reasonable cause to believe that a matter may be material to the regulator. Although this additional duty on auditors relates to their role as auditors, if the firm also undertakes non-audit services, those responsible for the audit work should request assurances from their colleagues that they are not aware of any matters that would require disclosure to the regulator.

All individuals providing accountancy or legal services as a business are required to make a report to the National Crime Agency (NCA) of any circumstances where they know or suspect that money laundering is taking or has taken place, or that an individual or company is benefiting from the proceeds of a crime (POCA2002 ss. 327–329, TA2000 ss. 15–18).

Removal and resignation

The appointment of an auditor may be terminated by resignation of the auditor, removal by the members or on application to the court or by not being reappointed by the members.

Resignation of auditors

Under s. 516, an auditor may resign their office by giving notice in writing to the company at its registered office. Where the company is a PIE, the notice of resignation must be accompanies by a statement of reasons as required by s. 519. Without this statement of reasons the resignation is not effective (s. 516(2)).

An auditor resigning from a non-PIE company needs to provide a statement only in certain circumstance, as considered below.

Notwithstanding their resignation, the auditor is entitled to receive notice and to attend and speak at a general meeting convened at their requisition or at any general meeting at which their term of office would otherwise have expired or at which it is proposed to fill the casual vacancy caused by their resignation (s. 518(10)). Accordingly, where an auditor of a public company resigns during the year, notice of the next general meeting at which accounts are laid before the members must be sent to the previous auditor, and the appointment of auditors to fill the casual vacancy will require special notice to be given to the company, usually by a director.

Removal of auditor

The provisions under which members may remove an auditor are almost identical to the provisions under which directors may be removed. As with directors, the members have the right to remove an auditor from office at any time by ordinary resolution (s. 510). Additonally the auditor of a PIE may be removed by application to the court (see below).

Special notice of the proposed removal must be given to the company and a copy must be forwarded to the auditor. Removal requires an ordinary resolution. The auditor can have a statement circulated or read out at the meeting. If an auditor is removed from office, this does not prevent them from seeking compensation or damages as result of the removal from office and termination of the appointment (s. 511).

Where a resolution to remove an auditor is approved, the company must forward a copy of that resolution to Companies House within 14 days (s. 512).

An auditor removed from office retains the rights to attend and speak at the general meeting at which their term of office would have otherwise expired or at which it is proposed to fill the vacancy caused by their removal (s. 513).

Removal of PIE auditor by application to court

Section 511A provides for the removal of the auditor of a PIE by application to the court either by the competent authority or members representing 5% or more of the voting rights or the nominal value of the share capital of the company. If the court is satisfied that there are proper grounds for the removal of the auditor, it may make an order to remove the auditor from office. There is no guidance on what might constitute proper grounds; however, s. 511A(6) states that divergence of opinions on accounting treatments or audit procedures shall not be proper grounds.

Non-reappointment of auditors

An auditor can be replaced by a new auditor by written resolution of the members in place of an auditor whose appointment has expired or would expire at the end of the period for appointing auditors.

If the proposed change occurs outside of the period allowed for appointing auditors, the company must send a copy of the proposed resolution to both the current and proposed auditors. The current auditor may, within 14 days, make a statement and request its circulation to members. Unless a court order is obtained, this statement must be circulated to the members (ss. 514, 515).

Rights of auditors who are removed or not reappointed

Where a resolution is to be proposed at a general meeting or by written resolution for removing an auditor before the expiration of their term of office, or for appointing as auditor a person other than a retiring auditor, the following requirements must be adhered to.

1 Copies of the special notice or of the written resolution must be sent as soon as practical by the company to the persons proposed to be removed as auditor, to be appointed as auditor and to the retiring auditor, as appropriate (ss. 514(3), 515(3)).
2 The auditor proposed to be removed or not reappointed may make representations in writing to the company on the proposed resolution and may ask the company to circulate that representation to the shareholders of the company (ss. 514(4), 515(4)).
3 The company must comply with that request. If it is too late to include the representation with the notice of the meeting, a note that a representation has been made should be included and a copy of the representations should then be sent to all the shareholders entitled to receive notice of the meeting (ss. 514(5), 515(5)).
4 If the representation is received too late to be circulated to shareholders, or if the representation is not sent out, the auditor concerned may require the representation to be read out at the meeting (s. 515(6)).
5 The auditor proposed to be removed or not reappointed is also entitled to receive notice of, and to attend and speak at, the general meeting at which the resolution for their removal or non-reappointment is to be considered.
6 The representations need not be sent out or be read at the meeting if, on the application of either the company or any other person claiming to be aggrieved, the court is satisfied that the rights conferred on the auditor proposed to be removed or not reappointed are being abused to secure needless publicity of a defamatory nature (ss. 514(7), 515(7)). In these circumstances, the court may also direct that the company's costs in making the application be met in whole or in part by the auditor.

Auditors' statement on ceasing to hold office

If the auditor to a company leaves office, depending on whether the company is a PIE or not and, if not, the circumstances of the auditor ceasing to hold that office, the auditor may be required to send to the company a statement of the reasons for their ceasing to hold office (s. 519).

PIE companies

An auditor ceasing to hold office as auditor to a PIE must always send the company a statement of the reason(s) for their ceasing to hold office (s. 519(1).

If the auditor considers that there are matters connected with their ceasing to hold office that need to be brought to the attention of of the company's members or creditors, the statement must include details of those matters.

In addition to the details connected to their resignation, if any, the statement must include the name and address of the auditor, the auditor's registration number in the register of auditors and the name and registered number of the company of which they are ceasing to act (s. 519(3)).

The statement must be sent:

- with the notice of resignation;
- where the auditor is not seeking reappointment not less that 14 days prior to the date for appointing a new auditor; or in any other circumstances not more than 14 days after the date of cessation.

(s. 519(4))

Non-PIE companies

A statement of reasons on cessation as appointment as an auditor to a non-PIE company is not required if either 1 or 2 below is satisfied:

1. the auditor is ceasing to hold office:
   a. in the case of a private company at the end of the period for appointing auditors; or
   b. in the case of a public company at the end of a a general meeting at which the accounts are laid before the members.
2. that:
   a. the auditor's reasons for ceasing to hold office are all exempt reasons; and
   b. there are no matters connected with their ceasing to hold office that the auditor considers needs to be brought to the attention of the company's members or creditors.

A reason is an exempt reason if:

- the auditor is no longer to carry out statutory audit work;
- the company is, or is to become, exempt from audit under s. 477, 479A or 480;
- the company is a subsidiary undertaking of a parent undertaking that is incorporated in the United Kingdom and:
  - the parent undertaking prepares group accounts; and
  - the auditor is being replaced as auditor of the company by the auditor who is conducting, or is to conduct, an audit of the group accounts; or
- the company is being wound up under Part 4 of the Insolvency Act 1986 or Part 5 of the Insolvency (Northern Ireland) Order 1989.

If a company receives from their auditor a statement in connection with their ceasing to hold office, pursuant to s. 519, unless the company is both a non-PIE company and the statement notes that there are no matters to be brought to the attention of the members or creditors, the company must, within 14 days of receipt of the statement, send a copy of it to every person entitled to receive copies of the accounts or apply to the court for a direction not to do so. If an application to court is made, the auditor must be notified. If the court determines that the statement should be circulated, the company must comply within 14 days of that decision (s. 520).

Unquoted companies

Where, for any reason, an auditor of an unquoted company ceases to hold office, they must send the company at its registered office a statement of any circumstances connected with their ceasing to hold office that they consider should be brought to the attention of the members or creditors of the company. If there are no circumstances to be reported to them, this must be stated (s. 519(1) and (2)).

Quoted company

Where, for any reason, an auditor of a quoted company ceases to hold office, they must send the company at its registered office a statement of the circumstances connected with their ceasing to hold office (s. 519(3)).

Time allowed to provide statement

In the case of a resigning auditor, the statement must be deposited with the notice of resignation. If the auditor does not seek reappointment at the next annual general meeting, the statement should be delivered not less than 14 days before the end of the period allowed for next appointing auditors. In any other circumstances, the statement should be deposited not later than the end of 14 days beginning with the date on which the auditor ceases to hold office (s. 519(4)).

Notification to Companies House

If the auditor is not notified within 21 days that an application is to be made to the court, pursuant to s. 520(2)(b) they must send a copy of their statement to the Registrar of Companies within seven days. If an application to the court is made and rejected, the auditor must send a copy of their statement to the Registrar of Companies within seven days of being notified of the court's decision by the company (s. 521).

Notification to audit authority

Where an auditor ceases to hold office before the end of their term of office and sends a statement to the company pursuant to s. 519, the auditor must send a copy of the statement to the appropriate audit authority (s. 522).

Where an auditor ceases to hold office to a private company at any time other than at the end of the period for appointing auditors or to a public company at any time other than at the end of an accounts meeting, the company must, within 28 days, give notice to the appropriate audit authority that the auditor is ceasing to hold office (s. 523). Notification is not required if the company believes the reasons for the cessation of appointment are exempt reasons (see above).

The notice must set out what the company considers are the reasons for the auditor ceasing to hold office. If the auditor has deposited a statement of circumstances with which the company agrees, a copy of that statement may be submitted by the company.

The appropriate audit authority will depend on whether the company is a PIE or not (s. 525). If the company is a PIE, notification should be made to the Financial Reporting Council (FRC), otherwise notification should be made to the auditor's recognised supervisory body.

Audit partner rotation

Although the Act does not place any restrictions on the period that one audit engagement partner has with a particular company, the Auditing Practices Board (APB) recognises that long engagement by key audit partners as well as senior staff can pose a threat to the auditor's objectivity and independence.

The APB regularly reviews and updates its ethical guidance to auditors, including the period during which any individual partner or senior member of staff is associated with the same audit client.

Generally it is for audit firms to establish their own procedures and maximum period of association with the same audit client, but the APB notes that any association of ten years or more needs careful consideration to ensure the continued integrity, objectivity and independence of the persons involved in an audit.

For a PIE, the APB recommends that the maximum period a key audit partner is responsible for carrying out the statutory audit should cease after a period of not more than five years, and that a further period of five years should elapse before they participate again in that statutory audit.

Auditors' liability

Any provision in a contract to exempt the auditors from any liability is void, except where such a clause is permitted by ss. 533–538A.

Indemnity

Section 533 permits companies to indemnify an auditor in defending proceedings in which judgement is given in favour of the auditor or relief is granted by the court.

Limitation of liability

Auditors and companies may agree to limit the liability of the auditor provided:

1 the limitation agreement only applies to acts or omissions in respect of the audit of one financial year;
2 the financial year is specified; and
3 it is approved by the members.

Any audit liability limitation must be fair and reasonable in all the circumstances, and in particular must have regard to the auditor's responsibilities under the Companies Act, the nature and purpose of the agreement to provide audit services, and the professional standards expected of the auditor (s. 537).

Private company

A liability limitation agreement may be approved by members:

- in advance by waiving the need for approval;
- in advance by approving the agreement's main terms; or
- after the agreement is entered into by agreeing to its terms (s. 536(2)).

Public company

A liability limitation agreement may be approved by members in advance by approving the agreement's main terms or after the agreement is entered into by agreeing to its terms (s. 536(3)).

12 – Share capital, debentures and loan stock

Introduction

A company is owned by its members. Companies without a share capital will have some other method of determining ownership, but the overwhelming majority of companies have a share capital consisting of one or more classes of shares.

Authorised capital

The Act abolished the concept of an authorised share capital. On application for registration of a new company that has a share capital, a statement of capital and initial shareholdings must be submitted to the Registrar of Companies. The information that must be contained in the statement of capital includes: the total number of shares to be taken on incorporation by the subscribers to the memorandum; the aggregate nominal value of those shares; for each class of shares, the rights attached to those shares, the total number of shares in that class and the aggregate nominal value of the shares of that class; and the amount to be paid up and the amount to be unpaid on each share.

For existing companies, authorised share capital will continue to act as a ceiling on the number of shares that can be allotted and will be considered as a restriction in the articles of association of the company. If the company wishes to allot shares beyond this ceiling, the shareholders will be able to remove the deemed restriction by ordinary resolution, rather than by special resolution, which would normally be required to amend the articles of association (see precedent 36).

Allotted capital

The Act defines 'allotted share capital' as shares that it has allotted (s. 546(1)(b)). Section 558 states that shares are taken as allotted when a person acquires the unconditional right to be included in the company's register of members in respect of the shares. Allotted shares includes shares taken by the subscribers on incorporation (s. 546(2)).

There is no guidance as to when an unconditional right exists, but it is generally accepted that this will be once the contract of allotment is completed and that acceptance of the application has been notified to the applicant.

Issued capital

Issued capital is the total capital that has been issued and taken up by the members of the company, after it has been issued for cash or for a consideration other than cash, and is expressed by reference to the aggregate nominal value of the shares issued. Accordingly, a company which issues 250 shares of £1 each has an issued share capital of £250. Provided there are no restrictions in the articles of association, a company can increase its issued share capital by allotting new shares.

Although there is no statutory definition of when a share is issued, it is generally accepted that this is when the shares are entered in the register of members and this was confirmed in *National Westminster Bank plc v Inland Revenue Commissioners 1995*. Issued shares includes shares taken by the subscribers on incorporation (s. 546(2)).

Paid-up capital

Paid-up capital refers to the nominal amounts that have been paid up on the company's issued capital. For example, if a company has 500 shares of 50p each in issue, then the issued capital is £250. If they are fully paid, the paid-up share capital will be £250. However, if, for example, the shares are issued only partly paid, with 25p paid up on each share, with the balance due at some point in the future, the paid-up capital will be £125.

Called-up capital

Called-up capital means the amount equal to the aggregate amount of calls made on the shares (whether paid or not), together with any amounts paid up without being called and any share capital to be paid on a specific future date under the articles of association, the terms of allotment or other arrangements for payment (s. 547).

Equity capital

Equity capital means the issued capital of the company, excluding any shares that have the right to participate in a dividend or return of capital only up to a specified amount (s. 548).

Changes to capital

Chapter 8 of Part 17 of the Act sets out the provisions relating to the alteration of share capital. Section 617 provides that a limited company with a share capital may not alter its share capital except as provided in Parts 17 and 18 of the Act.

Under Parts 17 and 18 of the Act, a company may:

1. increase its share capital by allotting new shares;
2. subdivide or consolidate all or any of its share capital;
3. reconvert stock into shares;
4. redeem shares;
5. purchase its own shares;
6. redenominate its share capital;
7. cancel its shares (duty to cancel shares held by or for a public company); and
8. reduce its share capital (s. 617).

No other alterations are permitted.

One alteration that may be requested by directors, but not permitted, is the conversion of non-redeemable shares into redeemable shares. There is no power under the Companies Act to convert non-redeemable shares into redeemable shares. Furthermore, s. 684 states that a company may issue shares that are, or are liable to be, redeemed. It can be seen that shares can only be issued as redeemable and not converted to be redeemable after issue. This problem can usually be overcome by undertaking a purchase of own shares by the company and by the shareholder(s) making application for the issue of redeemable shares and using the consideration monies to effect the purchase. It is also worth noting that a private company need no longer be authorised by its articles to allot redeemable shares, although the articles can restrict or exclude their issue. A public company wishing to allot redeemable shares will still need to be authorised to do so by its articles of association.

The 2006 Act removes the requirement for prior authorisation in the company's articles in relation to the following alterations of capital:

- reduction of share capital;
- subdivision and consolidation of share capital;
- redemption of shares;
- share buybacks; and
- reconversion of stock into shares.

A company will be authorised to pass resolutions to effect the above alterations to its share capital, unless it is specifically restricted by its articles of association.

Procedure for increase of authorised capital

As stated above, the Act abolished the requirement for new companies to have an authorised share capital. Under s. 617(2)(a), a company may increase its share capital by allotting new shares. Shareholders wishing to restrict the number of shares that can be issued in the company will need to amend the articles of association by special resolution of the members (see Chapter 8) to include suitable provisions, if the articles do not already contain such restrictions.

For companies existing before 1 October 2009, authorised share capital will continue to operate as a restriction in the company's articles of association. Any company wishing to allot shares beyond this ceiling will need shareholder approval to remove or increase the restriction from the company's articles, although this can be done by ordinary resolution rather than special resolution.

Consolidation of shares

The Act removed the requirement for a company's articles of association to permit the consolidation of shares, but the articles may restrict or exclude the exercise of such power under s. 618. Consolidation means that the shares of the company will be divided into shares of a larger nominal value, e.g. five shares of 10p each would be consolidated into one share of 50p each.

Consolidation does not often arise, but if a company has issued a large number of ordinary shares that are below the normal denominations of 25p, 50p or £1, it might be found convenient to consolidate the shares. However, many companies with shares having a nominal value of 10p, 5p or even fractions of a penny exist.

Subject to the company's articles of association, the share capital may be consolidated by ordinary resolution of the members following the procedure for written resolutions or holding general meetings set out in Chapter 8 (see precedent 38).

When the resolution to consolidate the specified shares has been approved by the members, the company must give notice within one month to the Registrar, specifying the shares affected. It is not necessary to file a copy of the resolution if it is an ordinary resolution.

The notice must be accompanied by a statement of capital on Form SH02, which must state, with respect to the company's share capital immediately following the passing of the resolution:

- the total number of shares in the company;
- the prescribed particulars of the rights attached to the shares;
- the total number of shares of that class;
- the aggregate nominal value of shares of that class; and
- the amount paid up and the amount (if any) unpaid on each share (whether on account of the nominal value of the share or by way of premium).

In the case of a Listed company, two copies of the resolution should be sent to the Financial Conduct Authority (FCA) (*LR 9.6.2*).

The register of members will need to be updated to show the holdings of each member in the new nominal value.

Some holdings of members will not consolidate into an exact number of new shares, and those members will 'lose' that fraction of their holding. In a Listed company, the directors will aggregate and sell all these fractional shares on the market, and distribute the proceeds to the appropriate member(s), subject to a minimum amount of, say, £5. Any proceeds amounting to less than this would be retained by the company.

In the case of Listed companies, it is necessary to apply to the FCA for the listing to be amended, while AIM and NEX companies will need to amend their admission particulars with the London Stock Exchange or NEX as appropriate. In each case, it will also be necessary to coordinate the change with Euroclear UK and Ireland Ltd relating to the maintenance of the electronic sub-register (CREST).

Share certificates may be called in for amendment, but it is more usual to send members a notice that the consolidation has taken place and enclosing a new share certificate, all existing certificates being cancelled.

Subdivision of shares

The Act removed the requirement for a company's articles of association to permit the subdivision of shares, but the articles may restrict or exclude the exercise of such power under s. 618. Subject to provision in the articles, an ordinary resolution (see precedent 39) of the company in general meeting may be passed, subdividing the company's shares into shares of a smaller nominal amount, to make them more marketable. This process is also referred to as splitting shares. For example, if the company has £1 shares quoted on the market at £10 each, these could be subdivided into four shares of 25p each, which would then carry a market value of just 250p each. If the shares are partly paid, the proportion between the amount paid and unpaid would remain as before.

The procedure for subdividing shares is similar to that for the consolidation described above, except that fractions of shares cannot arise. Notice must be sent to the Registrar of Companies within one month of the passing of the resolution, along with a statement of capital.

Following a subdivision, the register of members will have to be rewritten to show the number of shares held in the new nominal value by each member.

In the case of Listed companies, as for consolidated shares, it is necessary to apply to the FCA for the listing to be amended, while AIM and NEX companies will need to amend their admission particulars with the London Stock Exchange or NEX as appropriate. In each case, it will also be necessary to coordinate the change with Euroclear UK and Ireland Ltd relating to the maintenance of the electronic sub-register (CREST).

Share certificates may be called in for amendment, but it is more usual to send members a notice that the consolidation has taken place and enclosing a new share certificate, all existing certificates being cancelled.

Conversion of shares into stock

The Act abolished the power to convert shares into stock.

Reconversion of stock into shares

The Act removed the requirement for a company's articles of association to permit the reconversion stock into shares, but the articles may restrict or exclude the exercise of such power under s. 620. The Act allows the reconversion of existing stock back into paid-up shares of any nominal value by means of ordinary resolution (s. 620, see precedent 40).

If a company exercises its powers to reconvert stock into shares, it must give notice to the Registrar within one month, specifying the stock affected. The notice must be accompanied by a statement of capital on Form SH02 (see 'Consolidation of shares' above for details of what this should include).

Duty to cancel shares (public companies only)

Section 662 applies in the case of a public company, where:

1. shares in the company are forfeited, or surrendered to the company in lieu of forfeiture, in pursuance of the articles, for failure to pay any sum payable in respect of the shares;
2. any shares in the company are surrendered to the company in pursuance of s. 102C(1)(b) of the Building Societies Act 1986 (c.53);
3. shares in the company are acquired by it and the company has a beneficial interest in the shares;
4. a nominee of the company acquires shares in the company from a third party without financial assistance being given directly or indirectly by the company and the company has a beneficial interest in the shares; or
5. a person acquires shares in the company, with financial assistance given to them, directly or indirectly, by a company for the purpose of or in connection with the acquisition, and the company has a beneficial interest in the shares.

Unless the shares or any interest of the company in them are previously disposed of, the company must cancel the shares and reduce the amount of the company's share capital by the nominal value of the shares cancelled. Where the nominal value of the company's allotted share capital is brought below the authorised minimum, it must apply for re-registration as a private company, stating the effect of the cancellation. The company must cancel the shares and apply for re-registration (if applicable) no later than three years from the date of forfeiture or surrender in relation to points 1 and 2, no later than three years from the date of acquisition in respect of points 3 and 4, and no later than one year from the date of acquisition in relation to point 5.

The company must, within one month of cancellation, give notice to the Registrar, specifying the shares cancelled. The notice must be accompanied by a statement of capital on Form SH07 (see 'Consolidation of shares' for details of what this should include).

Effect of alterations of capital on voting rights

At the time an alteration of capital is made, the effect that it might have on the existing voting rights of shareholders should be taken into account, so that, if appropriate, suitable action may be taken to keep the voting rights between the different classes of shares in the same proportion that applied prior to the alteration. It may be necessary to hold meetings to obtain the consent of each class of shareholder (see precedent 43). If the voting or other rights of different classes are being changed, it will be necessary to hold separate class meetings of the affected classes in addition to the general meeting. This is so even if any particular class has no vote at general meetings. Class rights cannot be changed without approval of the class members whose rights are being changed.

Serious loss of capital

There is one other provision to be noted in connection with the capital of a public company. If the net assets of a public company become equal to one half or less of its called-up share capital, the directors must convene a general meeting of the company (s. 656) (see precedent 44). The notices must be issued within 28 days of the deficiency becoming known. The purpose of the meeting is to allow shareholders to consider what measures should be taken to deal with the situation. There is no requirement for a resolution to be put to the meeting, merely that the meeting be convened.

Because s. 656 stipulates that the directors must convene a general meeting, it is not possible for the resolution to be added to the business of an annual general meeting. However, it would be possible to convene a general meeting to be held at the conclusion of the AGM.

Shares and stock

References to shares should also be taken as including references to stock, unless inappropriate in the context. The Act abolished the power to convert shares into stock, but allows the reconversion of existing stock back into paid-up shares of any nominal value by means of ordinary resolution (s. 620).

Share premiums

A share premium is the amount of the issue price of a share in excess of its nominal value, e.g. in the case of a 50p share issued for £1.60, 50p is the nominal value and £1.10 is the premium. In a statement of a company's share capital, only the nominal amount of the shares is included. The amount of any share premium must be credited to a share premium account (s. 610). This is a special form of capital reserve which can be used only for paying up unissued shares to be offered to members as fully paid shares and for certain other purposes stated in s. 610. However, the share premium account is treated as part of the company's paid-up share capital, and provisions applicable to the reduction of capital apply to this account (s. 610).

It should be noted, however, that ss. 611 and 612 provide for a number of exemptions from the strict application of s. 610 following a merger or reconstruction where this is effected by an exchange of shares, and the company issuing its shares in exchange for shares in the other company issues its shares at a premium.

Where two companies merge and the acquiring company purchases the shares of the second company in consideration of the issue of fully paid shares, relief from s. 610 is given by s. 612, provided at least 90% of the target company's shares are acquired. Relief from s. 610 applies also to the issue of consideration shares for non-equity shares of the target acquired at the same time as the equity shares, whether the consideration is effected by the issue of new shares in the acquiring company or by the cancellation of shares in the target company not held by the acquiring company. For the purposes of the section, the 90% holding may include shares held before the transaction took place and shares held by the acquiring company's holding company, or any subsidiary or any fellow subsidiary of its holding company.

Where a group reconstruction is being undertaken, relief from s. 610 is given by s. 611 when the issuing company is a wholly owned subsidiary and allots shares to its holding company or a fellow subsidiary in exchange for the transfer of non-cash assets, provided the transferor company is a member of the same group. For the purposes of this section, the group means the holding company and any wholly owned subsidiaries.

The value of the premium on which relief has been given by ss. 611 or 612 is disregarded for the purposes of valuing the consideration shares in the company's balance sheet (s. 615).

Classes of shares

The articles of association will set out the division of shares into different classes, with the respective rights of each of the classes being stated. The most common classes into which shares of a company may be divided are:

1. ordinary shares which rank after the preference shares as regards dividends and return of capital but carry voting rights not normally given to holders of preference shares unless their preferential dividend is in arrears;
2. ordinary shares, which are non-voting shares, usually distinguished from the voting shares by calling them 'A' shares;

3 preference shares;
4 cumulative preference shares;
5 redeemable preference shares or cumulative redeemable preference shares; and
6 debentures and loan stocks.

See page 57, for more detail on these.

Payment of the interest on debentures and loan stocks ranks ahead of the payment of preference dividends and ordinary dividends. They would also rank ahead of preference and ordinary shares in repayment of capital in a liquidation. It should be noted, however, that debentures and loan stocks do not form part of the company's capital, although quite often they are colloquially referred to as 'loan capital'. The company's capital is confined to the company's share capital, which includes preference shares as well as ordinary shares.

Rights attaching to a class of shares

The rights attaching to all shares will be stated in the articles of association. The most common rights differentiating one class from another are the:

- right to vote;
- right to receive dividend;
- right to capital on a winding-up or a return of capital;
- right of pre-emption on transfer and allotment;
- right of redemption; and
- right to conversion, normally to ordinary shares.

See page 57, for more detail on these.

A company can create classes of shares with as many or few rights as it wishes. The rights will often depend on the investor where new capital is being invested to enable an existing business to expand. Although the majority of rights attaching to shares can be altered whether the shares have been issued or not, it is not possible to convert issued shares that were not redeemable into redeemable shares.

Variation of rights

The Act provides that the rights attached to a class of shares or members shall be varied in accordance with the provisions of the company's articles of association, or, if the company's articles do not make provision for the variation of class rights, in accordance with the provisions of Chapter 9 of Part 17 of the Act. This allows a company to specify less demanding procedures for varying class rights in its articles of association.

Section 630 provides that class rights may only be varied by either the written consent of the holders of at least three-quarters in nominal value of the issued shares of the relevant class, or a special resolution passed by the holders of that class sanctions the variation. Where the company's articles impose a higher threshold for consent to the variation of class rights, the company must comply with the more onerous regime. Section 631 provides that for companies without a share capital, consent in writing from at least three-quarters of the members of that class or a special resolution passed at a separate general meeting of the members of that class sanctioning the variation will be required to vary class rights.

Members together holding not less than 15% of the issued shares of a class (or 15% of the members of a class, in the case of a company without a share capital) who did not consent to, or vote in favour of, the variation may apply to the court for it to be cancelled within 21 days of the resolution consenting to the variation being passed. In this case, the variation will not take effect until it is confirmed by the court. The application may be made by one or more of these shareholders (or members) on behalf of those entitled to make the application. The court will disallow the variation if it is satisfied that the variation would unfairly prejudice the holders (or members) concerned; otherwise, the court will confirm the alteration (ss. 633 and 634). A copy of the court order must be filed with the Registrar within 15 days of it being made.

Companies creating new classes of shares or members, or varying the rights of existing classes of shares or members, are required to notify the Registrar of the particulars of the rights created or affected within one month of the date of variation (ss. 636–640).

Membership

The subscribers to the memorandum of association are deemed to have agreed to become members of the company and, on registration of the company, their names should be entered in the register of members. A person may subsequently become a member by applying for new shares or by the transfer or transmission to them of shares already in issue and the entry of their name in the register of members. Two criteria must be met to become a member: first, the person must agree to be a member; and second, they must be entered as a member in the register of members (s. 112). Both requirements must be met before a person is regarded as a member of the company.

Single-member companies

A company need have only one shareholder. Public companies are required to issue at least £50,000 in nominal value of shares, with each share at least 25% paid up as to its nominal value and 100% of any premium before commencing to trade, and to maintain this minimum capital at all times. The Companies (Single Member Private Limited Companies) Regulations 1992, SI 1992/1699 reduced the minimum number of shareholders required for a private limited company from two to one. The Companies Act 2006 dropped the requirement for a public company to have at least two members with effect from 1 October 2007. Any company incorporated prior to the coming into effect of these provisions may need to amend its articles of association if these specifically state that the company must have two or more members. Any rule of law requiring a private company to have two members has been modified by the statutory instrument.

Any sole shareholder may also be a sole director of a private company. Any company reducing its membership to one must, when updating the register of members, add a note stating that the company has only one member and the date on which the change occurred (s. 123). If a company with only one member increases its membership, a note should be added to the register of members stating this fact, together with the date on which the change occurred (s. 123, see precedent 81).

Section 318 provides that for a single-member company, notwithstanding any provision in a company's articles, one member present by person or by proxy shall constitute a valid quorum. Additionally, as the discipline of duly convening meetings for a single-member company is cumbersome, it is in order for a single member to take decisions normally requiring a meeting, provided that any decisions are formally recorded in writing (s. 357). Any agreements made between a single member and a sole director who is also the member must be set out in a written memorandum or recorded in the minutes of the next meeting of the board of directors (s. 231). Although this provision applies only to contracts other than in the normal course of business, to prevent any innocent omission it is recommended that a written record be kept of all contracts between the company and a sole member/director. It may also be appropriate for the director to declare their interest in the matter pursuant to the articles of association.

As long as there is no provision to the contrary in the articles, any legal person such as a company may hold shares in a company. The articles of some companies, however, exclude certain categories of person from membership, e.g. persons who are not able to give a declaration of British nationality. At the same time, it is necessary to ensure that in the case of a registered company, for example, the company's articles of association do not preclude the holding of shares in other companies.

However, an unincorporated body like a partnership, club or association not registered under the Act should not be accepted as a member of the company, because it does not possess legal personality. If such a body wishes to hold shares, the shares should be registered in the name of an individual or individuals, or a person having a legal personality such as a bank nominee or a trustee company.

Similarly, the holder of an office should not be accepted as a member in that capacity unless it is an office created by statute, such as the Treasury Solicitor or the Accountant General. Some public officers are legally deemed to be a corporation, e.g. the Public Trustee, and these may be registered as members of companies.

Shares should not be registered in the name of an English partnership. They should be held in the names of two or more partners, and no reference should be made in the register of members to the partnership. Scottish partnerships, however, have legal personality and may, therefore, be registered in the firm name as members of the company. Shares held by a limited liability partnership can be registered in the name of the LLP, as it is a corporate body with a legal persona. Shares in a company may be held by a number of persons in a joint account. However, some articles of association limit the number of persons who may be so registered.

In the case of a Listed company, the maximum number of joint holders is not permitted to be fewer than four.

Unless a subsidiary company is acting only as personal representative or trustee without having any beneficial interest in the shares or acting as an authorised dealer in securities, a subsidiary company is not permitted to be a member of its holding company (s. 136). Section 139 makes provisions to enable a company's subsidiary company to act as trustee for a group employee share scheme or pension scheme. There is, however, no prohibition on the holding of shares by a subsidiary in its holding company if it held shares in the company that acquired it (which thereby became its holding company) prior to its becoming a subsidiary of that company. However, in this case, the subsidiary is not permitted to vote at meetings of the holding company (s. 137(4)). It would not be lawful for any further shares in the holding company to be allotted to such a subsidiary company, a situation which could arise if the holding company undertook a capitalisation issue.

Minors as members of a company

See page 55, for details of minors as members of a company.

Warrants

A warrant is a document rather like a share certificate which entitles the holder to subscribe for equity capital in the company at some future date or dates at a price which is determined at the time of issue of the warrant. It should not be confused with a share warrant to bearer, which is a document evidencing title to shares already issued. Warrants to subscribe may be Listed and traded on the Stock Exchange or NEX, and the company would normally have a register of holders of the warrants. However, the warrants do not form part of the company's capital and holders are not entitled to receive dividends or interest.

If warrants are to be issued, they must be permitted by the company's articles of association. They should not be confused with the rights to convert into ordinary shares attached to convertible loan stocks, which cannot be bought or sold separately. Warrants may, however, be bought and sold on the Stock Exchange or NEX separately from other securities of the company. Warrants are often issued in connection with takeover offers in order to make the terms more attractive without immediate cost to the bidding company.

A register of holders is usually maintained in a form similar to that of the register of members. It will be necessary in the statement of the terms of issue to include the procedures regarding transfer of warrants, inspection of the register, requests for copies of the register and the dispatch of annual reports and accounts to warrant holders, although there are no statutory provisions covering these matters. Stamp duty is payable on transfers of warrants in the same way and at the same rate as transfers of shares.

Subscription rights

Sometimes the issue of a loan stock includes an associated right to subscribe for shares in the company concerned. This is not the same as the conversion rights under a convertible loan stock, where the loan stock is surrendered in exchange for shares. With subscription rights, the loan stock remains in issue and holders subscribe additional money in order to exercise their subscription rights. An alternative method of giving subscription rights is by the issue of option certificates. The exercise of subscription rights does not affect the company's register of loan stock holders, as it does in the case of a convertible loan stock where a person's holding of convertible loan stock would be reduced by the amount of stock which they converted into equity capital.

Debentures and loan stocks

The legislation governing the registration of charges is contained in s. 859A–Q.

The directors have implied power to borrow money on behalf of the company under their general powers to manage the business of the company, subject to the provisions of the Act and the articles of the company (Private and Public Model Articles 3 and 4).

However, the articles of some companies are more specific and impose restrictions on the amounts that may be borrowed, and it is necessary for the company in general meeting to alter the appropriate article if it is considered desirable that the directors' borrowing powers should be amended. A common provision in the articles is that the amount of monies borrowed or secured on the undertaking and property of the company (apart from temporary loans obtained by way of overdraft from the company's bankers) for the time being remaining undischarged, shall not, without the previous sanction of the company in general meeting, exceed the nominal amount of the share capital of the company for the time being issued.

If the company's articles contain an article restricting the directors' borrowing powers, it must be carefully followed, since if they were to borrow in excess of the limit specified, they might find themselves personally liable. The position of third parties acting in good faith would not, however, be affected by any restriction imposing a limit on the directors' powers to borrow on behalf of the company.

The ways in which the company borrows money may be in the form of debentures of various types, unsecured loan stocks and convertible loan stocks, apart from borrowing from the bank by way of overdraft for the company's day-to-day business.

Types of debenture

A debenture is defined in s. 738 as debenture stock, bonds and any other securities of the company, whether or not constituting a charge on the assets of the company. In effect, a debenture is a document that creates a debt or acknowledges a debt. It may, therefore, be an unsecured promise to pay or a promise to pay secured by a mortgage or charge over the property of the company.

Occasionally, debentures may be issued in bearer form similar to the share warrants to bearer, which may be issued in respect of shares. Arrangements for the payment of interest on bearer debentures are similar to those that apply in the case of the payment of dividends on **bearer shares**. In practice, issue of bearer debentures by companies is rare, although euro currency securities may be in this form.

The more common method is to issue a series of debentures in registered form. The conditions relating to interest, redemption or security will be printed on the reverse of each debenture issued. Registered debentures may be transferable on **stock transfer forms** under the Stock Transfer Act 1963 and such transfers are exempt from stamp duty (with a few exceptions). When a debenture or one of a series of debentures is transferred, the name and address of the new holder are endorsed on the debenture itself by the company.

If the company keeps a register of debenture holders, the transfer should be recorded in the register. If it creates a charge over the undertaking or any property of the company, an entry should be made in the company's register of charges and the charge registered with the Registrar of Companies. The period allowed for registration of particulars of a series of debentures is 21 days beginning with the day after the day on which the charge is created, if there is a deed containing the charge, or, if there is no such deed, 21 days beginning with the day after the day on which the first debenture of the series is created (s. 859B(6)). Registered debentures are normally issued only in the case of private companies, although a public company may issue such a debenture to its bank by way of security for a loan.

Public companies normally issue their debentures in the form of debenture stock secured on the company's assets and constituted by a trust deed between the company and a corporate trustee, e.g. an insurance company or a trust company. Where debenture stock is not secured by a charge over the undertaking or property of the company, it is described as 'unsecured loan stock'.

Secured debentures

The security for a mortgage debenture may be fixed or floating, or a combination of the two. **Fixed charges** are equivalent to mortgages and the company is restricted in dealing with the asset or assets charged without the prior consent of the debenture holder or of the trustee for the debenture stock. The difference in the case of a floating charge is that this extends over the whole of the undertaking of the company and is not restricted to particular assets. This enables the company to deal with its assets in the ordinary course of its business. It is possible for a fixed charge to be given over an asset that is already the subject of a **floating charge**. This would then take priority over the floating charge, although it would be usual to expect the terms of issue of a debenture creating a floating charge to prohibit the company from doing this.

A floating charge crystallises and becomes a fixed charge if an event should happen that allows the debenture holders or the trustee to take possession of the security or to appoint a receiver. The circumstances in which this may happen will be specified in the debenture or the trust deed. Usually, of course, one of these circumstances will be the non-payment of interest within a specified time from the due date or if a resolution should be passed to wind up the company. Subject to the rights of preferential creditors specified in IA1986 s. 386 and Sch. 6, the debenture holders have priority, to the extent of the security held, over the ordinary and other secured creditors on the crystallisation of a floating charge. In Scotland, a floating charge only crystallises on the commencement of a winding-up or the appointment of a receiver. Notice of the appointment of a receiver or manager of a company's property must also be notified to the Registrar within seven days of the appointment (s. 859K).

Particulars of a charge to secure any issue of debentures in Great Britain must be registered with the Registrar of Companies on Form MR03. The period allowed for registration is 21 days beginning with the day after the day on which the charge is created – if there is a deed containing the charge, this is the date of execution – or, if there is no such deed, 21 days beginning with the day after the day on which the first debenture of the series is created (s. 859E). If there is a deed, this must be delivered along with the form.

If there is no deed, one of the debentures must be delivered with the form.

Further, the company must deliver to the Registrar particulars of an issue of secured debentures in a series in the prescribed Form MR03.

It is necessary to send to the Registrar a certified copy of the charge document with the particulars. The Registrar will not check the particulars, although they may reject particulars that they consider to be unregistrable. Copies of instruments creating or evidencing a charge over the company's property must be kept at the company's registered office or a place specified under s. 1136 (s. 859P) and be available for inspection by any creditor or member of the company without fee, or by any other person on payment of such fee as may be prescribed (s. 859Q). It is important to the debenture holders that the particulars of a charge created by an issue of debentures are registered with the Registrar of Companies, since a charge is void unless particulars are filed with the Registrar within 21 days of its creation (s. 859H). It is usual, therefore, for the trustee for the debenture holders to attend to the registration under the authority contained in s. 859A(2), which provides that registration of a charge may be effected on the application of any person interested in it.

Unsecured loan stock

Unsecured loan stock carries a higher risk for investors. To compensate for this, it is usual for such stocks to bear a higher rate of interest than if it were a secured debenture stock. Sometimes it is also necessary to offer options in the form of a right to convert the stock into equity shares of the company at certain dates in the future (i.e. convertible loan stock; see below). The ratio is determined at the time of issue of the stock; alternatively, a right to subscribe for equity shares at a future date in a ratio and price determined at the time of issue is agreed. With regard to the latter, it should be noted that the loan stock continues in existence after the holder has exercised the subscription rights to which they are entitled. In the case of a convertible loan stock, the exercise of the holder of their right to convert into ordinary shares extinguishes their holding of the convertible loan stock to the extent that it is exercised.

The trust deed constituting unsecured loan stock will usually cover:

1. details of the terms of issue, payment of principal and interest and any conversion or subscription rights which may be attached to the stock;
2. restrictions on issuing further unsecured loan stock;
3. restrictions on further borrowing;
4. restrictions on disposal of the business or specified assets;
5. a covenant by the company to maintain sufficient equity capital to satisfy any conversion or subscription rights, further issues of equity capital and in regard to the business generally;
6. events in which the whole of the stock becomes immediately payable (e.g. default in payment of interest or ceasing to carry on business);
7. the remuneration of the trustees;
8. schedules which will be attached to the trust deed containing the form of stock certificate, the detailed conditions for redemption by drawings or purchase and of any conversion or subscription rights;
9. regulations regarding the register of holders of the stock;
10. arrangements for transfer and transmission of the stock; and
11. regulations governing meetings of holders of the stock.

If the loan stock is Listed, a summary of the conditions, instead of the full conditions, may be printed on the reverse of the certificate, provided that the trust deed does not prohibit this. The holder of the stock is entitled to be supplied with a copy of the trust deed at their request on payment of a fee (s. 749).

Convertible loan stock

Convertible loan stock is a form of loan stock, usually unsecured, which includes provision for the stock to be converted into equity shares at ratios determined at the time of issue of the stock. There is a requirement for the company to give the stockholders notice of their right to exercise the conversion rights in every year in which the right exists.

The company secretary or the company's registrar will be concerned with the proper procedure for dealing with applications from holders to exercise their conversion rights.

Bearer shares

UK companies are no longer permitted to have bearer shares and SBEE2015 contained a mandatory process for the compulsory conversion of any existing bearer shares either into register from or in the absence of the holders making themselves known for the bearer shares to be cancelled and an amount equal to their value to be paid into court.

13 – Share issues

Introduction

When issuing new shares, care must be taken to ensure that there are sufficient unissued shares in the authorised share capital to satisfy the issue, ensure that there is sufficient current authority in terms of ss. 550 or 551 for the directors to approve the issue and that any rights of pre-emption, whether as set out in the Act or in the company's own articles, are observed.

The terms 'share issue' and 'share allotment' refer to very slightly different aspects of the process of issuing shares, and for most purposes are intended to mean the same thing. When issuing shares, these are first allotted by the directors between those applying for them, and then they are issued to those successful applicants.

Once a company has issued shares, there are only limited circumstances under which they can be returned to the company. Failure to pay calls on partly paid shares can lead to them being forfeited (see page 225). Under strict conditions, a company can purchase its own shares or redeem shares, provided they were issued as redeemable (see page 237). Companies can also undertake a reduction of capital which might include a payment to shareholders (see page 245).

Whether shares are admitted to trading on a public exchange or not, most shares are transferable. Many private companies' articles contain pre-emption rights on transfer designed to ensure that the pool of issued shares is retained within a relatively small number of owners who are usually directly involved in the management of the company. The model articles, however, do not contain pre-emption rights on transfer of shares.

Public companies with traded shares will generally be prohibited by the exchange/market operator from imposing any restriction on the transferability of the shares. The main exception is where certain companies, such as British Airways, are required to maintain UK residents holding a minimum percentage of their issued shares.

Authority for allotment

In general, directors must not exercise the company's power to allot shares or grant rights to subscribe for shares unless authorised by ss. 550 or 551 (s. 549). This requirement does not apply to the:

- allotment of shares under an employee share scheme;
- grant of rights to subscribe for shares allotted under an employee share scheme; or
- allotment of shares arising on the conversion of a security into shares (s. 549(2) and (3)).

The directors of a private company with only one class of shares can exercise the company's power to allot shares or grant rights to subscribe for shares without any additional shareholder consent subject to any restrictions in the company's articles (s. 550).

In all other cases, directors may only exercise the company's power to allot shares if authorised to do so by the articles or by resolution of the shareholders (s. 551(1), see precedent 45). The authority may be given in general terms or made subject to conditions, but must state the maximum amount of the relevant securities that may be issued and specify the date on which the authority will expire. Authority may be given for a maximum of five years from the date of the resolution or date of incorporation if contained in the articles on incorporation (s. 551(3)). Companies with few shareholders will often adopt the longest period permissible and, to safeguard existing shareholders, will have pre-emption rights in their articles, as discussed below. Companies with a large number of shareholders, and Listed companies, will renew the authority in respect of all the then unissued shares (see precedent 19). The authority to allot relevant securities may be revoked, varied or renewed by ordinary resolution, even if the authority was given by a special resolution or contained in the articles of association. A resolution renewing an earlier authority must state the amount of shares that may be allotted and an expiry date, within five years. Securities may be allotted after the expiry of the authority, provided that the allotment is in pursuance of an offer or agreement made prior to the expiry of the authority. A copy of a resolution giving authority to directors to allot relevant securities must be filed with the Registrar of Companies within 15 days after it is passed (ss. 30 and 551(9)).

Pre-emption rights

The Act provides that, unless disapplied in whole or in part by the articles, where new shares are to be allotted, they must first be offered to existing shareholders in proportion to their existing holdings (s. 561).

In the case of a Listed company, the Financial Conduct Authority (FCA) requires that any new issues of shares for cash should first be offered to existing holders as in a rights issue (*LR 9.3.11*). Listed companies will routinely seek a waiver of the pre-emption provisions from members at each AGM for small issues of new shares (see page 216).

Pre-emption rights for existing shareholders are provided in ss. 561–573. These provisions may be excluded by the articles of a private company or by special resolution of the members (see precedent 46). Equity securities are defined in s. 560 as relevant shares in the company – i.e. basically the ordinary share capital of the company on which the rate of dividend varies according to the profits of the company and which carry no preferential right in the repayment of the capital in the event of winding-up. Securities that can be converted into relevant shares (i.e. convertible loan stocks) are also included, but the following are excluded:

1 shares taken by subscribers to the memorandum;
2 shares that as regards dividends and capital carry right to participate only up to a specified amount in a distribution;
3 shares held by a person acquired through an employees' share scheme or which are to be allotted in pursuance of such a scheme;
4 shares allotted under a capitalisation issue; and
5 shares allotted wholly or partly paid otherwise than in cash (ss. 560, 564–566).

This last exception effectively restricts pre-emption provisions to issues for cash. This is particularly useful where a company is looking to acquire another business or assets in exchange for the issue of its own shares, credited as fully paid.

Any pre-emption rights contained in a company's articles of association take precedence over the statutory pre-emption rights. The requirement of the Act is that no equity securities may be allotted unless they have first been offered to the holders of all the relevant shares in the company in proportion to their existing shareholdings. The detailed provisions with regard to the communication of the offer to the existing shareholders, who must be given a period of not less than 14 days in which to accept the offer, are laid down in s. 562. A record date to determine the holders entitled to receive the offer must be set in a period of 28 days before the date of the offer (s. 574).

The company and every officer who knowingly permits an allotment of shares to be made in contravention of the statutory pre-emption provisions are jointly and severally liable to compensate any person who may suffer loss as a result.

Disapplication of pre-emption rights

Private companies may exclude the statutory provisions by provisions contained in their articles. These will prevail even if they are inconsistent with the statutory provisions. It is also possible for both public and private companies to exclude the operation of the statutory pre-emption rights in s. 561 if the directors obtain authority by a special resolution of the members, either in respect of a general waiver in conjunction with a general authority to issue shares or for a specific share issue (ss. 570, 571). If the company's articles do not already contain a suitable provision, an alteration to the articles would be necessary and would require the approval of shareholders by special resolution in a general meeting.

The authority to disapply pre-emption rights is contained in ss. 569–573. It is also quite common for the special resolution required by s. 570, giving the directors power to disapply the Act's requirements with regard to pre-emption rights in respect of the allotment of securities up to a limit specified in the resolution, to be proposed as part of the regular business at the annual general meeting of a Listed company. In most cases, Listed companies will seek the waiver of pre-emption rights of up to an additional 5% of the issued share capital.

Established in 2005, the Pre-emption Group provides guidance and has issued a statement of principles on acceptable practice for Listed companies seeking waivers of pre-emption rights. The statement of principles was updated in March 2015 and permits the annual disapplication of pre-emption rights under s. 570, provided that:

- the general authority is restricted to an additional 5% of the issued ordinary share capital; and
- this additional 5% of the issued ordinary share capital is only used in connection with an acquisition or specified capital investment which is announced at the same time as the issue, or which has taken place in the preceding six-month period and is disclosed in the announcement of the issue.

The authority lapses at the earlier of the next AGM or 15 months after the date of the resolution.

In addition, the statement of principles notes that in any three-year rolling period, use of pre-emption waivers should be restricted to 7.5% of the issued ordinary share capital, excluding any specific waivers or use of the additional 5% general waiver for an acquisition or capital investment.

The pre-emption group reviewed application of the revised statement of principles in May 2016, and has recommended that the waiver be sought by two separate resolutions and has provided specimen wording for those resolutions. The group also recommended that where the additional 5% waiver is used, companies should, at the time of the share issue, provide details of the circumstances that have led to its use and describe the consultation process undertaken.

The grant of the power to directors to disapply the pre-emption rights makes it possible for the company to make a rights issue of its shares and exclude or make such other arrangements for certain (usually overseas) shareholders. Otherwise, it may be impossible to allot equity securities to all shareholders of the company in proportion to the respective numbers of shares held by them. This arises because in some countries (e.g. the United States), it would not be possible to offer the securities to residents of those countries without going through lengthy and costly procedures required by the local legislation. The rights of the persons concerned would, whenever practicable, be sold for their benefit. Circumstances may also arise where the company might wish to make small allotments of equity shares for cash to persons other than existing shareholders. The disapplication of the pre-emption rights would cease when the general authority of the directors to issue equity securities under s. 551 lapses. However, an offer made before the expiry of the authority to disapply the pre-emption rights would remain valid, notwithstanding the fact that the actual allotment did not take place until after that date.

Allotment procedure

The required steps are as follows.

1 It may be necessary for the authorised capital of the company to be increased or removed because the present unissued authorised capital is insufficient to cover the proposed allotment (see Chapter 16, and precedents 36 and 37).
2 The person wishing to subscribe for shares completes a form of application and returns it with the required payment (see precedent 47).
3 The directors should pass a resolution to allot the shares to the persons applying for them and, if the company has a seal, authorise the sealing of the share certificates and their issue to the applicants (see precedent 48).
4 A share certificate is then prepared for each applicant on the company's printed share certificate forms. In the case of small companies, blank certificates for completion by hand may be obtained from law stationers. In many cases, a stock of such certificates is included in the combined statutory registers supplied upon incorporation by the registration agents. In the case of a traded company, the shares may be issued in uncertificated form and the company's registrars will deal with the necessary formalities.
5 The share certificates after sealing (if appropriate) are sent to the applicant, informing them of the allotment. All these steps should be taken as soon as possible since, until the applicant is notified that their application for shares has been accepted, they may, subject to the terms of application, be free to withdraw it. In any event, the company is required to issue certificates within two months of allotment (s. 769).
6 The names of the persons allotted shares must be entered in the register of members of the company, and they thereupon become members of the company.
7 Return of allotments on Form SH01 must be filed with the Registrar within one month of the date of allotment.

Shares allotted for non-cash consideration

A public company is prohibited from allotting shares either fully or partly paid up for a non-cash consideration unless the consideration has been valued in the previous six months and a copy of the valuer's report has been sent to the proposed allottee (ss. 593, 596 and 597). There are, however, exemptions from this provision in the following cases:

1 allotments of shares made in a takeover by way of share exchange if the offer is open to all holders of the class of shares concerned (s. 594);

2 allotments of shares made in a merger by way of issue of shares in exchange for all the assets and liabilities of another company (s. 595); and
3 where the shares are allotted under a capitalisation issue by the capitalisation of reserves or sums standing to the credit of the profit and loss account (s. 593(2)).

The valuation report must be made by an independent person who would be qualified to be an auditor of the company, unless they consider that it would be appropriate for some other person with the required knowledge and experience to make the report. That person should not be an officer or servant of the company. The valuer's report must state:

1 the nominal value of the shares being allotted wholly or partly paid for a consideration other than cash;
2 the amount of any premium payable on the shares;
3 the consideration which has been valued and the method used to value it; and
4 the amount of the nominal value of the shares and any premium treated as paid up for a consideration other than cash.

If the person appointed to make the valuation has appointed someone else to make it, the valuer's report must mention this and state:

1 the name of the other person with details of their knowledge and experience; and
2 a description of the consideration that was valued by the other person and the method used to value it. The report must include a statement that the value of the consideration, together with any cash payable, is not less than the aggregate of the nominal value and any premium of the shares to be issued, and that there has been no material change in its value since the date of the valuation.

A copy of the report must be sent to the Registrar of Companies when the return of allotments is filed (s. 597). The person making the report is entitled to call for such information from officers of the company as they may require and it is an offence for misleading or false information to be given (s. 1153).

It is also an offence to contravene the requirements for the allotment of shares for a non-cash consideration, including failure to send the allottee a copy of the report. The allottee and any subsequent holder of the shares will be liable to pay the company the amount equal to the nominal value and premium treated as paid up for a consideration other than cash on the shares allotted to them if they knew, or should have known, of the contravention. A subsequent holder of the shares, purchasing the shares for value without knowledge of the contravention, will not be liable and will also not be liable if the previous holder was not themselves liable.

Procedure for the transfer of non-cash consideration

Usually, a formal contract is entered into for the transfer of the non-cash consideration to the company and for the allotment by it of shares in consideration for the assets transferred. This formal contract should be approved by the board of directors. The agreement must be stamped and sent to the Registrar of Companies with the return of allotments. This should be accompanied by a certified copy of the agreement if the Registrar is to be requested to return the original agreement.

If there is no written contract, particulars of the agreement must be set out on Form SH01.

It will be seen that the issue of shares for a consideration other than cash involves certain formalities and expense, and arrangements may be made for the transaction to be structured so as to constitute an allotment for cash.

Allotments by public companies

Special provisions apply in the case of allotment of shares to the public by public companies. These are as follows.

An allotment cannot be made unless the amount stated in the prospectus, if any, as the minimum amount required to be raised has, in fact, been subscribed and the sum payable on application for the shares concerned has been received by the company.

There can be no allotment if the amount of capital offered for subscription is not fully subscribed, unless there is an express term in the offer that an allotment may be made notwithstanding that there has not been a full subscription. This applies in the case of offers of shares for cash and offers of shares for a consideration other than cash.

If these two requirements are not met, the cash subscribed or other consideration paid must be returned to the applicants.

Other procedural matters arising in connection with the allotment of shares pursuant to offers to the public are covered more fully in Chapter 15.

Nominee shareholding

These arise where the beneficial owner of shares does not wish to have them registered in their own name. The shares may be registered instead in the name of a person or group of people or a company (the nominee). Historically, the beneficial owner of the shares had no contact with the company, since the company was required to address all communications to the registered shareholder – in this case, the nominee. Following implementation of ss. 145 and 146, this is no longer the case. Even though there must also be no reference in the company's register of members to the identity of the beneficial owner, since by s. 126 a company is not permitted to recognise any trust affecting any of its shares, nominee shareholders of Listed, AIM and NEX companies may give notice that beneficiaries are to enjoy 'information rights'. For all other companies, registered shareholders may nominate others to exercise specified rights provided the necessary procedures are set out in the company's articles. The model articles do not contain provisions to allow members to nominate others to exercise any of their rights.

This rule prohibiting the recognition of trusts is not contravened if a company accepts a body corporate as a member with the word 'nominees' or 'trustees' in its name. At the same time, notwithstanding s. 126, public companies are required by s. 808 to keep a register of responses to enquiries made under s. 793. Section 126 does not apply in Scotland. This is dealt with in more detail in Chapter 18.

The need for a nominee shareholding can arise in the case of wholly owned subsidiary companies if the articles require two or more shareholders or the company is a public limited company. In practice, one or more of the shares in the subsidiary must be registered in the name of a nominee on behalf of the company. This requirement is often met by arranging for one share to be registered in the joint name of a director of the holding company as the first named holder and the holding company as the second named holder. The second shareholder (i.e. the holding company) would hold the balance of the shares in the subsidiary company.

The nominee should provide a dividend mandate requesting that all dividends be paid to the holding company and should also execute a transfer of the shares, the name of the transferee and date being left blank. Thus, if the director were to leave the company, it would be possible for their nominee share to be transferred to another director who remained a director of the holding company. A short declaration of trust should also be executed by the director declaring that the share they hold is held by them as a nominee for the holding company and that they have no beneficial interest in it (see precedent 49). The declaration of trust will often include the following provisions:

1 The nominee will pay any dividends on the shares as the beneficial owner may direct.
2 The nominee will transfer or deal with the shares as the beneficial owner may direct.
3 The nominee will vote at general meetings as the beneficial owner shall direct or execute proxies as required, and, if any rights or options should be offered to them as holder of the nominee share, they will act in relation to the offer as directed by the beneficial owner.

If the declaration of trust is executed, there is no need for a blank transfer or dividend mandate. However, it may still be prudent to obtain a blank transfer signed by the nominee in case they are dismissed by the company and are unwilling to cooperate in giving up the nominee shares.

Payment for shares

There are two ways in which shares may be paid for:

1 in money or money's worth, including goodwill and knowhow; or
2 by way of capitalisation of the company's existing reserves.

The following methods are prohibited:

1 Payment for shares or any premium on them by a person undertaking to do work or perform services for the company, being a public company, or any other person (s. 585).
2 The allotment of shares at a discount, i.e. at an issue price for a share below its nominal value (s. 580). However, a company may pay commission as consideration for a person subscribing or procuring the subscription for shares in the company, since this is not treated as a discount (ss. 552 and 553).
3 Shares may not be allotted by a public company (other than under an employees' share scheme) unless at least one-quarter of their nominal value and the whole of their premium is paid up (s. 586).
4 Public companies may not allot shares as fully or partly paid up (both as to their nominal value and any premium on the shares) if the consideration for the allotment includes an undertaking which is to be, or may be, performed more than five years after the date of the allotment (s. 587). If an allotment is made for a consideration that includes an undertaking to be performed within five years and the undertaking is not performed within that period, the allottee becomes liable to pay the company an amount equal to the agreed issue price plus interest.

Shares taken up by a subscriber to the memorandum of association of a public company must be paid for in cash, as to both nominal value and any premium (s. 584). Subsequent holders of shares may incur liability if any of the above provisions relating to the payment for shares are contravened (s. 588).

The model articles for a private company do not permit the company to issue nil or partly paid shares (Private Model Article 21).

Acquisition of non-cash assets from subscribers or from certain shareholders

Special requirements apply if a public company proposes to acquire non-cash assets from a subscriber to the memorandum of a company formed as a public company (or from any person who was a member of the company at the date of the re-registration of the company as a public company) within the period of two years from the date on which the company became entitled to commence business (or the date of re-registration) (ss. 598–604).

Unless the provisions of ss. 599 and 601 have been complied with, a public company may not accept the transfer of a non-cash asset to it during a period of two years from the date of issue of the certificate authorising the company to commence business, or if the company was formed as a private company from the date of its re-registration, if the transferor was a subscriber to the memorandum and articles of association, or the value of the consideration represents 10% or more of the nominal value of the company's issued share capital at the time of the transaction.

The conditions of s. 599 are as follows:

1 The asset must be independently valued pursuant to s. 600.
2 A report of the valuer must be made to the company during the period of six months immediately preceding the date of the transaction.
3 The proposed transaction must be approved by the members of the company (see precedent 50).
4 A copy of the report and resolution must be circulated to the members and the person with whom the transaction is being made no later than the date of issue of the notice convening the shareholders' meeting to consider the transaction.
5 The transfer of assets carried out in the normal course of business or under the supervision of the court or an authorised officer of the court is exempted from the provision of s. 606.

Where an agreement is entered into in contravention of s. 598 and the person with whom the arrangement is made does not receive a copy of the report of the valuer, or is aware or should have been aware of any other contravention of s. 598, the company may recover from that person any consideration given under the agreement or an amount equal to the value of the consideration. In such a case, the agreement, or those parts of it not carried out, are void. If the agreement includes the allotment of shares, the allotment will stand; however, the allottee is liable to pay to the company an amount equal to the aggregate nominal value of the shares and any premium together with interest (5%) (s. 609).

Exemption from liability

Where a person is liable to a company in relation to a payment for shares, that person may apply to the court for exemption from liability in whole or in part. The court may grant exemption only if it appears just and equitable to do so under the circumstances set out in s. 606.

Calls and instalments on shares

Calls on shares

Calls on shares arise when shares have been issued on a partly paid basis and a further payment of all or part of the balance becomes due.

Calls on partly paid shares are made by a resolution of the directors under provisions contained in the company's articles (e.g. Public Model Articles 54–62). The resolution will specify the amount of the call, the due date for payment and where payment should be sent. Where shares are registered in two or more names, the joint holders are jointly and severally liable for the calls. In the case of deceased shareholders, the estate continues to be liable for outstanding calls unless the shares have been transferred into the personal names of the personal representatives, in which case the personal representatives are personally liable. The company's articles will also make provision for action to be taken in the event of default of payment of a call. As the Private Model Articles do not allow for the issue of shares other than as fully paid, there are no provisions for the making of calls or forfeiture for non-payment.

A general point to note is that registration of transfers of shares on which a call is unpaid should not be accepted for registration. This is because liability for payment of the call remains with the holder of the shares who was registered on the date that the call was made, unless the transferee assumes liability for the unpaid call. It is necessary to draw a distinction between shares issued by companies as partly paid and the issue of new shares payable in instalments, as in some privatisation issues, where the procedure in the case of non-payment of the instalments as they fall due is different from the non-payment of calls made by the directors on partly paid shares. The procedure for dealing with the payment of a call made by the directors on partly paid shares (i.e. other than the payment of predetermined instalments on shares) of a Listed company is shown below. A similar procedure with suitable changes would be used by an unlisted public company or a private company.

Procedure

1. The directors pass the appropriate resolution making the call (see precedent 51).
2. (*Listed company only*) The FCA must be sent a copy of the resolution and the proposed call letter.
3. Bulk printing of the call letters is arranged.
4. The call letters are prepared to be sent to the individual members, specifying the number of shares and the total amount of the calls to be paid, and the date and place of payment of the calls (see precedent 52).
5. The call letters are dispatched to the shareholders.
6. It is common for a receiving agent (usually the company's share registrar) to be appointed to receive the money for the calls.
7. Reminder letters are sent out to the members who have not paid the call, stating that immediate payment must be made and that interest may be charged on the amount left outstanding (see precedent 52).
8. If payment is still not received within a reasonable period, such as seven days, a further letter should be sent to the shareholders concerned, warning them

that unless the call is paid promptly, the directors will consider the possibility of forfeiting the shares under the company's articles (see precedent 53).

9 (*Listed, AIM and NEX companies only*) The company's stockbrokers should be requested to arrange for the listing of the shares to be amended as regards the further amount called up.

10 The partly paid share certificate should be endorsed with the payment of the call or a fresh share certificate issued and returned to the person lodging the certificate, i.e. the shareholder or an agent acting on behalf of the shareholder.

11 The accounts of the shareholders in the register of members should be noted with the payment of the call.

12 A note must be included in the company's balance sheet or annual return if there are any unpaid calls at the time when these documents are prepared.

Instalments on shares

Although partly paid shares are rare, payment for shares by instalments is frequently used in the case of an offer for sale of shares where the price is substantial, as was the case of some privatisation issues. It is usual in such cases for the shares, which may already be fully paid, to be held by a custodian bank, which in turn offers the shares to the public for payment by instalments. In these cases, non-payment of an instalment may result in the loss of the shares and the forfeiture procedure described below does not have to be followed. The terms of issue will provide for the payment of a first instalment on application and for a second instalment (and perhaps a third instalment) to be paid at a subsequent date (or dates) which is/are determined in advance. Accordingly, there is no need for the call to be formally made by the directors, since information regarding the amount(s) of the instalment(s) and the due date(s) for payment are mentioned in the letter of acceptance sent to the shareholder on receipt of their application payment.

The shares may be sold by the holder of a letter of acceptance before payment of the second instalment by signing the form of renunciation on the back of the letter of acceptance. About two months after dispatch of the letters of acceptance, however, holders become registered and the shares may then only be transferred by completion of a transfer form. Holders wishing to sell their shares must return the completed transfer form to their stockbroker, accompanied by the letter of acceptance.

The usual arrangement for the payment of the second instalment is for reminder notices to be sent out by the custodian bank about four weeks before the instalment is due, setting out the procedures for payment and transfer of shares. An interim certificate is sent with the reminder notice, which will be duly receipted and returned to the registered holder (or to their agent) by the receiving bank, following payment. The procedure for the payment of a third instalment, if there is one, would be similar. After payment of the final instalment, a fully paid share certificate will be issued.

The letters of acceptance and interim certificates make it clear that, in the event of the non-payment of any instalment, the entitlement of the registered holder may be cancelled and the related shares sold. Instalments previously paid will be returned to the registered holder less expenses and any loss suffered by the custodian bank in disposing of the shares. It should be noted, therefore, that in such cases, there is no need to go through the forfeiture procedure described below.

Forfeiture

It may become necessary to forfeit shares, if the articles so permit, because of non-payment of calls made by the directors on shares offered by companies for subscription on a partly paid basis. In this situation, it is important to ensure strict compliance with the requirements of the company's articles since, if these are not followed, the forfeiture could be declared invalid. The power is rarely exercised in practice, and it is recommended that legal advice should be taken before setting up forfeiture arrangements. When the shares have been forfeited, the person concerned ceases to be a member of the company and the forfeiture should be entered in the register of members.

Subject to the articles, a forfeiture of shares may be cancelled if the call should subsequently be received (with or without interest), assuming that at that time, the shares have not been sold by the directors under the powers given to the company in its articles of association (e.g. Public Model Article 60(4)).

To protect the company where forfeited shares are sold, a statutory declaration on the lines set out in Public Model Article 61 should be sworn. It should be noted that forfeiture does not apply in the case of failure to pay instalments on shares (see above), since the shares would have been issued as fully paid to the custodian bank.

Procedure

The following is the company secretarial procedure to follow in connection with the forfeiture of shares:

1. Send a reminder letter to the relevant shareholders within seven days of the due date for payment requesting that payment be made immediately and that interest may be charged from the due date for the payment.
2. Send a second reminder if no payment is received after seven days.
3. If after a further period of seven days, the amounts remain unpaid, send a final warning notice by recorded delivery requesting payment with interest not earlier than 14 days from the date of the notice and stating that in the event of non-payment by the specified date, the shares will be liable to be forfeited.
4. If the amounts continue to be unpaid, the directors pass a resolution without further notice which includes the names of the members and the numbers of

shares held by each shareholder which are forfeited, and giving authority to the directors to sell or reissue the forfeited shares (see precedent 41).

5 When the resolution has been passed, send a notification of the forfeiture by recorded delivery to the shareholders concerned requesting surrender of their share certificates or, if appropriate, allotment letters or letters of acceptance.
6 Amend the register of members to remove the shares that have been forfeited and place the appropriate shares to the credit of a 'forfeited shares' account.
7 Sell or reissue the shares, debit the forfeited shares account and credit the account of the purchaser of the shares in the register of members with the number of shares purchased.
8 A note should be made in the company's balance sheet or annual return of any forfeited shares remaining unissued at the time of preparation of the balance sheet or annual return.
9 The articles may allow the directors to accept surrender of shares. This power can be used only to avoid the formal forfeiture procedure, and can be accepted only if the shares are liable to forfeiture. Surrender of shares may not be used to avoid an uncalled liability on partly paid shares.
10 Any member whose shares have been forfeited is still liable to pay the unpaid amount, although the directors may waive such liability in full or in part, or may seek to recover such sums and need not take into account the value of the shares on forfeiture or any proceeds from their sale.

Company's lien on its shares

As well as rights to forfeiture, the articles of most companies (e.g. Public Model Articles 52 and 53) give the company a lien on its shares and on dividends payable thereon for all money due in respect of the shares. The lien would be enforced by sale of the member's shares after they had been given due notice of the debt owing to the company which remained unpaid, the notice being given in a similar manner to that described above in the case of forfeiture. If the amount realised by the sale exceeds the amount of debt, the surplus must be paid to the shareholder upon the surrender of the share certificate. Additionally, the lien can be used only for amounts owed by a shareholder as a shareholder and not for debts incurred in another capacity, i.e. commercial debt.

It should be noted that a public company can create a charge on its own shares only in respect of amounts payable on partly paid shares, unless it lends money or gives credit during the normal course of business. A private company that has re-registered as a public company may have a charge over fully paid shares provided the charge was registered prior to its re-registration.

Exercise of subscription rights and warrants

The company secretarial procedure for the exercise of subscription rights and warrants is similar to that which applies in the case of convertible loan stock, but additional matters require attention, as follows.

1 The cash received for shares subscribed is recorded and banked.
2 New loan stock certificates without the subscription rights are prepared and sent out with the share certificates.
3 The register of holders of the loan stock should be divided into two parts, one containing holders who still possess subscription rights exercisable at some future date and the other part the names of holders of loan stock to which subscription rights are no longer attached. If the loan stock is Listed, there will be two prices on the Stock Exchange: one for the stock which still has subscription rights attached and the other for the stock on which the subscription rights have been exercised.
4 A return of allotments on Form SH01 must be prepared and sent to the Registrar of Companies.

In the case of the exercise of warrants to subscribe for shares, a similar procedure will be followed as in the case of the exercise of subscription rights attached to loan stock, but there is no need to issue new warrant certificates since, once the right under it has been exercised, it is cancelled. Balance certificates for warrants, however, may be required if the holder does not exercise the whole of their rights, and some rights remain exercisable at a future date.

Bonus issues

A capitalisation issue is often referred to as a **bonus issue**, and is referred to as such by the Act. This is misleading, however, since the total value of a member's holding in shares of the company will not change because of the issue of 'bonus shares'. All that happens is that the member has more shares of a lower value. A capitalisation issue is often used to make shares with a high value easier to sell or to improve the ratio between retained profit and capital when securing loan finance. For a private company proposing to re-register as a public company, it is an ideal way to ensure that the minimum capital requirement is met without requiring the shareholders to inject additional funds to the company. The following procedures should be followed by private and unlisted companies. There are additional requirements for Listed companies set out in the *Listing Rules* considered in Chapter 16. The capitalisation issue may be made out of distributable profit, the share premium account or the revaluation account, and requires approval of the members by ordinary resolution.

1 Ensure that the articles permit the issue of bonus shares, that the directors have authority to allot additional shares in terms of s. 549 and, if the company has an authorised share capital, that there are sufficient unissued shares. If any of these requirements is lacking, the appropriate resolutions will need to be added to the notice of the general meeting being issued to approve the bonus issue.
2 Convene a board meeting to recommend the bonus issue to the shareholders (see precedent 54), to determine the basis of the issue and the method for dealing with fractions, if any. The directors must also decide whether the allotment will be renounceable by the existing members in favour of any third parties. For a private company, it is not normally desirable for the right to bonus shares to be renounceable other than to existing shareholders, except under strictly controlled conditions. It should be noted that the holding of any members not taking up their rights will be diluted and the aggregate value of their shares will fall. The directors will also convene an extraordinary general meeting to approve the necessary resolution(s).
3 Following the board meeting, the company secretary prepares, signs and issues a notice convening a general meeting, enclosing proxy forms if wished. The meeting will require 14 days' notice (s. 307). A private company may authorise the resolutions using the written resolution procedure (see Chapter 8).
4 Once the members have approved the issue, letters of allotment or renounceable letters of allotment, as appropriate, are issued (see precedent 55). In the case of renounceable allotments, it will be necessary to wait for registration of any renouncements, following which a directors' meeting must approve the final allotment of shares and approve the issue of share certificates evidencing the additional shares. Form SH01 must be filed with the Registrar within one month of the date of issue of the shares. Where amendments to the articles, an increase in authorised capital or an increase in the directors' authority to allot shares are also necessary, appropriate resolutions and forms should be filed within 15 days of the general meeting, together with a reprint of the articles incorporating the changes (s. 18).

Issue of debenture stock

The issues in relation to public issues of shares (see Chapter 15) apply equally in the case of a public issue of debenture stock and, subject to the provisions of the trust deed, arrangements for the transfer, payment of interest, meetings of holders, etc. will also be similar. There are additional requirements contained in the Prospectus Rules to be met if the debenture stock is to be Listed.

A trust deed to secure the issue of debenture stock will usually cover:

1 details of the stock, terms of issue, payment of principal and interest, any conversion rights and stock certificates;
2 the provisions constituting the charges of assets of the company in favour of the trustee, stipulating the events on which the security becomes enforceable;

3 the trustees' powers to concur with the company in dealings with the charged assets;
4 covenants by the company in relation to its business and to the charged assets;
5 the remuneration of the trustees;
6 where a floating charge is constituted, a prohibition on the issue of any other security ranking ahead of the stock without the consent of the holder; and
7 schedules to the trust deed containing the form of stock certificate, the detailed conditions of redemption in whole or in part by drawings or purchase and of any conversion rights, regulations with regard to the register of holders, provisions governing the transfer and transmission of the stock, and regulations governing meetings of holders of the stock.

If the debenture stock is Listed, the reverse of the certificate will have printed on it a summary of the conditions rather than the full conditions, unless this is prohibited by the trust deed. The holder of debenture stock is entitled to be supplied with a copy of the trust deed at their request on payment of a fee (s. 749).

The trust deed for Listed companies that intend that the debt security will also be Listed must contain the details set out in the *Prospectus Rules* and *Listing Rules*. These include:

- repayment dates;
- conversion rights;
- rights to attend and vote at meetings;
- rights of transfer;
- the fact that if the security is unsecured it must be designated as 'unsecured';
- appointment and powers of the trustees; and
- power to forfeit unclaimed interest, not to be used until 12 years from the date of payment.

Conversion of loan stock

The company secretary or the company's registrar will be concerned with the proper procedure for dealing with applications from holders to exercise their conversion rights. The following is a summary of the procedure to be followed:

1 Send a letter prior to each conversion date in each year to those holders of the loan stock who have not yet converted, reminding them of the opportunity to convert into ordinary shares (see precedent 63). Enclose a form of nomination and acceptance to convert or instruct them that if they wish to convert, they should complete the form printed on the reverse of the convertible loan stock certificate. Where the company is a Listed company, the circular reminding holders of the loan stock of their conversion rights should follow the format set out in the *Listing Rules*. If this format is followed, approval from the FCA is not required, although two copies of the circular must be submitted to the

FCA no later than their issue to the holders of the loan stock (*LR 9.6.1*). If the circular is not in the prescribed format, approval will be required and two draft copies of the circular together with the documents required by *LR 13.2.4* must be submitted to the FCA at least ten days prior to the intended date of publication (*LR 13.2.5*). Once agreed, two copies of the final version must be submitted to the FCA, as above.

2 Unless the board has delegated its powers, submit the documents to be approved by the board.
3 The circular and form of nomination and acceptance must be sent to the holders of the loan stock.
4 On receipt of loan stock certificates from holders, check that the form of acceptance, or the notice of conversion on the back, has been properly completed and is accompanied by a completed form of nomination and acceptance if the holder has nominated another person to receive the allotment of shares.
5 When the last day for the receipt of notice of conversion has passed, notify the FCA (if the stock is Listed) and the trustee for the holders of loan stock of the amount of stock converted and the number of ordinary shares to be allotted.
6 The board or an allotment committee of the directors formally allot the shares to the holders of the loan stock who have converted, or to their nominees if they have nominated another person to receive the shares arising out of the conversion. The certificates relating to the loan stock converted are cancelled. If the company has a common seal or a security seal, the share certificates and balance certificates are sealed. The certificates are sent with any remittance for fractions of loan stock that have been redeemed. The company will typically retain fractional remittances of less than £5.
7 Prepare the new share certificates or arrange for CREST accounts to be credited for those members holding shares in uncertificated form, together with any balance certificates for unconverted loan stock and cheques drawn for any amounts for fractions.
8 (*Listed, AIM and NEX companies only*) Apply for the new shares to be Listed and admitted to trading as appropriate.
9 Make the necessary entries in the register of members and loan stock register.
10 Within one month of the allotment, a return of allotments must be delivered to the Registrar of Companies on Form SH01.

Redemption of debentures

Although debentures may be reissued (s. 739), this is unusual. In practice, debentures and debenture stock are redeemable not later than a fixed future date. The title of the stock will give the date of redemption, e.g. '5% Mortgage Debenture Stock 2019/2029', in which case the whole of the stock outstanding is redeemable between specific dates in 2019 and 2029, usually at par, but possibly with a small premium.

The company should give notice of its intention to redeem the stock to every holder. The money for the redemption may come from a new issue of securities, out of profits or out of a combination of the two. Where redemption is out of profits of the company, the proceeds will usually have come from a sinking fund or similar arrangement. It is not unusual for the trust deed to provide for partial redemptions of the stock during the course of its life in advance of the final redemption date, by making annual drawings or by making market purchases at prices not exceeding those laid down in the trust deed. In addition to funding any redemption out of distributable profit or the issue of new shares, a private company may redeem debentures out of capital subject to the provisions of s. 709.

The procedure for the redemption of loan stocks and debentures is similar to the procedure for the redemption of redeemable shares issued by the company under the provisions of ss. 684–689.

Where debentures or debenture stock, secured by a charge over the company's property, are redeemed or converted in whole or in part, a memorandum of satisfaction that the property ceases to be affected by the charge may be filed with the Registrar of Companies, signed on behalf of the company and the chargee (s. 872). Although this procedure is not obligatory, it is in the best interests of the company for charges to be deleted from the public register immediately they are satisfied in whole or in part, to avoid misleading any banks or other creditors who would otherwise form an unduly adverse view of the company's credit. The appropriate entries in the company's own register of charges should also be made for any legacy charges contained in the company's own register of charges.

Financial assistance by a public company for the purchase of its own shares

Unless provided for in the Act, it is not lawful for a public company to provide financial assistance for the purchase of its own shares or the shares of its holding company whether at the same time as the acquisition of the shares or before (s. 678). Financial assistance is very widely defined as:

1 financial assistance by way of gift;
2 financial assistance given by way of guarantee, security or indemnity, other than an indemnity in respect of the indemnifier's own neglect or default, or by way of waiver or release;
3 financial assistance by way of loan or other agreement under which any of the obligations of the person giving the assistance are to be fulfilled at a time when in accordance with the agreement any obligation of another party remains unfulfilled or by way of novation of or assignment of rights arising under such loan or agreement; or

4 any other financial assistance given by a company, the net assets of which are thereby reduced by a material extent or which has no net assets (s. 677).

Various transactions not subject to the general prohibition of s. 678, including distribution of assets by way of lawful dividend, distribution on a winding-up, allotment of bonus shares or the redemption or repurchase by a company of its own shares, are set out in s. 681.

Financial assistance is not prohibited by s. 682 where:

1 the lending of money is part of the company's ordinary business and the loan is made in the ordinary course of business; or
2 the loan is given in good faith for the purposes of an employee share scheme or where the loan is made to an employee, but not a director, in good faith for the purpose of acquiring shares in the company or its holding company.

The relaxation of s. 678 provided by s. 682 is only available to a public company to the extent that its net assets are not reduced or, if they are reduced, that the payment is made out of distributable profit.

Financial assistance by private companies

The restriction on private companies providing financial assistance for the purchase of their own shares was repealed on 1 October 2008. Private companies are not permitted to provide financial assistance for the acquisition of shares in their public parent company. A subsidiary that is a public company may not provide financial assistance for the acquisition of shares in its private parent company.

14 – Purchase and redemption of shares

Introduction

A company may purchase its own shares that were not issued as redeemable shares provided that the purchase is authorised by ordinary resolution of the shareholders (ss. 690, 693(1)).

A private company may make a purchase of its own shares out of capital pursuant to s. 692(1ZA) and, if authorised by its articles of association, where the aggregate purchase price does not exceed the lower of £15,000 or 5% of the nominal value of the issued share capital in any financial year.

There are, however, certain procedural requirements to be followed. Generally, the procedures are similar to those applying when a company purchases its redeemable shares on the market. Unlike with redemption, the consideration for the purchase must be paid on completion and cannot be deferred or left outstanding on a loan account (s. 691(2)). However, for purposes of or pursuant to an employee share scheme, a private company is allowed to pay for its own shares in instalments with no time limits imposed (s. 691(3)).

It is advisable for a company contemplating purchasing its own shares to take legal advice at the outset. One of the points that arises is that if the amount paid by the company for the purchase of its shares exceeds the issue price of the shares, on general principle the excess is treated as a distribution by the company and is taxable as income in the hands of the vendor. A tax voucher should be issued in respect of the excess. If the company is not a Listed company or the subsidiary of a Listed company, s. 219 of the Income and Corporation Taxes Act 1988 (ICTA1988) contains a provision to the effect that the excess will not be treated as an income distribution, but will be treated as part of the capital proceeds of the sale of the shares.

Advance clearance that a proposed purchase will be treated in this way can be obtained from HM Revenue & Customs, but it is recommended that the company's taxation advisers are consulted before taking any action in this respect (ICTA1988 s. 225). A public company, whether Listed or not, may only purchase its own shares out of distributable profit or the proceeds of a new issue of shares made solely for that purpose.

Procedure for off-market purchases

The requirements for purchases by a company of its own shares are contained in ss. 694 and 701. Purchases would be either an off-market purchases or a market purchase. The latter is a purchase made on a recognised investment exchange (s. 693).

The following procedural steps must be complied with to effect an off-market purchase of shares by a company:

1 An ordinary resolution of the company must authorise the terms of the proposed contract of purchase before the company enters into the contract (s. 694(2)) (see precedents 57 and 58). The purchase may also be made under a contingent purchase whereby a company becomes entitled or obliged to purchase its own shares, provided this has been authorised by ordinary resolution. Authorities may be varied, revoked or renewed by an ordinary resolution. If the articles do not contain authority for the company to purchase its own shares, the articles should be amended by special resolution of the members. However, in the case of a public company, the ordinary resolution confirming or renewing authority for a company to purchase its own shares must specify a date for its expiry, which must be not later than 18 months from the date of passing the resolution (s. 694(5)).

2 The resolution will not be effective unless a copy of the proposed contract of purchase (or a written memorandum of its terms if it is not in writing) is made available for inspection by members of the company at the company's registered office for not less than 15 days prior to the meeting and is available for inspection at the meeting (s. 696). The memorandum must include the names of the members holding the shares to which the contract relates. If it is the contract itself that is available for inspection, it must have annexed to it a written memorandum specifying the names if they do not appear in the contract itself. Similar arrangements must be made in the case of the variation of an existing contract, which also has to be approved by an ordinary resolution. A private company may authorise the purchase of its own shares by written resolution under s. 288. To be valid, a copy of the proposed contract or a memorandum of its terms must be made available to each member no later than the date on which the written resolution is forwarded to them for approval and signature. In practice, it is normal to circulate a copy of the contract or the memorandum of its terms, together with the written resolution for signature and return.

3 The votes of any member whose shares are being repurchased should be disregarded for the purposes of establishing whether there is the necessary majority in favour of the resolution. The resolution will be ineffective if this provision is contravened (s. 698).

4 For the purposes of or pursuant to an employees' share scheme, a company may, by a single ordinary resolution, approve multiple share buyback contracts

in advance (s. 693A) and a private company may, subject to passing a special resolution of the company supported by a solvency statement provided by the directors, make payment for the shares out of capital (s. 720A(1)). As noted above, a private company may also make limited purchases out of capital under the much simpler process permitted by s. 692(1ZA). A copy of the solvency statement must be available to each eligible member whether the special resolution is proposed as a written resolution or at a general meeting of the company. The authority to purchase must specify the maximum number of shares to be acquired and determine the maximum and minimum prices that may be paid for the shares. The authority may be varied, revoked or renewed by an ordinary resolution, and must specify a date on which it is to expire, which must be not later than five years from the date of passing of the resolution. Payment out of capital must be made no earlier than five weeks and no later than seven weeks after the relevant shares are surrendered (s. 723 (1A)).

5 The same provisions as those set out in point 2 above apply to any resolution varying the terms of an existing agreement or the proposed release by the company of its rights to make a purchase under an existing agreement.

Procedure for market purchases by Listed companies

The conditions of the Act in respect of market purchases by a company of its own shares are less stringent than those that apply in the case of off-market purchases. It should be noted, however, that in the case of Listed companies, the requirements of Chapter 12 of the *Listing Rules* will need to be complied with. It will also be necessary to adhere to the best practice guidelines issued by institutional shareholder bodies such as the Investment Association. The following procedural points should be observed.

1 Other than where an existing authority is being renewed, a decision to seek authority for a market purchase must be notified to a regulatory information service (RIS) without delay (*LR 12.4.4*), together with notification of the result of the vote (*LR 12.4.5*). Although only an ordinary resolution is necessary, institutional shareholders have requested that the authority be sought by special resolution. The resolution must stipulate the maximum number of shares that may be purchased and the maximum and minimum purchase prices (see precedent 59).

2 The circular to shareholders must include, where appropriate, those details required by the *Listing Rules* (*LR 13.7.1*) in addition to the usual circular requirements (*LR 13.3*).

3 The circular will require approval by the FCA if the shares are to be acquired from a related party or are in respect of 25% or more of the issued share capital (*LR13.2.3*), unless a tender is made to all holders or the purchase from a related party is without prior agreement and pursuant to a general authority.

4 The company should not purchase shares at any time when the directors would not be free to do so on their own account.
5 Institutional shareholder bodies have issued guidance that they will support market purchases of up to 5%, and that purchases of up to 10% will be supported where circumstances make this appropriate. Proposals for the purchase of more than 10% are likely to be resisted unless specific proposals are put to shareholders for approval.
6 Purchases of more than 15% (excluding treasury shares) must be by way of a tender offer (*LR 12.4.2*). Purchases of less than 15% may be by way of a general authority, provided the price is not higher than 5% above the average market value over the previous five business days.
7 Details of any purchases made must be notified to a RIS no later than 7.30am on the business day following the purchase.

The ordinary resolution conferring, varying, revoking or renewing authority to make a market purchase of the company's own shares must be filed with the Registrar of Companies within 15 days of it being passed (ss. 30 and 701(8)).

The possible need to send tax vouchers to the vendors of the shares purchased should not be overlooked as the purchase of shares will usually be treated as a taxable distribution with tax payable on any excess consideration over the original issue price. Specialist advice on the tax consequences of any share purchases should be taken.

Procedural requirements for both off- and on-market purchases

Form SH03 must be filed with the Registrar of Companies, duly stamped, within 28 days of the delivery of the shares purchased by the company (s. 708). The return includes information on the number, class and nominal value of the shares purchased, the date of delivery to the company and, in the case of a public company, the aggregate amount paid by the company for the shares to which the return relates, together with the maximum and minimum prices paid. Stamp duty is payable by the company on the consideration paid by it on the purchase of its shares at the usual rate (currently 0.5%, rounded up to the nearest £5). A copy of a contract to purchase the company's shares (and a copy of any variation of it), or a memorandum of the terms if it is not in writing, must be kept at the registered office or SAIL (Single Alternative Inspection Location) address, if any, of the company from the conclusion of the contract for a period of ten years, commencing with the date on which the purchase of the shares was completed. This document must be kept open for inspection by any member without charge and, in the case of a public company, it may be inspected by any other person, also without charge (s. 702).

Details of any shares purchased must be included in the directors' report (Part 2 of Schedule 7 to the Large & Medium Sized Companies and Groups (Accounts and Reports) Regulations 2008 (SI 2008/410)) together, in the case of a Listed company, with details of any existing authority to purchase shares (*LR 9.8.6*). An amount equal to the nominal value of the shares purchased must be transferred to a capital redemption reserve and any premium paid in excess of the nominal value written off against distributable profits (s. 733).

Treasury shares

All companies may acquire their own shares and hold these in treasury (s. 724(3)). Unlike the provisions relating to purchase of own shares (see page 231), shares purchased under the treasury shares provisions are not cancelled on purchase but may be retained, sold or cancelled (ss. 727, 729).

The procedural steps for purchases into treasury are the same as for purchases of own shares, with the following additional provisions.

1. There is no maximum number of shares that may be held in treasury set out in the Companies Act. Companies considering a substantial purchase of shares into treasury will need to consider the impact on liquidity and notifiable interests of members, and the potential to trigger offers under the Takeover Code.
2. The company should not sell shares from treasury or transfer treasury shares to an employee share scheme at any time when the directors would not be free to do so on their own account.
3. Details of any allotments by way of capitalisation issue or the sale or transfer to an employee share scheme, or cancellation of treasury shares, must be notified to a RIS as soon as possible and no later than 7.30am on the first business day following the event (*LR 12.6.3, 4*).
4. Once the company has purchased the shares to be held in treasury, a return on Form SH03 must be submitted to the Registrar, stating the number of shares and the class of shares, together with the nominal value of the shares and the date on which they were repurchased (s. 707). The repurchase of shares to be held in treasury by a company is subject to stamp duty, the duty being payable on the consideration and not the nominal value at the rate of 0.5% (rounded up to the nearest £5).
5. If the shares are subsequently cancelled, sold or transferred, Form SH04 or SH05 must be filed (ss. 728, 730).
6. Shares held in treasury may be sold for cash, transferred to satisfy claims under employee share schemes or cancelled. Shares held in treasury have no voting or dividend rights but may take up rights in respect of bonus issues and may be redeemed if the shares are redeemable (s. 726).

Redeemable shares

Issue of redeemable shares

Redeemable shares, or shares that are liable to be redeemed at the option of the company or of the shareholder, may, if so authorised by the company's articles of association, be issued by a company limited by shares or limited by guarantee and having a share capital (ss. 684–689).

Redeemable shares may be issued by a company only if the following conditions are satisfied.

1 There must be provision in a public company's articles authorising it to issue redeemable shares. Private company articles may exclude or restrict the issue of redeemable shares.
2 At the time of issue of redeemable shares, the company must have other shares that are not redeemable (s. 684(4)).
3 Redeemable shares may not be redeemed unless they are fully paid (s. 686(1)).
4 The terms of redemption must provide for payment on redemption unless the terms of redemption specified at the time of allotment provide for payment at a later date (s. 686(2), (3)).
5 The redemption money must come only out of distributable profits or out of the proceeds of a fresh issue of shares made for the purpose. Private companies, however, subject to certain conditions, may make a redemption out of capital (s. 687).

Premium on redemption of shares

Any premium over the nominal value payable on redemption of redeemable shares must normally be paid out of the company's distributable profits (s. 687). If, however, the redeemable shares were issued at a premium, the premium payable on redemption may be paid from:

- the proceeds of a fresh issue of shares made for the purpose of the redemption up to an amount equal to the aggregate of the premiums received by the company on the issue of the shares redeemed; or
- the current amount of the company's share premium account (including any sum transferred to that account in respect of premiums on the new shares), whichever is the less. In this case, the company's share premium account must be reduced by the amount of the premium paid on the redemption out of the proceeds of the fresh issue (s. 687(3)). A private company may redeem redeemable shares out of capital (s. 687(1)) (see page 241).

Drawings of redeemable shares

A company's articles may require shares to be redeemed by a specified date, and in these circumstances, it is usual to establish a sinking fund for this purpose.

The fund is normally operated by annual drawings of shares to be redeemed at the redemption price, or by purchases on the market if they can be bought there at a lower price. If making market purchases, this should be done prior to the date on which the annual drawing would normally take place. It is much easier for the company to meet its target for annual redemptions by making market purchases.

The arrangements for making drawings are complicated and more costly since, in order to ensure impartiality, it is usual to arrange for the drawing to be supervised by two or more professional persons such as a solicitor, a chartered accountant or a notary public. Of course, if the price of shares to be redeemed is higher on the market than the redemption price, it is appropriate to effect the annual instalment of redemption by a drawing.

Where purchases are made on the market, the company's brokers are instructed to purchase the number of shares required for the annual instalment of redemption. However, if the price is favourable on the market, there is nothing to stop the company from continuing to make market purchases at prices lower than the redemption price to cover future annual instalments of redemption.

For a traded company, the process for undertaking a drawing would be undertaken by the company's share registrar. The following is a summary of the procedural points that arise where a drawing is to be undertaken:

1. A complete shareholder listing as at the record date is prepared.
2. Depending on the amount of shares to be repurchased, the holdings are broken down into parcels of (say) 5,000 shares, and each parcel is allocated a unique reference number. Where a particular shareholder's holding is not an exact multiple of 5,000, the balance is consolidated into composite parcels. Accordingly, a holder with 15,000 shares would have three parcels and a holder with 12,500 will have two parcels and the balance forming part of a third.
3. A schedule showing the allocation of the parcels and composite parcels among the shareholders is prepared and reconciled.
4. Tickets are prepared for each parcel, showing the reference number, to allow the draw to take place.
5. The date and place of drawing are arranged. The requirements of the articles must be observed in regard to the manner in which the drawing is to be made, e.g. in the presence of a notary public or solicitor.
6. (*Listed, AIM and NEX companies only*) A RIS should be advised of the date of drawing, the record date for the drawing, the number of shares to be drawn and the redemption price.
7. Holders whose shares have been drawn should be sent a formal notice of redemption, usually three to four weeks prior to the date the redemption payment is due (see precedent 56).
8. It is no longer possible to transfer the shares which have been drawn for redemption, and brokers instructed to sell shares in Listed companies should ascertain from the list posted by the FCA that they have not been drawn for redemption.
9. A letter giving details of the procedure for redemption and enclosing the form of payment authority and discharge form to be returned with the appropriate share certificate(s). The letter will explain that if the shares being redeemed are only part of the holding, and the shareholder cannot give certificate(s) covering the exact number, they should send certificate(s) to the nearest

number over the number of shares drawn for redemption and that a balance certificate for the excess (i.e. the shares not redeemed) will be sent to them. It will also explain that no further dividends will be paid on the shares redeemed.

10 A redemption account is opened and the necessary funds transferred to the account to cover the cheques to be issued.

11 When forms of authority are received from the shareholders, they should be checked to ensure that they have been properly completed and, if the certificate(s) lodged is (are) for more than the number of shares being redeemed, balance certificates should be prepared for issue to the shareholder.

12 Before sending cheques, the payment advice prepared under point 7 above should be checked against the official drawing list. The cheques should be sent out so as to arrive on the due redemption date.

13 Reminders should be sent to shareholders who have not returned their forms.

14 The shareholders' accounts in the register of members are debited with the number of shares redeemed.

15 The secretary formally reports to the board the completion of the redemption following the annual drawing for the sinking fund purpose.

16 Notice of the redemption must be sent to the Registrar of Companies on Form SH02.

17 If the shares redeemed are preference shares, holders will remain entitled to any dividend for the half-year ending on the redemption date and warrants should be prepared for the payment of the preference dividend to be dispatched to the holders in the ordinary way. Payment of the preference dividend should be dealt with quite separately from the payment of the redemption money.

18 If the shares are redeemed at a premium over the nominal value, the amount paid on redemption that exceeds the original issue price will be treated as a taxable distribution. The company should therefore issue a tax voucher to cover the amount of such distribution.

Shares that have been redeemed must be cancelled on redemption, and the amount of the issued share capital is diminished by the nominal value of the shares redeemed. If a company is about to redeem any shares, it may issue shares up to the nominal amount of the shares to be redeemed as if those shares had never been issued. Where redemption takes place wholly or partly out of distributable profits, a transfer must be made to the company's capital redemption reserve (s. 688).

Purchase of redeemable shares

The following summarises the procedure to be followed by Listed companies where the necessary shares to cover the sinking fund redemption instalment have been purchased on the market.

1 The company checks the contract notes received from its brokers in respect of the shares purchased.
2 The FCA must be advised of the number of shares purchased and the number still outstanding (*LR 9.6.4, 12.5.2*).
3 The company secretary arranges to pay the brokers for the shares purchased on the relevant settlement date against the contract notes.
4 Forms of discharge and certificates received from the brokers are checked.
5 If the shares have been purchased cum dividend, the holdings concerned must be withdrawn from the dividend list, since no dividend will be paid on them. If the shares have been purchased ex dividend, no special action is necessary.
6 The entries of the relevant shareholders in the register of members are debited with the shares purchased. These are transferred to a redemption account and on the redemption date, the shares will be utilised for the redemption instalment.

It should be noted that while the above procedure is described as a 'purchase' of redeemable shares, the operation is, in fact, another form of redemption of shares.

Procedure for redemption of loan stock and debentures

The procedure for the redemption of loan stocks and debentures through the operation of a sinking fund is similar to that described above in respect of the drawings of redeemable shares and purchase of redeemable shares. Debentures and loan stocks may be redeemed by annual drawings or by purchases on the market in order to meet the sinking fund requirements.

Redemption or purchases by private companies out of capital

As noted above, purchases by a public company of its own shares may be made only out of distributable profits or the proceeds of a fresh issue of shares.

In the case of private companies, however, ss. 709–723 provide a procedure to effect purchases or redemptions of shares out of capital. Very stringent and complicated additional procedures have to be complied with, to ensure the position of creditors is protected together with the appropriate protect of members rights especially where there are multiple share class each with differing rights or priority of rights to profit or capital.

The amount of the payment that may be made out of capital is known as the 'permissible capital payment'. The amount of the permissible capital payment is the amount to be paid for the shares after deduction of all distributable profits and the amount of any funds raised by the issue of new shares. Thus, no capital payment may be made until all available profit has been used. Capital is defined as any payment made other than out of distributable profit or the proceeds of a new issue. Accordingly, the use of funds raised by way of a loan will be treated as a capital payment (s. 710). The additional procedural steps to be followed in the case of the purchase or redemption by a private company of its own shares out of capital are contained in s. 713, as follows.

1 A statement must be made by the directors that specifies the amount of the permissible capital payment for the shares and the directors that must state that having made a full enquiry into the affairs of the company, they have formed the opinion that once the payment out of capital has been made, there are no grounds on which the company would then be unable to pay its debts and that, in the year following the payment, the company will be able to carry on its business as a going concern and pay its debts as they fall due. In stating their opinion the directors must take into account any contingent or prospective liabilities of the company at the time that the statement is made (s. 714(3), see precedent 60).
2 An auditor's report must be attached to the statutory declaration confirming that: the auditors have enquired into the company's state of affairs; the amount specified in the declaration as the permissible capital payment for the shares has been properly determined in accordance with s. 714(6); and the auditors do not consider that any opinion expressed by the directors in the declaration is unreasonable. A company that qualifies as small and has taken advantage of the exemption from appointing auditors will need to appoint auditors and have their accounts audited before this statement can be given (s. 714(5)).
3 A special resolution of the company must be passed on or within one week of the statutory declaration, approving the proposed payment out of capital, and copies of the statutory declaration must be available for inspection by members of the company at the meeting at which the resolution is passed (see precedents 57 and 61). A member whose shares are the subject of the special resolution may not vote on the resolution.
4 Publicity must be given to the proposed payment out of capital in the following manner:
   a. Within one week of the passing of the special resolution, a public notice must be published in the *London Gazette* or *Edinburgh Gazette*, together with a notice in a national newspaper or a notice in writing to each of the creditors of the company, stating that the company has approved a payment out of capital for the purpose of acquiring its own shares by redemption or purchase (see precedent 62).
   b. Within one week of the passing of the special resolution, copies of the statutory declaration and auditor's report must be filed with the Registrar of Companies, to be received not later than the date on which the public notice is given.
5 From the date of the public notice to the end of the fifth week following the date on which the special resolution was passed, the statutory declaration and auditor's report must be kept at the company's registered office and be open for inspection by any member or creditor of the company without charge.

6 Payment out of capital must be made within the period commencing five weeks after the date of passing the special resolution and terminating seven weeks after the date of the special resolution.
7 Up to the end of the fifth week following the date of passing the special resolution, any member of the company (other than a member who voted in favour of the resolution) and any creditor may apply to the court for the resolution to be cancelled on Form SH16 (s. 721). If such an application is made, notice must be given to the Registrar of Companies immediately on Form SH17. On the making of a court order, a copy must be filed with the Registrar within 15 days of it being made or a longer period, if the court allows (s. 722). The court has wide powers in considering any such application and may alter or extend the date or period specified in the resolution or in the Companies Act 2006.
8 For the purposes of or pursuant to an employees' share scheme, only reduced requirements for payment for shares out of capital apply to a private company. Subject to passing a special resolution of the company and supported by a solvency statement provided by the directors, a private company may make payment for the shares out of capital (s. 720A(1)).

The solvency statement must be made not more than 15 days before the date of passing of the special resolution. A copy of the solvency statement must be available to each eligible member whether the special resolution is proposed as a written resolution or at a general meeting of the company. The authority to purchase must specify the maximum number of shares to be acquired and determine the maximum and minimum prices that may be paid for the shares. Within 15 days from the date of passing of the special resolution, a copy of the special resolution, solvency statement, a statement of capital on Form SH03 and a statement of the directors confirming that the solvency statement was made not more than 15 days before the date of the passing of the special resolution and a copy of which was provided to the members must be delivered to the Registrar of Companies (s. 720B). Payment out of capital must be made no earlier than five weeks and no later than seven weeks after the relevant shares are surrendered (s. 723 (1A)).

Simplified procedure for small purchases

Private companies proposing to make small purchases of shares may take advantage of a simplified process under s. 692(1ZA).

To qualify for the simplified process, the company must satisfy the following criteria:

1 the aggregate purchase consideration in any financial year must not exceed the lower of £15,000 or 5% of fully paid share capital at the beginning of the financial year;

2 the articles of association must contain authority for the company to purchase its own shares; and
3 the purchase must be made out of capital.

The following procedural steps must be complied with to effect an off-market purchase of shares by a company under s. 692(1ZA):

1 An ordinary resolution of the company must authorise the terms of the proposed contract of purchase before the company enters into the contract (s. 694(2)) (see precedent 57). The purchase may also be made under a contingent purchase whereby a company becomes entitled or obliged to purchase its own shares, provided this has been authorised by ordinary resolution. Authorities may be varied, revoked or renewed by an ordinary resolution. If the articles do not contain authority for the company to purchase its own shares, the articles should be amended by special resolution of the members.
2 The resolution will not be effective unless a copy of the proposed contract of purchase (or a written memorandum of its terms if it is not in writing) is made available for inspection by members of the company at the company's registered office for not fewer than 15 days prior to the meeting and this is available for inspection at the meeting (s. 696). The memorandum must include the names of the members holding the shares to which the contract relates. If it is the contract itself that is available for inspection, it must have annexed to it a written memorandum specifying the names if they do not appear in the contract itself. Similar arrangements must be made in the case of the variation of an existing contract, which also has to be approved by an ordinary resolution. A private company may authorise the purchase of its own shares by written resolution under s. 288. To be valid, a copy of the proposed contract or a memorandum of its terms must be made available to each member no later than the date on which the written resolution is forwarded to them for approval and signature. In practice, it is normal to circulate a copy of the contract or the memorandum of its terms, together with the written resolution for signature and return.
3 The votes of any member whose shares are being repurchased should be disregarded for the purposes of establishing whether there is the necessary majority in favour of the resolution. The resolution will be ineffective if this provision is contravened (s. 698).

Failure to redeem or purchase shares

A company failing to redeem or purchase its shares under an agreement will not be liable to pay damages if other remedies could be available to the shareholder concerned (s. 735). The position if, at the commencement of the winding-up of the company, any shares have not been redeemed or purchased pursuant to the special resolution is also covered in s. 735.

Capital redemption reserve

Where purchase or redemption of shares is effected out of the company's distributable profits, the nominal value of the shares so redeemed or purchased must be transferred to the company's capital redemption reserve. If part of the redemption or purchase money comes from the proceeds of a fresh issue of shares, the amount transferred to the capital redemption reserve is the aggregate value of the proceeds of the new issue less the nominal value of the shares redeemed or purchased (s. 733).

The capital redemption reserve is treated as part of the capital of the company, but it may be used in connection with allotting fully paid shares to members under a capitalisation issue.

Reduction of share capital

Under s. 641, a limited company having a share capital may reduce its capital:

- in the case of a private company:
  - by special resolution supported by a solvency statement (ss. 642–644); or
  - following a simplified process for small purchases nor exceeding the lower £15,000 or 5% of the nominal value company's fully paid share capital (s. 691(1ZA));
- in the case of either a public or private company by a special resolution confirmed by the court (ss. 645–651).

A specific authorisation in a company's articles of association to reduce its share capital is not required for a capital reduction supported by either a solvency statement or where confirmed by the court. A company will be permitted to reduce its capital unless there is a specific prohibition or restriction in the articles. The following examples of undertaking a reduction are given in s. 641(4):

1. Extinguish or reduce the liability on any of its shares in respect of share capital not paid up.
2. Either with or without extinguishing or reducing liability on any of its shares:
   a. cancel any paid-up share capital which is lost or unrepresented by available assets; or
   b. repay any paid-up share capital in excess of the company's wants.

Following a reduction of capital, by whichever process, there must remain at least one share in issue.

Reduction of capital by private company supported by solvency statement

The Act provides for private companies to reduce their share capital by special resolution of the members, provided the resolution is supported by a solvency statement. No specific authority is required in the articles of association.

The solvency statement must be declared by the directors not more than 15 days prior to the date of the meeting at which the special resolution to authorise the reduction is considered. Where the resolution is not to be put to a general meeting but by way of a written resolution, a copy of the solvency statement must be sent to each member no later than the date of circulating the resolution (s. 642).

The solvency statement requires each director to confirm that, in their opinion, there are no grounds at the date of the statement that the company could not meets its debts and that during the period of 12 months following the statement, the company will be able to pay its debts as they fall due (s. 643).

The reduction of capital may also include a purchase of shares. If this is the case, the purchase of shares must also be approved following the purchase of shares process (see page 244).

The following procedure should be followed to approve the reduction of capital:

1 Convene a directors' meeting to approve giving of the solvency statement, recommending the reduction of capital to members and either to convene a general meeting or to circulate a written resolution to obtain members' approval.
2 Issue notice of general meeting, signed by director or company secretary, on 14 clear days' notice or circulate written resolution for members to consider special resolution(s). Included with the notice or written resolution must be a copy of the solvency statement unless it has been circulated in advance. The special resolution must be approved within 15 days of the date of the directors' solvency statement made under s. 642. See precedent 42 for sample special resolution.
3 Enclose with the notice a form of proxy if desired.
4 If a general meeting is held, ensure a valid quorum is present. The resolution should be put to vote either by show of hands or by poll and to be passed by a 75% majority).
5 Within 15 days of the passing of the resolution, file a copy of the special resolution, solvency statement, statement confirming the solvency statement made within 15 days prior to the resolution and circulated to members and Form SH19 with Companies House, together with filing fee of £10.
6 The reduction becomes effective upon registration of the documents by the Registrar of Companies.
7 Issue consideration cheques if appropriate and cancel share certificates relating to shares reduced. Update register of members. Issue balancing share certificates if appropriate.

Reduction of capital by company supported by court order

This process must be followed by public companies and any private company where a solvency statement cannot be made by the directors.

The initial company secretarial procedures are the same to those followed in a reduction of capital supported by a solvency statement with an appropriately worded resolution. The processes differ following the giving of members authority and relate to the court processes. The company secretary will be required to give an affidavit confirming that the necessary procedures have been followed. Accordingly, the date of issue of the notice, date and timing of meeting should be carefully recorded. Careful attention should be paid to procedural matters at the meeting to ensure that the proceedings cannot be challenged later. If the reduction is being undertaken to reflect a permanent loss of capital or shares no longer represented by assets and the company's share capital is divided into different classes, great care must be taken when deciding which class (if not all) should bear the reduction. While it may appear reasonable for preference shares with a limited right to participate in future profit to bear the reduction, leaving ordinary shares untouched, this is not necessarily the case. In a liquidation, it is the ordinary shares that rank last, rather than the preference shares. It may therefore be 'reasonable' for any loss in value of assets to be borne by the ordinary shares, as if in a liquidation.

Once a company has approved a resolution reducing its share capital, application to the court must be made for an order confirming the reduction (s. 645).

If the proposed reduction includes the diminution of any liability on unpaid share capital or the payment to a shareholder of any paid-up share capital or if directed by the court, any creditor of the company with an admissible claim in winding-up proceedings may object to the proposed reduction. The court will settle a list of creditors entitled to object. This list, depending on the particular circumstances, may be published. After publication, any other creditor may apply to be added to the list or removed from the list. Normally, the company will discharge or make provision for the debt. If, however, the debt in whole or in part is disrupted or the company is unwilling to make a provision, the court has power to appropriate such funds as it thinks fit to meet such claims, as if the company were being wound up by the court.

When the court is satisfied with the arrangements to protect the interests of the creditors and (if relevant) the members, the court will make an order confirming the reduction either as proposed or with any modifications deemed fit.

Where the court confirms the reduction, it may order the company to publish the reasons for the reduction of capital, or it may require the company to add the words 'and reduced' after its name for a specified period (s. 648(3) and (4)). The Registrar, on production of an order of court confirming the reduction of capital and the delivery of a copy of the order and a statement of capital (approved by the court), will register the order and the statement. The statement of capital must state, with respect to the company's share capital as altered by the order:

1 the total number of shares of the company;
2 the aggregate nominal value of those shares; and
3 for each class of shares:
   a. prescribed particulars of the rights attached to the shares;
   b. the total number of shares of that class;
   c. the aggregate nominal value of shares of that class; and
   d. the amount paid up and the amount (if any) unpaid on each share (whether on account of the nominal value of the share or by way of premium).

The resolution for reducing share capital, as confirmed by the court order, takes effect:

1 in the case of a reduction that forms part of a compromise or arrangement sanctioned by the court on delivery of the order and statement of capital to the Registrar, or if the court so orders, on the registration of the order and statement of capital; or
2 in any other case, on the registration of the order and statement of capital.

When the reduction takes place, the Registrar issues a certificate of registration in respect of the order and statement of capital. The certificate is conclusive evidence that the provisions of the Companies Act 2006 have been complied with and that the company's share capital is as set out in the statement of capital.

Where a public company proposes a reduction of share capital that will cause its issued share capital to fall below the authorised minimum (£50,000), the Registrar will not register the order unless directed to do so by the court, or unless the company re-registers as a private company. The court may authorise the company to be re-registered as a private company without a special resolution of the members having to be approved. If it does, the court must specify, in the order, the changes to the company's name and articles to be made in connection with the re-registration. The company can then be re-registered as a private company if an application to that effect is delivered to the Registrar along with a copy of the court's order, notice of the company's name and a copy of the articles of association as altered by the court order. A re-registration fee is also payable (£20 or same-day fee £50).

Reduction of capital by company using simplified process

Private companies proposing to make small value purchases of shares may take advantage of a simplified process. Unlike reduction of capital supporting by a solvency or one confirmed by the court, the simplified process requires authority in the articles of association.

The aggregate purchase consideration in any financial year must not exceed the lower of £15,000 or 5% of fully paid share capital, at the beginning of the financial year. The purchase must be made out of capital. As this type of reduction involves a payment to members, the necessary authority to approve a purchase of shares must be sought.

The following procedure should be followed to approve the reduction of capital:

1 Convene a directors' meeting recommending the reduction of capital and purchase of shares to members and either to convene a general meeting or to circulate a written resolution to obtain members' approval. Ensure a copy of the proposed contract of purchase (or a written memorandum of its terms if it is not in writing) is made available for inspection by members of the company at the company's registered office for not less than 15 days prior to the meeting and is available for inspection at the meeting.
2 Issue notice of general meeting, signed by director or company secretary, on 14 clear days' notice or circulate written resolution for members to consider special resolution(s). Included with the notice or written resolution must be a copy of the solvency statement unless it has been circulated in advance. The special resolution must be approved within 15 days of the date of the directors' solvency statement made under s. 642. See precedent 42 for sample special resolution.
3 Enclose with the notice a form of proxy if desired.
4 If a general meeting is held, ensure a valid quorum is present. The resolution should be put to vote either by show of hands or by poll and be approved by a 50% majority. The votes of any member whose shares are being repurchased should be disregarded for the purposes of establishing whether there is the necessary majority in favour of the resolution meeting.
5 Within 15 days of the passing of the resolution, file a copy of the ordinary resolutions and Form SH19 with Companies House, together with filing fee of £10.

The reduction becomes effective upon registration of the documents by the Registrar of Companies.

Issue consideration cheques if appropriate and cancel share certificates relating to shares reduced. Update register of members. Issue balancing share certificates if appropriate.

The purchase may also be made under a contingent purchase whereby a company becomes entitled or obliged to purchase its own shares, provided this has been authorised by ordinary resolution. Authorities may be varied, revoked or renewed by an ordinary resolution. If the articles do not contain authority for the company to purchase its own shares, the articles should be amended by special resolution of the members.

The memorandum of terms made available for inspection must include the names of the members holding the shares to which the contract relates. If it is the contract itself that is available for inspection, it must have annexed to it a written memorandum specifying the names if they do not appear in the contract itself.

Similar arrangements must be made in the case of the variation of an existing contract, which also has to be approved by an ordinary resolution.

A private company may authorise the purchase of its own shares by written resolution under s. 288. To be valid, a copy of the proposed contract or a memorandum of its terms must be made available to each member no later than the date on which the written resolution is forwarded to them for approval and signature. In practice, it is normal to circulate a copy of the contract or the memorandum of its terms, together with the written resolution for signature and return.

15 – Floating, listing and admission to trading

Introduction

Where a company requires significant additional, long-term funding, there are four main alternatives available:

1 long-term loans from a bank;
2 additional funding from existing members;
3 funding from a venture capital provider; and/or
4 additional funding from new shareholders.

Although company directors have a duty to manage the affairs of a company limited by shares for the benefit of its shareholders, they have no obligation to make provision for shareholders to be able to sell their shares.

However, if a company intends to raise additional funding from the public and/or institutional investors, this process will be more likely to succeed if the investors have an 'exit', so that there is a reasonable expectation that the investors can realise their investment at a future date.

This exit can be provided if the company buys back its shares, if it goes into liquidation or if it is sold to another company. However, these routes are not suitable for the majority of public companies, since they would not enable shares to be traded on a regular basis, allowing original investors to realise their investment or new investors to buy shares in the company at a time or times of their own choosing.

For many public companies, therefore, an appropriate exit route is provided by having the shares officially Listed and admitted to trading on either the Main Market, operated by the London Stock Exchange plc, or NEX Exchange Main Board, operated by NEX Exchange Limited. Both of these are Recognised Investment Exchanges (RIEs), which is the highest level of recognition under FSMA2000. As an alternative to listing, companies can have their shares admitted to trading on either AIM (Alternative Investment Market) or NEX Exchange Growth Market, which are Multi-lateral Trading Facilities (MTFs)) operated by the London Stock Exchange plc and NEX Exchange, respectively; these have lower levels of regulation than either the Main Market and NEX Exchange Main Board, and are comparatively cheaper to join. For smaller companies requiring an ability for members to buy and sell shares but no need for fund-raising, there are other opportunities for trading shares on trading platforms that are neither RIEs nor ERMs. The process of having shares admitted to trading, whether via a listing or not, is referred to as having the shares floated.

This chapter looks at the role of the Financial Conduct Authority (FCA), the regulatory environment, including the *Listing Rules*, and the process by which companies may be Listed and admitted to either the Main Market or the NEX Exchange Main Board, or to have their shares traded on AIM or NEX Exchange Growth Market.

There are, of course, both advantages and disadvantages of having a company's shares admitted to a public market, and the directors and existing members need to consider these carefully before embarking on the process to join one of the markets.

Table 15.1: Advantages and disadvantages of having a company's shares admitted to a public market

Advantages	*Disadvantages*
Access to the funding	Share price influenced by market conditions over which the company has no control
Providing a market for trading in the shares	Loss of control for existing management
Enables employee participation in ownership via employee share schemes	Continuing obligations and disclosure regimes require significant management time, policing and controls
Ability to acquire other businesses for paper (shares) rather than needing cash	Directors will lose autonomy and become accountable to external investors
Improved perception of financial strength and stability	Professional fees will increase as professional advisers, PR companies, share registrars, etc. will be required
Corporate governance regimes required of traded companies tend to improve management systems and controls	Increase in directors' responsibilities
Raising the profile of the company	

Listing and the FCA

Prior to May 2000, the London Stock Exchange was the 'competent authority' and exercised its powers under three EU directives regulating the admission of securities to official listing in the UK. Responsibility for these functions, exercised by the LSE under the guise of the UKLA, was transferred to the Financial Services Authority, and in 2013 to the Financial Conduct Authority. References to the UKLA are now references to the FCA (*LR 1.1.1*).

As the competent authority, the FCA establishes the listing rules for admission of securities to listing, the continuing obligations of the issuers of those securities and the enforcement of those continuing obligations.

Following the transfer, applications for admission to listing (i.e. for securities to be admitted to the Official List) must be made to the FCA, and a separate application must be made to either the London Stock Exchange plc or NEX Exchange Limited for those securities to be admitted to trading on either the Main Market or the NEX Exchange Main Market. The procedures for seeking a listing are set out in the *Listing Rules*.

These rules and the codes are not technically 'law'. The sanction for their breach is disciplinary action against the company and, ultimately, removal from the Official List so that the company's share price is no longer quoted on an exchange. Following implementation of the Financial Services and Markets Act 2000 (FSMA2000), breaches of the listing rules are now brought within the scope of civil prosecution, and the FCA has power to impose unlimited fines on companies, directors or other individuals breaching the rules.

The UK Listing Rules

To be Listed on the Official List, the company must comply with the *Listing Rules*, established by the FCA and amended from time to time. The *Listing Rules* contain the requirements and procedures for obtaining a listing, the continuing obligations of the company and its officers once the company is admitted to listing, and the circumstances giving rise to the suspension and termination of listing.

Objectives and principles

In applying the *Listing Rules*, the FCA will have regard to the following objectives and principles:

1 To seek a balance between providing issuers with ready access to the market for their securities and protecting investors.
2 To promote investor confidence in standards of disclosure, in the conduct of Listed companies' affairs and in the market as a whole.
3 Securities should be brought to the market in a way that is appropriate to their nature and number and which will facilitate an open and efficient market for trading in those securities.
4 An issuer must make full and timely disclosure about itself and its Listed securities, at the time of listing and subsequently.
5 Holders of equity securities should be given adequate opportunity to consider in advance and vote upon major changes in the company's business operations

and matters of importance concerning the company's management and constitution.

Recognised Investment Exchanges

Only Recognised Investment Exchanges (RIEs) may lawfully operate in Great Britain. To become a RIE, an investment exchange with its head office in the UK must apply to the FCA. An overseas investment exchange (i.e. an exchange with its head office outside the UK) must apply to the Treasury. There are eight RIEs currently operating in Great Britain. The two better-known markets are the Main Market operated by the London Stock Exchange plc, which until July 2007 had a monopoly on trading Listed shares.

The regulatory regime

Offers of fully 'listed' securities are governed by FSMA2000 and the *Listing Rules*. These rules and regulations apply to securities that are Listed or are the subject of an application for listing or are being offered for sale conditional on their being admitted to listing. Trading on the Stock Exchange is subject to the Stock Exchange Rules, while trading on NEX Exchange Main Board is subject to the NEX Rules (NR). Members of the Exchanges must also comply with the rules of the self-regulatory organisation to which they belong.

The regime is supervised by the FCA, to which most of the powers of the Secretary of State under the FSMA2000 have been transferred. The main feature of this regime is that, subject to certain exceptions, only authorised or exempt persons may carry on a regulated activity (FSMA2000 s. 19).

Regulated activity

Regulated activities are defined in FSMA2000, ss. 21 and 22 and Sch. 2. In particular, it must be noted that financial promotion and investment activity includes giving any form of investment promotion and advice and investment management, as well as undertaking securities transactions as broker-dealer and/or principal within the UK.

Authorised persons

The status of being an authorised or exempt person is conferred on application to the FSA by an individual or firm. Members of professional bodies such as solicitors and accountants may be authorised by their relevant professional body (FSMA2000, Part XX, ss. 325–333).

Unauthorised business

A person carrying on a regulated activity who is not authorised or not exempted commits an offence (FSMA2000 s. 20). Agreements made in respect of the regulated activity may be unenforceable by the unauthorised person (FSMA2000 ss. 26, 27 and 28), and they may be restrained by injunction or be made subject to a restitution order.

Differences between the markets

Market regulation

The London Stock Exchange operates both the Main Market and AIM. The Main Market is a regulated market for EU purposes and AIM is a 'non-regulated' or 'exchange-regulated' market. Having EU-regulated market status means that the Main Market is subject to EU legislation in the form of the *Listing Rules* issued by the UKLA. AIM, on the other hand, is subject to regulations issued by the Exchange. Accordingly AIM is better suited to the needs of smaller and newer market entrants, and subject to a lighter-touch regulation than is possible under the *Listing Rules*.

Premium or standard listing?

The requirements for admission and the continuing obligations will depend on whether a premium or standard listing is sought. A premium listing is only available for equity shares of commercial companies, closed-ended investment funds and open-ended investment companies that meet the full set of requirements for a premium listing (*LR 1.5.1G(3)*). All other securities, such as securities convertible into equity shares, depository receipts and shares that do not meet the full set of premium listing requirements, can only have a standard listing. A company that meets the criteria for a premium listing may, however, choose a standard listing for its shares.

A premium listing obliges the company to comply with more onerous requirements than it would for a standard listing. These more onerous requirements are often referred to as 'super-equivalent' requirements. These super-equivalent requirements are imposed by the FCA and go further than the minimum standard listing requirements imposed by the EU. Such super-equivalent standards are intended to provide additional investor protection and so promote shareholder confidence in the London Stock Exchange as a good place to make their investments and, as a result, maintain London as a key market for providing companies with access to capital.

Some of the continuing obligations under the *AIM Rules* are more onerous, and so provide better investor protection, than those required for a standard listing.

Table 15.2: Comparison of the requirements for admission and continuing obligations for companies seeking a premium or standard listing or trading on AIM

AIM	*Premium*	*Standard*
No minimum market capitalisation requirement (except investing companies which must raise at least £3m by a share issue on, or immediately prior to, admission (*AR* 8))	Expected minimum market capitalisation of £700,000 (*LR 2.2.7R(1)*)	Expected minimum market capitalisation of £700,000 (*LR 2.2.7R(1)*)
Admission document required (*AR* 3) (except for fasttrack admissions)	Prospectus required for admission (*LR 2.2.10R, LR 3.3.2R(2)* and FSMA s. 85)	Prospectus required for admission (*LR 2.2.10R, LR 3.3.2R(2)* and FSMA s. 85)
Admission document need not be approved by the FSA or the Exchange (although the Nominated Adviser (Nomad) must confirm that it complies with the AIM Rules (*AR 20*))	Prospectus must be approved by the FSA (*LR 2.2.10R, LR 3.3.2R(2)* and FSMA s. 85)	Prospectus must be approved by the FSA (*LR 2.2.10R, LR 3.3.2R(2)* and FSMA s. 85)
No pre-emption rights requirement	Shareholders must have pre-emption rights (*LR 2.2.15R*)	No pre-emption rights requirement
Audited information covering the last three financial years (or such shorter period as the issuer has been in operation) and the audit report for each year must be disclosed in the admission document (*AR* 3)	Must have published or filed accounts that cover at least the last three years ending no more than six months before the date of the prospectus and have been independently audited and reported on by the auditors without modification (*LR 6.1.3R(1)*) *	Audited information covering the last three financial years (or such shorter period as the issuer has been in operation) and the audit report for each year must be disclosed in the prospectus (*LR 20.1, Annex I, PRR 2.1.5*)
No trading record requirement (lock-in may be required where business not independent or revenue earning (*AR 7*))	At least 75% of the issuer's business must be supported by a historic revenue earning record covering the period for which the audited accounts are required (*LR 6.1.4R(1)*) *	No trading record requirement

AIM	*Premium*	*Standard*
No control of assets requirement	The issuer must control the majority of its assets and have done so for at least the period for which the audited accounts are required (*LR 6.1.4R(2)*) *	No control of assets requirement
No independent business requirement (lock-in may be required where business not independent or revenue earning (*AR 7*))	The issuer must carry on an independent business as its main activity (*LR 6.1.4R(3)*)*	No independent business requirement
'Clean' **working capital** statement required (*AR 3* and Sch. 2)	'Clean' working capital statement required (*LR 6.1.16R* and *item 3.1, Annex III, PRR 2.1.5*)	Working capital statement required (*LR item 3.1, Annex III, PRR 2.1.5*)
No free float requirement	25% minimum free float for each class of shares (*LR 6.1.19R*)	25% minimum free float for each class of shares (*LR 14.2.2R*)
No restriction on amount of warrants or options	Warrants or options to subscribe for equity shares must not exceed 20% of the issued equity share capital at the time of issue of the warrants or options (*LR 6.1.22R*)	No restriction on amount of warrants or options
Nomad (and broker) required (*AR 1 and 35*)	Sponsor required (*LR 8.2.1R(1)*)	No adviser requirement

* Mineral companies and scientific research companies are subject to different requirements (*LR 6.1.8R* to *LR 6.1.12R*).

Eligibility criteria

The criteria set out under the *Listing Rules* and the Admission and Disclosure Standards for shares to be admitted to the official list and to trading on the Main Market are more onerous than the criteria for the admission of shares to trading on AIM.

A key differences between the Main Market and AIM criteria is that for an AIM company, its nomad is required to confirm that it is satisfied that the applicant and its shares are appropriate to be admitted to AIM (*AR 20*).

The London Stock Exchange

The London Stock Exchange was for many years the only RIE headquartered in Great Britain.

The Exchange enables companies from global giants to smaller enterprises around the world to raise the capital they need to grow, with a choice of four primary markets:

1 Main Market – regarded by many investors and companies as the world's most prestigious listing and trading environment. Companies can have either a premium or standard listing on the Main Market.
2 AIM – equities market for smaller growing companies.
3 Professional Securities Market – for Listed debt and depository receipt securities.
4 Specialist Fund Segment – dedicated to specialised investment entities.

The London Stock Exchange provides two forms of market: the primary market gives companies wishing to raise working capital access to investors, who provide working capital in the knowledge that there is also a secondary market enabling investors to trade securities with other investors.

NEX Exchange (NEX)

NEX operates two markets:

1 two primary markets, one for Listed securities on the NEX Exchange Main Board and unlisted securities admitted to trading on the NEX Exchange Growth Market; and
2 a secondary market, the NEX Exchange Traded, for trading both Listed or quoted securities admitted to trading on other EU markets.

Types of public issue

There are several methods by which securities may be floated, including the following.

- *Offers for sale or subscription*. The company issues a prospectus in the form of listing particulars inviting application for its shares from investors. An offer for subscription is in the form of new securities issued directly by the company to the applicants. An offer for sale relates to new or existing securities, which are first acquired by an issuing house, which then offers the securities for sale to the public by issuing listing particulars and inviting applications.
- *Placings*. As in an offer for sale, securities are subscribed or purchased by the sponsoring firm of stockbrokers or issuing house, but these are then 'placed' with investment clients, a proportion also being sold through the market.

- *Intermediaries offers*. An intermediaries offer is a marketing of new securities to 'intermediaries' for them to allocate to their own clients, principally private client investors.
- *Vendor consideration issues*. A company that acquires a business or other assets may issue securities to the vendor instead of, or in addition to, cash.
- *Introductions*. This is where existing securities are Listed for the first time.
- *Rights issues*. This is where a company offers new shares to its existing shareholders in proportion to the number of shares they already hold. The rights issue may be underwritten so that the company is assured of raising the full amount of the working capital it requires. The right to the new shares can itself be traded.
- *Open offers*. Essentially this is the same as a rights issue; however, the benefit of the right is not permitted to be traded.
- *Capitalisation (or bonus) issues*. The directors of a company may arrange for fully paid shares of the same class to be allotted free of charge to existing holders in proportion to their holdings, following the capitalisation of the company's existing reserves. This is usually undertaken where the company's share price has risen to a level that is reducing the liquidity of the shares. The share price will fall approximately in line with the ratio of new shares issued.
- *Exchanges and conversions*. New securities may be Listed as the result of existing securities being exchanged for, or converted into, new securities.
- *Exercise of options or warrants*. Securities may carry rights for the holder to subscribe cash for further securities, which are issued when the rights are exercised.
- *Other issues*. Securities issued in circumstances other than those described above may be Listed, provided the relevant conditions are fulfilled. Shares issued under employees' share schemes are a common example.

Eligibility for listing

There are a number of conditions that must be met before the UKLA will consider an application for listing, the principal ones being as follows.

- The applicant must be an incorporated entity and operating in accordance with its constitution (the articles of association for a UK company) (*LR 2.2.1*).
- The securities (shares, debt instruments, etc.) to be Listed must be consistent with the law of the applicant incorporation, and be duly established and authorised by the applicant's constitution (*LR 2.2.2*).
- To be Listed, the securities must also be admitted to trading on a RIE market (Main Market or NEX Exchange Main Board) (*LR 2.2.3*).
- Securities must be fully paid and freely transferable (*LR 2.2.4*). The exception to transferability is that transfer may be restricted in accordance with s. 793 where a request for information on the identity of the beneficial owner of shares has not been complied with.

- For shares, the expected market value of the entire class must be at least £700,000 (*LR 2.2.7*).
- The application for listing must be in respect of the entire class or additional shares of an existing Listed class (*LR 2.2.9*).
- A prospectus complying with the prospectus rules must be approved (by the FCA for UK companies) and published (*LR 2.2.10*).
- If applicable, listing particulars must be approved (by the FCA) and published (*LR 2.2.11* and *LR 4*).

The listing process

The minimum time between submission of an application for listing, approval and admission to trading on a market is 20 working days. However, in practice, the period is usually between 12 and 24 weeks, and for many companies the process will have started up to two years prior to admission, as it may be necessary to undertake preliminary stages first, including choosing advisers, appointing non-executive directors, establishing appropriate management and corporate governance structures, making changes to the executive board and establishing the correct valuation for the company.

It should be noted that although documents are submitted to the FCA for approval, this is only formally given on the last day, at the same time as the shares are admitted to trading on a market, as both admission and listing are conditional on each other.

Once the decision to seek a listing has been taken, it is usual to convene a meeting at which the various advisers are present, to set out the general structure of the application process. This meeting would decide the amount of any working capital required, an approximate issue price, the structure of the issue, advisers' fees, abort costs and commissions payable on applications, the timing of the listing and other general matters.

It is likely that some 'housekeeping' will be required prior to the listing, including appointment of non-executive directors, adoption of new articles, adoption of employee share option scheme(s) and undertaking a bonus issue or share split to increase the number of shares in issue. If the company has only a few shareholders, it may also be necessary, either before or at the time of the listing, for these original shareholders to dispose of part of their holdings to ensure that there are at least 25% of the issued shares available for trading (*LR 6.1.19*). The following appointments will be required before the listing application is made:

- sponsor and financial adviser;
- brokers to the issue;
- solicitors;
- reporting accountants; and
- CREST eligible share registrar (and receiving agent if there is to be a share offer).

Some companies may also need to appoint experts to produce expert technical reports on aspects of the company's trade or proposed trade.

The London Stock Exchange and NEX normally expect new applicants and their advisers to attend a meeting with them prior to submission of the final application for trading, and not later than the time when they first contact the FCA regarding their application for admission to the Official List. The meeting is used to discuss matters such as the admission process (including timing) and the issuer's plans to develop the market in its securities after admission.

Drafting the listing particulars

The listing particulars will contain the information by which the investors will judge the issue. The solicitors and/or sponsors will prepare the first draft of the listing particulars, which must comply with the *Listing Rules*. The listing particulars will undergo several drafts and finally detailed verification so that all parties are satisfied that the information is complete, accurate, complies with the *Listing Rules* and gives a complete and accurate report of the company, its history and its future plans. The requirements for the listing application are set out in *LR 3, 4* and *6*.

Professional advisers

It will be necessary to appoint additional advisers, including the following.

The sponsor to the issue

The sponsor's main duties in the issue are:

1. to obtain approval from the FCA for the listing particulars and other documents, which the broker will submit on the company's behalf to the FCA in draft and, later, in final form;
2. to apply to the FCA for admission to the Official List and to the London Stock Exchange or NEX for admission to trading, and to ensure the CREST securities application form is submitted (the CREST securities application form is most often submitted by the company's share registrars rather than the broker) and (where a new line of stock is involved) a CREST enablement letter, which must be set on the company's headed paper but which will be submitted by the broker or share registrar;
3. to advise on the timing and pricing of the issue;
4. to place a proportion of the sub-underwriting with their clients; and
5. to advise on the company's continuing regulatory obligations.

Corporate broker

The broker acts as link between the company and potential investors, and following admission to the market in general. Most brokers retain analysts who will issue research notes on companies, and it is important to select a broker with appropriate expertise in your company's sector.

Table 15.3: Listing timetable

Period before admission	*Objective*
12–24 weeks prior to admission	Appoint advisers Timetable agreed
6–12 weeks prior to admission	Assess problem areas Draft prospectus and other documents Initial pricing review Draft documents submitted to the UKLA Initial meeting with LSE/NEX Draft PR presentations Presentations to analysts
1–6 weeks prior to admission	Due diligence and verification starts PR meetings and roadshow for potential investors Formally submit and agree documents with the UKLA (does not constitute approval) Print pathfinder if required
1 week prior to admission	All documents agreed by the UKLA Share price agreed Prospectus registered Subscription and underwriting agreements signed
48 hours prior to admission	'48 hour' documents submitted to the UKLA Formal applications for listing and admission UKLA and exchange fees paid
Admission date	Shares Listed and admitted to trading New shares issued Trading commences

Many firms can act as both sponsor and broker, and this may be appropriate. However, one firm acting in both capacities can cause difficulties where the sponsoring arm has information which, if passed to the broking arm, would put them in the position of not being able to trade the company's shares, as they would be in possession of price-sensitive information which would give them an unfair advantage when trading shares.

The broker will also actively market the shares to secure the success of the issue. This process is often referred to as book building. During the book-building phase, non-binding commitments to invest are obtained for an aggregate amount of money, as until the last day or so of any offer, the actual share price will not be known.

If there is to be a share offer, the brokers may well underwrite the offer, which means that they will purchase any shares that have not been sold to investors by the closing date. This has obvious advantages for the company, as it is guaranteed to raise the funds it requires; the disadvantage is the underwriting fees can be expensive, particularly if the offer is fully subscribed without recourse to the underwriter.

Reporting accountant

Although this is a separate and distinct function from that of the company auditor, the reporting accountant is often the company auditor, albeit staffed from the corporate finance department rather than the audit department. The reporting accountant's role is to review the company's financial history, accounting systems and internal controls, and to prepare a report for the benefit of potential investors.

Depending on the nature of the transaction, there are three forms of report that might be required.

1. A long form report is a detailed analysis of past financial performance and management structures, strengths and weaknesses. The long form report is not published but is provided to both directors and the sponsor, and is used to draft the prospectus.
2. The short form report, as the name implies, is an abridged version of the long form report and is reproduced in the prospectus.
3. The last report that is usually prepared where additional funds are being raised is a working capital report for the sponsor, covering the period 12–24 months following admission. This is to provide comfort to the sponsor that the company will have sufficient working capital for the period covered by the report, assuming any funds to be raised are actually raised. Additionally, although it is preferable to raise slightly more funds than are required, raising surplus capital has a detrimental effect on share price.

Lawyers

Typically there will be two firms appointed, the first advising the company and the second advising the sponsor. The company's lawyers will often lead the process of drafting documents in conjunction with the sponsor and with all other interested parties commenting on those drafts.

The company lawyers will also undertake verification of the documents. This is the process under which factual statements within the documents are verified to prove that they are based on fact. Verification is a painstaking task dreaded by all involved requiring companies to search their archives for old documents, agreements, research notes, etc.

PR consultants

Although some companies will already retain a firm of advertising and marketing consultants, it is often advisable to retain a firm of specialist financial PR consultants. Financial PR consultants play a crucial role in raising and maintaining a company profile during the book-building and fund-raising phases leading up to a flotation and after flotation, and maintaining awareness of the company to maintain liquidity once the initial flurry of activity associated with the float has subsided. Financial PR consultants will also ensure, in conjunction with the company lawyers, that statements issued by the company comply with FSMA2000 and UKLA disclosure requirements.

Share registrars

Whether the shares are to be Listed and traded on the Main Market or NEX Exchange Main Board, or admitted to trading on AIM or NEX Exchange Growth Market, the company will need to retain the services of a CREST-compliant share registrar to maintain the share register. CREST compliance is required in order to facilitate electronic share trading and settlement via CREST. Under this system, a company's share register is split between the electronic sub-register maintained by CREST and the certificated register maintained by the share registrar. The share registrar will update the full register by a real-time link to CREST, to ensure that at any particular time they have an accurate and current record of the ownership of the company's shares.

Other advisers

Additional advisers that may be required include surveyors to value properties and other material assets, security printers for the secure and rapid turnaround of the documents, insurance brokers, and trademark and patent attorneys.

Company approval

On the penultimate day, a completion board meeting is held to approve all the documentation (including verification notes), the procedures for listing and any share issue being undertaken. If the issue is being underwritten, the underwriting agreement(s) is usually signed at this late stage. The listing particulars are then submitted to the FCA and application for admission to trading is made to the London Stock Exchange or NEX as appropriate.

Listing timetable

Although each listing is slightly different, a typical timetable will be as follows.

Prospectus Regulation Rules

The Prospectus Regulation Rules derive from European legislation (Regulation (EU) No 2017/1129) and replaced the Prospectus Rules with effect from 21 July

2019. Unlike the Prospectus Rules, which derived from an EU Directive and consequently required UK legislation to be implemented, the Prospectus Regulation Rules derive from an EU Regulation and are implemented directly in the UK. Due to the differing implementation methods to bring this legislation into effect, various consequential changes required UK legislation in the form of the Financial Services and Markets Act 2000 (Prospectus) Regulations 2019.

The relevant Articles for the Prospectus Regulations are reproduced in the Prospectus Regulation Rules and form part of the FCA Handbook. The rules cover the format and detailed content of a prospectus, the period during which a prospectus remains valid and the manner in which a prospectus must be published. They reiterate the general rule that a person may not make an offer of securities to the public, or seek admission to trading on a regulated market, unless a prospectus has been prepared, approved by the FCA and published. Subject to certain qualifying criteria, a prospectus of a company incorporated in another EU state, approved by the competent authority of that state, may be acceptable for circulation in the UK without additional consent. Certain types of offers or specialist securities are exempt from the general rule to prepare a prospectus.

The Prospectus Rules stipulate the criteria by which the FCA will consider a prospectus and, where appropriate, allow the FCA to authorise the omission of information that a prospectus would otherwise have to contain.

What is an offer to the public?

Broadly speaking, any offer that is not restricted to a defined, small selection, of potential investors will be a public offer. The definition is very broad and can include offers by private companies. Under the Prospectus Regulation Rules, there is an offer to the public if there is a communication to persons in any form and by any means, presenting sufficient information on the terms of the offer and the securities to be offered, so as to enable an investor to decide to purchase or subscribe for those securities. This definition also applies to the placing of securities through financial intermediaries (PRR App 1.1).

The communication may be in any form and by any means, and includes placing through financial intermediaries.

Exemptions

The key exemptions from the requirement to publish a prospectus under the prospectus regime are:

- offers addressed to fewer than 150 people (other than qualified investors) in any 12-month period per EEA state;
- offers to 'qualified investors' – i.e. broadly institutions as at present and companies that are not SMEs; there is to be a self-certification procedure whereby SMEs and certain others can register as qualified investors as well, based on certain conditions;

- offers to persons outside the UK (although local laws would then apply);
- offers where the total consideration for securities in any period of 12 months is under €8 million or equivalent;
- offers where the minimum subscription and the denomination of the unit amounts is not less that €100,000; and
- a takeover effected by way of a share exchange.

Prospectus approval

If a prospectus is required, the prospectus must be drawn up in accordance with the Prospectus Rules and submitted to the FCA for approval, together with the appropriate fee. The FCA has 10 working days to approve the document if the company's shares are already admitted to the Main Market or NEX Exchange Main Board. If the shares are not Listed, the FCA is permitted 20 days in which to approve or reject the prospectus.

The Prospectus Rules contain detailed requirements for the contents of a prospectus, including:

- a declaration by those responsible for the prospectus that they have taken all reasonable care to ensure the information is, to the best of their knowledge, in accordance with the facts and contains no omission likely to affect its import;
- information about the issuer;
- financial information;
- information regarding the investment objective, policy and restrictions;
- information regarding managers, advisers and other service providers, organisational structure and management details; and
- risk factors.

Disclosure and Transparency Rules (DTR)

A Listed company must observe the disclosure requirements of the DTR. In addition, DTR 5 applies to AIM and NEX Exchange Growth Market companies. The main DTR provisions are as follows.

DTR 2: Disclosure and control of inside information by issuers

The general obligation to disclose price-sensitive inside information and the circumstances under which disclosure can be delayed, selective and holding announcements made in place of full disclosure, the obligation to compile and maintain insider lists and the control of inside information.

DTR 3: Transactions by persons discharging managerial responsibilities and their connected persons

The obligation to notify transactions in the company's securities by those exercising management responsibilities and their connected persons.

DTR 4: Periodic financial reporting

The obligation to publish annual financial reports, half-yearly reports and interim statements.

DTR 5: Vote holder and issuer notification rules

The obligation for shareholders to notify UK companies of the percentage of voting rights held, whether direct or indirect, reaches, exceeds or falls below 3% or any whole percentage point above 3%. Companies are obliged to make public details of their total voting rights and any changes to enable shareholders to meet their obligations under *DTR 5*.

DTR 6: Continuing obligations and access to information

These contain the rules on dissemination of information by companies.

DTR 7: Corporate governance

DTR 7.1 contains obligations regarding audit committees. *DTR 7.2* contains obligations relating to the corporate governance statement required in the company's directors' report or as a separate statement.

DTR 2 and *3* in particular have been amended by the Market Abuse Regulations with effect from 4 July 2016. The broad effect of the regulations is unchanged; however, there is an increased need for record keeping and the scope of some regulations has widened. For more information, see Chapter 16.

The London Stock Exchange as a secondary market

Dealings on the London Stock Exchange are conducted in accordance with the rules, regulations and usages of the LSE and the conduct of business rules of the FCA (or a self-regulatory organisation (SRO), as appropriate).

Trading systems

The London Stock Exchange operates various trading services to enable trading in constituent company shares.

1. *SEAQ* – SEAQ is London Stock Exchange's non-electronically executable quotation service that allows market makers to quote prices in AIM securities (not traded on SETS or SETSqx) as well as a number of fixed interest securities.
2. *SETS* (or the 'Order book') – SETS is the London Stock Exchange's premier electronic trading service that combines electronic order-driven trading with integrated market maker liquidity provision, delivering guaranteed two-way prices.
3. *SETS Intra-day Auction* – Introduced in March 2016, this is a new scheduled daily SETS Intra-day auction for equities; midday prices form an auction mechanism for trading larger-sized orders.

4 *SETSqx* – SETSqx (Stock Exchange Electronic Trading Service – quotes and crosses) is a trading service for securities less liquid than those traded on SETS. SETSqx combines a periodic electronic auction book with standalone non-electronic quote-driven market making. Electronic orders can be named or anonymous, and for the indicated securities, order book executions will be centrally cleared.
5 *International Order Book (IOB)* – The IOB enables investors to unlock the potential of some of the world's fastest-growing markets through a single central electronic order book. It offers easy and cost-efficient direct access to securities via depositary receipts from more than 44 countries, including those in Central and Eastern Europe, Asia and the Middle East.
6 *European Quoting Service (EQS)* – EQS allows quote-driven-market making on an extensive range of non-london, equity and equity-like securities defined by ESMA as liquid.

NEX as a secondary market

In addition to Listed shares admitted to its own market, NEX offers an alternative market for Listed shares or traded on AIM as well as European stocks.

The NEX trading platform was originally developed in 2005 to offer trading in Listed and unlisted UK equity securities. It is a quote-driven trading system, supported by competing market-makers.

The quote-driven system is favoured by many retail brokers, as it can facilitate immediate execution and lead to less volatility in share prices. Competing market-makers offer consistent and improved two-way prices in increased sizes for smaller companies, which are typically less liquid, ensuring that there is always the ability to deal in any smaller company share.

Continuing obligations

Listed companies are subject to further regulation and must comply with the general continuing obligations contained in the Listing Rules, Chapter 9 and supplemented by event specific obligations set out in the Listing Rules, Chapters 10–13. These ongoing requirements are considered necessary to ensure the maintenance of an orderly market in securities and providing all users of the market with access to the same information at the same time.

These continuing obligations are considered in Chapter 16.

London Stock Exchange Admission and Disclosure Standards

A company whose securities are admitted to trading on the London Stock Exchange's main market must also comply with the continuing obligations contained in the Exchange's Admission and Disclosure Standards. For the moment, these replicate the general disclosure obligations contained in Chapter 9 of the *Listing Rules*. Accordingly, compliance with the *Listing Rules* should also ensure compliance with the London Stock Exchange Standards. The Exchange has adopted these Standards to enable it to enforce its market supervision function. The Company Services team at the Exchange processes applications for admission to trading and deals with all other aspects of the Exchange's relationship with companies. The team does not review draft prospectuses, listing particulars or any other circulars. These reviews are carried out by the FCA.

Eligibility criteria

1 An application for admission to trading of any class of securities must relate to all securities of that class, issued or proposed to be issued or further securities of a class that is already admitted, issued or proposed to be issued.
2 The company must be in compliance with the requirements of any securities regulator by which it is regulated and/or any stock exchange on which it has securities admitted to trading.
3 In the case of transferable securities, all such securities must be freely negotiable.
4 Securities that are admitted to trading by the Exchange must be capable of being traded in a fair, orderly and efficient manner.
5 The Exchange may refuse an application for the admission if it considers that the applicant's situation is such that admission of the securities may be detrimental to the orderly operation or integrity of its markets, or the applicant does not or will not comply with the standards or with any special condition imposed by the Exchange.
6 Companies must confirm that they meet the criteria and requirements of the market to which they are applying.

Settlement

To be admitted to trading, securities must be eligible for electronic settlement.

Communication

Companies must provide details of a contact within their organisation who will be responsible for communications between the Exchange and the company. A company may wish to use a nominated representative.

NEX Exchange Main Board Admission and Disclosure Standards

A company whose securities are admitted to trading on the NEX Exchange Main Board must also comply with the continuing obligations contained in the NEX Exchange *Main Board – admission and disclosure standards*. As with the admission and disclosure standards of the London Stock Exchange, these replicate the general disclosure obligations contained in Chapter 9 of the *Listing Rules*. Accordingly, compliance with the *Listing Rules* should also ensure compliance with the NEX Exchange *Main Board – admission and disclosure standards*.

Eligibility criteria

1 An application for the admission of securities must relate to securities which are Listed or for which an application for listing has been made and cover all securities, whether issued or proposed to be issued, of the class to which they belong.
2 The company must be in compliance with the law of its place of incorporation and the requirements of any regulatory authority to which it is subject.
3 The securities to which the application relates must be freely transferable and eligible for electronic settlement within a relevant system or other system approved by NEX allowing for the expeditious settlement of transactions.
4 The applicant must make arrangements with a regulatory information service for the dissemination of regulatory announcements.
5 An applicant must submit the prescribed application fee.

Prospectus requirement

The NEX Exchange Main Board is a regulated market. Consequently, the admission of securities requires the publication of an approved prospectus, unless the applicant is exempt from such requirement under an applicable provision of PRR and FSMA.

An applicant who has produced an approved prospectus within a 12-month period preceding the expected date of admission or whose securities have been admitted to trading on a EU-regulated market for more than 18 months may qualify for an exemption under PRR, subject to specific requirements in relation to the production of a supplementary prospectus or summary document in certain circumstances. An applicant must seek appropriate professional advice on its disclosure obligations under PRR.

Issues of unlisted securities

Public offers of shares and other company securities that are not Listed and admitted to trading on the London Stock Exchange Main Market or NEX Exchange Main Board are governed by the Prospectus Regulation Rules (see page 264).

Alternative Investment Market

As the London Stock Exchange's market for smaller companies, the Alternative Investment Market (AIM) is intended to appeal to a wider range of companies.

Admission requirements

The requirements for admission to AIM set out in the *AIM Rules* (AR) are much less onerous than the requirements for admission to the Exchange's Main Market. In particular, there are no requirements for minimum market capitalisation, the percentage of shares which must be in public hands, or length of trading record.

If the company does not have a two-year trading record, any directors or employees who individually hold 1% or more of its AIM securities must agree not to dispose of any of their own holdings in the company for at least 12 months from the date of admission (*AR 7*).

Any type of security of a public company may be admitted to AIM. The securities to be admitted must be freely transferable and all securities of the class must be admitted (*AR 32* and *33*).

An applicant to AIM must produce an admission document, which must be freely available (AR 3).

A company seeking admission to trading on AIM must make an announcement through a regulatory information service at least 10 business days prior to the date on which it wishes its securities to be admitted (*AR 2*). It must also make a written application to the Exchange at least three business days prior to its proposed admission date (*AR 5*).

NEX Exchange Growth Market

NEX Exchange admits companies to its NEX Exchange Growth Market in accordance with the NEX Exchange Growth Market – Rules for Issuers (NE RFI). These rules contain the application requirements for admission to the NEX Exchange Growth Market and the continuing obligations of Growth Market companies, once admitted.

Admission requirements

A company seeking admission to trading on the NEX Exchange Growth Market must appoint and retain a NEX Exchange Corporate Adviser.

The application for admission is made on the company's behalf by its corporate adviser, who is responsible for ensuring that the company and the securities meet the eligibility criteria, that satisfactory guidance has been given to the directors to ensure they understand their obligations under the rules and that the information provided to NEX is accurate and complete.

To be eligible, the company must be lawfully incorporated, have securities that are allotted and freely transferable, have arrangements in place for electronic settlement following admission and have sufficient shares in public hands (10%) to ensure an orderly market (*NE RFI 5*). If there will be insufficient shares in public hands on admission, the company can seek a derogation provided the Exchange is satisfied that there will be an adequate market for the securities.

If any securities are to be issued to the public, a prospectus complying with the Prospectus Rules must be published, if appropriate. If a prospectus is not required, the company must publish an admission document (*NE RFI 10*).

NEX Exchange may authorise omissions from the admission document that are minor or relate to matters already in the public domain (*NE RFI 15*).

Advertising, marketing and promotion

Regardless of whether or not a public company is proposing to make an offer of Listed or unlisted securities, the advertising and marketing of those securities, other than the issue of prospectuses, supplemental prospectuses and announcements concerning their issue, is subject to the provisions of the FSMA2000, s. 21 and a number of statutory instruments including: the Financial Services and Markets Act 2000 (Financial Promotion) (Amendment) Order 2001, SI 2001/2633; the Financial Services and Markets Act 2000 (Miscellaneous Provisions) Order 2001, SI 2001/3650; and the Financial Services and Markets Act 2000 (Financial Promotion) (Amendment No. 2) Order 2001, SI 2001/3800.

16 – Continuing obligations of Listed, AIM and NEX Exchange Growth Market companies

Introduction

In addition to any legislative duties and responsibilities they have, directors of companies whose shares are admitted to trading on the London Stock Exchange Main Market, NEX Exchange Main Board, AIM or NEX Exchange Growth Market are required to comply with continuing obligations requirements. These are set out in Chapter 9 of the *Listing Rules* for Main Market and NEX Exchange Main Board companies, the *AIM Rules* for AIM companies and NEX Exchange Growth Market *Rules for Issuers* for NEX Exchange Growth Market companies. In addition, there are disclosure obligations set out in the *Disclosure and Transparency Rules*.

As with eligibility criteria, there are different continuing obligations for a premium or standard listing. In general, the continuing obligations for a company with a premium listing are more onerous than for an AIM or NEX Exchange Growth Market admission, which in turn may be more onerous than for a company with a standard listing.

Companies Act obligations of Listed companies

There are a number of requirements that only apply to Listed companies under the Companies Act 2006.

Definition of quoted company

Section 385 defines a 'quoted company' for the purpose of Part 15 (Accounts and Reports) of the 2006 Act as a company whose equity share capital has been Listed in the UK, officially Listed in an EEA state or admitted to dealing on the New York Stock Exchange or Nasdaq.

Strategic report

For a quoted company, the strategic report must also include (s. 414C (7–10)) information on:

- main trends and factors likely to affect future development, performance or position of the company;
- environmental matters;

- company employees;
- social and community interests;
- the company's strategy;
- the company's business model;
- the genders of its directors, senior managers and employees; and
- those third parties with which the company has contracts or arrangements essential to its business.

The directors may exclude and not disclose information if, in their opinion, disclosure would be seriously prejudicial to the interests of the company.

Directors' report

The directors of a quoted company must also disclose details on the acquisition of own shares (Sch. 7.9) in their directors' report.

Directors' remuneration report

Section 420 contains the directors' duty to prepare a remuneration report. The duty applies to every person who was a director of the quoted company immediately before the period for filing the accounts, and failure to comply constitutes an offence punishable by a fine.

The Large and Medium-sized Companies and Groups (Accounts and Reports) (Amendment) Regulations 2013 (SI 2013/1981) specify the extent to which the directors' remuneration report should be subject to audit. The 'auditable' part of a directors' remuneration report is the part containing the information required by paragraphs 4–17 of Part 3 of Schedule 8 to the Regulations, which includes the amount of each director's emoluments and compensation in the relevant financial year, and details on share options, long-term incentive schemes and pensions.

A quoted company must put, at the same meeting convened to receive the annual accounts, a resolution approving the directors' remuneration report. The resolution is an advisory one and, if lost, does not invalidate the payment of directors' remuneration (s. 439).

Auditor's report

The auditors of a quoted company must include details on the auditable sections of the directors' remuneration report, strategic report, directors' report and the corporate governance statement.

Summary information

Companies were previously permitted to circulate summary financial statements in place of their full report and accounts. This has now been withdrawn, and instead companies may issue the strategic report and supplemental material to their members in place of the full statutory accounts. Any member receiving the strategic report and supplemental material may request that the full accounts are sent to them (s. 426). Although available to any company preparing unabridged accounts (i.e. not small or medium sized), the issue of the strategic report and supplemental information is generally only taken up by Listed companies, as the full annual report and accounts are also readily available where required.

Quoted companies must include, in addition to the supplemental material set out in s. 426A, a copy of that part of the remuneration report which sets out the single total figure table in respect of the remuneration of its directors (s. 426A(2)(e).

Additional disclosures

The annual financial report of a Listed company must include the following additional information (*DTR 4.1.5*):

- Management report containing (*DTR 4.1.8-11*):
  - a fair review of the company's business and a description of the principal risks and uncertainties facing it. The business review must be a balanced and comprehensive analysis of the development and performance of the company during the financial year, and the position of the company at the end of the year. The review must also contain sufficient analysis, using financial key performance and other key performance indicators including environmental and employee matters, to demonstrate the development, performance and position of the company during the financial year;
  - details of any important events since the end of the financial year, likely future development, any activities in research and development, details of any acquisition(s) of own shares and the existence of any overseas branches; and
  - in relation to the company's use of financial instruments or where required for the assessment of its assets, liabilities, financial position and profit or loss, details of its financial risk management objectives and policies, and the company's exposure to price risk, credit risk, liquidity risk and cash flow risk.
- Responsibility statements: the annual financial report must include a responsibility statement made by those responsible confirming that, to the best of their knowledge and belief, the financial statements have been prepared in accordance with applicable accounting standards and give a true and fair view of the assets, liabilities, financial position and profit or loss of the company, and that the management report contains a fair review of the information required to be reviewed (*DTR 4.1.12*).

If the company is required to prepare consolidated accounts, the financial statements must comprise (*DTR 4.1.6R*):

- consolidated accounts prepared in accordance with IFRS; and
- parent company accounts prepared in accordance with the law of the country of its incorporation.

If the company is not required to prepare consolidated accounts, its financial statements must comprise accounts prepared in accordance with the law of the country of its incorporation (*DTR 4.1.6(2)*).

The financial statements must be audited, and the full text of the audit report made public (*DTR 4.1.7R*).

In addition to the requirements set out in *DTR 4.1*, Listed companies must include in their annual financial report (*LR 9.8.4*):

- a statement of the amount of interest capitalised by the group with an indication of the amount and treatment of any related tax relief;
- if the company has published unaudited financial information in a class 1 circular or prospectus since its previous annual financial report, it must reproduce that information and explain any variance of 10% or more between any profit forecast or estimate and the actual profit *LR 9.2.18 R*;
- details of any long-term incentive schemes as required by *LR 9.4.3 R*;
- details of any arrangements under which a director of the company has waived or agreed to waive any emoluments from the company or any subsidiary undertaking;
- where a director has waived or agreed to waive emoluments, details of such waiver;
- in the case of any allotment for cash of equity securities otherwise than to the holders of the company's equity shares in proportion to their holdings and any similar issues of shares in a major unlisted subsidiary, neither of which has been specifically authorised by the company's shareholders:
  - the classes of shares allotted and for each class of shares, the number allotted, their aggregate nominal value and the consideration received by the company for the allotment;
  - the names of the allottees, if fewer than six in number, and in the case of six or more allottees a brief generic description of each new class of equity holder;
  - the market price of the allotted securities on the date on which the terms of the issue were fixed; and
  - the date on which the terms of the issue were fixed;
- where a Listed company has Listed shares in issue and is a subsidiary undertaking of another company, details of the participation by the parent undertaking in any placing of its shares;
- details of any contract of significance subsisting during the period under review:
  - to which the Listed company, or one of its subsidiary undertakings, is a party and in which a director of the Listed company is or was materially interested; and
  - between the Listed company, or one of its subsidiary undertakings, and a controlling shareholder;

- details of any contract for the provision of services to the Listed company or any of its subsidiary undertakings by a controlling shareholder, subsisting during the period under review, unless:
  - it is a contract for the provision of services which it is the principal business of the shareholder to provide; and
  - it is not a contract of significance;
- details of any arrangement under which a shareholder has waived or agreed to waive any dividends or future dividends; and
- a statement made by the board:
  - whether the company has entered into any controlling shareholder agreement required under *LR 9.2.2ADR*; or
  - where the company has not entered into an agreement as required under *LR 9.2.2ADR*:
    - a statement that the FCA has been notified of that non-compliance in accordance with LR 9.2.23 R; and
    - a brief description of the background to and reasons for failing to enter into the agreement that enables shareholders to evaluate the impact of non-compliance on the company; and
  - that:
    - the company has complied with the undertakings in *LR 6.5.4R* or *LR 9.2.2ADR*;
    - so far as the company is aware, the undertakings in *LR 6.5.4R* or *LR 9.2.2AD R(1)* have been complied with by the controlling shareholder or any of its associates; and
    - so far as the company is aware, the procurement obligation (as set out in *LR 6.5.5R(2)(a)* or *LR 9.2.2BR (2)(a))* included in any agreement entered into under *LR 6.5.4R* or *LR 9.2.2AD R(1)* has been complied with by a controlling shareholder; or
  - where an undertaking in *LR 6.5.4R* or *LR 9.2.2AD R(1)* or a procurement obligation (as set out in *LR 6.5.5R(2)(a)* or *LR 9.2.2BR (2)(a))* included in any agreement entered into under *LR 6.5.4R* or *LR 9.2.2AD R(1)* has not been complied with:
    - a statement that the FCA has been notified of that non-compliance in accordance with *LR 9.2.24 R*; and
    - a brief description of the background to and reasons for failing to comply with the relevant undertaking or procurement obligation that enables shareholders to evaluate the impact of non-compliance on the company.

Where an independent director declines to support any of the statements relating to controlling shareholders, the statement must record this fact.

Where a Listed company's annual financial report contains a statement relating to non-observance of a controlling shareholder agreement, the FCA may still take any action it considers necessary in relation to the underlying breach by the Listed company of *LR 9.2.2AD R(1)* or *LR 9.2.2G R*.

The Listed company's annual financial report must include the information required under LR 9.8.4 R in a single identifiable section, unless the annual financial report includes a cross reference table indicating where that information is set out.

A Listed company need not include with the annual report and accounts details of waivers of dividends of less than 1% of the total value of any dividend provided that some payment has been made on each share of the relevant class during the relevant calendar year.

In the case of a company incorporated in the UK, the following additional items must be included in its annual financial report (*LR 9.8.6R*):

- details of all the interests notifiable under MAR 19 of each director of the company as at the end of the financial period, including any changes in the interests between the end of the financial period and a date not more than one month prior to the date of the notice of the AGM; if there have been no changes in a statement to that effect, (*LR 9.8.6A*);
- a statement showing, as at a date not more than one month prior to the date of the notice of the AGM:
  - interests in voting shares disclosed to the company; or
  - if no disclosures have been made, a statement to that effect;
- a statement made by the directors that the business is a going concern, together with supporting assumptions or qualifications as necessary, that has been prepared in accordance with the *Guidance on Risk Management, Internal Control and Related Financial and Business Reporting* published by the FRC in July 2018 (for financial years beginning on or after 1 January 2019);
- a statement setting out:
  - details of any shareholders' authority for the purchase by the company of its own shares that remains valid at the end of the financial period;
  - in the case of purchases made otherwise than through the market or by tender to all shareholders, the names of sellers of any shares purchased, or proposed to be purchased, by the company during the financial period;
  - in the case of any purchases made otherwise than through the market or by tender or partial offer to all shareholders, or options or contracts to make such purchases, entered into since the end of the financial period; and
  - in the case of sales of treasury shares for cash made otherwise than through the market, or in connection with an employees' share scheme, or otherwise than pursuant to an opportunity which (so far as was practicable) was made available to all holders of the listed company's securities (or to all holders of a relevant class of its securities) on the same terms, particulars of the names of purchasers of such shares sold, or proposed to be sold;

- a statement of how the company has applied the main principles set out in the Governance Code;
- a statement as to whether the company has:
  - complied throughout the accounting period with all relevant provisions set out in the Governance Code; or
  - not complied throughout the accounting period with all relevant provisions set out in the Governance Code and if not, setting out: those provisions it has not complied with; in the case of provisions whose requirements are of a continuing nature, the period within which it did not comply with some or all of those provisions; the company's reasons for non-compliance; and
- a report to the shareholders by the board that contains all the matters set out in *LR 9.8.8R*:
  - the unexpired term of the service contract of any director proposed for election or re-election at the forthcoming AGM; and
  - if any director for election or re-election does not have a service contract, a statement to that effect.

Availability of annual accounts and reports

Section 430 requires quoted companies to make available, on their website, their annual accounts and reports during the period from their publication until at least the date of publication of the annual accounts and reports for the following year.

The annual accounts and reports must be made available as soon as reasonably practicable, on a website that is maintained by or on behalf of the company, and that identifies the company in question. Access to the website must be available to all members of the public and not just to members of the company, continuously and free of charge. Any member or holder of debentures of a quoted company is entitled to be provided, on demand and without charge, with a single copy (in addition to any copy they might be entitled to under s. 423) of the following documents:

- last annual accounts;
- last directors' remuneration report;
- last strategic report;
- last directors' report; and
- auditor's report on the accounts (s. 432).

Section 433(3) lists those accounts documents of a quoted company which, in relation to each published copy, are required to bear the name of the person who signed the document on behalf of the board. For a quoted company, those documents are:

- the company's balance sheet;
- the directors' remuneration report;
- the strategic report; and
- the directors' report.

Directors' remuneration policy

A quoted company must, at least every three years, put a resolution to the meeting held to receive the annual report and accounts, a resolution to approve the directors' remuneration policy or any revisions to the directors' remuneration policy.

Any changes to the directors' remuneration policy are not effective until approved by the members.

Filing obligation of quoted companies

Section 447 separates out the specific filing obligations of quoted companies and includes a requirement to file the directors' remuneration report with the Registrar of Companies together with the auditors' report on the auditable part of the directors' remuneration report, in addition to the company's annual accounts, the directors' report and any separate corporate governance statement.

Sections 497 and 498 relate to duties of auditors of quoted companies.

Resignation of auditors

Section 519(3) makes specific provision in relation to an auditor of a quoted company ceasing to hold office. On ceasing to hold office for any reason, the auditor is required to deposit, at the company's registered office, a statement of the circumstances connected with their ceasing to hold office. This differs from the obligation of an auditor of an unquoted company who ceases to hold office, where the auditor is not required to deposit a statement unless they consider there to be circumstances that need to be brought to the attention of members or creditors in connection with them ceasing to hold office, in which case a statement to that effect must be deposited at the company's registered office.

Section 519 provides that auditors leaving quoted companies will now always be required to make a statement of the circumstances.

It is the auditor's responsibility to file a copy of their statement connected with their resignation with Companies House (s. 521); companies that constitute major audits are required to notify the Financial Reporting Council (FRC). The notification must include the statement of circumstances from the auditor if they consider there are matters to be brought to the attention of members, or, if there are none, the company must itself state why the audit appointment has terminated (s. 523(2)).

Rights of members to raise audit concerns

Section 527(1) permits the members of a quoted company, either holding between them 5% of the total voting rights or from at least 100 members holding on average shares with a nominal paid-up capital of £100, to require the company to publish, on a website, a statement setting out any matter relating to the audit of the company's accounts that are to be laid before the next accounts meeting, or any circumstances connected with a departing auditor of the company since the previous accounts meeting, that the members propose to raise at the next accounts meeting of the company.

Section 527(5) protects the company if members abuse the right – for example, by requesting a defamatory statement to be published. It enables the company, or someone else such as the auditor or a director, to apply to the court, and the court can then determine whether the right is being abused, in which case the company is not obliged to publish the statement. Section 527(6) provides that the court can order the shareholders who requested publication to pay some or all of the costs of such proceedings.

Length of notice

For traded companies, the notice periods are set out in s. 307A as follows:

- general meetings where specified conditions met: 14 days;
- all other general meetings: 21 days.

In order for a general meeting of a traded company to be held on 14 days' notice, the circumstances specified in s. 307A must be met. This section was inserted into the Act by the Companies (Shareholders' Rights) Regulations 2009 (SI 2009/1632). These circumstances are as follows:

- the meeting is not an annual general meeting (AGM);
- members are offered an electronic voting facility; and
- a special resolution has been passed to reduce the notice period to 14 days. This must have happened at either the immediately preceding AGM or at a general meeting held since the last AGM.

If all three conditions are met, the notice period will be 14 days. In all other cases, 21 days' notice will be required.

Uncertificated Securities Regulations

Regulation 34 of the Uncertificated Securities Regulations 1995, SI 1995/3272 (USR 1995) provides for a time to be specified in the notice of meetings for establishing the entitlement of members who hold shares in uncertificated form to attend and vote at general meetings. This cannot be more than 48 hours prior to the meeting. This takes account of the CREST settlement system, which operates on a real-time basis, with transactions being registered up to and indeed during the meeting. The specified cut-off time allows the entitlement to attend and vote, including by proxy, to be fixed. Current practice is to stipulate the close of business two days prior to the meeting. This results in a weekend cut-off date for meetings held on Mondays or Tuesdays, but as there are no settlements at weekends, it has no adverse effect.

USR 2001, reg. 41, paras. (3) and (4) provide for the company to stipulate a date not more than 21 days prior to the date of issue of the notice as the record date for the purposes of establishing the right to receive notice of the meeting.

Results of a poll

Section 341 requires quoted companies to disclose, on a website, the results of polls taken at general meetings, and includes a requirement for traded companies to publish the number of abstentions (if counted).

Section 353 sets out the requirements relating to the website on which the poll results must be published (see below).

Section 342 permits the members of a quoted company holding more than 5% of the total voting rights of all members who have a right to vote on the matter to which the poll relates (excluding any votes attaching to treasury shares), or more than 100 members with the right to vote on the matter to which the poll relates and who hold shares in the company on which there has been paid up an average sum per member of not less than £100, to require the directors to obtain an independent report on any poll taken or to be taken at a general meeting.

A request for an independent report on a poll must be received by the quoted company not later than one week after the poll is taken (s. 342(4)).

Listing rules and disclosure and transparency obligations of Listed companies

The continuing obligations in the listing rules, together with the disclosure and transparency rules, require and regulate:

- public announcements of certain matters affecting the company or its securities;
- circulars to be sent to shareholders informing them of imminent substantial transactions;
- the issue of the company's accounts;
- the purchase by the company of its own securities; and details regarding the directors and, in particular, their interests in the company's securities.

The obligations set out in the *Listing Rules*, Chapter 9 and the *Disclosure and Transparency Rules* are:

- general obligations (*LR 9.2*);
- obligations relating to proxies, sanctions relating to s. 793, pre-emption rights (*LR 9.3* and *DTR 6*);
- documents requiring prior approval (*LR 9.4*);
- share transactions such as rights issues, open offers and reconstructions (*LR 9.5* and *DTR 6*);
- notification of changes (*LR 9.6*);
- preliminary statement of annual results, dividends and half-yearly reports (*LR 9.7A* and *DTR 4*);
- annual report and account (*LR 9.8* and *DTR 4*);
- control and notification of inside information (*DTR 2*);
- notification of interests in shares (*DTR 3*); and
- notification of major interests in shares (*DTR 5*).

General obligations

A Listed company must, at all times, have its shares admitted to trading on a RIE and must notify the FCA that it has requested a RIE to admit or readmit any shares to trading, requested a RIE to cancel or suspend trading or that its shares have been cancelled or suspended from trading by a regulatory information service (RIS) (*LR* 2.2.3 and 9.2.2).

At least 75% of the company's shares business must be independent and controlled by the company (*LR* 6.1.4 and 9.2.2A).

The shares must be capable of being settled electronically (via CREST). A Listed company must comply with the *Disclosure and Transparency Rules* (*LR* 9.2.6 and 9.2.6B).

At least 25% of the issued shares excluding any shares held in treasury must be held by the public (*LR* 6.1.19 and 9.2.15).

Whenever a company publishes unaudited financial information in a class 1 circular or prospectus, it must reproduce that information in its next audited accounts and explain any variance of 10% or more between any profit forecast or estimate and the actual profit (*LR* 9.2 18).

Obligations relating to shareholders and exercise of rights

A Listed company must ensure that a proxy form allows for three-way voting and state that if there is no indication on how the proxy may vote, the proxy shall exercise their discretion as to whether and if so how to vote. Where there are five or more directors to retire by rotation, the proxy form may give shareholders the opportunity to vote on all elections as a whole, in addition to voting on each re-election individually (*LR* 9.3.6 and 9.3.7). Companies must not prevent shareholders from exercising their rights by proxy and must provide all shareholders with either a paper form of proxy or by electronic means. Forms of proxy must be available either with the notice of general meeting or following the announcement of the meeting (*DTR* 6.1.5).

Where a company has power in its articles of association to impose sanctions on a shareholder for non-compliance with a request for information under s. 793, those powers are restricted to:

- any sanction can only be implemented after 14 days' notice;
- for shareholdings of less than 0.25%, the sanctions are restricted to prohibition on attending meetings and exercise of voting rights;
- for shareholdings in excess of 0.25%, additional permitted sanctions are the withholding of dividend payments and restricting the right of transfer; and
- any sanctions imposed must cease to apply within seven days of the information requested being supplied or notice of a sale to an unconnected third party has been made through a RIS or overseas exchange or by the acceptance of a takeover offer (*LR* 9.3.9).

A company proposing to issue further equity shares or to sell treasury shares must offer them to existing shareholders in proportion to their holding, unless a general disapplication of the statutory pre-emption rights has been given pursuant to s. 561 or a rights issue is proposed and the disapplication relates to fractional entitlements and entitlements that are necessary or expedite (i.e. withholding entitlements from overseas shareholders), or where the sale is to an employee share scheme (*LR 9.3.11* and *12*).

Companies must disclose any changes in the rights attaching to shares (*DTR 6.1.9*).

Companies must ensure equal treatment of shareholders and provide all the facilities and information to enable such holders to exercise their rights (*DTR 6.1.3* and *4*). Companies must appoint a financial institution through which shareholders may exercise their financial rights (*DTR 6.1.6*). Companies may take advantage of electronic communications, but:

- any decision to do so must be taken in general meeting and the use of electronic communication must not be dependent on the location of the shareholder;
- identification arrangements must be made to ensure shareholders can exercise their rights and are informed;
- shareholders must be contacted in writing to request their consent to the dissemination of information by electronic means; and
- shareholders must be able to request information in written form (*DTR 6.1.8*).

Companies must provide information to the holders of loan stock or other debt instruments concerning the place, time and agenda of meetings, total number of shares and voting rights and the right of shareholders to participate in meetings (*DTR 6.1.12*).

Controlling shareholder agreements

A controlling shareholder of a Listed company is defined as any person together with any other persons they are acting in concert with who between them control at least 30% of the votes able to be cast at general meetings.

Companies with a controlling shareholder must enter into a legally binding controlling shareholder agreement or relationship agreement, in order to provide greater protection for minority shareholders. The agreement, as a minimum must contain the following undertakings by the controlling shareholder:

- that transactions and arrangement between the company and the controlling shareholder will be conducted on an arm's length basis on normal commercial terms;
- that the controlling shareholder will not take any action that would prevent the company from complying with its obligations under the *Listing Rules*; and

- that the controlling shareholder will not seek any shareholder resolutions the purpose of which is intended or appears to be intended to circumvent the proper application of the *Listing Rules*.

The FCA has confirmed that the intention is to ensure as far as possible that inappropriate relationships do not develop.

The consequence of a controlling shareholder failing to enter into a relationship agreement, or of non-compliance with the independence provisions, is that a Listed company will become subject to the related party requirements in Chapter 11 of the *Listing Rules* for any transaction with the controlling shareholder. The *Listing Rules* contain exceptions to normal related party requirements for ordinary course transactions, small transactions or other exempt transactions, which will not apply to transactions with a controlling shareholder, provided a relationship agreement is in place and adhered to.

Listed companies with a controlling shareholder must confirm in their annual report that they have entered into a controlling shareholders agreement, the extent to which the parties to the agreement have complied with the terms and explanation for any non-compliance.

When a premium listed company has a controlling shareholder, any directors proposed for election or re-election as independent directors will be subject to approval by both:

1. all shareholders; and
2. independent shareholders.

If this approval is not obtained, the company may propose a further resolution 90–120 days after the first, on which all shareholders will be entitled to vote – no separate approval by independent shareholders is required for this second vote.

Documents requiring prior approval of shareholders

Companies must ensure that the terms of any employees' share scheme or long-term incentive scheme are approved by ordinary resolution of shareholders in general meeting before being adopted (*LR 9.4.1*) other than schemes where all or substantially all employees are eligible to participate on similar terms provided that all or substantially all employees are not also directors (*LR 9.4.2*). There is also a limited exemption in circumstances where the only participant is a director and the arrangement is provided in unusual circumstances to facilitate their recruitment or retention as a director (*LR 9.4.2(2)*). In such circumstances, full disclosure must be made in the next annual report published after the date on which the individual is eligible to participate in the arrangement.

Companies must not issue options or warrants where the exercise price is less than the market value as determined in accordance with the scheme rules without the prior sanction of shareholders by ordinary resolution in general meeting (*LR 9.4.4*). This rule does not apply where the grant relates to options or warrants being granted in an employees' share scheme and participation is offered on substantially the same terms to all or substantially all employees, or in circumstances where the grant of options or warrants is pursuant to the issue of replacement options following a takeover or reconstruction (*LR 9.4.5*).

Share transactions such as rights issues, open offers and reconstructions

Where unsubscribed rights are to be placed prior to the commencement of dealings, a company must ensure that the placings account for at least 25% of the total shares issued under the rights issue, that placees are required to purchase any rights placed with them and that the purchase price of those rights does not exceed, by more than 50%, the difference between the offer price and the theoretical ex-rights price (*LR 9.5.1*).

Where any unsubscribed rights are sold by the company, any premium over the offer price less any expenses must be distributed to the holders of the shares to which the rights relate, except that amounts of £5 or less may be retained by the company (*LR 9.5.4*).

As soon as practical following completion of a rights issue, the company must notify a RIS of the issue price and principal terms of the offer, and the results of the issue including the date and price at which any unsubscribed rights were sold, if any. Rights issues must remain open for acceptances for at least 21 days (*LR 9.5.5 and 6*).

The timetable of an open offer of securities must be approved by the RIE on which the shares are traded. The terms of the open offer must contain a note that the terms are subject to shareholder approval, if this is the case, and the circular relating to the open offer must not imply that the offer gives the same entitlements as a rights issue (*LR 9.5.7* and 8).

If the company undertakes a vendor placing, it must ensure that all vendors have the opportunity to participate equally in the placing (*LR 9.5.9*).

An offer by a Listed company by way of open offer, placing, vendor placing, offer for subscription or issues out of treasury must not be at a discount of more than 10% to the mid-market price on the day the announcement of the offer or agreeing the placing takes place. The reference to mid-market price means the mid-market quotation for those shares published by the market on which the company's shares are admitted to trading (*LR 9.5.10*). A discount of more than 10% is permitted if the issue is subject to specific shareholder approval or made pursuant to a pre-existing general disapplication of pre-emption rights.

A company undertaking an offer for sale or offer for subscription must ensure that letters of allotment or acceptance are all issued simultaneously and numbered serially. There must be equality of treatment between certificated and uncertificated holdings. Letters of regret must be issued at the same time or not more than three business days later, provided that where letters of regret are not posted at the same time an advertisement is published in a national newspaper to be published on the day following posting of the letters of acceptance or allotment (*LR 9.5.11*).

If a Listed company issues a circular in connection with a reconstruction or refinancing, the circular must contain a working capital statement drawn up under the provisions of *LR 13.3* and on the basis that the reconstruction or refinancing is successful (*LR 9.5.12*).

If an issue of shares includes a fractional entitlement, the company must ensure that the fractions are sold for the benefit of holders of the shares to which the fractions relate and distribute such amounts to those holders where the net proceeds exceed £5 (*LR 9.5.13*).

Where a company issues additional shares of a class already Listed, application to have the new shares admitted to listing must be made as soon as possible and in any event within one month of allotment (*LR 9.5.14*).

Temporary documents of title relating to Listed shares must be serially numbered and include:

- name and address of first named holder and names of any joint holders;
- for fixed income shares, the amount of the next payment of interest or dividend;
- **pro-rata** entitlement;
- last date (past or future) for registering transfers to be eligible for participation in the issue;
- how the new shares rank for dividend or interest;
- nature of the document of title and proposed issue date;
- how fractions, if any, are to be dealt with; and
- for a rights issue, the period (minimum 21 days) during which the offer can be accepted and details of how any rights not subscribed will be dealt with, if at all.

If the offer is renounceable, the documents should also:

- state in the heading that the document is of value and negotiable;
- advise shareholders that if they are in any doubt about what to do to seek advice from an appropriate independent adviser;
- state that if the securities to which the offer relates have been sold to pass the documents to the person through whom the transfer was made for transmission to the purchaser;
- have the form of renunciation and registration instructions printed on the reverse or attached to the document;
- include provision for splitting and for the split form to be certified; and
- if, at the same time as shares are being offered for cash payment, shares are also being offered credited as fully paid, provide for the same period of renunciation (*LR 9.5.15*).

Definitive certificates of title must include the following details on the front:

- the authority under which the company is incorporated, the country of incorporation and its registered number, if any;

- the number of securities represented by the certificate in the top right-hand corner, including, if appropriate, the number and denomination of those securities;
- a footnote stating that transfer of all or part of the securities represented by the certificate cannot be registered without production of the certificate;
- if applicable, a note stating the minimum amount or multiples in which the securities may be transferred;
- the date of issue of the certificate;
- for a fixed income security, the interest payable and payment dates and a summary on the reverse of the redemption, repayment or conversion rights; and
- if the securities have preferential rights, a statement on the front, or, if this is not practical, on the reverse of the certificate of the rights to capital, dividends and conversion, if any (*LR 9.5.16*).

Announcements to FCA or a RIS

Documents

Companies must forward two copies of all circulars, notices, reports or other documents to which the listing rules apply to the FCA for publishing through the document-viewing facility. These copies must be forwarded to the FCA at the same time that they are issued. Other than routine business at their AGMs, companies must forward two copies of all resolutions passed in general meeting to the FCA for publication through the document-viewing facility as soon as possible after the meeting. Companies must notify a RIS when a document is available for viewing on the document-viewing facility, unless the full text of the document is also provided to the RIS (*LR 9.6.1–3* and *9.6.18*).

Capital

The FCA must be informed of the following information in relation to changes in capital:

- proposed changes to capital structure including any Listed debt securities;
- number of shares redeemed and the number remaining outstanding; and
- details of any extension to the validity of temporary documents of title.

Details of the results of a share issue must be notified as soon as known except that, subject to *DTR 2*, the announcement may be delayed by up to two business days, to enable underwriting commitments to be taken up or lapse (*LR 9.6.4* and *6*).

Directors

A RIS must be notified no later than the end of the business day following the decision or receipt of notice of any change in the board including (*LR 9.6.11*):

- name, position and function of any new director;
- resignation, removal or retirement of any director. Notification is not required where a director retires by rotation and is reappointed at a general meeting;

- significant changes to the role, functions or responsibilities of a director; and the effective date of any changes if not immediate and, if not known, that fact. Additional notification will be required once the date of change is known (*LR 9.6.12*).

In respect of the appointment of a new director, the following information must be disclosed within five business days of the decision to appoint them:

- details of all current directorships of publicly quoted companies held during the preceding five years distinguishing between current and past directorships;
- any unspent convictions in relation to indictable offences;
- details of any receiverships, **compulsory liquidations**, creditors' voluntary liquidations, administrations, company voluntary liquidations or compositions or arrangements with creditors or any class of creditors where the director was an executive director at the time or within 12 months preceding those events;
- details of any compulsory liquidations, administrations or partnership voluntary liquidations or compositions or arrangements with creditors or any class of creditors where the director was a partner at the time or within 12 months preceding those events;
- details of any receiverships of any asset of such person or partnership in which the director was a partner at the time or within 12 months preceding those events; and
- details of any public criticisms of the director by statutory or regulatory authorities and whether the director has ever been disqualified by a court from acting as a director or from fulfilling management duties or conducting the affairs of a company.

Any changes to these details and any new directorships in a publicly quoted company must be notified to a RIS as soon as possible (*LR 9.6.13* and *14*).

Lock-ups

Companies must notify a RIS as soon as possible of information relating the disposal of shares under an exemption to a lock-up arrangement previously disclosed in accordance with the prospectus regulations. Details of any variation to the terms of any lock-up arrangement must be notified as soon as possible (*LR 9.6.18* and *19*).

Change of name

When a company changes its name, it must notify a RIS, stating the date on which the change was effective, notify the FCA in writing and forward to the FCA a copy of the certificate of incorporation on change of name (*LR 9.6.19*).

Change of accounting date

A company must notify a RIS as soon as possible of any change in its accounting date, including the new accounting reference date. Where the effect of the change is to extend an accounting period to more than 14 months, the company will be required to issue a second interim report. The second interim report should be made up to either the old accounting reference date or a date not more than six months prior to the new accounting reference date (*LR 9.6.20–22*).

Preliminary statement of annual results, dividends, half-yearly reports and interim management statements

If a company prepares a preliminary statement of its annual results, the statement must be published as soon as possible after it has been approved by the board. The statement must be agreed with the company's auditor prior to publication (*LR 7A*).

The statement must include figures in the form of a table, including the items required for its interim report, and must be consistent with the presentation to be adopted in the annual report.

The statement must indicate any modification likely to be included in the auditor's report to the annual report, together with any significant additional information required to assess the results being announced.

A company must notify a RIS as soon as possible after the board meeting to approve a decision to pay or withhold a dividend or other distribution to shareholders, giving details of the net amount per share payable, the payment date, record (if applicable) and any foreign income dividend election, together with any income tax treated as payable at the lower rate and not repayable.

Listed companies are required to issue a half-yearly financial report covering the first six months of the financial year. The half-yearly report must be published as soon as possible and no later than two months after the end of the period to which it relates. Copies of the half-yearly report must be available to the public for at least ten years (*DTR 4.2.2*).

The half-yearly report must contain a condensed set of financial statements, interim management report and a statement of responsibilities (*DTR 4.2.3*). If the company is required to prepare consolidated accounts, the half-yearly report must be prepared in accordance with IAS 34 (*DTR 4.2.4*).

If the company is not required to prepare consolidated accounts, the condensed financial statements must contain a condensed balance sheet, condensed profit-and-loss account and explanatory notes. The half-yearly report must follow the same accounting policies and principles for recognising and measuring used when preparing the annual financial report and, for the balance sheet, show the same headings and subtotals included in the most recent annual financial statement together with any additional information required to ensure a true and fair view of the assets, liabilities, financial position and profit and loss of the company (*DTR 4.2.5* and *6*).

The interim management report included in the half-yearly report must include details of any important events during the period and their impact on the financial statements, and a summary of the principal risks and uncertainties for the remaining six months of the financial year (*DTR 4.2.7*).

The interim management report must also contain details of any related party transactions that have materially affected the financial position or performance of the company, and any changes in related party transactions disclosed in the previous financial report that could have a material effect on the financial position or performance of the company during the period covered by the interim management report.

If the half-yearly report has been audited, the auditor's report must be reproduced in full. If the half-yearly report has not been audited, a statement of this fact must be included in the report (*DTR 4.2.9*).

The half-yearly report must include a responsibility statement made by those responsible confirming that, to the best of their knowledge and belief, the financial statements have been prepared in accordance with applicable accounting standards and give a true and fair view of the assets, liabilities, financial position and profit or loss of the company, and that the interim management report contains a fair review of the information required to be revised by *DTR 4.2.7* and *8*. The responsibility statement must disclose the name and functions of those making the responsibility statement (*DTR 4.2.10*).

Annual report and accounts

A Listed company must publish its annual financial report within four months of the end of the financial year and ensure that its annual financial reports are freely available to the public for at least ten years after publication (*DTR 4.1.3* and *4*).

The annual financial report of a Listed company must include (*DTR 4.1.5*) the:

- audited financial statements;
- management report; and
- responsibility statements.

If the company is required to prepare consolidated accounts, the financial statements must comprise consolidated accounts prepared in accordance with IFRS (International Financial Reporting Standards) and parent company accounts prepared in accordance with the law of the country of its incorporation.

If the company is not required to prepare consolidated accounts, its financial statements must comprise accounts prepared in accordance with the law of the country of its incorporation (*DTR 4.1.6*).

The financial statements must be audited and the full text of the audit report made public (*DTR 4.1.7*).

The management report must contain (*DTR 4.1.8–11*):

- a fair review of the company's business and a description of the principal risks and uncertainties facing it. The business review must be a balanced and comprehensive analysis if the development and performance of the company during the financial year, and the position of the company at the end of the year. The review must also contain sufficient analysis, using financial key performance and other key performance indicators including environmental and employee matters, to demonstrate the development, performance and position of the company during the financial year (*DTR 4.1.8* and *9*);

- details of any important events since the end of the financial year, likely future development, any activities in research and development, details of any acquisition(s) of own shares and the existence of any overseas branches; and
- in relation to the company's use of financial instruments or where required for the assessment of its assets, liabilities, financial position and profit or loss, details of its financial risk management objectives and policies, and the company's exposure to price risk, credit risk, liquidity risk and cash flow risk.

The annual financial report must include a responsibility statement made by those responsible confirming that, to the best of their knowledge and belief, the financial statements have been prepared in accordance with applicable accounting standards and give a true and fair view of the assets, liabilities, financial position and profit or loss of the company, and that the management report contains a fair review of the information required to be reviewed. The responsibility statement must disclose the name and functions of those making the responsibility statement (*DTR 4.1.12*).

In addition to the requirements set out in *DTR 4.1*, Listed companies must include in their annual financial report (*LR 9.8.4*):

- a statement of the amount of interest capitalised during the financial year and an indication of the amount and treatment of any related tax relief;
- if the company has published unaudited financial information in a class 1 circular or prospectus since its previous annual financial report, it must reproduce that information and explain any variance of 10% or more between any profit forecast or estimate and the actual profit (*LR 9.2.18*);
- details of any small related party transaction (*LR 11.1.10*);
- details of any long-term incentive schemes required by *LR 9.4.3*; and
- details of any arrangements under which a director of the company has waived or agreed to waive any emoluments from the company or any subsidiary and relating to the period under review or any future year(s).

Where shares are issued for cash during the period under review otherwise than to shareholders in proportion to their holdings, and which has not been specifically authorised by the company in general meeting or where shares are issued in any major subsidiary undertaking, the following details must be provided:

- the classes of shares allotted and for each class of shares, the number allotted, their aggregate nominal value and the consideration paid;
- the names of the allottees, if there were six or fewer, and in the case of six or more allottees, a brief generic description of each new class of equity holder;
- the market price of the shares on the date on which the terms of the issue were fixed;
- the date on which the terms of the issue were fixed;

- where the company is a subsidiary undertaking, details of the participation by the parent undertaking in any placing made during the financial year;
- details of any material contract(s) subsisting during the financial year in which a director of the company is interested, or between the company, or any subsidiary, and a controlling shareholder;
- details of any contract for the provision of services to the company or any subsidiary by a controlling shareholder, subsisting during the financial year, unless it is a contract for the provision of services which it is the principal business of the shareholder to provide and it is not a material contract; and
- details of any arrangement under which a shareholder has waived or agreed to waive future dividends.

In the case of a company incorporated in the UK, the following additional items must be included in its annual financial report (*LR 9.8.6*):

- details of all the interests notifiable under article 19 of the Market Abuse Regulations of each director of the company as at the end of the financial period, including any changes in the interests between the end of the financial period and a date not more than one month prior to the date of the notice of the AGM; if there have been no changes in a statement to that effect, interests of each director include the interests of connected persons of which the company is, or ought upon reasonable enquiry to become, aware. If necessary, companies are expected to seek confirmation from directors of the interests, if any, of their connected persons, but are not expected to seek that confirmation directly from the connected person (*LR 9.8.6A*);
- a statement showing, as at a date not more than one month prior to the date of the notice of the AGM:
  - details of interests in voting shares disclosed to the company in accordance with *DTR 5*; or
  - if no disclosures have been made, a statement to that effect;
- a statement made by the directors that the business is a going concern, together with supporting assumptions or qualifications as necessary, that has been prepared in accordance with the *Guidance on Risk Management, Internal Control and Related Financial and Business Reporting* published by the FRC in September 2014;
- a statement setting out:
  - details of any shareholders' authority for the purchase by the company of its own shares that remains valid at the end of the financial period;
  - in the case of purchases made otherwise than through the market or by tender to all shareholders, the names of sellers of any shares purchased, or proposed to be purchased, by the company during the financial period;
  - in the case of any purchases made otherwise than through the market or by tender or partial offer to all shareholders, or options or contracts to make such purchases, entered into since the end of the financial period; and

  - in the case of sales of treasury shares for cash made otherwise than through the market, or in connection with an employees' share scheme, or otherwise than pursuant to an opportunity which (so far as was practicable) was made available to all holders of the Listed company's securities (or to all holders of a relevant class of its securities) on the same terms, particulars of the names of purchasers of such shares sold, or proposed to be sold;
- a statement of how the company has applied the main principles set out in the UK Corporate Governance Code;
- a statement as to whether the company has:
  - complied throughout the accounting period with all relevant provisions set out in the UK Corporate Governance Code; or
  - not complied throughout the accounting period with all relevant provisions set out in the UK Corporate Governance Code and if not, setting out: those provisions it has not complied with; in the case of provisions whose requirements are of a continuing nature, the period within which it did not comply with some or all of those provisions; and the company's reasons for non-compliance;
- a report to the shareholders by the board that contains all the matters set out in *LR 9.8.8*:
  - the unexpired term of the service contract of any director proposed for election or re-election at the forthcoming AGM; and
  - if any director for election or re-election does not have a service contract, a statement to that effect (*LR 9.8.8*).
- an overseas company with a primary listing must disclose in its annual report and accounts a statement of how the company has applied the main principles set out in the UK Corporate Governance Code, and provide a statement as to whether the company has:
  - complied throughout the accounting period with all relevant provisions set out in the UK Corporate Governance Code; or
  - not complied throughout the accounting period with all relevant provisions set out in the UK Corporate Governance Code and if not, setting out: those provisions it has not complied with; in the case of provisions whose requirements are of a continuing nature, the period within which it did not comply with some or all of those provisions; and the company's reasons for non-compliance;
- the unexpired term of the service contract of any director proposed for election or re-election at the forthcoming AGM; and, if any director for election or re-election does not have a service contract, a statement to that effect (*LR 9.8.8*).

Auditor's report

A Listed company must ensure that the auditors review each of the following before the annual report is published (*LR 9.8.10*):

- the statement by the directors that the business is a going concern;
- the parts of the statement relating to corporate governance that relate to the following provisions of the UK Corporate Governance Code: C1.1, C.2.1, C.2.3 and C3.1–C3.8; and
- any statements relating to corporate governance made in compliance with *DTR 7.2.5* and *7.2.6* and whether *DTR 7.2.2*, *7.2.3* and *7.2.7* have been complied with.

Any strategic report and additional material provided to members must disclose (*LR 9.8.13*) earnings per share, and the content of the strategic report and additional information set out in s. 426A (see Chapter 10).

AIM

Continuing obligations

The continuing obligations imposed on AIM companies by the AIM Rules (AR) include the following:

- Appoint and retain at all times a nominated adviser and a broker, although these roles may be combined (AR 1 and 35). The adviser is responsible for assisting the directors to comply with the rules of AIM (AR 1).
- Publish accounts to International Accounting Standards (AR 19). These accounts must be published and sent to members within six months of the year-end (AR 19). Prepare a half-yearly report within three months of the end of the relevant period and send a copy to a RIS (AR 18). There is no requirement to send the half-yearly accounts to members.
- Ensure that appropriate arrangements are in place for electronic settlement of the company's securities (AR 36).
- The board must adopt a code of dealing prohibiting directors and applicable employees from dealing in the company's shares during a close period and take all proper and reasonable steps to ensure compliance by its directors and applicable employees (AR 21).
- Documents sent to shareholders must be available to the public on a website notified to a RIS for a period of not less than 12 months from the date of the announcement; accounts for the previous three years must be made available (AR 26).
- Forward to a RIS copies of all announcements, circulars, notices, reports or other document at the same time as they are issued to shareholders (AR 10 and 20).

There are no additional requirements for AIM companies with regard to the content of annual accounts, corporate governance, purchase of own shares, etc. The *Listing Rules* do not apply to AIM companies, although some of its provisions are mirrored in the *AIM Rules*.

Announcements

An AIM company must notify a RIS without delay and in writing of (AR 17 except where shown otherwise):

- major developments in its sphere of activity and changes in its financial condition which are not public knowledge and may be price-sensitive (AR 11);
- details disclosed by directors in Schedule 5 regarding their interests in the company's securities and the interests of 'connected persons';
- any information disclosed to the company by significant shareholders;
- changes of directors or their details;
- publication of audited accounts (AR 19) and of any change in its accounting reference date (AR 17);
- the resignation, dismissal or change of any nominated adviser or nominated broker;
- any issue of new securities or cancellation of existing securities of a class already admitted to trading on AIM or the movement of shares into or out of treasury;
- details of any decision to pay a dividend or other distribution;
- details of substantial transactions (AR 12);
- details of changes to the company's legal name, registered office, accounting reference date or the website address required by AR 26;
- details of related party transactions where any ratio is 5% or more (AR 13); and
- any material change between the issuer's actual trading performance or financial condition and any profit forecast, estimate or projection included in its admission document.

NEX Exchange Growth Market

Continuing obligations and announcements

The continuing obligations imposed on NEX Exchange Growth Market companies are set out in Part 2 of the NE RFI and include the following:

- Appoint and retain at all times a NEX Corporate Adviser (NE RFI 31) and announce any resignation or appointment of corporate adviser as soon as possible (NE RFI 69).
- Announce, as soon as possible, any price-sensitive information relating to changes in its sphere of activity, financial position, performance or expected performance. Companies are not required to announce matters under negotiation (NE RFI 34).
- Companies must take reasonable care to ensure that any information announced to the market is relevant, accurate and complete, and that any information it is required to publish is announced no later than the date of publication (NE RFI 36 and 37).

- Electronic copies of documents sent to shareholders must also be forwarded to NEX as well as publicising the address or internet address where copies of the documents are available for inspection (NE RFI 38 and 71).
- Companies must disclose any change in the holdings of directors or significant shareholders notifiable to it under DTR 5 as soon as possible (NE RFI 41).
- Companies must announce their interim results within three months and their final results within five months of the year-end. Financial results must be prepared in accordance with UK or US GAAP or International Accounting Standards. If the annual accounts have had a modified audit opinion in respect of their preparation on a going concern basis, the company must publish quarterly accounts in respect of the first and third quarters of each financial year within one month of each period end (NE RFI 42–47) until such time as audited accounts have an unmodified audit opinion.
- Companies must announce, as soon as possible, the terms of any acquisition or disposal or material transaction which is or is likely to be price-sensitive or details of any reverse takeover (NE RFI 51 and 54).
- Companies must announce any changes in their issued share capital as soon as possible, except that where a series of issues are made, the announcements may be aggregated into monthly amounts. Where the issued share capital changes, the company must announce at the end of that month its issued share capital and that number of shares comprised in that issued share capital (NE RFI 58–62).
- Details of any proposed dividend (NE RFI 63).
- Any appointment, resignation or removal of directors or change in their executive responsibilities (NE RFI 66).
- Companies must have a policy to prohibit directors and their connected persons dealing shares during a close period or on considerations of a short-term nature (NE RFI 67).
- Any change of accounting reference date (NE RFI 70).
- Companies must maintain a website for the disclosure of information to members required by the NE RFI generally and in particular under NE RFI 71.

Market Abuse Regulations 2016 and the Disclosure and Transparency Rules

The Market Abuse Regulations 2016 (MAR) implement a common EU approach for preventing and detecting market abuse and ensuring a proper flow of information to the market. MAR, which came into force on 3 July 2016, introduced a number of changes to the disclosure rules. Although overall, the compliance requirements are largely unchanged, there has been a significant increase in the record keeping and reporting requirement.

In the UK, the most visible change for companies is the deletion of the Model Code from the Listing Rules and changes to the disclosure requirements of share dealing by persons discharging managerial responsibilities (PDMRs).

The primary obligation of companies under the Market Abuse Regulations relate to the control and disclosure of inside information and dealing by PDMRs (*MAR 17–21*). Investment firms have additional responsibilities to monitor and report investment transactions and suspicious activities for the prevention of market manipulation and other fraudulent activity.

MAR works in tandem with the Disclosure and Transparency Rules, and these have been updated to reflect changes introduced by MAR. *DTR 4* and *6* apply to Listed shares on a RIE (LSE Main Market or NEX Exchange Main Board), and *DTR 5* applies to companies with shares Listed on a RIE or on a prescribed market. Accordingly, *DTR 5* also applies to companies with shares admitted to AIM or NEX Growth Market.

DTR 1, *2* and *3* have been deleted and replaced by *MAR 16–19*.

Inside information: disclosure and control

Under *MAR 17*:

- companies must publish 'inside information', via a RIS, that directly concerns them as soon as possible and must post and keep on their website, for five years, copies of all inside information publicly disclosed (*MAR 17(1)*).
- disclosure of inside information may be delayed if:
  - immediate disclosure is likely to prejudice the company's legitimate interests;
  - delayed disclosure is unlikely to mislead the public; and
  - the company can ensure the information remains confidential until it is disclosed (*MAR 17(4)*);
- where a disclosure has been delayed, the company must notify the FCA of that fact immediately after the information has been disclosed, and provide an explanation if requested.

Inside information is information that:

- is precise;
- has not been made public;
- relates directly or indirectly to the company; and
- if made public, is likely to have a significant effect on the price of the company's shares or securities (that is, information that a reasonable investor would be likely to use as part of the basis of their investment decisions) (*MAR 7(1)(b)–(d)*).

Other than in situations where the recipient owes a duty of confidentiality where a company or a person acting on its behalf discloses inside information to a third party in the normal course of employment or profession, there must also be complete public disclosure of that information simultaneously in the case of a planned disclosure, or as soon as possible in the case of a non-intentional disclosure (*MAR 17(8)*).

The ability to share inside information with those owing a duty of confidentiality can only be relied on where the recipient needs that information to provide services or advice to the company (*DTR 2.5.7*). Where a selective disclosure has been made, a holding announcement should be prepared for release as soon as possible in the event of a leak (*DTR 2.6.3*). Any holding announcement should contain:

- as much detail on the subject matter as possible;
- the reasons why a fuller announcement cannot be given; and
- an undertaking to announce further details as soon as possible (*DTR 2.2.9*).

Companies should have a framework for the control of inside information and establish effective arrangements to restrict access to inside information to those persons who require access to perform their job. A company should maintain insider lists in relation to employees and advisers with access to inside information (*MAR 18*).

Companies must have deal-specific or event-based insider lists, and may have a permanent insider list. To be entered on a permanent insider list, the individual will be assumed to have access to all inside information at all times. As a result, any permanent insider list is likely to be very short.

Deal-specific or event-based insider lists must be kept in electronic form, must adhere to the format laid down by the regulations, must be retained for five years and must be capable of being provided to the FCA as soon as possible on request (*MAR 18(1)(c)*, *18(3)* and *18(5)*).

The minimum content for the insider lists is:

- identity of each person with access to the information;
- reason why the person is on the insider list;
- date and time that person obtained access to the information; and
- date on which the insider list was drawn up.

Companies are required to keep their insider lists up to date, and the list must also contain:

- date and time of any change in the reason for inclusion on the insider list;
- date and time any new person is added to the insider list; and
- date and time when a person ceases to have access to inside information.

All insiders must acknowledge in writing their legal and regulatory duties and that they are aware of the sanctions applicable to insider dealing and unlawful disclosure of inside information (*MAR 18(2)*).

Insider dealing

Dealing in shares on a regulated market while in possession of price-sensitive information ('**insider dealing**') is a criminal offence. The legislation is contained in Part V of the Criminal Justice Act 1993 (CJA1993).

Three offences were introduced by CJA1993, s. 52:

- dealing in company securities while in the possession of inside information;
- encouraging another person to deal while in possession of inside information; and
- disclosing information other than in the proper performance of an office, employment or profession.

The insider must either know that they possess inside information or knowingly acquire inside information from an inside source. It is no longer necessary for the insider to be connected with the particular company; a person can be an insider simply by having access to inside information. Accordingly, the husband or wife of a director could be convicted of using inside information passed on by their spouse, and any friends could also be guilty of an offence if they dealt in shares on the basis of inside information gained directly from the director or indirectly from the spouse or some other third party.

The definition of 'securities' has been expanded and now covers not only shares, debentures and debt securities, but also their derivatives (CJA1993 s. 54 and Sch. 2). Thus 'securities' include any asset that can be traded and not just the contract itself.

Similarly, the definition of 'dealing' has been expanded. Although deals of a purely private nature even on the basis of inside information will not normally be covered by the legislation, any transactions on a regulated market (e.g. the Stock Exchange) and any deals undertaken via professional intermediaries whether or not through a regulated market will be covered (CJA1993 s. 55).

The inside information must be specific, relate to the company whose securities have been dealt and must not be public knowledge. It must also be shown that if that information were to have been made public, it would have had a significant effect on the price of the securities concerned. There is, unfortunately, no definition or guidance as to the meaning of 'significant' in the legislation (CJA1993 s. 56).

The defences against a charge of insider dealing are set out in s. 53 of the CJA1993 and include that the person:

1. did not expect the dealing to result in a profit attributable to the information being price-sensitive;
2. had reasonable grounds for believing that the other party to the deal was also in possession of the information; and
3. would have dealt irrespective of whether or not they had been in possession of the price-sensitive information.

It should be emphasised that the provisions contained in CJA1993 are lengthy and complex, and many companies issue detailed notes of guidance for their directors and senior executives.

PDMRs

A person discharging managerial responsibilites (PDMR) is a natural or legal person in an issuer who is either (*MAR 1(13)* and *(25)*):

- a member of the administrative, management or supervisory body of that entity; or
- a senior executive who is not a member of the administrative, management or supervisory body of that entity, but who has regular access to inside information relating directly or indirectly to that entity and the power to make managerial decisions affecting the future developments and business prospects of that entity.

DTR 3.1.2 notes that an individual may be a 'senior executive' irrespective of the nature of any contractual arrangements between the individual and the issuer, and notwithstanding the absence of contractual arrangements, provided the individual has regular access to inside information relating (directly or indirectly) to the issuer, and has power to make managerial decisions affecting the future development and business prospects of the issuer.

It can be seen that the designation of a PDMR will vary from company to company, and that PDMRs might not be directors of the company.

PCA

A PDMR's persons closely associated (PCA) include (*MAR 3(1)(26)*):

- spouse or partner considered equivalent to a spouse under national law;
- dependent children of the PDMR;
- a relative of the PDMR who has shared the same residence for at least one year; and
- any legal person, trust or partnership, the managerial duties and responsibilities of which are carried out by the PDMR or PCA and:
  - is directly or indirectly controlled by the PDMR or PCA;
  - is established for the benefit of the PDMR or PCA; or
  - whose economic interests and substantially the same as the PDMR or PCA.

Disclosure of PDMR share transactions

MAR 19 contains details of the requirement for PDMRs to notify any transactions in shares undertaken by themselves or persons closely associated (PCA) with them. The provisions are very similar to the previous requirements of *DTR 3*.

In addition to notifying the company, PDMRs are now also required to notify the FCA of any transactions (*MAR 19(1)*).

There is a prescribed template for the PDMR disclosure to the FCA (*MAR 19(6)*), and this may be completed and submitted online from the FCA website.

Notifiable transactions must be disclosed within three business days:

- by the PDMR or PCA to the FCA and the company; and
- by the company to the market via a RIS (*MAR 19(2) and (3)*).

Companies must notify their PDMRs in writing of their obligations under *MAR 19* and draw up a list of their PDMRs and PCAs (*MAR 19(5)*).

PDMRs must notify their PCAs in writing of their obligations under *MAR 19* and keep a copy of that notification (*MAR 19(5)*).

Notifications by PDMRs need not be made until the aggregate of all transactions in any calendar year exceed €5,000, although notifications below this limit may be made on a voluntary basis (*MAR 19(8)*).

Closed periods

A PDMR must not conduct any transactions in the financial instruments of the company during a closed period, whether for themselves or for a third party, directly or indirectly (*MAR 19(11)*).

A closed period is the period of 30 days prior to an announcement of the company's full-year or half-year financial report. For this purpose, a preliminary announcement of full-year results will count as an announcement of the full-year results, provided the announcement contains all the key information expected to be included in the full year-end report.

Under MAR, there is no such prohibition on trading in the period prior to the announcement of quarterly results or trading updates; however, any transactions might well constitute insider dealing.

17 – Corporate governance

Introduction

Corporate governance is defined in the 1992 Cadbury Report as 'the system by which companies are directed and controlled'. Shareholders appoint the directors and the external auditors, and should satisfy themselves that an appropriate governance structure is in place. The board of directors sets the company's aims and has a responsibility to provide the leadership to put these into effect, to supervise the management of the business and to report to shareholders on its stewardship.

Although the principles lying at the heart of corporate governance can be applied to companies of all sizes and in particular those where the directors are no also the majority members, for many years reporting on corporate governance was the preserve of Listed companies. This, however, is changing not only with the introduction in 2018 of the Wates Principles but also with the requirement for some companies to report on their gender pay gap, supplier payment policies and policies and procedures to combat modern slavery (see Chapter 7).

The financial aspects of corporate governance are identified as the way in which the board sets financial policy and oversees its implementation (including the use of financial controls), and the process of reporting to the shareholders on the activities and development of the company.

Background

The economic success of the 1980s was followed by a downswing in the economic cycle, resulting in large numbers of unexpected corporate failures. Additionally, there were several high-profile cases of corporate failure involving fraud and/or spectacular lack of internal controls. In order to restore confidence in financial reporting, strengthening of accounting standards and the position of the external auditor in dealing with boards of directors was called for. Further revamps to corporate governance practices were prompted by the global financial crisis in 2007–08.

Cadbury

Following the Robert Maxwell/Mirror Group pension scandal and the collapse of the Bank of Credit and Commerce International (BCCI), there was concerted public pressure for reform. Against this background, in May 1992, Sir Adrian Cadbury's Committee issued a consultative document, the *Report of the Committee on the Financial Aspects of Corporate Governance*. The final report was issued in December 1992 and was generally perceived as a major advance.

A core element of the report was the Cadbury Code of Best Practice. Compliance with the Code was not mandatory, however, under the so-called 'comply or explain' regime where a company did not meet any particular code provision they had to explain in their annual report the reason for non-compliance. This key feature of UK corporate governance remains in place today. Cadbury understood that it was essential to keep the Code up to date and recommended that a new committee be appointed by 30 June 1995 in order to continue the process of review.

Greenbury

Published in July 1995, the report of the new committee, *Directors' Remuneration – Report of a Study Group chaired by Sir Richard Greenbury*, addressed the large salary increases and share option gains enjoyed by directors of the recently privatised utilities, which had led to the popular usage of the title 'fat cat' when describing apparently overpaid directors. The remuneration packages of high-profile directors in other sectors were also attracting attention.

The overriding objective of the Greenbury Committee was to establish a voluntary Code of Best Practice for directors' remuneration, and to impose a more onerous disclosure regime.

Increasing the disclosure requirements would ensure that shareholders were fully informed and able to make informed decisions on the performance of companies and their directors. A central plank of this disclosure regime was the promotion of the remuneration committee. The Report was founded upon three principles:

1 Accountability – directors are accountable to shareholders for the stewardship and performance of their company and responsibility for determining executive remuneration should be delegated to a disinterested body (i.e. the remuneration committee).
2 Transparency – corporate policy on executive remuneration should be reported on annually to shareholders and details of individual directors' packages should be set out in the annual report and accounts.
3 Performance – executive rewards should be linked to the performance of the company and of the individual, and the interests of directors should be aligned with those of shareholders.

Hampel

Following publication of the Greenbury Report, the Committee on Corporate Governance, chaired by Sir Ronald Hampel, was set up in mid-1995 to review progress of the implementation of the findings of the Cadbury and Greenbury Committees. Following wide consultation, the Hampel Committee's final report was issued in January 1998.

The Hampel Committee established a set of broad Principles of Corporate Governance concerning directors, their remuneration, shareholders and accountability and audit, bringing together elements of the earlier codes.

The Committee advocated a flexible approach to compliance, urging shareholders to take note of reasons given by companies for variations from best practice in corporate governance.

The Committee proposed that major changes in corporate governance should be dealt with by the London Stock Exchange and that the Financial Reporting Council should keep a watching brief on the necessity for further studies.

The Hampel Report proposed the consolidation of the Cadbury Code, the Greenbury Code and the Hampel Principles into one code. The Committee passed its proposals to the Stock Exchange, which published the Combined Code in June 1998.

Turnbull

Following publication of the Cadbury Code, guidance was issued concerning the disclosure required relating to internal controls. The disclosure requirements were restricted to financial controls.

After the Hampel Report, additional guidance on reporting on internal control under the Combined Code was issued in September 1999 by the Institute of Chartered Accountants in England and Wales (ICAEW). *Internal Control: Guidance for Directors on the Combined Code*, known as the Turnbull Report, sets out guidance for directors on:

- maintaining a sound system of internal control to safeguard the shareholders' investment and the company's assets;
- determining the extent of their compliance with the Code; and
- periodic consideration of whether an internal audit function should be established.

Higgs and Smith

Since the 1998 Hampel Report, the Financial Reporting Council (FRC) has acted as a focus for considering whether any developments in corporate governance call for further work. After the concerns raised by high-profile failures in the US and UK, and the increasing perception of directors receiving rewards for failure, the Department of Trade and Industry (DTI) (now the Department for Business, Energy & Industrial Strategy (BEIS)) sponsored a review of the role and effectiveness of non-executive directors. The review, chaired by Derek Higgs (the Higgs Review), published its report in January 2003.

On the same day, a second review into the role and responsibilities of audit committees under the chairship of Sir Robert Smith (the Smith Report) was also published. The two review bodies worked closely together and the Higgs Review included a draft of the Combined Code, incorporating both its own and the Smith Report's proposals.

Updated Turnbull: 2005

In October 2005, the Financial Reporting Council published an updated version of the Turnbull guidance. Publication of the updated guidance followed two consultation exercises, during the course of which the principles-based approach of the existing guidance was strongly endorsed by Listed companies, the investment community and the accountancy profession.

Walker Review of Corporate Governance of UK Banking Industry

Sir David Walker's report was published in November 2009 and, although primarily looking at the banking industry, it contained a number of recommendations that the FRC agreed should also apply to Listed companies. These were adopted in the current version of the code, which was also renamed as the UK Corporate Governance Code.

At the same time, the section of the code dealing with institutional shareholders was removed from the code and now forms a separate code: the **UK Stewardship Code**. Like the UK Corporate Governance Code, compliance is voluntary. UK authorised asset managers are required to report whether or not they apply the Code.

The main recommendations of the Walker report were:

- improve directors' induction and training, and provide support for non-executive directors;
- increase the time commitment for non-executive directors;
- board to be re-elected annually;
- external board performance evaluation once every three years;
- creation of a risk committee and chief risk officer, both reporting to the board; and
- re-election of the chair of the remuneration committee if the remuneration report secures less than 75% support from shareholders.

Diversity in the boardroom

Sir David Walker's report into corporate governance in the banking sector, contained recommendations to the FRC to consider incorporating into the Code provisions to promote diversity in the boardroom for all companies, not just those in the banking sector.

In 2010, women made up only 12.5% of the members of the corporate boards of FTSE 100 companies. This was up from 9.4% in 2004.

The importance of promoting a better gender and ethnicity balance on company boards is increasingly recognised across the world. Norway, Spain and Australia, among others, have made significant steps already.

Summary of recommendations

- Chairmen of FTSE 350 companies should set out the percentage of women they aim to have on their boards in 2013 and 2015. FTSE 100 boards should aim for a minimum of 25% female representation by 2015.
- Quoted companies should disclose in their annual report the proportion of women on the board, in senior executive positions and in the whole organisation.
- The Financial Reporting Council should amend the UK Corporate Governance Code to require Listed companies to establish a policy concerning boardroom diversity, including measurable objectives for implementing the policy, and disclose annually a summary of the policy and the progress made in achieving the objectives.
- The annual report should include meaningful information about the company's appointment process and how it addresses diversity, including details of the search and nominations processes used.
- Companies are encouraged to advertise non-executive board positions periodically, to generate greater diversity in applications.

UK Corporate Governance Code (2018)

The current version of the Code was published in July 2018 and applies to companies with a premium listing with financial years beginning on or after 1 January 2019. The 2018 Code has been completely re-written with much greater emphasis placed on the principles within the Code and a number of previous provisions, now forming accepted best practice, being moved to the accompanying guidance document.

The UK Corporate Governance Code is a guide to best practice; premium Listed companies should either comply with this or explain any departures from best practice.

The principles and provisions in the Governance Code are supported by guidance contained in *Guidance on Board Effectiveness* also updated and issued in July 2018. Many of the previous provisions of the Governance Code, although still relevant, are now well established and are no longer included in the Governance Code itself but contained in the guidance instead.

The 2018 update to the Governance Code has placed much more emphasis on the principles. Companies must effectively implement and audit compliance with those principles and provisions as well as reporting on how they have implemented them, in addition to actions taken to change behaviours and the outcome of those changes and their particular impact on and benefit to the reporting company.

Compliance with the UK Corporate Governance Code is not intended to be an exercise in 'box ticking', and compliance with certain aspects of the Code may not be appropriate for all companies.

The Governance Code is divided into five sections containing 18 main principles together with supporting provisions, as follows:

1. Board Leadership and Company Purpose

A. A successful company is led by an effective and entrepreneurial board, whose role is to promote the long-term sustainable success of the company, generating value for shareholders and contributing to wider society.

B. The board should establish the company's purpose, values and strategy, and satisfy itself that these and its culture are aligned. All directors must act with integrity, lead by example and promote the desired culture.

C. The board should ensure that the necessary resources are in place for the company to meet its objectives and measure performance against them. The board should also establish a framework of prudent and effective controls, which enable risk to be assessed and managed.

D. In order for the company to meet its responsibilities to shareholders and stakeholders, the board should ensure effective engagement with, and encourage participation from, these parties.

E. The board should ensure that workforce policies and practices are consistent with the company's values and support its long-term sustainable success. The workforce should be able to raise any matters of concern.

2. Division of Responsibilities

F. The chair leads the board and is responsible for its overall effectiveness in directing the company. They should demonstrate objective judgement throughout their tenure and promote a culture of openness and debate. In addition, the chair facilitates constructive board relations and the effective contribution of all non-executive directors, and ensures that directors receive accurate, timely and clear information.

G. The board should include an appropriate combination of executive and non-executive (and, in particular, independent non-executive) directors, such that no one individual or small group of individuals dominates the board's decision-making. There should be a clear division of responsibilities between the leadership of the board and the executive leadership of the company's business.

H. Non-executive directors should have sufficient time to meet their board responsibilities. They should provide constructive challenge, strategic guidance, offer specialist advice and hold management to account.

I. The board, supported by the company secretary, should ensure that it has the policies, processes, information, time and resources it needs in order to function effectively and efficiently.

3. Composition, Succession and Evaluation

J. Appointments to the board should be subject to a formal, rigorous and transparent procedure, and an effective succession plan should be maintained for board and senior management. Both appointments and succession plans should be based on merit and objective criteria and, within this context, should promote diversity of gender, social and ethnic backgrounds, cognitive and personal strengths.

K. The board and its committees should have a combination of skills, experience and knowledge. Consideration should be given to the length of service of the board as a whole and membership regularly refreshed.

L. Annual evaluation of the board should consider its composition, diversity and how effectively members work together to achieve objectives. Individual evaluation should demonstrate whether each director continues to contribute effectively.

4. Audit, Risk and Internal Control

M. The board should establish formal and transparent policies and procedures to ensure the independence and effectiveness of internal and external audit functions and satisfy itself on the integrity of financial and narrative statements.

N. The board should present a fair, balanced and understandable assessment of the company's position and prospects.

O. The board should establish procedures to manage risk, oversee the internal control framework, and determine the nature and extent of the principal risks the company is willing to take in order to achieve its long-term strategic objectives.

5. Remuneration

P. Remuneration policies and practices should be designed to support strategy and promote long-term sustainable success. Executive remuneration should be aligned to company purpose and values and be clearly linked to the successful delivery of the company's long-term strategy.

Q. A formal and transparent procedure for developing policy on executive remuneration and determining director and senior management remuneration should be established. No director should be involved in deciding their own remuneration outcome.

R. Directors should exercise independent judgement and discretion when authorising remuneration outcomes, taking account of company and individual performance, and wider circumstances.

The Wates Guiding Principles for Large Private Companies

The original corporate governance code was focused on providing additional safeguards for investors and holding directors to be more accountable. As a consequence, the guidance only applied to Listed companies, although it has been adopted with a number of changes by other non-listed organisations in order to demonstrate their corporate governance credentials.

Over the years, corporate governance has evolved and the scope of the protection has widened to include additional stakeholders relevant to both public and privately owned groups. During recent years there have been a number of high-profile collapses among large privately held companies, which has led to the call for a corporate governance regime specifically for such large private companies allowing for more meaningful comparison of their corporate governance processes and procedures.

Under the chairship of James Wates, the Coalition Group published six guiding principles for large private companies (the Wates Principles). As with the UK Corporate Governance Code, adherence to the Principles is not compulsory; however, any deviation should be explained. The Wates Principles are intended for use by private companies meeting the following criteria:

1 turnover of £200m or more and balance sheet value of more than £2 billion; and
2 more than 2,000 employees

The Wates Principles are:

1 **Purpose:** An effective board promotes the purpose of a company, and ensures that its values, strategy and culture align with that purpose.
2 **Composition:** Effective board composition requires an effective chair and a balance of skills, backgrounds, experience and knowledge, with individual directors having sufficient capacity to make a valuable contribution. The size of a board should be guided by the scale and complexity of the company.
3 **Responsibilities:** A board should have a clear understanding of its accountability and terms of reference. Its policies and procedures should support effective decision-making and independent challenge.
4 **Opportunity and risk:** A board should promote the long-term success of the company by identifying opportunities to create and preserve value and establishing oversight for the identification and mitigation of risks.
5 **Remuneration:** A board should promote executive remuneration structures aligned to the sustainable long-term success of a company, taking into account pay and conditions elsewhere in the company.
6 **Stakeholders:** A board has a responsibility to oversee meaningful engagement with material stakeholders, including the workforce, and have regard to that discussion when taking decisions. The board has a responsibility to foster good stakeholder relationships based on the company's purpose.

The UK Stewardship Code

The UK Stewardship Code was first published by the FRC in July 2010, with an updated version published effective on 1 October 2012. At the time of writing a further update to the Stewardship Code is being drafted and is expected to be released in late 2019. The FRC's aim is 'to enhance the quality of engagement between institutional investors and investee companies to help improve long-term returns to shareholders and efficient exercise of governance responsibilities by setting out good practice on engagement with investee companies'.

Like the UK Corporate Governance Code, the Stewardship Code operates on a 'comply or explain' basis, recognising that what constitutes best practice for most institutions may not be appropriate for all.

Like the UK Corporate Governance Code, the Stewardship Code contains seven main principles, as follows:

1. Institutional investors should publicly disclose their policy on how they will discharge their stewardship responsibilities.
2. Institutional investors should have a robust policy on managing conflicts of interest in relation to stewardship and this policy should be publicly disclosed.
3. Institutional investors should monitor their investee companies.
4. Institutional investors should establish clear guidelines on when and how they will escalate their activities as a method of protecting and enhancing shareholder value.
5. Institutional investors should be willing to act collectively with other investors where appropriate.
6. Institutional investors should have a clear policy on voting and disclosure of voting activity.
7. Institutional investors should report periodically on their stewardship and voting activities.

Annual Report Compliance Statement

Listed companies must disclose in their financial statements how they have met their obligations under the UK Corporate Governance Code. These are set out in three sets of rules:

- *DTR 7.1* and *7.2*, which set out certain mandatory disclosures;
- *LR 9.8.6*, *9.8.7* and *9.8.7A*, which include the 'comply or explain' requirement; and
- the UK Corporate Governance Code – in addition to companies providing an explanation where they choose not to comply with a provision, they must also disclose specified information in order to comply with certain provisions.

There is some overlap between the mandatory disclosures required under the DTR and those expected under the Code.

In respect of disclosures relating to the audit committee and the composition and operation of the board and its committees, compliance with the relevant provisions of the Code will result in compliance with the relevant Rules.

These requirements are summarised below.

Disclosure and Transparency Rules

- *DTR 7.1* concerns audit committees or bodies carrying out equivalent functions.
- *DTR 7.1.1*, *7.1.2* and *7.1.3* set out requirements relating to the composition and functions of the committee or equivalent body.
- *DTR 7.1.1* states that an issuer must have a body or bodies responsible for performing the functions set out in *DTR 7.1.3*.
- *DTR 7.1.1A* requires that a majority of the members of the relevant body must be independent, that at least one member must have competence in accounting or auditing, or both, and that members of the relevant body as a whole must have competence relevant to the sector in which the issuer is operating.
- *DTR 7.1.2* states that the requirements for independence and competence in accounting and/or auditing may be satisfied by the same members or by different members of the relevant body.
- *DTR 7.1.3* states that an issuer is required to ensure that, as a minimum, the relevant body must:
  - monitor the financial reporting process and submit recommendations or proposal to ensure its integrity;
  - monitor the effectiveness of the issuer's internal quality control and risk management systems and, where applicable, its internal audit, regarding the financial reporting of the issuer, without breaching its independence;
  - monitor the statutory audit of the annual and consolidated financial statements, in particular, its performance, taking into account any findings and conclusions by the competent authority under article 26(6) of the Audit Regulation;
  - review and monitor the independence of the statutory auditor, in accordance with articles 22, 22a, 22b, 24a and 24b of the Audit Directive and article 6 of the Audit Regulation, and in particular the appropriateness of the provision of non-audit services to the issuer in accordance with article 5 of the Audit Regulation;
  - inform the administrative or supervisory body of the issuer of the outcome of the statutory audit and explain how the statutory audit contributed to the integrity of financial reporting and what the role of the relevant body was in that process; and
  - except when article 16(8) of the Audit Regulation is applied, be responsible for the procedure for the selection of statutory auditor(s) and recommend the statutory auditor(s) to be appointed in accordance with article 16 of the Audit Regulation.
- *DTR 7.1.5* states that the issuer must make a statement available to the public disclosing which body carries out the functions required by *DTR 7.1.3* and how it is composed.

- *DTR 7.1.6* states that this can be included in the corporate governance statement required under *DTR 7.2*.
- *DTR 7.1.7* states that compliance with the relevant provisions of the Code will result in compliance with *DTR 7.1.1–7.1.5*.
- *DTR 7.2* concerns corporate governance statements. Issuers are required to produce a corporate governance statement that must be either included in the directors' report (*DTR 7.2.1*), or set out in a separate report published together with the annual report, or set out in a document on the issuer's website, in which case there must be a cross-reference in the directors' report (*DTR 7.2.9*).
- *DTR 7.2.2* requires that the corporate governance statement must contain a reference to the corporate governance code to which the company is subject (for companies with a premium listing, this is the Code).
- *DTR 7.2.3* requires that, where it departs from that code, the company must explain which parts of the code it departs from, and the reasons for doing so.
- *DTR 7.2.4* states that compliance with *LR 9.8.6 R (6)* (the 'comply or explain' rule in relation to the Code) will also satisfy these requirements.
- *DTR 7.2.5, 7.2.6* and *7.2.7* set out certain information that must be disclosed in the corporate governance statement as follows:
  - *DTR 7.2.5* states that the corporate governance statement must contain a description of the main features of the company's internal control and risk management systems in relation to the financial reporting process.
  - *DTR 7.2.6* states that the corporate governance statement must contain the information required by paragraph 13(2)(c), (d), (f), (h) and (i) of Schedule 7 to the Large and Medium-sized Companies and Groups (Accounts and Reports) Regulations 2008 (SI 2008/410) where the issuer is subject to the requirements of that paragraph.
  - *DTR 7.2.7* states that the corporate governance statement must contain a description of the composition and operation of the issuer's administrative, management and supervisory bodies and their committees.
  - *DTR 7.2.10 R* states that an issuer that is required to prepare a group directors' report within the meaning of s. 415(2) of the Companies Act 2006 must include in that report a description of the main features of the group's internal control and risk management systems in relation to the financial reporting process for the undertakings included in the consolidation, taken as a whole.

Listing Rules

LR 9.8.6 (for UK incorporated companies) and *LR 9.8.7* (for overseas incorporated companies) state that in the case of a company that has a premium listing of equity shares, the following items must be included in its annual report and accounts:

- a statement of how the Listed company has applied the Main Principles set out in the Code, in a manner that would enable shareholders to evaluate how the principles have been applied; and
- a statement as to whether the Listed company has:
  - complied throughout the accounting period with all relevant provisions set out in the Code; or
  - not complied throughout the accounting period with all relevant provisions set out in the Code, and if so, setting out:
    - those provisions, if any, it has not complied with;
    - in the case of provisions whose requirements are of a continuing nature, the period within which, if any, it did not comply with some or all of those provisions; and
    - the company's reasons for non-compliance.

LR 9.8.6 R (3) requires statements by the directors on:

- the appropriateness of adopting the going concern basis of accounting (containing the information set out in provision C.1.3 of the Code); and
- their assessment of the prospects of the company (containing the information set out in provision C.2.2 of the Code), prepared in accordance with the *Guidance on Risk Management, Internal Control and Related Financial and Business Reporting* published by the Financial Reporting Council in September 2014.

The UK Corporate Governance Code

In addition to the 'comply or explain' requirement in the LR, the Code includes specific requirements for disclosure which must be provided in order to comply. These are summarised below.

The annual report should include the following.

Section 1 – Board leadership and company purpose

- Provision 1: The board should assess the basis on which the company generates and preserves value over the long term. It should describe in the annual report how opportunities and risks to the future success of the business have been considered and addressed, the sustainability of the company's business model and how its governance contributes to the delivery of its strategy.
- Provision 2: The board should assess and monitor culture. Where it is not satisfied that policy, practices or behaviour throughout the business are aligned with the company s purpose, values and strategy, it should seek assurance that management has taken corrective action. The annual report should explain the board's activities and any action taken. In addition, it should include an explanation of the company's approach to investing in and rewarding its workforce.

- Provision 4: When 20% or more of votes have been cast against the board recommendation for a resolution, the company should explain, when announcing voting results, what actions it intends to take to consult shareholders in order to understand the reasons behind the result. An update on the views received from shareholders and action taken should be published no later than six months after the shareholder meeting. The board should then provide a final summary in the annual report, and, if applicable, in the explanatory notes to resolutions at the next shareholder meeting, on what impact the feedback has had on the decisions the board has taken and any actions or resolutions now proposed.
- Provision 5: The board should understand the views of the company's other key stakeholders and describe in the annual report how their interests and the matters set out in s. 172 of the Companies Act 2006 have been considered in board discussions and decision-making.
- If the board has not chosen one or more of these methods, it should explain what alternative arrangements are in place and why it considers that they are effective.

Section 2 – Division of Responsibilities

- Provision 9: The chair should be independent on appointment when assessed against the circumstances set out in Provision 10. The roles of chair and chief executive should not be exercised by the same individual. A chief executive should not become chair of the same company. If, exceptionally, this is proposed by the board, major shareholders should be consulted ahead of appointment. The board should set out its reasons to all shareholders at the time of the appointment and also publish these on the company website.
- Provision 10: The board should identify in the annual report each non-executive director it considers to be independent. Circumstances that are likely to impair, or could appear to impair a non-executive director's independence include, but are not limited to, whether a director:
  - is or has been an employee of the company or group within the last five years;
  - has, or has had within the last three years, a material business relationship with the company either directly, or as a partner, shareholder, director or senior employee of a body that has such a relationship with the company;
  - has received or receives additional remuneration from the company apart from a director's fee, participates in the company's share option or a performance-related pay scheme, or is a member of the company's pension scheme;
  - has close family ties with any of the company's advisers, directors or senior employees;
  - holds cross-directorships or has significant links with other directors through involvement in other companies or bodies;

- represents a significant shareholder; or
- has served on the board for more than nine years from the date of their first appointment.

Where any of these or other relevant circumstances apply, and the board nonetheless considers that the non-executive director is independent, a clear explanation should be provided.

- Provision 14: The responsibilities of the chair, chief executive, senior independent director, board and committees should be clear, set out in writing, agreed by the board and made publicly available. The annual report should set out the number of meetings of the board and its committees, and the individual attendance by directors.
- Provision 15: When making new appointments, the board should take into account other demands on directors' time. Prior to appointment, significant commitments should be disclosed with an indication of the time involved. Additional external appointments should not be undertaken without prior approval of the board, with the reasons for permitting significant appointments explained in the annual report. Full-time executive directors should not take on more than one non-executive directorship in a FTSE 100 company or other significant appointment.

Section 3 – Composition, Succession and Evaluation

- Provision 18: All directors should be subject to annual re-election. The board should set out in the papers accompanying the resolutions to elect each director the specific reasons why their contribution is, and continues to be, important to the company's long-term sustainable success.
- Provision 20: Open advertising and/or an external search consultancy should generally be used for the appointment of the chair and non-executive directors. If an external search consultancy is engaged, it should be identified in the annual report alongside a statement about any other connection it has with the company or individual directors.
- Provision 21: There should be a formal and rigorous annual evaluation of the performance of the board, its committees, the chair and individual directors. The chair should consider having a regular externally facilitated board evaluation. This should happen at least every three years. The external evaluator should be identified in the annual report and a statement made about other connection it has with the company or individual directors.
- Provision 23: The annual report should describe the work of the nomination committee, including:
  - the process used in relation to appointments, its approach to succession planning and how both support developing a diverse pipeline;
  - how the board evaluation has been conducted, the nature and extent of an external evaluator's contact with the board and individual directors, the

outcomes and actions taken, and how it has or will influence board composition;
  - the policy on diversity and inclusion, its objectives and linkage to company strategy, how it has been implemented and progress on achieving the objectives; and
  - the gender balance of those in the senior management and their direct reports.

Section 4 – Audit, Risk and Internal Control

- Principle N: The board should present a fair, balanced and understandable assessment of the company's position and prospects.
- Provision 26: The annual report should describe the work of the audit committee, including:
  - the significant issues that the audit committee considered relating to the financial statements, and how these issues were addressed;
  - an explanation of how it has assessed the independence and effectiveness of the external audit process and the approach taken to the appointment or reappointment of the external auditor, information on the length of tenure of the current audit firm, when a tender was last conducted and advance notice of any retendering plans;
  - in the case of a board not accepting the audit committee's recommendation on the external auditor appointment, reappointment or removal, a statement from the audit committee explaining its recommendation and the reasons why the board has taken a different position (this should also be supplied in any papers recommending appointment or reappointment);
  - where there is no internal audit function, an explanation for the absence, how internal assurance is achieved, and how this affects the work of external audit; and
  - an explanation of how auditor independence and objectivity are safeguarded, if the external auditor provides non-audit services.
- Provision 27: The directors should explain in the annual report their responsibility for preparing the annual report and accounts, and state that they consider the annual report and accounts, taken as a whole, are fair, balanced and understandable, and provide the information necessary for shareholders to assess the company's position, performance, business model and strategy.
- Provision 28: The board should carry out a robust assessment of the company's emerging and principal risks. The board should confirm in the annual report that it has completed this assessment, including a description of its principal risks, what procedures are in place to identify emerging risks, and an explanation of how these are being managed or mitigated.
- Provision 30: In annual and half-yearly financial statements, the board should state whether it considers it appropriate to adopt the going concern basis of accounting in preparing them, and identify any material uncertainties to the

company's ability to continue to do so over a period of at least 12 months from the date of approval of the financial statements.

- Provision 31: Taking account of the company's current position and principal risks, the board should explain in the annual report how it has assessed the prospects of the company, over what period it has done so and why it considers that period to be appropriate. The board should state whether it has a reasonable expectation that the company will be able to continue in operation and meet its liabilities as they fall due over the period of their assessment, drawing attention to any qualifications or assumptions as necessary.

Section 5 – Remuneration

- Provision 41: There should be a description of the work of the remuneration committee in the annual report, including:
  - an explanation of the strategic rationale for executive directors' remuneration policies, structures and any performance metrics; or reasons why the remuneration is appropriate using internal and external measures, including pay ratios and pay gaps;
  - a description, with examples, of how the remuneration committee has addressed the factors in Provision 40;
  - whether the remuneration policy operated as intended in terms of company performance and quantum, and, if not, what changes are necessary;
  - what engagement has taken place with shareholders and the impact this has had on remuneration policy and outcomes;
  - what engagement with the workforce has taken place to explain how executive remuneration aligns with wider company pay policy; and
  - to what extent discretion has been applied to remuneration outcomes and the reasons why.

Directors' remuneration report

For Listed companies, the reporting requirements for directors' remuneration fall into three categories:

1. **Companies Act requirements**: The requirements are set out in regulation 11 and schedule 8 of the Large and Medium-sized Companies and Groups (Accounts and Reports) Regulations 2008, as amended by the Large and Medium-sized Companies and Groups (Accounts and Reports) (Amendment) Regulations 2013, which came into force on 1 October 2013 (LMSR).
2. ***Listing Rules* and UK Corporate Governance Code requirements**: The requirements are set out in *LR 9.8.8* and provisions A.1.2, D.1.2 and D.2.1 of the Code.

3 **Best practice**: There are a number of best practice guides issued by various bodies, including:
   - *ABI Guidelines on Responsible Investment (2007)*;
   - *ABI position paper on Executive Remuneration (2009)*;
   - *ABI/NAPF Best Practice on Executive Contracts and Severance (2008)*;
   - *Investment Association Principles of Remuneration (2015)*; and
   - *PIRC Shareholder voting guidelines (2016)*.

The directors' remuneration report is split into two parts: an Annual Statement and Report on Remuneration ('Implementation Report'), and the Directors' Remuneration Policy ('Remuneration Policy'). Each part is subject to different shareholder voting requirements.

The Implementation Report must include:

- a statement from the chairperson of the Remuneration Committee, which will summarise major decisions on directors' remuneration, substantial changes relating to directors' remuneration and the context changes occurred and decisions were taken (para 3, sch. 8 LMSR);
- a report for each person who was a director during the period (set out in a prescribed tabular form), outlining payments to each director and providing a single figure for remuneration for each director (para 4, sch. 8 LMSR);
- total pension entitlements (para 13, sch. 8 LMSR);
- scheme interests awarded during the financial year (para 14, sch. 8 LMSR);
- payments to past directors (para 15, sch. 8 LMSR);
- payments for loss of office (para 16, sch. 8 LMSR);
- statement of directors' shareholding and share interests (para 17, sch. 8 LMSR);
- performance graph and table (para 18, sch. 8 LMSR);
- percentage change in remuneration of director undertaking the role of CEO (para 19, sch. 8 LMSR);
- relative importance of spend on pay (para 20, sch. 8 LMSR);
- statement of implementation of remuneration policy in the following financial year (para 21, sch. 8 LMSR);
- consideration by the directors of matters relating to directors' remuneration (para 22, sch. 8 LMSR); and
- statement of voting at general meeting (para 23, sch. 8 LMSR).

The Implementation Report must be put to an advisory shareholder vote, at the general meeting at which the financial report is to be received, by ordinary resolution (s. 439).

The second part of the report, the Remuneration Policy, is separate to the Implementation Report. The latter will be forward-looking and provide information on remuneration and potential payments (including exit payments) for each director. In contrast to the Implementation Report, the Remuneration Policy is subject to a binding shareholders' vote, at least once every three years, as an ordinary resolution (s. 439A).

The Remuneration Policy must include:

- all matters for which the company requires approval for the purposes of Chapter 4A of Part 10 of the Act. This chapter stipulates that no remuneration or payment for loss of office can be paid unless they are consistent with the approved policy. On approval of a new or amended policy, the previous policy ceases to have effect and accordingly any provisions being carried over from a previous policy must be restated in the new policy to be effective (para 24(3), sch. 8 LMSR);
- future policy table (para 25, sch. 8 LMSR);
- approach to recruitment remuneration (para 29, sch. 8 LMSR);
- service contracts (para 30, sch. 8 LMSR);
- illustrations of application of remuneration policy (para 33, sch. 8 LMSR);
- policy on payment for loss of office (para 36, sch. 8 LMSR);
- statement of consideration of employment conditions elsewhere in the company (para 38, sch. 8 LMSR); and
- statement of consideration of shareholder views (para 40, sch. 8 LMSR).

Where a company's Implementation Report is voted down, the Remuneration Policy must be put to shareholders, to vote on at the next AGM (s. 439A(2)(a)).

For years where a Remuneration Policy is not being put forward for voting on, it may be omitted from the Directors' Remuneration Report for that financial year. However, details should be included as to when the last policy was approved and where a copy of the policy may be found, for example, on the company's website (para 1, sch. 8 LMSR).

Guidance on the new regime was published by the GC100 in September 2013. Investor bodies such as the IA and NAPF have also updated their guidance.

Outlined below are the main points of the Regulations.

The role of the auditors

The *Listing Rules* require the directors to include a statement on compliance with the Code and a statement on going concern, and stipulate that these statements must be reviewed by the auditors (*LR 9.8.10*).

In the case of the compliance statement, the auditors are only required to review compliance with the following provisions:

- Statement by the directors that the business is a going concern (*LR 9.8.6(3)*).
- Explanation by directors and auditors of their responsibilities for preparing annual report and accounts (C.1.1).
- The directors should review the effectiveness of the company's system of internal control at least annually, and should report to shareholders that they have done so. The review should cover all controls, including financial, operational and compliance controls, and risk management (C.2.1).

- The board should establish an audit committee of at least three directors, all non-executive (smaller companies' audit committees may have two members). The members of the audit committee, a majority of whom should be independent non-executive directors, should be named in the annual report and accounts (C.3.1).
- The audit committee should have written terms of reference dealing clearly with its authority and duties. A separate part of the annual report should disclose how the audit committee discharges these responsibilities (C.3.2 and C.3.3).
- The audit committee should review procedures for members of staff to raise concerns over financial or other reporting irregularities (C.3.5).
- The audit committee should review the internal audit function and, if there is none, consider if that remains appropriate (C.3.6).
- Disclosure of circumstances and explanation if the board do not follow the audit committee's advice relating to the appointment, reappointment or removal of auditor (C.3.7).
- Details of the steps taken to safeguard independence if the auditor provides non-audit services (C.3.8).
- The auditable elements of the directors' remuneration report.
- A statement as to whether in their opinion the statements made in compliance with *DTR 7.2.5* and *7.2.6* are consistent with the accounts and whether, in their opinion and based upon their work, the requirements of *DTR 7.2.2, 7.2.3* and *7.2.7* have been complied with, if necessary.

18 – Share registration

Introduction

Most practitioners associate share registration with Listed, AIM and NEX companies. While it is true that, on the whole, it is only public companies with large numbers of external shareholders that use the services of share registrars, all companies with a share capital must maintain a register of members.

The register

The register of members of a company may be kept in manual form, either as bound or loose-leaf books, or may be kept on computer, whether on a simple spreadsheet or database, or using specialised share registration systems. Whatever form the register takes, it must include, as a minimum, the information set out in s. 113:

- the names and addresses of the members;
- the date on which each person was registered as a member;
- the date on which any person ceased to be a member; and
- if the company has share capital, the number of shares of each class or classes held and the amounts paid or agreed to be paid on the shares.

The register of members must be kept either in the registered office of the company or at the SAIL address.

Branch registers

Where a company has a substantial number of overseas shareholders, consideration should be given to establishing a branch register in terms of s. 129. It is not possible to establish a branch register in all countries and s. 129(2)(b) contains details of those countries where a branch register may be established, as follows:

- Bangladesh
- Cyprus
- Dominica
- The Gambia
- Ghana
- Kenya
- Guyana
- The Hong Kong Special Administrative Region of the People's Republic of China
- India
- Ireland
- Sierra Leone

- Kiribati
- Lesotho
- Malawi
- Malaysia
- Malta
- Nigeria
- Pakistan
- Seychelles
- Singapore
- South Africa
- Sri Lanka
- Swaziland
- Trinidad and Tobago
- Uganda
- Zimbabwe

Notice of the location or any change in the location of a branch register must be given to Companies House on Form AD06. A duplicate branch register must be kept at the same place as the main register and is treated as part of the main register for all purposes.

A branch register enables dealings of shares in that overseas country to be registered locally. This has the added benefit that such transfers will not be subject to UK stamp duty, although any local equivalent tax will be payable.

Unlike the main register a branch register must not contain details of any 'overseas' members with addresses outside the country where it is maintained.

Shares may be moved onto the branch register following receipt of an appropriate form of request, accompanied by the relative share certificate(s). A receipt is issued, which enables the member to apply direct to the keepers of the branch register for a new certificate evidencing the holding recorded on the branch register. A schedule of the requests is prepared and the transfers to the branch register are approved at a board or committee meeting (in a similar fashion to the approval of normal share transfers).

Copies of the schedules and requests should be notified to the holders of the branch register so that it can be brought up to date and requests for the issue of certificates checked. The share certificates issued by the branch register should clearly state that they are in respect of holdings recorded on the branch register and that documents transferring such shares should be forwarded to the branch registrar.

A similar procedure should be followed for transfers of shares from the branch register to the main register.

Name of registered holder

Only individuals or legal entities should be registered as members. Holders of an office can be registered provided it is a public office, such as the Official Receiver.

Names of English partnerships, trusts, share/investment clubs or settlements must not be registered as the holders of shares, as they have no legal capacity and accordingly valid instructions cannot be given. Scottish partnerships may be registered as, unlike English partnerships, these have legal capacity. If documentation is received to register shares in the name of a trust or partnership, it should be rejected. In such circumstances, the shares should be registered in the names of two or more of the partners or trustees. It is usual for the number of joint holders of shares to be restricted to a maximum of four.

Designated accounts

There is no obligation for a company to allow shareholder records to include account designations, unless required to do so by the company's articles of association. However, this is becoming increasingly common and companies rarely refuse to allow account designations. The designations will be in the form of an alphanumeric reference, but should not imply the existence of a trust over the shares. The use of designated accounts is increasing, particularly where shares are held in a CREST account on behalf of the beneficial owner. The designation of a CREST account may be up to eight characters and must not include punctuation or spaces.

A request for designation or a change of designation must be given by the shareholder on the standard form, which should indicate the number of shares to which the designation applies. The request should be submitted together with the appropriate share certificates for cancellation and the issue of new certificates bearing the designation(s). Alternatively, the designation details may be included on the transfer documents where a transfer of shares is taking place. If permitted by the articles, a company may charge for the designation or re-designation of accounts in respect of the same shareholder. A charge is not normally made where the designation details are included in the transfer details where a new shareholder account is being established.

Joint accounts

The articles of association usually place a limit of four on the number of joint holders for any particular holding. The *Listing Rules* and the CREST rules also impose a maximum number of joint holders of four. The following are suggested courses of action regarding various matters that arise from time to time in relation to joint accounts. These are subject to the provisions of the articles of association of the company and cannot be said to be statements of uniform practice:

1 If a request is received to divide an existing account into more than one account with the names of the joint holders in different orders, this may be processed provided that the request has been signed by each joint holder and confirmation has been given that, in each case, there is no change in beneficial ownership.
2 Equally, the order of the names of the joint holders for an existing joint account may be changed provided that the request is signed by each holder and confirmation is given that there has been no change in beneficial ownership.

3 The full names of all the holders on a joint account should be entered in the register and on share certificates. All communications will be sent to the address of the first-named holder, together with either the names or initials of the other joint holders. Although joint holders may request that correspondence should go to someone other than the first-named holder, companies will usually be reluctant to agree to this, due to the administrative complexities. Instead, the company may suggest that the order of the names of the joint holders be amended as set out in point 2.
4 Changes in address should, where possible, be recorded against all joint holders, not just the first-named holder. Otherwise, in the event of the death of the first-named holder, the address information for the surviving joint holder(s) may be out of date.

Inspection of the register

The register of members of a private company must be available for inspection for at least two hours between the hours of 9.00am and 3.00pm on a working day, upon request, provided sufficient notice is given. If the request is received during the notice period of a general meeting or the circulation period of a written resolution, two working days' notice is required. In all other circumstances, ten working days' notice is required.

For a public company, the register must be available for inspection for at least two hours on each working day between the hours of 9.00am and 5.00pm (Company (Company Records) Regulations 2008 (SI 2008/3006)).

Inspection of the register is free of charge to members and upon payment of the prescribed fee for non-members. Copies of the register must be supplied within five days of the receipt of the request on payment of the prescribed fee, unless application to the court is made on the grounds that the request is not for a proper purpose (ss. 116 and 117). The prescribed fees are set out in the Companies (Fees for Inspection and Copying of Company Records) Regulations 2007 (SI 2007/2612).

The fee is payable by both members and non-members according to the following scale.

Where a copy of the register is requested, this shall be provided in hard copy unless an electronic copy is requested (reg. 7 C(CR)R 2008). If the register is only kept in hard copy, an electronic copy need not be provided.

Where a copy of the register is being provided, the company may supply this in the format of its choice (reg. 8 C(CR)R 2008).

Share certificates

A sealed or executed share certificate is *prima facie* evidence of title to those shares (s. 768). The company is prohibited from denying the title of the person named in the certificate to the shares specified in it. Accordingly, it is essential that the details on the certificate are correct and that supplies of blank certificates are kept secure. However, if the certificate has been executed without the company's authority, this is void as a forgery and not binding on the company. The company is also prohibited from denying that shares are fully paid if they are so described in a share certificate. It is universal practice for public companies to effect an insurance policy against forged transfer. Liabilities in respect of the issue of certificates will usually be covered under the terms of the policy.

Small private companies commonly use certificate forms available from law stationers. Larger companies and/or Listed companies use specially printed share certificates. A share certificate should contain at least the following basic information:

- a unique certificate serial number;
- the name and registered number of the company;
- the name of the registered holder;
- the number and description of the shares to which the certificate relates, including a statement as to the extent to which the shares are paid up; and
- the date of the certificate.

Listed companies must also comply with the detailed requirements of the *Listing Rules* (*LR 9.5.16*). For security reasons, it is recommended that the number of shares should be shown twice on the certificates of Listed companies. This may be once in figures and once in words, or once in figures and once in figures contained in boxes referring to millions, hundreds of thousands, tens of thousands, thousands, hundreds, tens and units. The full names of the registered holder and of any joint holders must be given on certificates. There is no requirement to show decorations or professional qualifications. The full name of a corporate holder should be shown in the same form as on its certificate of incorporation.

If the address of the registered holder is shown on share certificates, the full address as recorded in the register of members should be shown. For joint holders, only the address of the first-named holder need be shown. However, it is not necessary to show addresses of shareholders on share certificates and this may be preferable, since this information is rarely kept up to date. On the other hand, an address shown on a share certificate may help to resolve a query as to the identity of a shareholder.

The certificates of companies with only a few shareholders will usually be signed by two directors or by one director and the company secretary, either under seal or as a deed. For companies with a large number of shareholders or a large number of transfers, arranging for certificates to be manually signed is not practical. In such circumstances, the board of directors should adopt a security seal (s. 50), which may be affixed to share certificates and also, in accordance with the authority given in the articles of association, omit signatures attesting the seal on share certificates.

Issue of certificates

Companies are required to issue share certificates to shareholders within two months after an issue of shares or the date when the documents necessary to effect a transfer have been received by the company (s. 769).

Listed, AIM or NEX companies are required to ensure that their shares are eligible for electronic settlement.

Certificates must be sent to addresses in the United Kingdom or elsewhere within the European Economic Area by first class post, or by an equivalent service that is no slower.

Certificates must be sent to addresses outside the EEA by airmail or an equivalent service. Where the company's securities have been admitted to CREST, certificates arising from withdrawals of stock from a dematerialised account will not be posted to the CREST members concerned, but will be sent via CCSS (the CREST courier and sorting service), usually within three business days of the stock withdrawal being requested. Articles of association generally provide that a company may replace a defaced or worn-out certificate on payment of a small fee. If a member requests the issue of more than one certificate for their total holding, if the articles so permit several certificates may be issued, subject to payment of any fee determined by the directors.

Lost certificates

Where a shareholder has lost their share certificate(s), the following procedure should be followed.

1 Ask the shareholder to make a careful search for the certificate(s).
2 If the shareholder confirms that the certificate(s) still cannot be found or it is known that the certificates have been destroyed (i.e. in the event of a fire or flood), it is recommended that the shareholder should be asked to complete an indemnity in respect of the lost certificate(s) (see precedent 70). This indemnity should be joined in by a bank, insurance or trust company. Some companies are prepared to dispense with a guarantee if the value of the shares comprised in the lost certificate is very small, although it should be borne in mind that the future value of the shares may rise significantly. If a certificate is lost in transit between an agent for the member and the member, it is usual to accept an indemnity from the agent, which will include the guarantee of a bank, insurance company or trust corporation, unless the agent itself comes within any of these categories.
3 On receipt of the duly completed indemnity, a duplicate certificate, clearly marked as a duplicate, is prepared and issued on payment of any fee required under the articles. The register is amended to note that the original certificate has been lost and a duplicate issued in its place.

Change of name of shareholder

Changes of name can arise in a number of ways.

1 A person may alter their name with or without formality. Provided there is no fraudulent intent, this is quite lawful. Before registering the change of name, the shareholder should be asked to provide a statutory declaration as to the change of name or a declaration of identity by some independent person of public standing.
2 By execution of a deed poll duly stamped, or a copy of the *London Gazette* or the *Edinburgh Gazette* containing the advertisement of the deed poll.
3 By marriage, in which case the marriage certificate provides the necessary evidence. The original should be requested, although companies may accept photocopies of certificates if certified as a true copy by a professional person such as a chartered secretary, accountant or solicitor, or a statutory declaration as to the shareholder's identity. In Scotland, however, a photocopy must be authenticated by signature of the District or Assistant Registrar. Clearly, a shareholder may not wish to submit the original marriage certificate and in this case, a certified copy or a statutory declaration is an acceptable alternative.
4 The grant of an honour, such as the conferment of a knighthood, may involve a change of name. This may be proved by a copy of the *London Gazette* containing the grant of the honour.
5 For a corporate shareholder, the certificate of incorporation on change of name or certificate of re-registration (or a certified photocopy) should be produced for registration.

On receiving appropriate evidence of change of name for registration, the change should be recorded as follows:

1 Check that there is complete identity between the document (which should be accompanied by the share certificate(s)) and the registered shareholding.
2 Make appropriate entries, including date, in the register of members.
3 Endorse the share certificate(s) validated by the company's registration stamp, and return it or them to the shareholder. Alternatively, issue a new share certificate showing the amended name details.
4 If a dividend mandate has previously been submitted, it may be appropriate for a revised mandate to be completed by the shareholder.

Change of address of shareholder

Changes of address notified by a shareholder should be signed by the shareholder wherever possible. If the notification is on a printed card, this should, if necessary, be returned for signature. Some companies are prepared to accept notifications of change of address given on behalf of a shareholder by a bank, solicitor or stockbroker. A notification of change of address purported to be given by a member of the shareholder's family should never be accepted. Ideally, notifications of change of address should give both the old and the new addresses, as this facilitates identification.

Upon receipt of an acceptable notification of change of address, the change should be noted in the register of members. It is not usually necessary for the share certificates to be amended. As discussed above, many companies no longer show address details on share certificates.

Although it is not necessary to issue acknowledgements of changes of address, this can prove useful to ensure that the new details been have been correctly entered and to help prevent fraud. If confirmation of the change is sent to both the old and new addresses, the true shareholder will have the opportunity to query a fraudulent change. This is particularly relevant if notification of a lost certificate is made a few weeks after a change of address.

Transfer of shares

Companies whose shares have been admitted to CREST will be authorised to accept electronic instructions to effect the transfer of shares (see page 336).

In the case of a private transaction in the shares of both private and public companies, a member wishing to dispose of their holding (i.e. the transferor) will complete a stock transfer form in the form contained in Sch. 1 to the Stock Transfer Act 1963. This is passed to the purchaser (i.e. the transferee) with a share certificate or certificates for at least the number of shares being transferred, in exchange for the agreed price. The transferee enters their name and address as transferee on the transfer form, dates it and has it stamped by HM Revenue & Customs. The transfer and share certificate(s) are then lodged with the company for registration. The transferee does not have to sign the stock transfer form, provided the shares are fully paid (see point 3 below).

Procedure on receipt of transfer

On receipt of the transfer, the following procedure should be followed:

1 Check that details of the transferor and shareholding transferred agree with the share certificate and with the appropriate entry in the register of members. See the following page on checking the validity of transfers.
2 If the company has several classes of shares in issue, check that the shares transferred are fully and correctly described. There should be a separate stock transfer form for each class of shares being transferred.
3 If the shares are only partly paid, the amount shown as paid up on each share on the share certificate must be correctly shown on the transfer. If the company has recently made a call on the shares, the transfer should not be accepted until the call has been paid. In the case of partly paid shares, the

transfer form should be in the old common form of transfer in general use prior to the Stock Transfer Act 1963, which must also be executed by the transferee.

4 The share certificate(s) accompanying the transfer must be the original or a duplicate. If an original certificate is lodged and a duplicate has also been issued, the duplicate must also be surrendered to the company prior to registration.

5 Check the execution of the transfer by the transferor (or by their attorney). If the transfer has been lodged with the company by a private individual, it may be desirable to obtain confirmation of the authenticity of the signature of the transferor.

6 Check the company's registration records to make sure that there is no lien or restraint on a transfer of the shares.

7 Check that the transfer has been duly stamped by HM Revenue & Customs, and that the duty is appropriate for the consideration shown. If not stamped, the transfer must be certified as exempt (s. 770).

8 If all the above matters are in order, cancel the share certificate(s) and prepare a new certificate in the name of the transferee. Where only part of the holding covered by a certificate is being transferred, prepare a balance certificate in the name of the transferor.

9 The transfer should be approved by the company's board and authority given for the new certificate to be sealed, if appropriate, after checking that the transfer does not contravene any pre-emption rights in the company's articles (see precedent 64). The directors of Listed, AIM and NEX companies are required to ensure that shares are freely transferable and a resolution authorising the company secretary or the registrars to process transfers as they are received will have been given (*LR 2.2.4*, *AIM Rule 32*, NEX *Rule 2*).

10 Where the articles of association of a company contain pre-emption provisions on the transfer of shares, these provisions must be strictly followed. The existing shareholders can waive their rights, whether in full or in part, either by letter or by the approval of a special resolution (see precedent 65). If a transfer is registered and pre-emption provisions have not been followed, the transfer can be challenged by the existing shareholders. If the directors resolve to refuse registration for any reason, the transferee must be informed within two months of lodgement of the transfer.

11 Enter the name of the transferee in the register of members, crediting the number of shares transferred to them. Debit the transferor's account in the register with the number of shares transferred.

12 File the transfer and cancelled share certificate(s).

13 Send the new certificate to the transferee or to their agent, after it has been sealed, if appropriate. If there is a balance certificate this should be sent direct to the transferor or their agent. Certificates should be ready within two months from the date on which the transfer is lodged (s. 776).

For Listed companies, the new certificate(s) should be dispatched by first class mail or equivalent to members resident within the EU, and by airmail to members not resident in the EU.

Checking the validity of transfers

The details on the transfer form and the share certificates must be carefully checked to ensure that they relate to the same holding. The register should also be checked to ensure that the certificate(s) is still valid and has not previously been reported as lost. The following points should be noted when checking the validity of transfers:

1 If the shareholding is in joint names, the names of the transferors should be shown on the transfer in the same order as they appear on the certificate and in the register of members. This avoids confusion if there are other holdings on the register in the same names but in a different order.
2 If the shareholder's account is designated, it should be checked that the correct designation appears on the transfer. It is clearly important to avoid the wrong account being debited in the register.
3 The transfer should deal with only one holding in the register as far as it concerns the transferor and transferee. If the same persons are concerned with other holdings with names in different order or bearing different designations, separate transfers will be necessary.
4 A transferor should be described as an executor or administrator only if they remain on the company's register in that capacity.
5 A transfer should deal with only one class of share unless the articles of association permit a single transfer to cover more than one class (which is unusual).
6 A transfer signed by the registered holder and lodged for registration after their death can be accepted for registration if otherwise in order, and if only a relatively short period has elapsed since the death, and provided that no grant of representation has been registered by the company.
7 A transfer signed by an attorney of a registered holder must not be accepted for registration if it is known that the shareholder has died (whether or not a grant of representation has been registered with the company). This is because the death of a principal automatically revokes any power of attorney unless the power is coupled with an interest of the donee.
8 If a transfer has been executed by mark because of infirmity or illiteracy, it should be attested to the effect that the transfer has been read and explained to the transferor and that it appeared to have been understood by them. The attestation should be made by two witnesses, one of whom should have medical, legal or religious qualification, or by some other person of public standing. If the transfers are executed in Scotland, the procedure for notarial execution should be observed.

9 Unless the articles of association provide otherwise, a transfer of shares may be registered up to the last moment before liquidation (regardless of the means or standing of the transferee), so long as the transfer is *bona fide* in the sense that the transferor retains no interest in the shares.

10 Transferees must be individuals or corporate bodies without qualification as to any representative or nominal or trustee capacity in which they may hold the shares. Unincorporated bodies such as partnerships (in England and Wales) or clubs are not acceptable.

11 Transfers to the holder of an office rather than to a named individual should be accepted only if the office is of an official and public nature.

12 If there are a number of transferees, the number should be checked to ensure that it does not exceed the limits specified in the articles of association. Listed companies are required to allow at least four joint holders of shares.

13 If the details of the transferee on the transfer have been altered (the alteration should in any event be initialled by the transferor), a 'no sub-sale' declaration should be obtained from the person lodging the transfer, unless it is clear that the alteration does not affect the identity of the transferee.

Stamp duty

The stock transfer form should be stamped by HM Revenue & Customs prior to being lodged with the company for registration. Stamp duty is currently payable on transfers with a value of £1,000 or more at the rate of 0.5% of the consideration paid for the shares, rounded up to the nearest £5. Stamp duty is payable within 30 days of the date of the transaction. If transfers, or other documents, are submitted for stamping late, interest and/or penalties may be payable.

The person responsible for maintaining the company's register of members (e.g. the company secretary or the company's registrar) is legally responsible for ensuring that all transfers accepted for registration are properly stamped or correctly certified as exempt (s. 770). There is no need to ascertain if the consideration is in accordance with the market value. It is only necessary to ensure that the stamp duty corresponds to the consideration stated on the transfer. Adjudication should be requested in any case where the transfer appears not to have been properly stamped. There is an arrangement between the UK and Eire to accept each other's stamps on transfers signed in either country.

Transfers exempt from stamp duty

The £5 fixed charge on certain instruments are also now exempt from stamp duty apart from duplicate or counterpart documents of substitute bearer instruments, both of which still need to be presented to HM Revenue & Customs for denoting of the relevant particulars. These changes do not affect electronic transfers of stock, which remain liable to stamp duty reserve tax.

Where the amount or value of the consideration is £1,000 or less, it will need to be certified on the reverse to confirm that the transaction does not form part of a larger transaction or series of transactions with an aggregate value in excess of £1,000. The certificate is printed on the reverse of the transfer form and, if completed, the form may be sent direct to the company or its registrar for processing.

Transfers to market makers in the ordinary course of business are also exempt from stamp duty. These must carry the HM Revenue & Customs supplementary stamp denoting that they are not chargeable to duty under s. 81 of the Finance Act 1986.

Where shares are being transferred under a reorganisation or on an acquisition, the transfers may be exempt from stamp duty. An appropriate application should be submitted to the stamp duty adjudication section claiming exemption from stamp duty. The most common exemptions from duty are given for transactions complying with the conditions of s. 42 of the Finance Act 1930 or s. 77 of the Finance Act 1986. Broadly speaking, these exemptions are available for transfers between companies within a group or, in the case of a share exchange, where the shareholders in the acquiring company after the transaction mirror the shareholders in the company being acquired prior to the transaction and they hold the shares in the same proportions.

The Finance Act 2014 introduced a new exemption from stamp duty. Stamp duty and Stamp Duty Reserve Tax were abolished for transfers of unlisted shares and securities traded on a recognised growth market. AIM and NEX are both recognised growth markets. The exemption applies to all shares traded on those markets, provided the shares are not also Listed on a Recognised Investment Exchange (RIE).

Forged transfers

A forged transfer is a nullity and can pass no rights whatsoever to any transferee. On discovery of the forgery, the purported transferor is entitled to receive a similar number of identical shares to those transferred. It is the company's responsibility to provide these, together with any dividends or other entitlements that their wrongful removal from the register has prevented them from receiving.

If, before the forgery is discovered, the shares are transferred for valuable consideration to a third party acting in good faith and without knowledge of the forgery, the company is liable in damages to that person to compensate them for any loss they may have suffered. This is in addition to the liability to restore the name of the defrauded owner to the register of members in respect of the shares. Because the third party relied on a certificate issued by the company under seal, the company is prohibited from denying the validity of its certificates under seal or executed as deeds.

The company has a corresponding right of action against the person lodging the transfer for registration as by lodging the transfer they imply that it is genuine.

This does not, however, absolve a company and its officers from exercising care in connection with the registration of transfers and consequential actions. Despite all practicable precautions, however, it is not possible to be certain that a company will not at some time incur liability in respect of a forged transfer. Under the Forged Transfer Acts 1891 and 1892, any company has power to make compensation by cash payment out of its funds for any loss arising from a forged transfer. Companies usually effect a forged transfer insurance policy to cover this risk. These will generally include cover for documents lodged for registration, dividend warrants, transfer receipts, etc.

Rectification of transferee details

Amendments to the register should be made only under the sanction of a court order for rectification (s. 125). In practice, however, minor clerical errors are informally corrected on the register under the authority of a responsible officer (such as the company secretary or registrar), following receipt by the company or its registrar of a duly completed form of request for rectification of transferee details.

Where a major alteration is requested affecting the identity of the transferee (e.g. a completely different name is to be substituted), the legal position as to whether rectification without recourse to the court is permitted is not entirely free from doubt.

Practical difficulties are, however, unlikely to arise if the following points are observed.

1 Particular care should be exercised if the circumstances suggest that some change of beneficial ownership or sub-sale has taken place or that there has been a change of mind on the part of the broker or the client as to the names in which the shares concerned should be registered. If there is any doubt, rectification without recourse to the court should be permitted only if satisfactory assurances that the circumstances permit such rectification are obtained from the lodging agent.
2 If the original certificate was issued more than three months before the receipt of the request for rectification or if, in the meantime, a dividend has been paid or accepted, or there is other evidence that the transferee has accepted the shares concerned, rectification without recourse to the court should not be permitted. In this event, rectification by the court is required or a duly executed and stamped transfer from the present registered holder to the 'correct transferee' should be obtained.

Transmission of shares

'Transmission' of shares has been defined as dispositions by operation of law, compared with 'transfers' of shares, which are dispositions by voluntary act. Transmissions are most commonly encountered upon death or upon bankruptcy or upon a member becoming of unsound mind and the subject of an order of the Court of Protection.

CREST: the electronic share settlement system

The Uncertificated Securities Regulations 2001 (SI 2001/3755) provide the basis and regulation of CREST. This is an electronic system whereby ownership of shares can be transferred by alterations in computer records, which serve as evidence of title. CREST is operated by Euroclear UK & Ireland Ltd.

Residual settlement

Although virtually all institutional transactions in Listed, AIM and NEX company shares are settled using CREST, shares that have not been admitted to CREST are usually settled through the residual settlement system established by Euroclear UK & Ireland.

Stock in the form of share certificates and executed stock transfer form is delivered through the CREST courier and sorting service (CCSS) to the buying member firm. The consideration is then made by the buying member firm through the CREST system.

The completed stock transfer form or, in the case of multiple transferees, broker transfer forms and the share certificates will be sent to the company's registrar for processing, either directly or via CCSS. The registrar will process the transfer(s) as set out on page 330. The certificates resulting from the transfer will be returned via CCSS if delivered that way or by post. Transfers effected this way settle on the basis of a rolling two-day settlement period known as 'T+2'.

Overview

Where the company's shares have been admitted to settlement in CREST, the register of members is split in two, with Euroclear UK & Ireland being responsible for the electronic sub-register enabling electronic transfer of title on settlement. An individual shareholder may have two accounts: one certificated and the other uncertificated. Movements between the uncertificated accounts are authorised by electronic messages from the system operator (without the use of paper transfers). Movements from uncertificated to certificated accounts (stock withdrawals) are also effected by electronic messages. A movement from a certificated account to an uncertificated account (stock deposit) is a paper-based transaction. The registrar may also initiate adjustments to the register, sending a registrar's adjustment message to the system operator, to correct errors or give effect to certain corporate actions involving the issue of further units of the security concerned.

At the end of each business day, there is reconciliation between the operator and the registrar and by the operator with the other system members. The system members include institutional investors and nominees' brokers and banks. Corporate or private investors who are unable or unwilling to meet the requirements of full membership may become sponsored members, appointing a full member to act on their behalf.

Listed, AIM and NEX companies are required to appoint CREST-compliant registrars to facilitate electronic settlement of their securities (*AIM Rule 36, NE RFI 2*).

CREST preserves much of the 'name on register' aspects of the former system, although it may become more difficult to identify shareholders if they move (because of CREST or shortening settlement times) to holding shares through nominees.

Where a nominee holds shares for a number of beneficial holders, the company can send just one aggregate dividend payment to the nominee, leaving the nominee to split the dividend between those entitled and to issue subsidiary tax vouchers. As regards reports and accounts, there is an obligation to supply only one copy to the nominee, although companies will usually make bulk deliveries available on request.

Joining CREST

Where a company's shares are being Listed (or admitted to AIM or NEX) for the first time, as part of the arrangements for the listing, the company will be required to apply for the shares to be admitted to CREST. The articles of the company should make provision for the shares to be held and transferred through CREST. The company's registrars will liaise with Euroclear UK & Ireland to ensure that the CREST functionality for the shares is enabled at the appropriate time. There are two alternative methods of ensuring a company's shares are capable of CREST settlement:

1 If the articles do not permit the company's securities to be transferred through CREST (as will usually be the case), they can be changed by special resolution to allow this form of transfer).
2 Alternatively, in the case of shares, a board resolution may be used for this purpose. This route will override provisions of the articles that are inconsistent with the holding or transfer of shares in uncertificated form (see precedent 66). There may, however, be other inconsistencies not covered by the directors' resolution, in which case amendment of the articles by special resolution will be necessary.

Notice of the directors' resolution is required to be given either before it is passed, or within 60 days of its being passed, to every member of the company. To save costs, it is desirable to include the notice in a routine mailing to shareholders.

A combined course of action may be taken as follows:

1 Pass the board resolution that title to the company's securities shall be transferred through CREST.
2 Explain the matter in the annual report and include in the annual general meeting notice a special resolution effectively ratifying the board's decision by

changing the articles as necessary. In this way, additional consequential changes may be made while enabling CREST settlement prior to the date of the annual general meeting. A copy of the directors' resolution must be filed at Companies House within 15 days of being passed. It must be included in or annexed to any copy of the articles of association issued after the resolution had been passed (reg. 40(3)).

As well as making itself eligible for electronic settlement, as described above, a security application form must be submitted to Euroclear UK & Ireland 48 hours prior to the commencement of settlement, usually by the registrar, for each class of securities to commence CREST settlement. Such securities are known as being 'CREST enabled'.

CREST transaction procedure

Once a security is enabled in CREST, all market transactions are settled through the system whether or not they are uncertificated. The procedures are as follows:

1 A member of CREST which wishes to move its certificated securities into its uncertificated CREST account does so by lodging the relevant certificates and a completed dematerialisation request form with the CCSS. Alternatively, if a CREST member acquires shares in certificated form and wishes them to be credited to their uncertificated account, the share certificate(s) are lodged with the CCSS, together with a signed stock deposit form. The CCSS passes these documents on to the company's registrar for action.

2 Prior to lodgement, the member sends an electronic data capture (EDC) message to the CREST operator. The CCSS forwards the member's EDC message to the registrar when it has accepted a stock deposit or dematerialisation request, which enables the registrar to check that the documentation is subsequently received. If, upon receipt of the documents, these are found to be in order, the securities concerned are transferred by the registrar from the certificated account of the client and credited to the uncertificated account of the CREST member. They will then be available for delivery through CREST under the usual settlement procedures. Such CREST transfers are exempt from stamp duty, although the underlying transaction may itself have attracted an SDRT (Stamp Duty Reserve Tax) charge, collected through the CREST system.

3 If a CREST member wishes securities held on its uncertificated account to be held in certificated form, the member sends a stock withdrawal request electronically to the registrar through the CREST system. This message includes full details of both parties to the transaction as well as the number of shares involved. The registrar moves the securities into the relevant (existing or new) account in the certificated part of the register and issues a certificate in the required name, which is forwarded to the CREST member via the CCSS. These stock movements are exempt from stamp duty and SDRT (though the

settlement of the underlying purchase of the securities for the client may itself have attracted an SDRT charge, collected through the system).

Shareholder visibility

Due to the structure of CREST, there is a growing trend for private shareholders to hold through CREST member nominees. One way of preserving the direct link between the company and its shareholders is by means of designated accounts in the register. Under company law as it currently stands, however, this does not in itself give any membership rights to the underlying owner of the shares. The company must treat the nominee on the register as the legal owner of the shares (s. 126). The use of multiple designation of accounts involves extra costs for the CREST member concerned and would seem also to compromise much of the welcome simplicity of the CREST system. It is, however, increasingly being used by brokers with substantial private clients, as it facilitates quicker dealing and settlement, and significantly reduces the amount of paperwork.

Sponsored members

These obstacles to shareholder visibility are partially overcome by the adoption of the concept of sponsored membership.

CREST allows investors who are not connected electronically to the CREST system to become sponsored members. Their accounts are operated on their behalf by a full institutional member of CREST (a participating member). A sponsored member communicates with the CREST system via the relevant participating member. Clearly, for those investors who wish to take this route, this will resolve the questions of visibility and rights of shareholders, as they will appear on the register in their own names. However, a sponsored member needs to have their own (debit capped) assured payment arrangement with a payment bank, although the arrangement will be operated by the relevant participating member. The investor must apply to be a member of CREST, a nominal subscription being payable.

Information rights

Section 146 permits registered members holding shares on behalf of another to nominate that person to exercise 'information rights' over those shares.

Information rights means:

1. the right to receive a copy of all communications that the company sends to its members generally or class meetings; and
2. the right to require copies of the accounts and reports and the right to require hard copy versions of documents provided in another form.

An election under s. 146 must relate to all communications, not just some of them.

In order to exercise their rights, the beneficial owner of the shares must notify the nominee that they wish to exercise their rights and provide an address for the receipt of the communications (s. 147).

The nominee must then inform the company that the nominated person wishes to receive hard copies of all communications and provide the company with the address provided by the beneficial owner of the shares. If the member holds shares on behalf of more than one other person when notifying the company of the details of any nominated persons, the member must also notify the number of their shares to which each nomination relates.

In the absence of a notification to receive hard copies of the documents or where no address is supplied, the nominated person is deemed to have agreed to the receipt of documents in electronic form or via a website (ss. 152 and 153).

The arrangement may be terminated by either the nominee or the nominated person. The arrangement will also cease upon the death or bankruptcy of the nominated person, being a person, or if a body corporate by their dissolution or commencement of winding-up (s. 148).

If a member nominates more persons than the number of shares they hold, the right to exercise information rights is terminated.

The company may enquire of a nominated person if they wish to retain the information rights they hold. If no reply is received with 28 days, the information rights lapse. The company may not make such an enquiry more than once in any 12-month period (s. 148(7)).

Where a company sends a copy of a communication to a nominated person, there must be included a statement that (s. 149):

1. the nominated person may be entitled to be appointed or have someone else appointed as proxy for the meeting; and
2. if there is no such right to be appointed as proxy, they may have the right to give instructions as to the exercise of the voting instructions.

The right under s. 146 to nominate a person and the enjoyment of those rights by the nominated person are enforceable only by the member against the company, not by the nominated person (s. 150).

Corporate actions

For securities that have been admitted to CREST, the system has an impact on a number of possible corporate actions or stock events. Specialist advice will be required and consideration given to the use of CREST when a company contemplates:

- rights issues;
- takeover offers;
- issue of loan stocks;
- conversion or redemption of shares;
- new issues and placings;
- payment of dividends, etc.; or
- consolidation or share splits.

Court orders and transmission of shares

The procedures outlined on pages 343–358 cannot be applied to a CREST holding, as most individuals will hold through a nominee and the issuer will not be concerned with the beneficial ownership. Where such matters are appropriate to the uncertificated holding of a CREST member, the following procedural points will apply:

1. A member is required to notify Euroclear UK & Ireland immediately if the member is aware that a stop notice or other court order affecting a security held by it through CREST is to be granted or served or if application is being made for such an order. When Euroclear UK & Ireland becomes aware of any such order inhibiting the transfer of a member's holding through CREST, it will immediately transfer the securities concerned to an escrow account under the control of Euroclear UK & Ireland.
2. A member is required to notify Euroclear UK & Ireland of any event by which it becomes incapacitated as regards transfer of securities held by it through CREST. In this situation, Euroclear UK & Ireland will suspend the member from CREST membership to prevent any further processing of transactions affecting the member. Euroclear UK & Ireland will then liaise with the relevant authorities regarding further action.
3. If a member who is an individual dies, on receipt of the death certificate Euroclear UK & Ireland will arrange for the relevant holdings to be re-certificated. The usual procedure detailed on page 343 can be followed.

Registration of documents

Recording of documents

In this section, reference is made only to 'shares' and 'shareholdings', but the procedures indicated apply to any class of shares, stock, debentures, loan stocks or other securities of a company. Where reference is made to a document register, this may be a loose-leaf register containing copies of original documents or a bound register in which the relevant information is extracted or summarised from the document being registered. Additionally, where the register is kept in electronic form, notes on the register would also be in electronic form.

General points regarding documents

The following general points should be noted:

1. Any person lodging a document with the company is deemed to represent to the company that the document is genuine.
2. Where only a small shareholding is involved, some relaxation of the strict requirements may be accepted if the person lodging the document is a professional person such as an accountant, solicitor, etc.

3 The particular shareholding must be clearly and precisely identified, and include the full name and address of the shareholder as registered. In the case of joint holdings, the names in the documents should be in the same order as they appear in the register of members. If there is any discrepancy between the names in the document and the names in the register, a declaration of identity should be obtained before registration of the document.
4 A company registered in England and Wales may not note in the register any nominee or trustee capacity in which registered shareholders hold their shares (s. 126). However, this does not preclude the use of designations or the use of words such as 'nominee' or 'trustee' in a corporate shareholder's name.
5 It may be necessary to make endorsements or alterations to existing share certificates. These should be signed and marked with an official stamp, so as to prevent unauthorised alterations or endorsements being made.
6 If authorised by the articles of association, a fee may be charged for the registration of documents. Listed companies are not permitted to make such a charge.

Differences between English and Scottish practice

There are substantial differences between the law of England and the law of Scotland on both matters of private company law and common law. For example, a grant of probate or letters of administration in England generally establishes the right of the executor or administrator to deal with the whole of the estate. In the case of a Scottish confirmation, however, the executor is given power to deal only with such part of the estate to which they have been confirmed; other assets not included in the confirmation may be the subject of a further grant to the executor or of a grant to other persons.

The Administration of Estates Act 1971 permits a company registered in England and Wales or in Northern Ireland to register a confirmation issued in Scotland without further formality. Some documents issued by the English courts are acceptable in Scotland, although in some cases, validation by a Scottish court is required. In all other cases, however, documents issued by English courts are totally unacceptable in Scotland.

Apart from confirmations, some documents issued by Scottish courts are acceptable in England. In some cases, validation by an English court may be required, while other Scottish documents are unacceptable in England. For example, in the case of shares, in Scotland a majority of the holders in a joint account may sign a transfer for the shares registered in their names when registered as trustees. However, in England, all the holders would be required to sign a transfer of the shares without reference to their trustee capacity.

Documents issued by other jurisdictions

Orders or documents issued by courts outside England and Wales and Scotland are not acceptable for registration either by English or Scottish companies, and consequently should not be accorded any recognition. It is possible for such orders to be validated for use here, but if there are no such equivalent procedures, a fresh English or Scottish order must be obtained.

Common registration procedures

Death of a shareholder

There is a strict process to follow when registering the death of a shareholder.

In order to provide evidence of death, the original or certified copy of the death certificate must be produced. The name on the register should be amended by the insertion of 'deceased' after the person's name.

When a shareholder has died, the shares form part of the deceased's estate and it is only their executors who have authority to give instruction regarding those assets. The identity of the executors is confirmed by the grant of probate. The issue of a grant of probate can, in some instances, take many months and, until issued, nothing can happen with the shares and any dividends should be retained.

Once the grant of probate has been issued, the original or an office copy (one bearing the seal of the court) must be obtained and the executors' details inserted in the register of members.

The executors can then either transfer the shares directly to beneficiaries or, if distribution cannot be made, have the shares registered in their names under a letter of request (see precedent 71).

Probate

Grants of probate are issued by the High Court in England to the person or persons named in a will of a deceased person as their executor(s). It is usual for probate to be granted to all the executors (or surviving executors named in the will), although one or more may renounce probate or reserve power to prove subsequently, in which case a further grant known as a double probate would be issued. Where a sole surviving executor dies before the estate is completely distributed and without themselves having named an executor by will, application should be made to the court by a person or persons interested in the original estate for the grant of letters of administration. However, where a deceased sole or surviving executor has named an executor in their own will, then upon such an executor obtaining a grant of probate to the estate of the deceased executor, they are entitled to continue executorship of the original estate. This is known as the 'chain of representation'.

A probate includes a copy of the will and is issued over an impressed seal of the High Court. In order to speed up the process of administration of the estate, executors or their advisers may obtain additional office copies of the grant of probate, bearing an impressed seal of the court which does not include a copy of the will but does include the names of the persons authorised to deal with the estate. These 'office copies' are extremely useful where the deceased held shares in a number of companies and it is desired to avoid delay in registering the probate with those companies.

In the case of grants of probate issued overseas, in the Commonwealth or in the Republic of South Africa, the court will, on application of the executor, reseal grants of probate. Companies should only accept such grants for registration that have been resealed. The availability of resealing grants is set out in the Colonial Probate Act 1892 and the full list of territories is:

- Alberta
- Antigua
- Australian Capital Territory
- Bahamas
- Barbados
- Belize
- Bermuda
- Botswana
- British Antarctic Territory
- British Columbia
- Brunei
- Cayman Islands
- Christmas Island
- Cocos Island
- Republic of Cyprus
- Dominica
- Falkland Islands
- Fiji
- Gambia
- Ghana
- Gibraltar
- Grenada
- Guyana
- Hong Kong
- Jamaica
- Kenya
- Kiribati
- Lesotho
- Malawi
- Malaysia
- Manitoba
- Montserrat
- New Brunswick
- New Guinea Territory
- New Hebrides
- New South Wales
- New Zealand
- Newfoundland
- Nigeria
- Norfolk Island
- North West Territories of Canada
- Nova Scotia
- Ontario
- Papua New Guinea
- Prince Edward Island
- Queensland
- St Kitts, Nevis and Anguilla
- St Helena
- St Lucia
- St Vincent
- Saskatchewan
- Seychelles
- Sierra Leone
- Solomon Islands
- South Africa
- South Australia
- Sri Lanka
- Swaziland
- Tanzania
- Tasmania
- Tortola (British Virgin Islands)
- Trinidad and Tobago
- Turks and Caicos Islands
- Tuvalu
- Uganda
- Victoria
- Western Australia
- Zambia

Grants of probate issued in Northern Ireland and confirmations issued in Scotland do not require to be resealed in England. A separate English grant of probate must be obtained, however, in the case of the Isle of Man, Channel Islands and the Republic of Ireland, since probates issued in these countries cannot be resealed in England. The original grant of probate or an office copy should be submitted to the company for registration, together with the share certificate(s) relating to the holding. Although the probate can be registered without production of the share certificates, these should be endorsed with the details of the probate by the company.

The procedure for registering probates is as follows:

1 Check that there is complete identity between the deceased named in the probate and the registered shareholder. If there is any doubt, a declaration of identity should be obtained from the person lodging the document, who would usually be the solicitor acting for the estate, or from the bank at which the account of the deceased executor was held.
2 Record the names of the executors named in the probate in the document register.
3 Record in the register of members the date of death and the date of registration of the probate, with the name and address of the executor(s) named in the probate and with the word 'deceased' added after the name of the deceased shareholder.
4 Endorse the share certificate(s) with the fact and date of death, the date of registration of probate and the name and address of the executor(s), and validate the endorsement by the company's registration stamp.
5 Impress the registration stamp on the back of the probate, which should then be returned to the person who lodged it with the company, together with the endorsed share certificate(s). If appropriate, include a new dividend mandate form for completion by the executors, since the mandate lodged by the shareholder will have been revoked by their death.
6 It is also usual to send a form known as a letter of request with the returned documents (see precedent 71). The executors can complete this form to register the share-holding in their names. This is helpful to the company, as it is then no longer concerned with the 'chain of representation' if any of the named executors should die before the shares are sold or transferred to a beneficiary. A letter of request need not be sent if the person lodging the transfer indicated that the shareholding was to be disposed of by transfer.
7 Registering the shares in the name of the executor(s) also has the added benefit of removing the deceased shareholder from the mailing list. If this is not done, as the deceased shareholder's estate is still the legal owner of the shares until the shares are transferred, correspondence must still be addressed to that shareholder with the words 'deceased' after the shareholder's name. This can cause understandable distress to family members.

8 Registration of a double probate should be accepted only if the original executors are still registered in their representative capacity, i.e. if they have not been registered in their own names following submission of a letter of request.

Communications from the company would be sent to the first-named executor.

Letters of request

Letters of request are addressed to the company by executors or administrators of a deceased shareholder, and request the company to enter their names in the register of members as the holders of the shares held by the deceased. The letter may only be registered by the company if a grant of representation in respect of the deceased shareholder has already been registered, appointing the persons who signed the letter of request as the executors or administrators of the deceased's estate. The letter must be signed by all the executors and administrators, but their signatures need not be witnessed. The executor or administrator may be a body corporate, in which case a letter must be executed under its seal unless an officer of the company has authority to execute such documents. If so, the authority under which it is signed should be produced to the company.

When a letter of request is received (see precedent 71), the procedure for registering it is similar to that which applies in the case of non-market transfers, considered earlier in this chapter.

Letters of administration

Letters of administration are granted by the High Court, appointing a person or persons to administer the estate of a person who died without having made a valid will.

Like probates, grants of administration bear the stamp of the High Court and sealed office copies may be obtained to facilitate registration with a number of companies.

As regards the Commonwealth, Isle of Man, Channel Islands, Republic of Ireland and foreign probates, the points made above regarding probates originating in those countries apply equally to grants of letters of administration.

The procedure for registering letters of administration is also similar to that set out in the case of probates, administrators taking the place of the executors.

There are a number of different forms of grant of letters of administration and entries in the register of members, and endorsements on certificates should indicate the exact form of the grant. Usually a letter of request for the administrator(s) to be personally registered as holder(s) of shares is appropriate only in the case of a grant of letters of administration with the will annexed. This is issued by the High Court in cases where the deceased left a will but did not name any executor, where the executor may have predeceased the shareholder or where the executor has renounced probate.

Confirmation

Confirmation is the Scottish document issued by the Sheriff Court. It has similar effect to an English probate or letters of administration, and the procedure for registration by companies in England and Wales is the same as in the case of probates. It is granted to the executors named in the will, who are termed 'executors nominate'. If there are no surviving executors or if the deceased left no will, the court makes a grant to a person or persons to administer the estate who are termed 'executors dative' (called administrators in England).

The chief difference to note between English probates and letters of administration is that the Scottish confirmation has annexed to it an inventory of the deceased's property to which the executors have been confirmed. The executors may deal only with the property Listed. Consequently, companies must check that the list includes the securities of the company. If not included, they can be added by the court. Extracts are issued, to assist companies and others, under the seal of the court and signed by the clerk. Reference should be made to the Institute's Manual for guidance as to the procedure to be followed where a sole or surviving executor dies before the estate has been completely administered, as Scottish practice is quite different from that in England.

Death of a holder in joint account

If shares are registered in the names of two or more joint shareholders, upon the death of one of the holders, the shares remain registered in the name(s) of the surviving holder or holders and no executors or administrators are involved. All that the company requires is the production of the certificate of death of the joint holder. This should be the original, although some companies will accept photocopies if they are lodged by a person of professional standing. This does not apply in Scotland, where any photocopy must be authenticated by signature of the District or Assistant Registrar or, alternatively, the death may be proved by a decree of the Court of Session.

A grant of probate or grant of letters of administration or confirmation to the estate of the deceased joint holder may be submitted instead of a death certificate and this is equally acceptable as evidence of the death. Upon receipt of a death certificate or other evidence of death of a joint holder, the following procedure should be adopted:

1 Check that there is complete identity between the person named in the certificate and the registered shareholder, obtaining a declaration of identity in the event of doubt.
2 Record the particulars of the document (i.e. death certificate, probate or confirmation) in the document register.
3 Enter the fact and date of death and date of registration in the register of members, deleting the name and address of the deceased joint holder. If the deceased joint holder was the first named in the account, then the person who

was second named in the account will become the first-named holder, involving transfer of the account to a different part of the register of members.

4 Endorse the share certificate, validated by the company's registration stamp, and return it to the surviving shareholder accompanied by the document submitted to prove death. If the latter was a probate or confirmation, it should be endorsed as registered as 'proof of death only'.
5 Continue to pay dividends on the holding in accordance with any existing mandate unless the surviving shareholder executes a new mandate.
6 If there is no dividend mandate in force, dividends are paid to the first-named survivor in the account, to whom all communications are also addressed.
7 Where the first-named holder has died, care must be taken to ensure that correct and up-to-date addresses for the surviving joint holder(s) are recorded on the register.

Bona vacanta

If a person dies domiciled in England and Wales without having made a will and no one has lawful rights of succession, the High Court will issue a grant of administration (known as *bona vacanta*), appointing officers of the Government Legal Department (previously called the Treasury Solicitor) or officers of the Duchy of Lancaster or the Duke of Cornwall to administer the estate. The procedure for registration is the same as in the case of a probate. In such cases, it would be usual for the shareholding to be disposed of forthwith and consequently no letter of request would be issued. The appropriate Scottish document is *ultimus haeres*; in this case, the Queen's and Lord Treasurer's Remembrancer takes possession of the estate.

Small estates

There is no statutory definition of a small estate in relation to shareholdings in companies, but many companies permit concessionary procedures where the total estate does not exceed £20,000 in value and the value of the shares does not exceed £5,000. Many companies are prepared to dispense with the formalities of obtaining a full probate or confirmation where the total value does not justify the expense of obtaining a grant of representation from the court. However, some risk is involved and some companies may specify a lower limit.

Applications to waive such formalities are normally considered individually. If it is decided that it would be appropriate in the circumstances to dispense with the formalities, the personal representative or beneficiary should be required to submit:

- the death certificate;
- a statutory declaration as to the identity of the person claiming to deal with the shareholding and of their entitlement to deal with it;
- a letter from the Capital Taxes Office confirming that on the information

supplied to it, no liability to inheritance tax arises in connection with the holding;

- the share certificate(s); and
- a letter of indemnity under which the applicant undertakes to indemnify the company if any liability on the company should arise by permitting the concessionary procedure and also undertaking to obtain and produce a formal grant of probate, confirmation or letters of administration, should the company require these at any time.

Occasionally it may be appropriate to dispense with the production of a letter from the Capital Taxes Office, where the applicant is an elderly widow or widower, because of difficulties the applicant would experience in providing the necessary information to obtain the letter. If this concession is granted, a paragraph concerning the absence of liability to inheritance tax should be included in the indemnity referred to above. Care is needed, because the reason why the estate is small may be that the deceased made substantial gifts in their lifetime to try to avoid inheritance tax.

Powers of attorney

Powers entered into before 1 October 2007

A power of attorney is an appointment by an individual or body corporate of a person or persons to act on their or its behalf to the extent and for the time specified in the power. Such appointments are usually made when the person granting the power is going to be absent abroad for a considerable period or is facing a long illness, or just because they wish to free themselves from dealing with matters of routine.

Schedule 1 of the Powers of Attorney Act 1971 sets out a short form of general power of attorney. This may conveniently be used to confer wide powers on the attorney. This form is most suitable for use by individuals, as it is short and simple.

Powers of attorney granted by bodies corporate would generally be in more extended form, setting out in detail the precise extent of the powers granted. This would also apply in Scotland, as the short form of general power of attorney under the 1971 Act is not available for powers created in Scotland.

It is advisable for the power of attorney to be executed under seal, since the attorney themselves may have to execute documents under seal on behalf of the principal, i.e. the 'donor' of the power. It is not necessary for powers of attorney to be stamped by HM Revenue & Customs. The signature of the principal on the power of attorney should be witnessed; one witness is needed in the case of powers executed in England and Wales, and two if executed in Scotland. A power of attorney given by a company should be under its common seal or executed as a deed. When completed abroad, powers of attorney require notarial attestation or consular legalisation.

The person granting a power of attorney may be unable to execute it because of physical infirmity. In this case, the power may be signed and sealed by some other person in the presence of two other persons as witnesses, who must also sign the document. Companies may register copies of powers of attorney instead of the original, if they are copies certified by the principal or by a solicitor or stockbroker. The certificate should certify that the copy is a true and complete copy of the original. Power of attorney is sometimes expressed to be irrevocable for a period of one year, after which it may be revoked by the donor of the power. The power is automatically revoked on the donor's death. The Powers of Attorney Act 1971 gives some protection to companies which have registered powers of attorney in relation to a shareholder. It provides that where a power has been revoked and a person without knowledge of revocation deals with the donee of the power, the transaction is as valid as if the power had continued in existence.

This applies only in England and Wales. Where the power of attorney is not in the general simple form provided by the Powers of Attorney Act 1971, the company should read it carefully before acting, in order to ensure that the action to be taken is within the powers set out. Companies will be particularly concerned with the provisions in the power regarding the purchase and sale of investments, receipt of dividends, interest or capital monies, attendance and voting at meetings, and completion of such documents as may be issued in connection with the share-holding. An attorney may not delegate their powers or appoint a substitute unless the power granted to them specifically provides for this. It is emphasised that the law governing powers of attorney is wide and complex, and in cases of doubt, reference should be made to the more detailed information given in the Institute's Manual.

Procedure

The following procedure should be followed when a power of attorney is received for registration:

1. The document must be either the original power, bearing a 50p impressed stamp if it was executed before 26 March 1985, or an authenticated copy.
2. Check that there is complete identity between the donor of the power and either a registered shareholder or a person in the course of acquiring shares for registration, evidenced by a stock transfer form, a CREST stock withdrawal, a renounced allotment letter or a renounced certificate lodged for registration.
3. Photocopy the complete power for the company's records.
4. Carefully scrutinise the execution, continued validity, scope and the general interpretation of the power.
5. Note whether the power appoints more than one person as the attorneys; if so, check whether the appointment is joint, in which case all the attorneys must act together, or whether it is joint and several, where any of the attorneys may act individually.

6 Check whether the power affects the registered address of the shareholding or manner of payment of dividends. If not, the registered address remains as before, as do any instructions for payment of dividends.
7 Affix the company's registration stamp to the power and return it to the sender.
8 It is not usual practice to send a protective notice to the donor of the power informing them that the power of attorney has been received and that it will be assumed to be in order and registered unless they notify the company otherwise. Such a notice should, however, be sent where the person executing the power by the direction of the donor because of physical infirmity is themselves the attorney appointed by the power.
9 Every time a document executed by the attorney is lodged with the company, the validity of the particular transaction should be verified by reference to the copy of the power of attorney held by the company.

If the power of attorney is revoked or lapses, the company's copy should be marked accordingly and moved to a separate file for lapsed powers of attorney.

No entry need be made in the register of members regarding the registration of a power of attorney, nor should any alteration be made in the heading of the relevant account in the register of members.

The Mental Capacity Act 2005

The Mental Capacity Act 2005 (MCA2005) came into force on 1 October 2007 and applies to England and Wales only. Enduring powers of attorney made prior to 1 October 2007 that have not been revoked remain valid, provided that in the case of a donor who has become mentally incapable, the enduring power has been registered under MCA2005 with the Public Guardian.

Under MCA2005, individuals may give a lasting power of attorney in the form prescribed in the appropriate regulations which will continue in force even if the donor should become mentally incapable, subject to the power being registered with the Public Guardian. If the power is in the prescribed form, the following further points arise:

1 The company may act on the power even though not registered by the Court of Protection, if it is unaware that the donor has become mentally incapable. This protection derives from the Powers of Attorney Act 1971, s. 5(2).
2 The company may not act on the power if it is aware that the donor has become mentally incapable but no application has been made to the Public Guardian for registration of the power.
3 The company may act on the power if it is aware that the donor has become mentally incapable and has evidence produced to it that an application for registration has been made to the Court of Protection, even though the registration has not been completed. The Enduring Powers of Attorney Act 1985

(EPA1985) gives certain powers of maintenance and for the prevention of loss to the estate of the donor of the power. It also gives statutory protection to a company acting under a power governed by EPA1985, provided that it is not aware of any irregularity in the exercise of the powers by the attorney.

4 The company may act on the power if it has documentary evidence of the registration of the power with the Public Guardian. The documentary evidence that the company should require to see are office copies of the fact of registration by the Public Guardian. The company is protected in this instance if there should be any irregularity concerning the power or if it should have been revoked by the court provided that the company is unaware of the irregularity or the revocation. Companies or their registrars may consider it prudent to obtain legal advice before dealing with powers created under MCA2005 if they have not had previous experience of these provisions. It has already been ruled by the court that the appointment by a person (i.e. the donor of the power) already suffering from a degree of mental illness and, therefore, unable to manage their affairs, is valid if the person making the appointment was aware of what they were doing.

Court of Protection orders

A receiver may be appointed by order of the Court of Protection to manage the income of a person described as 'the patient' if, based on medical evidence, the court is satisfied that the patient is incapable, by reason of mental disorder, of administering their own property and affairs. These orders authorise the receiver to receive all income of the patient. The order will contain such other directions as are appropriate in the circumstances. Accordingly, the effect of orders varies and care must be taken to ensure that all acts by the receiver are within their powers as set out in the order. All orders bear the seal of the court. The equivalent Scottish document is known as an appointment of judicial factor, guardian or curator bonis.

Procedure

If a protection order is received, the following procedure should be adopted:

1 There must be complete identity between the documents submitted and a registered shareholding in the company. In the case of doubt, a declaration of identity should be obtained from the person lodging the document (usually a solicitor); alternatively, a declaration may be given by the receiver.
2 The details should be recorded and a copy of the order retained for future reference.
3 Future communications to the shareholder are addressed to the receiver, who should be described as 'receiver for . . .'. The issuing of a Court of Protection order does not change the beneficial ownership of the shares.
4 The order should be endorsed on the reverse with the company's registration stamp.

5 The shareholder's share certificates need not be endorsed and they need not be submitted to the company.
6 It may be appropriate for a revised dividend mandate to be completed by the receiver.
7 The order will continue in force until either it is revoked or the death of the shareholder. On the death of the shareholder, the order automatically lapses and the powers of the receiver terminate, whereupon the company may then take the usual action in relation to a deceased shareholder (see page 343).

Directions in addition to or varying existing directions may be issued under the seal of the court from time to time. If further directions are received, the same steps as noted above should be followed.

Notice of lien

A notice of lien is not an official document or court order, but is written advice given usually by a bank to the effect that certificates representing a shareholding have been deposited with the person giving the notice by way of security for a loan or advance. If the notice is given by a bank or other corporate body, it will be signed on its behalf by an authorised official.

Such notices should not be acknowledged, as acceptance would be contrary to s. 126. Rather than taking possession of the physical share certificates, banks will often require that the shares are registered in the name of their own nominee on behalf of the shareholder. There is no equivalent Scottish document.

Stop notice

A stop notice is an official notice given under rules of court, which is usually submitted to the company by a solicitor, restraining the transfer of (and in some cases the payment of dividends on) a specified shareholding because of the interest of a third party in the shares. The original documents evidencing the debt due will have been previously filed with the court. The notice will identify the shareholding and must be signed by the person who gave the affidavit. There is no equivalent Scottish document.

Procedure

If a stop notice is received for registration, the following procedure should be adopted:

1 There must be complete identity between the holding specified in the notice and a shareholding in the company. Service of the notice should be acknowledged to the sender, unless the shareholding cannot be identified, in which case it should be returned to the sender. The office copy will be retained by the company for future reference.

2 Details of the stop notice should be entered in the register of members.
3 The details should also be entered on the 'stop list'.
4 If any transfer (or redemption) of the shareholding or part of it is lodged for registration, 'warning-off' letters should be sent both to the person who lodged the notice and to the person on whose behalf it was lodged, who then have 14 days in which to obtain an injunction restraining the transfer.
5 If no injunction is served within the 14-day period, the stop notice lapses in respect of the shares being transferred and the transfer or redemption notice may be processed.
6 The details in the register of members and the 'stop list' should then be amended as appropriate. The notice should be endorsed with the details of the transfer (or redemption) if there is any balance of the holding to which the stop notice still applies.
7 A stop notice may be withdrawn in which case the register of members, stop list and copy of the stop notice would be amended or noted appropriately.
8 If a stop notice is received for registration relative to a holding in uncertificated form within the CREST system, the notice should immediately be transmitted to the operator of the CREST system, Euroclear UK & Ireland, so that it may initiate the necessary changes to the register (this will result in the holding being moved into a CREST escrow account).

Charging order

This is a court order securing a shareholding for the benefit of a **judgement creditor**. The order is made in two parts. First, there is an *order nisi*, which acts as a stop notice (see above). If the settlement of the debt is made, the order will be discharged. If settlement is not made, the order may be made absolute. If made absolute, the judgement creditor is empowered to realise the shareholding to settle the debt. The duly sealed order or an office copy will identify the relevant shareholding. The equivalent Scottish document is a letter of arrestment, which cannot be registered by English companies.

Procedure

If a charging order is received, the following procedure should be adopted:

1 There must be complete identity between the holding specified in the order and a shareholding in the company. Service of the order should be acknowledged to the sender unless the holding cannot be identified, in which case the order should be returned to the sender.
2 The order or office copy submitted to the company is retained by the company.
3 An appropriate entry in the register of members should be made to indicate the existence of the order.
4 Details of the order should be entered on a 'stop list'.

5 If any transfers of the relevant shareholding are lodged for registration, a 'warning-off' letter must be sent to the judgement creditor detailed in the order, who may then perfect their security by obtaining a further order of the court making the charging order absolute. The terms of the order must be strictly followed.
6 If an order absolute is made, these details should be entered in the register of members, the 'stop list' should be amended and the order absolute retained with the original order.
7 An order absolute usually authorises the sale of the shares with payment of the proceeds into the court.
8 If debt due to the judgement creditor is settled, the charging *order nisi* must be withdrawn. The advice of withdrawal must be made personally by the judgement creditor before a practising solicitor. The discharge of the *order nisi* should be acknowledged, the details recorded in the register of members and the 'stop list' amended. The notice of discharge should be retained with the original order.

Garnishee order

A garnishee order is a court order attaching all debts for the benefit of a judgement creditor. The debts will be amounts due from the company to a shareholder and the judgement creditor will be a person owed money by that shareholder and who has obtained judgement from the court to that effect. The terms of the order usually include rights to income (dividends) as well as capital. The order does not restrict the transfer of securities. As with a charging order, the order is made in two parts. An *order nisi* is made requiring the company to attend (through a representative) a court hearing. If, before that time, the judgement debt has been satisfied, the order is discharged. If the debt is not satisfied, the order is made absolute. If the order is made absolute, the company is under an obligation to pay the judgement creditor the amount of any debts due by the company to the shareholder concerned. The judgement creditor will be empowered to give to the company a discharge of its debt to the shareholder. The sealed court order or duly authorised office copy will identify the shareholder concerned and the amount of the debt. There is no equivalent Scottish document.

Procedure

The procedure for registration of a garnishee order is the same as that for registering a charging order. As the order attaches to income and not just capital, any dividends must be paid to the creditor until such time as the debt is settled and the order is discharged.

Bankruptcy order

A company may be required to register a court order adjudicating a shareholder bankrupt. The effect of a bankruptcy order is to transfer the shares to a trustee for the benefit of the shareholder's creditors generally. Trustees are usually appointed following the issue of the adjudication order, and this is evidenced by a certificate of the Department for Business, Energy & Industrial Strategy (BEIS) (formerly the Department for Business, Innovation and Skills) naming the trustee and confirming details of the appointment. Either the original order bearing the seal of the court or a duly authenticated office copy of the order or a copy of the *London Gazette* notifying the order with the relevant certificate from BEIS should be submitted to the company, together with the shareholder's share certificate(s).

The equivalent Scottish document is an act and warrant appointing a trustee in sequestration.

Procedure

The following procedure should be adopted:

1 There must be complete identity between the person named in the order or ***Gazette*** advertisement and a registered shareholding.
2 Relevant details of the documents submitted should be recorded and a copy retained for future reference.
3 The heading of the account should be changed to 'the trustee of the estate of . . ., a bankrupt', adding the name and address of the trustee by way of note. The shares of the bankrupt vest in this case in the trustee by operation of law without the need for any instrument of transfer (IA1986 s. 306).
4 The share certificate(s) should be endorsed with the details of the order and the certificates and the order or *Gazette* advertisement validated with the company's registration stamp.
5 All further communications should be addressed to the trustee in their representative capacity or as directed by the trustee.
6 It may be appropriate for a dividend mandate to be completed by the trustee.

Order for rectification of register

An order may be made by a court under s. 125 for the rectification of the register of members. The rectification can take any form, including removals or additions to the register or the substitution of one person for another whether in respect of the entire holding or only part of it. Original orders will bear the seal of the court or an office copy may be presented for registration. The order will identify the shareholding to which it relates, which should be submitted together with the share certificates where appropriate.

An order for rectification of the register may only be made by a court in the country of registration of the company concerned. Accordingly, an order made by a Scottish court may not be registered by English companies and an order made by an English court may not be registered by a Scottish company.

Procedure

On receipt of such an order, the following procedure should be adopted:

1 There must be complete identity between the holding referred to in the order and a shareholding in the company.
2 The amendment authorised in the order should be made in the register of members, and the date of the order and its registration should be entered as the authority for such amendment, and there may be consequential changes to other company records. A copy of the order should be retained for future reference.
3 Although the share certificate(s) could be endorsed, preferably a new certificate should be issued.
4 The order should be endorsed with the company's registration stamp and returned to the sender with the new share certificate.
5 It may be appropriate for a dividend mandate to be completed.

Appointment of receiver

The company may receive notice of the appointment of a receiver, or a receiver and manager in relation to a shareholder which is a body corporate. The appointee may act only within the terms of the relevant court order, debenture or trust deed under which they were appointed.

The equivalent Scottish document is the appointment of a receiver.

Procedure

The following procedure should be adopted:

1 There must be complete identity between the body corporate in respect of which a receiver is being appointed and a shareholding in the company.
2 Service of the order or notice should be acknowledged to the sender unless the holding cannot be identified, in which case the order should be returned to the sender.
3 The details of the appointment, name and address of the receiver and date of registration should be entered in the register of members. The account in the register should be amended to the name and address of the receiver, described as 'receiver of . . . Limited/plc'.
4 Where a notice is received, this should be retained. If the appointment is made by court order, this should be endorsed and returned. A copy of the order should be kept for future reference.
5 Share certificates do not need to be endorsed.
6 All future communications should be addressed to the receiver or as directed by the receiver.

7 It may be appropriate for a dividend mandate to be completed.

8 The receivership may be brought to an end, following which the entries in the register of members should be amended accordingly. Any dividend mandate in favour of the receiver should be terminated. The notice or order ending the appointment should be retained with the original notice or copy order.

Appointment of liquidator

The company may receive notice of the appointment of a liquidator in relation to a shareholder which is a body corporate. The person appointed liquidator assumes the functions of the board of directors of that body corporate to facilitate the realising of its assets, collection of debts and distribution of any surplus to creditors and, if the surplus is sufficient, to shareholders.

The company may receive notice in the form of a copy of the resolution appointing the liquidator in the case of a voluntary liquidation or in the form of an original court order or an office copy in the case of a compulsory liquidation.

In either instance, a copy of the *London Gazette* containing notification of the appointment may also be accepted.

If the company receives notice of appointment of a liquidator, the procedure is the same as that for the appointment of a receiver. In the case of the appointment of a liquidator, the company will also receive a stock transfer form when the liquidator realises the shareholder company's assets.

19 – Dividends

Introduction

Dividends represent a distribution of accumulated profit to shareholders in proportion to the number of shares they hold. The company can only pay a dividend to its shareholders if it has sufficient distributable profits under s. 830.

Dividends are declared by the directors. For Listed, AIM and NEX companies, there is a timetable for the declaration and subsequent payment of dividends. This is to ensure the smooth operation of the market. Once the record date is reached, the share price will be reduced to reflect that the purchaser of the shares will not be entitled to receive the dividend payment. This is known as the ex date, as the shares are sold excluding the dividend.

Dividends

Responsibility for the arrangements for the payment of dividends on a company's shares or interest on its debentures and loan stocks lies with the company secretary's department or with its registrar. Before dealing with the procedures to be followed and the related documents used, consideration should be given to the statutory powers and restrictions imposed on companies by the Companies Acts in regard to making distributions, as defined in the Acts.

There is an implied power for trading companies to distribute their profits to the members subject to any limitations included in the memorandum and articles of association and subject also to the provisions of the Companies Act 2006 (Part 23 – Distributions) and the general law. In the case of shares (both ordinary shares and preference shares), the distributions are made in the form of dividends, which are expressed as a specified amount of money per share.

In the case of a company with different classes of shares, the articles may provide for the priority of dividend payments, e.g. the fixed rate of dividend on the preference shares must be paid before any dividend is paid on the ordinary shares. Unless there are provisions to the contrary, the preference dividends are presumed to be cumulative. This means that if, in any year, the profits of the company are insufficient to pay the fixed preference dividends, the entitlement will be carried forward to the next year or following years when the company is able to make the payment. Some companies have participating preference shares, which may be cumulative or non-cumulative; these shares give entitlement to a specified share in the profits related to the level of dividends paid on the ordinary shares, in addition to the fixed annual preferential dividend.

The model articles provide that the company may declare dividends by ordinary resolution (Private Model Articles reg. 30, Public Model Articles reg. 70). These dividends are usually referred to as final dividends and are considered as part of the business of the annual general meeting. The articles will also usually provide that the directors may declare interim dividends without seeking authority from the shareholders (Private Model Articles reg. 30, Public Model Articles reg. 70). An interim dividend is one decided solely and approved by the directors between general meetings. Final dividends are declared by shareholders following a recommendation from the board of directors. Whether the dividend is a final dividend or an interim dividend, the ability of the company to pay dividends is governed by the provisions of the Act on the distribution of profit.

Mandates

Form and completion

Shareholders can lodge mandates with the company authorising it to pay dividends on their shares direct to their individual bank accounts. The ICSA has prepared a standard form of dividend mandate known as 'Request for payment of interest or dividends' (see precedent 67). The dividend mandate is the authority from the shareholder to the company to pay dividends becoming due to a specified branch of a specified bank. It incorporates an authority to send dividends to a new branch of the bank if the company receives notice that the shareholder's account has been transferred.

Dividend mandates must be signed by the shareholder. If there are joint holders, the dividend mandate should be signed by all the joint holders. In the case of a corporate body, the mandate may be signed by an official who should state their office. In the case of administrators, attorneys, executors, receivers, trustees in bankruptcy, etc., or any other person acting on behalf of the shareholder, the authority under which they sign the dividend mandate must be registered with the company.

Bank mandates

Companies should, ideally, not receive mandates direct from shareholders. Any mandate so received should be returned to the shareholder with a request that it is lodged with the company by the shareholder's bank. The submission of the mandate through the bank, authenticated by the stamp of the branch of the bank on the mandate form, ensures that the mandate contains the correct address and title of the branch, the branch's sorting code number and the account number to which the dividend is to be credited. Most banks and building societies accept full liability in respect of the customers' bank account numbers shown on the dividend mandate form and bearing their stamp, and for this reason, mandates should ideally not be accepted direct from shareholders. Companies should also make sure that they receive mandates on the accepted standard form of mandate approved by the ICSA.

The sorting code and a customer's account number are used in connection with the payment of dividends through the Bankers' Automated Clearing System (BACS). Occasionally, it may be necessary to send individual warrants direct to other banks, and in such cases the numbers should also be given on the warrants to ensure that the dividend reaches its correct destination.

Registration of mandates

It is not usual to send acknowledgements to shareholders when dividend mandates are received, especially in the case of the larger companies. The shareholder will be aware that their instructions have been received by the crediting of the next dividend to their bank account.

Dividend mandates must be recorded when received by the company. Although it may be convenient to record this information in the register of members, it should not be made available for inspection of the register by the public. Accordingly, mandate information should be recorded separately in a manual system and where a computerised register is used, this information must be suppressed where inspection is afforded to members of the public. When notification of marriage is received from a shareholder, it is desirable to obtain confirmation of any existing mandate instruction in case the shareholder also has a new address and/or bank account. The lodgement of a power of attorney with the company does not affect the payment of dividends in accordance with any existing mandate, unless the attorney has been given specific authority under the power to give a dividend mandate. In this situation, the attorney may lodge a revised mandate form.

To encourage shareholders to agree to mandate their dividends to a bank, some companies include a form of mandate on the back of the dividend warrants sent out direct to the shareholders whose dividends are not mandated.

Third party mandates

For personal reasons, a shareholder may wish dividends to be paid to some other person instead of to a bank, e.g. a firm of solicitors or accountants. However, this is not common. Most common forms of articles of association do not contain any provision for a company to refuse to accept a dividend mandate, no matter in whose favour it may be given.

Revocation of mandates

A mandate may be revoked at any time by the shareholder giving notice in writing to the company. It also lapses automatically upon the death of the shareholder, when the company should withhold payment of further dividends until the appointment of executors or administrators has been registered. It would then be in order for the company to accept instructions from the personal representative for the payment of dividends.

If one of the holders in a joint account dies, the dividend mandate continues to apply. There may, however, be a separate account in the name(s) of the survivor(s), in which case the accounts would normally be merged in the register of members. If it is desired to keep the two accounts separate, it will be necessary to designate one of the accounts, since the accounts will both be in the same name. It should be noted that a bankruptcy or protection order (or their Scottish equivalent) does not terminate a dividend mandate, although the receiver, trustee, curator or factor may give their own instructions that supersede any existing mandate.

In the case of a small company with few shareholders, the closing of an account in the register of members does not involve the lapse of the dividend mandate, which would be revived if the account were to be re-opened. However, it is impracticable to follow this procedure in large companies, since the accounts in question will be moved to a closed section of the register, either by the removal of the account cards or appropriate computer instructions. Consequently, if a new account is opened, fresh dividend instructions will be required.

Change of branch notice

Banks may issue change of branch notices if a customer transfers their account to another branch of the same bank. A company will frequently receive change of branch notices shortly after the payment of a dividend, since the payment of the dividend to the old branch will bring to light the need for a change.

The existing branch prepares and signs the notice, which is then passed on to the new branch, which inserts and verifies the details of its sorting code number and account number of the customer. The notice is then stamped by the bank in confirmation of this information and forwarded to the company to be recorded, as in the case of an original mandate form.

Like the ordinary dividend mandate, the change of branch notice applies to all shares and stocks of any class that are currently registered or may in future be registered in the name(s) of the shareholder(s) concerned. A change of branch notice limited to a particular holding or class of shares or stocks should not be accepted by a company, although the existing holding may be mentioned for reference and identification purposes.

It should be noted that a change of branch notice may not be used if the customer transfers their account to a different bank altogether, as this would be outside the authority given in the original mandate by the shareholder to the company. In this case, the shareholder should be given a new mandate for completion.

A change of branch notice should not be accepted if it is not possible to identify the notice with the original mandate given by the shareholder. The procedure for recording an acceptable bank change of branch notice on receipt by the company is the same as that which applies in the case of an original mandate.

BACS

The Bankers' Automated Clearing System (BACS) is the system used by many companies to pay dividends direct to banks and buildings societies.

Under this system, a computer file containing details of the shareholders, their bank account details and the amounts due must be submitted to BACS at least three working days before the due date.

BACS will verify the data and transmit instructions to the banks, who then credit the shareholders' accounts with the amount of the dividend. The company will issue a separate tax voucher direct to the shareholders. Any errors in the BACS payment details in respect of incorrect account numbers or accounts that have been closed are notified to the company or registrar and the amounts unpaid credited to the dividend account. The reasons for the error can then be investigated and manual cheques issued.

BACS payments are often preferred by shareholders, as they are simple and do not require any further action. The use of BACS also eliminates the possibility of cheques being lost in the postal system or being intercepted.

Where a company proposes to use BACS for the first time to distribute dividend payments, the articles of association should be checked to ensure that the articles do not provide that payment be made by cheque or warrant in which case they will require amendment (see page 33). Reg. 31 of the Model Articles for Private Companies or reg. 72 of the Model Article for Public Companies do provide the flexibility that the payment can be made in any other means as agreed by the directors with the recipient, either in writing or by such other means as the directors decide.

CREST

For those who hold their shares through CREST, it is possible for dividends to be paid via CREST. Tax vouchers can be sent electronically and can be transmitted through CREST. The company's articles must be checked to see if the payment by CREST is permitted, otherwise it can be changed to include the provision to enable dividends to be paid through this method. CREST members may also make dividend elections through CREST by indicating to the issuer that the holder wishes to receive payment in a particular currency, or wishes to take up a scrip dividend or participate in a dividend reinvestment plan. Please refer to further information on the Euroclear UK & Ireland Ltd website (see Directory).

Dividend warrants

There is a standard form of dividend/interest warrant that has been agreed by all parties concerned, including the ICSA, the banks and the Stock Exchange.

The FCA requires that, in the case of limited securities, the full ISIN code of the company be printed in a box to be located as close as possible to the top right-hand corner of the warrant. ISINs are published against the names of companies in the Official List as well as companies admitted to AIM or NEX. The UKLA has special requirements in the case of warrants and dividend confirmations for convertible loan stocks or stocks carrying subscription rights.

Because of the large number of shareholders and the increase in the number of warrants to be issued, it is now usual for warrants to bear printed facsimile signatures of the persons authorised by the company to sign them. In this case, the banks require an indemnity from the company to protect them against the issue of unauthorised warrants. The banks also require the indemnity to cover the issue of warrants if the amount is shown in figures only instead of in both words and figures, as fraudulent alteration on figures only is potentially easier.

Dividend confirmation

Under the autumn budget 2015, the rules relating to the taxation were changed; as part of this, the tax credit on dividends was withdrawn. However, companies are still required to provide a statement of tax deducted in dividends and the dividend confirmation replaced the tax voucher from March 2016. The dividend confirmation is a statement and explanation to the shareholder or stockholder, and shows the number of shares (or the amount of stock) on which payment has been made and the amount payable.

There is a form of wording for the dividend confirmation issued by the ICSA Registrars' Group (see precedent 68).

Some countries have double taxation agreements with the United Kingdom, and residents of those countries who are holders of debentures or loan stocks of UK companies may receive their interest payments without deduction of income tax at the basic rate or under deduction of tax at a reduced rate.

Payment procedure

The payment of a dividend needs to be carefully planned and it is of great assistance if, in advance of the payment of each dividend, a control sheet or timetable is prepared setting out all the various steps which have to take place so as to ensure that nothing is overlooked.

1 (*Listed, AIM and NEX companies only*) Immediately after the board meeting at which a dividend is declared or recommended, a regulatory information service should be informed (*LR 9.7A.2*). The announcement of the dividend will usually be accompanied by the company's half yearly report or preliminary figures for the year, and this is sent to the UKLA at the same time.
2 Announcements of dividends should follow the Stock Exchange's recommended record dates, a list of which is published every year for the guidance of companies. Dividend timetables that fall outside these guidelines must be cleared in advance by the LSE. Adherence to these dates facilitates the Stock Exchange's dividends claims procedure, enabling the shares to be dealt with on

the Stock Exchange in ex-dividend form at the earliest possible date after the announcement. This reduces the number of dividend claims that have to be made against the seller of shares who may have sold their shares xd (ex dividend), but whose shares are still registered in their name on the company's record date (see below) for the payment of the dividend. It is also helpful to include in the announcement the actual date of payment of the dividend.

3 (*Listed, AIM and NEX companies only*) In the case of dividends on preference shares and interest payments on debentures and loan stocks that fall due for payment on fixed dates each year, the FCA should be advised of the record date for each payment.

4 Model Articles, reg. 31 (Private companies) or reg. 71 (Public companies), and most companies' articles, provide that in the case of joint holders of shares, the company is legally bound to pay the dividend to the first-named shareholder in the joint account.

5 If, prior to the record date, a shareholder has disposed of all or part of their holding and the transfer has not been registered by the record date, the company is bound to pay the dividend to the registered shareholder at the record date. It is the responsibility of the purchaser's stockbrokers to claim the dividend from the seller. The dividend confirmation for the dividend will have gone to the seller of the shares together with the dividend payment. When they receive the dividend, the purchaser's stockbrokers will provide the purchaser with their own form of certificate. Claims arise only if the shareholder has purchased their shares cum dividend. No claim arises if the shareholder purchased their shares ex dividend, since the amount of the dividend would have been taken into account by adjustment of the share price on the Stock Exchange on the first day on which the shares were quoted ex dividend. In this case the dividend belongs to the seller, who may retain the dividend on receiving it although they have sold their shares. The schedule of dates, referred to above, should be adhered to in order to minimise claims.

6 If a transaction in shares is effected outside the Stock Exchange, the right to any current or pending dividend will have to be settled between the parties concerned. This is of no concern to the company, who will pay the dividend to the registered holder on the record date.

7 The draft of the dividend warrant and tax voucher should be prepared in good time, to allow for any corrections necessary to the proof. The bulk order for printing can be given to the printers when the rate of dividend is known. At the time of the Budget, it is necessary to bear in mind the possibility of a change in the basic rate of income tax. When part of the dividend will be paid through BACS, a separate supply of tax vouchers should be ordered. It is usual for warrants to be serially numbered and also for each dividend payment to be given its own identifying number. This assists in reconciling different dividend accounts. If there are several classes of stock on which dividends are to be paid, it is a good idea to use different-coloured paper for each class of security.

8 Arrangements should be made to ensure that all transfers, transmission documents, probates, confirmations, letters of administration, marriage certificates, changes of address, dividend mandates, etc. received up to the close of business on the record date are duly processed, so that the dividends or interest payments may be correctly dispatched. It should also be checked whether there are any stop notices or other restraints on dividends; if so, the relevant payments must be withheld.

9 With a manual system, each shareholder's holding has to be entered on the dividend sheets with the amount of dividend and tax credit alongside their name. The overall total of the number of shares on which the dividend is paid should agree with the company's issued capital and the columns relating to the tax credits and net dividends balanced to the total amount of the payment. It will, of course, be necessary to round off net payments resulting in odd fractions of a penny, but the total of the dividends to be paid should not exceed the total cost of the dividend when calculated by reference to the company's issued capital. In the case of a manual system, the warrants and confirmations will need to be fully addressed from plates or stencils for dispatch. The information on the warrants and confirmations should agree with that shown on the dividend sheets and, to make sure that they have been accurately completed, the warrants should be totalled and agreed with the totals on the dividend sheets.

10 If payments are being made through BACS the necessary computer file must be sent or transferred electronically to BACS at least three working days before the due date.

11 In the case of warrants sent direct to shareholders who have not mandated their dividends, each one should be signed. The signature may be applied either autographically (i.e. handwritten) or with a machine-affixed facsimile signature, which involves passing each warrant through a machine for the signature to be applied. However, in the case of most large companies, the signatures will be pre-printed on the warrants, usually in facsimile form. Computer-based registers will automatically update the address details to be printed on the warrants. There may be other queries in relation to a holding, e.g. the advice of a death in respect of which the grant of probate has not yet been received by the company with the names and addresses of the executors or administrators. In these circumstances, the warrants concerned should be withdrawn and retained until lodgement of probate or letters of administration. If it is known that the shareholder's previous dividend warrant has remained uncashed, a reminder letter about the uncashed warrant could be sent with the new dividend warrant, although it may be necessary to request a shareholder to return the warrant to the company or to the registrar for re-dating. It may be found that a number of earlier warrants have remained unpaid, despite the reminder; in this case it would be advisable to withdraw and retain further warrants until the matter of the shareholder's whereabouts can be clarified. However, this may be prohibited by the provisions of the company's articles of association

with regard to the dispatch of dividend warrants. In the case of Listed companies, it is usual to take power in their articles to cease sending dividend warrants by post where warrants have been returned undelivered or left uncashed. This power may not be exercised until such warrants have been returned or left uncashed on two consecutive occasions, or where after the first occasion enquiries have not established any new address.

12 Although some companies only maintain one dividend account, it may be convenient to ask the bank to open a separate account for each dividend designated with the title and the identifying number of the dividend payment. The total amount of the dividend can be credited to this account on the payment date by transfer from the company's current or deposit account. If only one dividend account is maintained – i.e. in respect of the current dividend in course of payment – it will be necessary to open an unclaimed dividend account into which any amounts which remained unclaimed at the time of funding the dividend account are transferred to pay a new dividend. Even if more than one dividend account is maintained, it is undesirable to leave separate dividend accounts open indefinitely. Balances on earlier separate dividend accounts may be transferred to an unclaimed dividend account when the quantity of old warrants being presented for payment reduces to a trickle.

13 Most Listed companies arrange for their registrars to deal with the printing and dispatch of warrants. The envelopes should be dispatched in time to be received by shareholders on the payment date, the date of posting being dependent on whether first-class or second-class post is used.

14 Inevitably, a number of envelopes containing warrants will be returned by Royal Mail as undeliverable, usually because the shareholder has not notified the company of a change of address.

15 Some warrants may be returned because the shareholder has died. These should be retained until probate or letters of administration are received, in the case of a sole shareholder, or the death certificate relating to a shareholder who was the first named in a joint account. These warrants may then be appropriately endorsed and, if necessary, re-dated and reissued to the persons entitled to receive them.

Unclaimed dividends

When dividends are paid direct to shareholders, warrants may occasionally be lost in the post or they may be mislaid by the shareholder. Outstanding unpaid dividend warrants are a nuisance to the company and it is usual for them to indicate on the warrants that unless they are paid within six months (or sometimes 12), they will have to be returned to the company for re-dating or verification.

A reminder may be sent to shareholders who have not yet banked their warrants about a month before the expiration of the six-month period. If the warrants are banked, they may then be debited against the current dividend account before that account is closed and the balance transferred to the unclaimed dividend account.

If there is no response to the first reminder notice, it may be followed by a further reminder notice with the next dividend payment sent out to the shareholder, to the effect that the previous warrant is still unpaid and requesting that it be returned for re-dating if more than six months have elapsed.

If the shareholder indicates that the warrant has been lost, a duplicate can be issued against signature of a simple form of indemnity or, if the dividend is not of a large amount, by signature of an undertaking. The difference between the indemnity and an undertaking is that, in the case of an indemnity, the shareholder undertakes to indemnify the company against any losses that it may incur as a result of the issue of a duplicate warrant. In the case of the undertaking, the shareholder merely agrees that if the original warrant is found, it will be returned to the company for cancellation. Before the issue of a duplicate warrant, payment of the original warrant should be stopped at the bank and an appropriate note made on the dividend sheets.

If it is found that the shareholder has died, the usual procedure followed on receipt of notice of death of a shareholder should be followed, i.e. the dividend withheld until probate, letters of administration or confirmation is lodged.

It is in the company's interests to clear outstanding dividends as quickly as possible, since the queries arising may result in a need to alter the register of members and it is desirable for this to be kept as up to date as possible. Similarly, prompt action should be taken in the event of the return as undeliverable of copies of the company's report and accounts sent to shareholders.

At least two dividend warrants should be sent to shareholders before action is taken to withhold the dispatch of further warrants. In the case of Listed companies, the UKLA requires that dividend warrants should not be withheld unless two consecutive dividend payments have been returned as undeliverable or left uncashed.

However, if the company's articles follow Table A, reg. 106, it could be argued that the company has no right to withhold the dispatch of dividend warrants to shareholders. Clearly, from the security point of view, it is unwise to continue to send out dividend warrants when it is known that they will not be received by the shareholder or, if received, will not be acted upon by them. Dividends become statute barred (in England) under the Limitation Act 1980 after 12 years from the date of declaration, although some courts have held that the period may be six years. In the case of Scotland, the Prescription and Limitation (Scotland) Act 1973 applies and the limitation period is five years after the date of declaration. However, most companies do not dispute dividend payments, since the publication in the company's accounts of the unclaimed dividends may be held to be an acknowledgement of the debt by the company. This means that the limitation periods start afresh each time an entry is made in the accounts. In order to deal with this matter, therefore, the FCA allows Listed companies to include the following powers in their articles of association:

- to forfeit dividends which have not been claimed for 12 years or more after the date of declaration; and
- to sell shares of untraceable shareholders, the company retaining the net sale proceeds of the shares pending the possible receipt of claims from the shareholders concerned.

To meet the FCA's requirements in this respect, however, the articles must stipulate the following:

- during a period of 12 years, at least three dividends in respect of the shares in question have become payable and no dividend during that period has been claimed; and
- on expiry of the 12 years, the company gives notice by advertisement in two national newspapers of its intention to sell the shares and notifies the FCA of that intention.

Scrip dividends

Some companies allow shareholders to elect whether to receive dividends in the form of shares instead of in cash. This is effected by the issue of fully paid shares to equity shareholders in lieu of cash dividends, but authority to do this must be contained in the company's articles. The shareholder is thus able to build up their shareholding in the company without incurring brokerage expenses and stamp duty, and the money that would otherwise be distributed in cash as dividends is retained in the business for the benefit of the company. However, the value of the shares issued is still taxed as a distribution of income in the same way as a cash dividend, which means that the shareholder must be provided with a tax voucher. Many companies now follow the practice of offering scrip dividends. The Investment Committee of the Association of British Insurers, now forming part of the Investment Association, requires that any authority in the articles of Listed companies should be subject to renewal by an ordinary resolution of the members at least once every five years.

The procedure for dealing with a scrip dividend is as follows:

1. Ensure that the company's articles give power to the board to offer shareholders the right to elect to receive new ordinary shares in the company instead of receiving a dividend in cash. If not, the company's articles will require changing by a special resolution (see page 33; see precedent 69).
2. At a general meeting of the company (usually the annual general meeting), pass an ordinary resolution for the board to offer shareholders the right to elect to receive new ordinary shares instead of cash for all or any part of any interim and final dividends for the financial period of the company ending on the next accounting date (see precedent 69).
3. When the board declares an interim dividend or recommends a final dividend on the company's shares, it should also resolve to make the offer of new shares

to shareholders as an alternative to the cash dividend. This is subject, of course, in the case of the final dividend, to that dividend being approved by shareholders at the annual general meeting.

4 Entitlement to the alternative scrip dividend instead of a cash dividend will be to those shareholders on the company's register of members on the record date for the dividend.

5 In the case of a Listed company, the price of the new shares will be determined by taking the average of the middle market quotations for the company's shares for the five business days commencing on the date when the company's shares were first quoted ex dividend on the Stock Exchange. For non-listed companies, the price of the new shares would be calculated by the directors and may include reference to recent share issues or transfers and/or the net asset value disclosed in the latest accounts.

6 Prepare a circular letter to be sent to shareholders giving the price of the new shares and explaining the action they should take if they wish to receive new shares instead of the whole or any part of the cash dividend to which they are entitled. Also state in the circular that shareholders who do not wish to elect to receive any new shares need not take any action, and that their dividend will be paid in cash in the usual way on the payment date.

7 Prepare a form of election, which must be signed by the shareholder(s), to accompany the circular letter. This will be personalised with the following information:
   (a) number of shares held on the dividend record date;
   (b) maximum number of shares on which election may be made (this number will be an exact multiple of the number of shares required to be elected to receive one new share);
   (c) number of shares on which the dividend will be paid in cash if the maximum number of shares is elected as in (b) above (i.e. the balance of the shares being less than the multiple required for one new share);
   (d) the maximum number of new shares to be issued if the maximum number of shares is elected as in (b) above; and
   (e) the number of shares which the shareholder wishes to elect for new shares if they wish to elect fewer than the maximum in (b) above.

8 Special dividend warrants will be prepared with boxes to show the number of elected shares and the number of non-elected shares on which the normal full cash dividend will be paid. On these dividend warrants the pence per share, tax credit and amount payable boxes will be as usual.

9 New share certificates will be prepared or CREST accounts credited for each shareholder for the number of shares issued in lieu of cash dividend. It is usual to attach an explanatory note explaining how the number of shares, tax credit information, etc. have been determined.

10 A sum equal to the aggregate nominal amount of the new ordinary shares allotted pursuant to the elections for new shares made by shareholders will be

capitalised out of any amount standing to the credit of any reserve or fund (including the profit and loss account), as determined by the directors.

11 (*Listed, AIM and NEX companies only*) Application is made to the FCA and the Stock Exchange for any new shares issued as scrip dividends to be Listed and admitted to trading.

Enhanced scrip dividends, under which the value of the shares being offered exceeds the value of the cash payment, are becoming increasingly popular. They are used by companies to encourage shareholders to take up the scrip dividend alternative. If an enhanced scrip dividend is to be offered, prior approval from HM Revenue & Customs is required. If the company's shares are Listed, the price of the shares must be calculated with reference to a period as close as practical to the first dealing day of the new shares.

It is usual for companies offering scrip dividends to notify shareholders on the occasion of each dividend payment of the terms on which scrip dividends may be elected for that particular dividend. This is because the terms depend upon the rate of dividend and the price of the company's shares at the time in question. This also gives shareholders the opportunity of deciding on each occasion whether or not they wish to receive that particular dividend in the form of shares, rather than in cash. This does not arise, of course, in the case of those shareholders who have given the company continuing scrip dividend mandates (see below).

If the shareholder signs a scrip dividend mandate, all their future dividends will be in the form of shares, until they cancel the mandate. This will exclude any part of the dividend paid in cash in respect of any balance of their holding of shares that does not make up the multiple required for a new share. Alternatively, the company may carry forward to the next dividend payment any balance of the cash dividend on shares that are insufficient in number to make up the multiple required for a new share, to be added to the amount of the next dividend payment. The total is then used for the purpose of the scrip dividend on that occasion, any further balance of cash again being carried forward. The procedure described for the implementation of a scrip dividend scheme must be appropriately modified in the case of shareholders who have signed scrip dividend mandates.

If shareholders have signed ordinary dividend mandates for dividends to be paid into a bank, the payment made will comprise the cash dividend on the balance of their shareholding that did not add up to the multiple required for the allocation of a new share under the scrip dividend scheme. The bank mandates still operate for a dividend which is paid in cash, irrespective of whether or not the shareholder has signed a scrip dividend mandate.

When prices on the Stock Exchange are volatile, companies may afford protection to their shareholders by providing that all share elections will be automatically withdrawn if, due to a price fall, the market value of the shares received is substantially less than the cash dividend forgone. Some companies may propose a specific amount for this purpose, e.g. a fall of 15% or more in the company's share price. Most scrip dividend schemes give the director wider powers to suspend or terminate the offer at any time (where the price of the company's shares has fallen dramatically).

Dividend reinvestment schemes

Dividend reinvestment schemes should not be confused with scrip dividend schemes, described above. Under these schemes, a shareholder signs a mandate to the effect that all dividends on their shares in future be paid to the company or its registrar to be used in the purchase of shares in the company on the market and added to their existing holding. The shares are purchased as a single transaction on the day the dividend is paid at the current market price, taking advantage of the lower dealing costs involved in a bulk purchase. The shareholder will be taxed as if they had received a cash dividend and, in addition, the shareholder will have to pay a minimum of £5 stamp duty on the transaction.

A few weeks after each purchase, particulars of the transaction are sent to the shareholder with a certificate for the additional shares purchased. Any balance of dividend that is insufficient to buy one new share is carried forward in the shareholder's dividend reinvestment account and added to the next dividend paid.

As the shares are not new shares, there is no dilution of the company's share capital, but at the same time the cash saved on the dividends that are not paid in cash is not retained in the company for its benefit, as in the case of a scrip dividend scheme.

Waivers of dividends

Shareholders with substantial holdings, particularly directors of small companies, may elect to waive future dividend payments by executing a form of waiver as a deed which, to be effective, must be received by the company prior to the declaration or payment of an interim dividend or the approval by shareholders of a recommended final dividend. If the waiver is dated after the declaration of the dividend, the shareholder will still be liable to the income tax on the dividend that would have been paid. This is because, once declared, the dividend becomes a debt due by the company. As a matter of tax law, a dividend is taxed in the tax year in which it becomes payable, rather than the year in which it is declared.

In the case of Listed companies, the FCA requires that particulars of waivers be given in the company's annual report unless the amount(s) are minor (less than 1%) and that some payment has been made on each share of the relevant class during the relevant calendar year (*LR 9.8.4(13)* and *LR 9.8.5*).

Disclosure of any waiver(s) of dividends must also be made in any prospectus or listing particulars where a UK listing is sought and must be reported upon by the auditors in their report accompanying such prospectus.

20 – Mortgages and charges

Introduction

Companies sometimes create a mortgage or charge over their assets as security for loans and guarantees provided by a third party. In order to protect potential creditors and others doing business with the company, details of all charges and mortgages must be registered with the Registrar of Companies.

Charges

A charge is security for the payment of a debt or other obligation, such as future rent payments. The charge does not pass title to the assets charged or any right to possession to the person who has been given the charge (the chargee).

Mortgages

A mortgage is security for the payment of a debt or other obligation that does pass title to the assets charged, but does not pass the right to possession to the chargee.

Legislation

The charges regime was amended by the Companies Act 2006 (Amendment of Part 25) Regulations 2013, which repealed Chapters 1 and 2 of Part 25 of CA2006.

Registration of charges

Most charges granted by a company registered in the UK over any of its property (wherever situated in the UK and regardless of the law under which the charge was created) can be registered at Companies House, unless there is an express exclusion specified in the Regulations. With effect from 6 April 2013, where a charge is evidenced by an instrument, a company need only submit a certified copy of the instrument to the Registrar of Companies (s. 859A(3)). An important point is that the 21-day time limit for registration remains under the new regime.

Below are details of charges which cannot be registered:

- A charge in favour of a landlord on a cash deposit given as a security in connection with the lease of land.

- A charge created by a member of Lloyd's (within the meaning of the Lloyd's Act 1982) to secure its obligations in connection with its underwriting business at Lloyd's.
- A charge that any other Act specifically excludes from registration (for example, the Financial and Collateral Arrangements (No. 2) Regulations 2003).

Under the new regime, penalties for failing to register a charge apply to a wider range of charges, as more charges are registrable. It is worth noting that the criminal sanction for the failure of registering a charge has now been abolished. The impact that this abolition will have in practice is likely to be minimal as, similar to previous requirements, a charge that has not been registered, that should have, will be void against a liquidator, administrator or creditor, and any money secured by the charge will become payable immediately.

The following table outlines the new forms for submission at Companies House and confirmation if the 21-day time limit applies.

Table 20.1: New forms and the 21-day time limit

Form Number	*Title*	*21-day time limit to deliver the form? (Y/N)*
MR01*	Particulars of a charge	Y
MR02*	Particulars of a charge subject to which property or undertaking has been acquired	N
MR03	Particulars for the registration of a charge to secure a series of debentures	Y
MR04*	Statement of satisfaction in full or part of a charge	N
MR05*	Statement that part or the whole of the property has been released from the charge or no longer forms part of the company's property	N
MR06	Statement of company acting as a trustee	N
MR07	Particulars of alteration of a charge (particulars of a negative pledge)	N
MR08	Particulars of a charge where there is no instrument	Y
MR09	Particulars of a charge subject to which property or undertaking has been acquired where there is no instrument	N
MR10	Particulars for the registration of a charge to secure a series of debentures where there is no instrument	Y

Form Number	Title	21-day time limit to deliver the form? (Y/N)
RM01	Notice of appointment of administrative receiver, receiver or manager	N
RM02	Notice of ceasing to act as an administrative receiver, receiver or manager	N

A filing fee of £23 applies when registering a charge, though where using WebFiling or electronic means, the fee is £15.

It should be noted that similar forms exist for limited liability partnerships.

Companies House register of charges

Following delivery to the Registrar of Companies of a charge, a unique reference code will be allocated. A note will also be placed on the register of this code, together with details of any documents delivered under the relevant CA2006 sections.

The Registrar of Companies must also issue a certificate of registration of the charge. The certificate will include details of the charge and the unique reference code (s. 859H).

Enforcement of security

If a chargee appoints or obtains an order for the appointment of a receiver or manager under the power contained in a mortgage or charge document, details of such appointment must be filed with the Registrar of Companies within seven days of such appointment (s. 859K(2)).

A person appointed as a receiver or manager to enforce any security must give notice upon ceasing to act as such receiver or manager (s. 859K(3)).

Company's register of charges

Companies are no longer required to keep a register of charges for charges created on or after 6 April 2013. In place of this requirement, copies of charges (and any amendments to them) and instruments creating a charge (if applicable) must be made available for inspection at either the company's registered office or SAIL address (s. 859P and Q).

In practice, companies will still need to maintain a record in order to monitor outstanding charges, and it is likely that some sort of register will be maintained. Such a register or record is not required to be made available for public inspection.

The requirement to keep and maintain a register of charges remains in place for charges created before 6 April 2013.

Satisfaction and release

As under the previous legislation, there is no requirement to notify the Registrar of Companies that a charge has been released or satisfied or if the property charged no longer belongs to the company. Despite this being the case, it is in the company's interests to ensure the records are accurate and that potential investors, bankers and creditors are aware that all or part of any previous loans or other obligations have been satisfied.

Where a company wishes to have such an event noted on the public record, notice must be given of the satisfaction of a mortgage in full or in part, by submitting Form MR04 to Companies House. Where notification is being provided of the fact that a company has been released from a charge or if the property no longer belongs to the company, Form MR05 must be submitted to Companies House.

On receipt of either Form MR04 or MR05, the Registrar of Companies will update the register of charges kept at Companies House (s. 859L).

Oversea companies

Companies registered outside of Great Britain, the Channel Islands and the Isle of Man that have either a place of business or branch in England or Wales must register details of any charges they create on any property in England or Wales or any such property which is already subject to a charge (the Overseas Companies (Execution of Documents and Registration of Charges) Regulations 2009). There is no longer a need for overseas companies that are not registered in Great Britain to register details of charges created, and the Slavenburg register has therefore been abolished.

21 – Takeovers, mergers and divisions

Introduction

The object of a takeover transaction is the acquisition usually by a company (the offeror or acquirer) of the whole or a majority of the issued share capital of another company (the target or offeree). The consideration for the acquisition may be the issue of shares or other securities in the acquiring company, the payment of cash or a combination of the two.

Types of takeover

The following are the main types of takeover transaction:

- A formal agreement may be made with the shareholders of the target company. This is practicable only where there is a small number of shareholders. This is the usual type of takeover transaction for private companies.
- Arrangements may be made to purchase, by private agreement or on a public market, blocks of shares in a company in order to build up a sizeable holding, which could form the basis on which to launch a bid for the remainder of the issued share capital. It is necessary, however, where the target company is a public company, to have regard to the provisions of the City Code on Takeovers and Mergers, compliance with both of which is supervised by the Panel on Takeovers and Mergers (the Takeover Panel).
- The acquiring company may make a public offer to the shareholders of the company to be acquired by sending documents to its shareholders making an offer to acquire their shares on stated terms.
- A takeover may be effected under a scheme of arrangement made under the provisions of ss. 895–901, although this is a more complicated procedure.

Takeover Panel

The Panel on Takeovers and Mergers (the 'Panel') is an independent body, established in 1968, whose main functions are to issue and administer the City Code on Takeovers and Mergers (the 'Code') and to supervise and regulate takeovers and other matters to which the Code applies in accordance with the Rules set out in the Code. It has been designated as the supervisory authority to carry out certain regulatory functions in relation to takeovers pursuant to the Directive on Takeover Bids (2004/25/EC) (the 'Directive'). Its statutory functions are set out in and under Chapter 1 of Part 28 of the Companies Act 2006.

The Panel regulates takeover bids and other merger transactions (however effected) for public companies or companies that have been public companies in the previous ten years that have their registered offices in the United Kingdom, the Channel Islands or the Isle of Man if any of their securities are admitted to trading on a regulated market in the United Kingdom or on any stock exchange in the Channel Islands or the Isle of Man. Its remit also extends to unlisted public companies and certain private companies that are resident in the UK.

In all cases, the Panel's function is to ensure that shareholders are treated fairly and not denied an opportunity to decide on the merits of a takeover, and that shareholders of the same class are afforded equivalent treatment by an offeror. The Code is not concerned with the financial or commercial advantages of a takeover. These are matters for the company and its shareholders.

The Code

The Code has been developed since 1968 to reflect the collective opinion of those professionally involved in the field of takeovers as to appropriate business standards and as to how fairness to shareholders and an orderly framework for takeovers can be achieved. Following the implementation of the Takeovers Directive (2004/25/EC) (the 'directive') by means of Part 28 of the Companies Act 2006 (the 'Act'), the rules set out in the Code have a statutory basis in relation to the UK and comply with the relevant requirements in the Directive.

General principles and rules

The Code is based upon a number of General Principles, which are essentially statements of standards of commercial behaviour. These General Principles are the same as the general principles set out in Article 3 of the Directive. They apply to takeovers and other matters to which the Code applies. They are expressed in broad general terms and the Code does not define the precise extent of, or the limitations on, their application. They are applied in accordance with their spirit in order to achieve their underlying purpose.

In addition to the General Principles, the Code contains a series of rules. Although most of the rules are expressed in less general terms than the General Principles, they are not framed in technical language, and like the General Principles, they are to be interpreted to achieve their underlying purpose. Therefore, their spirit must be observed as well as their letter.

The following is a brief summary of some of the most important Rules:

- When a person or group acquires interests in shares carrying 30% or more of the voting rights of a company, they must make a cash offer to all other shareholders at the highest price paid in the 12 months before the offer was announced (30% of the voting rights of a company is treated by the Code as the level at which effective control is obtained).

- When interests in shares carrying 10% or more of the voting rights of a class have been acquired by an offeror in the offer period and the previous 12 months, the offer must include a cash alternative for all shareholders of that class at the highest price paid by the offeror in that period. Further, if an offeror acquires for cash any interest in shares during the offer period, a cash alternative must be made available at that price at least.
- If the offeror acquires an interest in shares in a target company at a price higher than the value of the offer, the offer must be increased accordingly.
- The target company must appoint a competent independent adviser whose advice on the offer must be made known to all the shareholders, together with the opinion of the board.
- Favourable deals for selected shareholders are banned.
- All shareholders must be given the same information.
- Those issuing takeover circulars must include statements taking responsibility for the contents.
- Profit forecasts and asset valuations must be made to specified standards and must be reported on by professional advisers.
- Misleading, inaccurate or unsubstantiated statements made in documents or to the media must be publicly corrected immediately.
- Actions during the course of an offer by the target company that might frustrate the offer are generally prohibited unless shareholders approve these plans.
- Stringent requirements are laid down for the disclosure of dealings in relevant securities during an offer.
- Employees of both the offeror and the offeree must be informed about an offer.

Enterprise Act 2002

Regard should be paid to the provisions of Part 3 of the Enterprise Act 2002 (EA2002) affecting takeovers and mergers references to the Competition Commission. The Enterprise Act introduced a new merger regime, with decisions taken in most cases by independent competition authorities against a competition-based test rather than the previous public interest test.

From April 2014, the Competition Commission and most of the roles of the Office of Fair Trading were brought together under a unified structure known as the Competition and Markets Authority.

The main provisions of the Act provide for:

- final decisions on most mergers to be taken by the Office of Fair Trading (OFT) and the Competition Commission (CC) rather than by the Secretary of State;
- mergers to be considered against a new test of whether they result in a substantial lessening of competition (EA2002 s. 35). A number of matters may be potentially relevant to the assessment of whether a merger will result in a

substantial lessening of competition. The matters may include, but are not limited to:

- market shares and concentration;
- extent of effective competition before and after the merger;
- efficiency and financial performance of firms in the market;
- barriers to entry and expansion in the relevant market;
- availability of substitute products and the scope for supply or demand-side substitution;
- extent of change and innovation in a market;
- whether in the absence of the merger one of the firms would fail and, if so, whether its failure would cause the assets of that firm to exit the market; and
- the conduct of customers or of suppliers to those in the market;

- discretion for the competition authorities to clear a merger or allow it to proceed with less stringent competition remedies in circumstances where it is expected to result in defined types of customer benefit, even though there might be decreased competition (EA2002 s. 22);
- the Secretary of State to continue to decide mergers which raise defined public interest considerations;
- revisions to the special regime for mergers between water enterprises to align it where possible with the general regime while preserving the importance currently attached to the ability of the water regulator to make comparisons between different enterprises;
- the retention of the existing two-stage approach to merger control. The OFT will carry out the first stage investigation to decide whether a reference to the Competition Commission (CC) is required. The CC will carry out an in-depth investigation as required;
- the retention of the system of voluntary rather than compulsory pre-notification of mergers;
- statutory maximum timetables for competition authorities to reach final decisions (EA2002 ss. 24, 25);
- the replacement of the current worldwide assets-based criteria with a UK-based turnover test for determining whether a merger is subject to merger control (EA2002 s. 23) as follows:
  - the value of the turnover in the UK of the enterprise being taken over exceeds £70 million; or
  - the merger would result in the creation or enhancement of at least a 25% share of supply of goods or services in the UK. This would cover, for example, both a merger between two enterprises each having a 15% share of supply, and between two enterprises where one has a 22% share and the other has a 5% share; and
  - that between two enterprises where one which already has a 25% share of supply mergers with another having a 5% share.

Agreements with individual members

A simple way of effecting a transfer of ownership of a company is by making agreements with individual members. It can be effected merely by the exchange of the consideration for duly executed transfers with the share certificates. Usually, however, a formal agreement is entered into between the parties, which should be drawn up with legal advice. The agreement should cover such matters as full details of the shares to be acquired and the consideration to be paid for them with a time for completion, and set out who will be responsible for paying legal costs, duty and any other related expenses. Usually warranties are also required from the directors of the offeree company containing financial information about the offeree company, the title to its property, pending litigation, etc., including any changes affecting the company that may have occurred since the date of the last balance sheet.

The following procedural points arise in connection with the takeover of a company by agreement with individual members:

1 The purchase and sale agreement must be carefully drawn up with legal advice to ensure that the interests of both parties to the agreement are adequately protected.
2 The final agreement is executed and formally exchanged between the parties, and a date set for completion of the exchange of shares for the agreed consideration.
3 At the time of completion, the executed transfers, accompanied by the share certificates, are exchanged for the consideration. If any new shares have been issued as part of the consideration, the renounceable certificates for the new shares should be handed over with the forms of renunciation on the renounceable certificates duly signed.
4 The Registrar of Companies should be informed of any changes in director or secretary on Form TM01 and of any change in the registered office address on Form AD01. A return of allotments should also be submitted to the Registrar of Companies on Form SH01, covering the allotments of shares that have been made.
5 Entries should then be made in the various statutory registers, e.g. the register of members, reflecting the registration of any share transfers, and the register of directors and secretaries. The share transfers should, of course, be properly stamped or be duly certified as being exempt from stamp duty.
6 Announcements should be made to the FCA (for a Listed company), the press (if appropriate), the company's customers and its employees.
7 Once the stock transfer forms have been stamped by HM Customs & Revenue, details of the transfers should be entered into the target company's register of members and appropriate entries made in the PSC Register.

Purchases in the market

Arrangements may be made whereby a company obtains a significant proportion of the shares in a publicly quoted company by purchases of the company's shares on the market to which the company's shares have been admitted to trading. Fewer formalities are involved with this type of transaction, but care should be taken to ensure compliance with the rules of the City Code on Takeovers and Mergers. It is also important to remember that when the holding reaches 3% and each whole percentage point thereafter in nominal value of the company's issued share capital, notice must be given to the company and the FCA within two days as required by the *Disclosure and Transparency Rules* (see Chapter 16). The company receiving the notification is required to inform a regulatory information service. In the initial stages, in order to preserve confidentiality, the acquisitions are often made through a nominee or nominees.

However, when calculating the level of holding giving rise to an obligation to notify the company, e.g. 3%, purchases by persons acting in concert with the acquiring company must be included in the total, and there is an obligation for such persons to keep each other informed to ensure compliance with the notification requirements. It should also be remembered that the acquisition of certain levels of shareholdings may give rise to an obligation to make a general offer for all the shares of the company, which could also affect the price of the shares.

Public offers

A public offer is a takeover offer made to all the shareholders of a company to acquire all or a proportion of their holdings in the offeree company, either for cash or for shares and/or other securities in the offeror company. This is the usual form of takeover and usually receives wide publicity in the press.

Public offers involve many more procedural steps than takeovers by agreement with individual members or by purchases on the Stock Exchange. It is necessary to ensure strict compliance with the City Code, the FCA and, in the case of a Listed company, with the requirements of the FCA. To comply with the requirements of the FCA, the offer documents will usually be sent direct to the shareholders of the offeree company by a merchant bank or issuing house authorised under that Act. The secretaries and directors of both the offeror and offeree companies will be closely involved in the preparation of the draft documentation, which will require approval by the respective companies' boards.

Offer documentation for a public offer

Although the issuing house and the companies' solicitors will carry out most of the work in preparing the offer documents, the directors of the two companies concerned take legal responsibility for the accuracy of the documents. The secretary of the offeror company will be particularly concerned with the following matters.

1 If both or either the offeror or offeree company are Listed, the documentation must comply with the *Listing Rules* (Chapters 10 and 13). Appropriate documentation will require approval by the FCA.
2 If it is considered likely that the matter will be referred to the Competition Commission, the offer document must contain a term that the offer will lapse if the matter is referred to the CC before the first closing date for the offer or the date upon which the offer is declared unconditional, whichever occurs first. The offeror company will, in many instances, make the offer conditional on the matter not being referred to the CC and that any decision not to refer must be on terms acceptable to the offeror. If it is likely that a reference will be made, the offeror should consider the representations to be made to the CC in support of the merger and whether advance clearance should be sought. Any advance clearance will be the subject of publicity, which may cause the share price of the offeree to rise, making the proposed acquisition less likely, as the cost of acquisition may rise too high. The Secretary of State, rather than referring the matter, may accept undertakings from the parties relating to matters that may have an adverse effect on the public interest.
3 If the shares to be issued in connection with the offer are to be Listed on the Official List and admitted to trading on the Main Market or NEX Exchange Main Board, the offer documentation should also include the listing particulars contained in the *Listing Rules*.

The following practical matters arise in connection with a takeover by a public offer.

1 The document which the shareholder signs must constitute a transfer of the securities being acquired to the offeror company.
2 Unless contrary instructions are given, any existing dividend mandates applicable to the shares in the offeree company will be applied to the shares in the offeror company being issued in exchange.
3 The form of acceptance and transfer would be designed so that it can be used as a working form, with relevant boxes for various steps in the processing to be filled in as they are completed.
4 Companies whose shares are settled within CREST will need to liaise with their registrars at an early stage, to ensure that the appropriate corporate actions procedures are established to enable shareholders to accept the offer within CREST using an escrow account set up for that purpose.
5 Envelopes for the offer documents, with reply-paid envelopes for the return of forms of acceptance and transfer with the share certificates, should be prepared to be sent to the shareholders in the offeree company.
6 Envelopes should also be prepared for any circular letter to be sent to the offeror company's own shareholders, either to explain the reasons for the offer or in connection with the convening of an extraordinary general meeting to approve any necessary increase in capital.

7 Since events in takeover battles sometimes move fairly swiftly, it will be prudent to have available further sets of envelope labels, both to the offeror company's shareholders and to the offeree company's shareholders, in case further circulars are to be issued, e.g. perhaps following an improvement in the terms of the offer.

Acceptances of a public offer

Most shareholders, including institutional shareholders, will not accept the offer until the final few days before the closing date. The office of the offeror company, or its registrar's office or the receiving banker's office, should be prepared to deal with the last rush of acceptances. The Panel on Takeovers and Mergers requires stringent procedures to be followed to avoid possible double counting of acceptances and purchases of the same shareholding.

The following action should be taken on receipt of the acceptances:

1 Check that the form of acceptance and transfer has been properly completed, with relevant share certificate(s), against the copy of the register of members of the offeree company.
2 Acceptance forms are usually accepted even though not accompanied by the relevant share certificate(s), but such acceptances, although they may be treated as valid, should be set to one side so that they may be completed when the accompanying share certificate(s) is/are sent in.
3 Acceptances may also be certificated if the share certificates for a recent purchase have not yet been prepared.

If a shareholder has lost their certificate(s), it will be necessary to issue an indemnity in order that a duplicate certificate may be prepared to support the acceptance (see precedent 70). Also, if forms of acceptance have been signed by a personal representative or a power of attorney, it will be necessary to ensure that the appropriate documents have been duly registered and, if not, to request their submission.

During the period of the offer, the offeree company should notify the offeror company of transfers received for registration in order that the offer documents may be sent out to these new shareholders and the copy of the register of members of the offeree company updated. If no underwriting is involved, however, it may be extended indefinitely, subject to the offer being declared unconditional by the 60th day after the posting of the offer.

Action following the first closing date of a public offer

Totals of the complete and incomplete acceptances will be calculated and the board of the offeror company will then consider whether the level of acceptances is such that it may declare the bid to be unconditional or whether it will extend it for a further period. If the level of acceptances is small, the offeror company may decide to extend the period for acceptances and, perhaps, improve the terms of the offer.

Once the offer has been declared unconditional, however, it is necessary to prepare the consideration documents, i.e. the definitive certificates or crediting CREST accounts for shares and/or other securities in the offeror company to be issued in exchange for shares in the offeree company, and to draw cheques for those who have accepted a cash alternative. A committee of the board of the offeror company should be established in order to make the allotments of the consideration securities. It would be usual for the consideration to be sent out 21 days after the closing date or 21 days after the date on which valid acceptances are received by the offeror company or its agents. Also, upon an offer becoming unconditional, share options including those under SAYE and other employee share schemes may become exercisable.

Transfers to offeror company

The transfer that is executed by or on behalf of the offeror company (i.e. the company making the takeover offer) covering the shares in respect of which duly executed forms of acceptance and transfer have been received in order to put these shares into the name of the offeror company is known as a 'bulk transfer'. It is used in conjunction with the individual forms of acceptance and transfer for each separate accepting shareholder. The bulk transfer is obviously more convenient than dealing separately with the many individual forms of acceptance and transfer, each of which has been signed by each accepting shareholder and each of which would have to be duly stamped by HMRC before registration.

The bulk transfer itself must be duly stamped by HMRC in the usual way. In order that this may be assessed, a schedule giving details of the forms of acceptance is attached to the bulk transfer. This is necessary because HMRC calculates the amount of stamp duty separately for each holding transferred and these amounts are then aggregated to ascertain the amount of stamp duty payable on the bulk transfer. The completed forms of acceptance and transfer, together with the covering share certificates and the duly stamped bulk transfer, are lodged with the offeree company.

Compulsory acquisition

Compulsory acquisition is dealt with in ss. 974–987. These sections are designed to protect the rights of the minority to resist compulsory acquisition if they have reasonable grounds to do so and to ensure that they are treated no less fairly than shareholders who have accepted the offer.

The Companies Act provides a procedure for the offeror company to acquire compulsorily certain non-assented minority shareholdings (squeeze-out provisions). If the offeror company has, by virtue of acceptances to the offer, acquired or contracted to acquire not less than nine-tenths in value of the shares to which the offer relates, it may give notice to the holder of any shares that it has not so acquired, or contracted to acquire, that it desires to acquire their shares (s. 979).

The notice must be issued during the period of three months after the last date for acceptance of the offer, but cannot be given later than six months from the date of commencement of the offer (s. 980).

Even where the acquiring company, having acquired 90% of the shares, does not wish to enforce its right to buy out the minority holders, notice must be given to those holders so that they may exercise their right to be bought out by the acquiring company on the same terms as the offer (sell-out provisions). The notice must be issued within one month of reaching the 90% acceptance level. The non-assenting shareholders can exercise their right to be bought out, provided they give notice within three months of the end of the period for acceptance under the offer or, if earlier, within three months of the date of the notice issued by the company pursuant to s. 984(3) (s. 984).

Shares already held by the offeror company – i.e. registered in its name at the date the offer was made – including any shares contracted to be acquired but not registered in the offeror company's name at that date, are excluded from calculation of the nine-tenths minimum. However, shares the holders of which are subject to a contract for no consideration to accept the offer after it is made are not excluded. Shares acquired by the offeror company, by market purchases or private agreement subsequent to the date of making the offer, may also count towards the nine-tenths minimum subject to the price paid for the shares not exceeding the value of the offer or revised offer.

The notice that it wishes to acquire shares must be given to a non-assenting shareholder on Form 984. A copy of the notice together with a statutory declaration confirming that the conditions for giving the notice are satisfied must be sent to the offeree company (s. 980(4)). Section 981 deals with the effects of giving a notice under s. 980, the principal ones being as follows:

1 Where the offeror company has given a choice of consideration that may be taken by the offeree company's shareholders for their shares, a non-assenting shareholder must be given the same alternatives as shareholders who have accepted the offer, even if some of these may have lapsed. The offeror may stipulate in the s. 980 notice the terms that will apply if the non-assenting shareholder does not respond to the notice within six weeks from the date of the notice. This provision prevents those dissenting from blocking the compulsory acquisition.
2 At the end of six weeks from the date of the compulsory acquisition notice, the compulsory acquisition is effected by the offeror company sending the offeree company a copy of the notice, together with a form of transfer for each dissenting shareholder, covering their shares in the offeree company which have not been assented to the offer. This is accompanied by a share certificate for the total number of consideration shares in the offeror company for the non-assenting shareholders or a cheque for the total cash consideration, as appropriate. Each such transfer is executed by a person appointed by the offeror company on behalf of the shareholders concerned (s. 981(7)).

3 These transfers will then be registered by the offeree company, thereby putting the dissenting shareholders' shares in the offeree company into the name of the offeror company. The shares in the offeror company received as consideration will be held by the offeree company on trust for the former shareholders. Any cash consideration should be held in a separate interest-bearing bank account.
4 The offeree company is required to hold the consideration for the non-assenting shareholders for a period of 12 years. At the end of this period, providing that it has, at intervals during that period, made reasonable enquiries to trace the non-assenting shareholders, shares in the offeror company received as consideration may be sold and the proceeds, together with any consideration received in cash being held in the bank account, paid into court. Similar action would be taken on the winding-up of the offeree company. The company's costs in making the enquiries may be recovered from such proceeds or money held in the separate bank account.

The right of a minority (i.e. non-assenting) shareholder to be bought out by the offeror company is provided by s. 983. When the offeror company has, in pursuance of a takeover offer, acquired by acceptances not less than nine-tenths in value of all the shares in issue of the offeree company (including any shares which it has otherwise acquired or contracted to acquire since the date of the offer), the holder of any shares who has not accepted the offer may send a written communication to the offeror company, requiring it to acquire their shares.

The offeror company must, within one month of having acquired nine-tenths of all the shares, send a notice to any shareholders who have not assented to the offer, informing them of their right to be bought out and they may within three months of the notice, or, if later, within three months of the deadline for acceptance of the offer, require the offeror company to acquire their shares. The notice is sent on Form 984.

Where the terms of the offer give a choice of consideration that may be taken by the offeree company's shareholders for their shares, the notice under s. 984 to the non-assenting shareholder must give particulars of the choices available and which option is to apply if the shareholder does not indicate a choice when requiring the offeror company to acquire their shares (s. 985).

It should be noted that where there is a choice of consideration between shares in the offeror company, or a sum in cash for each share in the offeree company, the underwriting arrangements will usually stipulate that the cash offer is open for a certain period only, at the end of which the consideration may be taken only in shares. However, in the case of compulsory acquisition under s. 979, and whether or not any time limit was applicable to any of the terms of the offer, e.g. a cash offer, the offeror is bound to pay cash for the non-assenting shareholder's shares or if the choice chosen is shares and the offeror company is no longer able to provide these, the consideration paid to the non-assenting shareholder must consist of an amount of cash which at the date of the compulsory acquisition notice under s. 979 is equivalent to the chosen consideration (s. 981(5)). In the case of the exercise of shareholders' rights to be bought out under s. 983, the same provisions regarding a cash offer apply, but where the offeror company is no longer able to provide the share alternative, the amount of cash payable is equivalent to the chosen consideration as at the date that the non-assenting shareholder requires the offeror company to acquire their shares (s. 985(5)).

It will be seen, therefore, that the window for the dissenting shareholders to take the cash offer, should they so desire, is reopened. Care must be taken to ensure that the notices are correctly sent, e.g. by recorded delivery in the UK or by airmail outside the UK.

Where the offeror company gives notice of compulsory acquisition under s. 979, the court may, on the application of a non-assenting shareholder within six weeks of the date of the s. 979 notice, order that the offeror is not be entitled to acquire their shares or that the shares will be acquired on terms different from those of the offer (s. 986(1)). In the case of the exercise of the rights of a non-assenting shareholder under s. 983, on the application of either the shareholder or the offeror, the court may order such terms as it thinks fit on which the offeror is entitled and bound to acquire the shares. Compulsory acquisition under s. 979 may be impossible where a company has numerous untraceable shareholders. Under subsections (2) or (4) of s. 979 where a takeover has not been accepted to the extent necessary to effect compulsory acquisition under s. 979, the court may, on the application of the offeror company, authorise the company to proceed to give s. 979 compulsory acquisition notices to shareholders who have not accepted the offer, if it is satisfied that the offeror company has taken all reasonable steps to trace the shareholders concerned and if the total of the shares assented to the offer added to the total of the shares held by the untraceable shareholders amounts to not less than the minimum required to implement the s. 979 compulsory acquisition procedure (s. 986(9)).

The consideration held by the offeree company on trust for the dissenting shareholders may subsequently be claimed by them on surrender of the documents of title to shares in the offeree company or giving an indemnity if they can no longer be found. Quite often the claim will be made by the executors of a deceased non-assenting shareholder's estate who, in winding-up their affairs, find that they held shares in the offeree company and had not accepted the offer.

When a claim is received, any cash will be paid out, or, if the consideration is in the form of shares in the offeror company, the offeree company will execute a transfer in the name of the entitled holder and send this to the offeror company for registration, accompanied by the share certificate for shares in the offeror company being held by the offeree company. The offeror company will prepare a share certificate in the holder's name and send a balance certificate in the name of the offeree company for the shares in the offeror company still to be claimed.

Stamp duty exemptions

Takeovers (and schemes of arrangements) are sometimes arranged in such a way that there is exemption from stamp duty on the transfer of shares to the offeree company. These exemptions are usually only available where the 'takeover' relates to a re-structuring of a company or group of companies and where ultimate ownership does not change as a result of the acquisition. Under FA1986 s. 77, exemption from stamp duty may be claimed under circumstances where there has been no change in ownership. The following conditions must be met for a claim for exemption to succeed:

1. The acquiring company must acquire the whole or a part of the target undertaking as part of a scheme of reconstruction.
2. The acquiring company must be a UK-registered company.
3. The consideration must consist only of shares to be issued to the shareholders of the target company.
4. There must be no consideration other than the discharge or assumption of any liabilities of the target company by the acquirer.
5. The transaction must be for *bona fide* commercial reasons and not just a scheme for the avoidance of tax or stamp duty.
6. The shares must be issued to the shareholders of the target company *pro rata* to their existing holdings, so that the shareholders of the acquiring company are in the same proportions after the transaction as their holdings of shares in the target company prior to the transaction.

Reconstruction

Schemes of arrangement

A takeover of one company by another may be effected by a liquidation under the provisions of IA1986 s. 110 or a scheme of arrangement under the provisions of ss. 895–901. These arrangements are, however, more complicated than the forms of takeover described above and involve the incorporation of a new holding company to takeover both the offeree and the offeror companies in order to merge their operations.

Alternatively, the offeror company may acquire the undertaking of the offeree company for cash or the issue of shares in the acquiring company. Schemes of arrangement may be useful where it is desired to acquire 100% of the offeree company but, because of the nature of the business, it would not be possible to obtain the required 90% level of acceptances that would enable the offeror company to effect compulsory acquisition. The approval of the court is required and consequently the legal advisers of both companies will be involved in settling the necessary documentation.

Reconstruction by liquidation

A takeover by means of a reconstruction is effected by winding-up the offeree company. This effects the sale of the company's assets to another company in exchange for shares in that company, which are then distributed to the shareholders of the offeree company in proportion to their holdings. Reconstruction by liquidation and sale of the offeree company's assets is appropriate only in cases where the continued existence of the offeree company is not desired. The liquidation is effected as a members' or **creditors' voluntary winding-up** and the detailed provisions governing the procedure are laid down in IA1986 s. 110. In view of the many complications that may arise, legal and taxation advice should be taken.

Reconstruction may be suitable where there is to be a reduction of capital combined with the provision of fresh capital for a new company by the members of the reconstructed company. For example, a company with an adverse balance on its profit and loss account but with good prospects could be wound up and its assets sold to a new company (after paying off creditors) in exchange for partly paid shares in the new company allotted to members of the old company in proportion to their existing holdings. The calling up of the unpaid liability on the new shares would provide working capital for the future operations of the business. In the case of a public company, it would be usual for the provision of new capital to be underwritten, in case there are shareholders who do not assent to the scheme for reconstruction or assenting shareholders who fail to pay up the calls on the partly paid shares. However, the total holdings of the dissenting shareholders should not exceed an agreed percentage because, under IA1986 s. 111(2), the underwriters would have to buy out the interests of the dissenting shareholders in order that the scheme could be implemented. A dissenting shareholder is a member of the transferor company who does not vote in favour of the special resolution to wind up the company and who notifies the liquidator that they should either abstain from carrying the resolution into effect or purchase their interest at an agreed price.

It is desirable that resolutions for approving a reconstruction under IA1986 s. 110 be submitted to two meetings, the first meeting to approve the reconstruction and the second meeting to put the company into liquidation. If both resolutions were passed at the same meeting, the company would still have to be wound up even if the number of dissenting shareholders made the implementation of the scheme of reconstruction impracticable.

The procedural steps for a reconstruction are as follows:

1 A board meeting of the company to be liquidated is convened to:
   a. make the necessary declaration of solvency;
   b. settle the draft agreement to be entered into by the liquidator for the sale of the company to the new company;
   c. approve the articles of the new company;
   d. approve that the draft underwriting contract be executed by the liquidator or for the company to execute with adoption by the liquidator later;

e. approve the circular letter to the shareholders informing them of the reasons for the proposed reconstruction and the terms; and
f. approve the notice of general meeting and form of proxy (which must be a three-way proxy in the case of a Listed company).

2 Special resolutions for reconstruction and liquidation are passed at a general meeting.
3 The business of the offeree company (i.e. the old company) is continued by the liquidator from the date of the resolution to wind up to the date when the business is acquired by the new company.
4 When the sale agreement has been executed, the liquidator transfers the assets to the new company. They must ensure that they retain sufficient assets to pay off the creditors of the old company unless the creditors have agreed that liability for these debts may be transferred to the new company by means of a novation agreement. They must also retain assets to purchase the interests of any dissenting shareholders and to pay the expenses of the liquidation and their own remuneration.
5 A letter is sent to shareholders giving details of their rights to shares in the newly formed company, which will be issued in exchange for their shares in the old company on receipt of their share certificates. As noted above, the shares in the new company would be offered as partly paid shares in proportion to shareholders' existing holdings in the old company; the additional capital would then be called up and thus provide working capital for the future operation of the business by the new company.
6 The liquidator continues to complete the liquidation of the old company in accordance with the usual procedure. On completion of the liquidation, it is usual for the liquidator to execute a conveyance transferring all the residual property of the old company to the new company.

22 – Insolvency, dissolution and restoration

Introduction

The law on corporate insolvency is contained mainly in the Insolvency Act 1986, which came into force with effect from 29 December 1986 as amended by the Insolvency Act 2000 and the Enterprise Act 2002. The insolvency provisions of the Enterprise Act came into force on 15 September 2003. In view of the complexity of the subject, a company secretary faced with a situation in which the company may not be able to pay its debts as they fall due is strongly advised to seek specialist advice.

A company becomes insolvent when it is unable to pay its debts as they fall due. Once this stage has been reached, in order to protect the interest of creditors, employees and shareholders, the directors must take steps for the company's affairs to be wound up. Winding-up involves the realisation of the company's assets. This process is undertaken on behalf of creditors by a licensed insolvency practitioner, who is appointed as the liquidator of the company. As a result, winding-up is frequently referred to as liquidation.

Section 123 of the Insolvency Act 1986 sets out the criteria under which a company will be deemed to be unable to pay its debts:

- failing to comply with a statutory demand for a debt in excess of £750;
- failing to satisfy enforcement of a judgement debt;
- the court is satisfied that the company is unable to pay its debts as they fall due; or
- the court is satisfied that the liabilities of the company exceed the assets of the company.

In circumstances where the directors realise that the company will become insolvent, but has not yet reached that point, they might wish to appoint an administrator to manage the company until it is able to continue, to be sold or, if all else fails, to be wound up. Administration is considered on page 402.

The **statute law** is principally contained in the Insolvency Act 1986 and the Company Directors Disqualification Act 1986. The Enterprise Act 2002 introduced a number of initiatives in respect of both corporate and individual insolvency. Implementation of the Enterprise Act provisions required a substantial amount of secondary legislation including, most recently, The Insolvency

(Amendment) Rules 2010, a number of orders relating to transitional provisions and consequential amendments.

Methods of winding-up

There are three methods of winding-up:

1 members' **voluntary winding-up**;
2 creditors' voluntary winding-up; and
3 winding-up by the court.

Members' voluntary winding-up

A members' voluntary winding-up is a solvent winding-up under which the directors must have prepared a statutory declaration within the five weeks immediately preceding the resolution to wind up. This states that, having made full enquiry, they are of the opinion that the company will be able to pay its debts in full with interest at the official rate within a period not exceeding 12 months from commencement of the winding-up (IA 1986 ss. 89 and 90). If a director makes such declaration without reasonable grounds and the debts and interest are not paid within the specified period, they are liable to a fine or imprisonment, or both, and the burden of proof of innocence is on the director (IA1986 s. 89(4)).

The resolution to wind up is coupled with a resolution to appoint a liquidator. If during the course of the administration the liquidator forms the opinion that the company is unlikely to be able to pay its liabilities in full within the stipulated time, they are required to call a meeting of creditors within 28 days. This converts the administration into a creditors' winding-up.

Creditors' voluntary winding-up

This may be appropriate where a declaration of solvency cannot be made, and the company is wound up as a creditors' voluntary winding-up. A meeting of the creditors must be called and held within 14 days after the meeting of the members of the company at which a resolution to wind up is passed (IA1986 s. 98). The liquidation commences at the time of passing the resolution to wind up (IA1986 s. 86).

Winding-up by the court

A company may be wound up by the court if:

1 the company so resolves by special resolution;
2 a judgement creditor or a creditor petitions the court where an amount in excess of £750 has not been paid following written demand for payment (IA1986 s. 123);
3 it is just and equitable for the company to be wound up; or
4 the company fails to comply with certain statutory requirements, e.g. the minimum number of members (IA1986 ss. 122 and 124).

The most usual ground for a petition to the court is the inability of the company to pay its debts. A contributory, the Official Receiver, the Secretary of State, the Bank of England and the Attorney General may present a petition under various statutory provisions even if the company is solvent.

Initial procedures

Members' voluntary winding-up

The procedure for a members' voluntary winding-up is as follows:

1 The company's board resolve to make a declaration of solvency, which must embody a statement of assets and liabilities and be made up to a date within five weeks immediately before the passing of the resolution to wind up. The declaration has to be filed with the Registrar of Companies within 15 days of the passing of the resolution to wind up (IA1986 ss. 89 and 90).
2 The board authorises the calling of a general meeting at which a special resolution to wind up will be considered (see precedent 84). An ordinary resolution will suffice if the period of life of the company has expired or an event has occurred on the happening of which the articles provide that the company should be wound up (IA1986 s. 84).
3 If the resolution is passed, it will be necessary to appoint a liquidator. This may be done by an ordinary resolution of the company.
4 The resolution to wind up, signed by the chair of the meeting, should be published in the *London Gazette* or the *Edinburgh Gazette*, as appropriate, within 14 days of being passed (IA1986 s. 85). The resolution and all documents for publication in each *Gazette* must be authenticated by a solicitor or a member of an established body of accountants or secretaries. The resolution to wind up must also be filed within 15 days with the Registrar of Companies (s. 30 and IA1986 s. 84).
5 The liquidator must, within 14 days of their appointment, advertise their appointment in each *Gazette* and give notice to the Registrar of Companies on Form LQ01.
6 The Insolvency Rules 1986 (IR1986) reg. 4.148A set out provisions for determination of the liquidator's remuneration.

The subsequent procedure is similar to that for a creditors' voluntary winding up set out below, except that meetings of, and notices to, creditors are not required.

Creditors' voluntary winding-up

The procedure for a creditors' voluntary winding-up is as follows.

1 A meeting of the board authorises the calling of a general meeting to consider a special resolution that the company, by reason of its liabilities, cannot continue and that it is advisable to wind up (IA1986 s. 84(1)(c)) (see precedent 84).

2 A meeting of the creditors must be called by the company to be held within 14 days of the members' meeting to consider the resolution to wind up (IA1986 s. 98). At least seven days' notice of the meeting must be given to the creditors. Notice of the creditors' meeting should be advertised in the appropriate *Gazette* and two local newspapers (IA1986 s. 98(1)(b)(c)).
3 The notice must state either:
4 (a) the name and address of the insolvency practitioner who will give such information to the creditors before the meeting takes place as they may reasonably require; or
5 (b) a place in the principal area of business of the company where a list of names and addresses of the company's creditors will be available for inspection without charge.
6 The creditors' meeting will be presided over by one of the directors, who should prepare a statement of affairs in the prescribed form, verified by affidavit, to be laid before the creditors' meeting.
7 At the general meeting, a special resolution is passed to wind up and an ordinary resolution is passed to nominate the liquidator.
8 At the creditors' meeting, which must be attended by the liquidator, the directors may answer questions put to them by the creditors concerning the administration of the company, although there is no legal requirement for them to do so.
9 The liquidator is the person nominated by the creditors or, where no other person has been so nominated, the person (if any) nominated by the company. Where a different person is nominated by the creditors, any member or creditor of the company may apply to the court within seven days for an order that the members' nomination shall remain liquidator instead of, or jointly with, the creditors' nomination, or that some other person be appointed liquidator (IA1986 s. 100).
10 On the appointment of a liquidator, all the powers of the directors cease.
11 The creditors have the power to appoint a liquidation committee, which may sanction the continuation of some of the directors' powers (IA1986 ss. 101 and 103).
12 The remuneration of the liquidator is fixed by the liquidation committee or, if there is no committee, by the creditors, failing which it is based on the scales applicable to the Official Receiver under IR1986 sch. 6.
13 Upon their appointment, the liquidator should immediately:
   (a) arrange for the redirection of mail, if not already done;
   (b) if thought necessary, change the registered office address;
   (c) take over all books and records of the company;
   (d) make a formal report to each creditor enclosing a copy of the directors' statement of affairs, and a copy of any statement made by the directors at the creditors' meeting. Creditors must be informed of the liquidator's appointment and be invited to forward a statement of their claims;

(e) advertise for claims at the appropriate time;
(f) inform the appropriate sheriffs and bailiffs of the winding-up resolution and of the appointment of the liquidator;
(g) take into protective custody the company's assets and ensure that there is adequate insurance cover;
(h) open, in the name of the liquidator, separate bank accounts (any sums not immediately required may and should be transferred into a deposit account in the liquidator's name or in other suitable interest-bearing security);
(i) disclaim onerous property or unprofitable contracts as soon as practicably possible;
(j) consider the position of secured creditors and, if necessary, discuss and negotiate with them;
(k) consider the position of any landlords, particularly any distress warrants;
(l) consider the most appropriate way of disposing of the company's assets and discuss this with appointed agents;
(m) make a demand for the company's outstanding **book debts** and consider the position as to work in progress; and
(n) consider and discuss any pending or future litigation outstanding against the company with the company's solicitors.

Winding-up by the court

The procedure for winding-up by the court is as follows:

1 When the court makes a winding-up order, the Official Receiver becomes the liquidator (IA1986 s. 136(2)).
2 The Official Receiver may require officers of the company, or other persons as specified, to prepare, swear and submit a statement of affairs within 21 days (IA1986 s. 131).
3 Separate meetings of creditors and contributories may be summoned by the Official Receiver at their discretion for the appointment of some other person to be liquidator of the company (IA1986 s. 136(4)). Contributions are defined by IA1986 s. 79, but are usually synonymous with the term 'members'. The Official Receiver remains the liquidator if another person is not appointed. The Official Receiver must summon a meeting for the appointment of another liquidator if one-quarter in value of the creditors requisition them to do so on IR1986, Form 4.21 ('Request by creditor(s) for a meeting of the company's creditors and contributories') in accordance with IA1986 s. 136(5) and IR1986 reg. 4.57.
4 The court may make any appointment or order to give effect to the wishes of the meetings or make any other order that it may think fit.
5 The creditors and contributories may nominate as liquidator any person who is qualified to act as an insolvency practitioner (IA1986 s. 139) and, in the absence of a nomination by the creditors, the contributories' nominee (if any) will be the liquidator.

6 At any time the Official Receiver may apply to the Secretary of State for the appointment of a liquidator in their place. Any such liquidator must send notice of their appointment as the court may direct (IA1986 s. 137(3), (4)).

Liquidator

The liquidator should:

1 take over responsibility for the assets of the company, together with its books and records;
2 take other necessary steps to protect and realise the assets, as indicated above in the case of a creditors' voluntary winding-up;
3 disclaim any onerous property or unprofitable contracts (IA1986 s. 178 and IR1986 reg. 4.187–4.194);
4 ensure the winding-up order halts any proceedings against the company, except by leave of the court (IA1986 s. 130(2)); and
5 provide the Official Receiver with information, access to books or such other assistance as they may reasonably require.

The liquidator's qualifications

A liquidator must be a person who is qualified to act as an insolvency practitioner (IA1986 s. 390). The Secretary of State may give authority for a person to act as an insolvency practitioner or authorise another competent authority to do so (IA1986 s. 392). IR1986 reg. 390(3) requires every insolvency practitioner who is appointed office-holder in any formal insolvency proceeding to have insurance cover ('bond') for the proper performance of their duties, the value of which may not be less than the value of the relevant assets, subject to a minimum of £5,000 and a maximum of £5,000,000.

Duties and powers of a liquidator

The duties and powers of a liquidator are specified in IA1986 ss. 165–170 and IA1986 Sch. 4.

Report on conduct of directors

A report must be made immediately to the Secretary of State under s. 7(3) of the Company Directors Disqualification Act 1986 (CDDA1986) if, in the winding-up proceedings, it appears to a liquidator or the Official Receiver that the conduct of a director of the company is such as to render them unfit to be concerned in the management of a limited company. Under the provisions of the Insolvent Companies (Reports on Conduct of Directors) No. 2 Rules 1986, SI 1986/2134, a return must be submitted to the Secretary of State within six months of appointment of the liquidator or the Official Receiver, stating whether or not there is any such knowledge of the conduct of director(s) or if the conduct return will be delayed beyond that date. If subsequent to the conduct return further information about the conduct of director(s) should come to notice, a further return must be submitted. Appropriate forms for making these returns are annexed to the Rules mentioned above, which also apply to administrative receivers and administrators. The matters determining the unfitness of directors are set out in CDDA1986 Sch. 1. A court of summary jurisdiction may impose a disqualification order for a maximum of five years, or in the case of superior courts, 15 years.

Investigations, preferences, fraud and criminal offences

The liquidator must investigate the records of the company to establish whether any of the following have occurred:

1. transactions at an undervalue and preferences (IA1986 s. 238);
2. floating charges created in favour of a connected person within two years of commencement of the liquidation or within one year if created in favour of any other person or created between the time of presentation of a petition for an **administration order** and the making of the order (IA1986 s. 245);
3. fraudulent trading (s. 993 and IA1986 ss. 213 and 215);
4. wrongful trading (IA1986 ss. 214 and 215);
5. any misfeasance by any director or manager (IA1986 s. 212); or
6. failure to register any charge under CA2006.

Under IA1986 s. 218(4), the liquidator has a statutory duty, in a voluntary winding-up, to report any fraud or criminal act they discover to the Director of Public Prosecutions.

The Enterprise Act 2002 introduced new rules under which the liquidator must seek the sanction of the creditors' committee, creditors or the court before bringing proceedings for wrongful or fraudulent trading, to attack preferential payments or transactions at undervalue. Additionally, the costs of these and any related actions are to be costs of the liquidation.

Employees

The employees' contracts of employment are terminated by the winding-up order of the court. In a voluntary winding-up the subsequent failure by the liquidator to maintain the terms of the employment terminates the employment. Under the Employment Rights Act 1996, the liquidator acts as the employer's representative so far as claims are concerned. The employer's representative, with certain limits, is provided with funds from the Department for Work and Pensions to meet the claims of employees, which they then distribute to the employees concerned. The claims of the employees against the insolvent company paid in this way are then assigned to the Department for Work and Pensions, which may claim in the liquidation of the company. The Department for Work and Pensions will also probably claim any sums that have been paid for redundancy.

Tax implication of liquidation

A separate record should be kept of tax liabilities incurred by the liquidator during the course of the liquidation, these being part of the costs of the liquidation as distinct from tax liabilities arising up to the date of commencement of the winding-up, which would be subject of a claim in the liquidation. Any VAT arising is treated similarly.

Determination of creditors' claims

In a winding-up by the court, creditors must submit their claims in writing on IR1986 Form 4.25 ('Proof of debt – general form') (IR1986 reg. 4.73). In the case of voluntary liquidations, the liquidator may require a creditor to submit their claim in writing, but no specific form is provided for this. If the liquidator rejects a claim in whole or in part, they must give their reasons in writing to the creditor. A creditor has 21 days to require the matter to be put before the court if they are dissatisfied with the liquidator's decision (IR1986 reg. 4.83).

Winding-up in Scotland

Certain provisions relating to winding-up are peculiar to Scottish law and are described in various sections of IA1986. These are ss. 120–121, 122(2), 142, 157, 161–162, 169, 185, 193, 198–199, 204 and 243.

Company voluntary arrangements

Until the Insolvency Act 1986 came into force, a company could enter into a binding arrangement with some or all of the creditors to compromise their claims by means of a scheme of arrangement under ss. 895–901. However, a scheme under this section is extremely complex to put into effect: for example, it is necessary to identify correctly, and call separate meetings of, the various classes of creditors affected by the scheme. The scheme also has to be approved by the court before it comes into effect. As a result, this course has been followed relatively rarely.

The Insolvency Act 1986 Part I ss. 1–7 introduced a new procedure enabling the directors of a company, an administrator or a liquidator, as appropriate, to make a proposal to the company's creditors for a composition in satisfaction of its debts or a scheme of arrangement of its affairs, known as a 'voluntary arrangement'.

A proposal containing details outlined in Rule 1.3 must provide for some person ('the nominee'), who is qualified to act as an insolvency practitioner in relation to the company, to act in relation to the voluntary arrangement either as trustee or for the purpose of supervising its implementation.

Procedure

Where the nominee is not the liquidator or administrator of the company, the following procedure must be followed:

1 The directors prepare a document setting out the terms of the proposed voluntary arrangement incorporating a statement of affairs and give formal notice of the same to the nominee. The nominee endorses the notice with their consent to act and submits a report to the court, within 28 days, stating whether, in their opinion, the meetings of the members and creditors should be summoned to consider the proposal and, if applicable, the date, time and place at which the meetings should be held. The date on which the meetings are to be held may not be less than 14 or more than 28 days from the date on which the nominee's report is filed in court. The nominee is required to send notice of the meetings of the members and the creditors, at least 14 days before the day for them to be held, to all creditors of whom they are aware and to all members. Where the nominee is the liquidator or the administrator, they may summon the meetings of the members and creditors, without any application to the court, by giving at least 14 days' notice. With the notice of the respective meeting, the nominee must send:
   a. a proposal;
   b. a statement of affairs; and
   c. the nominee's comments.

2 At the creditors' meeting, a majority in excess of three-quarters in value of those present in person or by proxy is required for approval of the proposal (IR1986 regs. 1.19 and 1.20). At the members' meeting, a majority in excess of one half of those present in person or by proxy is required for approval of the proposal. Either meeting may propose modifications, which may include another person qualified to act as an insolvency practitioner in relation to the company as nominee. Neither meeting may approve a proposal or any modification under which the rights of preferential creditors are altered without their concurrence.

3 The votes of certain creditors must be left out of account, as specified in IR1986 reg. 1.19(3), and any resolution is invalid if those voting against it include more than one half in value of qualifying votes (IR1986 reg. 1.19(4)).

4 Approval of the voluntary arrangement by both meetings binds every person who had notice of, and was entitled to vote at, either of the meetings (IA1986 s. 5(2)(b)).

5 If, on the day of the meetings of the creditors and the members, the requisite majority is not obtained, the chair may, and shall if so resolved, adjourn the meetings for not more than 14 days (IR1986 reg. 1.21(2)).

6 If the company is being wound up or an administration order is in force, the court may stay the winding-up proceedings or discharge the administration order so as to facilitate the voluntary arrangement (IA1986 s. 5(3)).

7 An application may be made to the court by a member, a creditor, the nominee, the liquidator or an administrator if the voluntary arrangement is

unfairly prejudicial or if there has been material irregularity in relation to either of the meetings (IA1986 s. 6).

Remuneration, expenses and completion of the voluntary arrangement

The following fees, costs, charges and expenses may be incurred in connection with the voluntary arrangement:

1 disbursements by the nominee prior to approval of the arrangement and agreed remuneration for their services;
2 disbursements, remuneration, expenses and any payments sanctioned by the terms of the arrangement or which would be payable in an administration or winding-up.

The supervisor shall, within 28 days of full implementation of the arrangement, or within such time as may be allowed by court, send notice to that effect to the Registrar of Companies, the court, and all creditors and members of the company who were bound by it. With the notice there must be a report by the supervisor summarising all receipts and payments in the arrangement and, if applicable, an explanation of any material disparity between the anticipated and the actual result.

Administration orders

The Enterprise Act 2002 replaced Part II of the Insolvency Act 1986 under which the court could make an administration order in relation to a company if it is satisfied that the company is or is likely to become unable to pay its debts. Under the new provisions, there are three entry routes into administration:

1 application to court by the company, a majority of the directors of the company, a qualifying floating charge holder or one or more creditors;
2 out-of-court appointment by a qualifying floating charge holder; or
3 out-of-court appointment by the company or a majority of its directors.

An administration order directs that, during the period for which it is in force, the affairs, business and property of the company shall be managed by an administrator. Regardless of which of the three entry routes is used, the administrator remains as a court-appointed officer. According to the definition in IA1986 s. 123, a company is deemed to be unable to pay its debts if any of the following holds:

- It is unable to pay a debt exceeding £750 within a period of 21 days commencing on the date of delivery of a demand for payment made in the prescribed form.
- In England and Wales, execution issued on a judgement remained unsatisfied in whole or in part.

- The court is satisfied that the company is unable to pay its debts as they fall due.
- The court is satisfied that the value of the company's assets is less than the amount of its liabilities.
- In Scotland, a charge for payment on an extract decree, or an extract registered bond, or an extract registered process, has expired without payment.
- In Northern Ireland, a certificate of unenforceability has been granted in respect of a judgement.

The purpose of the administration has also been amended. In place of the previous four purposes are three objectives:

1 to rescue the company (not necessarily the business) as a going concern;
2 to achieve a better result for creditors than would be likely in a liquidation; and
3 to realise property in order to make distributions to secured or preferential creditors.

Appointment of administrator

By court

Application to the court is the only way in which creditors (other than the holder of a qualifying floating charge) or the supervisor of a **company voluntary arrangement** can initiate the appointment of an administrator. Application to court will also be required where the company is in liquidation or administrative receivership or there is an outstanding winding-up petition.

The application is made on a prescribed form and requires an affidavit setting out details of the company's financial position, any security held by creditors and other matters relevant to the application. The proposed administrator must give written consent to act.

By qualifying floating charge holder

The holder of a qualifying floating charge can effect the appointment of an administrator by giving notice of an intention to appoint an administrator to the relevant court. Qualifying floating charges are defined in paragraph 14 of Sch. B1 to the Insolvency Act 1986. A qualifying floating charge is one that:

- states that paragraph 14 of Sch. B1 applies to it;
- purports to empower the holder to appoint an administrator; or
- purports to empower the holder to make an appointment as an administrative receiver.

Where there is more than one holder of qualifying floating charges, each must consent to the appointment of an administrator. A copy of the notice of intention to appoint an administrator must also be given to all other holders of qualifying floating charges.

Provided there are no objections or an application is made for a court order and all holders of qualifying floating charges have consented, the proposed administrator is appointed five days after the notice of intention to appoint by the filing of a notice of appointment.

By the company or directors

The company itself or its directors can effect the appointment of an administrator by giving notice of an intention to appoint an administrator to the relevant court.

Where there is one or more qualifying floating charges, each charge holder must be sent a copy of the notice of the intention to appoint an administrator.

Provided there are no objections or an application is made for a court order and all holders of qualifying floating charges have consented, the proposed administrator is appointed ten days after the notice of intention to appoint by the filing of a notice of appointment. If there are no qualifying floating charges, there is no need to file a notice of intention to appoint and the appointment can be made by filing the notice of appointment alone.

Administration process

Once a company is in administration, all business documents issued by it must state the name of the administrator and contain a statement to the effect that the affairs and the business of the company are being managed by the administrator.

Ending administration

Administration is no longer an open-ended process and the administration will end 12 months after its commencement, subject to any extension sanctioned by the creditors and/or the court. On cessation of the administration, the administrator must circulate a copy of their final report and the notice of cessation to each person who received a copy of the original proposal, to the court and to the Registrar of Companies.

Administrator

An administrator must be a person authorised to act as an insolvency practitioner. Any person acting as an administrator who is not so qualified is liable to imprisonment or to a fine, or both (IA1986 s. 389). An administrator's remuneration may be determined by a creditors' committee or, if there is no creditors' committee, or the committee does not make the requisite determination, the administrator's remuneration may be fixed by a resolution of a meeting of creditors or, ultimately, by the court.

Powers of an administrator

In general, an administrator of a company has power to do all things necessary for the management of the affairs, business and property of the company. The powers are specified in IA1986 ss. 14 and 15 and Sch. 1.

Receiverships

The law governing receiverships is considerable and in this book only general matters affecting the appointment and procedures to be followed when a receiver is appointed are considered. Consequently, further reference should be made to appropriate books on the subject and expert advice sought, if necessary.

Definition of an administrative receiver

An administrative receiver is a receiver or manager of the whole or substantially the whole of a company's property and business, appointed by or on behalf of the holders of debentures of the company secured by a floating charge (IA1986 s. 29(2)(a)). An appointee under a fixed charge will normally have no power to manage the business and is, as such, known as a 'receiver'.

The legislation relating to receivers in England and Wales is contained in IA1986 s. 439(1) Sch. 13 Part I), ss. 403 and 405, IA1986 ss. 29–49 and s. 72 and in IR1986 regs. 3.1–3.38. The law relating to receivers in Scotland is different and is found in IA1986 ss. 50–72.

The position in England and Wales is dealt with first, followed by the position in Scotland.

The Enterprise Act 2002 restricts the use of administrative receivership. Holders of floating charges created on or after 15 September 2003 will no longer be able to appoint an administrative receiver unless they fall within a limited number of exemptions. These are: capital market arrangements, public–private partnerships, utility projects, project finance and financial market contracts and registered social landlords.

Qualification of an administrative receiver

Under IA1986 s. 390, only a qualified practitioner may act as an administrative receiver of a floating charge and any person acting as such who is not so qualified is liable to imprisonment or a fine, or both (IA1986 s. 389). There are detailed provisions in IA1986 ss. 396–398 as to who may be regarded as a fit and proper person, and as to the education, practical training and experience required for the appointment as a licensed insolvency practitioner.

Appointment by the court

A court may appoint a receiver on the application of a mortgagee or a debenture holder:

- where repayment of principal and/or interest is in arrears;
- when the security has become crystallised into a specific charge by the making of a winding-up order or passing of a resolution to wind up; or
- where the security of the mortgagee or the debenture holder is in jeopardy.

A receiver may also be appointed by the court on the application either of a contributory (i.e. a person liable to contribute to the assets of the company in the event of its being wound up) or of the company. The court will sometimes appoint a receiver and a manager on a short-term basis if the directors are not fulfilling their functions – for instance, because of a dispute between them, and pending a general meeting where there has been no governing body.

A court will not appoint a receiver if winding-up would be more appropriate.

Appointment by debenture holders

The appointment is made under a deed executed by the debenture holder and is, together with the debenture, evidence of their capacity.

The appointment of a receiver usually arises in the following circumstances:

- failure to pay the principal and/or interest in accordance with the terms of the debenture;
- where a borrowing limit has been exceeded and has not been reduced within a specified period; or
- a breach of some other provisions in the debenture or trust deed.

The debenture usually confers fixed and floating charges on the assets of a company. It is possible, however, for the security to be simply a fixed or a floating charge.

It is therefore important to consider the following at the commencement of a receivership:

1. Under a fixed charge, a receiver will not normally have power to manage the business and may call in and realise the relevant assets only for the purpose of redeeming the debt due to the debenture holder.
2. An appointment under a floating charge may be made as 'receiver' or 'administrative receiver'. The former cannot be appointed with the powers of the latter unless the deed contains such provision.
3. A 'receiver' will have power to manage if such right is given to them by the debenture deed containing a charge on the goodwill of business of the company.

The employees' legal position

The appointment of a receiver does not automatically terminate the employment of the company's employees and, unless the receiver negotiates new terms, they will be taken to have adopted any contract of employment not terminated within 14 days after their appointment (IA1986 s. 44).

Powers, liabilities and responsibilities

An administrative receiver has the powers which the debenture holders have conferred on them which are deemed to include the powers Listed in IA1986 Sch. A (IA1986 s. 42). On application to the court, a receiver may seek authority to dispose of any of the company's properties as if it were not subject to the security (IA1986 s. 43(1)).

An administrative receiver is deemed to be the company's agent until the commencement of liquidation and, unless the contract provides otherwise, is personally liable on any contract entered into by them in carrying out their functions albeit that they are normally entitled to indemnity out of the assets of the company (IA1986 s. 43(5)). If the administrative receiver enters into contracts without authority, their liability is unlimited and they have no right of indemnity.

Taxation

Tax on any income arising during the receivership – for instance, from trading profits, deposit interest and capital gains – is usually considered to be assessable on the company and is not a liability of the receiver. If the assessment relates to a period after liquidation, it is an expense in the liquidation, but otherwise it is merely a claim against the company.

Phoenix companies

Directors of an insolvent company cannot be appointed as directors of a company with a prohibited name. A prohibited name is one that is the same as that of the insolvent company, or so similar as to suggest an association with that company.

Dissolution

The Registrar of Companies is authorised pursuant to s. 1000 to remove from the Register companies that they believe are defunct – for example, where a company has failed to file accounts and annual returns, and no response is received to letters sent to the company's registered office.

Under s. 1003, a private company which is not trading may make a voluntary application to have the company's name struck off the Register. This procedure may not be used if, within three months of the proposed application, the company has changed its name, traded, disposed of property or rights for value, or engaged in any activity other than that required to effect the dissolution or where application for a scheme of arrangement or petition or order under the Insolvency Act has been made.

Dissolution may not be appropriate in circumstances where the company has any assets or liabilities, even if there is no chance of payment being either made or sought.

Procedure

One of the most common causes for an application for dissolution to be stopped is on application of HM Revenue & Customs. HMRC will object in any circumstances where they believe there is or might be any tax due. Accordingly, unless the company has been dormant for some years, clearance from HMRC should be sought and any liability to tax settled.

Application is made on Form DS01, signed by the director(s) or a majority of directors, together with the filing fee (£10).

A copy of the application must be sent within seven days to any person who, at any time on or after the date of application but prior to dissolution, was an employee, a member, a creditor, a director or a manager or trustee of any pension fund established for the employees. On receipt of the application, the Registrar will publish a notice in the *Gazette* inviting any objections as to why the company should not be struck off. If no objections are made within two months of publication, the Registrar will strike off the company and publish a further notice in the *Gazette* notifying that the company has been dissolved.

The directors may halt the dissolution process by submitting Form DS02 and are obliged to do so if any of the events set out in s. 1009 occur.

Restoration

Under ss. 1024–1028, application may be made to the Registrar by a former director or member of the company to restore the company to the register under an administrative restoration procedure. The procedure is only available for companies struck off and dissolved by the Registrar under CA2006 ss. 1000 or 1001 and in the circumstances prescribed by CA2006 s. 1025, and it is envisaged that the procedure will be used primarily by companies that were dissolved for default in complying with filing requirements, but which continued to trade at the time of strike-off.

A procedure for restoration to the register by way of court order is also provided under CA2006 ss. 1029–1032. The procedure is available to companies struck off and dissolved for any reason whether at the instigation of the Registrar, on application by the directors or as a result of formal winding-up proceedings.

The Secretary of State may also apply to the court for restoration if this is justified in the public interest. Applications for administrative restoration must be made within the period of six years from the date of dissolution (CA2006 s. 1024(4)).

Applications to the court must be made:

- at any time for the purpose of bringing proceedings against the company for personal injury; or
- within the period of six years from the date of dissolution.

The six-year period does not apply in circumstances where an application for administration restoration has been validly submitted and rejected by the Registrar. In these circumstances the application to the court must be made within 28 days of the date of the notice of the Registrars decision even if the normal six-year period has expired.

The court may order restoration if it is satisfied that:

- the person was not given a copy of the company's application;
- the company's application involved a breach of the conditions of the application; or
- for some other reason it is just to do so.

The Secretary of State may also apply to the court for restoration if this is justified in the public interest.

Applications are made to the High Court. The Registrar of the Companies Court in London usually hears restoration cases in chambers once a week on Friday afternoons. Cases are also heard at the District Registries. For more detailed guidance on restoration, see *A Guide to Company Restoration*, available online from the Treasury Solicitor's Department (see Directory).

The court will require an affidavit or a witness statement confirming that:

- the originating document was served; and
- the solicitor dealing with the *bona vacantia* assets has no objection to the restoration of the company.

The affidavit or witness statement should also cover, as appropriate to the application:

- details of the company's original incorporation and objects;
- members, directors and company secretary;
- its trading activities;
- an explanation of any failure to file accounts, annual returns or other documents at Companies House;
- details of the striking-off and dissolution;
- details concerning the company's solvency; and/or
- the purpose for the application.

Before the order can be granted, the company will need to file all documents required to bring the company's statutory filing up to date.

All costs of the restoration are met by the applicant including the Government Legal Department's costs, fees payable to the Registrar and any late filing penalties due in respect of accounts. The penalties are those that had already been imposed but not paid prior to dissolution or in respect of any accounts that were overdue for filing when the company was dissolved. The period when the company was dissolved is ignored for the purposes of calculating the amount of penalties due.

An office copy of the court order with the court seal impressed must be delivered to the Registrar of Companies. The company is regarded as restored when the order is delivered.

23 – Investigations

Introduction

All companies are required to allow access to documents and records on request by individuals and organisations. Certain organisations – principally the Department of Business, Energy & Industrial Strategy (BEIS) (formerly the Department for Business, Innovation and Skills) – have power to investigate a company's affairs. Very few individuals have the right of entry to premises. Where a warrant to enter and search premises is given, this is valid only if served by a police officer. Accordingly, entry can be refused to, for example, representatives from HM Revenue & Customs, BEIS inspectors and FCA investigators.

Table 23.1 summarises the powers and rights of entry of the various regulatory bodies covered by this chapter.

Table 23.1: Regulatory bodies: powers and rights of entry

Body/Person	*Power to require production of documents or information*	*Right of entry without warrant*	*Power of entry and search by warrant (exercised by police)*
Directors	Access to all documents	No	No
Shareholders	Access to statutory records	No	No
Auditors	Yes	No	No
BEIS Inspectors	Yes	No	Yes
HMRC – direct taxes	Yes	Yes To review NI records provided reasonable notice but not conduct search	Yes
HMRC – indirect taxes	Yes	Yes To review VAT records but not conduct search	Yes

Body/Person	*Power to require production of documents or information*	*Right of entry without warrant*	*Power of entry and search by warrant (exercised by police)*
FCA	Yes	No	Yes
CMA	Yes	Yes Two days' notice might be required, to review documents but not conduct search	Yes
Panel	Yes	No	No

Types of access

Directors

All directors, whether executive or non-executive, have the right to review all of the company's records.

Shareholders

Shareholders are entitled to inspect or receive copies of any of the company's statutory registers and minutes of general meetings. They are entitled to receive a copy of the company's unabridged annual accounts.

Shareholders have no right of access to a company's premises. Shareholders are entitled to attend general meetings of the company. However, as there is no right to enter the premises, unruly shareholders can be excluded or removed from meetings.

Members of the public

Members of the public are entitled to inspect or receive copies of any of the company's statutory registers upon payment of a fee. There is no right to receive copies of the company's accounts, although they may obtain a copy of the accounts filed with the Registrar of Companies, which may be abridged. There is no right of access to company premises.

Auditors

As noted in Chapter 11, in preparing their report, the auditor must carry out whatever investigations are necessary in order to be able to state whether proper accounting records have been maintained by the company and whether the company's accounts are in agreement with those records. If the auditor is not able to make such a statement, this fact must be stated in their report giving such details of the omissions or inconsistencies as are appropriate in the circumstances (s. 498(3)).

Auditor's access to information

An auditor of a company enjoys certain statutory rights to information in connection with the exercise of their duties. These include the following:

1 A right of access at all times to the company's books, accounts and vouchers, and to require from the company's directors and officers such information and explanations as the auditor thinks necessary for the performance of their duties (s. 499(1)).
2 The auditor is entitled to attend any general meetings of the company and to receive all notices and other communications relating to any general meeting. They may also speak on any business of the meeting that concerns them as auditor (s. 502).
3 It is the duty of subsidiary undertakings incorporated in Great Britain and their auditors to give the auditors of the parent company such information and explanations as those auditors may reasonably require for the purposes of their duties as auditors of the parent company (s. 499(2)).

Auditors' right of entry

Auditors have no right of access to company premises.

Investigations, review of records and production of records

A number of regulatory bodies have rights to require production of documents, provision of information and/or power to investigate.

Department of Business, Energy & Industrial Strategy (BEIS)

All companies are regulated by BEIS which has authority, given by the Companies Act 1985 ss. 431–453, as amended by ss. 1035–1039, to investigate companies. These investigations provisions of the Companies Act 1985 are among the few provisions that remain in force following full implementation of the Companies Act 2006. Investigations can be made in a variety of ways and there are levels of investigation common to all investigations. BEIS will either appoint inspectors, usually an accountant and a barrister, with power to examine witnesses under caution, or require the production of documents and records for examination by BEIS officials.

Right of entry

Inspectors or competent persons appointed to enquire into the affairs of a company have no right of entry or right to undertake a search of business or other premises.

A justice of the peace may issue a warrant under CA1985 s. 448 for the entry and search of premises if there are reasonable grounds for believing that there are documents in the premises whose production has not been complied with.

A justice of the peace may issue a warrant under CA1985 s. 448 for the entry and search of premises if there are reasonable grounds for believing that: there are documents in the premises relating to an offence of which the penalty on conviction is not less than two years; the Secretary of State, or a person appointed by them, has the power to require the production of those documents; and if production was requested, the documents would be removed or destroyed.

A warrant issued under CA1985 s. 448 authorises a police officer and any named persons with them to:

1 enter the specified premises;
2 search and take possession of documents appearing to be relevant;
3 take copies of any such documents; and
4 require explanations concerning the documents from any persons in the premises.

Appointment of inspectors

There are six categories of inspection:

1 appointment of inspectors to investigate the affairs of the company;
2 investigations into ownership of company;
3 investigations of directors' share dealings;
4 production of documents;
5 investigations to assist overseas regulatory authorities; and
6 investigations under the Financial Services and Markets Act 2000.

To investigate the affairs of a company

Appointment of inspectors by the Secretary of State can be requested by the company itself, by a minimum of 200 shareholders or, if the company does not have a share capital, by not less than one-fifth of the company's members (CA1985 s. 431). Such applications are, however, very rare.

The Secretary of State will appoint inspectors to investigate the affairs of a company, if the court by order declares the affairs should be investigated, if it appears to them that there are circumstances to indicate that:

- the company's affairs are or have been undertaken with intent to defraud creditors, or the creditors of another person, for fraudulent or unlawful purpose or in such a way that is unfairly detrimental to some part of its members;
- any act or intended act or omission or intended omission whether by or on behalf of the company would be prejudicial to some part of the members, or that the company was formed for any fraudulent or unlawful purpose;

- persons forming the company or connected with its management have in that regard been guilty of fraud, misconduct or misfeasance towards the company or its members; or
- the members have not been given information concerning the affairs of the company which they might reasonably expect.

The terms of appointment will determine the report required and may stipulate that the report will not be made public: CA1985 s. 432(2A). Inspectors appointed under CA1985 s. 431 or 432 to investigate the affairs of a company have power to extend their investigation to any subsidiary or holding company without the need for any specific appointment by the Secretary of State (CA1985 s. 433).

Once inspectors are appointed under CA1985 ss. 431 and 432, it is the duty of all officers and agents of the company and of any person who is or may be in possession of information or documents relating to the company under investigation to:

- produce to the inspectors all documents of or relating to the company in their custody or power;
- attend before the inspectors when required; inspectors may examine any person on oath and may administer an oath accordingly; and
- give all assistance in connection with the investigation that they are reasonably able to give (CA1985 s. 434, as amended by s. 1038).

The right to silence has been excluded and the inspectors may compel a witness to answer questions; any answers may be given in evidence against that person. Where a witness refuses to answer any question or refuses to assist in the investigation, the inspectors may certify that fact to the court. On enquiry, the court may punish the person as if they are guilty of contempt of court (CA1985 s. 436).

The inspectors report to the Secretary of State on the conclusion of their investigation. The publication of the inspectors' report is at the discretion of the Secretary of State and it is the policy of BEIS to publish a report only if it is in the public interest (CA1985 s. 437).

If matters have come to light during the course of an investigation that suggest that a criminal offence has been committed, those facts are referred to the appropriate prosecuting authority. Once referred, the inspectors need take no further action (CA1985 s. 437(1B)).

If there is evidence to suggest that civil proceedings ought to be brought, in the public interest, by any company, the Secretary of State may bring such proceedings in the name of and on behalf of the company and will indemnify the company for the costs of such action (CA1985 s. 438).

The expenses of an investigation under CA1985 s. 431 or 432 will be borne by the Secretary of State, who may recover those costs, or part of them, from any person convicted as a result of the investigation. Where the appointment was made at the request of shareholders, the company may be liable for some or all of the costs (CA1985 s. 439).

Power to investigate ownership

Where it appears to the Secretary of State that there are good reasons for doing so, inspectors or BEIS officials may be appointed to investigate the true identity of those financially interested in the success or failure of a company or able to control or materially influence its management (CA1985 ss. 442 and 444).

The terms of appointment may limit the investigation to matters connected with specified shares or holdings. Such investigations are usually used to investigate the circumstances where there is potential takeover and there are circumstances to suggest the existence of undisclosed arrangements or undertakings between groups of shareholders (CA1985 s. 442(2)).

Inspectors appointed under CA1985 s. 442 have the same powers as inspectors appointed under CA1985 ss. 431 and 432. As noted above, such powers are, however, restricted to those persons who are or have been or appear to be or have been interested in the shares or debentures, together with those other persons it appears to the inspectors possess information relevant to their investigation (CA1985 s. 443).

Where the matter to be investigated does not require the appointment of inspectors under CA1985 s. 442, the Secretary of State may require the production of documents or information concerning present or past interests in shares or debentures from any person they reasonably believe might have it (CA1985 s. 444(1)). Any person failing to provide the information or supplying false information is liable to fine, imprisonment or both (CA1985 s. 444(3)).

Production of documents

The majority of investigations initiated by BEIS do not require the appointment of inspectors. Instead, the Secretary of State may, if they think there are good reasons, give a direction requiring the production of specified documents and records. A competent person may also be authorised to require any company or person to produce specified documents (CA1985 s. 447).

The power to require the production of documents extends to the taking of copies and requesting explanation of any matter in those documents from any person. Failure to produce the documents or provide an explanation without good reason is an offence under CA1985 s. 447(6). Making false or reckless statements is an offence under CA1985 s. 451. Documents can be withheld if they are covered by professional privilege (CA1985 s. 452). Some banking records may also be withheld. Information obtained under CA1985 s. 447 may not be published or disclosed without the consent of the company, and unauthorised publication or disclosure is an offence (CA1985 s. 449). Disclosure may, however, be made to a competent authority as set out in CA1985 s. 449, including the Secretary of State, the Treasury, the Bank of England, Financial Conduct Authority and any police officer. HM Revenue & Customs is not a competent authority for the purposes of CA1985 s. 449 and Sch. 15C.

Overseas regulatory authorities

BEIS was given power under CA1989 ss. 82–91 to assist overseas authorities investigating UK companies. The power permits investigation, interviews under oath and seeking documents and records. In deciding whether to provide assistance, regard must be given to whether reciprocal assistance would be forthcoming.

HM Revenue & Customs

Following the merger of the Inland Revenue and HM Customs & Excise in April 2005, all officers of HM Revenue & Customs (HMRC) have the same powers. In practice, however, investigations relating to direct taxes are undertaken by former Inland Revenue officers using their pre-existing powers, and investigations into indirect taxes are undertaken by former customs and excise officers using their pre-existing powers.

Direct tax investigations

Generally speaking, HMRC can give notice requiring the production of documents and the provision of information. This must be complied with in a specified period of not less than 30 days. Relevant legislation includes: the Taxes Management Act 1970, s. 20; the Finance Act 1998 para. 27, Sch. 18; the Corporation Tax (Instalment Payments) Regulations 1998, SI 1998/3175 regs. 10, 11 and 12; and the Income and Corporation Taxes Act 1988, ss. 708 and 767A.

HMRC also has power to review company PAYE and NI records. This power is given by: the Income Tax (Employments) Regulations 1993, SI 1993/744 reg. 53; the Social Security (Contributions) Regulations 2001, SI 2001/1004 para. 26, Part III, Sch. 4; and the Income Tax (Sub-contractors in the Construction Industry) Regulations 1975, SI 1975/1960 reg. 41.

In terms of investigation of National Insurance records, s. 110ZA of the Social Security Administration Act 1992 provides broad information-gathering powers of entry at all reasonable times to premises where it is believed either a trade or business or the records of a trade or business are kept. This right of entry is limited to reasonable times, and entry can be refused if the request or time etc. is unreasonable in the circumstances.

HMRC officials have no automatic right of entry. They may, however, obtain a warrant under s. 20C of the Taxes Management Act 1970, signed by a circuit judge, to enter and search premises. The warrant is valid if served by a police officer. To obtain a warrant, the circuit judge must be satisfied that there are reasonable grounds for suspecting that evidence of an offence involving serious tax fraud is to be found on the premises. Certain documents are privileged and cannot be seized. These include personal, medical or religious records, and the property of any tax adviser.

Indirect tax investigations

The Customs & Excise Management Act 1979 and Sch. 11 to the VAT Act 1994 gave the Commissioners of Customs wide-reaching powers of investigation and information gathering.

HMRC is moving away from the previous system of periodic VAT visits with visits now generated by:

- VAT returns showing an unusual level of sales or purchases compared to industry norms;
- information received;
- information obtained during the course of an inspection of another company's records;
- information from other government departments.

Unannounced visits do still take place and customs officers have the right of entry to premises to inspect records at any reasonable time. The right of entry to inspect records does not permit a search for records to be undertaken. Visits are usually by appointment and the HMRC officer has the right to call for any books and records. Where the visit is by appointment and the business owner is therefore on notice of the visit, they are obliged to answer the officer's questions. This is not the case for unannounced visits.

Where there has been an unannounced visit and, for genuine business or personal reasons, it is inconvenient, the officer(s) can be asked to leave. If the officer(s) insist(s) on their right of entry, they should be given access to a clear room and should be accompanied at all times. They should not be given uncontrolled access to business records.

Although rarely used, HMRC officers have the power to arrest. In order to search premises, a search warrant must be obtained.

Financial Conduct Authority

Part XI of the FSMA2000 sets out the powers of the Financial Conduct Authority (FCA) to gather information and carry out investigations.

Production of documents

The FCA has authority under s. 165 of the FSMA2000 to require the production of document or information from:

- an authorised or formerly authorised person;
- a person connected with an authorised person;
- the operator, trustee or depository of an open-ended investment company;
- a recognised investment exchange; or
- a recognised clearing house.

Power to commission reports

The FCA may require an authorised, formerly authorised or connected person to commission and provide a report into any relevant matter (FSMA2000 s. 166). A relevant matter is one about which the FCA could require information under FSMA2000 s. 165. The person making the report must be nominated by or approved by the FCA. Authorised persons and firms are required to cooperate with any person writing the report. Under FSMA2000 s. 167, the FCA may appoint a competent person to conduct a general investigation into the business of an authorised person or appointed representative or into the ownership or control of an authorised person. Written notice of any investigation must be given to the person or firm under investigation in terms of FSMA2000 s. 170(2). The competent person appointed to carry out the investigation may be an employee of the FCA or some other person engaged for that purpose.

Under FSMA2000 s. 168, the FCA may appoint a competent person to conduct an investigation where it appears there are circumstances to suggest that a specific contravention or offence may have taken place. Such specific investigations would include breaches of the general prohibition to provide investment advice, breaches of any rules or regulations made under the FSMA2000, commission of misleading statements and practices in terms of FSMA2000 s. 397, market abuse in terms of FSMA2000 s. 188, insider dealing in terms of Part V of the Criminal Justice Act 1993 or suspected breach of the money laundering regulations.

FSMA2000 s. 169 gives the FCA power to investigate authorised persons and firms on behalf of an overseas regulator.

Investigators' powers

Investigators appointed under FSMA2000 s. 167 have power to require persons to attend before them and answer questions, provide information and to provide documents. This power is restricted to information relevant to the investigation and to the person under investigation or a connected person of that person (FSMA2000 s. 171).

Investigators appointed under FSMA2000 s. 168 have additional powers set out in FSMA2000 ss. 172 and 173. These powers do not apply in all cases and care must be taken to establish the appropriate power in any given case. Generally, the investigators' powers of interview and information gathering are extended to persons not under investigation but who might have relevant information.

FSMA2000 s. 175 permits investigators appointed by the FCA or the Secretary of State to compel the production of relevant documents from any person, together with any explanation of the document where needed. Banking documents may be withheld without the consent of the person to whom they relate, unless their disclosure has been specifically authorised by the FCA or the Secretary of State.

Right of entry

An investigator appointed under the terms of the FSMA2000 has no right of entry or search; accordingly, entry may be refused. The investigator may, however, obtain a warrant to enter and search premises from a justice of the peace or, in Scotland, from a sheriff. A warrant to enter and search must be executed by a police officer. To obtain a warrant, the justice of the peace or sheriff must be satisfied that there are grounds for believing that:

- a request for the production of documents has not been complied with and that the documents are on the premises;
- there are grounds to believe that any request to provide documents found on the premises would not be complied with or the documents would be moved, altered or destroyed; or
- a serious offence has been or is being committed and that there is information or documents on the premises relevant to the offence and that a request for their production would not be complied with or might result in the documents being removed, altered or destroyed.

Offences

Where any person fails, without good reason, to comply with a request made under Part XI of the FSMA2000 for information or the production of documents, that fact may be certified to the court. On enquiry, the court may punish the person as if they were guilty of contempt of court (FSMA2000 s. 177). A person who recklessly provides false or misleading information or who falsifies, withholds or destroys any documents or information is guilty of an offence and, on conviction, is liable to a fine of up to £5,000 or six months' imprisonment, or both.

Competition and Markets Authority

On 1 April 2014, the Competition and Markets Authority took over all functions of the Competition Commission and the Office of Fair Trading, and their powers of investigation contained in the Competition Act 1998 and the Enterprise Act 2002.

Sections 194–201, 224 and 225 of the Enterprise Act 2002 (EA2002) set out the investigation and surveillance powers of the CMA.

Production of documents

EA2002 ss. 193 and 224 give the CMA power to require persons to attend interviews to answer questions or to provide documents or other written evidence. The power under EA2002 s. 193 relates to the investigation of cartels; EA2002 ss. 224 and 225 relate to consumer protection.

Power of entry

EA2002 s. 194 allows the CMA to obtain a warrant from the High Court (procurator fiscal in Scotland) to allow a named CMA officer to enter premises and conduct searches for documents or other evidence in connection with investigations into cartels. This power is for use where the CMA believes that:

- a request for the production of documents has not been complied with and that the documents are on the premises;
- there are grounds to believe that any request to provide documents found on the premises would not be complied with or the documents would be moved, altered or destroyed; or
- a serious offence has or is being committed and that there is information or documents on the premises relevant to the offence and that a request for their production would not be complied with or might result in the documents being removed, altered or destroyed.

EA2002 ss. 31, 109 and 176 give the CMA authority to require the production of specified documents or to require individuals to attend interviews and to give evidence. These powers are in respect of the CMA's investigations into mergers and abuse of market dominance.

The CMA has power to launch competition investigations and in carrying out these investigations, CMA officials have the power to enter and in some circumstances search premises for relevant documents.

CMA officials have power under CA1998 s. 27 to enter business and residential premises without a warrant and require production of documents or provision of information and to take copies of documents. Section 27 of CA1998 does not permit a search of the premises or forced entry.

Under CA1998 s. 28, CMA officials can obtain a warrant from the High Court of the Competition Authority Tribunal to enter, by force if necessary, business premises and search and take possession of documents. Section 28A provides the power of entry and search by warrant in respect of domestic premises.

The CMA has similar powers of entry with or without a warrant where it is acting on behalf of another EU member state. These powers are confirmed by ss. 65E–65H.

Takeover Panel

Sections 947–965 set out the investigation and other powers of the Takeover Panel (the Panel).

Production of documents

Section 947 empowers the Panel to require, by notice in writing, a person to produce specified or described documents and/or to provide in such form or manner as may be specified such information as is specified or described.

The requirement to produce documents or information must be supplied at a specified place and within a reasonable period specified by the Panel, and may be required to be authenticated in such manner as the Panel may reasonably require.

The documents or information that the Panel may require are those that they may reasonably require to enable it to exercise its functions (s. 947(3)).

The Panel may authorise any person to exercise its powers to require the production of documents or information (s. 947(5)).

The Panel or their authorised representative cannot require the production of documents or information in respect of which a claim for legal professional privilege (confidentiality of communication in Scotland) could be maintained in legal proceedings (s. 947(10)).

Section 948 prohibits the Panel from disclosing documents or information, other than those already in the public domain, provided to it in the exercise of its functions that relate to a private individual during their lifetime or a business for as long as the business continues without their consent. This protection does not apply to any disclosure made for the purpose of facilitating the Panel of carrying out its functions, is made to a person, is of a description and is in accordance with CA2006 Sch. 2 (s. 948(3)).

Right of entry

The Panel and their representatives have no right of entry to premises.

24 – Overseas and non-Companies Act companies

Introduction

Any overseas company which opens a UK establishment must register with the Registrar of Companies within one month (SI 2009/1801).

An 'establishment' is defined as being a branch within the meaning of the Eleventh Company Law Directive or a place of business that is not such a branch. A 'UK establishment' is defined as being an establishment in the UK. From the legislation, it is clear that a UK establishment is a permanent place of business and part of the structure of the overseas company. A UK establishment may well have its own management and have delegated responsibility for its actions.

Registration of a UK establishment

Every overseas company that is incorporated outside the United Kingdom (England and Wales, Scotland and Northern Ireland) and that wishes to open a UK establishment within the UK is required to register with the Registrar of Companies.

An overseas company may have more than one UK establishment within the UK. If they each have management independence, each UK establishment will require to be registered. If there is a main office to which the other offices report, it is only necessary for the main UK establishment to register. If two UK establishments both report direct to the overseas parent, both must register.

An overseas company that opens a UK establishment or new UK establishment must register the necessary details with the Registrar, submitting Form OS IN01 containing the following details in respect of the overseas company:

1 the company's registered name;
2 details of an alternative name, if the company wishes to carry on business under an alternative name;
3 its registered number and the identity of the register of the country of incorporation;
4 its legal form (public, private, etc.);

5 address of principal place of business or registered office in the country of incorporation, if not included in the constitutional documents;
6 details of directors and secretary or equivalent;
7 the authority of the directors to represent the company and their capacity to bind the company in dealings with third parties, together with a statement of whether this authority may be exercised solely or jointly with other directors;
8 whether the company is a credit or financial institution; and
9 if the overseas company is not incorporated in a Member State of the EU, additional information is required: namely, the legislation under which the company was incorporated, confirmation that any sensitive words within the corporate name have been authorised, and a copy of that authorisation and accounting period together with time period for public disclosure.

In respect of the UK establishment itself, the following information should be registered:

1 The address of the UK establishment.
2 The date on which it was established.
3 The business carried on by the UK establishment.
4 The trading name, if different from the parent's registered name.
5 The name and address of all persons resident in the UK authorised to accept service on behalf of the parent company in respect of that branch.
6 The name and address of all persons authorised to represent the company as permanent representatives for the business of that UK establishment.
7 The authority of the permanent representatives to contract on behalf of the UK establishment and whether they may exercise such authority solely or if jointly the name of the joint authorised representatives (reg. 7(1)).

If an overseas company has more than one establishment in the UK, there is no need to repeat all the information on each Form OS IN01, as reference may be made to a Form OS IN01 previously filed. Only information exclusive to the particular UK establishment need be disclosed.

In addition to Form OS IN01, a certified copy of the constitutional document of the overseas company and, if not in English, a certified translation must be submitted. This document need only be submitted once and must be referred to for other UK establishment registrations. Any alterations to the constitutional documents must be notified on Form OS CC01.

If the UK establishment for which full registration was made is subsequently closed, the constitutional documents may be 'transferred' to another UK establishment using Form OS AD01. A UK establishment registration fee of £20 is payable (£100 for same-day registration). Any change in the details of the UK establishment must be notified within 21 days, or, if they are changes to the details of the overseas company, within 21 days of the date on which notice could have been made in the normal course of post from the overseas country, using the applicable form available at Companies House (www.companieshouse.gov.uk).

Each overseas company with registered UK establishments must register its annual report and accounts. The full accounts of the overseas company are required and not just accounts relating to the UK establishment(s). The form of accounts required will depend on the requirements in the overseas company's country of incorporation. If the overseas company is required to publish audited accounts, those accounts and any other accounting information published must be filed with the Registrar within three months of their publication in their home country. If the accounts are not in English, a certified translation must also be filed. If, however, the overseas company is not required in its own country to publish audited accounts, then it must publish accounts as if it were incorporated under the Companies Acts, as amended by Part 5 of the Regulations (see page 426).

The effect of this legislation is to allow any overseas company to file the accounts prepared for its host country, with a certified translation if necessary. If the overseas company is not required by the laws of its country of incorporation to publish accounts, then accounts must be prepared as if the company were registered under the Companies Act.

A filing fee of £20 is payable on submission of the accounts.

A UK establishment that owns property over which charges have been given is required to register details with the Registrar.

Every UK establishment of an overseas company must state the following information on all business letters, order forms and websites that are used in carrying on business in the UK:

- country of incorporation;
- identity of the registry (if applicable);
- the company number;
- location of its head office;
- legal form of the company;
- whether the liability of the members is limited and whether the company is limited;
- where applicable, whether the company is being wound up or subject to insolvency proceedings; and
- if there is a reference to share capital, the reference must be to paid-up share capital.

Where an overseas company has more than one registered UK establishment and is being wound up, it must, within 14 days of the commencement of the winding-up, give details of its name, particulars of the winding-up and the date on which the winding-up is or will be effective (Form OS LQ03 or OS LQ02). Within 14 days of appointment, the liquidator must notify their name and address, the date of their appointment and a description of their powers (Form OS LQ01). Following the termination of the winding-up, for whatever reason, the liquidator must file details of the termination within 14 days (Form OS DS02 or OS LQ04).

Details must be given for each UK establishment, although one return may be made, provided the registered UK establishment numbers of each UK establishment are stated on the return. These provisions do not apply to any winding-up under the provisions of Part V of IA1986.

Filing requirements

An overseas company with registered UK establishments must register its annual report and accounts. The full accounts of the overseas company are required, not the accounts relating to the UK establishment(s). The form of accounts required will depend on the requirements in the overseas company's country of incorporation. If the overseas company is required to publish audited accounts, those accounts and any other accounting information published must be filed with the Registrar within three months of their publication in their home country. If the accounts are not in English, a certified translation must also be filed.

If the overseas company is not required in its own country to publish audited accounts, then it must prepare and file accounts in respect of each financial period as if it were a company formed under the Companies Acts. The accounts of the overseas company as a whole entity are required, not simply accounts relating to the trade within UK. Again, if the accounts are not in English, a certified translation is also required to be filed.

There is a filing fee of £20 for the submission of UK establishment accounts.

European Economic Interest Groupings (EEIGs)

EEIGs were established by Council Regulation (EEC) No. 2137/85. The appropriate legislation was brought into effect in England and Wales and Scotland by the European Economic Interest Grouping Regulations 1989, SI 1989/638.

EEIGs are designed to help businesses in different Member States establish and maintain links. The EEIG provides an alternative to takeover, merger or joint venture where the costs involved usually preclude smaller companies from participating. An EEIG enables such links to be established without losing the identity and independence of the members.

What is an EEIG?

The EEIG is an association between corporate bodies, firms or individuals from different Member States so as to operate together across national borders. Its aim is to facilitate or develop the commercial activities of its members. Although an EEIG carries out activities on behalf of its members, its activities are separate from those of its members.

An EEIG may be registered in any Member State, can operate in any Member State and can contract with people outside the EU. Only corporate bodies, firms or individuals resident in the EU can become members of an EEIG. An EEIG registered in the UK is a corporate body.

An EEIG cannot:

1 be formed with the object of making a profit (an EEIG can make a profit, however, as a consequence of its operations);
2 exercise control over any other undertaking and/or its members;
3 hold shares or own part or all of any of its members;
4 issue shares or receive investment from the public;
5 be a member of another EEIG;
6 employ more than 500 people; or
7 be used for the transfer of any property between a company and a director, or a connected person, other than allowed by national law.

Advantages of an EEIG

An EEIG has the following advantages:

1 legal capacity;
2 tax transparency;
3 flexibility regarding financing;
4 no capital requirement; and
5 no requirement to prepare or file accounts.

Disadvantages of an EEIG

An EEIG has the following disadvantages:

1 unlimited joint and several liability of the members;
2 it cannot seek funds from the public; and
3 it cannot buy a share in another EEIG.

Registration

An EEIG must be registered in the Member State where its official address is situated. The official address must be either where its central administration is carried out or where one of its members has its central administration.

If an EEIG opens an establishment in another Member State, that establishment must be registered in that other State.

The official address may be transferred within the EU. If the transfer is to another Member State, a transfer proposal must be drawn up and filed with Companies House. The transfer may not take place until two months after publication of the proposal.

The formation and termination of an EEIG must be published in the *London*, *Edinburgh* or *Belfast Gazette* (as appropriate) and in the *Official Journal of the European Union* within one month of formation or termination as appropriate.

There are three different types of registration:

1 A new EEIG which is to have its official address in the UK must register:
   a. Form EE FM01; and
   b. the contract of formation with a certified translation if not in English.

2 An existing EEIG that is moving its official address to the UK must register:
   a. Form EE FM01, formation contract and certified translation (if appropriate);
   b. evidence of the publication of the transfer proposal; and
   c. a statement that no competent authority has opposed the transfer.
3 An EEIG setting up an establishment in the UK but which will continue to have its official address outside the UK must register:
   a. Form EE FM02; and
   b. certified copies of all documents registered in the Member State where the EEIG has its official address together with certified translations, if appropriate.

Regardless of which type of registration is being effected, there is a filing fee of £20.

Formation contract

The contract of formation of an EEIG must include:

1 its registered name;
2 its official address;
3 the objects for which it was formed;
4 the names, business names, legal form and address or registered office of its members;
5 the number and place of registration (if any) of its members; and
6 if formed for a specific event or period, the length of that period.

Name of an EEIG

The name of an EEIG must include the words 'European Economic Interest Grouping' or 'EEIG'. With this exception, the rules and restrictions on names for EEIGs are substantially the same as those for companies formed and registered under the Companies Act 2006.

Changes in registered information

1 Notice of changes to the registered details of an EEIG must be registered as follows.
2 Notice of the appointment and removal of managers on Form EE AP01 or EE TM01 where the official address is in Great Britain, and Form EE AP02 or MP01 where it is elsewhere.
3 Form EE MP01 must also be used to file the following documents and particulars:
   a. amendment to the formation contract;
   b. any judicial or members' decision ordering or establishing the winding-up of the EEIG;
   c. any judicial decision nullifying the EEIG;

  d. notice of a member's assignment of all or part of its participation in the EEIG;
  e. notice of the appointment or termination of appointment of a liquidator of the EEIG;
  f. notice of the conclusion of liquidation of the EEIG;
  g. a proposal to transfer the official address to another Member State; and
  h. notice of any proposal exempting new member(s) from liabilities incurred prior to their admission.

4 Form EE MP02 must be used to register the setting up or closing of any establishment other than where registration on Form EE FM02 is required.

Structure of an EEIG

An EEIG must be formed by at least two members from different Member States, and a manager or managers must be appointed to manage the day-to-day affairs of the EEIG.

Membership of an EEIG is intended to be open to as many people and organisations as possible within the EU. The main requirement is that each member should have been engaged in an economic activity in the EU before becoming a member of the EEIG.

To be eligible for membership, companies, firms and other legal bodies must:

- have been formed according to the law of one of the Member States and have their registered or statutory office (if applicable) within the EU; and
- have their central administration and control within the EU.

Individuals may become members if they carry on any industrial, commercial, craft or agricultural activity, or provide professional or other services within the EU.

The members decide how the EEIG will be run and this provision will normally be set out in the formation contract. There is no requirement for regular meetings of the members.

Each member has at least one vote and no one member can hold a majority of the votes.

The members are free to decide the voting procedures to be set down in the contract of formation. Certain decisions require a unanimous decision of the members, as follows:

- alteration of the objects of the EEIG;
- changes to the votes allotted to members;
- extension to the duration of the EEIG;
- changes to members' financing of the EEIG;
- changes to members' obligations;
- changes to the formation contract; and
- transfer of the official address to another Member State.

Management of an EEIG

The members appoint managers who run the EEIG and make normal daily decisions. At least one manager must be appointed. EEIGs registered in the UK may appoint a corporate as manager, provided that an individual is then registered as the manager's representative. The actions of the managers are binding on the EEIG and the members are jointly liable for those actions. The only limitation that can be applied to the managers by the members is a requirement for dual signatories, provided that this requirement is published in the appropriate *Gazette*.

Funding

Members of an EEIG are not required to subscribe any capital. EEIGs can be financed by capital invested, by loans or donations from members or others. The contribution may be in the form of the services and skills. EEIGs may not seek investment from the public.

Accounts

The EEIG is not subject to any accounting requirements and does not have to file an annual return with Companies House. A return to HM Revenue & Customs, however, is required.

Taxation

Taxation operates under a system of fiscal transparency with any profits, losses or gains shared between the members according to their capital share. These profits, losses or gains are then taxed in the hands of the members according to the relevant taxation treatment in their own Member State. In the UK these provisions are set out in the Finance Act 1990, Sch. 11.

This tax transparency does not extend to taxes such as VAT and stamp duty. An EEIG will have to register for VAT purposes if it makes taxable supplies in the same way as any other company, firm or person.

Societas Europaea

The European Company Statute Regulation (Council Regulation (EC) No. 2157/2001) was adopted on 8 October 2001 and came into force with effect from 8 October 2004. The statute created a new type of company that can operate on a Europe-wide basis and be governed by community law directly applicable in Member States, rather than by national law. The European company or 'Societas Europaea' is available to businesses operating in more than one Member State, and can be formed in a number of ways:

- by the merger of two or more existing public limited companies from at least two different EU Member States;
- by the formation of a holding company promoted by public or private limited companies from at least two EU Member States;

- by the formation of the subsidiary of companies from at least two different Member States;
- by the transformation of an existing public limited company with an EU-registered office and head office and which has for at least two years had a subsidiary in another Member State; or
- as a subsidiary of an existing Societas Europaea.

There is no central European registry and registration will be published in the *Official Journal*. Registration must be made in one of the Member States and will need to comply with national registration requirements of the country in which the administrative office is located. For a Societas Europaea with a registered office in England or Wales, this would require filing and registering at Companies House in Cardiff.

Companies House has issued a series of statutory forms for SE companies; these are Listed below. Additional advice is available in the Companies House guidance booklet GPO6, *The European Company: Societas Europaea (SE)*.

The five methods of forming an SE company in the UK are:

1. formation by merger of SE (Form SE FM01);
2. formation of a holding SE (Form SE FM02);
3. formation of a subsidiary SE under article 2(3) (Form SE FM03);
4. formation of a subsidiary SE under article 3(2) (Form SE FM05); and
5. conversion of a plc to an SE (Form SE FM04).

The registration fee for all forms of SE formation is £20.

Name of an SE

The name of an SE must be preceded or followed by the abbreviation 'SE'. With this exception, the rules and restrictions on names for SEs are substantially the same as those for companies formed and registered under the Companies Act 2006.

Appendix I – Model Articles of Association

Introduction

The Companies (Model Articles) Regulations 2008 prescribe model articles for private companies limited by shares, public companies and guarantee companies. The relevant model articles will automatically be the articles for companies formed under the Companies Act 2006 which do not register their own articles of association, or which register their own articles but do not exclude the model articles in whole or in part.

Model Articles for a public company

Companies (Model Articles) Regulations 2008 Schedule 3(SI 2008/3229)

MODEL ARTICLES FOR PUBLIC COMPANIES

PART 1: INTERPRETATION AND LIMITATION OF LIABILITY

Defined terms

1. In the articles, unless the context requires otherwise:

'alternate' or 'alternate director' has the meaning given in article 25;

'appointor' has the meaning given in article 25;

'articles' means the company's articles of association;

'bankruptcy' includes individual insolvency proceedings in a jurisdiction other than England and Wales or Northern Ireland which have an effect similar to that of bankruptcy;

'call' has the meaning given in article 54;

'call notice' has the meaning given in article 54;

'certificate' means a paper certificate (other than a share warrant) evidencing a person's title to specified shares or other securities;

'certificated' in relation to a share, means that it is not an uncertificated share or a share in respect of which a share warrant has been issued and is current;

'chairman' has the meaning given in article 12;

'chairman of the meeting' has the meaning given in article 31;

'Companies Acts' means the Companies Acts (as defined in section 2 of the Companies Act 2006), in so far as they apply to the company;

'company's lien' has the meaning given in article 52;

'director' means a director of the company, and includes any person occupying the position of director, by whatever name called;

'distribution recipient' has the meaning given in article 72;

'document' includes, unless otherwise specified, any document sent or supplied in electronic form;

'electronic form' has the meaning given in section 1168 of the Companies Act 2006;

'fully paid' in relation to a share, means that the nominal value and any premium to be paid to the company in respect of that share have been paid to the company;

'hard copy form' has the meaning given in section 1168 of the Companies Act 2006;

'holder' in relation to shares means the person whose name is entered in the register of members as the holder of the shares, or, in the case of a share in respect of which a share warrant has been issued (and not cancelled), the person in possession of that warrant;

'instrument' means a document in hard copy form;

'lien enforcement notice' has the meaning given in article 53;

'member' has the meaning given in section 112 of the Companies Act 2006;

'ordinary resolution' has the meaning given in section 282 of the Companies Act 2006;

'paid' means paid or credited as paid;

'participate', in relation to a directors' meeting, has the meaning given in article 9;

'partly paid' in relation to a share means that part of that share's nominal value or any premium at which it was issued has not been paid to the company;

'proxy notice' has the meaning given in article 38;

'securities seal' has the meaning given in article 47;

'shares' means shares in the company;

'special resolution' has the meaning given in section 283 of the Companies Act 2006;

'subsidiary' has the meaning given in section 1159 of the Companies Act 2006;

'transmittee' means a person entitled to a share by reason of the death or bankruptcy of a shareholder or otherwise by operation of law;

'uncertificated' in relation to a share means that, by virtue of legislation (other than section 778 of the Companies Act 2006) permitting title to shares to be evidenced and transferred without a certificate, title to that share is evidenced and may be transferred without a certificate; and

'writing' means the representation or reproduction of words, symbols or other information in a visible form by any method or combination of methods, whether sent or supplied in electronic form or otherwise.

Unless the context otherwise requires, other words or expressions contained in these articles bear the same meaning as in the Companies Act 2006 as in force on the date when these articles become binding on the company.

Liability of members

2. The liability of the members is limited to the amount, if any, unpaid on the shares held by them.

PART 2: DIRECTORS

DIRECTORS' POWERS AND RESPONSIBILITIES

Directors' general authority

3. Subject to the articles, the directors are responsible for the management of the company's business, for which purpose they may exercise all the powers of the company.

Members' reserve power

4. (1) The members may, by special resolution, direct the directors to take, or refrain from taking, specified action.
(2) No such special resolution invalidates anything which the directors have done before the passing of the resolution.

Directors may delegate

5. (1) Subject to the articles, the directors may delegate any of the powers which are conferred on them under the articles:
(a) to such person or committee;
(b) by such means (including by power of attorney);
(c) to such an extent;
(d) in relation to such matters or territories; and
(e) on such terms and conditions,
as they think fit.
(2) If the directors so specify, any such delegation may authorise further delegation of the directors' powers by any person to whom they are delegated.
(3) The directors may revoke any delegation in whole or part, or alter its terms and conditions.

Committees

6. (1) Committees to which the directors delegate any of their powers must follow procedures which are based as far as they are applicable on those provisions of the articles which govern the taking of decisions by directors.
(2) The directors may make rules of procedure for all or any committees, which prevail over rules derived from the articles if they are not consistent with them.

DECISION-MAKING BY DIRECTORS

Directors to take decisions collectively

7. Decisions of the directors may be taken:
(a) at a directors' meeting; or
(b) in the form of a directors' written resolution.

Calling a directors' meeting

8. (1) Any director may call a directors' meeting.
(2) The company secretary must call a directors' meeting if a director so requests.
(3) A directors' meeting is called by giving notice of the meeting to the directors.
(4) Notice of any directors' meeting must indicate:
(a) its proposed date and time;
(b) where it is to take place; and
(c) if it is anticipated that directors participating in the meeting will not be in the same place, how it is proposed that they should communicate with each other during the meeting.
(5) Notice of a directors' meeting must be given to each director, but need not be in writing.
(6) Notice of a directors' meeting need not be given to directors who waive their entitlement to notice of that meeting, by giving notice to that effect to the company not more than seven days after the date on which the meeting is held. Where such notice is given after the meeting has been held, that does not affect the validity of the meeting, or of any business conducted at it.

Participation in directors' meetings

9. (1) Subject to the articles, directors participate in a directors' meeting, or part of a directors' meeting, when:
(a) the meeting has been called and takes place in accordance with the articles; and
(b) they can each communicate to the others any information or opinions they have on any particular item of the business of the meeting.
(2) In determining whether directors are participating in a directors' meeting, it is irrelevant where any director is or how they communicate with each other.

(3) If all the directors participating in a meeting are not in the same place, they may decide that the meeting is to be treated as taking place wherever any of them is.

Quorum for directors' meetings

10. (1) At a directors' meeting, unless a quorum is participating, no proposal is to be voted on, except a proposal to call another meeting.
(2) The quorum for directors' meetings may be fixed from time to time by a decision of the directors, but it must never be less than two, and unless otherwise fixed it is two.

Meetings where total number of directors less than quorum

11. (1) This article applies where the total number of directors for the time being is less than the quorum for directors' meetings.
(2) If there is only one director, that director may appoint sufficient directors to make up a quorum or call a general meeting to do so.
(3) If there is more than one director:
(a) a directors' meeting may take place, if it is called in accordance with the articles and at least two directors participate in it, with a view to appointing sufficient directors to make up a quorum or calling a general meeting to do so; and
(b) if a directors' meeting is called but only one director attends at the appointed date and time to participate in it, that director may appoint sufficient directors to make up a quorum or call a general meeting to do so.

Chairing directors' meetings

12. (1) The directors may appoint a director to chair their meetings.
(2) The person so appointed for the time being is known as the chairman.
(3) The directors may appoint other directors as deputy or assistant chairmen to chair directors' meetings in the chairman's absence.
(4) The directors may terminate the appointment of the chairman, deputy or assistant chairman at any time.
(5) If neither the chairman nor any director appointed generally to chair directors' meetings in the chairman's absence is participating in a meeting within ten minutes of the time at which it was to start, the participating directors must appoint one of themselves to chair it.

Voting at directors' meetings: general rules

13. (1) Subject to the articles, a decision is taken at a directors' meeting by a majority of the votes of the participating directors.
(2) Subject to the articles, each director participating in a directors' meeting has one vote.
(3) Subject to the articles, if a director has an interest in an actual or proposed transaction or arrangement with the company:

(a) that director and that director's alternate may not vote on any proposal relating to it; but
(b) this does not preclude the alternate from voting in relation to that transaction or arrangement on behalf of another appointor who does not have such an interest.

Chairman's casting vote at directors' meetings

14. (1) If the numbers of votes for and against a proposal are equal, the chairman or other director chairing the meeting has a casting vote.
(2) But this does not apply if, in accordance with the articles, the chairman or other director is not to be counted as participating in the decision-making process for quorum or voting purposes.

Alternates voting at directors' meetings

15. A director who is also an alternate director has an additional vote on behalf of each appointor who is:
(a) not participating in a directors' meeting; and
(b) would have been entitled to vote if they were participating in it.

Conflicts of interest

16. (1) If a directors' meeting, or part of a directors' meeting, is concerned with an actual or proposed transaction or arrangement with the company in which a director is interested, that director is not to be counted as participating in that meeting, or part of a meeting, for quorum or voting purposes.
(2) But if paragraph (3) applies, a director who is interested in an actual or proposed transaction or arrangement with the company is to be counted as participating in a decision at a directors' meeting, or part of a directors' meeting, relating to it for quorum and voting purposes.
(3) This paragraph applies when:
(a) the company by ordinary resolution disapplies the provision of the articles which would otherwise prevent a director from being counted as participating in, or voting at, a directors' meeting;
(b) the director's interest cannot reasonably be regarded as likely to give rise to a conflict of interest; or
(c) the director's conflict of interest arises from a permitted cause.
(4) For the purposes of this article, the following are permitted causes:
(a) a guarantee given, or to be given, by or to a director in respect of an obligation incurred by or on behalf of the company or any of its subsidiaries;
(b) subscription, or an agreement to subscribe, for shares or other securities of the company or any of its subsidiaries, or to underwrite, sub-underwrite, or guarantee subscription for any such shares or securities; and
(c) arrangements pursuant to which benefits are made available to employees and directors or former employees and directors of the company or any of its

subsidiaries which do not provide special benefits for directors or former directors.

(5) Subject to paragraph (6), if a question arises at a meeting of directors or of a committee of directors as to the right of a director to participate in the meeting (or part of the meeting) for voting or quorum purposes, the question may, before the conclusion of the meeting, be referred to the chairman whose ruling in relation to any director other than the chairman is to be final and conclusive.

(6) If any question as to the right to participate in the meeting (or part of the meeting) should arise in respect of the chairman, the question is to be decided by a decision of the directors at that meeting, for which purpose the chairman is not to be counted as participating in the meeting (or that part of the meeting) for voting or quorum purposes.

Proposing directors' written resolutions

17. (1) Any director may propose a directors' written resolution.

(2) The company secretary must propose a directors' written resolution if a director so requests.

(3) A directors' written resolution is proposed by giving notice of the proposed resolution to the directors.

(4) Notice of a proposed directors' written resolution must indicate:

(a) the proposed resolution; and

(b) the time by which it is proposed that the directors should adopt it.

(5) Notice of a proposed directors' written resolution must be given in writing to each director.

(6) Any decision which a person giving notice of a proposed directors' written resolution takes regarding the process of adopting that resolution must be taken reasonably in good faith.

Adoption of directors' written resolutions

18. (1) A proposed directors' written resolution is adopted when all the directors who would have been entitled to vote on the resolution at a directors' meeting have signed one or more copies of it, provided that those directors would have formed a quorum at such a meeting.

(2) It is immaterial whether any director signs the resolution before or after the time by which the notice proposed that it should be adopted.

(3) Once a directors' written resolution has been adopted, it must be treated as if it had been a decision taken at a directors' meeting in accordance with the articles.

(4) The company secretary must ensure that the company keeps a record, in writing, of all directors' written resolutions for at least ten years from the date of their adoption.

Directors' discretion to make further rules

19. Subject to the articles, the directors may make any rule which they think fit about how they take decisions, and about how such rules are to be recorded or communicated to directors.

APPOINTMENT OF DIRECTORS

Methods of appointing directors

20. Any person who is willing to act as a director, and is permitted by law to do so, may be appointed to be a director:
(a) by ordinary resolution; or
(b) by a decision of the directors.

Retirement of directors by rotation

21. (1) At the first annual general meeting all the directors must retire from office.
(2) At every subsequent annual general meeting any directors:
(a) who have been appointed by the directors since the last annual general meeting; or
(b) who were not appointed or reappointed at one of the preceding two annual general meetings,
must retire from office and may offer themselves for reappointment by the members.

Termination of director's appointment

22. A person ceases to be a director as soon as:
(a) that person ceases to be a director by virtue of any provision of the Companies Act 2006 or is prohibited from being a director by law;
(b) a bankruptcy order is made against that person;
(c) a composition is made with that person's creditors generally in satisfaction of that person's debts;
(d) a registered medical practitioner who is treating that person gives a written opinion to the company stating that that person has become physically or mentally incapable of acting as a director and may remain so for more than three months; or
(e) notification is received by the company from the director that the director is resigning from office as director, and such resignation has taken effect in accordance with its terms.

Directors' remuneration

23. (1) Directors may undertake any services for the company that the directors decide.
(2) Directors are entitled to such remuneration as the directors determine:
(a) for their services to the company as directors; and
(b) for any other service which they undertake for the company.

(3) Subject to the articles, a director's remuneration may:
(a) take any form; and
(b) include any arrangements in connection with the payment of a pension, allowance or gratuity, or any death, sickness or disability benefits, to or in respect of that director.
(4) Unless the directors decide otherwise, directors' remuneration accrues from day to day.
(5) Unless the directors decide otherwise, directors are not accountable to the company for any remuneration which they receive as directors or other officers or employees of the company's subsidiaries or of any other body corporate in which the company is interested.

Directors' expenses

24. The company may pay any reasonable expenses which the directors properly incur in connection with their attendance at:
(a) meetings of directors or committees of directors;
(b) general meetings; or
(c) separate meetings of the holders of any class of shares or of debentures of the company,
or otherwise in connection with the exercise of their powers and the discharge of their responsibilities in relation to the company.

ALTERNATE DIRECTORS

Appointment and removal of alternates

25. (1) Any director (the 'appointor') may appoint as an alternate any other director, or any other person approved by resolution of the directors, to:
(a) exercise that director's powers; and
(b) carry out that director's responsibilities,
in relation to the taking of decisions by the directors in the absence of the alternate's appointor.
(2) Any appointment or removal of an alternate must be effected by notice in writing to the company signed by the appointor, or in any other manner approved by the directors.
(3) The notice must:
(a) identify the proposed alternate; and
(b) in the case of a notice of appointment, contain a statement signed by the proposed alternate that the proposed alternate is willing to act as the alternate of the director giving the notice.

Rights and responsibilities of alternate directors

26. (1) An alternate director has the same rights, in relation to any directors' meeting or directors' written resolution, as the alternate's appointor.
(2) Except as the articles specify otherwise, alternate directors:

(a) are deemed for all purposes to be directors;
(b) are liable for their own acts and omissions;
(c) are subject to the same restrictions as their appointors; and
(d) are not deemed to be agents of or for their appointors.
(3) A person who is an alternate director but not a director:
(a) may be counted as participating for the purposes of determining whether a quorum is participating (but only if that person's appointor is not participating); and
(b) may sign a written resolution (but only if it is not signed or to be signed by that person's appointor).
No alternate may be counted as more than one director for such purposes.
(4) An alternate director is not entitled to receive any remuneration from the company for serving as an alternate director except such part of the alternate's appointor's remuneration as the appointor may direct by notice in writing made to the company.

Termination of alternate directorship

27. An alternate director's appointment as an alternate terminates:
(a) when the alternate's appointor revokes the appointment by notice to the company in writing specifying when it is to terminate;
(b) on the occurrence in relation to the alternate of any event which, if it occurred in relation to the alternate's appointor, would result in the termination of the appointor's appointment as a director;
(c) on the death of the alternate's appointor; or
(d) when the alternate's appointor's appointment as a director terminates, except that an alternate's appointment as an alternate does not terminate when the appointor retires by rotation at a general meeting and is then reappointed as a director at the same general meeting.

PART 3: DECISION-MAKING BY MEMBERS

ORGANISATION OF GENERAL MEETINGS

Members can call a general meeting if not enough directors

28. If:
(a) the company has fewer than two directors; and
(b) the director (if any) is unable or unwilling to appoint sufficient directors to make up a quorum or to call a general meeting to do so,
then two or more members may call a general meeting (or instruct the company secretary to do so) for the purpose of appointing one or more directors.

Attendance and speaking at general meetings

29. (1) A person is able to exercise the right to speak at a general meeting when that person is in a position to communicate to all those attending the meeting, during the meeting, any information or opinions which that person has on the business of the meeting.

(2) A person is able to exercise the right to vote at a general meeting when:

(a) that person is able to vote, during the meeting, on resolutions put to the vote at the meeting; and

(b) that person's vote can be taken into account in determining whether or not such resolutions are passed at the same time as the votes of all the other persons attending the meeting.

(3) The directors may make whatever arrangements they consider appropriate to enable those attending a general meeting to exercise their rights to speak or vote at it.

(4) In determining attendance at a general meeting, it is immaterial whether any two or more members attending it are in the same place as each other.

(5) Two or more persons who are not in the same place as each other attend a general meeting if their circumstances are such that if they have (or were to have) rights to speak and vote at that meeting, they are (or would be) able to exercise them.

Quorum for general meetings

30. No business other than the appointment of the chairman of the meeting is to be transacted at a general meeting if the persons attending it do not constitute a quorum.

Chairing general meetings

31. (1) If the directors have appointed a chairman, the chairman shall chair general meetings if present and willing to do so.

(2) If the directors have not appointed a chairman, or if the chairman is unwilling to chair the meeting or is not present within ten minutes of the time at which a meeting was due to start:

(a) the directors present; or

(b) (if no directors are present), the meeting,

must appoint a director or member to chair the meeting, and the appointment of the chairman of the meeting must be the first business of the meeting.

(3) The person chairing a meeting in accordance with this article is referred to as 'the chairman of the meeting'.

Attendance and speaking by directors and non-members

32. (1) Directors may attend and speak at general meetings, whether or not they are members.

(2) The chairman of the meeting may permit other persons who are not:

(a) members of the company; or

(b) otherwise entitled to exercise the rights of members in relation to general meetings,

to attend and speak at a general meeting.

Adjournment

33. (1) If the persons attending a general meeting within half an hour of the time at which the meeting was due to start do not constitute a quorum, or if during a meeting a quorum ceases to be present, the chairman of the meeting must adjourn it.

(2) The chairman of the meeting may adjourn a general meeting at which a quorum is present if:

(a) the meeting consents to an adjournment; or

(b) it appears to the chairman of the meeting that an adjournment is necessary to protect the safety of any person attending the meeting or ensure that the business of the meeting is conducted in an orderly manner.

(3) The chairman of the meeting must adjourn a general meeting if directed to do so by the meeting.

(4) When adjourning a general meeting, the chairman of the meeting must:

(a) either specify the time and place to which it is adjourned or state that it is to continue at a time and place to be fixed by the directors; and

(b) have regard to any directions as to the time and place of any adjournment which have been given by the meeting.

(5) If the continuation of an adjourned meeting is to take place more than 14 days after it was adjourned, the company must give at least seven clear days' notice of it (that is, excluding the day of the adjourned meeting and the day on which the notice is given):

(a) to the same persons to whom notice of the company's general meetings is required to be given; and

(b) containing the same information which such notice is required to contain.

(6) No business may be transacted at an adjourned general meeting which could not properly have been transacted at the meeting if the adjournment had not taken place.

VOTING AT GENERAL MEETINGS

Voting: general

34. A resolution put to the vote of a general meeting must be decided on a show of hands unless a poll is duly demanded in accordance with the articles.

Errors and disputes

35. (1) No objection may be raised to the qualification of any person voting at a general meeting except at the meeting or adjourned meeting at which the vote objected to is tendered, and every vote not disallowed at the meeting is valid.

(2) Any such objection must be referred to the chairman of the meeting whose decision is final.

Demanding a poll

36. (1) A poll on a resolution may be demanded:
(a) in advance of the general meeting where it is to be put to the vote; or
(b) at a general meeting, either before a show of hands on that resolution or immediately after the result of a show of hands on that resolution is declared.
(2) A poll may be demanded by:
(a) the chairman of the meeting;
(b) the directors;
(c) two or more persons having the right to vote on the resolution; or
(d) a person or persons representing not less than one tenth of the total voting rights of all the members having the right to vote on the resolution.
(3) A demand for a poll may be withdrawn if:
(a) the poll has not yet been taken; and
(b) the chairman of the meeting consents to the withdrawal.

Procedure on a poll

37. (1) Subject to the articles, polls at general meetings must be taken when, where and in such manner as the chairman of the meeting directs.
(2) The chairman of the meeting may appoint scrutineers (who need not be members) and decide how and when the result of the poll is to be declared.
(3) The result of a poll shall be the decision of the meeting in respect of the resolution on which the poll was demanded.
(4) A poll on:
(a) the election of the chairman of the meeting; or
(b) a question of adjournment,
must be taken immediately.
(5) Other polls must be taken within 30 days of their being demanded.
(6) A demand for a poll does not prevent a general meeting from continuing, except as regards the question on which the poll was demanded.
(7) No notice need be given of a poll not taken immediately if the time and place at which it is to be taken are announced at the meeting at which it is demanded.
(8) In any other case, at least seven days' notice must be given specifying the time and place at which the poll is to be taken.

Content of proxy notices

38. (1) Proxies may only validly be appointed by a notice in writing (a 'proxy notice') which:
(a) states the name and address of the member appointing the proxy;
(b) identifies the person appointed to be that member's proxy and the general meeting in relation to which that person is appointed;
(c) is signed by or on behalf of the member appointing the proxy, or is authenticated in such manner as the directors may determine; and

(d) is delivered to the company in accordance with the articles and any instructions contained in the notice of the general meeting to which they relate.

(2) The company may require proxy notices to be delivered in a particular form, and may specify different forms for different purposes.

(3) Proxy notices may specify how the proxy appointed under them is to vote (or that the proxy is to abstain from voting) on one or more resolutions.

(4) Unless a proxy notice indicates otherwise, it must be treated as:

(a) allowing the person appointed under it as a proxy discretion as to how to vote on any ancillary or procedural resolutions put to the meeting; and

(b) appointing that person as a proxy in relation to any adjournment of the general meeting to which it relates as well as the meeting itself.

Delivery of proxy notices

39. (1) Any notice of a general meeting must specify the address or addresses ('proxy notification address') at which the company or its agents will receive proxy notices relating to that meeting, or any adjournment of it, delivered in hard copy or electronic form.

(2) A person who is entitled to attend, speak or vote (either on a show of hands or on a poll) at a general meeting remains so entitled in respect of that meeting or any adjournment of it, even though a valid proxy notice has been delivered to the company by or on behalf of that person.

(3) Subject to paragraphs (4) and (5), a proxy notice must be delivered to a proxy notification address not less than 48 hours before the general meeting or adjourned meeting to which it relates.

(4) In the case of a poll taken more than 48 hours after it is demanded, the notice must be delivered to a proxy notification address not less than 24 hours before the time appointed for the taking of the poll.

(5) In the case of a poll not taken during the meeting but taken not more than 48 hours after it was demanded, the proxy notice must be delivered:

(a) in accordance with paragraph (3); or

(b) at the meeting at which the poll was demanded to the chairman, secretary or any director.

(6) An appointment under a proxy notice may be revoked by delivering a notice in writing given by or on behalf of the person by whom or on whose behalf the proxy notice was given to a proxy notification address.

(7) A notice revoking a proxy appointment only takes effect if it is delivered before:

(a) the start of the meeting or adjourned meeting to which it relates; or

(b) (in the case of a poll not taken on the same day as the meeting or adjourned meeting) the time appointed for taking the poll to which it relates.

(8) If a proxy notice is not signed by the person appointing the proxy, it must be accompanied by written evidence of the authority of the person who executed it to execute it on the appointor's behalf.

Amendments to resolutions

40. (1) An ordinary resolution to be proposed at a general meeting may be amended by ordinary resolution if:

(a) notice of the proposed amendment is given to the company secretary in writing by a person entitled to vote at the general meeting at which it is to be proposed not less than 48 hours before the meeting is to take place (or such later time as the chairman of the meeting may determine); and

(b) the proposed amendment does not, in the reasonable opinion of the chairman of the meeting, materially alter the scope of the resolution.

(2) A special resolution to be proposed at a general meeting may be amended by ordinary resolution, if:

(a) the chairman of the meeting proposes the amendment at the general meeting at which the resolution is to be proposed; and

(b) the amendment does not go beyond what is necessary to correct a grammatical or other non-substantive error in the resolution.

(3) If the chairman of the meeting, acting in good faith, wrongly decides that an amendment to a resolution is out of order, the chairman's error does not invalidate the vote on that resolution.

RESTRICTIONS ON MEMBERS' RIGHTS

No voting of shares on which money owed to company

41. No voting rights attached to a share may be exercised at any general meeting, at any adjournment of it, or on any poll called at or in relation to it, unless all amounts payable to the company in respect of that share have been paid.

APPLICATION OF RULES TO CLASS MEETINGS

Class meetings

42. The provisions of the articles relating to general meetings apply, with any necessary modifications, to meetings of the holders of any class of shares.

PART 4: SHARES AND DISTRIBUTIONS

ISSUE OF SHARES

Powers to issue different classes of share

43. (1) Subject to the articles, but without prejudice to the rights attached to any existing share, the company may issue shares with such rights or restrictions as may be determined by ordinary resolution.

(2) The company may issue shares which are to be redeemed, or are liable to be redeemed at the option of the company or the holder, and the directors may determine the terms, conditions and manner of redemption of any such shares.

Payment of commissions on subscription for shares

44. (1) The company may pay any person a commission in consideration for that person:

(a) subscribing, or agreeing to subscribe, for shares; or

(b) procuring, or agreeing to procure, subscriptions for shares.

(2) Any such commission may be paid:

(a) in cash, or in fully paid or partly paid shares or other securities, or partly in one way and partly in the other; and

(b) in respect of a conditional or an absolute subscription.

INTERESTS IN SHARES

Company not bound by less than absolute interests

45. Except as required by law, no person is to be recognised by the company as holding any share upon any trust, and except as otherwise required by law or the articles, the company is not in any way to be bound by or recognise any interest in a share other than the holder's absolute ownership of it and all the rights attaching to it.

SHARE CERTIFICATES

Certificates to be issued except in certain cases

46. (1) The company must issue each member with one or more certificates in respect of the shares which that member holds.

(2) This article does not apply to:

(a) uncertificated shares;

(b) shares in respect of which a share warrant has been issued; or

(c) shares in respect of which the Companies Acts permit the company not to issue a certificate.

(3) Except as otherwise specified in the articles, all certificates must be issued free of charge.

(4) No certificate may be issued in respect of shares of more than one class.

(5) If more than one person holds a share, only one certificate may be issued in respect of it.

Contents and execution of share certificates

47. (1) Every certificate must specify:

(a) in respect of how many shares, of what class, it is issued;

(b) the nominal value of those shares;

(c) the amount paid up on them; and

(d) any distinguishing numbers assigned to them.

(2) Certificates must:

(a) have affixed to them the company's common seal or an official seal which is a facsimile of the company's common seal with the addition on its face of the word 'Securities' (a 'securities seal'); or
(b) be otherwise executed in accordance with the Companies Acts.

Consolidated share certificates

48. (1) When a member's holding of shares of a particular class increases, the company may issue that member with:
(a) a single, consolidated certificate in respect of all the shares of a particular class which that member holds, or
(b) a separate certificate in respect of only those shares by which that member's holding has increased.
(2) When a member's holding of shares of a particular class is reduced, the company must ensure that the member is issued with one or more certificates in respect of the number of shares held by the member after that reduction. But the company need not (in the absence of a request from the member) issue any new certificate if:
(a) all the shares which the member no longer holds as a result of the reduction; and
(b) none of the shares which the member retains following the reduction,
were, immediately before the reduction, represented by the same certificate.
(3) A member may request the company, in writing, to replace:
(a) the member's separate certificates with a consolidated certificate; or
(b) the member's consolidated certificate with two or more separate certificates representing such proportion of the shares as the member may specify.
(4) When the company complies with such a request, it may charge such reasonable fee as the directors may decide for doing so.
(5) A consolidated certificate must not be issued unless any certificates which it is to replace have first been returned to the company for cancellation.

Replacement share certificates

49. (1) If a certificate issued in respect of a member's shares is:
(a) damaged or defaced; or
(b) said to be lost, stolen or destroyed,
that member is entitled to be issued with a replacement certificate in respect of the same shares.
(2) A member exercising the right to be issued with such a replacement certificate:
(a) may at the same time exercise the right to be issued with a single certificate or separate certificates;
(b) must return the certificate which is to be replaced to the company if it is damaged or defaced; and

(c) must comply with such conditions as to evidence, indemnity and the payment of a reasonable fee as the directors decide.

SHARES NOT HELD IN CERTIFICATED FORM

Uncertificated shares

50. (1) In this article, 'the relevant rules' means:

(a) any applicable provision of the Companies Acts about the holding, evidencing of title to, or transfer of shares other than in certificated form; and

(b) any applicable legislation, rules or other arrangements made under or by virtue of such provision.

(2) The provisions of this article have effect subject to the relevant rules.

(3) Any provision of the articles which is inconsistent with the relevant rules must be disregarded, to the extent that it is inconsistent, whenever the relevant rules apply.

(4) Any share or class of shares of the company may be issued or held on such terms, or in such a way, that:

(a) title to it or them is not, or must not be, evidenced by a certificate; or

(b) it or they may or must be transferred wholly or partly without a certificate.

(5) The directors have power to take such steps as they think fit in relation to:

(a) the evidencing of and transfer of title to uncertificated shares (including in connection with the issue of such shares);

(b) any records relating to the holding of uncertificated shares;

(c) the conversion of certificated shares into uncertificated shares; or

(d) the conversion of uncertificated shares into certificated shares.

(6) The company may by notice to the holder of a share require that share:

(a) if it is uncertificated, to be converted into certificated form; and

(b) if it is certificated, to be converted into uncertificated form,

to enable it to be dealt with in accordance with the articles.

(7) If:

(a) the articles give the directors power to take action, or require other persons to take action, in order to sell, transfer or otherwise dispose of shares; and

(b) uncertificated shares are subject to that power, but the power is expressed in terms which assume the use of a certificate or other written instrument,

the directors may take such action as is necessary or expedient to achieve the same results when exercising that power in relation to uncertificated shares.

(8) In particular, the directors may take such action as they consider appropriate to achieve the sale, transfer, disposal, forfeiture, re-allotment or surrender of an uncertificated share or otherwise to enforce a lien in respect of it.

(9) Unless the directors otherwise determine, shares which a member holds in uncertificated form must be treated as separate holdings from any shares which that member holds in certificated form.

(10) A class of shares must not be treated as two classes simply because some shares of that class are held in certificated form and others are held in uncertificated form.

Share warrants

51. (1) The directors may issue a share warrant in respect of any fully paid share.
(2) Share warrants must be:
(a) issued in such form; and
(b) executed in such manner,
as the directors decide.
(3) A share represented by a share warrant may be transferred by delivery of the warrant representing it.
(4) The directors may make provision for the payment of dividends in respect of any share represented by a share warrant.
(5) Subject to the articles, the directors may decide the conditions on which any share warrant is issued. In particular, they may:
(a) decide the conditions on which new warrants are to be issued in place of warrants which are damaged or defaced, or said to have been lost, stolen or destroyed;
(b) decide the conditions on which bearers of warrants are entitled to attend and vote at general meetings;
(c) decide the conditions subject to which bearers of warrants may surrender their warrant so as to hold their shares in certificated or uncertificated form instead; and
(d) vary the conditions of issue of any warrant from time to time,
and the bearer of a warrant is subject to the conditions and procedures in force in relation to it, whether or not they were decided or specified before the warrant was issued.
(6) Subject to the conditions on which the warrants are issued from time to time, bearers of share warrants have the same rights and privileges as they would if their names had been included in the register as holders of the shares represented by their warrants.
(7) The company must not in any way be bound by or recognise any interest in a share represented by a share warrant other than the absolute right of the bearer of that warrant to that warrant.

PARTLY PAID SHARES

Company's lien over partly paid shares

52. (1) The company has a lien ('the company's lien') over every share which is partly paid for any part of:
(a) that share's nominal value; and
(b) any premium at which it was issued,

which has not been paid to the company, and which is payable immediately or at some time in the future, whether or not a call notice has been sent in respect of it.
(2) The company's lien over a share:
(a) takes priority over any third party's interest in that share; and
(b) extends to any dividend or other money payable by the company in respect of that share and (if the lien is enforced and the share is sold by the company) the proceeds of sale of that share.
(3) The directors may at any time decide that a share which is or would otherwise be subject to the company's lien shall not be subject to it, either wholly or in part.

Enforcement of the company's lien

53. (1) Subject to the provisions of this article, if:
(a) a lien enforcement notice has been given in respect of a share; and
(b) the person to whom the notice was given has failed to comply with it,
the company may sell that share in such manner as the directors decide.
(2) A lien enforcement notice:
(a) may only be given in respect of a share which is subject to the company's lien, in respect of which a sum is payable and the due date for payment of that sum has passed;
(b) must specify the share concerned;
(c) must require payment of the sum payable within 14 days of the notice;
(d) must be addressed either to the holder of the share or to a person entitled to it by reason of the holder's death, bankruptcy or otherwise; and
(e) must state the company's intention to sell the share if the notice is not complied with.
(3) Where shares are sold under this article:
(a) the directors may authorise any person to execute an instrument of transfer of the shares to the purchaser or a person nominated by the purchaser; and
(b) the transferee is not bound to see to the application of the consideration, and the transferee's title is not affected by any irregularity in or invalidity of the process leading to the sale.
(4) The net proceeds of any such sale (after payment of the costs of sale and any other costs of enforcing the lien) must be applied:
(a) first, in payment of so much of the sum for which the lien exists as was payable at the date of the lien enforcement notice; and
(b) second, to the person entitled to the shares at the date of the sale, but only after the certificate for the shares sold has been surrendered to the company for cancellation or a suitable indemnity has been given for any lost certificates, and subject to a lien equivalent to the company's lien over the shares before the sale for any money payable in respect of the shares after the date of the lien enforcement notice.
(5) A statutory declaration by a director or the company secretary that the declarant is a director or the company secretary and that a share has been sold to satisfy the company's lien on a specified date:

(a) is conclusive evidence of the facts stated in it as against all persons claiming to be entitled to the share; and
(b) subject to compliance with any other formalities of transfer required by the articles or by law, constitutes a good title to the share.

Call notices

54. (1) Subject to the articles and the terms on which shares are allotted, the directors may send a notice (a 'call notice') to a member requiring the member to pay the company a specified sum of money (a 'call') which is payable in respect of shares which that member holds at the date when the directors decide to send the call notice.
(2) A call notice:
(a) may not require a member to pay a call which exceeds the total sum unpaid on that member's shares (whether as to the share's nominal value or any amount payable to the company by way of premium);
(b) must state when and how any call to which it relates it is to be paid; and
(c) may permit or require the call to be paid by instalments.
(3) A member must comply with the requirements of a call notice, but no member is obliged to pay any call before 14 days have passed since the notice was sent.
(4) Before the company has received any call due under a call notice the directors may:
(a) revoke it wholly or in part; or
(b) specify a later time for payment than is specified in the notice,
by a further notice in writing to the member in respect of whose shares the call is made.

Liability to pay calls

55. (1) Liability to pay a call is not extinguished or transferred by transferring the shares in respect of which it is required to be paid.
(2) Joint holders of a share are jointly and severally liable to pay all calls in respect of that share.
(3) Subject to the terms on which shares are allotted, the directors may, when issuing shares, provide that call notices sent to the holders of those shares may require them:
(a) to pay calls which are not the same; or
(b) to pay calls at different times.

When call notice need not be issued

56. (1) A call notice need not be issued in respect of sums which are specified, in the terms on which a share is issued, as being payable to the company in respect of that share (whether in respect of nominal value or premium):

(a) on allotment;
(b) on the occurrence of a particular event; or
(c) on a date fixed by or in accordance with the terms of issue.

(2) But if the due date for payment of such a sum has passed and it has not been paid, the holder of the share concerned is treated in all respects as having failed to comply with a call notice in respect of that sum, and is liable to the same consequences as regards the payment of interest and forfeiture.

Failure to comply with call notice: automatic consequences

57. (1) If a person is liable to pay a call and fails to do so by the call payment date:
(a) the directors may issue a notice of intended forfeiture to that person; and
(b) until the call is paid, that person must pay the company interest on the call from the call payment date at the relevant rate.

(2) For the purposes of this article:
(a) the 'call payment date' is the time when the call notice states that a call is payable, unless the directors give a notice specifying a later date, in which case the 'call payment date' is that later date; and
(b) the 'relevant rate' is:
  (i) the rate fixed by the terms on which the share in respect of which the call is due was allotted;
  (ii) such other rate as was fixed in the call notice which required payment of the call, or has otherwise been determined by the directors; or
  (iii) if no rate is fixed in either of these ways, 5% per annum.

(3) The relevant rate must not exceed by more than 5 percentage points the base lending rate most recently set by the Monetary Policy Committee of the Bank of England in connection with its responsibilities under Part 2 of the Bank of England Act 1998(2).

(4) The directors may waive any obligation to pay interest on a call wholly or in part.

Notice of intended forfeiture

58. A notice of intended forfeiture:
(a) may be sent in respect of any share in respect of which a call has not been paid as required by a call notice;
(b) must be sent to the holder of that share or to a person entitled to it by reason of the holder's death, bankruptcy or otherwise;
(c) must require payment of the call and any accrued interest by a date which is not less than 14 days after the date of the notice;
(d) must state how the payment is to be made; and
(e) must state that if the notice is not complied with, the shares in respect of which the call is payable will be liable to be forfeited.

Directors' power to forfeit shares

59. If a notice of intended forfeiture is not complied with before the date by which payment of the call is required in the notice of intended forfeiture, the directors may decide that any share in respect of which it was given is forfeited, and the forfeiture is to include all dividends or other moneys payable in respect of the forfeited shares and not paid before the forfeiture.

Effect of forfeiture

60. (1) Subject to the articles, the forfeiture of a share extinguishes:
(a) all interests in that share, and all claims and demands against the company in respect of it; and
(b) all other rights and liabilities incidental to the share as between the person whose share it was prior to the forfeiture and the company.
(2) Any share which is forfeited in accordance with the articles:
(a) is deemed to have been forfeited when the directors decide that it is forfeited;
(b) is deemed to be the property of the company; and
(c) may be sold, re-allotted or otherwise disposed of as the directors think fit.
(3) If a person's shares have been forfeited:
(a) the company must send that person notice that forfeiture has occurred and record it in the register of members;
(b) that person ceases to be a member in respect of those shares;
(c) that person must surrender the certificate for the shares forfeited to the company for cancellation;
(d) that person remains liable to the company for all sums payable by that person under the articles at the date of forfeiture in respect of those shares, including any interest (whether accrued before or after the date of forfeiture); and
(e) the directors may waive payment of such sums wholly or in part or enforce payment without any allowance for the value of the shares at the time of forfeiture or for any consideration received on their disposal.
(4) At any time before the company disposes of a forfeited share, the directors may decide to cancel the forfeiture on payment of all calls and interest due in respect of it and on such other terms as they think fit.

Procedure following forfeiture

61. (1) If a forfeited share is to be disposed of by being transferred, the company may receive the consideration for the transfer and the directors may authorise any person to execute the instrument of transfer.
(2) A statutory declaration by a director or the company secretary that the declarant is a director or the company secretary and that a share has been forfeited on a specified date:
(a) is conclusive evidence of the facts stated in it as against all persons claiming to be entitled to the share; and

(b) subject to compliance with any other formalities of transfer required by the articles or by law, constitutes a good title to the share.

(3) A person to whom a forfeited share is transferred is not bound to see to the application of the consideration (if any) nor is that person's title to the share affected by any irregularity in or invalidity of the process leading to the forfeiture or transfer of the share.

(4) If the company sells a forfeited share, the person who held it prior to its forfeiture is entitled to receive from the company the proceeds of such sale, net of any commission, and excluding any amount which:

(a) was, or would have become, payable; and

(b) had not, when that share was forfeited, been paid by that person in respect of that share,

but no interest is payable to such a person in respect of such proceeds and the company is not required to account for any money earned on them.

Surrender of shares

62. (1) A member may surrender any share:

(a) in respect of which the directors may issue a notice of intended forfeiture;

(b) which the directors may forfeit; or

(c) which has been forfeited.

(2) The directors may accept the surrender of any such share.

(3) The effect of surrender on a share is the same as the effect of forfeiture on that share.

(4) A share which has been surrendered may be dealt with in the same way as a share which has been forfeited.

TRANSFER AND TRANSMISSION OF SHARES

Transfers of certificated shares

63. (1) Certificated shares may be transferred by means of an instrument of transfer in any usual form or any other form approved by the directors, which is executed by or on behalf of:

(a) the transferor; and

(b) (if any of the shares is partly paid) the transferee.

(2) No fee may be charged for registering any instrument of transfer or other document relating to or affecting the title to any share.

(3) The company may retain any instrument of transfer which is registered.

(4) The transferor remains the holder of a certificated share until the transferee's name is entered in the register of members as holder of it.

(5) The directors may refuse to register the transfer of a certificated share if:

(a) the share is not fully paid;

(b) the transfer is not lodged at the company's registered office or such other place as the directors have appointed;

(c) the transfer is not accompanied by the certificate for the shares to which it relates, or such other evidence as the directors may reasonably require to show the transferor's right to make the transfer, or evidence of the right of someone other than the transferor to make the transfer on the transferor's behalf;
(d) the transfer is in respect of more than one class of share; or
(e) the transfer is in favour of more than four transferees.
(6) If the directors refuse to register the transfer of a share, the instrument of transfer must be returned to the transferee with the notice of refusal unless they suspect that the proposed transfer may be fraudulent.

Transfer of uncertificated shares

64. A transfer of an uncertificated share must not be registered if it is in favour of more than four transferees.

Transmission of shares

65. (1) If title to a share passes to a transmittee, the company may only recognise the transmittee as having any title to that share.
(2) Nothing in these articles releases the estate of a deceased member from any liability in respect of a share solely or jointly held by that member.

Transmittees' rights

66. (1) A transmittee who produces such evidence of entitlement to shares as the directors may properly require:
(a) may, subject to the articles, choose either to become the holder of those shares or to have them transferred to another person; and
(b) subject to the articles, and pending any transfer of the shares to another person, has the same rights as the holder had.
(2) But transmittees do not have the right to attend or vote at a general meeting in respect of shares to which they are entitled, by reason of the holder's death or bankruptcy or otherwise, unless they become the holders of those shares

Exercise of transmittees' rights

67. (1) Transmittees who wish to become the holders of shares to which they have become entitled must notify the company in writing of that wish.
(2) If the share is a certificated share and a transmittee wishes to have it transferred to another person, the transmittee must execute an instrument of transfer in respect of it.
(3) If the share is an uncertificated share and the transmittee wishes to have it transferred to another person, the transmittee must:
(a) procure that all appropriate instructions are given to effect the transfer; or
(b) procure that the uncertificated share is changed into certificated form and then execute an instrument of transfer in respect of it.
(4) Any transfer made or executed under this article is to be treated as if it were made or executed by the person from whom the transmittee has derived rights in

respect of the share, and as if the event which gave rise to the transmission had not occurred.

Transmittees bound by prior notices

68. If a notice is given to a member in respect of shares and a transmittee is entitled to those shares, the transmittee is bound by the notice if it was given to the member before the transmittee's name has been entered in the register of members.

CONSOLIDATION OF SHARES

Procedure for disposing of fractions of shares

69. (1) This article applies where:
(a) there has been a consolidation or division of shares; and
(b) as a result, members are entitled to fractions of shares.
(2) The directors may:
(a) sell the shares representing the fractions to any person including the company for the best price reasonably obtainable;
(b) in the case of a certificated share, authorise any person to execute an instrument of transfer of the shares to the purchaser or a person nominated by the purchaser; and
(c) distribute the net proceeds of sale in due proportion among the holders of the shares.
(3) Where any holder's entitlement to a portion of the proceeds of sale amounts to less than a minimum figure determined by the directors, that member's portion may be distributed to an organisation which is a charity for the purposes of the law of England and Wales, Scotland or Northern Ireland.
(4) The person to whom the shares are transferred is not obliged to ensure that any purchase money is received by the person entitled to the relevant fractions.
(5) The transferee's title to the shares is not affected by any irregularity in or invalidity of the process leading to their sale.

DISTRIBUTIONS

Procedure for declaring dividends

70. (1) The company may by ordinary resolution declare dividends, and the directors may decide to pay interim dividends.
(2) A dividend must not be declared unless the directors have made a recommendation as to its amount. Such a dividend must not exceed the amount recommended by the directors.
(3) No dividend may be declared or paid unless it is in accordance with members' respective rights.

(4) Unless the members' resolution to declare or directors' decision to pay a dividend, or the terms on which shares are issued, specify otherwise, it must be paid by reference to each member's holding of shares on the date of the resolution or decision to declare or pay it.
(5) If the company's share capital is divided into different classes, no interim dividend may be paid on shares carrying deferred or non-preferred rights if, at the time of payment, any preferential dividend is in arrears.
(6) The directors may pay at intervals any dividend payable at a fixed rate if it appears to them that the profits available for distribution justify the payment.
(7) If the directors act in good faith, they do not incur any liability to the holders of shares conferring preferred rights for any loss they may suffer by the lawful payment of an interim dividend on shares with deferred or non-preferred rights.

Calculation of dividends

71. (1) Except as otherwise provided by the articles or the rights attached to shares, all dividends must be:
(a) declared and paid according to the amounts paid up on the shares on which the dividend is paid; and
(b) apportioned and paid proportionately to the amounts paid up on the shares during any portion or portions of the period in respect of which the dividend is paid.
(2) If any share is issued on terms providing that it ranks for dividend as from a particular date, that share ranks for dividend accordingly.
(3) For the purposes of calculating dividends, no account is to be taken of any amount which has been paid up on a share in advance of the due date for payment of that amount.

Payment of dividends and other distributions

72. (1) Where a dividend or other sum which is a distribution is payable in respect of a share, it must be paid by one or more of the following means:
(a) transfer to a bank or building society account specified by the distribution recipient either in writing or as the directors may otherwise decide;
(b) sending a cheque made payable to the distribution recipient by post to the distribution recipient at the distribution recipient's registered address (if the distribution recipient is a holder of the share), or (in any other case) to an address specified by the distribution recipient either in writing or as the directors may otherwise decide;
(c) sending a cheque made payable to such person by post to such person at such address as the distribution recipient has specified either in writing or as the directors may otherwise decide; or
(d) any other means of payment as the directors agree with the distribution recipient either in writing or by such other means as the directors decide.

(2) In the articles, 'the distribution recipient' means, in respect of a share in respect of which a dividend or other sum is payable:
(a) the holder of the share; or
(b) if the share has two or more joint holders, whichever of them is named first in the register of members; or
(c) if the holder is no longer entitled to the share by reason of death or bankruptcy, or otherwise by operation of law, the transmittee.

Deductions from distributions in respect of sums owed to the company

73. (1) If:
(a) a share is subject to the company's lien; and
(b) the directors are entitled to issue a lien enforcement notice in respect of it,
they may, instead of issuing a lien enforcement notice, deduct from any dividend or other sum payable in respect of the share any sum of money which is payable to the company in respect of that share to the extent that they are entitled to require payment under a lien enforcement notice.
(2) Money so deducted must be used to pay any of the sums payable in respect of that share.
(3) The company must notify the distribution recipient in writing of:
(a) the fact and amount of any such deduction;
(b) any non-payment of a dividend or other sum payable in respect of a share resulting from any such deduction; and
(c) how the money deducted has been applied.

No interest on distributions

74. The company may not pay interest on any dividend or other sum payable in respect of a share unless otherwise provided by:
(a) the terms on which the share was issued; or
(b) the provisions of another agreement between the holder of that share and the company.

Unclaimed distributions

75. (1) All dividends or other sums which are:
(a) payable in respect of shares; and
(b) unclaimed after having been declared or become payable,
may be invested or otherwise made use of by the directors for the benefit of the company until claimed.
(2) The payment of any such dividend or other sum into a separate account does not make the company a trustee in respect of it.
(3) If:
(a) 12 years have passed from the date on which a dividend or other sum became due for payment; and
(b) the distribution recipient has not claimed it,

the distribution recipient is no longer entitled to that dividend or other sum and it ceases to remain owing by the company.

Non-cash distributions

76. (1) Subject to the terms of issue of the share in question, the company may, by ordinary resolution on the recommendation of the directors, decide to pay all or part of a dividend or other distribution payable in respect of a share by transferring non-cash assets of equivalent value (including, without limitation, shares or other securities in any company).
(2) If the shares in respect of which such a non-cash distribution is paid are uncertificated, any shares in the company which are issued as a non-cash distribution in respect of them must be uncertificated.
(3) For the purposes of paying a non-cash distribution, the directors may make whatever arrangements they think fit, including, where any difficulty arises regarding the distribution:
(a) fixing the value of any assets;
(b) paying cash to any distribution recipient on the basis of that value in order to adjust the rights of recipients; and
(c) vesting any assets in trustees.

Waiver of distributions

77. Distribution recipients may waive their entitlement to a dividend or other distribution payable in respect of a share by giving the company notice in writing to that effect, but if:
(a) the share has more than one holder; or
(b) more than one person is entitled to the share, whether by reason of the death or bankruptcy of one or more joint holders, or otherwise,
the notice is not effective unless it is expressed to be given, and signed, by all the holders or persons otherwise entitled to the share.

CAPITALISATION OF PROFITS

Authority to capitalise and appropriation of capitalised sums

78. (1) Subject to the articles, the directors may, if they are so authorised by an ordinary resolution:
(a) decide to capitalise any profits of the company (whether or not they are available for distribution) which are not required for paying a preferential dividend, or any sum standing to the credit of the company's share premium account or capital redemption reserve; and
(b) appropriate any sum which they so decide to capitalise (a 'capitalised sum') to the persons who would have been entitled to it if it were distributed by way of dividend (the 'persons entitled') and in the same proportions.
(2) Capitalised sums must be applied:

(a) on behalf of the persons entitled; and
(b) in the same proportions as a dividend would have been distributed to them.

(3) Any capitalised sum may be applied in paying up new shares of a nominal amount equal to the capitalised sum which are then allotted credited as fully paid to the persons entitled or as they may direct.

(4) A capitalised sum which was appropriated from profits available for distribution may be applied:

(a) in or towards paying up any amounts unpaid on existing shares held by the persons entitled; or
(b) in paying up new debentures of the company which are then allotted credited as fully paid to the persons entitled or as they may direct.

(5) Subject to the articles the directors may:

(a) apply capitalised sums in accordance with paragraphs (3) and (4) partly in one way and partly in another;
(b) make such arrangements as they think fit to deal with shares or debentures becoming distributable in fractions under this article (including the issuing of fractional certificates or the making of cash payments); and
(c) authorise any person to enter into an agreement with the company on behalf of all the persons entitled which is binding on them in respect of the allotment of shares and debentures to them under this article.

PART 5: MISCELLANEOUS PROVISIONS

COMMUNICATIONS

Means of communication to be used

79. (1) Subject to the articles, anything sent or supplied by or to the company under the articles may be sent or supplied in any way in which the Companies Act 2006 provides for documents or information which are authorised or required by any provision of that Act to be sent or supplied by or to the company.

(2) Subject to the articles, any notice or document to be sent or supplied to a director in connection with the taking of decisions by directors may also be sent or supplied by the means by which that director has asked to be sent or supplied with such notices or documents for the time being.

(3) A director may agree with the company that notices or documents sent to that director in a particular way are to be deemed to have been received within a specified time of their being sent, and for the specified time to be less than 48 hours.

Failure to notify contact details

80. (1) If:

(a) the company sends two consecutive documents to a member over a period of at least 12 months; and
(b) each of those documents is returned undelivered, or the company receives notification that it has not been delivered,

that member ceases to be entitled to receive notices from the company.
(2) A member who has ceased to be entitled to receive notices from the company becomes entitled to receive such notices again by sending the company:
(a) a new address to be recorded in the register of members; or
(b) if the member has agreed that the company should use a means of communication other than sending things to such an address, the information that the company needs to use that means of communication effectively.

ADMINISTRATIVE ARRANGEMENTS

Company seals

81. (1) Any common seal may only be used by the authority of the directors.
(2) The directors may decide by what means and in what form any common seal or securities seal is to be used.
(3) Unless otherwise decided by the directors, if the company has a common seal and it is affixed to a document, the document must also be signed by at least one authorised person in the presence of a witness who attests the signature.
(4) For the purposes of this article, an authorised person is:
(a) any director of the company;
(b) the company secretary; or
(c) any person authorised by the directors for the purpose of signing documents to which the common seal is applied.
(5) If the company has an official seal for use abroad, it may only be affixed to a document if its use on that document, or documents of a class to which it belongs, has been authorised by a decision of the directors.
(6) If the company has a securities seal, it may only be affixed to securities by the company secretary or a person authorised to apply it to securities by the company secretary.
(7) For the purposes of the articles, references to the securities seal being affixed to any document include the reproduction of the image of that seal on or in a document by any mechanical or electronic means which has been approved by the directors in relation to that document or documents of a class to which it belongs.

Destruction of documents

82. (1) The company is entitled to destroy:
(a) all instruments of transfer of shares which have been registered, and all other documents on the basis of which any entries are made in the register of members, from six years after the date of registration;
(b) all dividend mandates, variations or cancellations of dividend mandates, and notifications of change of address, from two years after they have been recorded;
(c) all share certificates which have been cancelled from one year after the date of the cancellation;

(d) all paid dividend warrants and cheques from one year after the date of actual payment; and
(e) all proxy notices from one year after the end of the meeting to which the proxy notice relates.

(2) If the company destroys a document in good faith, in accordance with the articles, and without notice of any claim to which that document may be relevant, it is conclusively presumed in favour of the company that:
(a) entries in the register purporting to have been made on the basis of an instrument of transfer or other document so destroyed were duly and properly made;
(b) any instrument of transfer so destroyed was a valid and effective instrument duly and properly registered;
(c) any share certificate so destroyed was a valid and effective certificate duly and properly cancelled; and
(d) any other document so destroyed was a valid and effective document in accordance with its recorded particulars in the books or records of the company.

(3) This article does not impose on the company any liability which it would not otherwise have if it destroys any document before the time at which this article permits it to do so.

(4) In this article, references to the destruction of any document include a reference to its being disposed of in any manner.

No right to inspect accounts and other records

83. Except as provided by law or authorised by the directors or an ordinary resolution of the company, no person is entitled to inspect any of the company's accounting or other records or documents merely by virtue of being a member.

Provision for employees on cessation of business

84. The directors may decide to make provision for the benefit of persons employed or formerly employed by the company or any of its subsidiaries (other than a director or former director or shadow director) in connection with the cessation or transfer to any person of the whole or part of the undertaking of the company or that subsidiary.

DIRECTORS' INDEMNITY AND INSURANCE

Indemnity

85. (1) Subject to paragraph (2), a relevant director of the company or an associated company may be indemnified out of the company's assets against:
(a) any liability incurred by that director in connection with any negligence, default, breach of duty or breach of trust in relation to the company or an associated company;
(b) any liability incurred by that director in connection with the activities of the company or an associated company in its capacity as a trustee of an

occupational pension scheme (as defined in section 235(6) of the Companies Act 2006), and

(c) any other liability incurred by that director as an officer of the company or an associated company.

(2) This article does not authorise any indemnity which would be prohibited or rendered void by any provision of the Companies Acts or by any other provision of law.

(3) In this article:

(a) companies are associated if one is a subsidiary of the other or both are subsidiaries of the same body corporate; and

(b) a 'relevant director' means any director or former director of the company or an associated company.

Insurance

86. (1) The directors may decide to purchase and maintain insurance, at the expense of the company, for the benefit of any relevant director in respect of any relevant loss.

(2) In this article:

(a) a 'relevant director' means any director or former director of the company or an associated company;

(b) a 'relevant loss' means any loss or liability which has been or may be incurred by a relevant director in connection with that director's duties or powers in relation to the company, any associated company or any pension fund or employees' share scheme of the company or associated company; and

(c) companies are associated if one is a subsidiary of the other or both are subsidiaries of the same body corporate.

Model Articles for a private company

Companies (Model Articles) Regulations 2008 Schedule 1 (SI 2008/3229)

MODEL ARTICLES FOR PRIVATE COMPANIES LIMITED BY SHARES

PART 1: INTERPRETATION AND LIMITATION OF LIABILITY

Defined terms

1. In the articles, unless the context requires otherwise:

'articles' means the company's articles of association;

'bankruptcy' includes individual insolvency proceedings in a jurisdiction other than England and Wales or Northern Ireland which have an effect similar to that of bankruptcy;

'chairman' has the meaning given in article 12;

'chairman of the meeting' has the meaning given in article 39;

'Companies Acts' means the Companies Acts (as defined in section 2 of the Companies Act 2006), in so far as they apply to the company;

'director' means a director of the company, and includes any person occupying the position of director, by whatever name called;

'distribution recipient' has the meaning given in article 31;

'document' includes, unless otherwise specified, any document sent or supplied in electronic form;

'electronic form' has the meaning given in section 1168 of the Companies Act 2006;

'fully paid' in relation to a share, means that the nominal value and any premium to be paid to the company in respect of that share have been paid to the company;

'hard copy form' has the meaning given in section 1168 of the Companies Act 2006;

'holder' in relation to shares means the person whose name is entered in the register of members as the holder of the shares;

'instrument' means a document in hard copy form;

'ordinary resolution' has the meaning given in section 282 of the Companies Act 2006;

'paid' means paid or credited as paid;

'participate', in relation to a directors' meeting, has the meaning given in article 10;

'proxy notice' has the meaning given in article 45;

'shareholder' means a person who is the holder of a share;

'shares' means shares in the company;

'special resolution' has the meaning given in section 283 of the Companies Act 2006;

'subsidiary' has the meaning given in section 1159 of the Companies Act 2006;

'transmittee' means a person entitled to a share by reason of the death or bankruptcy of a shareholder or otherwise by operation of law; and

'writing' means the representation or reproduction of words, symbols or other information in a visible form by any method or combination of methods, whether sent or supplied in electronic form or otherwise.

Unless the context otherwise requires, other words or expressions contained in these articles bear the same meaning as in the Companies Act 2006 as in force on the date when these articles become binding on the company.

Liability of members

2. The liability of the members is limited to the amount, if any, unpaid on the shares held by them.

PART 2: DIRECTORS

DIRECTORS' POWERS AND RESPONSIBILITIES

Directors' general authority

3. Subject to the articles, the directors are responsible for the management of the company's business, for which purpose they may exercise all the powers of the company.

Shareholders' reserve power

4. (1) The shareholders may, by special resolution, direct the directors to take, or refrain from taking, specified action.
(2) No such special resolution invalidates anything which the directors have done before the passing of the resolution.

Directors may delegate

5. (1) Subject to the articles, the directors may delegate any of the powers which are conferred on them under the articles:
(a) to such person or committee;
(b) by such means (including by power of attorney);
(c) to such an extent;
(d) in relation to such matters or territories; and
(e) on such terms and conditions,
as they think fit.
(2) If the directors so specify, any such delegation may authorise further delegation of the directors' powers by any person to whom they are delegated.
(3) The directors may revoke any delegation in whole or part, or alter its terms and conditions.

Committees

6. (1) Committees to which the directors delegate any of their powers must follow procedures which are based as far as they are applicable on those provisions of the articles which govern the taking of decisions by directors.
(2) The directors may make rules of procedure for all or any committees, which prevail over rules derived from the articles if they are not consistent with them.

DECISION-MAKING BY DIRECTORS

Directors to take decisions collectively

7. (1) The general rule about decision-making by directors is that any decision of the directors must be either a majority decision at a meeting or a decision taken in accordance with article 8.
(2) If:
(a) the company only has one director; and
(b) no provision of the articles requires it to have more than one director,
the general rule does not apply, and the director may take decisions without regard to any of the provisions of the articles relating to directors' decision-making.

Unanimous decisions

8. (1) A decision of the directors is taken in accordance with this article when all eligible directors indicate to each other by any means that they share a common view on a matter.
(2) Such a decision may take the form of a resolution in writing, copies of which have been signed by each eligible director or to which each eligible director has otherwise indicated agreement in writing.
(3) References in this article to eligible directors are to directors who would have been entitled to vote on the matter had it been proposed as a resolution at a directors' meeting.
(4) A decision may not be taken in accordance with this article if the eligible directors would not have formed a quorum at such a meeting.

Calling a directors' meeting

9. (1) Any director may call a directors' meeting by giving notice of the meeting to the directors or by authorising the company secretary (if any) to give such notice.
(2) Notice of any directors' meeting must indicate:
(a) its proposed date and time;
(b) where it is to take place; and
(c) if it is anticipated that directors participating in the meeting will not be in the same place, how it is proposed that they should communicate with each other during the meeting.
(3) Notice of a directors' meeting must be given to each director, but need not be in writing.
(4) Notice of a directors' meeting need not be given to directors who waive their entitlement to notice of that meeting, by giving notice to that effect to the company not more than seven days after the date on which the meeting is held. Where such notice is given after the meeting has been held, that does not affect the validity of the meeting, or of any business conducted at it.

Participation in directors' meetings

10. (1) Subject to the articles, directors participate in a directors' meeting, or part of a directors' meeting, when:

(a) the meeting has been called and takes place in accordance with the articles; and

(b) they can each communicate to the others any information or opinions they have on any particular item of the business of the meeting.

(2) In determining whether directors are participating in a directors' meeting, it is irrelevant where any director is or how they communicate with each other.

(3) If all the directors participating in a meeting are not in the same place, they may decide that the meeting is to be treated as taking place wherever any of them is.

Quorum for directors' meetings

11. (1) At a directors' meeting, unless a quorum is participating, no proposal is to be voted on, except a proposal to call another meeting.

(2) The quorum for directors' meetings may be fixed from time to time by a decision of the directors, but it must never be less than two, and unless otherwise fixed it is two.

(3) If the total number of directors for the time being is less than the quorum required, the directors must not take any decision other than a decision:

(a) to appoint further directors; or

(b) to call a general meeting so as to enable the shareholders to appoint further directors.

Chairing of directors' meetings

12. (1) The directors may appoint a director to chair their meetings.

(2) The person so appointed for the time being is known as the chairman.

(3) The directors may terminate the chairman's appointment at any time.

(4) If the chairman is not participating in a directors' meeting within ten minutes of the time at which it was to start, the participating directors must appoint one of themselves to chair it.

Casting vote

13. (1) If the numbers of votes for and against a proposal are equal, the chairman or other director chairing the meeting has a casting vote.

(2) But this does not apply if, in accordance with the articles, the chairman or other director is not to be counted as participating in the decision-making process for quorum or voting purposes.

Conflicts of interest

14. (1) If a proposed decision of the directors is concerned with an actual or proposed transaction or arrangement with the company in which a director is

interested, that director is not to be counted as participating in the decision-making process for quorum or voting purposes.
(2) But if paragraph (3) applies, a director who is interested in an actual or proposed transaction or arrangement with the company is to be counted as participating in the decision-making process for quorum and voting purposes.
(3) This paragraph applies when:
(a) the company by ordinary resolution disapplies the provision of the articles which would otherwise prevent a director from being counted as participating in the decision-making process;
(b) the director's interest cannot reasonably be regarded as likely to give rise to a conflict of interest; or
(c) the director's conflict of interest arises from a permitted cause.
(4) For the purposes of this article, the following are permitted causes:
(a) a guarantee given, or to be given, by or to a director in respect of an obligation incurred by or on behalf of the company or any of its subsidiaries;
(b) subscription, or an agreement to subscribe, for shares or other securities of the company or any of its subsidiaries, or to underwrite, sub-underwrite, or guarantee subscription for any such shares or securities; and
(c) arrangements pursuant to which benefits are made available to employees and directors or former employees and directors of the company or any of its subsidiaries which do not provide special benefits for directors or former directors.
(5) For the purposes of this article, references to proposed decisions and decision-making processes include any directors' meeting or part of a directors' meeting.
(6) Subject to paragraph (7), if a question arises at a meeting of directors or of a committee of directors as to the right of a director to participate in the meeting (or part of the meeting) for voting or quorum purposes, the question may, before the conclusion of the meeting, be referred to the chairman whose ruling in relation to any director other than the chairman is to be final and conclusive.
(7) If any question as to the right to participate in the meeting (or part of the meeting) should arise in respect of the chairman, the question is to be decided by a decision of the directors at that meeting, for which purpose the chairman is not to be counted as participating in the meeting (or that part of the meeting) for voting or quorum purposes.

Records of decisions to be kept

15. The directors must ensure that the company keeps a record, in writing, for at least 10 years from the date of the decision recorded, of every unanimous or majority decision taken by the directors.

Directors' discretion to make further rules

16. Subject to the articles, the directors may make any rule which they think fit about how they take decisions, and about how such rules are to be recorded or communicated to directors.

APPOINTMENT OF DIRECTORS

Methods of appointing directors

17. (1) Any person who is willing to act as a director, and is permitted by law to do so, may be appointed to be a director:
(a) by ordinary resolution; or
(b) by a decision of the directors.
(2) In any case where, as a result of death, the company has no shareholders and no directors, the personal representatives of the last shareholder to have died have the right, by notice in writing, to appoint a person to be a director.
(3) For the purposes of paragraph (2), where two or more shareholders die in circumstances rendering it uncertain who was the last to die, a younger shareholder is deemed to have survived an older shareholder.

Termination of director's appointment

18. A person ceases to be a director as soon as:
(a) that person ceases to be a director by virtue of any provision of the Companies Act 2006 or is prohibited from being a director by law;
(b) a bankruptcy order is made against that person;
(c) a composition is made with that person's creditors generally in satisfaction of that person's debts;
(d) a registered medical practitioner who is treating that person gives a written opinion to the company stating that that person has become physically or mentally incapable of acting as a director and may remain so for more than three months; and
(e) notification is received by the company from the director that the director is resigning from office, and such resignation has taken effect in accordance with its terms.

Directors' remuneration

19. (1) Directors may undertake any services for the company that the directors decide.
(2) Directors are entitled to such remuneration as the directors determine:
(a) for their services to the company as directors; and
(b) for any other service which they undertake for the company.
(3) Subject to the articles, a director's remuneration may:
(a) take any form; and
(b) include any arrangements in connection with the payment of a pension, allowance or gratuity, or any death, sickness or disability benefits, to or in respect of that director.
(4) Unless the directors decide otherwise, directors' remuneration accrues from day to day.
(5) Unless the directors decide otherwise, directors are not accountable to the company for any remuneration which they receive as directors or other officers or

employees of the company's subsidiaries or of any other body corporate in which the company is interested.

Directors' expenses

20. The company may pay any reasonable expenses which the directors properly incur in connection with their attendance at:
(a) meetings of directors or committees of directors;
(b) general meetings; or
(c) separate meetings of the holders of any class of shares or of debentures of the company,
or otherwise in connection with the exercise of their powers and the discharge of their responsibilities in relation to the company.

PART 3 SHARES AND DISTRIBUTIONS

SHARES

All shares to be fully paid up

21. (1) No share is to be issued for less than the aggregate of its nominal value and any premium to be paid to the company in consideration for its issue.
(2) This does not apply to shares taken on the formation of the company by the subscribers to the company's memorandum.

Powers to issue different classes of share

22. (1) Subject to the articles, but without prejudice to the rights attached to any existing share, the company may issue shares with such rights or restrictions as may be determined by ordinary resolution.
(2) The company may issue shares which are to be redeemed, or are liable to be redeemed at the option of the company or the holder, and the directors may determine the terms, conditions and manner of redemption of any such shares.

Company not bound by less than absolute interests

23. Except as required by law, no person is to be recognised by the company as holding any share upon any trust, and except as otherwise required by law or the articles, the company is not in any way to be bound by or recognise any interest in a share other than the holder's absolute ownership of it and all the rights attaching to it.

Share certificates

24. (1) The company must issue each shareholder, free of charge, with one or more certificates in respect of the shares which that shareholder holds.
(2) Every certificate must specify:
(a) in respect of how many shares, of what class, it is issued;
(b) the nominal value of those shares;

(c) that the shares are fully paid; and
(d) any distinguishing numbers assigned to them.
(3) No certificate may be issued in respect of shares of more than one class.
(4) If more than one person holds a share, only one certificate may be issued in respect of it.
(5) Certificates must:
(a) have affixed to them the company's common seal; or
(b) be otherwise executed in accordance with the Companies Acts.

Replacement share certificates

25. (1) If a certificate issued in respect of a shareholder's shares is:
(a) damaged or defaced; or
(b) said to be lost, stolen or destroyed,
that shareholder is entitled to be issued with a replacement certificate in respect of the same shares.
(2) A shareholder exercising the right to be issued with such a replacement certificate:
(a) may at the same time exercise the right to be issued with a single certificate or separate certificates;
(b) must return the certificate which is to be replaced to the company if it is damaged or defaced; and
(c) must comply with such conditions as to evidence, indemnity and the payment of a reasonable fee as the directors decide.

Share transfers

26. (1) Shares may be transferred by means of an instrument of transfer in any usual form or any other form approved by the directors, which is executed by or on behalf of the transferor.
(2) No fee may be charged for registering any instrument of transfer or other document relating to or affecting the title to any share.
(3) The company may retain any instrument of transfer which is registered.
(4) The transferor remains the holder of a share until the transferee's name is entered in the register of members as holder of it.
(5) The directors may refuse to register the transfer of a share, and if they do so, the instrument of transfer must be returned to the transferee with the notice of refusal unless they suspect that the proposed transfer may be fraudulent.

Transmission of shares

27. (1) If title to a share passes to a transmittee, the company may only recognise the transmittee as having any title to that share.
(2) A transmittee who produces such evidence of entitlement to shares as the directors may properly require:

(a) may, subject to the articles, choose either to become the holder of those shares or to have them transferred to another person; and
(b) subject to the articles, and pending any transfer of the shares to another person, has the same rights as the holder had.

(3) But transmittees do not have the right to attend or vote at a general meeting, or agree to a proposed written resolution, in respect of shares to which they are entitled, by reason of the holder's death or bankruptcy or otherwise, unless they become the holders of those shares.

Exercise of transmittees' rights

28. (1) Transmittees who wish to become the holders of shares to which they have become entitled must notify the company in writing of that wish.
(2) If the transmittee wishes to have a share transferred to another person, the transmittee must execute an instrument of transfer in respect of it.
(3) Any transfer made or executed under this article is to be treated as if it were made or executed by the person from whom the transmittee has derived rights in respect of the share, and as if the event which gave rise to the transmission had not occurred.

Transmittees bound by prior notices

29. If a notice is given to a shareholder in respect of shares and a transmittee is entitled to those shares, the transmittee is bound by the notice if it was given to the shareholder before the transmittee's name has been entered in the register of members.

DIVIDENDS AND OTHER DISTRIBUTIONS

Procedure for declaring dividends

30. (1) The company may by ordinary resolution declare dividends, and the directors may decide to pay interim dividends.
(2) A dividend must not be declared unless the directors have made a recommendation as to its amount. Such a dividend must not exceed the amount recommended by the directors.
(3) No dividend may be declared or paid unless it is in accordance with shareholders' respective rights.
(4) Unless the shareholders' resolution to declare or directors' decision to pay a dividend, or the terms on which shares are issued, specify otherwise, it must be paid by reference to each shareholder's holding of shares on the date of the resolution or decision to declare or pay it.
(5) If the company's share capital is divided into different classes, no interim dividend may be paid on shares carrying deferred or non-preferred rights if, at the time of payment, any preferential dividend is in arrears.

(6) The directors may pay at intervals any dividend payable at a fixed rate if it appears to them that the profits available for distribution justify the payment.
(7) If the directors act in good faith, they do not incur any liability to the holders of shares conferring preferred rights for any loss they may suffer by the lawful payment of an interim dividend on shares with deferred or non-preferred rights.

Payment of dividends and other distributions

31. (1) Where a dividend or other sum which is a distribution is payable in respect of a share, it must be paid by one or more of the following means:
(a) transfer to a bank or building society account specified by the distribution recipient either in writing or as the directors may otherwise decide;
(b) sending a cheque made payable to the distribution recipient by post to the distribution recipient at the distribution recipient's registered address (if the distribution recipient is a holder of the share), or (in any other case) to an address specified by the distribution recipient either in writing or as the directors may otherwise decide;
(c) sending a cheque made payable to such person by post to such person at such address as the distribution recipient has specified either in writing or as the directors may otherwise decide; or
(d) any other means of payment as the directors agree with the distribution recipient either in writing or by such other means as the directors decide.
(2) In the articles, 'the distribution recipient' means, in respect of a share in respect of which a dividend or other sum is payable:
(a) the holder of the share; or
(b) if the share has two or more joint holders, whichever of them is named first in the register of members; or
(c) if the holder is no longer entitled to the share by reason of death or bankruptcy, or otherwise by operation of law, the transmittee.

No interest on distributions

32. The company may not pay interest on any dividend or other sum payable in respect of a share unless otherwise provided by:
(a) the terms on which the share was issued; or
(b) the provisions of another agreement between the holder of that share and the company.

Unclaimed distributions

33. (1) All dividends or other sums which are:
(a) payable in respect of shares; and
(b) unclaimed after having been declared or become payable,
may be invested or otherwise made use of by the directors for the benefit of the company until claimed.

(2) The payment of any such dividend or other sum into a separate account does not make the company a trustee in respect of it.
(3) If:
(a) 12 years have passed from the date on which a dividend or other sum became due for payment; and
(b) the distribution recipient has not claimed it,
the distribution recipient is no longer entitled to that dividend or other sum and it ceases to remain owing by the company.

Non-cash distributions

34. (1) Subject to the terms of issue of the share in question, the company may, by ordinary resolution on the recommendation of the directors, decide to pay all or part of a dividend or other distribution payable in respect of a share by transferring non-cash assets of equivalent value (including, without limitation, shares or other securities in any company).
(2) For the purposes of paying a non-cash distribution, the directors may make whatever arrangements they think fit, including, where any difficulty arises regarding the distribution:
(a) fixing the value of any assets;
(b) paying cash to any distribution recipient on the basis of that value in order to adjust the rights of recipients; and
(c) vesting any assets in trustees.

Waiver of distributions

35. Distribution recipients may waive their entitlement to a dividend or other distribution payable in respect of a share by giving the company notice in writing to that effect, but if:
(a) the share has more than one holder; or
(b) more than one person is entitled to the share, whether by reason of the death or bankruptcy of one or more joint holders, or otherwise,
the notice is not effective unless it is expressed to be given, and signed, by all the holders or persons otherwise entitled to the share.

CAPITALISATION OF PROFITS

Authority to capitalise and appropriation of capitalised sums

36. (1) Subject to the articles, the directors may, if they are so authorised by an ordinary resolution:
(a) decide to capitalise any profits of the company (whether or not they are available for distribution) which are not required for paying a preferential dividend, or any sum standing to the credit of the company's share premium account or capital redemption reserve; and

(b) appropriate any sum which they so decide to capitalise (a 'capitalised sum') to the persons who would have been entitled to it if it were distributed by way of dividend (the 'persons entitled') and in the same proportions.

(2) Capitalised sums must be applied:

(a) on behalf of the persons entitled; and

(b) in the same proportions as a dividend would have been distributed to them.

(3) Any capitalised sum may be applied in paying up new shares of a nominal amount equal to the capitalised sum which are then allotted credited as fully paid to the persons entitled or as they may direct.

(4) A capitalised sum which was appropriated from profits available for distribution may be applied in paying up new debentures of the company which are then allotted credited as fully paid to the persons entitled or as they may direct.

(5) Subject to the articles the directors may:

(a) apply capitalised sums in accordance with paragraphs (3) and (4) partly in one way and partly in another;

(b) make such arrangements as they think fit to deal with shares or debentures becoming distributable in fractions under this article (including the issuing of fractional certificates or the making of cash payments); and

(c) authorise any person to enter into an agreement with the company on behalf of all the persons entitled which is binding on them in respect of the allotment of shares and debentures to them under this article.

PART 4: DECISION-MAKING BY SHAREHOLDERS

ORGANISATION OF GENERAL MEETINGS

Attendance and speaking at general meetings

37. (1) A person is able to exercise the right to speak at a general meeting when that person is in a position to communicate to all those attending the meeting, during the meeting, any information or opinions which that person has on the business of the meeting.

(2) A person is able to exercise the right to vote at a general meeting when:

(a) that person is able to vote, during the meeting, on resolutions put to the vote at the meeting; and

(b) that person's vote can be taken into account in determining whether or not such resolutions are passed at the same time as the votes of all the other persons attending the meeting.

(3) The directors may make whatever arrangements they consider appropriate to enable those attending a general meeting to exercise their rights to speak or vote at it.

(4) In determining attendance at a general meeting, it is immaterial whether any two or more members attending it are in the same place as each other.

(5) Two or more persons who are not in the same place as each other attend a general meeting if their circumstances are such that if they have (or were to have)

rights to speak and vote at that meeting, they are (or would be) able to exercise them.

Quorum for general meetings

38. No business other than the appointment of the chairman of the meeting is to be transacted at a general meeting if the persons attending it do not constitute a quorum.

Chairing general meetings

39. (1) If the directors have appointed a chairman, the chairman shall chair general meetings if present and willing to do so.
(2) If the directors have not appointed a chairman, or if the chairman is unwilling to chair the meeting or is not present within 10 minutes of the time at which a meeting was due to start:
(a) the directors present; or
(b) (if no directors are present) the meeting,
must appoint a director or shareholder to chair the meeting, and the appointment of the chairman of the meeting must be the first business of the meeting.
(3) The person chairing a meeting in accordance with this article is referred to as 'the chairman of the meeting'.

Attendance and speaking by directors and non-shareholders

40. (1) Directors may attend and speak at general meetings, whether or not they are shareholders.
(2) The chairman of the meeting may permit other persons who are not:
(a) shareholders of the company; or
(b) otherwise entitled to exercise the rights of shareholders in relation to general meetings,
to attend and speak at a general meeting.

Adjournment

41. (1) If the persons attending a general meeting within half an hour of the time at which the meeting was due to start do not constitute a quorum, or if during a meeting a quorum ceases to be present, the chairman of the meeting must adjourn it.
(2) The chairman of the meeting may adjourn a general meeting at which a quorum is present if:
(a) the meeting consents to an adjournment; or
(b) it appears to the chairman of the meeting that an adjournment is necessary to protect the safety of any person attending the meeting or ensure that the business of the meeting is conducted in an orderly manner.
(3) The chairman of the meeting must adjourn a general meeting if directed to do so by the meeting.

(4) When adjourning a general meeting, the chairman of the meeting must:
(a) either specify the time and place to which it is adjourned or state that it is to continue at a time and place to be fixed by the directors; and
(b) have regard to any directions as to the time and place of any adjournment which have been given by the meeting.
(5) If the continuation of an adjourned meeting is to take place more than 14 days after it was adjourned, the company must give at least seven clear days' notice of it (that is, excluding the day of the adjourned meeting and the day on which the notice is given):
(a) to the same persons to whom notice of the company's general meetings is required to be given; and
(b) containing the same information which such notice is required to contain.
(6) No business may be transacted at an adjourned general meeting which could not properly have been transacted at the meeting if the adjournment had not taken place.

VOTING AT GENERAL MEETINGS

Voting: general

42. A resolution put to the vote of a general meeting must be decided on a show of hands unless a poll is duly demanded in accordance with the articles.

Errors and disputes

43. (1) No objection may be raised to the qualification of any person voting at a general meeting except at the meeting or adjourned meeting at which the vote objected to is tendered, and every vote not disallowed at the meeting is valid.
(2) Any such objection must be referred to the chairman of the meeting, whose decision is final.

Poll votes

44. (1) A poll on a resolution may be demanded:
(a) in advance of the general meeting where it is to be put to the vote; or
(b) at a general meeting, either before a show of hands on that resolution or immediately after the result of a show of hands on that resolution is declared.
(2) A poll may be demanded by:
(a) the chairman of the meeting;
(b) the directors;
(c) two or more persons having the right to vote on the resolution; or
(d) a person or persons representing not less than one tenth of the total voting rights of all the shareholders having the right to vote on the resolution.
(3) A demand for a poll may be withdrawn if:
(a) the poll has not yet been taken; and
(b) the chairman of the meeting consents to the withdrawal.

(4) Polls must be taken immediately and in such manner as the chairman of the meeting directs.

Content of proxy notices

45. (1) Proxies may only validly be appointed by a notice in writing (a 'proxy notice') which:
(a) states the name and address of the shareholder appointing the proxy;
(b) identifies the person appointed to be that shareholder's proxy and the general meeting in relation to which that person is appointed;
(c) is signed by or on behalf of the shareholder appointing the proxy, or is authenticated in such manner as the directors may determine; and
(d) is delivered to the company in accordance with the articles and any instructions contained in the notice of the general meeting to which they relate.
(2) The company may require proxy notices to be delivered in a particular form, and may specify different forms for different purposes.
(3) Proxy notices may specify how the proxy appointed under them is to vote (or that the proxy is to abstain from voting) on one or more resolutions.
(4) Unless a proxy notice indicates otherwise, it must be treated as:
(a) allowing the person appointed under it as a proxy discretion as to how to vote on any ancillary or procedural resolutions put to the meeting; and
(b) appointing that person as a proxy in relation to any adjournment of the general meeting to which it relates as well as the meeting itself.

Delivery of proxy notices

46. (1) A person who is entitled to attend, speak or vote (either on a show of hands or on a poll) at a general meeting remains so entitled in respect of that meeting or any adjournment of it, even though a valid proxy notice has been delivered to the company by or on behalf of that person.
(2) An appointment under a proxy notice may be revoked by delivering to the company a notice in writing given by or on behalf of the person by whom or on whose behalf the proxy notice was given.
(3) A notice revoking a proxy appointment only takes effect if it is delivered before the start of the meeting or adjourned meeting to which it relates.
(4) If a proxy notice is not executed by the person appointing the proxy, it must be accompanied by written evidence of the authority of the person who executed it to execute it on the appointor's behalf.

Amendments to resolutions

47. (1) An ordinary resolution to be proposed at a general meeting may be amended by ordinary resolution if:
(a) notice of the proposed amendment is given to the company in writing by a person entitled to vote at the general meeting at which it is to be proposed not

less than 48 hours before the meeting is to take place (or such later time as the chairman of the meeting may determine); and

(b) the proposed amendment does not, in the reasonable opinion of the chairman of the meeting, materially alter the scope of the resolution.

(2) A special resolution to be proposed at a general meeting may be amended by ordinary resolution, if:

(a) the chairman of the meeting proposes the amendment at the general meeting at which the resolution is to be proposed; and

(b) the amendment does not go beyond what is necessary to correct a grammatical or other non-substantive error in the resolution.

(3) If the chairman of the meeting, acting in good faith, wrongly decides that an amendment to a resolution is out of order, the chairman's error does not invalidate the vote on that resolution.

PART 5: ADMINISTRATIVE ARRANGEMENTS

Means of communication to be used

48. (1) Subject to the articles, anything sent or supplied by or to the company under the articles may be sent or supplied in any way in which the Companies Act 2006 provides for documents or information which are authorised or required by any provision of that Act to be sent or supplied by or to the company.

(2) Subject to the articles, any notice or document to be sent or supplied to a director in connection with the taking of decisions by directors may also be sent or supplied by the means by which that director has asked to be sent or supplied with such notices or documents for the time being.

(3) A director may agree with the company that notices or documents sent to that director in a particular way are to be deemed to have been received within a specified time of their being sent, and for the specified time to be less than 48 hours.

Company seals

49. (1) Any common seal may only be used by the authority of the directors.

(2) The directors may decide by what means and in what form any common seal is to be used.

(3) Unless otherwise decided by the directors, if the company has a common seal and it is affixed to a document, the document must also be signed by at least one authorised person in the presence of a witness who attests the signature.

(4) For the purposes of this article, an authorised person is:

(a) any director of the company;

(b) the company secretary (if any); or

(c) any person authorised by the directors for the purpose of signing documents to which the common seal is applied.

No right to inspect accounts and other records

50. Except as provided by law or authorised by the directors or an ordinary resolution of the company, no person is entitled to inspect any of the company's accounting or other records or documents merely by virtue of being a shareholder.

Provision for employees on cessation of business

51. The directors may decide to make provision for the benefit of persons employed or formerly employed by the company or any of its subsidiaries (other than a director or former director or shadow director) in connection with the cessation or transfer to any person of the whole or part of the undertaking of the company or that subsidiary.

DIRECTORS' INDEMNITY AND INSURANCE

Indemnity

52. (1) Subject to paragraph (2), a relevant director of the company or an associated company may be indemnified out of the company's assets against:

(a) any liability incurred by that director in connection with any negligence, default, breach of duty or breach of trust in relation to the company or an associated company;

(b) any liability incurred by that director in connection with the activities of the company or an associated company in its capacity as a trustee of an occupational pension scheme (as defined in section 235(6) of the Companies Act 2006); and

(c) any other liability incurred by that director as an officer of the company or an associated company.

(2) This article does not authorise any indemnity which would be prohibited or rendered void by any provision of the Companies Acts or by any other provision of law.

(3) In this article:

(a) companies are associated if one is a subsidiary of the other or both are subsidiaries of the same body corporate; and

(b) a 'relevant director' means any director or former director of the company or an associated company.

Insurance

53. (1) The directors may decide to purchase and maintain insurance, at the expense of the company, for the benefit of any relevant director in respect of any relevant loss.

(2) In this article:

(a) a 'relevant director' means any director or former director of the company or an associated company;

(b) a 'relevant loss' means any loss or liability which has been or may be incurred by a relevant director in connection with that director's duties or powers in relation to the company, any associated company or any pension fund or employees' share scheme of the company or associated company; and
(c) companies are associated if one is a subsidiary of the other or both are subsidiaries of the same body corporate.

Table A

Previous Companies Acts incorporated Tables A to F which were the model forms for both the memorandum and articles of association. Accordingly the previous model articles are referred to as Table A even though in reality there were 19 different versions of Table A from 1856 until the final version created in 2008.

REGULATIONS FOR MANAGEMENT OF A COMPANY LIMITED BY SHARES

The 1985 Table A is contained in the Companies (Tables A to F) Regulations 1985. These Regulations were amended on 22 December 2000 by the Companies Act 1985 (Electronic Communications) Order 2000. The amendments made by the Order have been incorporated in the following text and are highlighted in italics. Where necessary, the text of the unamended version of the 1985 Table A is given by way of notes.

Companies which adopted the 1985 Table A prior to 22 December 2000 will need to refer to these notes. However, if a company with Articles which make no provision for electronic communications takes advantage of the new statutory procedures, it must in certain circumstances comply with the relevant provisions of the amended Table A, even though they do not form part of its Articles.

In relation to companies incorporated on or after 1 October 2007, Table A has been further amended by the Companies (Tables A to F) (Amendment) Regulations 2007 (SI 2007/2541) and the Companies (Tables A to F) (Amendment) (No.2) Regulations 2007 (SI 2007/2826). The revised text of Table A incorporating these amendments (as they apply to private and public companies respectively) is available via the Companies House website (see Directory).

Interpretation

1. In these regulations:

'the Act' means the Companies Act 1985 including any statutory modification or re-enactment thereof for the time being in force.

'the articles' means the articles of the company.

'clear days' in relation to the period of notice means that period excluding the day when the notice is given or deemed to be given and the day for which it is given or on which it is to take effect.

'communication' means the same as in the Electronic Communications Act 2000.

'electronic communication' means the same as in the Electronic Communications Act 2000.[1]

'executed' includes any mode of execution.

'office' means the registered office of the company.

'the holder' in relation to shares means the member whose name is entered in the register of members as the holder of the shares.

'the seal' means the common seal of the company.

'secretary' means the secretary of the company or any person appointed to perform the duties of the secretary of the company, including a joint, assistant or deputy secretary.

'the United Kingdom' means Great Britain and Northern Ireland.

Unless the context otherwise requires, words or expressions contained in these regulations bear the same meaning as in the Act but excluding any statutory modification thereof not in force when these regulations become binding on the company.

Share capital

2. Subject to the provisions of the Act and without prejudice to the rights attached to any existing shares, any share may be issued with such rights or restrictions as the company may by ordinary resolution determine.

3. Subject to the provisions of the Act, shares may be issued which are to be redeemed or are to be held liable to be redeemed at the option of the company or the holder on such terms and in such manner as may be provided by the articles.

4. The company may exercise the powers of paying commissions conferred by the Act. Subject to the provisions of the Act, any such commissions may be satisfied by the payment of cash or by the allotment of fully or partly paid shares or partly in one way and partly in the other.

5. Except as required by law, no person shall be recognised by the company as holding a share upon any trust and (except as otherwise provided by the articles or by law) the company shall not be bound by or recognise any interest in any share except an absolute right to the entirety thereof in the holder.

Share certificates

6. Every member, upon becoming the holder of any shares, shall be entitled without payment to one certificate for all the shares of each class held by him (and, upon transferring part of his holding of shares of any class, to a certificate for the balance of such holding) or several certificates each for one or more of his shares upon payment for every certificate after the first of such reasonable sum as the directors may determine. Every certificate shall be sealed with the seal and

shall specify the number, class and respective amounts paid thereon. The company shall not be bound to issue more than one certificate for shares held jointly by several persons and delivery of a certificate to one joint holder shall be sufficient delivery to all of them.
7. If a share certificate is defaced, worn-out, lost or destroyed, it may be renewed on such terms (if any) as to evidence and indemnity and payment of the expenses reasonably incurred by the company in investigating evidence as the directors may determine but otherwise free of charge, and (in the case of defacement or wearing-out) on delivery up of the old certificate.

Lien

8. The company shall have a first and paramount lien on every share (not being a fully paid share) for all moneys (whether presently payable or not) payable at a fixed time or called in respect of that share. The directors may at any time declare any share to be wholly or in part exempt from the provisions of this regulation. The company's lien on a share shall extend to any amount payable in respect of it.
9. The company may sell in such manner as the directors determine any shares on which the company has a lien if a sum in respect of which the lien exists is presently payable and is not paid within 14 clear days after notice has been given to the holder of the share or to the person entitled to it in consequence of the death or bankruptcy of the holder, demanding payment and stating that if the notice is not complied with the shares may be sold.
10. To give effect to a sale the directors may authorise some person to execute an instrument of transfer of the shares sold to, or in accordance with the directions of, the purchaser. The title of the transferee to the shares shall not be affected by any irregularity in or invalidity of the proceedings in reference to the sale.
11. The net proceeds of the sale, after payment of the costs, shall be applied in payment of so much of the sum for which the lien exists as is presently payable, and any residue shall (upon surrender to the company for cancellation of the certificate for the shares sold and subject to a like lien for any moneys not presently payable as existed upon the shares before the sale) be paid to the person entitled to the shares at the date of the sale.

Calls on shares and forfeiture

12. Subject to the terms of allotment, the directors may make calls upon the members in respect of any moneys unpaid on their shares (whether in respect of nominal value or premium) and each member shall (subject to receiving at least 14 clear days' notice specifying when and where payment is to be made) pay to the company as required by the notice the amount called on his shares. A call may be required to be paid by instalments. A call may, before receipt by the company of any sum due thereunder, be revoked in whole or part and payment of a call may be postponed in whole or part. A person upon whom a call is made shall remain liable for calls made upon him notwithstanding the subsequent transfer of the shares in respect whereof the call was made.

13. A call shall be deemed to have been made at the time when the resolution of the directors authorising the call was passed.

14. The joint holders of a share shall be jointly and severally liable to pay all calls in respect thereof.

15. If a call remains unpaid after it has become due and payable the person from whom it is due and payable shall pay interest on the amount unpaid from the day it became due and payable until it is paid at the rate fixed by the terms of allotment of the share or in the notice of the call or, if no rate is fixed, at the appropriate rate (as defined by the Act) but the directors may waive payment of the interest wholly or in part.

16. An amount payable in respect of a share on allotment or at any fixed date, whether in respect of nominal value or premium or as an instalment of a call, shall be deemed to be a call and if it is not paid the provisions of the articles shall apply as if the amount had become due and payable by virtue of a call.

17. Subject to the terms of allotment, the directors may make arrangements on the issue of shares for a difference between the holders in the amounts and times of payment of calls on their shares.

18. If a call remains unpaid after it has become due and payable the directors may give to the person from whom it is due not less than 14 clear days' notice requiring payment of the amount unpaid together with any interest which may have accrued. The notice shall name the place where payment is to be made and shall state that if the notice is not complied with the shares in respect of which the call was made will be liable to be forfeited.

19. If the notice is not complied with any share in respect of which it was given may, before the payment required by the notice has been made, be forfeited by a resolution of the directors and the forfeiture shall include all dividends or other moneys payable in respect of the forfeited shares and not paid before the forfeiture.

20. Subject to the provisions of the Act, a forfeited share may be sold, re-allotted or otherwise disposed of on such terms and in such manner as the directors determine either to the person who was before the forfeiture the holder or to any other person and at any time before sale, re-allotment or other disposition, the forfeiture may be cancelled on such terms as the directors think fit. Where for the purposes of its disposal a forfeited share is to be transferred to any person the directors may authorise some person to execute an instrument of transfer of the shares to that person.

21. A person any of whose shares have been forfeited shall cease to be a member in respect of them and shall surrender to the company for cancellation the certificate for the shares forfeited but shall remain liable to the company for all moneys which at the date of forfeiture were presently payable by him to the company in respect of those shares with interest at the rate at which interest was payable on those moneys before the forfeiture or, if no interest was so payable, at the appropriate rate (as defined by the Act) from the date of forfeiture until payment but the directors may waive payment wholly or in part or enforce payment without any allowance for the value of the shares at the time of forfeiture or for any consideration received on their disposal.

22. A statutory declaration by a director or the secretary that a share has been forfeited on a specified date shall be conclusive evidence of the facts stated in it as against all persons claiming to be entitled to the share and the declaration shall (subject to the execution of an instrument of transfer if necessary) constitute a good title to the share and the person to whom the share is disposed of shall not be bound to see to the application of the consideration, if any, nor shall his title to the share be affected by any irregularity in or invalidity of the proceedings in reference to the forfeiture or disposal of the share.

Transfer of shares

23. The instrument of transfer of a share may be in any usual form or in any other form which the directors may approve and shall be executed by or on behalf of the transferor and, unless the share is fully paid, by or on behalf of the transferee.

24. The directors may refuse to register the transfer of a share which is not fully paid to a person of whom they do not approve and they may refuse to register the transfer of a share on which the company has a lien. They may also refuse to register a transfer unless:

(a) it is lodged at the office or at such other place as the directors may appoint and is accompanied by the certificate for the shares to which it relates and such other evidence as the directors may reasonably require to show the right of the transferor to make the transfer;

(b) it is in respect of only one class of shares; and

(c) it is in favour of not more than four transferees.

25. If the directors refuse to register a transfer of a share, they shall within two months after the date on which the transfer was lodged with the company send to the transferee notice of the refusal.

26. The registration of transfers of shares or of transfers of any class of shares may be suspended at such times and for such periods (not exceeding 30 days in any year) as the directors may determine.

27. No fee shall be charged for the registration of any instrument of transfer or other document relating to or affecting the title to any share.

28. The company shall be entitled to retain any instrument of transfer which is registered, but any instrument of transfer which the directors refuse to register shall be returned to the person lodging it when notice of the refusal is given.

Transmission of shares

29. If a member dies the survivor or survivors where he was a joint holder, and his personal representatives where he was a sole holder or the only survivor of joint holders, shall be the persons recognised by the company as having any title to his interest; but nothing herein contained shall release the estate of a deceased member from any liability in respect of any share which had been jointly held by him.

30. A person becoming entitled to a share in consequence of the death or bankruptcy of a member may, upon such evidence being produced as the directors may properly require, elect either to become the holder of the share or to have some other person nominated by him registered as the transferee. If he elects to become the holder he shall give notice to the company to that effect. If he elects to have another person registered he shall execute an instrument of transfer of the share to that person. All the articles relating to the transfer of shares shall apply to the notice or instrument of transfer as if it were an instrument of transfer executed by the member and the death or bankruptcy of the member had not occurred.

31. A person becoming entitled to a share in consequence of the death or bankruptcy of a member shall have the rights to which he would be entitled if he were the holder of the share, except that he shall not, before being registered as the holder of the share, be entitled in respect of it to attend or vote at any meeting of the company or at any separate meeting of the holders of any class of shares in the company.

Alteration of share capital

32. The company may by ordinary resolution:

(a) increase its share capital by new shares of such amount as the resolution prescribes;

(b) consolidate and divide all or any of its share capital into shares of larger amount than its existing shares;

(c) subject to the provisions of the Act, sub-divide its shares, or any of them, into shares of smaller amount and the resolution may determine that, as between the shares resulting from the subdivision, any of them may have any preference or advantage as compared with the others; and

(d) cancel shares which, at the date of the passing of the resolution, have not been taken or agreed to be taken by any person and diminish the amount of its share capital by the amount of the shares so cancelled.

33. Whenever as a result of a consolidation of shares any members would become entitled to fractions of a share, the directors may, on behalf of those members, sell the shares representing the fractions for the best price reasonably obtainable to any person (including, subject to the provisions of the Act, the company) and distribute the net proceeds of sale in due proportion among those members, and the directors may authorise some person to execute an instrument of transfer of the shares to, or in accordance with the directions of, the purchaser. The transferee shall not be bound to see to the application of the purchase money nor shall his title to the shares be affected by any irregularity in or invalidity of the proceedings in reference to the sale.

34. Subject to the provisions of the Act, the company may by special resolution reduce its share capital, any capital redemption reserve and any share premium account in any way.

Purchase of own shares

35. Subject to the provisions of the Act, the company may purchase its own shares (including any redeemable shares) and, if it is a private company, make a payment in respect of the redemption or purchase of its own shares otherwise than out of distributable profits of the company or the proceeds of a fresh issue of shares.

General meetings

36. All general meetings other than annual general meetings shall be called extraordinary general meetings.

37. The directors may call general meetings and, on the requisition of members pursuant to the provisions of the Act, shall forthwith proceed to convene an extraordinary general meeting for a date not later than eight weeks after receipt of the requisition. If there are not within the United Kingdom sufficient directors to call a general meeting, any director or any member of the company may call a general meeting.

Notice of general meetings

38. An annual general meeting and an extraordinary general meeting called for the passing of a special resolution or a resolution appointing a person as a director shall be called by at least 21 clear days' notice. All other extraordinary general meetings shall be called by at least 14 clear days' notice but a general meeting may be called by shorter notice if it is so agreed:

(a) in the case of an annual general meeting, by all the members entitled to attend and vote thereat; and

(b) in the case of any other meeting by a majority in number of the members having a right to attend and vote being a majority together holding not less than 95% in the nominal value of the shares giving that right.

The notice shall specify the time and place of the meeting and the general nature of the business to be transacted and, in the case of an annual general meeting, shall specify the meeting as such.

Subject to the provisions of the articles and to any restriction imposed on any shares, the notice shall be given to all members, to all person entitled to a share in consequence of the death or bankruptcy of a member and to the directors and auditors.

39. The accidental omission to give notice of a meeting to, or the non-receipt of notice of a meeting by, any person entitled to receive notice shall not invalidate the proceedings at that meeting.

Proceedings at general meetings

40. No business shall be transacted at any meeting unless a quorum is present. Two persons entitled to vote upon the business to be transacted, each being a member or a proxy for a member or a duly authorised representative of a corporation, shall be a quorum.

41. If such a quorum is not present within half an hour from the time appointed for the meeting, or if during a meeting such a quorum ceases to be present, the meeting shall stand adjourned to the same day in the next week at the same time and place or to such time and place as the directors may determine.

42. The chairman, if any, of the board of directors or in his absence some other director nominated by the directors shall preside as chairman of the meeting, but if neither the chairman nor any such other director (if any) be present within fifteen minutes after the time appointed for holding the meeting and willing to act, the directors present shall elect one of their number to be chairman and, if there is only one director present and willing to act, he shall be chairman.

43. If no director is willing to act as chairman, or if no director is present within fifteen minutes after the time appointed for holding the meeting, the members present and entitled to vote shall choose one of their number to be chairman.

44. A director shall, notwithstanding that he is not a member, be entitled to attend and speak at any general meeting and at any separate meeting of the holders of any class of shares in the company.

45. The chairman may, with the consent of a meeting at which a quorum is present (and shall if so directed by the meeting), adjourn the meeting from time to time and from place to place, but no business shall be transacted at an adjourned meeting other than that business which might properly have been transacted at the meeting had the adjournment not taken place. When a meeting is adjourned for 14 days or more, at least seven days' notice shall be given specifying the time and place of the adjourned meeting and the general nature of the business to be transacted. Otherwise it shall not be necessary to give any such notice.

46. A resolution put to the vote of a meeting shall be decided on a show of hands unless before, or on the declaration of the result of, the show of hands a poll is duly demanded. Subject to the provisions of the Act, a poll may be demanded:

(a) by the chairman; or

(b) by at least two members having the right to vote at the meeting; or

(c) by a member or members representing not less than one-tenth of the total voting rights of all the members having the right to vote at the meeting; or

(d) by a member or members holding shares conferring a right to vote at the meeting being shares on which an aggregate sum has been paid up equal to not less than one-tenth of the total sum paid up on all the shares conferring that right;

and a demand by a person as proxy for a member shall be the same as a demand by the member.

47. Unless a poll is duly demanded a declaration by the chairman that a resolution has been carried unanimously, or by a particular majority, or lost, or not carried by a particular majority and an entry to that effect in the minutes of the meeting shall be conclusive evidence of the fact without proof of the number or proportion of the votes recorded in favour or against the resolution.
48. The demand for a poll may, before the poll is taken, be withdrawn but only with the consent of the chairman and a demand so withdrawn shall not be taken to have invalidated the result of a show of hands declared before the demand was made.
49. A poll shall be taken as the chairman directs and he may appoint scrutineers (who need not be members) and fix a time and place for declaring the result of the poll. The result of the poll shall be deemed to be the resolution of the meeting at which the poll was demanded.
50. In the case of an equality of votes, whether on a show of hands or on a poll, the chairman shall be entitled to a casting vote in addition to any other vote he may have.
51. A poll demanded on the election of a chairman or on a question of adjournment shall be taken forthwith. A poll demanded on any other question shall be taken either forthwith or at such time and place as the chairman directs not being more than 30 days after the poll is demanded. The demand for a poll shall not prevent the continuance of a meeting for the transaction of any business other than the question on which the poll was demanded. If a poll is demanded before the declaration of the result of a show of hands and the demand is duly withdrawn, the meeting shall continue as if the demand had not been made.
52. No notice need be given of a poll not taken forthwith if the time and place at which it is to be taken are announced at the meeting at which it is demanded. In any other case at least seven clear days' notice shall be given specifying the time and place at which the poll is to be taken.
53. A resolution in writing executed by or on behalf of each member who would have been entitled to vote upon it if it had been proposed at a general meeting at which he was present shall be as effectual as if it had been passed at a general meeting duly convened and held and may consist of several instruments in the like form executed by or on behalf of one or more members.

Votes of members

54. Subject to any rights or restrictions attached to any shares, on a show of hands every member who (being an individual) is present in person or (being a corporation) present by a duly authorised representative, not being himself a member entitled to vote, shall have one vote and on a poll every member shall have one vote for every share of which he is the holder.
55. In the case of joint holders the vote of the senior who tenders a vote, whether in person or by proxy, shall be accepted to the exclusion of the votes of the other

joint holders; and seniority shall be determined by the order in which the names of the holders stand in the register of members.

56. A member in respect of whom an order has been made by any court having jurisdiction (whether in the UK or elsewhere) in matters concerning mental disorder may vote, whether on a show of hands or on a poll, by his receiver, curator bonis or other person authorised in that behalf appointed by that court, and any such receiver, curator bonis or other person may, on a poll, vote by proxy. Evidence to the satisfaction of the directors of the authority of the person claiming to exercise the right to vote shall be deposited at the office, or at such other place as is specified in accordance with the articles for the deposit of instruments of proxy, not less than 48 hours before the time appointed for holding the meeting or adjourned meeting at which the right to vote is to be exercised and in default the right to vote shall not be exercisable.

57. No member shall vote at any general meeting or at any separate meeting of the holders of any class of shares in the company, either in person or by proxy, in respect of any share held by him unless all moneys presently payable by him in respect of that share have been paid.

58. No objection shall be raised to the qualification of any voter except at the meeting or adjourned meeting at which the vote objected to is tendered, and every vote not disallowed at the meeting shall be valid. Any objection made in due time shall be referred to the chairman whose decision shall be final and conclusive.

59. On a poll votes may be given either personally or by proxy. A member may appoint more than one proxy to attend on the same occasion.

60. *The appointment of a proxy shall be executed by or on behalf of the appointor and shall be in the following form (or in a form as near thereto as circumstances allow or in any other form which is usual or which the directors may approve)*:[2]

' PLC/Limited

I/We, , of , being a member/members of the above-named company, hereby appoint of , or failing him, of , as my/our proxy to vote in my/our name[s] and on my/our behalf at the annual/extraordinary general meeting of the company to be held on 20 , and at any adjournment thereof.

Signed on 20 .'

61. Where it is desired to afford members an opportunity of instructing the proxy how he shall act the *appointment of*[3] a proxy shall be in the following form (or in a form as near thereto as circumstances allow or in any other form which is usual or which the directors may approve):

' PLC/Limited

I/We, , of , being a member/members of the above-named company, hereby appoint of , or failing him, of , as my/our proxy to vote in my/our name[s] and on my/our behalf at the annual/extraordinary general meeting of the company to be held on 20 , and at any adjournment thereof.

This form is to be used in respect of the resolutions mentioned below as follows:

Resolution No 1 *for *against
Resolution No 2 *for *against.
*Strike out whichever is not desired.
Unless otherwise instructed, the proxy may vote as he thinks fit or abstain from voting.
Signed this day of 20 .'

62. *The appointment of a proxy and any authority under which it is executed or a copy of such authority certified notarially or in some other way approved by the directors may:*

(a) in the case of an instrument in writing, be deposited at the office or such other place within the United Kingdom as is specified in the notice convening the meeting or in any instrument of proxy sent out by the company in relation to the meeting not less than 48 hours before the time for holding the meeting or adjourned meeting at which the person named in the instrument proposes to vote; or (aa) in the case of an appointment contained in an electronic communication, where an address has been specified for the purpose of receiving electronic communications:
   - *(i) in the notice convening the meeting, or*
   - *(ii) in any instrument of proxy sent out by the company in relation to the meeting, or*
   - *(iii) in any invitation contained in an electronic communication to appoint a proxy issued by the company in relation to the meeting, be received at such address not less than 48 hours before the time for holding the meeting or adjourned meeting at which the person named in the appointment proposes to vote;*

(b) in the case of a poll taken more than 48 hours after it is demanded, be deposited or received as aforesaid after the poll has been demanded and not less than 24 hours before the time appointed for the taking of the poll; or

(c) where the poll is not taken forthwith but is taken not more than 48 hours after it was demanded, be delivered at the meeting at which the poll was demanded to the chairman or to the secretary or to any director;

and an appointment of proxy which is not deposited, delivered or received in a manner so permitted shall be invalid.

In this regulation and the next, 'address', in relation to electronic communications, includes any number or address used for the purposes of such communications.[4]

63. A vote given or poll demanded by proxy or by the duly authorised representative of a corporation shall be valid notwithstanding the previous determination of the authority of the person voting or demanding a poll unless notice of the determination was received by the company at the office or at such other place at which the instrument of proxy was duly deposited or, where the appointment of the proxy was *contained in an electronic communication, at the address at which the appointment was duly received*[5] before the commencement of the meeting or adjourned meeting at which the vote is given or the poll demanded or (in the case of a poll taken otherwise than on the same day as the meeting or adjourned meeting) the time appointed for taking the poll.

Number of directors

64. Unless otherwise determined by ordinary resolution, the number of directors (other than alternate directors) shall not be subject to any maximum but shall be not less than two.

Alternate directors

65. Any director (other than an alternate director) may appoint any other director, or any other person approved by resolution of the directors and willing to act, to be an alternate director and may remove from office an alternate director so appointed by him.

66. An alternate director shall be entitled to receive notice of all meetings of directors and of all meetings of committees of directors of which his appointor is a member, to attend and vote at any such meeting at which the director appointing him is not personally present, and generally to perform all the functions of his appointor as a director in his absence but shall not be entitled to receive any remuneration from the company for his services as an alternate director. But it shall not be necessary to give notice of such a meeting to an alternate director who is absent from the United Kingdom.

67. An alternate director shall cease to be an alternate director if his appointor ceases to be a director; but if a director retires by rotation or otherwise but is reappointed or deemed to have been reappointed at the meeting at which he retires, any appointment of an alternate director made by him which was in force immediately prior to his retirement shall continue after his reappointment.

68. Any appointment or removal of an alternate director shall be by notice to the company signed by the director making or revoking the appointment or in any other manner approved by the directors.

69. Save as otherwise provided in the articles, an alternate director shall be deemed for all purposes to be a director and shall alone be responsible for his own acts and defaults and he shall not be deemed to be the agent of the director appointing him.

Powers of directors

70. Subject to the provisions of the Act, the memorandum and the articles and to any directions given by special resolution, the business of the company shall be managed by the directors who may exercise all the powers of the company. No alteration of the memorandum or articles and no such direction shall invalidate any prior act of the directors which would have been valid if that alteration had not been made or that direction had not been given. The powers given by this regulation shall not be limited by any special power given to the directors by the articles and a meeting of directors at which a quorum is present may exercise all powers exercisable by the directors.

71. The directors may, by power of attorney or otherwise, appoint any person to be the agent of the company for such purposes and on such conditions as they determine, including authority for the agent to delegate all or any of his powers.

Delegation of directors' powers

72. The directors may delegate any of their powers to any committee consisting of one or more directors. They may also delegate to any managing director or any director holding any other executive office such of their powers as they consider desirable to be exercised by him. Any such delegation may be made subject to any conditions the directors may impose, and either collaterally with or to the exclusion of their own powers and may be revoked or altered. Subject to any such conditions, the proceedings of a committee with two or more members shall be governed by the articles regulating the proceedings of directors so far as they are capable of applying.

Appointment and retirement of directors

73. At the first annual general meeting all the directors shall retire from office, and at every subsequent annual general meeting one-third of the directors who are subject to retirement by rotation or, if their number is not three or a multiple of three, the number nearest to one third shall retire from office; but, if there is only one director who is subject to retirement by rotation, he shall retire.

74. Subject to the provisions of the Act, the directors to retire by rotation shall be those who have served longest in office since their last appointment or reappointment, but as between persons who became or were last reappointed directors on the same day those to retire shall (unless they otherwise agree among themselves) be determined by lot.

75. If the company, at the meeting at which a director retires by rotation, does not fill the vacancy the retiring director shall, if willing to act, be deemed to have been reappointed unless at the meeting it is resolved not to fill the vacancy or unless a resolution for the reappointment of the director is put to the meeting and lost.

76. No person other than a director retiring by rotation shall be appointed or reappointed a director at any general meeting unless:

(a) he is recommended by the directors; or

(b) not less than 14 nor more than 35 clear days before the date appointed for the meeting, notice executed by a member qualified to vote at the meeting has been given to the company of the intention to propose that person for appointment or reappointment stating the particulars which would, if he were so appointed or reappointed, be required to be included in the company's register of directors together with notice executed by that person of his willingness to be appointed or reappointed.

77. Not less than seven nor more than 28 clear days before the date appointed for holding a general meeting notice shall be given to all who are entitled to receive notice of the meeting of any person (other than a director retiring by rotation at the meeting) who is recommended by the directors for appointment or reappointment as a director at the meeting or in respect of whom notice has been duly given to the company of the intention to propose him at the meeting for appointment or reappointment as a director. The notice shall give particulars of that person which would, if he were so appointed or reappointed, be required to be included in the company's register of directors.

78. Subject as aforesaid, the company may by ordinary resolution appoint a person who is willing to act to be a director either to fill a vacancy or as an additional director and may also determine the rotation in which any additional directors are to retire.

79. The directors may appoint a person who is willing to act to be director, either to fill a vacancy or as an additional director, provided that the appointment does not cause the number of directors to exceed the number fixed by or in accordance with the articles as the maximum number of directors. A director so appointed shall hold office only until the next following annual general meeting and shall not be taken into account in determining the directors who are to retire by rotation at the meeting. If not reappointed at such annual general meeting, he shall vacate office at the conclusion thereof.

80. Subject as aforesaid, a director who retires at an annual general meeting may, if willing to act, be reappointed. If he is not reappointed, he shall retain office until the meeting appoints someone in his place, or if it does not do so, until the end of the meeting.

Disqualification and removal of directors

81. The office of director shall be vacated if:

(a) he ceases to be a director by virtue of any provision of the Act or becomes prohibited by law from being a director; or

(b) he becomes bankrupt or makes any arrangement or composition with his creditors generally; or

(c) he is, or may be, suffering from mental disorder and either:

  (i) he is admitted to hospital in pursuance of an application for treatment under the Mental Health Act 1983 or, in Scotland, an application for admission under the Mental Health (Scotland) Act 1960; or

  (ii) an order is made by a court having jurisdiction (whether in the United Kingdom or elsewhere) in matters concerning mental disorder for his detention or for the appointment of a receiver, curator bonis or other person to exercise powers with respect to his property or affairs; or

(d) he resigns his office by notice to the company; or

(e) he shall for more than six consecutive months have been absent without permission of the directors from meetings of the directors held during that period and the directors resolve that his office be vacated.

Remuneration of directors

82. The directors shall be entitled to such remuneration as the company may by ordinary resolution determine and, unless the resolution provides otherwise, the remuneration shall be deemed to accrue from day to day.

Directors' expenses

83. The directors may be paid all travelling, hotel, and other expenses properly incurred by them in connection with their attendance at meetings of directors or committees of directors or general meetings or separate meetings of the holders of any class of shares or of debentures of the company or otherwise connection with the discharge of their duties.

Directors' appointments and interests

84. Subject to the provisions of the Act, the directors may appoint one or more of their number to the office of managing director or to any other executive office under the company and may enter into an agreement or arrangement with any director for his employment by the company or for the provision by him of any services outside the scope of the ordinary duties of a director. Any such appointment, agreement or arrangement may be made on such terms as the directors determine and they may remunerate any such director for his services as they think fit. Any appointment of a director to an executive office shall terminate if he ceases to be a director but without prejudice to any claim for damages for breach of the contract of service between the director and the company. A managing director and a director holding any other executive office shall not be subject to retirement by rotation.

85. Subject to the provisions of the Act, and provided that he has disclosed to the directors the nature and extent of any material interest of his, a director notwithstanding his office:

(a) may be a party to, or otherwise interested in, any transaction or arrangement with the company or in which the company is otherwise interested;

(b) may be a director or other officer of, or employed by, or party to any transaction or arrangement with, or otherwise interested in, any body corporate promoted by the company or in which the company is otherwise interested; and

(c) shall not, by reason of his office, be accountable to the company for any benefit which he derives from any such office or employment or from any such transaction or arrangement or from any interest in any such body corporate and no such transaction or arrangement shall be liable to be avoided on the ground of any such interest or benefit.

86. For the purposes of regulation 85:

(a) a general notice given to the directors that a director is to be regarded as having an interest of the nature and extent specified in the notice in any transactions or arrangement in which a specified person or class of persons is interested shall be deemed to be a disclosure that the director has an interest in any such transaction of the nature and extent so specified; and

(b) an interest of which a director has no knowledge and of which it is unreasonable to expect him to have knowledge shall not be treated as an interest of his.

Director's gratuities and pensions

87. The directors may provide benefits, whether by payment of gratuities or pensions or by insurance or otherwise, for any director who has held but no longer holds any executive office or employment with the company or with any body corporate which is or has been a subsidiary of the company or a predecessor in business of the company or of any such subsidiary, and for any member of his family (including a spouse and a former spouse) or any person who is or was dependent upon him, and may (as well before as after he ceases to hold such office or employment) contribute to any fund and pay premiums for the purchase of any such benefit.

Proceedings of directors

88. Subject to the provisions of the articles, the directors may regulate their proceedings as they think fit. A director may, and the secretary at the request of a director shall, call a meeting of the directors. It shall not be necessary to give notice of a meeting to a director who is absent from the United Kingdom. Questions arising at a meeting shall be decided by a majority of votes. In the case of an equality of votes, the chairman shall have a second or casting vote. A director who is also an alternate director shall be entitled in the absence of his appointor to a separate vote on behalf of his appointor in addition to his own vote.

89. The quorum for the transaction of business of the directors may be fixed by the directors and unless so fixed at any other number shall be two. A person who holds office only as an alternate director shall, if his appointor is not present, be counted in the quorum.

90. The continuing directors or a sole continuing director may act notwithstanding any vacancies in their number, but, if the number of directors is less than the number fixed as the quorum, the continuing directors or director may act only for the purpose of filling vacancies or of calling a general meeting.

91. The directors may appoint one of their number to be the chairman of the board of directors and may at any time remove him from that office. Unless he is unwilling to do so, the director so appointed shall preside at every meeting of directors at which he is present. But if there is no director holding that office, or if the director holding it is unwilling to preside or is not present within five minutes after the time appointed for the meeting, the directors present may appoint one of their number to be chairman of the meeting.

92. All acts done by a meeting of directors, or of a committee of directors, or by a person acting as a director shall, notwithstanding that it be afterwards discovered that there was a defect in the appointment of any director or that any of them were disqualified from holding office, or had vacated office, or were not entitled to vote, be as valid as if every such person had been duly appointed and was qualified and had continued to be a director and had been entitled to vote.

93. A resolution signed in writing by all the directors entitled to receive notice of a meeting of directors or of a committee of directors shall be as valid and effectual as if it had been passed at a meeting of directors or (as the case may be) a committee of directors duly convened and held and may consist of several documents in the like form each signed by one or more directors; but a resolution signed by an alternate director need not also be signed by his appointor and, if it is signed by a director who has appointed an alternate director, it need not be signed by the alternate in that capacity.

94. Save as otherwise provided by the articles, a director shall not vote at a meeting of directors or a committee of directors on any resolution concerning a matter in which he has, directly or indirectly, an interest or duty which is material and which conflicts or may conflict with the interests of the company unless his interest or duty arises only because the case falls within one or more of the following paragraphs:

(a) the resolution relates to the giving to him of a guarantee, security, or indemnity in respect of money lent to, or an obligation incurred by him for the benefit of, the company or any of its subsidiaries;

(b) the resolution relates to the giving to a third party of a guarantee, security, or indemnity in respect of an obligation of the company or any of its subsidiaries for which the director has assumed responsibility in whole or in part and whether alone or jointly with others under a guarantee or indemnity or by the giving of security;

(c) his interest arises by virtue of his subscribing or agreeing to subscribe for any shares, debentures or other securities of the company or any of its subsidiaries, or by virtue of his being, or intending to become, a participant in the underwriting or sub-underwriting of an offer of any such shares, debentures or other securities by the company or any of its subsidiaries for subscription, purchase or exchange;

(d) the resolution relates in any way to a retirement benefits scheme which has been approved, or is conditional upon approval, by the Board of Inland Revenue for taxation purposes.

For the purposes of this regulation, an interest of a person who is, for any purpose of the Act (excluding any statutory modification thereof not in force when this regulation becomes binding on the company), connected with a director shall be treated as an interest of the director and, in relation to an alternate director, an interest of his appointor shall be treated as an interest of the alternate director without prejudice to any interest which the alternate director has otherwise.

95. A director shall not be counted in the quorum present at a meeting in relation to a resolution on which he is not entitled to vote.

96. The company may by ordinary resolution suspend or relax to any extent, either generally or in respect of any particular matter, any provision of the articles prohibiting a director from voting at a meeting of directors or of a committee of directors.

97. Where proposals are under consideration concerning the appointment of two or more directors to offices or employments with the company or any body corporate in which the company is interested the proposals may be divided and considered in relation to each director separately and (provided he is not for another reason precluded from voting) each of the directors concerned shall be entitled to vote and be counted in the quorum in respect of each resolution except that concerning his own appointment.

98. If a question arises at a meeting of directors or of a committee of directors as to the right of a director to vote, the question may, before the conclusion of the meeting, be referred to the chairman of the meeting and his ruling in relation to any director other than himself shall be final and conclusive.

Secretary

99. Subject to the provisions of the Act, the secretary shall be appointed by the directors for such term, at such remuneration and upon such conditions as they may think fit; and any secretary so appointed may be removed by them.

Minutes

100. The directors shall cause minutes to be made in books kept for the purpose:

(a) of all appointments of officers made by the directors; and

(b) of all proceedings at meetings of the company, of the holders of any class of shares in the company, and of the directors, and of committees of directors, including the names of the directors present at each such meeting.

The seal

101. The seal shall only be used by the authority of the directors or of a committee of directors authorised by the directors. The directors may determine who shall sign any instrument to which the seal is affixed and unless otherwise so determined it shall be signed by a director and by the secretary or by a second director.

Dividends

102. Subject to the provisions of the Act, the company may by ordinary resolution declare dividends in accordance with the respective rights of members, but no dividend shall exceed the amount recommended by the directors.

103. Subject to the provisions of the Act, the directors may pay interim dividends if it appears to them that they are justified by the profits of the company available for distribution. If the share capital is divided into different classes, the directors may pay interim dividends on shares which confer deferred or non-preferred rights with regard to dividend as well as on shares which confer preferential rights with regard to dividend, but no interim dividend shall be paid on shares carrying deferred or non-preferred rights if, at the time of payment, any preferential dividend is in arrear. The directors may also pay at intervals settled by them any dividend payable at a fixed rate if it appears to them that the profits available for distribution justify the payment. Provided the directors act in good faith they shall not incur any liability to the holders of shares conferring preferred rights for any loss they may suffer by the lawful payment of an interim dividend on any shares having deferred or non-preferred rights.

104. Except as otherwise provided by the rights attached to shares, all dividends shall be declared and paid according to the amounts paid up on the shares on which the dividend is paid. All dividends shall be apportioned and paid proportionately to the amounts paid up on the shares during any portion or portions of the period in respect of which the dividend is paid; but, if any share is issued on terms providing that it shall rank for dividend from a particular date, that share shall rank for dividend accordingly.

105. A general meeting declaring a dividend may, upon the recommendation of the directors, direct that it shall be satisfied wholly or partly by the distribution of assets and, where any difficulty arises in regard to the distribution, the directors may settle the same and in particular may issue fractional certificates and fix the value for distribution of any assets and may determine that cash shall be paid to any member upon the footing of the value so fixed in order to adjust the rights of members and may vest assets in trustees.

106. Any dividend or other moneys payable in respect of a share may be paid by cheque sent by post to the registered address of the person entitled or, if two or more persons are the holders of the share or are jointly entitled to it by reason of the death or bankruptcy of the holder, to the registered address of that one of those persons who is first named on the register of members or to such person and to such address as the person or person entitled may in writing direct. Every cheque shall be made payable to the order of the person or persons entitled or to such other person as the person or persons entitled may in writing direct and payment of the cheque shall be a good discharge to the company. Any joint holder or other person jointly entitled to a share as aforesaid may give receipts for any dividend or other moneys payable in respect of the share.

107. No dividend or other moneys payable in respect of a share shall bear interest against the company unless otherwise provided by the rights attached to the share.

108. Any dividend which has remained unclaimed for 12 years from the date when it became due for payment shall, if the directors so resolve, be forfeited and cease to remain owing by the company.

Accounts

109. No member shall (as such) have any right of inspecting any accounting records or other book or document of the company except as conferred by statute or authorised by the directors or by ordinary resolution of the company.

Capitalisation of profits

110. The directors may with the authority of an ordinary resolution of the company:

(a) subject as hereinafter provided, resolve to capitalise any undivided profits of the company not required for paying any preferential dividend (whether or not they are available for distribution) or any sum standing to the credit of the company's share premium account or capital redemption reserve;

(b) appropriate the sum resolved to be capitalised to the members who would have been entitled to it if it were distributed by way of dividend and in the same proportion and apply such sum on their behalf either in or towards paying up the amounts, if any, for the time being unpaid on any shares held by them respectively, or in paying up in full unissued shares or debentures of the company of a nominal amount equal to that sum, and allot the shares or debentures credited as fully paid to those members, or as they may direct, in those proportions, or partly in one way and partly in the other: but the share premium account, the capital redemption reserve, and any profits which are not available for distribution may, for the purposes of this regulation, only be applied in paying up unissued shares to be allotted to members credited as fully paid;

(c) make such provision by the issue of fractional certificates or by payment in cash or otherwise as they determine in the case of shares or debentures becoming distributable under this regulation in fractions; and

(d) authorise any person to enter on behalf of all members concerned into an agreement with the company providing for the allotment to them respectively, credited as fully paid, of any shares or debentures to which they are entitled upon such capitalisation, any agreement made under such authority being binding on all such members.

Notices

111. Any notice to be given to or by any person pursuant to the articles (other than a notice calling a meeting of the directors) shall be in writing or shall be given using electronic communications to an address for the time being notified for that purpose to the person giving the notice.

In this regulation, 'address', in relation to electronic communications, includes any number or address used for the purposes of such communications.[6]

112. The company may give any notice to a member either personally or by sending it by post in a prepaid envelope addressed to the member at his registered address or by leaving it at that address or by giving it using *electronic communications to an address for the time being notified to the company by the member.* In the case of joint holders of a share, all notices shall be given to the joint holder whose name stands first in the register of members in respect of the joint holding and notice so given shall be sufficient notice to all the joint holders.

A member whose registered address is not within the United Kingdom and who gives to the company an address within the United Kingdom at which notices may be given to him, or an address to which notices may be sent by electronic communications, shall be entitled to have notices given to him at that address, but otherwise no such member shall be entitled to receive any notice from *the company. In this regulation and the next, 'address', in relation to electronic communications, includes any number or address used for the purposes of such communications.*[7]

113. A member present, either in person or by proxy, at any meeting of the company or of holders of any class of shares in the company shall be deemed to have received notice of the meeting and, where requisite, of the purposes for which it was called.

114. Every person who becomes entitled to a share shall be bound by any notice in respect of that share which, before his name is entered in the register of members, has been duly given to a person from whom he derives his title.

115. Proof that an envelope containing a notice was properly addressed, prepaid and posted shall be conclusive evidence that the notice was given. Proof that notice contained in an electronic communication *was sent in accordance with guidance issued by the Institute of Chartered Secretaries and Administrators shall be conclusive evidence that the notice was given.* A notice shall be deemed to be given at the expiration of 48 hours after the envelope containing it was posted *or, in the case of a notice contained in an electronic communication, at the expiration of 48 hours after the time it was sent.*[8]

116. A notice may be given by the company to the persons entitled to a share in consequence of death or bankruptcy of a member by sending or delivering it, in any manner authorised by the articles for the giving of notice to a member, addressed to them by name, or by the title of representatives of the deceased, or trustee of the bankrupt or by any description at the address, if any, within the United Kingdom supplied for that purpose by the persons claiming to be so entitled. Until such an address has been supplied, a notice may be given in any manner in which it might have been given if the death or bankruptcy had not occurred.

Winding-up

117. If the company is wound up, the liquidator may, with the sanction of an extraordinary resolution of the company and any other sanction required by the Act, divide among the members in specie the whole or any part of the assets of the company and may, for that purpose, value any assets and determine how the division shall be carried out as between members or different classes of members. The liquidator may, with the like sanction, vest the whole or any part of the assets in trustees upon such trusts for the benefit of the members as he with the like sanction determines, but no member shall be compelled to accept any assets upon which there is a liability.

Indemnity

118. Subject to the provisions of the Act, but without prejudice to any indemnity to which a director may otherwise be entitled, every director or other officer or auditor of the company shall be indemnified out of the assets of the company against any liability incurred by him in defending any proceedings, whether civil or criminal, in which judgement is given in his favour or in which he is acquitted or in connection with any application in which relief is granted to him by the court from liability for negligence, default, breach of duty or breach of trust in relation to the affairs of the company.

Footnotes

1. The italicised words were inserted by Sch.1 to the Companies Act 1985 (Electronic Communications) Order 2000 on 22 December 2000. Prior to that date Table A did not include a definition of an 'electronic communication' or a 'communication'.
2. Regulation 60 was amended by Sch.1 to the Companies Act 1985 (Electronic Communications) Order 2000 on 22 December 2000. Prior to that date it read as follows: 'An instrument appointing a proxy shall be in writing, executed by or on behalf of the appointor and shall be in the following form...'
3. The words 'appointment of ' were inserted in reg.61 by Sch.1 to the Companies Act 1985 (Electronic Communications) Order 2000 on 22 December 2000. Prior to that date it read as follows: 'Where it is desired to afford members an opportunity of instructing the proxy how he shall act the instrument appointing a proxy...'
4. Regulation 62 was amended by Sch.1 to the Companies Act 1985 (Electronic Communications) Order 2000 on 22 December 2000. Prior to that date it read as follows: 'The instrument appointing a proxy and any authority under which it is executed or a copy of such authority certified notarially or in some other way approved by the directors may:
   (a) be deposited at the office or such other place within the United Kingdom as is specified in the notice convening the meeting or in any instrument of proxy sent out by the company in relation to the meeting not less than 48 hours before the time for holding the meeting or adjourned meeting at which the person named in the instrument proposes to vote; or
   (b) in the case of a poll taken more than 48 hours after it is demanded, be deposited as aforesaid after the poll has been demanded and not less than 24 hours before the time appointed for the taking of the poll; or
   (c) where the poll is not taken forthwith but is taken not more than 48 hours after it was demanded, be delivered at the meeting at which the poll was demanded to the chairman or to the secretary or to any director; and an instrument of proxy which is not deposited or delivered in a manner so permitted shall be invalid.'
5. The words in italics in reg.63 were inserted by Sch.1 to the Companies Act 1985 (Electronic Communications) Order 2000 on 22 December 2000.
6. Regulation 111 was amended by Sch.1 to the Companies Act 1985 (Electronic Communications) Order 2000 on 22 December 2000. Prior to that date it read as follows: 'Any notice to be given to or by any person pursuant to the articles shall be in writing except that notice calling a meeting of directors need not be in writing.'
7. The words in italics in reg.112 were inserted by Sch.1 to the Companies Act 1985 (Electronic Communications) Order 2000 on 22 December 2000.
8. The words in italics in reg.115 were inserted by Sch.1 to the Companies Act 1985 (Electronic Communications) Order 2000 on 22 December 2000.

Appendix 2 – The UK Corporate Governance Code

Introduction

The first version of the UK Corporate Governance Code (the Code) was published in 1992 by the Cadbury Committee. It defined corporate governance as 'the system by which companies are directed and controlled. Boards of directors are responsible for the governance of their companies. The shareholders' role in governance is to appoint the directors and the auditors and to satisfy themselves that an appropriate governance structure is in place.' This remains true today, but the environment in which companies, their shareholders and wider stakeholders operate continues to develop rapidly.

Companies do not exist in isolation. Successful and sustainable businesses underpin our economy and society by providing employment and creating prosperity. To succeed in the long term, directors and the companies they lead need to build and maintain successful relationships with a wide range of stakeholders. These relationships will be successful and enduring if they are based on respect, trust and mutual benefit. Accordingly, a company's culture should promote integrity and openness, value diversity and be responsive to the views of shareholders and wider stakeholders.

Over the years the Code has been revised and expanded to take account of the increasing demands on the UK's corporate governance framework. The principle of collective responsibility within a unitary board has been a success and – alongside the stewardship activities of investors – played a vital role in delivering high standards of governance and encouraging long-term investment. Nevertheless, the debate about the nature and extent of the framework has intensified as a result of financial crises and high-profile examples of inadequate governance and misconduct, which have led to poor outcomes for a wide range of stakeholders.

At the heart of this Code is an updated set of Principles that emphasise the value of good corporate governance to long-term sustainable success. By applying the Principles, following the more detailed Provisions and using the associated guidance, companies can demonstrate throughout their reporting how the governance of the company contributes to its long-term sustainable success and achieves wider objectives.

Achieving this depends crucially on the way boards and companies apply the spirit of the Principles. The Code does not set out a rigid set of rules; instead it offers flexibility through the application of Principles and through 'comply or explain' Provisions and supporting guidance. It is the responsibility of boards to use this flexibility wisely and of investors and their advisers to assess differing company approaches thoughtfully.

Reporting on the Code

The 2018 Code focuses on the application of the Principles. The Listing Rules require companies to make a statement of how they have applied the Principles, in a manner that would enable shareholders to evaluate how the Principles have been applied. The ability of investors to evaluate the approach to governance is important. Reporting should cover the application of the Principles in the context of the particular circumstances of the company and how the board has set the company's purpose and strategy, met objectives and achieved outcomes through the decisions it has taken.

It is important to report meaningfully when discussing the application of the Principles and to avoid boilerplate reporting. The focus should be on how these have been applied, articulating what action has been taken and the resulting outcomes. High-quality reporting will include signposting and cross-referencing to those parts of the annual report that describe how the Principles have been applied. This will help investors with their evaluation of company practices.

The effective application of the Principles should be supported by high-quality reporting on the Provisions. These operate on a 'comply or explain' basis and companies should avoid a 'tick-box approach'. An alternative to complying with a Provision may be justified in particular circumstances based on a range of factors, including the size, complexity, history and ownership structure of a company. Explanations should set out the background, provide a clear rationale for the action the company is taking, and explain the impact that the action has had. Where a departure from a Provision is intended to be limited in time, the explanation should indicate when the company expects to conform to the Provision. Explanations are a positive opportunity to communicate, not an onerous obligation.

In line with their responsibilities under the UK Stewardship Code, investors should engage constructively and discuss with the company any departures from recommended practice. In their consideration of explanations, investors and their advisors should pay due regard to a company's individual circumstances. While they have every right to challenge explanations if they are unconvincing, these must not be evaluated in a mechanistic way. Investors and their advisors should also give companies sufficient time to respond to enquiries about corporate governance.

Corporate governance reporting should also relate coherently to other parts of the annual report – particularly the Strategic Report and other complementary information – so that shareholders can effectively assess the quality of the company's governance arrangements, and the board's activities and contributions. This should include providing information that enables shareholders to assess how the directors have performed their duty under s. 172 of the Companies Act 2006 (the Act) to promote the success of the company. Nothing in this Code overrides or is intended as an interpretation of the statutory statement of directors' duties in the Act.

The Code is also supported by the *Guidance on Board Effectiveness* (the Guidance). We encourage boards and companies to use this to support their activities. The Guidance does not set out the 'right way' to apply the Code. It is intended to stimulate thinking on how boards can carry out their role most effectively. The Guidance is designed to help boards with their actions and decisions when reporting on the application of the Code's Principles. The board should also take into account the Financial Reporting Council's *Guidance on Audit Committees* and *Guidance on Risk Management, Internal Control and Related Financial and Business Reporting.*

Application

The Code is applicable to all companies with a premium listing, whether incorporated in the UK or elsewhere. The new Code applies to accounting periods beginning on or after 1 January 2019.

For parent companies with a premium listing, the board should ensure that there is adequate cooperation within the group to enable it to discharge its governance responsibilities under the Code effectively. This includes the communication of the parent company's purpose, values and strategy.

Externally managed investment companies (which typically have a different board and company structure that may affect the relevance of particular Principles) may wish to use the Association of Investment Companies' Corporate Governance Code to meet their obligations under the Code. In addition, the Association of Financial Mutuals produces an annotated version of the Code for mutual insurers to use.

1 Board leadership and company purpose

Principles

A. A successful company is led by an effective and entrepreneurial board, whose role is to promote the long-term sustainable success of the company, generating value for shareholders and contributing to wider society.

B. The board should establish the company's purpose, values and strategy, and satisfy itself that these and its culture are aligned. All directors must act with integrity, lead by example and promote the desired culture.

C. The board should ensure that the necessary resources are in place for the company to meet its objectives and measure performance against them. The board should also establish a framework of prudent and effective controls, which enable risk to be assessed and managed.

D. In order for the company to meet its responsibilities to shareholders and stakeholders, the board should ensure effective engagement with, and encourage participation from, these parties.
E. The board should ensure that workforce policies and practices are consistent with the company's values and support its long-term sustainable success. The workforce should be able to raise any matters of concern.

Provisions

1. The board should assess the basis on which the company generates and preserves value over the long-term. It should describe in the annual report how opportunities and risks to the future success of the business have been considered and addressed, the sustainability of the company's business model and how its governance contributes to the delivery of its strategy.
2. The board should assess and monitor culture. Where it is not satisfied that policy, practices or behaviour throughout the business are aligned with the company's purpose, values and strategy, it should seek assurance that management has taken corrective action. The annual report should explain the board's activities and any action taken. In addition, it should include an explanation of the company's approach to investing in and rewarding its workforce.
3. In addition to formal general meetings, the chair should seek regular engagement with major shareholders in order to understand their views on governance and performance against the strategy. Committee chairs should seek engagement with shareholders on significant matters related to their areas of responsibility. The chair should ensure that the board as a whole has a clear understanding of the views of shareholders.
4. When 20% or more of votes have been cast against the board recommendation for a resolution, the company should explain, when announcing voting results, what actions it intends to take to consult shareholders in order to understand the reasons behind the result. An update on the views received from shareholders and actions taken should be published no later than six months after the shareholder meeting. The board should then provide a final summary in the annual report and, if applicable, in the explanatory notes to resolutions at the next shareholder meeting, on what impact the feedback has had on the decisions the board has taken and any actions or resolutions now proposed.[1]
5. The board should understand the views of the company's other key stakeholders and describe in the annual report how their interests and the matters set out in s. 172 of the Companies Act 2006 have been considered in board

1 Details of significant votes against and related company updates are available on the Public Register maintained by The Investment Association – www.theinvestmentassociation.org/publicregister.html

discussions and decision-making.[2] The board should keep engagement mechanisms under review so that they remain effective. For engagement with the workforce,[3] one or a combination of the following methods should be used:

- a director appointed from the workforce;
- a formal workforce advisory panel;
- a designated non-executive director.

If the board has not chosen one or more of these methods, it should explain what alternative arrangements are in place and why it considers that they are effective.

6. There should be a means for the workforce to raise concerns in confidence and – if they wish – anonymously. The board should routinely review this and the reports arising from its operation. It should ensure that arrangements are in place for the proportionate and independent investigation of such matters and for follow-up action.
7. The board should take action to identify and manage conflicts of interest, including those resulting from significant shareholdings, and ensure that the influence of third parties does not compromise or override independent judgement.
8. Where directors have concerns about the operation of the board or the management of the company that cannot be resolved, their concerns should be recorded in the board minutes. On resignation, a non-executive director should provide a written statement to the chair, for circulation to the board, if they have any such concerns.

2 Division of responsibilities

Principles

F. The chair leads the board and is responsible for its overall effectiveness in directing the company. They should demonstrate objective judgement throughout their tenure and promote a culture of openness and debate. In addition, the chair facilitates constructive board relations and the effective contribution of all non-executive directors, and ensures that directors receive accurate, timely and clear information.

G. The board should include an appropriate combination of executive and non-executive (and, in particular, independent non-executive) directors, such that no one individual or small group of individuals dominates the board's decision-making. There should be a clear division of responsibilities between the

2 The Companies (Miscellaneous Reporting) Regulations 2018 require directors to explain how they have had regard to various matters in performing their duty to promote the success of the company in s. 172 of the Companies Act 2006. The Financial Reporting Council's Guidance on the Strategic Report supports reporting on the legislative requirement.

3 See the Guidance on Board Effectiveness Section 1 for a description of 'workforce' in this context.

leadership of the board and the executive leadership of the company's business.

H. Non-executive directors should have sufficient time to meet their board responsibilities. They should provide constructive challenge, strategic guidance, offer specialist advice and hold management to account.

I. The board, supported by the company secretary, should ensure that it has the policies, processes, information, time and resources it needs in order to function effectively and efficiently.

Provisions

9. The chair should be independent on appointment when assessed against the circumstances set out in Provision 10. The roles of chair and chief executive should not be exercised by the same individual. A chief executive should not become chair of the same company. If, exceptionally, this is proposed by the board, major shareholders should be consulted ahead of appointment. The board should set out its reasons to all shareholders at the time of the appointment and also publish these on the company website.
10. The board should identify in the annual report each non-executive director it considers to be independent. Circumstances that are likely to impair, or could appear to impair, a non-executive director's independence include, but are not limited to, whether a director:
    - is or has been an employee of the company or group within the last five years;
    - has, or has had within the last three years, a material business relationship with the company, either directly or as a partner, shareholder, director or senior employee of a body that has such a relationship with the company;
    - has received or receives additional remuneration from the company apart from a director's fee, participates in the company's share option or a performance-related pay scheme, or is a member of the company's pension scheme;
    - has close family ties with any of the company's advisers, directors or senior employees;
    - holds cross-directorships or has significant links with other directors through involvement in other companies or bodies;
    - represents a significant shareholder; or
    - has served on the board for more than nine years from the date of their first appointment.

    Where any of these or other relevant circumstances apply, and the board nonetheless considers that the non-executive director is independent, a clear explanation should be provided.
11. At least half the board, excluding the chair, should be non-executive directors whom the board considers to be independent.

12. The board should appoint one of the independent non-executive directors to be the senior independent director to provide a sounding board for the chair and serve as an intermediary for the other directors and shareholders. Led by the senior independent director, the non-executive directors should meet without the chair present at least annually to appraise the chair's performance, and on other occasions as necessary.
13. Non-executive directors have a prime role in appointing and removing executive directors. Non-executive directors should scrutinise and hold to account the performance of management and individual executive directors against agreed performance objectives. The chair should hold meetings with the non-executive directors without the executive directors present.
14. The responsibilities of the chair, chief executive, senior independent director, board and committees should be clear, set out in writing, agreed by the board and made publicly available. The annual report should set out the number of meetings of the board and its committees, and the individual attendance by directors.
15. When making new appointments, the board should take into account other demands on directors' time. Prior to appointment, significant commitments should be disclosed with an indication of the time involved. Additional external appointments should not be undertaken without prior approval of the board, with the reasons for permitting significant appointments explained in the annual report. Full-time executive directors should not take on more than one non-executive directorship in a FTSE 100 company or other significant appointment.
16. All directors should have access to the advice of the company secretary, who is responsible for advising the board on all governance matters. Both the appointment and removal of the company secretary should be a matter for the whole board.

3 Composition, succession and evaluation

Principles

J. Appointments to the board should be subject to a formal, rigorous and transparent procedure, and an effective succession plan should be maintained for board and senior management.[4] Both appointments and succession plans should be based on merit and objective criteria[5] and, within this context, should promote diversity of gender, social and ethnic backgrounds, cognitive and personal strengths.

K. The board and its committees should have a combination of skills, experience

4 The definition of 'senior management' for this purpose should be the executive committee or the first layer of management below board level, including the company secretary.

5 Which protect against discrimination for those with protected characteristics within the meaning of the Equalities Act 2010.

and knowledge. Consideration should be given to the length of service of the board as a whole and membership regularly refreshed.

L. Annual evaluation of the board should consider its composition, diversity and how effectively members work together to achieve objectives. Individual evaluation should demonstrate whether each director continues to contribute effectively.

Provisions

17. The board should establish a nomination committee to lead the process for appointments, ensure plans are in place for orderly succession to both the board and senior management positions, and oversee the development of a diverse pipeline for succession. A majority of members of the committee should be independent non-executive directors. The chair of the board should not chair the committee when it is dealing with the appointment of their successor.
18. All directors should be subject to annual re-election. The board should set out in the papers accompanying the resolutions to elect each director the specific reasons why their contribution is, and continues to be, important to the company's long-term sustainable success.
19. The chair should not remain in post beyond nine years from the date of their first appointment to the board. To facilitate effective succession planning and the development of a diverse board, this period can be extended for a limited time, particularly in those cases where the chair was an existing non-executive director on appointment. A clear explanation should be provided.
20. Open advertising and/or an external search consultancy should generally be used for the appointment of the chair and non-executive directors. If an external search consultancy is engaged, it should be identified in the annual report alongside a statement about any other connection it has with the company or individual directors.
21. There should be a formal and rigorous annual evaluation of the performance of the board, its committees, the chair and individual directors. The chair should consider having a regular externally facilitated board evaluation. In FTSE 350 companies this should happen at least every three years. The external evaluator should be identified in the annual report and a statement made about any other connection it has with the company or individual directors.
22. The chair should act on the results of the evaluation by recognising the strengths and addressing any weaknesses of the board. Each director should engage with the process and take appropriate action when development needs have been identified.
23. The annual report should describe the work of the nomination committee, including:

- the process used in relation to appointments, its approach to succession planning and how both support developing a diverse pipeline;
- how the board evaluation has been conducted, the nature and extent of an external evaluator's contact with the board and individual directors, the outcomes and actions taken, and how it has or will influence board composition;
- the policy on diversity and inclusion, its objectives and linkage to company strategy, how it has been implemented and progress on achieving the objectives; and
- the gender balance of those in the senior management[6] and their direct reports.

4 Audit, risk and internal control

Principles

M. The board should establish formal and transparent policies and procedures to ensure the independence and effectiveness of internal and external audit functions and satisfy itself on the integrity of financial and narrative statements.[7]

N. The board should present a fair, balanced and understandable assessment of the company's position and prospects.

O. The board should establish procedures to manage risk, oversee the internal control framework, and determine the nature and extent of the principal risks the company is willing to take in order to achieve its long-term strategic objectives.

Provisions

24. The board should establish an audit committee of independent non-executive directors, with a minimum membership of three, or in the case of smaller companies, two.[8] The chair of the board should not be a member. The board should satisfy itself that at least one member has recent and relevant financial experience. The committee as a whole shall have competence relevant to the sector in which the company operates.

6 See footnote 4.

7 The board's responsibility to present a fair, balanced and understandable assessment extends to interim and other price-sensitive public records and reports to regulators, as well as to information required to be presented by statutory instruments.

8 A smaller company is one that is below the FTSE 350 throughout the year immediately prior to the reporting year.

25. The main roles and responsibilities of the audit committee should include:
    - monitoring the integrity of the financial statements of the company and any formal announcements relating to the company's financial performance, and reviewing significant financial reporting judgements contained in them;
    - providing advice (where requested by the board) on whether the annual report and accounts, taken as a whole, is fair, balanced and understandable, and provides the information necessary for shareholders to assess the company's position and performance, business model and strategy;
    - reviewing the company's internal financial controls and internal control and risk management systems, unless expressly addressed by a separate board risk committee composed of independent non-executive directors, or by the board itself;
    - monitoring and reviewing the effectiveness of the company's internal audit function or, where there is not one, considering annually whether there is a need for one and making a recommendation to the board;
    - conducting the tender process and making recommendations to the board, about the appointment, reappointment and removal of the external auditor, and approving the remuneration and terms of engagement of the external auditor;
    - reviewing and monitoring the external auditor's independence and objectivity;
    - reviewing the effectiveness of the external audit process, taking into consideration relevant UK professional and regulatory requirements;
    - developing and implementing policy on the engagement of the external auditor to supply non-audit services, ensuring there is prior approval of non-audit services, considering the impact this may have on independence, taking into account the relevant regulations and ethical guidance in this regard, and reporting to the board on any improvement or action required; and
    - reporting to the board on how it has discharged its responsibilities.
26. The annual report should describe the work of the audit committee, including:
    - the significant issues that the audit committee considered relating to the financial statements, and how these issues were addressed;
    - an explanation of how it has assessed the independence and effectiveness of the external audit process and the approach taken to the appointment or reappointment of the external auditor, information on the length of tenure of the current audit firm, when a tender was last conducted and advance notice of any retendering plans;
    - in the case of a board not accepting the audit committee's recommendation on the external auditor appointment, reappointment or removal, a statement from the audit committee explaining its recommendation and

the reasons why the board has taken a different position (this should also be supplied in any papers recommending appointment or reappointment);
- where there is no internal audit function, an explanation for the absence, how internal assurance is achieved, and how this affects the work of external audit; and
- an explanation of how auditor independence and objectivity are safeguarded, if the external auditor provides non-audit services.

27. The directors should explain in the annual report their responsibility for preparing the annual report and accounts, and state that they consider the annual report and accounts, taken as a whole, is fair, balanced and understandable, and provides the information necessary for shareholders to assess the company's position, performance, business model and strategy.
28. The board should carry out a robust assessment of the company's emerging and principal risks.[9] The board should confirm in the annual report that it has completed this assessment, including a description of its principal risks, what procedures are in place to identify emerging risks, and an explanation of how these are being managed or mitigated.
29. The board should monitor the company's risk management and internal control systems and, at least annually, carry out a review of their effectiveness and report on that review in the annual report. The monitoring and review should cover all material controls, including financial, operational and compliance controls.
30. In annual and half-yearly financial statements, the board should state whether it considers it appropriate to adopt the going concern basis of accounting in preparing them, and identify any material uncertainties to the company's ability to continue to do so over a period of at least 12 months from the date of approval of the financial statements.
31. Taking account of the company's current position and principal risks, the board should explain in the annual report how it has assessed the prospects of the company, over what period it has done so and why it considers that period to be appropriate. The board should state whether it has a reasonable expectation that the company will be able to continue in operation and meet its liabilities as they fall due over the period of their assessment, drawing attention to any qualifications or assumptions as necessary.

5 Remuneration

Principles

P. Remuneration policies and practices should be designed to support strategy and promote long-term sustainable success. Executive remuneration should

9 Principal risks should include, but are not necessarily limited to, those that could result in events or circumstances that might threaten the company's business model, future performance, solvency or liquidity and reputation. In deciding which risks are principal risks, companies should consider the potential impact and probability of the related events or circumstances, and the timescale over which they may occur.

be aligned to company purpose and values, and be clearly linked to the successful delivery of the company's long-term strategy.

Q. A formal and transparent procedure for developing policy on executive remuneration and determining director and senior management[10] remuneration should be established. No director should be involved in deciding their own remuneration outcome.

R. Directors should exercise independent judgement and discretion when authorising remuneration outcomes, taking account of company and individual performance, and wider circumstances.

Provisions

32. The board should establish a remuneration committee of independent non-executive directors, with a minimum membership of three, or in the case of smaller companies, two.[11] In addition, the chair of the board can only be a member if they were independent on appointment and cannot chair the committee. Before appointment as chair of the remuneration committee, the appointee should have served on a remuneration committee for at least 12 months.
33. The remuneration committee should have delegated responsibility for determining the policy for executive director remuneration and setting remuneration for the chair, executive directors and senior management.[12] It should review workforce[13] remuneration and related policies and the alignment of incentives and rewards with culture, taking these into account when setting the policy for executive director remuneration.
34. The remuneration of non-executive directors should be determined in accordance with the articles of association or, alternatively, by the board. Levels of remuneration for the chair and all non-executive directors should reflect the time commitment and responsibilities of the role. Remuneration for all non-executive directors should not include share options or other performance-related elements.
35. Where a remuneration consultant is appointed, this should be the responsibility of the remuneration committee. The consultant should be identified in the annual report alongside a statement about any other connection it has with the company or individual directors. Independent judgement should be exercised when evaluating the advice of external third parties and when receiving views from executive directors and senior management.[14]
36. Remuneration schemes should promote long-term shareholdings by executive directors that support alignment with long-term shareholder interests.

10 See footnote 4.
11 See footnote 8.
12 See footnote 4.
13 See the *Guidance on Board Effectiveness* Section 5 for a description of 'workforce' in this context.
14 See footnote 4.

Share awards granted for this purpose should be released for sale on a phased basis and be subject to a total vesting and holding period of five years or more. The remuneration committee should develop a formal policy for post-employment shareholding requirements encompassing both unvested and vested shares.

37. Remuneration schemes and policies should enable the use of discretion to override formulaic outcomes. They should also include provisions that would enable the company to recover and/or withhold sums or share awards, and specify the circumstances in which it would be appropriate to do so.
38. Only basic salary should be pensionable. The pension contribution rates for executive directors, or payments in lieu, should be aligned with those available to the workforce. The pension consequences and associated costs of basic salary increases and any other changes in pensionable remuneration, or contribution rates, particularly for directors close to retirement, should be carefully considered when compared with workforce arrangements.
39. Notice or contract periods should be one year or less. If it is necessary to offer longer periods to new directors recruited from outside the company, such periods should reduce to one year or less after the initial period. The remuneration committee should ensure compensation commitments in directors' terms of appointment do not reward poor performance. They should be robust in reducing compensation to reflect departing directors' obligations to mitigate loss.
40. When determining executive director remuneration policy and practices, the remuneration committee should address the following:
    - clarity – remuneration arrangements should be transparent and promote effective engagement with shareholders and the workforce;
    - simplicity – remuneration structures should avoid complexity and their rationale and operation should be easy to understand;
    - risk – remuneration arrangements should ensure reputational and other risks from excessive rewards, and behavioural risks that can arise from target-based incentive plans, are identified and mitigated;
    - predictability – the range of possible values of rewards to individual directors and any other limits or discretions should be identified and explained at the time of approving the policy;
    - proportionality – the link between individual awards, the delivery of strategy and the long-term performance of the company should be clear. Outcomes should not reward poor performance; and
    - alignment to culture – incentive schemes should drive behaviours consistent with company purpose, values and strategy.
41. There should be a description of the work of the remuneration committee in the annual report, including:
    - an explanation of the strategic rationale for executive directors' remuneration policies, structures and any performance metrics;

- reasons why the remuneration is appropriate using internal and external measures, including pay ratios and pay gaps;
- a description, with examples, of how the remuneration committee has addressed the factors in Provision 40;
- whether the remuneration policy operated as intended in terms of company performance and quantum, and, if not, what changes are necessary;
- what engagement has taken place with shareholders and the impact this has had on remuneration policy and outcomes;
- what engagement with the workforce has taken place to explain how executive remuneration aligns with wider company pay policy; and
- to what extent discretion has been applied to remuneration outcomes and the reasons why.

Appendix 3 – Statutory forms and filing periods

Introduction

Set out below are the main forms used by private and public companies showing the section to which the form relates, the relevant filing period and whether the form may be filed using the web filing service.

Type	*Description*	*CA2006 section(s)*	*Form code*	*Filing period*	*Web filing available*
Accounts					
	Change of accounting reference date	392	AA01	Effective on registration	Yes
	Dormant company accounts (DCA)	441	AA02	9 months	Yes
	Notice of resolution removing auditors from office AA03	512	AA03	14 days	
	Statement of guarantee by a parent undertaking of a subsidiary company	394A, 448A, 479A	AA06	On submission of unaudited subsidiary accounts	
Change of constituion					
	Notice of restriction on the company's articles	23	CC01	Effective of registration	
	Notice of removal of restriction on the company's articles	23	CC02	Effective of registration	
	Statement of compliance where amendment of articles restricted	24	CC03	Effective of registration	

Type	*Description*	*CA2006 section(s)*	*Form code*	*Filing period*	*Web filing available*
	Statement of company's objects	31	CC04	Effective of registration	
	Change of constitution by enactment	34	CC05	Effective of registration	
	Change of constitution by order of court or other authority	35	CC06	Effective of registration	
Change of name					
	Exemption from requirement as to use of 'limited' or 'cyfyngedig' on change of name	60	NE01	On application	
	Notice of change of name by resolution	78	NM01	On application	Yes
	Notice of change of name by conditional resolution	78	NM02	On application	
	Notice confirming satisfaction of the conditional resolution for change of name	78	NM03	On application	
	Notice of change of name by means provided for in the articles	79	NM04	On application	
	Notice of change of name by resolution of directors	64 or 1033	NM05	On application	
	Request to seek comments of government department or other specified body on change of name	56	NM06	On application	
Change of registered office					
	Change of registered office address	87	AD01	Effective on registration	Yes
	Notice to change the situation of an England and Wales company or a Welsh company	88	AD05	Effective on registration	

Type	*Description*	*CA2006 section(s)*	*Form code*	*Filing period*	*Web filing available*
Company records					
	Notification of Single Alternative Inspection Location (SAIL)	114, 162, 228, 237, 275, 358, 702, 805, 809, 877, 859Q, 892	AD02	Effective on registration	Yes
	Change of location of the company records to the single alternative inspection location (SAIL)	114, 128D, 162, 228, 237, 275, 358, 702, 720, 743, 790N, 790Z, 805, 809, 859Q, 877, 892	AD03	Effective on registration	Yes
	Change of location of the company records to the registered office	114, 128D, 162, 228, 237, 275, 358, 702, 720, 743, 790N, 790Z, 805, 809, 859Q, 877, 892	AD04	Effective on registration	Yes
	Election to keep information from register of directors on the central (public) register	167A	EH01	Effective on registration	Yes
	Election to keep information from register of directors' residential addresses on the central (public) register	167A	EH02	Effective on registration	Yes
	Election to keep information from register of secretaries on the central (public) register	279A	EH03	Effective on registration	Yes

Type	*Description*	*CA2006 section(s)*	*Form code*	*Filing period*	*Web filing available*
	Election to keep information from register of people with significant control (PSC) on the central (public) register	790X	EH04	Effective on registration	Yes
	Election to keep information from register of members on the central (public) register	128B	EH05	Effective on registration	Yes
	Update to members' information held on the central (public) register	128E	EH06	As soon as possible once obligation to notify commences	
	Withdrawal of election to keep information from register of directors on the central (public) register	167E	EW01	Effective on registration	Yes
	Withdrawal of election to keep information from register of directors' usual residential addresses on the central (public) register	167E	EW02	Effective on registration	Yes
	Withdrawal of election to keep information from register of secretaries on the central (public) register	279E	EW03	Effective on registration	Yes
	Withdrawal of election to keep information from register of people with significant control (PSC) on the central (public) register	790ZD	EW04	Effective on registration	Yes
	Withdrawal of election to keep members' information on the central (public) register	128J	EW05	Effective on registration	Yes

Type	Description	CA2006 section(s)	Form code	Filing period	Web filing available
Confirmation statement					
	Confirmation statement	853A	CS01	14 days	Yes
Directors and secretaries					
	Appointment of director	167, 167D	AP01	14 days	Yes
	Appointment of corporate director	167, 167D	AP02	14 days	Yes
	Appointment of secretary	276, 279D	AP03	14 days	Yes
	Appointment of corporate secretary	276, 279D	AP04	14 days	Yes
	Change of director's details	167, 167D	CH01	14 days	Yes
	Change of corporate director's details	167, 167D	CH02	14 days	Yes
	Change of secretary's details	276, 279D	CH03	14 days	Yes
	Change of corporate secretary's details	276	CH04	14 days	Yes
	Termination of appointment of director	167, 167D	TM01	14 days	Yes
	Termination of appointment of secretary	276, 279D	TM02	14 days	Yes
Incorporation					
	Application to register a company	9	IN01	On application	Yes
Investment companies					
	Notice of intention to carry on business as an investment company	833(1)	IC01	Effective on registration	
	Notice that a company no longer wishes to be an investment company	833(4)	IC02	Effective on registration	
Mortgage					
	Particulars of an instrument of alteration to a floating charge created by a company registered in Scotland	ss. 410, 466 CA 1985	466 (Scot)	21 days	

Type	*Description*	*CA2006 section(s)*	*Form code*	*Filing period*	*Web filing available*
	Particulars of a charge	859A & 859J	MR01	21 days	Yes
	Particulars of a charge subject to which property or undertaking has been acquired	859C & 859J	MR02	Effective on registration	Yes
	Particulars for the registration of a charge to secure a series of debentures	859B & 859J	MR03	21 days	
	Statement of satisfaction in full or in part of a charge	859L	MR04	Effective on registration	Yes
	Statement that part or the whole of the property charged (a) has been released from the charge (b) no longer forms part of the company's property or undertaking	859L	MR05	Effective on registration	Yes
	Statement of company acting as a trustee	859J	MR06	Effective on registration	
	Particulars of alteration of a charge (particulars of a negative pledge)	859O	MR07	Effective on registration	
	Particulars of a charge where there is no instrument	859A, 859J	MR08	21 days	
	Particulars of a charge subject to which property or undertaking has been acquired where there is no instrument	859C, 859J	MR09	Effective on registration	
	Particulars for the registration of a charge to secure a series of debentures where there is no instrument	859B, 859J	MR10	21 days	

Type	Description	CA2006 section(s)	Form code	Filing period	Web filing available
Opening of overseas branch register					
	Notice of opening of overseas branch register	130	AD06	0	
	Notice of discontinuance of overseas branch register	135	AD07	0	
Other appointments					
	Appointment of a manager under section 47 of the Companies (Audit, Investigations and Community Enterprise) Act 2004 or receiver and manager under section 18 of the Charities Act 1993 or judicial factor (Scotland)	1154	AP05	14 days	
	Change of service address for manager appointed under section 47 of the Companies (Audit, Investigations and Community Enterprise) Act 2004 or receiver and manager under section 18 of the Charities Act 1993 or judicial factor (Scotland)	1154	CH05	14 days	
	Termination of appointment of manager under section 47 of the Companies (Audit, Investigations and Community Enterprise) Act 2004 or receiver and manager under section 18 of the Charities Act 1993 or judicial factor (Scotland)	1154	TM03	14 days	

Type	*Description*	*CA2006 section(s)*	*Form code*	*Filing period*	*Web filing available*
People with significant control					
	Notice of individual person with significant control (PSC)	790K, 790ZA	PSC01	As soon as possible once obligation to notify arises	Yes
	Notice of relevant legal entity (RLE) with significant control	790K, 790ZA	PSC02	As soon as possible once obligation to notify arises	Yes
	Notice of other registrable person (ORP) with significant control	790K, 790ZA	PSC03	As soon as possible once obligation to notify arises	Yes
	Change of details of individual person with significant control (PSC)	790M, 790ZA	PSC04	As soon as possible once obligation to notify arises	Yes
	Change of details of relevant legal entity (RLE) with significant control	790M, 790ZA	PSC05	As soon as possible once obligation to notify arises	Yes
	Change of details of other registrable person (ORP) with significant control	790M, 790ZA	PSC06	As soon as possible once obligation to notify arises	Yes
	Notice of ceasing to be an individual person with significant control (PSC), relevant legal entity (RLE), or other registrable person (ORP)	790M, 790ZA	PSC07	As soon as possible once obligation to notify arises	Yes
	Notification of PSC statements	790M, 790ZA	PSC08	As soon as possible once obligation to notify arises	Yes
	Update to PSC statements	790M, 790ZA	PSC09	As soon as possible once obligation to notify arises	

Type	*Description*	*CA2006 section(s)*	*Form code*	*Filing period*	*Web filing available*
Receiver/Manager					
	Notice of appointment of an administrative receiver, receiver or manager	859K	RM01	7 days	
	Notice of ceasing to act as an administrative receiver, receiver or manager	859K	RM02	Effective on registration	
Registrar's powers					
	Replacement of document not meeting requirements for proper delivery	1076	RP01	As specified in request from Companies House	
	Application for rectification by the Registrar of Companies	1095 and regs 4, 5 Registrar of Companies and Applications for Striking off Regulations 2009	RP02A	On application	
	Application for rectification of a registered office or UK establishment address by the Registrar of Companies	1095 and regs 4, 5 Registrar of Companies and Applications for Striking off Regulations 2009	RP02B	On application	

Type	*Description*	*CA2006 section(s)*	*Form code*	*Filing period*	*Web filing available*
	Notice of an objection to a request for the Registrar of Companies to rectify the Register	1095 and regs 4, 5 Registrar of Companies and Applications for Striking off Regulations 2009	RP03	Within 28 days of application	
	Second filing of a document previously delivered		RP04	Effective on registration	
	Application for removal of material about directors who have not consented to act	1095(4A) and regs 4, 5 Registrar of Companies and Applications for Striking off Regulations 2009	RP06	Effective on registration	
	Application to change a company's disputed registered office address	The Companies (Address of Registered Office) Regulations 2016	RP07	Effective on registration	
	Correction of a director's date of birth which was incorrectly stated on incorporation	167	RPCH01	Effective on registration	
	Certified voluntary translation of an original document that is or has been delivered to the Registrar of Companies	1106, reg 4 Companies (Cross-Border Mergers) Regulations 2007	VT01	Effective on registration	

Type	Description	CA2006 section(s)	Form code	Filing period	Web filing available
Re-registration					
	Application by a private company for re-registration as a public company	94 and 765(4)	RR01	15 days	
	Application by a public company for re-registration as a private limited company	100	RR02	15 days	
	Notice by the company of application to the court for cancellation of resolution for re-registration	99(2)	RR03	15 days	
	Notice by the applicants of application to the court for cancellation of resolution for re-registration	99(1)	RR04	On application to Court	
	Application by a private limited company for re-registration as an unlimited company	103	RR05	15 days	
	Application by an unlimited company for re-registration as a private limited company	106	RR06	15 days	
	Application by a public company for re-registration as a private unlimited company	110	RR07	15 days	
	Application by a public company for re-registration as a private limited company following a court order reducing capital	651	RR08	15 days	
	Application by a public company for re-registration as a private company following cancellation of shares	664	RR09	15 days	
	Statement of capital	108	SH19	15 days	

Type	*Description*	*CA2006 section(s)*	*Form code*	*Filing period*	*Web filing available*
Restoration					
	Application for administrative restoration to the Register	1024	RT01	On application	
Share capital					
	Notice to non-assenting shareholders	984(3)	984	1 month, to shareholders only	
	Notice to non-assenting shareholders	980(1)	980(1)	Within 3 months after the last day the offer can be accepted, or 6 months after the date of the offer where not governed by the Takeover Code	
	Statutory declaration relating to a notice to non-assenting shareholders	980(4)(b)	980dec	When offeror gives notice under s. 979	
	Notice of application to court to cancel share warrants	s. 5(5), sch. 4 SBEEA 2015	NAC01	On application	
	Return of allotment of shares	555	SH01	1 month	Yes
	Notice of consolidation, sub-division, redemption of shares or re-conversion of stock into shares	619, 621, 689	SH02	1 month	
	Return of purchase of own shares	707	SH03	28 days	
	Notice of sale or transfer of treasury shares	728	SH04	28 days	

Type	*Description*	*CA2006 section(s)*	*Form code*	*Filing period*	*Web filing available*
	Notice of cancellation of treasury shares	730	SH05	28 days	
	Notice of cancellation of shares	708	SH06	28 days	
	Notice of cancellation of shares held by or for a public company	663	SH07	1 month	
	Notice of name or other designation of class of shares	636	SH08	1 month	
	Return of allotment by unlimited company allotting a new class of shares	556	SH09	1 month	
	Notice of particulars of variation of rights attached to shares	637	SH10	1 month	
	Notice of new class of members	638	SH11	1 month	
	Notice of particulars of variation of class rights	640	SH12	1 month	
	Notice of name or other designation of class of members	639	SH13	1 month	
	Notice of redenomination	625	SH14	1 month	
	Notice of reduction of capital following redenomination	627	SH15	15 days	
	Notice by the applicants of application to court for cancellation of the special resolution approving a redemption or purchase of shares out of capital	722(1)	SH16	On application to court	

Type	*Description*	*CA2006 section(s)*	*Form code*	*Filing period*	*Web filing available*
	Notice by the company of application to court for cancellation of the special resolution approving a redemption or purchase of shares out of capital	722(2)	SH17	On receipt of notice that an application has been made	
	Statement of capital for reduction supported by solvency statement or court order	644 and 649	SH19	15 days	
	Statement of capital on cancellation of share warrants	s. 7(2), sch. 4 SBEEA 2015	SH19	15 days	
	Application for trading certificate for a public company	761 and 762	SH50	On application	
Strike off and dissolution					
	Striking off application by a company	1003	DS01	On application	
	Withdrawal of striking off application by a company	1010	DS02	On application	Yes

Appendix 4 – Sensitive words

Introduction

As set out in Chapter 4, companies will not be incorporated within or be permitted to change their name to a name which gives the impression that the company is connected to central or local government, or uses a word or expression that requires consent of the Secretary of State without written justification or consent as appropriate.

The list of sensitive words are set out in Schedules 1 and 2 of the Company, Limited Liability Partnership and Business Names (Sensitive Words and Expressions) Regulations 2014 (SI 2014/3140), reproduced below.

SCHEDULE 1

SPECIFIED WORDS AND EXPRESSIONS

PART 1

Words and Expressions specified for the purposes of sections 55(1) and 1194(1) of the 2006 Act.

Accredit
Accreditation
Accredited
Accrediting
Adjudicator
Association
Assurance
Assurer
Audit office
Auditor General
*Banc
Bank
Banking
Benevolent
*Breatannach
*Breatainn
*Brenhinol
*Brenin
*Brenhiniaeth
Britain
British
Chamber of commerce
Charitable
Charity
Charter
Chartered
Child maintenance
Child support
*Coimisean
*Comhairle
*Comisiwn
Commission
Co-operative
Council
*Cyngor
Dental
Dentistry
*Diùc
*Dug
Duke
Ei Fawrhydi
England
English
Federation
Friendly Society

Foundation
Fund
Government
*Gwasanaeth iechyd
Health centre
Health service
Health visitor
His Majesty
HPSS
HSC
Inspectorate
Institute
Institution
Insurance
Insurer
Judicial appointment
King
Licensing
*Llywodraeth
Medical centre
Midwife
Midwifery
*Mòrachd
Mutual
NHS
Northern Ireland
Northern Irish
Nurse
Nursing
Oifis sgrùdaidh
*Oilthigh
Ombudsman
*Ombwdsmon
*Parlamaid
Parliament
Parliamentarian
Parliamentary
Patent
Patentee
Police
Polytechnic
Post office
*Prifysgol
Prince
*Prionnsa
*Prydain
*Prydeinig
Queen
Reassurance
Reassurer
Registrar
Regulator
Reinsurance
Reinsurer
*Riaghaltas
*Rìgh
*Rìoghachd Aonaichte
*Rìoghail
*Rìoghalachd
Royal
Royalty
Scotland
Scottish
*Senedd
Sheffield
*Siambr fasnach
Social service
Society
Special school
Standards
Stock exchange
*Swyddfa archwilio
*Teyrnas Gyfunol
*Teyrnas Unedig
Trade union
Tribunal
Trust
*Tywysog
Underwrite
Underwriting
University
Wales
Welsh
Windsor

*Restrictions also apply to the grammatically mutated forms of these words and expressions.

PART 2

Words and Expressions specified for the purposes of section 55(1) of the 2006 Act

Alba
Albannach
Na h-Alba
*Cymru
*Cymraeg
*Cymreig

SCHEDULE 2

LIST OF GOVERNMENT DEPARTMENTS AND OTHER BODIES WHOSE VIEWS MUST BE SOUGHT

PART 1

Applications Where Situation of Registered Office or Principal Place of Business is Irrelevant

Column (1) *Word or expression specified under regulation 3*	*Column (2)* *Specified Government department or other body whose view must be sought*
Accredit	Department for Business, Energy & Industrial Strategy
Accreditation	Department for Business, Energy & Industrial Strategy
Accredited	Department for Business, Energy & Industrial Strategy
Accrediting	Department for Business, Energy & Industrial Strategy
Assurance	Financial Conduct Authority
Assurer	Financial Conduct Authority
Banc	Financial Conduct Authority
Bank	Financial Conduct Authority
Banking	Financial Conduct Authority
Brenhinol	The Welsh Assembly Government
Brenin	The Welsh Assembly Government
Brenhiniaeth	The Welsh Assembly Government
Child maintenance	Department for Work and Pensions
Child support	Department for Work and Pensions
Dental	General Dental Council
Dentistry	General Dental Council
Diùc	The Scottish Government
Dug	The Welsh Assembly Government
Ei Fawrhydi	The Welsh Assembly Government
Friendly Society	Financial Conduct Authority
Fund	Financial Conduct Authority
Gwasanaeth iechyd	The Welsh Assembly Government
Health visitor	Nursing & Midwifery Council
HPSS	Department of Health, Social Services and Public Safety
HSC	Department of Health, Social Services and Public Safety
Insurance	Financial Conduct Authority
Insurer	Financial Conduct Authority
Judicial appointment	Ministry of Justice
Llywodraeth	The Welsh Assembly Government
Medical centre	Department of Health, Social Services and Public Safety

Column (1) *Word or expression specified under regulation 3*	*Column (2)* *Specified Government department or other body whose view must be sought*
Midwife	Nursing & Midwifery Council
Midwifery	Nursing & Midwifery Council
Mòrachd	The Scottish Government
Mutual	Financial Conduct Authority
NHS	Department of Health
Nurse	Nursing & Midwifery Council
Nursing	Nursing & Midwifery Council
Oifis sgrùdaidh	Audit Scotland
Oilthigh	The Scottish Government
Parlamaid	The Scottish Parliamentary Corporate Body
Parliament	The Corporate Officer of the House of Lords and The Corporate Officer of the House of Commons
Parliamentarian	The Corporate Officer of the House of Lords and The Corporate Officer of the House of Commons
Parliamentary	The Corporate Officer of the House of Lords and The Corporate Officer of the House of Commons
Patent	The Patent Office
Patentee	The Patent Office
Polytechnic	Department for Business, Energy & Industrial Strategy
Prifysgol	The Welsh Assembly Government
Prionnsa	The Scottish Government
Reassurance	Financial Conduct Authority
Reassurer	Financial Conduct Authority
Reinsurance	Financial Conduct Authority
Reinsurer	Financial Conduct Authority
Riaghaltas	The Scottish Government
Rìgh	The Scottish Government
Rìoghail	The Scottish Government
Rìoghalachd	The Scottish Government
Senedd	The National Assembly for Wales
Sheffield	The Company of Cutlers in Hallamshire
Swyddfa archwilio	Auditor General for Wales
Tywysog	The Welsh Assembly Government
Underwrite	Financial Conduct Authority
Underwriting	Financial Conduct Authority

PART 2

Applications Where Situation of Registered Office or Principal Place of Business is Relevant

Column (1)	*Column (2)*	*Column (3)*	*Column (4)*	*Column (5)*
	Specified Government department or other body whose view must be sought			
Word or expression specified under regulation 3	*under regulation 6(a)*	*under regulation 6(b)*	*under regulation 6(c)*	*under regulation 6(d)*
Audit office	Comptroller & Auditor General	Auditor General for Wales	Audit Scotland	Northern Ireland Audit Office
Charitable, Charity	The Charity Commission	The Charity Commission	Office of the Scottish Charity Regulator	The Charity Commission
Duke, His Majesty, King, Prince, Queen, Royal, Royalty, Windsor	Ministry of Justice	The Welsh Assembly Government	The Scottish Government	Ministry of Justice
Health centre Health service	Department of Health	The Welsh Assembly Government	The Scottish Government	Department of Health, Social Services and Public Safety
Police	The Home Office	The Home Office	The Scottish Government	Department of Justice in Northern Ireland
Special school	Department for Education	The Welsh Assembly Government	The Scottish Government	Department of Education
University	Department for Business, Energy & Industrial Strategy	The Welsh Assembly Government	The Scottish Government	Department for Employment and Learning

Appendix 5 – Recommended retention periods for documents

Type of document	Period of retention
Certificate of incorporation	Original should be kept permanently
Certificate to commence business (public company)	Original to be kept permanently
Board minutes	Originals to be kept permanently
Minutes of general and class meetings, directors' minutes, written resolutions	Originals to be kept permanently
Annual report and accounts	Signed copy to be kept permanently (a stock of spare copies should be maintained for up to five years to meet casual requests)
Trust deeds	Originals to be kept permanently
Circulars to shareholders including notices of meetings	Master copy to be kept permanently
Memorandum and articles of association	Original copy to be kept permanently
Seal book/register	Original to be kept permanently
Proxy forms/polling cards	One month if no poll demanded; one year if poll demanded
Register of directors and secretaries, register of directors' interests, register of interests in voting shares, register of charges, register of members	Originals to be kept permanently
Register of debenture or loan stock holders	Seven years after redemption of stock
Forms for application of shares, debentures, etc., forms of acceptance and transfer, renounceable letters of acceptance and allotment, renounceable share certificates	Originals to be kept permanently

Type of document	Period of retention
Request for designation or re-designation of accounts, letters of request, allotment sheets	Originals to be kept permanently
Letters of indemnity for lost share certificates	All originals to be kept permanently
Stop notices and other court orders	Originals to be kept permanently
Powers of attorney	Copies to be retained permanently
Dividend and interest bank mandate forms	Original to be kept until account closed
Cancelled share or stock certificates	One year
Notification of change of address	Two years
Any contract or memorandum to purchase the company's own shares	Ten years
Report of an interest in voting shares for investigations requisitioned by members	Six years
Register of interest in shares when company ceases to be a public company	Six years
Contracts with customers, suppliers or agents	Six years after expiry
Licensing agreements	Six years after expiry
Rental and hire purchase agreements	Six years after expiry
Indemnities and guarantees	Six years after expiry
Deeds of title	Permanently
Leases	Twelve years after lease has terminated
Agreements with architects, builders, etc.	Six years after contract completion
Patent and trademark records	Permanently
Accounting records required by the Companies Acts	Six years for a public company; three years for a private company
Taxation returns and records	Six years
Internal financial reports	Five years
Statements and instructions to banks	Six years
Staff personnel records	Seven years after employment ceases
Patent agreements with staff	Twenty years after employment ceases

Type of document	Period of retention
Applications for jobs	Up to twelve months
Payroll records	Twelve years
Salary registers	Six years
Tax returns	Permanently
Expense accounts	Seven years
Employment agreements	Permanently
Time cards and piece-work records	Two years
Wages records	Six years
Medical records	Twelve years
Industrial training records	Six years
Accident books	Twelve years
Trustees and rules (pension schemes)	Permanently
Trustees' minute book	Permanently
Pension fund annual accounts and HMRC approvals	Permanently
Investment records	Permanently
Actuarial valuation records	Permanently
Contribution records	Permanently
Records of ex-pensioners	Six years after cessation of benefit
Pension scheme investment policies	Twelve years after cessation
Group health policies	Twelve years after final cessation of benefit
Group personal accident policies	Twelve years after cessation of benefit
Public liability policies	Permanently
Product liability policies	Permanently
Employers' liability policies	Permanently
Sundry insurance policies	Three years after lapse
Claims correspondence	Three years after settlement
Accident reports and relevant correspondence	Three years after settlement
Insurance schedules	Ten years

Type of document	Period of retention
Customs & Excise returns	Six years
Vehicle registration records, MOT certificates and vehicle maintenance records	Two years after disposal of vehicle
Certificates and other documents of title	Permanently or until investment disposed of

Precedents

Precedent 1 Pro forma directors' minute

ANY COMPANY LIMITED
('the Company')
Company Number: 987654321

Minutes of a Meeting of the Board of Directors of the Company held at Company Office, 1 The Street, Any Town, This County on 1st January 2016 at 10.00 am

Present:	J Smith T Jones
Attending:	J Doe – company secretary

Chairman

It was noted that John Smith was chairman of the meeting.

Notice and Quorum

The chairman reported that notice of the meeting had been given to all of the directors and noted that the quorum necessary for a meeting of the board of directors was present.

1st Topic heading

Brief introduction of matter being discussed, synopsis of discussion and decision reached.

2nd Topic heading

Brief introduction of matter being discussed, synopsis of discussion and decision reached.

Close of Meeting

There being no further business the chairman declared the meeting closed.

____

CHAIRMAN

Notes:
Section 172 of the Companies Act 2006

(1) A director of a company must act in the way he considers, in good faith, would be most likely to promote the success of the company for the benefit of its members as a whole, and in doing so have regard (amongst other matters) to –
   (a) the likely consequences of any decision in the long term,
   (b) the interests of the company's employees,
   (c) the need to foster the company's business relationships with suppliers, customers and others,
   (d) the impact of the company's operations on the community and the environment,
   (e) the desirability of the company maintaining a reputation for high standards of business conduct, and
   (f) the need to act fairly as between members of the company.

(2) Where or to the extent that the purposes of the company consist of or include purposes other than the benefit of its members, subsection (1) has effect as if the reference to promoting the success of the company for the benefit of its members were to achieving those purposes.

(3) The duty imposed by this section has effect subject to any enactment or rule of law requiring directors, in certain circumstances, to consider or act in the interests of creditors of the company.

Precedent 2 Pro forma directors' resolution to convene general meeting

General Meeting

The meeting considered the matter and **IT WAS RESOLVED THAT** a general meeting of the Company be convened and held on [•] 20 [•] at [•][on short notice immediately following this meeting] to consider and if deemed fit to approve a [special/ordinary] resolution to [•] **AND THAT** the company secretary be and is hereby authorised to sign and issue to the shareholders a notice convening the said meeting.

Precedent 3 Pro forma general meeting minute

[•] LIMITED
('the Company')
Company Number: [•]

Minutes of a General Meeting of the Company
held at [•]
on [•] 20[•] at [•] am/pm

Present:

Attending:

Chairman
It was noted that [•] was chairman of the meeting.

Notice and Quorum
[The chairman reported that all the Company's shareholders had consented to the meeting being held on short notice.] The chairman noted that a quorum was present. The notice convening the meeting was taken as read.

Business of the Meeting
The Chairman proposed [resolution 1 as set out in the notice of the meeting] / [that (text of resolution here)] and enquired if any members present had any questions.

There being no questions the resolution was put to the meeting, as an ordinary resolution, and passed unanimously on a show of hands.

Close of Meeting
There being no further business the chairman declared the meeting closed.

____

CHAIRMAN

Precedent 4 Pro forma members' written resolution

Company Number: [•]

The Companies Act 2006
PRIVATE COMPANY LIMITED BY SHARES
WRITTEN RESOLUTION[S]

[•] LIMITED
('the Company')

We, the undersigned, being members of the Company eligible to attend and vote at general meetings of the Company, hereby pass the following resolution[s] designated as [an ordinary] [a special] resolution[s] and agree that the said resolution[s] shall be as valid and effective as if it [they] had been passed at a general meeting the Company duly convened and held.

IT IS RESOLVED:

[•]

Signed:

.... Date: ....20[•]

[Name]

.... Date: ....20[•]

[Name]

Notes:

1. These written resolutions have been proposed by the directors of the Company. The purpose of these resolutions is [ ].
2. The circulation date of these written resolutions is [•] 20[•].
3. Please signify your agreement to those resolutions which you do agree to by signing against your name where indicated, enter the date on which you signed the document and initial those boxes relating to the corresponding resolutions to which you agree. Please then return the document to the Company.
4. If you sign the document and return it to the Company without indicating whether you agree to all the resolutions or any particular resolution being passed, it will be assumed by the Company that you agree to all of the resolutions being passed.
5. If you return the document signed, but undated, it will be assumed by the Company that you signed the document on the day immediately preceding the day on which it was received by the Company.
6. If not passed by the requisite majority of the total voting rights of eligible members, these written resolutions shall lapse on the [•] 20[•].
7. As the resolution is [an ordinary] [a special] resolution, the requisite majority needed to pass the resolution is a [simple majority] [three-fourths] of the total voting rights of eligible members.
8. Once these resolutions have been signed and returned to the Company, your agreement to them may not be revoked.

Precedent 5 Pro forma general meeting notice

[•] LIMITED

('the Company')

Company Number: [•]

Notice of General Meeting

NOTICE IS HEREBY GIVEN THAT a General Meeting of the Company will be held at [•] on [•] 20[•] at [•] am/pm to consider and if deemed fit to approve the following resolutions, resolution [•] being proposed as an ordinary resolution and resolution [•] being proposed as a special resolution:

Resolutions

1. Text of resolution 1 here
2. Text of resolution 2 here

Date: [•] 20[•] **BY ORDER OF THE BOARD**
Registered Office:

____
COMPANY SECRETARY
Notes:

1. A member entitled to attend and vote at the meeting is entitled to appoint more than one proxy, to exercise all or any of his rights to attend, speak and vote in his place on a show of hands or on a poll provided that each proxy is appointed to a different share or shares, or to a different £10.00 or multiple of £10.00 of stock. Such proxy need not be a member of the Company.
2. To be valid, the completed and signed form of proxy must be returned to [•] not less than 48 hours (excluding weekends, Christmas Day, Good Friday or recognised public and bank holidays) before the time fixed for the meeting. Lodging a form of proxy does not preclude a member from attending and voting at the meeting.

Precedent 6 Members' resolution to change company name

Special Resolution

THAT the name of the Company be changed to:

[•]

Precedent 7 Three-way form of proxy

[Company Name]

Company No. [ ]

FORM OF PROXY

Please use a **black** pen. Mark with an **X** inside the box as shown in the example. ☒

I/We hereby appoint the Chairman of the meeting OR the following person

[ ]

Please leave this box blank if you have selected the chairman. Do not insert your own name.

as my/our proxy to exercise all or any of my/our rights to attend, speak and vote in respect of my/our voting entitlement* on my/our behalf at the general meeting of [Company Name] to be held at [Address] on [Date] at [Time] am/pm and at any adjourned meeting.

Please tick here if this proxy appointment is one of multiple appointments being made* ☐

* For the appointment of more than one proxy please refer to note 2 below.

Ordinary Resolutions:

	For	Against	Vote Withheld
1. To [summary of resolution here]	☐	☐	☐
2. To [summary of resolution here]	☐	☐	☐
Special Resolution:			
3. To [summary of resolution here]	☐	☐	☐

I/We would like my/our proxy to vote on the resolution proposed at the meeting as indicated on this form.

Signature	**Date**

Explanatory Notes:

1. You may appoint a proxy or proxies to exercise all or any of your rights to attend, speak and vote on your behalf at the meeting. If you wish to appoint a person other than the chairman, please insert the name of your chosen proxy holder in the space provided.
2. To appoint more than one proxy you may photocopy this form. Please indicate in the box next to the proxy holder's name the number of shares in relation to which they are authorised to act as your proxy. Please also indicate by ticking the box provided if the proxy instruction is one of multiple instructions being given. All forms must be signed and should be returned together in the same envelope.
3. Unless otherwise indicated the proxy may vote as he or she sees fit or abstain in relation to any business of the meeting.
4. The 'Vote Withheld' option is provided to enable you to abstain on a resolution. Please note that a 'Vote Withheld' is not a vote in law and will not be counted in the votes 'For' and 'Against' a resolution.
5. If the appointor is a corporation, this form must be under its common seal or under the hand of some officer or attorney duly authorised in that behalf.
6. In the case of joint holders, the signature of any one holder will be sufficient, but the names of all the joint holders should be stated.
7. If this form is returned without indication as to how the person appointed proxy shall vote, he will exercise his discretion as to how he votes or whether he abstains from voting.
8. To be valid, this form must be completed and deposited at the Company's registered office not less than 48 hours (excluding any day that is not a working day) before the time fixed for holding the meeting.

Precedent 8 Copy of resolution for Companies House

Company Number: [•]

THE COMPANIES ACT 2006

SPECIAL RESOLUTION

OF

[•] LIMITED

COMPANY LIMITED BY SHARES

At a general meeting of the above-named Company, duly convened and held at [•] on the [•] day of 20[•], the following **SPECIAL RESOLUTION** was duly passed:

THAT the name of the Company be changed to:

[•]

____

DIRECTOR/COMPANY SECRETARY

Precedent 9 Directors' resolution to adopt company seal, overseas seal or security seal

[Company/Securities/Overseas] Seal

IT WAS RESOLVED THAT the seal, an impression of which is made in the margin of these minutes be adopted as the [company/security/overseas] seal of the company. In respect of the use of the overseas seal its use is authorised under the hand of Mr James Smith.

Precedent 10 Directors' resolution to change location of registered office

Registered Office

IT WAS RESOLVED THAT the registered office of the Company be changed to [•] and that the company secretary be instructed to file Form AD01 with the Registrar of Companies.

Precedent 11 Members' resolution to amend/adopt new articles of association

Special Resolution

THAT the articles of association of the Company be amended in the manner following, that is to say, by the deletion of the present clause [•] and the adoption of a new clause [•] namely:-

(see attached sheet)

OR

THAT the regulation attached hereto and initialled by the chairman for the purposes of identification be adopted as the articles of association of the company in substitution for and to the exclusion of the existing articles.

Precedent 12 Members' resolution to re-register a ltd company as a plc

Special Resolutions

(1) **THAT:**

(a) the Company be re-registered as a public company limited by shares within the meaning of the Companies Act 2006;

(b) the name of the Company be changed to [•] Plc; and

(c) with the exception of the subscriber clause the memorandum of association of the Company be deleted.

(2) **THAT** the regulations produced to the meeting and signed by the Chairman for the purposes of identification be adopted as the articles of association of the Company in substitution for and to the exclusion of the existing articles of association.

(*see attached copy*)

Precedent 13 Members' resolution to re-register a plc as a ltd company

Special Resolutions

(1) **THAT:**

(a) the Company be re-registered as a private company limited by shares within the meaning of the Companies Act 2006;

(b) the name of the Company be changed to **[•]** Limited; and

(c) with the exception of the subscriber clause the memorandum of association of the Company be deleted.

(2) **THAT** the regulations produced to the meeting and signed by the Chairman for the purposes of identification be adopted as the articles of association of the Company in substitution for and to the exclusion of the existing articles of association.

(*see attached copy*)

Precedent 14 Directors' resolution to appoint additional director

Appointment of Director

IT WAS RESOLVED THAT [•] having consented to act, be appointed as a director of the Company with [immediate effect][effect from [•] 20[•]] and that the company secretary be instructed to file form [AP1/AP02] with the Registrar of Companies.

Precedent 15 Director's general notice of interests

General notice of interests by a director

Director's Name
Director's Address

The Directors
[ ] [Limited][Plc]

Pursuant to section 185 of the Companies Act 2006, I give notice that I have the interest in each of the companies or firms Listed below which is shown against its name below and that I am to be regarded as interested in any transaction or arrangement which may, after the date hereof, be made with any of those companies or firms.

Name of company or firm		Nature and extent of interest
[XYZ Ltd]	[Shareholder]	[• % holding via family trust]

I also give notice that under that section I am connected with [each of] the person[s] Listed below and am to be regarded as interested in any transaction or arrangement which may, after the date hereof, be made with [any of] the undermentioned person[s].

Name of person	Nature and connection with that person
[ ]	[ ]
[ ]	[ ]

[date]
Signed:

____
[name of director]

Precedent 16 Directors' resolution to approve appointment of alternate director

Alternate Director

There was produced to the meeting a letter from [•] appointing [•] as their alternate director with effect from [•] 20[•]. It was noted that in accordance with article [•] of the Company's articles of association it was necessary for the directors to approve the appointment.

After due consideration **IT WAS RESOLVED THAT** the appointment of [•] as alternate director to [•] be approved and that the company secretary be instructed to file form [AP01/AP02] with the Registrar of Companies and make an appropriate entry in the Register of Directors.

Precedent 17 Members' resolution to approve director's service contract where more than two years' notice of termination required

Ordinary resolution

THAT the service contract proposed to be entered into between the company and Mr Smith, a director, as set out in the memorandum of terms attached to the notice convening this meeting be approved in terms of s. 188 Companies Act 2006.

Precedent 18 Directors' resolution to approve another director's conflict of interest

At this point Mr Smith formally declared his interest in the matter. It was noted that, in accordance with article [•] of the Company's articles of association, having declared his interest Mr Smith was entitled to consider and vote upon the matter.

In reaching their decision, the Directors considered the need to promote the success of the Company for the benefit of its members as a whole and, in doing so, had regard to the specific requirements of s. 172 of the Companies Act 2006.

Precedent 19 Pro forma AGM notice for an unlisted plc

[•] PLC

('the Company')

Company Number: [•]

Notice of Annual General Meeting

NOTICE IS HEREBY GIVEN THAT the 20[•] Annual General Meeting of the Company will be held at [•] on [•] 20[•] at [•]am/pm to consider and, if deemed fit, to approve the following resolutions, all of which are being proposed as ordinary resolutions:

Ordinary Resolution

1. To receive [and adopt] the accounts of the Company for the year ended/period to [•] 20[•] together with the reports thereon of the directors and the auditors of the Company.

2. To [receive the statement of the auditors made pursuant to Section 837(4) of the Companies Act 2006 ('the 2006 Act') and to] approve the recommendation of the directors that a final dividend of [ ]p per ordinary share be declared in respect of the year ended/period to [•] 20[•].
3. To reappoint [•] retiring as a director in accordance with the Company's articles of association and, being eligible, offering [himself/herself] for reappointment as a director of the Company.
4. To reappoint [•] retiring as a director due to [his/her] appointment having been made since the last annual general meeting of the Company in accordance with the Company's articles of association and, being eligible, offering [himself/herself] for reappointment as a director of the Company.
5. To [re]appoint [•] as auditors of the Company in accordance with Section 489 of the 2006 Act, until the conclusion of the next general meeting of the Company at which audited accounts are laid before members and to authorise the Directors to determine their remuneration.
6. That the Directors of the Company be and they are hereby authorised generally and unconditionally pursuant to and in accordance with section 551 of the Companies Act 2006 ('the 2006 Act') to exercise all the powers of the Company to allot relevant securities (within the meaning of section 560 of the 2006 Act up to an aggregate nominal amount of £[•] [(representing [•] per cent of the Company's issued ordinary share capital on [•] 20[•]) [specify applicable reference date] provided that this authority shall expire [on [•] 20[•]]/[on whichever is earlier of the date of the Company's next Annual General Meeting (and at the conclusion thereof) or 15 months from the date on which this resolution is passed] save that the Company may, pursuant to this authority, make offers or agreements before the expiry of this authority which would or might require relevant securities to be allotted after such expiry and the Directors may allot relevant securities in pursuance of such offers or agreements as if the authority conferred by this resolution had not expired *[and all authorities previously conferred upon the Directors pursuant to section 80 of the 1985 Act shall be revoked but without prejudice to any exercise of such other authorities prior to the date on which this resolution is passed]*.
7. That:
   (a) [subject to the passing of resolution [6] above,] the Directors be and they are hereby empowered pursuant to section 570 of the 2006 Act to allot equity securities (within the meaning of section 560 of the 2006 Act) for cash pursuant to the authority conferred by [resolution [6] above] as if section 561 of the 2006 Act did not apply to such allotment, provided that this power shall be limited to the allotment of equity securities:
      (i) in connection with an offer of equity securities by way of rights to the holders of ordinary shares [and/or any other persons entitled to participate therein] [(other than the Company itself in respect of any shares held by it as treasury shares within the meaning of section 573 of the 2006 Act)] in proportion (as nearly as may be) to their respective

holdings of ordinary shares [(or, as appropriate, the number of ordinary shares which such other persons are, for the purposes of such offer, deemed to hold)] on a record date fixed by the Directors but subject to such exclusions or other arrangements as the Directors may consider necessary or expedient to deal with [any legal or practical] problems under the laws of any territory or the requirements of any regulatory body or any stock exchange in any territory or in connection with fractional entitlements or otherwise howsoever; or

(ii) [pursuant to the terms of any share scheme for directors and employees of the Company and/or its subsidiaries approved by the shareholders of the Company in general meeting; or]

(iii) (other than pursuant to paragraph[s] (i) [or (ii)] above) having (in the case of relevant shares (as defined in section 560 of the 2006 Act)) a nominal amount or (in the case of any other equity securities) giving the right to subscribe for or convert into relevant shares having a nominal amount, not exceeding in aggregate £[•] [(the 'Relevant Amount')] [(representing [•] per cent of the Company's issued ordinary share capital on [•] 20[•], being *[specify applicable reference date]*;

(b) [the Directors be and they are hereby empowered pursuant to section 573 of the 2006 Act to effect a sale of relevant shares held by the Company as treasury shares for cash as if section 561 of the 2006 Act did not apply to such sale[, provided that this power shall be limited to the sale of relevant shares held by the Company as treasury shares having a nominal amount which, when aggregated with the nominal amount of any relevant shares allotted or the subject of rights of subscription or conversion pursuant to paragraph (a)(iii) above, does not exceed the Relevant Amount].]

[Each of] the power[s] conferred by paragraph[s (a) [and (b)]] above shall expire [on [•] 20[•]]/[on whichever is earlier of the date of the Company's next Annual General Meeting (and at the conclusion thereof) or 15 months from the date on which this resolution is passed] save that the Company may, before the expiry of such power[s], make offers or agreements which would or might require equity securities to be allotted [and/or relevant shares held as treasury shares to be sold] after such expiry and the Directors may allot equity securities [and/or sell relevant shares held as treasury shares] in pursuance of such offers or agreements as if the power[s] conferred hereby had not expired [and all powers previously conferred upon the Directors pursuant to section 570 [and section 573] of the 2006 Act shall be revoked but without prejudice to any exercise of such other powers prior to the date on which this resolution is passed].

8. That, pursuant to section 366 of the 2006 Act, the Company and all companies that are subsidiaries of the Company [at the time this resolution is passed at any time during the period for which this resolution has effect] be and are hereby authorised to make/incur (in aggregate):

(a) political donations to political parties or independent election candidates not exceeding in total the amount of £[•];

(b) political donations to political organisations other than political parties not exceeding in total the amount of £[•];
(c) political expenditure not exceeding in total the amount of £[•], during the period beginning with the date of this resolution and ending [on [•] 20[•]]/[on whichever is the earlier of the date of the Company's next Annual General Meeting (and at the conclusion thereof) or [12 months] from the date on which this resolution is passed].

For the purposes of this resolution, the terms 'political donations', 'political parties', 'independent election candidates', 'political organisation' and 'political expenditure' have the meanings set out in Part 14 of the 2006 Act.]

Date: [•] 20[•] **BY ORDER OF THE BOARD**

Registered Office:

____

COMPANY SECRETARY

[insert notice notes here - see precedent 5]

Precedent 20 Members' resolution to remove a director

Ordinary Resolution

THAT [•] be removed as a director of the company with immediate effect.

Precedent 21 Special notice of proposed removal of director

[Proposer's name and address]

The Directors
[Company Name]
[Company Registered Office Address]

Date: [•] 20[•]

Dear Sirs

I hereby give notice pursuant to section 168(2) of the Companies Act 2006 of my intention to propose the following resolution as an ordinary resolution at the next annual general meeting of the company.

Ordinary Resolution

THAT [•] be removed as a director of the company with immediate effect.

Yours faithfully

____

[Name]
[Address]

Precedent 22 Draft article where all directors have died

In the event of the Company having no members and no directors as the result of the death or deaths of the members and/or directors, the personal representative of the last member or director to die has the right by notice in writing to appoint a director of the Company and this appointment shall have the same effect as if made in a general meeting. Where due to circumstances resulting in the death of two or more members or directors it is uncertain which of them survived the longest it shall be assumed that death occurred in the order of seniority, thus the younger will be assumed to have outlived the elder.

Precedent 23 Directors' resolution to note director resignation

Resignation of Director

It was noted that a letter of resignation had been received from [•] resigning as a director with [immediate effect][effect from [•] 20[•]] and **IT WAS RESOLVED THAT** the company secretary be instructed to file form TM01 with the Registrar of Companies.

Precedent 24 Directors' resolution to establish board committee

Board committee

IT WAS RESOLVED THAT [•] and [•] be appointed as a board committee to consider [•] and that the committee shall have all the powers of the board [subject to any regulations or resolutions or restrictions that may be imposed upon them by the board from time to time/subject to the terms of reference produced to the meeting and forming part of these minutes].

Precedent 25 Pro forma notice of directors' meeting and agenda

[•] LIMITED
('the Company')
Company Number: [•]

Notice is given that a Meeting of the Board of Directors of the Company will be held at [•] on [•] 20[•] at [•] am/pm

AGENDA

1. Minutes of the meeting held on [•] 20[•]
2. Matters arising
3. Operations report
4. Finance report
5. Project overview
6. Other business
   Change of registered office
   Meeting dates for 2016

Precedent 26 Directors' resolution to appoint chairman, vice chairman or deputy chairman

Chairman/Deputy chairman/Vice chairman

IT WAS RESOLVED THAT [•] be and is hereby appointed as [chairman/deputy chairman/vice chairman] of the board of directors until [further notice/for a period of three years] upon the terms set out in the letter of appointment attached.

Precedent 27 Sole director's resolution to appoint additional director(s)

Director

It was resolved that in accordance with regulation 1(3) of the Model Articles and forming part of the articles of association of the company that **[•]** be and is hereby appointed as an additional director with immediate effect.

Precedent 28 Draft article to vest all powers in a sole director

A sole Director shall have authority to exercise all the powers and discretions by the Model Articles for Private Companies (the Model Articles) or these articles expressed to be vested in the directors generally and the quorum for the transaction of the business of the directors shall be one and the provisions of regulation 11 in the Model Articles shall be modified accordingly. Regulation 11(3) of the Model Articles shall not apply to the Company.

Precedent 29 Pro forma directors' resolution in writing

[•] LIMITED

('the Company')

Company Number: [•]

Resolutions in writing of the sole director of the Company in accordance with [Regulation 8 of the model articles for private companies OR Regulation 7 of the model articles for public companies] that forms part of the Articles of Association of the Company.

____

20[•]

____

[subject heading]

IT WAS RESOLVED THAT [•].

In reaching their decision, the Directors considered the need to promote the success of the Company for the benefit of its members as a whole and, in doing so, had regard to the specific requirements of s. 172 of the Companies Act 2006.

____

(Director's Name)

Notes:
Section 172 of the Companies Act 2006

(1) A director of a company must act in the way he considers, in good faith, would be most likely to promote the success of the company for the benefit of its members as a whole, and in doing so have regard (amongst other matters) to:
  - (a) the likely consequences of any decision in the long term,
  - (b) the interests of the company's employees,
  - (c) the need to foster the company's business relationships with suppliers, customers and others,
  - (d) the impact of the company's operations on the community and the environment,
  - (e) the desirability of the company maintaining a reputation for high standards of business conduct, and
  - (f) the need to act fairly as between members of the company.

(2) Where or to the extent that the purposes of the company consist of or include purposes other than the benefit of its members, subsection (1) has effect as if the reference to promoting the success of the company for the benefit of its members were to achieving those purposes.

(3) The duty imposed by this section has effect subject to any enactment or rule of law requiring directors, in certain circumstances, to consider or act in the interests of creditors of the company.

Precedent 30 Company secretary's certification of minutes

I hereby certify that the following is an extract of the minutes of the board of directors of the Company held on [•] 20[•].

____

Company secretary

Precedent 31 Members' resolution to approve substantial property transaction

Ordinary Resolution

THAT in accordance with ss. 190(1) and (2) of the Companies Act 2006 the sale by the Company to [•] Limited, a company in which Mr [•], Director of the company is interested by virtue of being a director and shareholder, of the freehold property situated at [•] for the sum of [•] be approved.

Precedent 32 Members' resolution to approve political donation by company

THAT, pursuant to section 366 of the 2006 Act, the Company and all companies that are subsidiaries of the Company [at the time this resolution is passed at any time during the period for which this resolution has effect] be and are hereby authorised to make/incur (in aggregate):

(a) political donations to political parties or independent election candidates not exceeding in total the amount of £[•];
(b) political donations to political organisations other than political parties not exceeding in total the amount of £[•];
(c) political expenditure not exceeding in total the amount of £[•], during the period beginning with the date of this resolution and ending [on [•] 20[•]]/[on whichever is the earlier of the date of the Company's next Annual General Meeting (and at the conclusion thereof) or [12 months] from the date on which this resolution is passed].

For the purposes of this resolution, the terms 'political donations', 'political parties', 'independent election candidates', 'political organisation' and 'political expenditure' have the meanings set out in Part 14 of the 2006 Act.]

Precedent 33 Directors' resolution to appoint company secretary or joint company secretary

Appointment of Company Secretary

IT WAS RESOLVED THAT [•] having consented to act, be appointed as the [joint] company secretary of the Company with [immediate effect][effect from [•] 20[•]] and that [•] be instructed to file form [AP03/AP04] with the Registrar of Companies.

Precedent 34 Directors' resolution to note resignation of company secretary

Resignation of Company Secretary

It was noted that a letter of resignation had been received from [•] resigning as the company secretary with [immediate effect][effect from [•] 20[•]] and that Form TM02 be filed with the Registrar of Companies.

Precedent 35 Directors' resolution to remove company secretary and appoint replacement

Removal and Appointment of Company Secretary

IT WAS RESOLVED THAT [•] be removed as company secretary with immediate effect and that [•] having consented to act, be appointed as the company secretary of the Company with [immediate effect][effect from [•] 20[•]] and that the new company secretary be instructed to file Forms [AP03/AP04] and TM02 with the Registrar of Companies.

Precedent 36 Members' resolution to remove restriction of issuing shares by virtue of legacy authorised share capital statement

THAT clause [•] formerly contained in the company's memorandum of association and now forming part of the articles of association be deleted and that subject to section [550 [and 551]] of the Companies Act 2006 there be no restriction on the number of shares that the Company can issue.

Precedent 37 Draft article to restrict issue of share over specified amount

THAT the articles of association be amended by the adoption of a new clause [•] as set out below:

The Directors shall have power to issue or allot shares up to a maximum issued and allotted share capital of £[•].

Precedent 38 Members' resolution to consolidate shares

Ordinary Resolution

THAT the 5,000 issued ordinary shares of £10 each in the capital of the Company be consolidated into 2,500 ordinary shares of £20 each on the basis that no member shall be entitled to a fraction of a share and fractional entitlements shall be aggregated and sold and purchased by the Company in accordance with resolution [•] the proceeds of sale, exceeding £3.00 will be distributed to the members concerned.

Precedent 39 Members' resolution to subdivide shares

Ordinary Resolution

THAT the 50 issued ordinary shares of £100 each in the capital of the Company be subdivided into 5,000 ordinary shares of £1.00 each on the basis of 100 new shares for each share currently held.

Precedent 40 Members' resolution to reconvert stock into shares

Ordinary Resolution

THAT £[•] of the principal amount outstanding on the 20[•] loan stock be converted into fully paid ordinary shares on the basis of 10 ordinary shares of £1.00 for each £10 unit of loan stock converted.

Precedent 41 Directors' resolution to cancel shares forfeited/ purchased

IT WAS RESOLVED THAT [•] ordinary shares of 50 pence each in the capital of the company, unpaid, and registered in the name of [•] be forfeited for non-payment of the call of 50 pence per share payable on or before [•] due notice of which was given to the said member on [•] in accordance with the resolution of the board dated [•] and that the said shares be sold, disposed of, reissued or cancelled in such manner as the directors may determine.

Precedent 42 Members' resolutions to authorise reduction of capital

Ordinary Resolution

THAT the issued capital of the company comprising 25,000 ordinary shares of £1.00 each be reduced to 5,000 ordinary shares of £1.00 each by the cancellation of 20,000 shares and the return of £20,000 to the members.

OR

THAT the issued capital of the company comprising 25,000 ordinary shares of £1.00 each be reduced to 25,000 ordinary shares of £0.10 each by the cancellation of £22,500 from the share premium account.

Precedent 43 Draft notice to convene class meeting to vary class rights

[•] LIMITED
('the Company')
Company Number: [•]

Notice of Class Meeting

NOTICE IS HEREBY GIVEN THAT a Class Meeting of the holders of Preference shares of the Company will be held at [•] on [•] 20[•] at [•]am/pm to consider and, if deemed fit, to approve the following resolution being proposed as a special resolution:

Special Resolution

THAT [•]

Date: [•] 20[•] **BY ORDER OF THE BOARD**

Registered Office:

____

COMPANY SECRETARY

Notes:

1. A holder of preference shares entitled to attend and vote at the meeting is entitled to appoint more than one proxy, to exercise all or any of his rights to attend, speak and vote in his place on a show of hands or on a poll provided that each proxy is appointed to a different share or shares, or to a different £10.00 or multiple of £10.00 of stock. Such proxy need not be a member of the Company.
2. To be valid, the completed and signed form of proxy must be returned to **[•]** not less than 48 hours (excluding weekends, Christmas Day, Good Friday or recognised public and bank holidays) before the time fixed for the meeting. Lodging a form of proxy does not preclude a member from attending and voting at the meeting.

Explanatory notes on the resolution

Resolution 1

[•]

Precedent 44 Draft notice to consider serious loss of capital

[•] LIMITED

('the Company')

Company Number: [•]

Notice of General Meeting

NOTICE IS HEREBY GIVEN THAT a General Meeting of the Company will be held at [•] on [•] 20[•] at [•]am/pm pursuant to s. 656 of the Companies Act 2006, to consider whether any, and if so what steps should be taken to deal with the situation arising by virtue of the fact that the net assets of the Company are half or less than half of its called-up share capital.

Date: [•] 20[•] **BY ORDER OF THE BOARD**

Registered Office:

____

COMPANY SECRETARY

Notes:

1. A member entitled to attend and vote at the meeting is entitled to appoint more than one proxy, to exercise all or any of his rights to attend, speak and vote in his

place on a show of hands or on a poll provided that each proxy is appointed to a different share or shares, or to a different £10.00 or multiple of £10.00 of stock. Such proxy need not be a member of the Company.

Explanatory notes on the resolution

Resolution 1

The directors are required to convene a general meeting to consider what action to take, if any, if the company's net assets are half or less than half of its called up share capital. There is no resolution to be put to the meeting.

Precedent 45 Members' resolution to give directors authority to issue shares

Ordinary Resolution

THAT with effect from the time of the passing of this resolution the directors are unconditionally authorised, pursuant to s. 551 of the Companies Act 1985, to allot shares at any time or times during the period of five years from the date hereof.

Precedent 46 Members' resolution to waive pre-emption provisions on issue of new shares

Ordinary Resolution

THAT the provisions of s. 561 of the Companies Act 2006 shall not apply to the issue of up to 25,000 ordinary shares of £1.00 each provided such allotment shall take place within 12 months of the date of this resolution.

OR

THAT pursuant to the provisions of s. 570 of the Companies Act 2006 (the Act) the provisions of s. 561 of the Act shall not apply to the allotment of any shares where the directors have general authority in terms of s. 551 of the Act to allot shares.

Precedent 47 Application for new shares

[Applicant's address]

The Directors
[Company Name Limited
Company Number
Company Address]

Dear Sirs

I/We hereby apply for the issue of [•] ordinary shares of £[•] each in the capital of [•] Limited (the Company) to be issued at £[•] per share fully paid and hereby request you to allot such shares to me/us.

I/We enclose herewith a cheque in the sum of £[•] in full payment for the said shares. I/We agree to take the said shares subject to the articles of association of the Company and authorise you to enter my/our name in the register of members as the holder of the said shares.

Dated this [•] day of [•] 20[•]

Yours faithfully

____

[Print Name]

Precedent 48 Directors' resolution to issue new shares

Application for Shares

The chairman reported that the following application[s] had been received for the allotment of [a] share[s] in the capital of the Company:

[•] ordinary shares of £1.00 each from [•].
[•] ordinary shares of £1.00 each from [•].

Declaration of Interest

At this point [•] formally declared [his/her] interest in the matter as one of the applicants for the issue of shares. It was noted that having declared [his/her] interest [•] [was/was not] permitted by article [•] of the articles of association of the Company to consider and vote upon the matter.

Waiver of Pre-emption Rights

The chairman reported that the rights of pre-emption on allotment of these new shares, set out in the Company's articles of association, had been waived by the existing shareholders.

Allotment of Shares

After due consideration **IT WAS RESOLVED THAT** pursuant to the authority conferred upon the directors by the articles of association, the said applications be and are hereby approved and that the said shares be allotted to the applicants fully paid at [par value/a price of £[•] per share] for cash.

In reaching their decisions, the Directors considered the need to promote the success of the Company for the benefit of its members as a whole and, in doing so, had regard to the specific requirements of s. 172 of the Companies Act 2006.

Share Certificates

IT WAS RESOLVED THAT any two directors or one director and the company secretary be and are hereby authorised to issue appropriate share certificates to the allottees signed on behalf of the Company.

Filing of Forms

IT WAS RESOLVED THAT the company secretary be instructed to file a form SH01 with the Registrar of Companies.

Precedent 49 Declaration of trust by nominee for shares

To: [•]
[•]

[•] Limited

I, the undersigned [•] hereby acknowledge that I am a nominee and trustee for you in respect of [•] ordinary shares of £[•] each fully paid and held by me in the capital of [•] Limited (hereinafter called 'the Company').

I hand you herewith the share certificate for the said shares together with a transfer duly executed by me and I hereby irrevocably authorise you to complete such transfer by filling in the date and the name and address of the transferee and the amount of the consideration for the transfer and to pass the duly completed document to the Company for registration.

I will pay all dividends, bonuses and other payments received by me in respect of the said shares to you and I will, so long as I remain as registered holder of the said shares, vote in respect thereof as you may from time to time direct and not otherwise.

Dated this [•] day of [•] 20[•]

Signed as a Deed and delivered
by the above named

____
[•]

Witnessed by:

Witness Signature	]	______________________
Witness Name	]	______________________
Witness Address	]	______________________
		______________________
Witness Occupation	]	______________________
Date	]	______________________

Precedent 50 Members' resolution to approve acquisition of non-cash asset from subscribers

Ordinary Resolution

THAT in accordance with the provisions of s. 601 of the Companies Act 2006 the terms of the proposed acquisition of [•] from [•], a subscriber to the company's memorandum, be approved.

Precedent 51 Directors' resolution to call unpaid amounts on shares

IT WAS RESOLVED THAT a call of [•] pence per share be made on the [•] issued ordinary shares of £1.00 of the company, such call to be paid on or before [•] and that the company secretary be instructed to issue call letters on [•] 20[•].

Precedent 52 Call letter and reminder

[Company Name Limited
Company Number
Company Address]

[Member's name and address]

Dear Sir/Madam

Call letter for a call of [•] pence per ordinary share

I am instructed to inform you that pursuant to a resolution of the Board of Directors made on [•] 20[•], a call of [•] p per ordinary share in the capital of the Company has been made, such call to be paid on or before [•] 20[•].

Accordingly you are requested to pay the total amount of the call, shown above, in respect of the shares registered in your name(s) at this date to [•] by the due date. Upon payment of the call you should lodge this call letter and the relevant share certificate(s) with the Company to allow the certificates to be endorsed and returned.

Interest may be charged on the call at the rate of [•]% per annum if payment is not made by the due date. Failure to pay the call by such date will render the shares liable to forfeiture. You will remain liable for this call notwithstanding any subsequent transfer of the shares hereafter.

Yours faithfully

Company Secretary

[Company Name Limited
Company Number
Company Address]

[Member's name and address]

Dear Sir/Madam

Call Letter Ref:

I am instructed to bring to your attention your failure to comply with the notice sent to you on [•] 20[•] requiring payment of the call upon your partly-paid shares amounting to £[•].

The call was due on [•] 20[•]. You are required to pay to the company the amount of your call, together with interest at the rate of [•] per cent per annum from [•] 20[•] up to and including the date of payment, on or before [•] 20[•]. Payment, accompanied by the original call notice, must be sent to the company. Should you fail to pay the call (together with the interest on it) within this time, the shares are, under the articles of association, liable to be forfeited. I must remind you, however, that forfeiture of the shares in no way releases you from liability for the call and the interest, and that, under its articles of association, the company is entitled to enforce its claims without any deduction or allowance for the value of the shares at the time of forfeiture.

The company also holds a first and paramount lien over the [•] fully paid shares of the company of which you are the registered holder, for all monies due to the company.

No transfer of any shares of which you are the registered holder can be accepted by the company until the call and interest have been paid.

By order of the Board

Company Secretary

Precedent 53 Letter to confirm forfeiture of shares by director(s)

Dear Sir/Madam

I am directed to inform you that the [•] ordinary shares of £[•] each in the above company, of which you were the registered holder, have, by a resolution of the directors passed at a board meeting held on [•] 20[•] been duly forfeited in consequence of your having failed to pay the call due on them on [•] 20[•].

[I am also to request you to pay such call amounting to £[•] with interest at [•] per cent from [•] 20[•] up to the day of actual payment, and to inform you that in default of your complying with this request before [•] 20[•] proceedings will be taken against you to enforce such payment without further notice.]

By order of the Board

Company Secretary

Precedent 54 Directors' resolution to recommend bonus issue

Bonus Issue of Shares

The Chairman reported the proposal to undertake a capitalisation issue to increase the Company's issued share capital from [•] to [•] Ordinary Shares of £1.00 each. It was noted that the increase would be effected by capitalising £[•] from revenue reserves.

It was further noted that a General Meeting of the shareholders of the Company would need to be convened and held to approve resolutions authorising the Directors to allot additional shares and declaring a capitalisation issue. There was produced to the meeting a Notice convening a General Meeting of the Shareholders to be held immediately upon short notice and IT WAS RESOLVED THAT:

1. The Directors do recommend to the shareholders that the sum of £[•] be capitalised and appropriated to the holders of the Ordinary Shares in the Capital of the Company pro rata to their existing holdings.
2. The Secretary be and is hereby instructed to sign and issue to the shareholders a Notice convening a General Meeting of the members.

At this point, the meeting was adjourned to enable the General Meeting of the shareholders to be held upon short notice. Upon resumption of the meeting the Chairman reported that the General Meeting of the shareholders had been duly held and that the resolutions set out in the notice of the meeting had been approved unanimously.

The meeting now considered the proposed capitalisation issue and IT WAS RESOLVED THAT:

1. Pursuant to the authority given by and the directions contained in the resolution of the Company passed at the General Meeting held this day, the sum of £[•] therein referred to, be capitalised and appropriated as therein set out.
2. [•] Ordinary Shares of £1.00 each credited as fully paid be and are hereby provisionally allotted to the persons and in the numbers set out in the respective renounceable entitlement forms now produced to the meeting, such allotments being as follows:
   a. [•] Ordinary Shares of £1.00 each fully paid to [•].
   b. [•] Ordinary Shares of £1.00 each fully paid to [•].
3. The company secretary be and is hereby authorised to issue renounceable letters of allotment to the provisional allottees, renunciations to be made within 14 days of the date hereof.

Precedent 55 Letter of provisional allotment for bonus issue

Dear Sir/Madam

I am instructed to inform you that you have been allotted [•] ordinary shares of £[•] each in the capital of the Company, credited as fully paid, subject to the Articles of Association of the Company. The shares will rank for all dividends declared and paid after the date hereof.

If you wish to have all the shares comprised herein registered in your name, you need do nothing with this letter until [•] 20[•] when it should be exchanged for a definitive share certificate at the registered office of the Company. If you wish to dispose of the shares comprised in this letter, you should complete and sign the form of renunciation and hand this letter to the renouncee on or before [•] 20[•].

(*Note:* If you are the person in whose favour this letter has been renounced you must complete the registration application form and lodge this allotment letter at the [registered office] of the Company not later than [•] to be exchanged for a definitive share certificate.)

BY ORDER OF THE BOARD

Company Secretary

Precedent 56 Notice to members of redemption of shares

Formal notice of shares to be redeemed

Dear

Redemption [•] [Preference] Shares

In accordance with the terms of issue and the Company's articles of association, [there have been drawn for redemption and] the Company will redeem at [•] pence per share on [•] 20[•], [•] of the preference shares held by you.

A payment authority and discharge form will be sent to you in due course.

Yours faithfully,

Company Secretary

Letter detailing procedure and payment and discharge forms

Dear

Redemption [•] Shares

Further to the notice sent to you on [•] 20[•] advising that the above [Preference] Shares held by you will be redeemed on [•] 20[•], I enclose payment authority and discharge form for your signature and return.

Please complete the form and return it together with appropriate share certificate(s) not later than [•] 20[•]. Subject to receipt of the form and appropriate share certificate(s) a cheque for the value of the preference shares will be posted on [•] 20[•].

In accordance with the terms of issue of the shares the value has been calculated as follows:

[*insert valuation details here*]

If the preference shares now being redeemed are only part of your holding, and you do not have a certificate for the exact number a balance certificate will be issued.

There will be no further dividend payments in respect of the preference shares being redeemed.

Yours faithfully,

Company Secretary

Payment authority and discharge form

To the Directors
[•] Limited

I hereby authorise and request you to send a cheque for the sum of [•] pounds being the amount due to me/us on redemption of [•] preference shares to:

and I confirm that your compliance with this request shall discharge the company's liability for such payment.

I enclose [•] preference share certificate(s) for cancellation.

Signed:

[*Insert shareholder's name*]

Precedent 57 Members' resolution to approve share purchase contract

Ordinary Resolution

THAT the contract proposed to be made between the Company and [•] for the purchase by the Company of [•] Ordinary Shares of £1.00 each fully paid in the capital of the Company upon the terms of the draft attached hereto and initialled by the Chairman for the purposes of identification be and is hereby approved.

Precedent 58 Simple share purchase contract – by company

THIS AGREEMENT is made the [•] day [•] 20[•] BETWEEN [•] of [•] (hereinafter called 'the Vendor') and [•] Limited whose registered office is at [•] (hereinafter called 'the Company').

WHEREAS:

(a) The Company was incorporated in England and Wales on [ ] with a registered number of and has an issued share capital of £[•] divided into [•] ordinary shares of £[•] each all of which are fully paid.

(b) The Vendor is the beneficial owner of [•] ordinary shares of £[•] each ('the shares') in the capital of the Company.

(c) The parties have proposed that the Vendor shall sell and the Company shall purchase the shares on the terms set out in this agreement and in accordance with all applicable laws.

NOW IT IS HEREBY AGREED THAT:

1 The Vendor shall sell and the Company shall purchase the shares beneficially held by the Vendor, free of all liens, charges and encumbrances.
2 The consideration for the shares shall be £[•] payable in full upon completion.
3 Completion of the sale and purchase of the shares hereby agreed shall take place at [•] on [•] 20[•] at [•] am/pm when:
   (a) the Vendor shall deliver to the Company the share certificate(s) in respect of the shares to be sold by him pursuant to this agreement;
   (b) the Company shall deliver to the Vendor a draft for the purchase monies due.
4 This agreement shall be governed by the laws of England.

AS WITNESS the hands of the parties hereto the day and year first before written.

Precedent 59 Members' resolution to approve market purchase of shares

Ordinary Resolution

THAT the company be authorised to make market purchases (as defined by Section 693(4) of the Companies Act 2006) of ordinary shares of 25p each in its capital be renewed provided that:

(a) the maximum aggregate number of ordinary shares hereby authorised to be purchased is 5,000,000;
(b) the minimum price which may be paid for each such ordinary share is the nominal value of such share and the maximum price which may be paid for such ordinary shares is not more than 5%. above the average of the middle market quotations for such shares taken from the Daily Official List of The London Stock Exchange plc for the five business days in respect of which such Daily Official List is published immediately preceding the date of purchase (in each case excluding expenses);
(c) unless previously revoked or varied the authority hereby conferred is to expire at the conclusion of the annual general meeting of the Company to be held in 2018 or on 31 March 2018, whichever is the earlier; and
(d) the Company may make a contract to purchase ordinary shares under the authority hereby conferred prior to the expiry of such authority which may be or will be executed wholly or partly after the expiry of such authority, and may make a purchase of ordinary shares in pursuance of any such contract notwithstanding such expiry.

Precedent 60 Directors' statement to support purchase out of capital

[•] Limited (the Company)

Directors' Statement under Section 714 of the Companies Act 2006 (the Act)

The amount of the permissible capital payment for the shares to be purchased by the

Company in accordance with the share buyback agreement proposed to be entered into between the Company and [•] whose shares are to be purchased [wholly/partly] out of capital] as set out in the [notice of general meeting/draft written resolution] circulated on [•] is £[•].

We, the undersigned being all the directors of the Company as at the date of this statement, having made full inquiry into the affairs and prospects of the company and having taken account of all of the Company's liabilities (including any contingent or prospective liabilities), have formed the opinion that:

(a) As regards the Company's initial situation immediately following the date on which the payment out of capital is proposed to be made, there will be no grounds on which the Company could be found to be unable to pay its debts; and
(b) As regards the Company's prospects for the year immediately following the date on which the payment out of capital is proposed to be made that:
    (i) taking into account our current intentions with respect to the management of the Company business during this year; and
    (ii) the amount and character of the financial resources that will, in our view, be available to the Company during this year, the Company will be able to continue to carry on business as a going concern (and will accordingly be able to pay its debts as they fall due) throughout this year.

An auditor's report from [•] dated [•] in accordance with s. 714(6) of the Act is attached to this statement.

The Company's business does not include that of a banking company or an insurance company.

Signed by:
[all directors must sign the statement]

Precedent 61 Members' resolution to approve purchase of shares out of capital

Ordinary Resolution

THAT the payment of £[•] out of the capital of the Company as defined in Sections 710 to 712 of the Companies Act 2006 in respect of the purchase of [•] Ordinary Shares of £1.00 each under Section 709 of the said Act from [•] be and is hereby approved.

Precedent 62 London Gazette notice re purchase out of capital

[•] Limited

NOTICE IS HEREBY GIVEN THAT:

1 By a special resolution of the shareholders of the above-named Company approved at a general meeting of the shareholders held on [•] 20[•] the payment out of capital of £[•] for the purpose of the Company acquiring [•] ordinary shares of £1.00 each from [•] was authorised.

2 The amount of the permissible capital repayment as defined by Sections 711 and 772 of the Companies Act 2006 was £[•].
3 The directors' statement and the auditors' report required by Section 714 of the said Act are available for inspection at the registered office of the Company situated at [•].
4 Any creditor of the Company may at any time within the period of five weeks immediately following [•] 20[•] (being the date of the above mentioned special resolution) apply to the High Court under Section 721 of the said Act for an order prohibiting the payment.

Precedent 63 Letter re conversion of loan stock

Notice of conversion of loan stock

Dear Sir

Conversion of [•] Loan Stock of the Company

In accordance with the terms of issue of the convertible loan stock created by a resolution of the Board of Directors approved on [•] 20[•] you are entitled to convert all or part of your holding of convertible loan notes during the period [•] to [•] by giving notice to the company. According to our records you are the registered holder of 100,000 such convertible loan notes.

The convertible loan notes are convertible into [•] ordinary shares for each £100 of loan stock held.

If you want to convert any of your loan stock please complete the attached form of conversion and return it together with your loan stock certificate no later than [•].

By order of the Board

Company Secretary

Notice to company by loan stock holder requiring conversion

Dear Sirs

Take notice that in exercise of the power conferred upon me by the terms of issue of the [•] Convertible Loan Stock I require £[•] of the convertible loan stock held by me to be converted on [•] on the terms fixed for their conversion, for which purpose I enclose a loan stock certificate comprising such loan stock. Kindly acknowledge receipt and forward to me a certificate for any unconverted balance of such loan stock and a share certificate for the new shares allotted to me as a result of this conversion.

[signature
full name and address of loan stock holder]

Precedent 64 Directors' resolution to approve transfer of shares

Transfer of shares

There was produced to the meeting [a] stock transfer form[s] transferring shares in the capital of the Company as follows:

[•] ordinary shares of £[•] each fully paid from [•] to [•].

[•] ordinary shares of £[•] each fully paid from [•] to [•].

The meeting considered the matter and **IT WAS RESOLVED THAT** the said transfer[s] be and [is/are] hereby approved and, [subject to stamping by HM Revenue & Customs, OR being certified exempt from stamp duty be] registered in the books of the Company and that any two directors [or one director and the company secretary] be and are hereby authorised to issue the share certificate[s] to the transferee[s] signed on behalf of the Company.

In reaching their decision, the Directors considered the need to promote the success of the Company for the benefit of its members as a whole and, in doing so, had regard to the specific requirements of s. 172 of the Companies Act 2006.

Precedent 65 Members' waiver of pre-emption rights on transfer

I/We, [name[•]] of [address[•]] being the registered holder of [•] ordinary shares of £[•] each in the capital of [•] (the 'Company') do hereby waive all rights of pre-emption on the transfer of shares conferred upon [me/us] by article [•] of the articles of association of the Company so as to permit the transfer and registration of [•] ordinary shares of £[•] each in the capital of the Company from [•] to [•].

EXECUTED AS A DEED this [•] day of [•] by the said

Precedent 66 Directors' resolution to amend articles to enable electronic settlement of shares

IT WAS RESOLVED THAT pursuant to Regulation 16(2) of the Uncertified Securities Regulations 2001 ('the Regulations'):

(a) title to the ordinary shares of £1.00 each in the capital of the Company ('the Shares'), in issue or to be issued, may be transferred by means of a relevant system (as defined in the Regulations);

(b) such relevant system shall include the relevant system of which Euroclear UK & Ireland Limited is to be the Operator (as defined in the Regulations);

(c) the Shares shall not include any shares referred to in Regulation 18; and

(d) this resolution ('the Resolution') shall become effective immediately prior to Euroclear UK & Ireland Limited granting permission for the Shares to be transferred by means of the CREST system.

It was noted that, upon the Resolution becoming effective in accordance with its terms, and for as long as it is in force, the Articles of Association of the Company in relation to the Shares will not apply to any uncertificated shares to the extent that they are inconsistent with:

(a) the holding of any Shares in uncertificated form;
(b) the transfer of title to any Shares by means of the CREST system; and
(c) any provision of the Regulations.

There was produced to the meeting a notice of the passing of the resolution ('the Notice').

IT WAS RESOLVED THAT the Notice, as set out below, be approved and sent to every member of the Company in accordance with the Company's Articles of Association within 60 days of the passing of the Resolution as required by Regulation 16(4).

TO: ALL THE MEMBERS OF THE COMPANY

Notification of directors' resolution relating to
the CREST system.

This is to give you notice, in accordance with the Uncertificated Securities Regulations 2001 ('the Regulations'), that on [*date*], the Company resolved by a resolution of its directors that title to the ordinary shares of £1.00 each in the capital of the Company, in issue or to be issued, may be transferred by means of a relevant system. The resolution of the directors will become effective immediately prior to Euroclear UK & Ireland Limited granting permission for the shares concerned to be transferred by means of the CREST system.

Precedent 67 Dividend bank mandate

**REQUEST FOR PAYMENT OF INTEREST OR DIVIDENDS
TO BANK OR BUILDING SOCIETY**

PLEASE COMPLETE IN BLOCK CAPITALS

1. Name of Company in which you hold shares
2. Shareholder Ref
3. Full name and address of shareholder (first named holder for joint holdings)
   If being completed by POA, executor or administrator for deceased shareholder please state name of full name of shareholder
4. Account designation (if any shown on share certificate)
5. Full names of joint holders (in same order as shown on share certificate)
6. Signature of shareholders (or executors, administrators, POA etc)

   ____
7. Name and address of bank or building society

   ____

   Building society reference/roll number
8. Account name, account number and sort code

   Account name __________ Account number __________ Sort code _____

If holder is corporate body, the stamp of your bank or building society is required. For personal shareholders their stamp is only required if payment is not being made to an account in the first holder's name. The branch stamp is required to confirm the signature in box 6 is that of the shareholder or authorised signatory.

Payments made in accordance with this instruction discharges the company and registrar from further liability whether the form is stamped by your branch or not.

Precedent 68 Pro forma dividend tax confirmation

DIVIDEND CONFIRMATION

[Co Name]

[Shareholder Name]

Shareholder Ref: [ ]

[Shareholder address]

Holding Designation: [Desig]

Joint Holder(s) (if any):

[•]

[•]

[•]

Number of shares held	*Dividend payable per share*
Total amount payable	*Tax deducted £nil*

Precedent 69 Members' resolution to authorise scrip dividend

Special Resolution

THAT the articles of association of the company be amended in the following manner that is to say by the adoption of a new clause [•], as set out below, and by the renumbering of the existing clauses [•] to [•] (inclusive) as clauses [•] to [•] (inclusive).

'[•] With the prior approval of an Ordinary Resolution of the Company the Directors may, in respect of any dividend proposed to be paid or declared thereafter on any particular class or classes offer the shareholders the right to elect to receive in lieu of such dividend (or part thereof) an allotment of additional shares of the same class credited as fully paid. In any such case the following provisions shall apply:

		Rate per Share:	[ ]
Share Class:	[ ]	Record Date:	[ ]
ISIN (if any):	[ ]	Pay Date:	[ ]
Payment Ref:	[ ]	Interim or Final:	[Interim] / [Final]
Holding:	[ ]	Amount Payable	£[ ]

(a) the basis of allotment shall be determined by the Directors, in their absolute discretion;

(b) no fraction of any share shall be allotted. The Directors may make such provisions as they think fit for any fractional entitlements including provisions whereby, in whole or in part, the benefit thereof accrues to the Company and/or under which fractional entitlements are accrued and/or retained and in each case accumulated on behalf of any shareholder and such accruals or retentions are applied to the allotment by way of bonus to or cash subscription on behalf of such shareholder of fully paid shares and/or under which fractional entitlements and/or accruals or retentions are paid as cash dividends;

(c) if the Directors determine to allow such right of election on any occasion they shall give notice in writing to the shareholders of the right of election offered to them and shall issue forms of election and shall specify the procedure to be followed and the place at which, and the latest date and time by which, duly completed forms of election must be lodged in order to be effective; the Directors may also issue forms under which shareholders may elect to receive shares instead of cash both in respect of the relevant dividend and in respect of future dividends not yet declared or resolved (and accordingly in respect of which the basis of allotment shall not have been determined);

(d) the dividend (or that part of the dividend in respect of which a right of election has been accorded) shall not be payable on shares in respect whereof the share election has been duly exercised ('the Elected Shares'), and in lieu thereof additional shares (but not any fraction of a share) shall be allotted to the holders of the Elected Shares on the basis of allotment determined as aforesaid. For such purpose the Directors shall capitalise, out of such of the sums standing to the credit of reserves (including any share premium account or capital redemption reserve fund) or profit and loss account as the Directors may determine, a sum equal to the aggregate nominal amount of additional shares to be allotted on such basis and shall apply the same in paying up in full the appropriate number of unissued shares for allotment and distribution to and amongst the holders of the Elected Shares on such basis;

(e) the additional shares so allotted shall rank *pari passu* in all respects with the fully paid shares of the same class then in issue save only as regards participation in the relevant dividend;

(f) the provisions of regulation 36 of the Model Articles for private companies shall apply (*mutatis mutandis*) to any capitalisation made pursuant to this [Article [•]];

(g) the Directors may on any occasion determine that rights of election shall not be made available to any shareholders with registered addresses in any territory where in the absence of a registration statement or other special formalities the circulation of an offer of rights of election would or might be unlawful, and in such event the provisions aforesaid shall be read and construed subject to such determination; and

(h) in relation to any particular proposed dividend the Directors may in their absolute discretion withdraw the offer previously made to shareholders to elect to receive additional Shares in lieu of the cash dividend (or part thereof) at any time prior to the allotment of the additional Shares.'

Ordinary Resolution
THAT pursuant to Clause [•] of the Articles of Association of the Company adopted by resolution [•] above the Directors be authorised to offer the holders of ordinary shares the right to elect to receive an allotment of new ordinary shares credited as fully paid in lieu of any dividend proposed to be paid or declared hereafter.

Precedent 70 Indemnity for lost share certificate

INDEMNITY
FOR LOST
CERTIFICATE

(above this line for Registrar's use only)

To the Directors of [•] Limited (Company Number [•])

The original certificate of title relating to the under-mentioned securities of the above-named Company has been lost or destroyed.

Neither the securities nor the certificate of title thereto have been transferred, charged, lent or deposited or dealt with in any manner affecting the absolute title thereto and the person named in the said certificate is the person entitled to be on the register in respect of such securities.

I request you to issue a duplicate certificate of title for such securities and in consideration of your doing so, undertake (jointly and severally) to indemnify you and the Company against all claims and demands (and any expenses thereof) which may be made against you or the Company in consequence of your complying with this request and of the Company permitting at any time hereafter a transfer of the said securities, or any part thereof, without the production of the said original certificate.

I undertake to deliver to the Company for cancellation the said original certificate should the same ever be recovered.

PARTICULARS OF CERTIFICATE LOST OR DESTROYED

Particulars of Certificate	Amount and Class of Securities	In Favour of
Share Certificate No. [•]	[•] ordinary shares of £1.00 each	

Dated this [•] day of [•] 20[•].

Signature ______________________________

Precedent 71 Letter of request by executor

LETTER OF REQUEST	Above this line for Registrar's use only

REQUEST BY EXECUTORS OR ADMINISTRATORS OF A DECEASED HOLDER TO BE PLACED ON THE REGISTER AS HOLDERS IN THEIR OWN RIGHT

Full name and address of Undertaking	TO THE DIRECTORS OF	
*Full description of security		
Name or amount of Shares, Stock or other Security and, in figures column only, number and denomination of units if any.	WORDS ____________________	FIGURES (________ units of ______)
Full name of deceased	____________________ Deceased	
	late of____________________	

I/We, the undersigned, being the personal representative(s) of the above named deceased, hereby request you to register me/us in the books of the Company as the holder(s) of the above mentioned Stock/Shares now registered in the name of the said deceased.

Dated this............day of...20

Signature(s) of Personal Representative(s)

....

....

<table>
<tr><td rowspan="6">Full name(s) and address(es) of the Personal Representative(s) (IN THE ORDER IN WHICH THEY ARE TO BE REGISTERED) (TYPEWRITTEN OR IN BLOCK CAPITALS)</td><td></td></tr>
<tr><td></td></tr>
<tr><td></td></tr>
<tr><td></td></tr>
<tr><td></td></tr>
<tr><td></td></tr>
<tr><td colspan="2">IF AN ACCOUNT ALREADY EXISTS IN THE ABOVE NAME(S) THE ABOVE-MENTIONED HOLDING WILL BE ADDED TO THAT ACCOUNT, <u>UNLESS INSTRUCTIONS ARE GIVEN TO THE CONTRARY</u>.</td></tr>
</table>

The Certificate(s) in the name of the deceased if not already with the Company's Registrars must accompany this form *A separate Letter of Request should be used for each class of Security.	Stamp or name and address of person lodging this form

Precedent 72 Members' consent to short notice

[•] LIMITED
('the Company')
Company Number: [•]

Agreement to Short Notice

We, the undersigned, [all the members for the time being of the Company/representing not less than 90% of the Company's members] having a right to attend and vote at general meetings of the Company hereby agree, in respect of the general meeting to be held on [•] 20[•] at [•] am/pm:

(a) to accept shorter notice of the said meeting than the period of notice prescribed by Section 307(1) of the Companies Act 2006; and
(b) to accept service of the documents specified in Section 424(3) of the Companies Act 2006, less than 21 days before the date of the said meeting.

Signed:

________________________ ________________________

Dated this [•] day of [•] 20[•].

Precedent 73 Members' resolutions to approve change in auditors (non-PIE company)

THAT [•] be [re]appointed as auditors of the Company in accordance with Section 485(4) of the Companies Act 2006, until such time that they resign from office or are removed by the members in accordance with the provisions of that Act or are deemed not reappointed in accordance with Section 488 of that Act, and to authorise the directors to fix the auditors' remuneration.

OR

THAT [•] be appointed auditors of the company in accordance with the provisions of s. 485(4) of the Companies Act 2006 in place of [•], the retiring auditors, until such time that they resign from office or are removed by the members in accordance with the provisions of that Act or are deemed not reappointed in accordance with Section 488 of that Act, and to authorise the directors to fix the auditors' remuneration.

OR

THAT [•] be appointed auditors of the company in accordance with the provisions of s. 485(4) of the Companies Act 2006 in the place of [•], who have resigned, until such time that they resign from office or are removed by the members in accordance with the provisions of that Act or are deemed not reappointed in accordance with Section 488 of that Act, and to authorise the directors to fix the auditors' remuneration.

OR

THAT [•] appointed during the year to fill the casual vacancy caused by the resignation of [•], be reappointed auditors of the company in accordance with the provisions of s. 485(4) of the Companies Act 2006 until such time that they resign from office or are removed by the members in accordance with the provisions of that Act or are deemed not reappointed in accordance with Section 488 of that Act, and to authorise the directors to fix the auditors' remuneration.

Precedent 74 Members' resolution to appoint third party in place of retiring director

Ordinary Resolution

THAT [•] be appointed as a director of the Company in place of [•] the retiring director who has indicated his unwillingness to continue as a director.

Precedent 75 Members' notice of requisition of members' meeting

To: The Board of Directors

[•] Limited

WE, the undersigned, being holders of more than one-tenth of the paid up capital of the Company, as at the date of this notice, and representing at least 10% of the right of voting at general meetings of the Company require you forthwith to proceed to convene a General Meeting of the Company for the purpose of considering and if thought fit approving the following resolution which will be proposed as an [Ordinary/Special] Resolution namely:

[ORDINARY/SPECIAL] RESOLUTION THAT [•]

Dated this [•] day of [•] 20[•]

Precedent 76 Directors' resolution to change accounting reference date

Accounting Reference Date

IT WAS RESOLVED THAT the accounting reference date of the Company be [shortened/extended] from [•] 20[•] to [•] 20[•] with the next financial Accounts to be finalised and filed at Companies House being drawn up for the period from [•] 20[•] to [•] 20[•]. The company secretary was instructed to file Form AA01 with the Registrar of Companies.

Precedent 77 Directors' resolution to approve accounts and circulation to members

Annual Accounts

The directors' report and the audited accounts for the year ended/period to [•] 20[•] produced to the meeting were signed and approved for submission to the Company's members.

Dividend

IT WAS RESOLVED THAT no dividend be declared in respect of the year ended/period to [•] 20[•].

OR

It was noted that an interim dividend of [•]p per ordinary share had been declared in respect of the year ending/period to [•] 20[•].

OR

The chairman reported the proposal to declare a final dividend of [•]p per ordinary share in respect of the year ended/period to [•] 20[•].

[There was produced to the meeting a letter from the Company's auditors confirming that the qualification to their report to the accounts for the year ended/period to [•] 20[•] was not material in determining whether the proposed dividend should be paid.]

IT WAS RESOLVED THAT the payment of a final dividend of [•]p per ordinary share be and is hereby recommended and that a resolution to this effect be put to the [sole] member[s] at the forthcoming annual general meeting.

Precedent 78 Directors' resolution to appoint auditors (non-PIE company)

Auditors

It was noted that [•] had indicated their willingness to continue as auditors of the Company and that a resolution for their reappointment would be proposed at the forthcoming [annual] general meeting in respect of the accounting period of the Company ending [•] 20[•].

OR

In accordance with s. 485(3)(a) of the Companies Act 2006 **IT WAS RESOLVED THAT** [•] be hereby appointed as auditors of the Company for the first accounting period of the Company ending [•] 20[•].

OR

As the Company was no longer exempt from appointing auditors in respect of the accounting period ending [•], in accordance with s. 485(3)(b) of the Companies Act 2006 **IT WAS RESOLVED THAT** [•] be and are hereby appointed as auditors of the Company.

OR

In accordance with s. 485(3)(c) of the Companies Act 2006 **IT WAS RESOLVED THAT** [•] be and are hereby appointed as auditors of the Company to fill a casual vacancy in respect of the first accounting period of the Company ending [•] 20[•].

Precedent 79 Directors' resolution not to appoint auditors where company exempt

It was noted that the Company was exempt from audit in respect of its accounts for the year ended [•]. The meeting considered the matter and **IT WAS RESOLVED THAT** pursuant to s. 487(1)(e) no auditors be appointed in respect of the year.

Precedent 80 Auditors' letter of resignation

Dear Sirs

We hereby resign as auditors of the Company with effect from the date hereof.

In accordance with Section 519(1) of the Companies Act 2006, we wish the following circumstances connected with our ceasing to hold office as auditors to be brought to the attention of the members and creditors of the company.

[statement of circumstances]

OR

In accordance with Section 519(2) of the Companies Act 2006, we hereby state that there are no circumstances connected with our resignation which we consider should be brought to the attention of the members or creditors of the Company.

Yours faithfully
(signature of auditors)

OR

Dear Sirs
We write to inform you that we are not willing to be reappointed as auditors of the company as from the conclusion of the next general meeting of the company at which the requirements of the Companies Act 2006 Section 437 are complied with. There are no circumstances connected with our ceasing to hold office as auditors which should be brought to the attention of the members or creditors of the company.

OR

We wish the following circumstances connected with our ceasing to hold office as auditors to be brought to the attention of the members and creditors of the company.
[statement of circumstances]

Yours faithfully
(signature of auditors)

Precedent 81 Statement in register of members where company has or ceases to have only one member

On [•] 20[•] [•] became the sole member of the Company.

OR

On [•] 20[•] [•] ceased to be the sole member of the Company.

Precedent 82 Company enquiry into interests in shares (s. 793 request)

Dear [•],

Interests in Ordinary Shares of £[•] each (the 'Shares') of [•] (the 'Company')

Pursuant to section 793 of the Companies Act 2006 (the 'Act') we require you to provide us in writing, by no later than 5pm (London, UK time) on [•] the [•] day of [•] 20[•], the following information concerning your interest (within the meaning of sections 820–825 of the Act) in the Shares:

1. The number of Shares in which you have an interest as at the date of your reply to this letter ('Current Interest') and the number of Shares in which you have had an interest at any time since the incorporation of the Company on [•] 20[•] but which no longer form part of your Current Interest ('Past Interest').
2. Confirmation as to the nature of your Current Interest or your Past Interest in the Shares including whether such interests are or were held legally and/or beneficially.
3. The dates upon which you acquired an interest in any Shares forming part of your Current Interest and your Past Interest.
4. If it is a Past Interest, please specify the dates on which an interest in any Shares forming part of your Past Interest was disposed of and, as far as lies within your

knowledge, the complete details of the identity of the person who held that interest immediately after your interest in the Shares ceased.

5. In relation to your Current Interest, as far as lies within your knowledge, the full name and address of each person (including but not limited to nominees and investment managers) who also has an interest in such Shares, together with particulars of the nature of each interest and the number of Shares in which each person had an interest.
6. Full details of any agreement to which section 824 of the Act applies (agreements or arrangements between persons to acquire interests in the Company) or any other agreement or arrangement known to you relating to the exercise of any rights conferred by the holding of the Shares.

Your response to this letter should be posted, faxed or e-mailed to the address set out below, marked for the attention of [•].

Yours faithfully

Company Secretary
[response address]

Precedent 83 Directors' resolution to approve use of company seal

IT WAS RESOLVED THAT [•] be and is hereby approved and that any two directors [or any one director and the company secretary] be and are hereby authorised to sign and seal the said document on behalf of the Company.

Precedent 84 Members' resolution to approve winding-up of company

Special resolution
THAT the company be wound up voluntarily, and that [•] of [•] be appointed liquidator for the purposes of such winding-up.

OR

Special resolution
THAT it has been proved to the satisfaction of this meeting that the company cannot, by reason of its liabilities, continue its business and that it is advisable to wind up the company and accordingly that the company be wound up voluntarily and that [•] of the firm of [•], Chartered Accountants of [•], be nominated liquidator for the purpose of such winding-up.

Precedent 85 Members consent to company adopting the audit exemption for a subsidiary

Dear sirs

Audit exemption

Pursuant to s. 479A Companies Act 2006, the undersigned, being the sole/ all the members of **[•] (the 'Company'), hereby give[s] notice of its/their consent to the Company adopting the exemption from audit available for subsidiary companies under s. 479A of the Act, in respect of the year ended** [•].

Yours faithfully

Must be signed by or on behalf of all members

Precedent 86 Statement re: subsidiary audit exemption to be made in parent company accounts.

The UK subsidiaries listed below have claimed audit exemption under Companies Act 2006 s. 497A with respect to the year ended [•]. The Company has given a statement of guarantee under Companies Act 2006 s. 479C, whereby the Company will guarantee all outstanding liabilities to which the respective subsidiary companies are subject as at [•].

[Subsidiary companies listed here]

Precedent 87 Members' resolution to re-register a limited company as an unlimited company

Special Resolutions

(1) **THAT:**

(a) the Company be re-registered as a private unlimited company [with/without a share capital] within the meaning of the Companies Act 2006;

(b) the name of the Company be changed to **[•]**; and

(2) **THAT** the regulations produced to the meeting and signed by the Chairman for the purposes of identification be adopted as the articles of association of the Company in substitution for and to the exclusion of the existing articles of association.

(*see attached copy*)

Precedent 88 Members' resolution to re-register a limited company as an unlimited company

Special Resolutions

(1) **THAT:**

(a) the Company be re-registered as a private company limited by [shares/ guarantee] within the meaning of the Companies Act 2006;

(b) the name of the Company be changed to **[•] Limited***; and

(2) **THAT** the regulations produced to the meeting and signed by the Chairman for the purposes of identification be adopted as the articles of association of the Company in substitution for and to the exclusion of the existing articles of association.

(*see attached copy*)

* If re-registering as a private company limited by guarantee the company may claim exemption from using the work Limited in its name if it meets the qualifying criteria.

Glossary

The following definitions are not intended to be legal definitions.

Abridged accounts A condensed version of the annual accounts which small and medium-sized companies (according to the specified size criteria) are allowed to file with the register of companies. They may not be used as a substitute for the full annual accounts for the circulation to members.

Administration order Court order to appoint an administrator to manage the affairs of a company in financial difficulty.

Administrator A person appointed by the court to manage a company in financial difficulties in order to protect creditors and, if possible, avoid liquidation. The administrator has the power to remove and appoint directors. Also a person who administers the estate of a deceased person in the absence of any executors.

Agent Someone who is authorised to carry out business transactions on behalf of another (the principal), who is thereby bound by such actions.

Allotment The issue of shares.

Allottee A person or company to whom shares have been allotted.

Alternate director A person appointed by a director to represent them, usually at board meetings, and who assumes the responsibilities and duties of their appointor when acting in their place.

Annual accounts The accounts which are prepared to fulfil the directors' duty to present audited accounts to members in respect of each financial year. Annual accounts of limited companies must be filed with the Registrar of Companies.

Annual general meeting A general meeting of the company's members, which must be held in each calendar year within 15 months of the previous AGM. Under the Companies Act 2006, private companies are (generally) no longer required to hold AGMs, although the requirement remains for public companies.

Annual return A form filed each year with the Registrar of Companies, containing specified information about the company's directors, secretary, registered office, shareholders, share capital, etc. Withdrawn from 1 July 2016.

Articles of association The constitutional document setting out the internal regulations of the company. Unless modified or excluded, the specimen Articles in the relevant version of Table A/model articles have effect.

Audit The independent examination of, and expression of opinion on, the company's accounts. All persons or firms offering audit services must be registered auditors and belong to one of the recognised accountancy bodies.

Bearer shares Shares that can be transferred simply by passing the certificate from one person to the next. The 'bearer' of the certificate having title to the shares represented by it.

Bonus issue Issue of additional shares to existing shareholders, in proportion to their current holding, already paid up in full out of the distributable reserves of the company.

Book debts Amounts owed to a company resulting from its trading activities, usually in the form of unpaid invoices rendered to customers.

Capital The money or money's worth used by a company to finance its business. *See also* working capital.

Certificate of incorporation A certificate issued by the Registrar of Companies on receipt of specified constitutional and other documents of the company. The company assumes its identity as a legal person on the date of incorporation shown on the certificate.

Charge A means by which a company offers its assets as security for a debt. A charge is a general term that includes, but is not limited to, a mortgage. A fixed charge relates to a specific asset or assets. A floating charge relates to whatever assets of a specified class are in the company's possession at the time the charge crystallises (if it does so).

Class rights Where a company has more than one class of shares, the rights attached to those different classes of shares.

Common law The body of law based on custom and usage and decision reached in previous cases. The principles and rules of common law derive but from judgements and judicial opinions and not legislation introduced by parliament.

Common seal A seal bearing a company's name for affixing to legal documents.

Company An association of persons which, on incorporation, becomes a legal entity entirely separate from the individuals comprising its membership. In the Companies Act 1985, 'company' is restricted to companies registered under that Act or previous Companies Acts.

Company secretary An officer of the company with a number of statutory duties, such as to sign the annual return and accompanying documents, and usually charged with a range of duties relating to the company's statutory books and records, filing requirements, etc. Under the Companies Act 2006, private companies are no longer required to appoint a company secretary.

Company voluntary arrangement An arrangement under the Insolvency Act 1986 between the company and its members.

Compulsory liquidation Winding-up of a company by order of the winding-up court.

Confirmation statement A form filed each year with the Registrar of Companies, confirming that specified information about the company's directors, secretary, registered office, shareholders, share capital, notified to Companies House is correct or that any updates are being provided with the statement. Replaced the annual return from 1 July 2016.

Contract An agreement between two or more persons creating a legally enforceable obligation between them.

Creditor A person or company owed money.

Creditors' voluntary winding-up Insolvent winding-up of a company by resolution of its members.

Debenture A written acknowledgement of a debt owed by a company, often – but not necessarily – secured. It is common practice for a debenture to be created by a trust deed by which company property is mortgaged to trustees for the debenture holders, as security for the payment of interest and capital.

Debt An amount of money owed by one person, the debtor, to another, the creditor.

Department for Business, Energy & Industrial Strategy (BEIS) The government department responsible for the administration of company law. The Companies Act confers certain powers on the Secretary of State. Formerly called the Department for Business, Innovation and Skills (BIS).

Director An officer of the company responsible for determining policy, supervising the management of the company's business and exercising the powers of the company. Directors must generally carry out these functions collectively as a board.

Directors' report A statement attached to the annual accounts containing certain information laid down in the Act.

Distributable profit Profit retained by a company which may be distributed to its members.

Distribution The transfer of some or all of a company's assets (usually cash) to its members, generally by way of dividend or on a winding-up.

Dividends The distribution of a portion of the company's assets (usually cash) to its members, generally by way of dividend or on a winding-up.

Dormant company A company which has not traded or has ceased trading.

Fiduciary Having a position of trust, such that the power and authority conferred by the position must be exercised solely in the interest of the person with whom the fiduciary relationship exists. Trustees are in a fiduciary position, as are solicitors in relation to their clients. Directors have a fiduciary duty to the company, obliging them to act always in good faith and not to derive a personal profit from their position.

Financial statements The term adopted by the joint accountancy bodies to signify 'balance sheet, profit and loss accounts, statements of source and application of funds, notes and other statement which collectively are intended to give a true and fair view of financial position and profit or loss'.

Financial year The period in respect of which the company's profits and loss accounts is drawn up; it need not coincide with the fiscal or calendar year and need not be a period of 12 months.

Fixed charge Security, usually for a loan, over a specific asset such as a building or equipment.

Floating charge Security, usually for a loan, over a class of assets the individual components of which vary over time, such as stock or book debts.

Formation *See* registration.

Gazette Official BEIS publication for formal announcements. Published daily.

General meeting Any general meeting of the company's members that is not an annual general meeting.

Guarantee A formal agreement under which a guarantor undertakes to meet the contractual obligations of one person to another in the event of default. A company limited by guarantee is one in which the liability of the members is limited to a specified amount in a winding-up.

Holding company A company which has subsidiaries.

Incorporation *See* registration.

Insider dealing Buying or selling shares on the basis of an unfair advantage derived from access to price-sensitive information not generally available. Insider dealing is a criminal offence.

Issued capital *See* share capital.

Judgement creditor A creditor who has obtained a court order in their favour.

Limited company The commonest form of company, in which the liability of members for the debts of the company is limited – either to the amount of share capital for which they have applied (a company limited by shares) or to a specific amount guaranteed in the event of a winding-up (a company limited by guarantee).

Limited liability partnership/LLP A corporate body where the members have limited liability but undertake the management themselves rather than appointing directors to manage the company on their behalf.

Liquidation The process under which a company ceases to trade and realises its assets for distribution to creditors and then shareholders. The term 'winding up' is synonymous.

Listed company A company whose shares are Listed by the Financial Services Authority on the Official List of the UK and admitted for trading on the London Stock Exchange or NEX Listed markets.

Members The company's shareholders, of which there must be at least two in a public company. A private company can have a single shareholder.

Members' voluntary winding-up Solvent winding-up of a company by resolution of its members.

Memorandum of association A constitutional document setting out details of the subscribers on incorporation.

NEX Exchange is a recognised investment exchange and operates the NEX Exchange Main Board for Listed securities and NEX Exchange Growth Market for unlisted securities

Officer Includes a director, manager or (where appointed) the secretary of a company. Not everyone with the title of manager is sufficiently senior to be regarded as an officer, who must have a level of supervisory control which reflects the general policy of the company. Also includes the company's auditor.

Ordinary resolution A resolution at a general meeting carried by a simple majority of votes actually cast.

Ordinary shares The most common form of share in a company, giving holders the right to share in the company's profits in proportion to their holdings and the right to vote at general meetings (although non-voting ordinary shares are occasionally encountered).

Paid-up capital Refers to the amounts actually paid up on any issued shares.

Partnership A business run by two or more persons where the owners share ownership (partners) and have unlimited liability for the business' debts.

Person with Significant Control an individual owning or exercising control over 25% or more of a company's equity shares or voting rights.

Pre-emption rights Preferential right of existing members to purchase new shares to be issued or existing shares being offered for sale by way of transfer by an existing member.

Preference shares Shares carrying the right to payment of a fixed dividend out of profits before the payment of an ordinary dividend or the preferential return of capital or both.

Prima facie On the face of it, at first sight.

Private company A company that is not a public company.

Pro rata In proportion, rateably.

Prospectus Any prospectus, notice, circular, advertisement or other invitation to the public to subscribe for purchase of a company's shares or debentures.

Proxy A person authorised by a member to vote on his behalf at a general meeting.

Public company (plc) A company which meets specified requirements as to its minimum share capital and which is registered as a public company. Only public companies are allowed to offer shares and debentures to the public.

Quasi-loan A loan where a company reimburses the director's creditor.

Redeemable shares Shares which are issued as redeemable may be bought back by the company at a future date.

Registrar of Companies The official responsible for maintaining the company records filed under the requirements of the Companies Act.

Registration Process by which companies are created by filing (or registering) a number of specified documents at Companies House.

Regulatory information service (RIS) An information provider approved by the FSA to disseminate information to the market.

Resolution A decision at a meeting reached by a majority of members actually voting.

Retirement by rotation The annual standing down of directors (usually one third) for re-election by members at an annual general meeting.

Service contract A director's contract of employment.

Shadow director A person, not appointed as a director, managing or directing the affairs of a company or who directs the actions of the directors.

Share A unit of ownership of the company, representing a fraction of the share capital and usually conferring rights to participate in distributions. There may be several kinds of shares each carrying different rights. Shares are issued at a fixed nominal value, although the company may actually receive a larger amount, the excess representing share premium. Members may not be required to subscribe the full amount immediately, in which case the shares are partly paid. The members then await calls, which require them to pay further amounts until the shares are fully paid.

Share capital The capital of a company contributed or to be contributed by members. Nominal capital represents the nominal value of the shares issued and excludes any premium paid.

Share premium The excess of the price at which shares are issued above their nominal value.

Special resolution A resolution required either by the Companies Act or a company's articles which must be carried by at least 75% of the members voting at a general meeting. Such resolutions tend to be required where the proposal would change the nature of the relationship between a company and its members, such as an amendment to the Articles.

Statute law The body of law represented by legislation, and thus occurring in authoritative written form. Statue law contrasts with common law, over which it takes precedence.

Stock transfer form Document used to transfer ownership of shares from one person (transferor) to another (transferee).

Subscriber A person who subscribes to the Memorandum of Association and agrees to take up shares in the company on incorporation.

Subsidiary A company controlled by another which usually holds a majority of the issued shares.

Table A (model articles) The specimen Articles of Association for a company limited by shares incorporated under former Companies Acts. Unless specifically modified or excluded, the version of Table A/model articles in force at the time of a company's incorporation automatically applies to the company.

Takeover The process under which one company acquires control of another usually by acquiring all the shares.

Three-way proxy A proxy form, which must be used by a Listed company, which allows a member to instruct his proxy how to vote on each resolution.

Transfer Process where ownership of shares passes from one person to another usually by way of a sale.

Transferee A person acquiring shares by way of transfer.

Transferor A person disposing of shares by way of transfer.

UK Corporate Governance Code The code on corporate governance that applies to UK Listed companies. It is a voluntary code rather than a legal requirement. The UK Listing Rules require Listed companies to disclose in their annual report the extent of their compliance and to explain any non-compliance.

UK Stewardship Code The code on best practice for engaging with investee companies by institutional investors. It is a voluntary code rather than a legal requirement.

Unlimited company A company in which the members have unlimited liability for the company's debts in the event of a winding-up.

Voluntary winding-up Winding-up of a company at the instigation of its members.

Working capital The capital required by a company on a day-to-day basis to meet its operating costs.

Written resolution Allows private companies to conduct – with some exceptions – business that requires member approval without having to convene a general meeting.

Directory

Advisory, Conciliation and Arbitration Service
www.acas.org.uk

Bar Council
www.barcouncil.org.uk

British and Irish Legal Information Institute
www.bailii.org

Chartered Institute of Management Accountants
www.cimaglobal.com/

Chartered Institute of Legal Executives
www.cilex.org.uk

Companies House
www.gov.uk/government/organisations/companies-house

Companies House forms
www.gov.uk/topic/company-registration-filing/forms

Company information
https://beta.companieshouse.gov.uk/

Company name checker
https://beta.companieshouse.gov.uk/company-name-availability

Competition & Markets Authority
www.gov.uk/government/organisations/competition-and-markets-authority

Confederation of British Industry
www.cbi.org.uk

Court of Justice of the European Union
https://curia.europa.eu

Courts and Tribunals Judiciary
www.judiciary.gov.uk

Department for Business, Energy & Industrial Strategy
www.gov.uk/government/organisations/department-for-business-energy-and-industrial-strategy

Domain name registrars
ICANN
www.icann.org
Nominet UK
www.nominet.uk
Internic
www.internic.net

European Business Register
www.ebr.org

European Court of Human Rights
http://echr.coe.int

European Patent Office
www.epo.org/index.html

European Union
https://europa.eu

Financial Conduct Authority
FCA Handbook
www.handbook.fca.org.uk/handbook
Listing rules
www.handbook.fca.org.uk/handbook/LR/
Financial Services Register
https://register.fca.org.uk
Mutuals Public Register
www.fca.org.uk/firms/mutuals-public-register

Financial Reporting Council
www.frc.org.uk/
Audit resources
www.frc.org.uk/auditors
Corporate governance
www.frc.org.uk/directors/corporate-governance-and-stewardship
www.frc.org.uk

HM Courts & Tribunals Service
www.gov.uk/government/organisations/hm-courts-and-tribunals-service

HM Land Registry
www.gov.uk/government/organisations/land-registry

HM Revenue & Customs
www.gov.uk/government/organisations/hm-revenue-customs
Stamp duty
www.gov.uk/topic/business-tax/stamp-taxes

Information Commissioner's Office
www.ico.org.uk

Institute of Chartered Accountants in England and Wales
www.icaew.com

Institute of Chartered Accountants in Ireland
www.charteredaccountants.ie

Institute of Chartered Accountants in Scotland
www.icas.com

Institute of Chartered Secretaries and Administrators
www.icsa.org.uk
Guidance material
www.icsa.org.uk/knowledge
Publications
www.companysecretarialpracticeonline.co.uk
www.icsa.org.uk/shop

Institute of Directors
www.iod.com

International Corporate Governance Network
www.icgn.org

Judicial Committee of the Privy Council
www.jcpc.uk

Law society
www.lawsociety.org.uk

London Stock Exchange
www.londonstockexchange.com/home/homepage.htm
Admission and disclosure standards
www.londonstockexchange.com/companies-and-advisors/main-market/documents/admission-and-disclosure-standards.pdf
AIM rules
www.londonstockexchange.com/companies-and-advisors/aim/advisers/rules/aim-rules-for-companies-updated-october-2018.pdf
Dividend timetable
www.londonstockexchange.com/traders-and-brokers/rules-regulations/dividend-procedure-timetable-2019.pdf

Panel on Takeovers and Mergers
www.thetakeoverpanel.org.uk

Patent/Trademark Office
www.gov.uk/government/organisations/intellectual-property-office

Practical law
www.uk.practicallaw.thomsonreuters.com

Prudential Regulation Authority
www.bankofengland.co.uk/prudential-regulation

Supreme Court of the United Kingdom
www.supremecourt.uk

Trade Union Congress
www.tuc.org.uk

UK Legislation
www.legislation.gov.uk

UK Listing Authority
www.fca.org.uk/markets/ukla

UK Parliament
www.parliament.uk

Further reading

Armour, Douglas, Company Secretary's Checklists, 11th edition (ICSA Publishing Ltd, 2019).

Barber, Bernadette and Allen, Barbara, Corporate Governance Handbook, 4th Ed (ICSA Publishing Ltd, NYP 2017).

Bruce, Martha, The ICSA Director's Guide, 5th edition (ICSA Publishing Ltd, 2013).

Company Secretary's Review (LexisNexis).

Coyle, B, The Non-Executive Directors' Handbook, 5th edition (ICSA Publishing Ltd, 2019).

Gillard, Cecile, Farman, Debbie Cotton, Angela and Goose, Helen, Jordans Company Secretarial Precedents (Jordans, 2016).

Governance and Compliance. ICSA magazine,

Hamer, Andrew C., The ICSA Guide to Document Retention, 3rd edition (ICSA Publishing Ltd, 2011).

Herbert Smith Freehills LLP, A Practical Guide to the UK Listing Regime, 4th edition (ICSA Publishing Ltd, NYP 2017).

Impey, D and Griffiths, M and Loose P, The Company Director: Powers, Duties and Liabilities, 12 edition (Jordan Publishing, 2015).

Impey, D and Montague, N, Running a Limited Company, 8 edition, (Jordan Publishing, 2013).

Jordans Company Administration and Governance (Jordans).

Lai, Jerry, Tolley's Company Secretary's Handbook (Tolley, annual editions).

Loose, Peter, Griffiths, Michael and Impey, David, The Company Director, 11th edition (Jordans, 2015).

Robson, R and Davis, P, Effective Minute Taking, 2 edition (ICSA Publishing Ltd, 2018).

The CSPOnline Newsletter. Available from ICSA Publishing Ltd.

The Law and Practice of Company Meetings (ICSA Publishing Ltd, 2013). A practical guide to running company meetings.

Walmeley, Keith, Butterworths Company Law Handbook (Butterworths, annual editions).

Walmsley, Keith and Hamer, Andrew, CSPOnline (ICSA Publishing Ltd) (online subscription service).

Other Information Sources

Companies House guidance

Companies House produce a range of guidance all available to view or download from their website (www.gov.uk/government/collections/companies-house-guidance-for-limited-companies-partnerships-and-other-company-types).

Topics covered include the following:

1 What information we [Companies House] make available to the public
2 Online filing
3 Company incorporation, names and officers
4 Confirmation statement
5 Accounts
6 Changes to the company
7 People with significant control (PSC)
8 Flat management companies
9 Mortgage charges
10 Company registers
11 Company strike off, dissolution and restoration
12 Late filing penalties (LFP)
13 Registrar's rules and powers
14 Restricting the disclosure of your information
15 Liquidation and insolvency
16 Limited liability partnerships (LLPs)
17 Overseas companies
18 European economic interest groupings (EEIGs)
19 European public companies Societas Europaea (SEs)
20 Limited partnerships (LPs)
21 Cross border mergers
22 Inconsistencies
23 Paper filing requirements
24 Guide to our official statistics
25 Webinars

The Chartered Governance Institute Guidance Notes

These are available for free for members and affiliate members of the Institute and can be downloaded from www.icsa.org.uk/knowledge/resources.

Index

www.ingramcontent.com/pod-product-compliance
Ingram Content Group UK Ltd.
Pitfield, Milton Keynes, MK11 3LW, UK
UKHW061933100926
8556IPUK00025B/1484

9 781860 727771